Business Information Systems
Analysis, Design and Practice

GRAHAM CURTIS
University of East London

and

DAVID COBHAM
University of Lincoln

 Prentice Hall
FINANCIAL TIMES

An imprint of **Pearson Education**
Harlow, England • London • New York • Boston • San Francisco • Toronto • Sydney • Singapore • Hong Kong
Tokyo • Seoul • Taipei • New Delhi • Cape Town • Madrid • Mexico City • Amsterdam • Munich • Paris • Milan

Pearson Education Limited

Edinburgh Gate
Harlow
Essex CM20 2JE
England
and Associated Companies throughout the world

Visit us on the World Wide Web at:

www.pearsoned.co.uk

First published 1989
Second edition published 1995
Third edition published 1998
Fourth edition published 2002
Fifth edition published 2005
Sixth edition published 2008

ISBN: 978-0-273-71382-1

British Library Cataloguing-in-Publication Data
A catalogue record for this book is available from the British Library

Library of Congress Cataloging-in-Publication Data
A catalog record for this book is available from the Library of Congress

10 9 8 7 6 5 4 3 2 1
12 11 10 09 08
Typeset in 10/12 Sabon by 73
Printed and bound in Great Britain by Ashford Colour Press Ltd, Gosport, Hampshire

The publisher's policy is to use paper manufactured from sustainable forests.

To Julia, Edmund and James

To Joan, and for Alan – a truly 'gentle man'

Brief Contents

Contents

Chapter 7   Business intelligence   227

Chapter 8   File organization and databases for business information systems   285

Chapter 16   Object oriented approaches   540

Chapter 17   Systems development: further tools, techniques and alternative approaches   590

Chapter 18   Expert systems and knowledge bases   631

Supporting resources

Visit **www.pearsoned.co.uk/curtis** to find the following valuable online resources:

Companion Website for students

- Self-assessment questions.
- Hints for answering the review questions in the book.
- A worked database solution for Figure 8.10 in the book.

For instructors

- An updated Instructor's Manual including guideline answers to the end of chapter exercises and the case study questions in the book.
- A comprehensive set of PowerPoint slides for supplementing your teaching.

For more information please contact your local Pearson Education sales representative or visit **www.pearsoned.co.uk/curtis.**

Preface

Information technology has permeated the organization at every level. There is a growing need for those interested in business, management or accountancy to understand the nature of this technology and the way it can best be harnessed to provide information for business functions. This text aims to examine and explain:

- the nature of information and its use in managerial decision making;
- the role of the information system within organizational strategy;
- how recent developments in information technology have been accompanied by the rise of end-user computing in business;
- the way that information is organized, stored and processed by modern information technology as viewed from the interests of a business user;
- how developments in networks and the Internet have made an impact on business; and
- the process of analysis and design of a business information system.

Readership

The book is designed as a core text for those undertaking an information systems course as part of a degree or HND in business studies or a related field. It is also recommended for second/third-year undergraduate business information systems modules in computer science courses. The book will be suitable for professional courses run by the major accountancy bodies and the Institute of Data Processing Management (IDPM). It is also appropriate for conversion courses at the Masters level or for MBA-level modules in information systems. It requires minimal prior knowledge of information technology, although an understanding of the basic functions of a business organization is assumed.

Content

It is impossible to appreciate the way that information systems can aid the realization of business objectives unless a basic understanding is obtained both of the information technology, in its broadest sense, and of the way information systems are designed. The level of understanding needed is not to the same depth as that required of a computer specialist. It must be sufficiently comprehensive, however, to enable those in business to assess the opportunities, limitations and major issues surrounding modern business information systems.

Chapter 1 introduces the reader to the idea of information and its relation to management decision making. After covering essential systems concepts, an overview of the structure and purpose of a management information system is explained.

Chapter 2 begins by explaining the central ideas behind business strategic planning. The role of the information system is identified in this process. Various strategic uses of information systems, such as their use as a competitive weapon, are explored.

Chapter 3 explains the basic hardware, software and communications components in a business information system. The reader who is familiar with elementary computer science to A-level may omit most of these sections.

Chapter 4 begins by examining the central notions behind distributed computing and its organizational benefits. The latter part of the chapter examines networks and their position within business. Electronic data interchange and its advantages are explored.

Chapter 5 concentrates on recent developments in global networks and distributed systems. The application of the Internet and the World Wide Web are examined.

Chapter 6 explores the world of e-commerce. It introduces new models for conducting business that exploit the Internet and the World Wide Web.

Chapter 7 covers how technology can provide business intelligence which in turn supports decision making in systems for planning, control and management. It explains the central ideas behind decision support systems and their development through prototyping. It introduces the concept of data warehouses and the techniques of data mining. The relation to and role of end-user computing is examined. Human–computer interaction is treated in later sections of the chapter.

Chapter 8 introduces files and file processing, file organization and access in a business system. The chapter highlights the limitations of a file-based approach to data storage and explains the role of databases and database technology in overcoming these.

Chapter 9 looks at the checks, balances and controls in the development, implementation and use of information systems. It considers the rights and responsibilities of individuals, organizations and society as a whole.

Chapters 10 to 15 explain, by use of a case study, the stages involved in the development of an information system. The emphasis is on analysis and overall design of the information system rather than detailed design and implementation. The approach taken is in line with many structured methodologies. Both process analysis and modelling and data analysis and modelling are treated extensively.

Chapter 16 introduces the object oriented paradigm as an alternative to structured approaches. Using the Unified Modelling Language (UML) the various stages of use case modelling, static modelling and dynamic modelling are explained.

Chapter 17 provides alternatives to the techniques covered in the previous chapters and introduces the important concept of project management. An introduction to CASE in the development of business systems is covered and rapid applications development is introduced as an important systems development framework. The 'hard' systems development approaches are then critically evaluated and, by way of an alternative paradigm, the 'soft' approaches of Checkland and of the socio-technical school of participative analysis and design are introduced. These are covered because it is felt important that the reader appreciate the scope and limitations of 'hard' methodologies.

Chapter 18 provides an explanation of the core ideas behind expert systems. The storage and use of knowledge in expert systems is described. The central ideas and uses of expert systems are first explained. More detailed aspects of knowledge representation and inferencing are covered in later sections of the chapter.

Structure

Each chapter contains an initial brief summary of the forthcoming chapter content. This is followed by the main body of the text and, finally, a more extensive summary of topics covered. There are numerous questions at the end of each chapter. These fall into two types. First, there are straightforward revision questions, which test the reader's basic understanding of the text; the solutions to these can be found in the contents of the chapter itself. Second, there are problems that require the reader to apply concepts or techniques covered in the text to a described situation, and there are discussion questions where the reader is expected to apply his or her understanding of the text to a wider business or social context. Solutions to these can be found on the instructors' website. Also at the end of each chapter are selected references for further reading. Each recommended text or article is generally accompanied by a short description indicating the area it covers and the type of reader for which it is most appropriate.

Three different routes to navigate the book's chapters

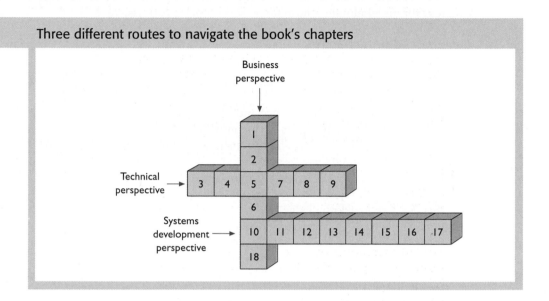

Reader perspectives

Although it is intended that the book be treated as a whole and read in sequence, different readers have different interests:

- *Business perspective:* Those interested in information systems and their development from a business perspective might well read Chapters 1, 2, 5, 6, 10 and 18 first.

- *Development perspective:* Chapters 10 to 17 can be taken as a more or less self-contained section on information systems analysis and design, with the reader being able to dip into previous chapters as is felt necessary.

- *Technical perspective:* For those wishing a technical introduction to business information technology, networks, data storage and control, Chapters 3, 4, 5, 7, 8 and 9 can be approached first.

Mini case studies

The book makes extensive use of mini case studies. These are used, particularly in the earlier chapters, to provide a context for the understanding of key concepts and also to inform the reader about current issues and latest developments. Brief questions prompt the reader to reflect on the content of the mini case study and then apply it to the text.

Longer case studies

Most chapters also conclude with a longer case study. These provide a greater depth of material with which to investigate the topic. They are possible candidates for group activities and can form the basis of productive project work and assignments.

Extended case study

The chapters containing the systems development perspective make use of a more extended case study, Kismet, which is developed progressively. This extended case study introduces a business problem and follows the project through the stages of feasibility, systems analysis and design then implementation and review to provide a realistic context for understanding the systems development process.

Sixth edition changes

This text differs from the fifth edition in a number of ways:

Many topics have been strengthened or rewritten to reflect recent changes and developments. Topics which have been given particular attention compared to the last edition include business intelligence and object oriented approaches. The chapter covering decision support systems has been completely overhauled to reflect the current interest in business intelligence. New topics such as document management systems, human resource systems, web services and digital dashboards have been introduced, existing topics such as customer relationship management have been enlarged, and topics such as on-line analytical processing, data warehousing and data mining have been relocated to this chapter to acknowledge the important contribution they make in providing business intelligence. A completely new chapter covering object oriented systems development has been added to reflect interest in these approaches and provide further opportunities for the reader to compare and evaluate different methodologies.

The presentation of current experience and practice and leading-edge developments in technology through mini case studies and longer case studies has been preserved; these have been completely updated to continue to provide that current point of reference.

There have also been numerous minor additions and amendments to bring the book into line with technological developments over the three years since the last edition.

Acknowledgements

We would like to thank colleagues at the University of East London, at the University of Lincoln and those elsewhere who have provided useful comments on earlier drafts. In particular, the comments of anonymous reviewers have been invaluable.

Graham Curtis
David Cobham
July 2007

Publisher's acknowledgements

We would like to thank the following reviewers for their valuable comments on the book:

Valerie Hill, Northumbria University

Vincent Ong, University of Bedfordshire

John Wateridge, Bournemouth University

Heather Fulford, Loughborough University

Andy Jones, Staffordshire University

Patricia Britten, The University of Buckingham

We are grateful to the following for permission to reproduce copyright material:

Figure 2.2 adapted from source material, Susan Gasson, the iSchool at Drexel University, USA; Table 2.1 and Figure 2.5 (adapted) from Information systems management and strategy formulation: the 'stages of growth' model revisited, *Journal of Information Systems*, Vol. 1 No. 2, Blackwell Publishing (Galliers R.D. and Sutherland A.R. 1991); Figure 2.9 adapted from *Corporate Information Systems Management: Text and Cases*, 5th Edn., Irwin/McGraw-Hill (Applegate L., McFarlan F.W., and McKenny J.L. 1999); Figure 5.2 (a) and (b) from Hobbes' Internet Timeline Copyright © 2006 Robert H Zakon http://www.zakon.org/robert/internet/timeline; Figures 5.6 and 5.7 from the International Committee of the Red Cross; Figures 5.10 and 5.11 courtesy of Google Inc; Figure 6.6 from www.ladybirdkids.com; Figure 6.7 from iMegaMall.com; Figure 6.9 RM Websites Screengrab are Trade Marks of Royal Mail Group Ltd Reproduced by kind permission of Royal Mail Group Ltd. All Rights Reserved; Figure 7.9 from Cognos 8; Figure 7.10 reprinted by permission of Harvard Business School Press. From *The Balanced Scorecard: Translating Strategy into Action*, by Kaplan, R.S and Norton, D.P. Boston, MA 1996. Copyright © 1996 by the Harvard Business School Publishing Corporation; all rights reserved. Figure 8.8 reprinted from *Information Systems*, Vol. 3, No. 3, D. Tsichritzis and A. Klug, (eds), The ANSI/X3/SPARC DBMS Framework Report of the Study Group on Database Management Systems, pp. 173–191. Copyright 1978, with permission from Elsevier; Figure 9.7 from British Computer Society (BCS). The BCS code of conduct can be found at www.bcs.org; Figure 17.1 from Fowler, UML DISTILLED: BRIEF GUIDE TO STANDARD OBJECT MODELING LANGUAGE, p. 14 Figure 2.1 Outline Development Process. © 2004 Pearson Education, Inc Reproduced by permission of Pearson Education, Inc. All rights reserved. Figure 16.1 from *Learning UML*, O'Reilly Media Inc. (Si Alhir, S. 2003). Figures 17.2 and 17.3 from LARMAN, CRAIG, APPLYING UML AND PATTERNS: AN INTRODUCTION TO OBJECT-ORIENTED ANALYSIS AND DESIGN AND ITERATIVE DEVELOPMENT, 3rd, © 2005. Electronically reproduced by permission of Pearson Education, Inc., Upper Saddle River, New Jersey. Figure 17.4 PRINCE® is a Registered Trade Mark of the Office of

Government Commerce in the United Kingdom and other countries, PRINCE2™ is a Trade Mark of the Office of Government Commerce. Mini Case Study 2.1 Vendors need new relationship with customers from *The Financial Times Limited*, 7 March 2006, © Lou Eccleston; Mini Case Study 3.3 Open source software – friend or foe from *The Financial Times Limited*, 10 November 2003, © Andy Mulholland; Mini Case Study 7.2 Olap from *The Financial Times Limited*, 29 October 2003, © Chloe Veltman; Mini Case Study 9.1 Diverting dangerous traffic from *The Financial Times Limited*, 11 July 2007, © Jessica Twentyman; Mini Case Study 9.4 Broadcast your details with and RFID passport from *The Financial Times Limited*, 28 February 2007, © Ken Munro. The screenshots in this book are reprinted by permission of Microsoft Corporation.

We are grateful to the Financial Times Limited for permission to reprint the following material:

Mini Case Study 1.1 Psychologists are busy digging around in a mountain of data, © *Financial Times*, 4 December 2006; Mini Case Study 1.2 Japan leaders join forces to head off new rules, © *Financial Times*, 29 March 2006; Mini Case Study 1.3 Electronic trading sparks a surge in LSE's profits, © *Financial Times*, 9 November 2006; Mini Case Study 1.4 A better way to restore faith in official statistics, © *Financial Times*, 25 July 2006; Case Study 1 A window on the life of a company, © *Financial Times*, 29 March 2007; Mini Case Study 2.3 Western IT consultancies take the fight to India, © *Financial Times*, 5 June 2007; Case Study 2 Keeping a close eye on the customer, © *Financial Times*, 30 May 2007; Mini Case Study 3.1 Business card scanners bring order to desktop in disarray, © *Financial Times*, 26 October 2006; Mini Case Study 3.2 Robot that redefines space, © *Financial Times*, 8 June 2007; Case Study 3 Airport check-in: Board your flight by mobile phone, © *Financial Times*, 14 May 2007; Mini Case Study 4.1 Programs written in old code pose business problem, © *Financial Times*, 22 November 2006; Mini Case Study 4.3 Asia is set to double its broadband customers by 2012, © *Financial Times*, 18 April 2007; Mini Case Study 4.4 Europe should reach for the sky, © *Financial Times*, 28 May 2007; Case Study 4 Storage needs met by networks, © *Financial Times*, 28 February 2007; Mini Case Study 5.1 Report warns of broadband complacency, © *Financial Times*, 16 April 2007; Mini Case Study 5.2 Use of .eu domain name grows rapidly, © *Financial Times*, 12 April 2007; Mini Case Study 5.3 Building blocks for the future, © *Financial Times*, 26 January 2005; Mini Case Study 5.4 New tools to vie with Google, © *Financial Times*, 30 May 2007; Mini Case Study 6.2 Blue Nile uses website to extend across the Atlantic, © *Financial Times*, 14 May 2007; Mini Case Study 6.3 Online tricks turn browsers to sales clicks, © *Financial Times*, 18 May 2007; Mini Case Study 6.4 E-procurement: History proves the greatest teacher, © *Financial Times*, 11 July 2007; Case Study 6 Internet shopping tops £100bn, © *Financial Times*, 18 May 2007; Mini Case Study 7.1 Performance for the public, © *Financial Times*, 6 October 2004; Mini Case Study 7.3 How to get rid of 'devil customers', © *Financial Times*, 13 June 2007; Case Study 7 Can mash-ups match up to business needs?, © *Financial Times*, 24 January 2007; Mini Case Study 8.1 Weatherbys bloodline runs into banking, © *Financial Times*, 2 June 2007; Mini Case Study 8.2 A maverick who used maths to make his clients a mint, © *Financial Times*, 4 June 2007; Mini Case Study 8.3 Battle to make sense of it all, © *Financial Times*, 6 August 2003; Case Study 8 Faulty customer data and the faux-royal slipper syndrome, © *Financial Times*, 7 December 2005; Mini Case Study 9.2 Mobile workers can be cleansed at the gate, © *Financial Times*, 11 July 2007; Mini Case Study 9.3 The

Great Firewall of China, © *Financial Times*, 15 March 2007; Mini Case Study 9.5 Phishing and skimming surge, © *Financial Times*, 27 June 2007; Case Study 9 Websites face more attacks, © *Financial Times*, 30 May 2006; Mini Case Study 10.1 Her Majesty's Prison Service, © *Financial Times*, 7 September 2006; Case Study 10 Enthusiasm and skill led to inflexibility, © *Financial Times*, 18 April 2007; Case Study 11 Partners, © *Financial Times*, 7 September 2006; Mini Case Study 18.1 Short cut to the cheapest deals, © *Financial Times*, 30 March 2007.

In some instances we have been unable to trace the owners of copyright material, and we would appreciate any information that would enable us to do so.

Chapter 1

Information systems

Learning outcomes

On completion of this chapter, you should be able to:

- Define information, systems and information systems
- Assess the information required to aid business decision making
- Distinguish between formal and informal information
- Contrast models of decision making
- Distinguish the managerial levels at which decisions are made
- Assess the cost and value of information
- Identify the characteristics of systems
- Employ the framework of a systems approach to evaluate the information requirements of more complex systems
- Explain what is meant by a management information system.

Introduction

This chapter covers three interrelated areas – information, systems and information systems. Information is considered in its role of aiding business decisions. By studying the nature of decisions, important characteristics of information can be identified. Models of decision making, the cognitive background of decision makers and the levels of managerial activity associated with management decisions are all considered. Properties of business information are developed in terms of the kinds of decision taken and the types of decision taker involved. The provision of information within an organization has an associated cost. To justify this expenditure the information must be of value. The idea of information value, both qualitative and quantitative, is covered.

The framework of a systems approach is used in understanding the information requirements of a complex organization. Characteristics of systems and a systems approach are explained in the second part of the chapter. The ideas of information and a system are put together in developing the concept of a **management information system (MIS)**. This is viewed as a collection of information subsystems interacting with a corporate database. Difficulties in the design of these information systems are considered by outlining five distinct approaches towards MIS design. Finally, the importance of informal information for decision taking within organizations is stressed.

1.1 Introduction

The pattern of employment has altered radically in the UK over the last two centuries (see Figure 1.1). There has been a decline in the importance of agriculture as a source of employment brought on by industrialization during the early and middle parts of the nineteenth century. This was followed by a steady increase in the percentage of the workforce employed in manufacturing, which reached a peak in the early decades of the twentieth century. Since the nineteenth century, the decline in manufacturing employment has been taken up by two sectors – the service sector and the information sector. By far the faster growing of these is the information sector.

Many occupations are now almost exclusively concerned with the handling, processing, provision or transmission of information. Included in these would be jobs in insurance, banking, accountancy, and central and local government. Anyone employed in the postal or telecommunications industries is directly or indirectly involved in the transmission of information. Other areas such as travel, retailing, the police and the armed forces all rely on a greater provision of information than at any time in the past. In manufacturing, a declining percentage of the workforce is involved in the production process, and an increasing percentage is employed in the processing of information. The increasing ownership of computers and the phenomenal growth in the use of the Internet and the World Wide Web have accompanied a much greater participation of businesses in the processing of information.

What has led to this burgeoning of the information sector? On the supply side, the development of faster, cheaper and more flexible technology for information processing (computers) and information transmission (telecommunications) has enabled the information sector to grow. More information can now be provided more quickly and cheaply than before. Access to information and to information systems has, particularly with the development of the Internet, become far easier. On the demand side, the complexity and volatility of market forces mean that businesses require more targeted and more current information to gain a competitive advantage and survive. Externally, they

Figure 1.1 Patterns of employment in the UK

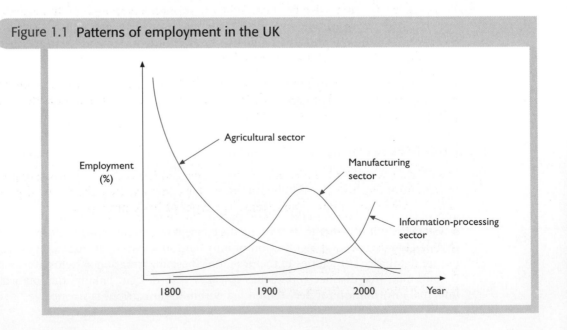

need to be up to date with market preferences, competitors' prices, and the supply and cost of finance. Internally, pressures to maintain profitability or efficiency require instant information to monitor and control the continuing functioning of the organization.

This book is about information systems for business. The purpose of this chapter is to provide a general understanding of the idea of information, the concept of a system and, putting the two together, to provide an understanding of the nature of an information system for a business.

1.1.1 Data and information

Before we can understand the idea of a business information system, it is necessary to look at both the concept of information and the concept of a system. In this section and the subsequent two sections, the topic of information and its general characteristics as applied to business are covered.

Many definitions have been proposed for the term **information**. The one that will be used here is that:

Information is data processed for a purpose.

A business deals with a wide variety of data. Some of this concerns financial transactions. An example of an item of transaction data is the record of the sale of a product to a customer by the business. This fact might be recorded on a piece of paper, such as in a sales day book, or as a series of laser-burned impressions on a compact disk. However, it is not information until it undergoes some sort of processing and the results of the processing are communicated for a particular purpose. For instance:

1. The record of the amount of the sale may be aggregated with other sales amounts and the result transferred to a debtors' control account. This in turn will form part of a trial balance sheet and a final balance sheet to be presented to shareholders. The purpose of this processing is to provide a summarized snapshot picture of the state of the assets and liabilities of the business.

2. The sales data may also be classified by customer, aggregated with the current balance of the customer and the result compared with a credit limit assigned to the customer. The purpose is to alert the credit control manager that action may be necessary if the credit limit is exceeded.

Data, as given in the example, is the record of an event or a fact. The information derived from this data is used for making decisions, of which planning decisions and control decisions are the most important.

1.1.2 Data processes

Data that is formally handled in a business may undergo complex processing prior to presentation and use as information. However complex, though, the total processing can be broken down into simple steps. The types of basic process are:

- classification of data;
- rearranging/sorting data;
- summarizing/aggregating data;
- performing calculations on data;
- selection of data.

Table 1.1 Examples of types of data process

Type of data process	Example
Classification of data	Transaction data may be classified as invoice data, payment data, order data
Rearranging/sorting data	Data on employees may be ordered according to ascending employee number
Summarizing/aggregating data	Data on the performance of various departments may be aggregated to arrive at a summary of performance
Performing calculations on data	Data on the total hours worked by an employee may be multiplied by the hourly wage rates to arrive at a gross wage
Selection of data	Total yearly turnover data on customers may be used to select high-spending customers for special treatment by sales personnel

Examples of each are shown in Table 1.1. In so far as these basic processes are governed by rules, they are therefore suitable for a computerized system.

1.2 Decisions

Information is data that has been processed for a purpose. That purpose might be to offer the information for sale or could be a statutory requirement, but invariably it is to aid some kind of decision. In order to understand more about the different types of information that are provided in business, it is necessary to look at the area of decision taking and decision takers and the way that information is used in decisions.

No decision is taken in isolation. Decisions are taken by decision takers who have certain organizational objectives in mind, a certain background, and a certain mental way of processing and appreciating information. Moreover, these individuals have personal interests that may affect the decision-taking process. From the corporate point of view, information needs to be supplied to these decision takers in order that the decision taken will be the most effective in the light of the organizational objectives.

1.2.1 Cognitive style and background

'Cognitive style' is a term used in psychology that broadly describes the way that individuals absorb information, process it and relate it to their existing knowledge, and use it to make decisions. Cognitive style and personal background act as filters to the information provided to a decision taker. In outline, one approach to cognitive style (Kilmann and Mitroff, 1976) regards individuals as falling into one of two categories in the way that they absorb information. At one extreme, some people take in information best if it is highly detailed and specific, often quantitatively based. The various elements of information need not be linked as a whole. The other group absorbs information in

Figure 1.2 Four cognitive styles for absorbing information and taking decisions

		Information-absorption style	
		Detailed	Holistic
Decision-making style	Analysis	I	2
	Intuition	3	4

a holistic way, that is, in a less concrete way, preferring general facts, suppositions and 'soft data' linked as a whole.

After obtaining information the decision must be taken. Once again there appear to be two distinctive styles. One group will involve itself in a high degree of analytic thought in reaching a decision. This group will be capable of providing detailed justifications often involving quantitative reasons in support of final decisions. The other group will rely more on intuition, experience, rules of thumb and judgement. There will be a concentration on looking at the situation as a whole rather than parts of it independently. This group will often find it difficult to provide justification for recommended decisions. The combination of these information-absorption and decision-taking styles is shown in Figure 1.2.

It is not claimed here that one or other of these styles of assimilating information or making decisions is superior. The point is that if information is presented in a way that is not conducive to the cognitive style of the recipient then it will not be fully utilized in a decision. When information systems are designed the designer, if at all possible, should take into account the range of cognitive styles of those for whom the information is provided. This important though obvious point is often overlooked or ignored when information systems are designed for business.

The background of a decision taker is also a powerful influence on the way that information is perceived. Differing subject specializations will lead individuals to judge different aspects of information as being more/less relevant or more/less important for making decisions. For instance, accountants will tend to concentrate on numerical information, with which they are familiar. They will require the numerical information to be compiled and presented in a standard manner compatible with their expectations and training. They may ignore details of organizational structure and management styles. It is quite possible that they may even fail to perceive the information when it is presented. In contrast, the organizational specialist may not understand the importance of the numerical, financial and cost aspects of the business organization. This is quite understandable as the specialisms of each only give them a limited model through which to perceive and organize information in a way that is relevant to making decisions.

Personal backgrounds and cognitive styles are not wholly independent of one another. The ability to work best with detailed quantitative information, for example, will not be unconnected with the occupation of an accountant or engineer.

1.2.2 A model of decision making

The process of taking a decision can be described as falling into several stages (Simon, 1965). These stages provide a framework within which decisions can be viewed. To be

Figure 1.3 Stages in making a decision

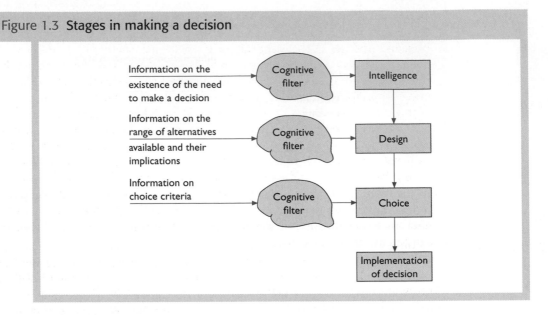

executed successfully, each of the stages will require different types of information. The stages, shown in Figure 1.3, are:

1. **Intelligence:** The decision maker needs to be made aware of the existence of a problem that requires some sort of decision. Information needs to be presented in a manner conducive to this recognition.

2. **Design:** Alternative solutions to the problem must be considered. This involves the recognition of the range of acceptable decisions and the implications of each. At this stage, information needs to be supplied to aid the decision maker in predicting and evaluating these implications.

3. **Choice:** This involves the choice between the various alternatives investigated in the previous stage. If there has been a full analysis of the options this should be a straightforward stage. Otherwise, the decision maker may have to choose between incomplete and perhaps incomparable alternatives.

4. **Implementation:** The chosen decision is carried out.

The stages are illustrated in the following case. A manufacturing company produces a range of modular kitchen units to supply various retail outlets. These outlets sell and fit the final kitchens for their own customers. The problem is that one of the major retail clients of the kitchen unit manufacturer is becoming dissatisfied with the quality of the delivered kitchen units. There is a problem, which may become a larger problem if nothing is done.

1. **Intelligence:** The decision maker in the kitchen units manufacturing company needs to be aware that a problem exists. This must be a person of sufficient rank to make an effective decision. One way is to wait until a customer complains before taking any decision. Then there is always the danger that notification of the problem will not reach the right level of management before it is too late. A more active form of intelligence gathering is to formally request information from customers on their view of the service that they are getting.

2. **Design:** Once aware of the problem, the decision maker can consider a range of possible options. One is to increase the quality of the product by buying in more expensive fitments. Another is to reschedule production and divert more labour resources to quality control and finishing of the units. Yet another is to do both of these things. The option of deciding to do nothing must always be considered. Each of these will have implications for costs, profits, the timing of production, what action competitors might or might not take, the order book with the client company, and a range of other areas. The decision maker needs to be able to evaluate each of these. Some implications can be assessed quite easily with the aid of computer support, especially if they rely on internally held quantitative information. For example, the use of a spreadsheet model will yield a fast, accurate and effective picture of the internal cost implications of buying more expensive fitments. Other options are more difficult to assess. This is particularly true where external and qualitative information is needed. The response of competitors may require an analysis of the market and the past history of the firms involved.

3. **Choice:** Once the implications of each of the options have been evaluated, the time will come to make a choice as to what to do. This might not be simple if the design stage is incomplete or has not yielded definite results. Rules of thumb and past experience may be used as a guide for choice. In the case of the kitchen manufacturer, two of the options considered were 'do nothing' and 'buy in fitments of higher quality'. The problems involved with choice can be seen by further investigation of the kitchen unit manufacturing organization. The 'do nothing' option has implications. There will be the possibility that the retail outlet may take its business elsewhere. On balance, this seems unlikely given the long-established trading relationship and the lack of mature competitors for the specific types of unit favoured by this outlet. But then again the retail outlet is advertising for a new purchasing manager. In contrast, the latter decision to purchase high-quality fitments has definite implications for profit and cost, which are to be balanced against the high probability that this will satisfy the customer complaints. Here the decision maker is required to choose between alternatives that have implications in different areas with different degrees of certainty.

In this organization, the power and responsibility to take the required decision rest with middle to upper management. Other types of decision would be taken at a lower level in the management hierarchy. The levels of managerial decision are explained in the next section.

The classic model of decision making described above defines a strictly linear sequence of stages. Although these stages are clearly essential in arriving at a decision, a more iterative model may be appropriate, particularly where the business environment is changing rapidly. To respond to, or to anticipate, these changes a decision maker might return to an earlier stage and refine or revise his or her view.

1.2.3 Levels of managerial decision taking

Three levels of managerial activity are important in understanding the way organizations take decisions (Anthony, 1965). These are strategic planning, tactical planning and control, and operational planning and control.

Strategic planning

This is carried out by the most senior management and will deal with broad issues concerning an organization's development over the long term. The planning may involve, for example, decisions on what markets to move into, whether to diversify production, how resources should be allocated to major functions or departments within the organization, how to structure the company's finances, or whether to undertake particular major investment projects or accept major contracts with long-term implications. The determination of organizational objectives is also within the scope of strategic planning.

In order to make strategic decisions senior management needs information. Because strategic planning has a long-term time horizon, much of this information will relate to the future rather than the present. The nature of many of the decisions requires information on the development of market forces, patterns of expenditure and the economy as a whole. This requires information to be supplied on matters external to the company from sources such as market surveys, trade publications, demographic studies, government reports and commissioned research from specialist suppliers. The fact that the information refers to external areas outside the control of the organization and that it applies to the future means that it is likely to be highly uncertain and will tend to be of a summarized or general nature rather than highly detailed.

Tactical planning and control

This is a managerial activity normally associated with the middle echelons of management. Tactical planning may involve the allocation of resources within departmental budgets, decisions on medium-term work scheduling and forecasting, and planning medium-term cash flows. Examples of control at this middle managerial level are the monitoring of actual production and expenditure against budgets, the analysis of variances and actions taken in response.

Information for decisions at the tactical level will refer to the medium term, between now and the next few months or a year. It will be mainly generated internally within the organization, although some external information may be necessary. As an example of the latter, it is difficult to set budgets if external raw material prices are the subject of uncertainty or wage rates are set in response to national union negotiations – in both cases external information may be of help. The information will generally be required in an aggregate form – for example, total production for the month of a certain product – though not as consolidated as that for a strategic decision. The internal nature of the information and its time horizon means that it is likely to be subject to less uncertainty than information supplied for strategic decisions.

Operational planning and control

This is concerned with the decisions made in the normal day-to-day operations within a business. Decisions in this area are designed to ensure the effective and efficient use of existing resources to realize budget objectives. These decisions may involve the treatment of personnel (for example, hiring and firing), the control of inventory and production levels, pricing decisions, aspects of credit control over customers and other forms of accounting and cash controls.

Information for operational planning and control is generated almost exclusively within the organization, and it is highly detailed, certain and immediately relevant. For instance, the operational decision as to whether to purchase more of an item that has fallen below its reorder stock level will be based on at least some of the following information:

- the number of requisition orders already placed for the item, the quantities ordered and the expected delivery dates;
- the expected future use of the item, including any outstanding customer commitments;

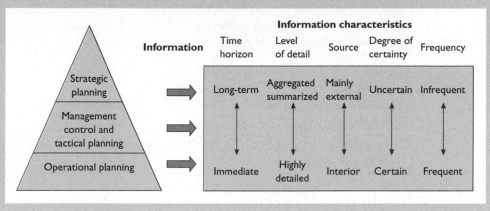

Figure 1.4 Information characteristics for managerial decisions

- the storage and handling facilities available; and
- the range of suppliers of the item, their prices and their expected delivery dates.

All this information will be held within the organization, and once it is recognized as relevant for the decision it can be retrieved and used. Figure 1.4 shows the characteristics of information supplied for the various levels of managerial activities. These activities need not necessarily be carried out by different people. Indeed, in a very small company decisions at these levels may all be carried out by the same person.

Mini case 1.1   FT

Decision making

The Internet was designed, and continues to be maintained, by technologists rather than psychologists and economists. This may be a good thing in terms of its robustness and efficiency, but does not make it simple to work with. So it is no surprise that a survey in the UK sponsored by Google, the world's leading Internet search company, and the employers' lobby, the CBI, found that most consumer companies were diffident about the effectiveness of their marketing online and felt they had a lot to learn about a medium that is still less than 20 years old.

There are five sciences important to understanding the future of the Internet. First, information management and retrieval, the essence of Internet search which Google has revolutionized. Second, machine learning, which makes possible predictive models: for example, how will a 19-year-old male living in New York respond to a particular advertisement? Third, large-scale computing systems: supercomputers built out of off-the-shelf components. Fourth, cognitive psychology: here is where the Internet comes into its own. On a good day, an anthropologist may find 100 people to take part in an experiment: 100m people may use Yahoo over the same period. Fifth, microeconomics: here there are similarities with the offline world. The way airlines price seats on aeroplane journeys, for example, involves yield management of a fundamentally similar nature to the way advertising slots are priced on Internet search services.

> Monetization has to be built into an Internet product from the beginning. The danger is that engineers will make what they believe to be engineering decisions but turn out to be deep revenue decisions. The cost can run into hundreds and millions of dollars.
>
> Adapted from: **Psychologists are busy digging around in a mountain of data**
> Alan Cane, *Financial Times*, 4 December 2006

Questions

1. How can the Internet assist in decision making at the strategic, tactical and operational levels?
2. What does the article mean when referring to engineering decisions and revenue decisions?
3. How do the five sciences referred to in the article relate to the models and levels of decision making described in the sections above?

1.2.4 The structure of decisions

Simon (1965, 1977) makes a simple yet important distinction between structured (programmable) and unstructured (non-programmable) decisions. **Structured decisions** are those governed by clear rules. The decision procedure can be expressed as a set of steps to be followed, can be incorporated in a decision table or can be revealed by a procedural logic flowchart. The information that is needed before a structured decision can be made is clearly specifiable and unambiguous, and once it is obtained the process of arriving at the decision action is straightforward.

An example of a structured decision would be the granting of credit to a customer where this is done on a points basis. Customers obtain points for having a job, the salary associated with it, the time the job has been held, whether they are married, have children, and whether they have other credit cards, loans or a mortgage. The points are assigned mechanically and totalled. If the total is above a certain threshold the customer is granted credit, otherwise not. Because structured decisions are governed by clear rules, they can often be left to low-grade personnel or even be fully automated in some cases.

With **unstructured decisions**, it is often unclear what information is needed and how it should be assessed in relation to the decision objectives. These objectives may themselves be unclear or the subject of disagreement. Unlike structured decisions, there will be no set procedure or rules for arriving at the decision. The use of rules of thumb (heuristics) and 'experience' is characteristic of unstructured decisions.

An example of an unstructured decision is the hiring of supervisory or senior staff. Here information such as qualifications and experience is obviously relevant, but what is not clear is how good qualifications in one candidate are to be measured against experience in a second, and how this is to be offset against the intelligence and adaptability revealed by a third candidate.

Gorry and Scott-Morton (1971) have developed the ideas of Anthony (1965) and Simon (1965, 1977) to provide a useful way of categorizing decisions by comparing managerial activities against the *degree* of structure in a decision. This is shown in Table 1.2. The degree of structure corresponds to the extent to which each of the decision-making stages is structured or unstructured. A decision that is highly structured at the stages of intelligence, design and choice would count as a highly structured decision. A lack of structure during each of these three stages would mean that the decision was regarded as highly unstructured. Many decisions lie between these two extremes, being structured in some stages but unstructured in others. These are termed **semi-structured**.

Table 1.2 Structure and managerial activity in decision making

	Strategic planning	*Management control*	*Operational control*
Unstructured	Company reorganization	Personnel management	Dealing with customer enquiries
Semi-structured	Introduction of new product	Analysis of performance	Short-term production scheduling
Structured	Financial structure planning	Allocating budgets	Stock reorder decisions

As the type of decision will determine the characteristics of the information that is required to make it, the analysis by structure provides a useful guide for the development of management information systems. In general, the more highly structured the decision the more likely it is that a computer system can provide useful information. In cases where the intelligence, design and choice elements are all structured the computer system may not only be used to provide information but also to automate the decision itself. In other cases, varying degrees of decision support can be given.

1.3 Value of information

Information produced for business purposes has a cost. The costs are associated with collection, processing and storage. These are present whether the information is produced by a manual or a computer system. In order to justify this cost the information must also have some value. The value is generally to be found in better decision making, whether this be in the area of control, planning or in some other area. How then is information to be valued?

1.3.1 Quantifiable value

Sometimes information provided to an organization or generated within it has measurable benefits in monetary terms. These benefits result from two factors. First, the information may reduce uncertainty surrounding the making of a decision. Second, a decision may be taken more quickly, and therefore be more timely, in the presence of the faster provision of information.

Figure 1.5 illustrates the way that information can reduce uncertainty and lead to a measurable financial benefit. Assume that a decision faces a farmer. Should turnips or wheat be planted? The matrix indicates the profits for planting turnips and wheat depending on whether the weather is dry or wet. Past records show that it is as likely to be wet as dry (probability = 0.5). The expected pay-off profits for planting turnips and for planting wheat can now be calculated as 60 and 50 arbitrary units, respectively. If the farmer is risk-neutral, they will go for the higher-yield option and plant turnips with an expected pay-off of 60. Let us now suppose that perfect information can be supplied to the farmer on the future state of the weather. Of what financial value is this information? If the information is that it is wet then turnips will be planted and if dry wheat will

Figure 1.5 An example of the value of information in reducing uncertainty

Weather

	Dry	Wet
Turnips	40	80
Wheat	100	0

Profit on crops

Probability of dry weather = 0.5
Probability of wet weather = 0.5

∴ expected pay-off profit for turnips = $0.5 \times 40 + 0.5 \times 80 = 60$
∴ expected pay-off profit for wheat = $0.5 \times 100 + 0.5 \times 0 = 50$

If risk neutrality is assumed, optimal expected pay-off profit = 60 for turnips

Assume that perfect weather forecasting information can be provided

If the weather is wet, plant turnips, pay-off profit = 80
If the weather is dry, plant wheat, pay-off profit = 100

∴ prior to buying information the expected pay-off profit = $0.5 \times 80 + 0.5 \times 100 = 90$

∴ the value of the information
= expected pay-off profit with information − expected pay-off profit without information
= 90 − 60
= **30**

be planted. The weather forecast will be as likely to show (accurately) that the weather is wet as to show that it is dry. Therefore, the expected pay-off profit for the farmer is 90. The value to the farmer of the information is the difference between the expected pay-offs with and without the information. Any rational farmer would be prepared to pay up to 30 for this weather forecasting information.

Although this example is highly simplified, it clearly illustrates the way information can be of aid in a decision. It is necessary to know:

- the range of decision alternatives (plant wheat or turnips);
- the range of factors affecting the results of the decision (dry or wet weather);
- the pay-offs that occur for each decision result (pay-off matrix);
- the probabilities that the factors will be operative (past weather records indicating the probability of wet or dry weather); and
- the reduction in uncertainty surrounding these factors as a result of the information (perfect weather forecast leading to elimination of uncertainty).

The calculations involved are much the same if the range of decisions and conditions is increased and we allow that information only reduces rather than eliminates uncertainty.

Another way that information can prove to be of financial benefit is by being up to date. This enables decisions to be taken more swiftly. Computerized transaction-processing systems and management information systems provide information more quickly than the manual systems that they replace. A computerized system can generate data concerning sales and information on a company's debtors more quickly. This may cut the average time between the sale of a product and the receipt of payment for it. This time is known as the **debtor period**.

Suppose that the average time taken for a customer to pay a debt is six weeks and the amount outstanding from debtors is £6000. If faster processing, such as the immediate generation of an invoice at the time of sale and quicker provision of information on non-payment, can cut the period to four weeks, the average outstanding debt will drop to £4000. This is equivalent to a cash injection of £2000.

Similarly, savings in **buffer stock** may be made. Buffer stock is held to prevent a stockout occurring. Better information can reduce the need to hold such large levels of this safety stock. Often much of this stock is held to counteract the effects of poor and slow stock control. If the levels of stock can be cut from a value equivalent to six weeks' turnover to a value represented by four weeks' turnover then this is equivalent to a cash injection equal to two weeks' turnover at cost prices.

The last two examples illustrate ways in which a computerized information system can lead to quantifiable benefits. However, it is unusual for information to have a total value that is precisely measurable. Generally, the advantages conferred will be unquantifiable. In many cases it may be difficult or impossible to place figures on the value of information simply because there may be no quantifiable benefits at all. A decision to obtain and provide the information will be based purely on its non-quantifiable value.

1.3.2 Non-quantifiable value

It is undeniable that information can provide benefits that are not strictly measurable. For example, better information provided to customers on available products and current prices is liable to increase customer confidence, attract new customers and prevent existing customers moving elsewhere. It is impossible to put a figure on this value. Why is this? Many other changes are occurring to alter customer preferences: advertising by the company, competitors, responses, changes in consumer expenditure patterns, and so on. It is difficult to isolate the effect of the provision of better information from these other factors.

Similar observations apply to information provided for internal decisions. It may be thought that the provision of information improves a type of decision, but it is difficult to separate the effect of this information on the decision from all the other influences.

Occasionally, information has other uses than to aid decision making. Performance information on sales representatives, for instance, may be used to motivate them to achieve greater levels of sales. Sometimes information is collected without any clear purpose in mind but merely to build up a background understanding of an area. Strictly this should be called **intelligence**. In both these cases, the information has value or, in the latter case, possible value. In neither is this value quantifiable.

It is a great temptation to restrict attention to the quantifiable benefits associated with the provision of information, especially when taking a decision on whether to undertake an investment in a business information system. However, a limited cost–benefit analysis on this narrow accounting basis would have meant that several information technology projects that have been undeniably successful would not have been given the 'go ahead'. It is important to recognize that even though benefits cannot be quantified this is no reason to ignore them in making investment decisions.

1.4 The idea of a system

We live in a world full of systems. There are central heating systems, telephone systems, computer systems, fuel injection systems and the human circulatory system, to name but a few. As well as these physical systems there are also more abstract systems.

Among these would be counted systems of logic and philosophical systems. Social systems containing men and women as social beings constitute a further class that includes, for example, economic systems, social security systems and legal systems. There are also business information systems – the subject of this book. The idea of a system provides a useful framework within which to view business information as it flows within an organization, is used for decisions or is processed by modern information technology. The question that this section addresses is: 'What is it that such a diverse range of things have in common by virtue of which they are all known as systems?' Before we can study business information systems, it is important that we have a clear understanding of the concept of a system.

A **system** can be defined as a collection of interrelated parts that taken together form a whole such that:

■ the collection has some purpose; and

■ a change in any of the parts leads to or results from a change in some other part(s).

This is a very broad definition. But then the concept of system is itself wide-ranging. The purpose of some systems, such as the solar system, could provide an interesting theological debate! The important point in the definition above is that a system is a collection of interrelated parts – it cannot be a single thing such as a potato but must be perceived as having an internal structure. Moreover, these parts must be dynamically interrelated through change rather than merely being geographically in close proximity. The system must also have some purpose, goal or objective, and the changes or processes in its parts will normally serve that goal. Most systems, and in particular the systems of interest to this book, have several additional characteristics. An understanding of these characteristics will enrich our concept of a system.

1.4.1 Characteristics of systems

The systems model

Most systems can be illustrated by the model in Figure 1.6. Inputs are accepted into the system and outputs are produced by the processes within the system. In many cases, there may be intermediate storage and control over the functioning of the system.

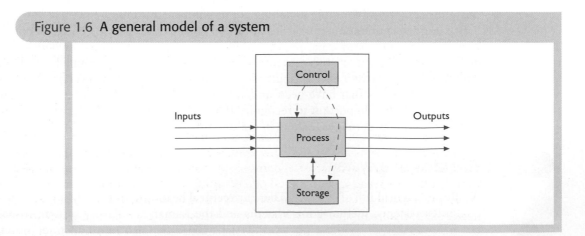

Figure 1.6 **A general model of a system**

To see how this model is exemplified by a simple familiar system, consider the example of a central heating system. The **input** is gas (energy) at a particular geographical point and electricity (energy) required for the electrical equipment. The **outputs** of the system are heat energy geographically dispersed throughout the house (together with the products of combustion in the boiler such as water vapour). The **process** is the combustion within the boiler, the transfer of the resultant heat energy to the water and the pumping of water through the pipes and radiators. The water within the system provides a temporary **storage** for the heat energy as it becomes geographically dispersed throughout the system. The output heat energy leaves the system and enters the environment by courtesy of Newton's law of cooling. The **control** is provided by the thermostat, which accepts a given standard, say 20 degrees Celsius. The thermostat turns off the input when the sensed temperature rises a given amount above this and turns on the input if it falls below it.

The systems model provides a useful framework within which to view a business organization as it concentrates attention on important aspects of its functioning. Imagine a manual order-processing system in a business. Its objective is to process customer orders accurately and quickly. It will help to increase understanding of this system if the inputs, outputs, control, process and storage aspects are clearly distinguished and identified. For instance, suppose for simplicity that the sole input is a customer order. By concentrating on this input we need to determine:

- the data held on a customer order;
- the source of the customer order (for example from salesperson, mail, phone);
- the frequency with which customer orders are received;
- the peaks and troughs in the volume of received orders (and how the processing element of the system deals with these); and
- controls and checks existing over acceptance of the order.

These are just a few questions suggested by looking at the inputs of the order-processing system. Viewing manual order processing as a system does not in itself generate these questions but rather directs attention in a way that is helpful in understanding and analysis.

Systems objectives

All systems have **objectives**, and in identifying a system the objectives must be specified. This may be easy in the case of a central heating system. The objective is to convert localized energy (for example, gas energy) into geographically dispersed heat energy in order to maintain the environmental temperature of a building or dwelling within a given range. The objective is clear, and there is a straightforward **measure of performance** that can be applied to establish whether the system is meeting its objective. The measure of performance is the temperature as sensed by a thermometer.

Other systems may have objectives that are less clear, or those objectives may be stated in such a way that no easy measure of performance is obvious. Systems that evolve, such as economic systems or business organizations, are less likely to have clear objectives than a system that has been designed. The latter are built to meet objectives specified in advance. In contrast, a national economic system probably has no clear objectives other than the vaguely stated one of satisfying the economic needs of (some of) those participating in it. Measures of performance are often not agreed. Is it gross national product, the rate of growth of national product, the percentage of the workforce employed, the rate of profit, the distribution of product, or what? Economists and politicians flourish and differ because these issues are not clearly defined. Business systems lie somewhere between these two extremes.

Inputs and outputs of a system

Although the inputs and outputs of systems can be almost anything, each falls into one of a number of distinct broad categories. They are:

- materials;
- energy;
- labour power;
- information;
- decisions;
- money.

Business information systems are mainly concerned with information/decision inputs and outputs, although they will have others – manual information systems need labour power, computerized information systems need energy.

The inputs and outputs of a system are connected to other systems. This is illustrated in Figure 1.7. The outputs of one system become the inputs to another. It is possible to view the world as being composed of systems. Then there are no outputs that 'disappear'. Of course, a person's interest is always restricted to only some of these systems.

Systems environment and boundary

Inputs come from and outputs are transferred to the **environment** of a system. The environment may be defined as whatever lies outside the boundaries of the system but interacts with the system. If something lies outside a system but does not affect the system's behaviour and changes in the state of the system do not affect it, then that thing would not be in the environment of the system. Environment is not a geographical concept – the central water pumping station is in the immediate environment of a domestic water system, although it is located five miles away, whereas the electrical system in the house next door does not lie in the environment of that domestic water system.

The notion of environment has been defined in terms of the concept of **boundary**. The features that delineate the scope of a system form its boundaries. What is perceived

Figure 1.7 Systems connected by inputs and outputs

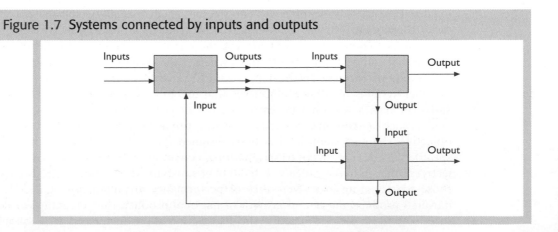

as a system with boundaries by one observer will be determined by what that perceiver identifies as the objectives of the system combined with the area over which that perceiver has interest and control. The idea of a system therefore involves not only 'facts' in the world but also the perceptions and interests of the observer.

To see this, consider the example of a manager whose objective it is to reorganize the stores within a manufacturing company in order to provide the most efficient service. Viewing the stores as a system, the manager will delineate the scope of the system in terms of the control that that manager has to reorganize the stores. The production of stock and its disposal by selling will be seen as lying outside the system. The manager has little or no control over these areas. However, the organization of the stores, their physical layout, personnel, documentation and procedures, will be within the scope of the manager's interest and therefore lie within the system. In contrast, to a member of senior management taking a larger view of the business the stores will be only one part of the system. Others will include production and sales. This manager will see the production and pricing of raw materials, for example, as lying outside the manager's control and so outside the system as perceived.

Closed systems do not have inputs or outputs – they have no environment. Strictly, there are no closed systems (except the universe as a whole), but the term is often used of systems that interact only weakly with their environment. Several command economies in the late twentieth century, such as Albania, were described as closed systems because they had few or no links with the outside world. **Open systems** are those systems that are not closed.

1.4.2 Subsystems and systems hierarchies

Systems are composed of subsystems that are interrelated with one another by means of their inputs and outputs. This gives the system an internal structure. Each subsystem is itself a system with objectives, inputs, outputs, and possibly control and storage elements, and so can be further decomposed into its subsystems. In the example above, the senior manager regarded the stores as a subsystem.

The process of decomposition can continue until the most basic elements are reached. Each of these is called a **black box**. A black box has inputs and outputs, but its internal structure is ignored. Whether something is a black box is not an objectively given fact. For most people a TV set is a black box with electrical energy and a signal (coded information via the aerial) as inputs, and variegated light (picture) and sound as outputs. For the TV repairer, however, it is a system composed of many interacting subsystems, which themselves may be composed of elements that to the repairer are black boxes. These are the basic electronic devices. A black box is defined entirely in terms of the relationships between its inputs and outputs. Each black box would be checked to establish which one did not produce the required outputs given known inputs. This faulty part would then be replaced. Although it is a black box for the TV repairer, it would not be so for the electronics expert.

The decomposition of a system into its subsystems may be shown with a **systems hierarchy chart**, as in Figure 1.8. This is a (partial) representation of a manufacturing organization as a hierarchy of subsystems. The subsystems are defined by the functions they perform. The chart gives a clear representation of the hierarchical relations between the various subsystems. At the first level, the system can be seen to be composed of accounts, sales order processing and other subsystems. At deeper levels, the breakdown of each of their constituents is shown. The purpose of decomposition is to break

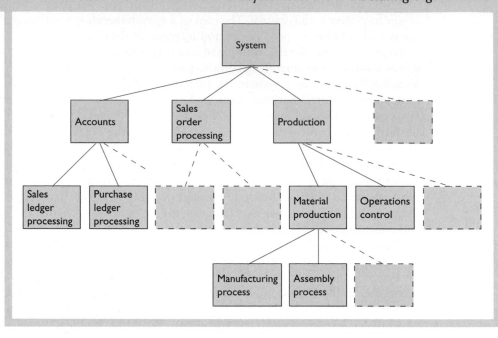

Figure 1.8 **Hierarchical relations between subsystems in a manufacturing organization**

the larger system into its constituent parts. The process continues until the subsystems obtained are of a manageable size for understanding.

Although the hierarchy chart reveals relations between subsystems, it does not illustrate the inputs and outputs to the various subsystems or their interconnection via these inputs and outputs. This is shown by a **flow block diagram**. A flow block diagram for the manufacturing company is shown in Figure 1.9. The subsystems are represented by

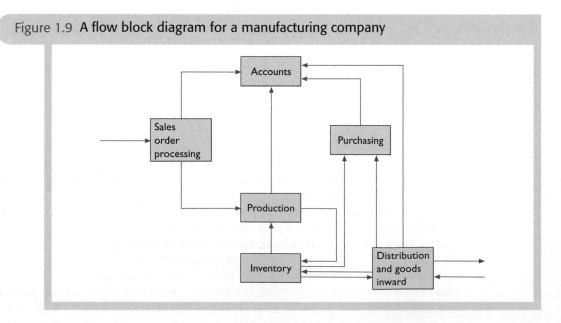

Figure 1.9 **A flow block diagram for a manufacturing company**

Figure 1.10 A flow block diagram for the production subsystem of a manufacturing company

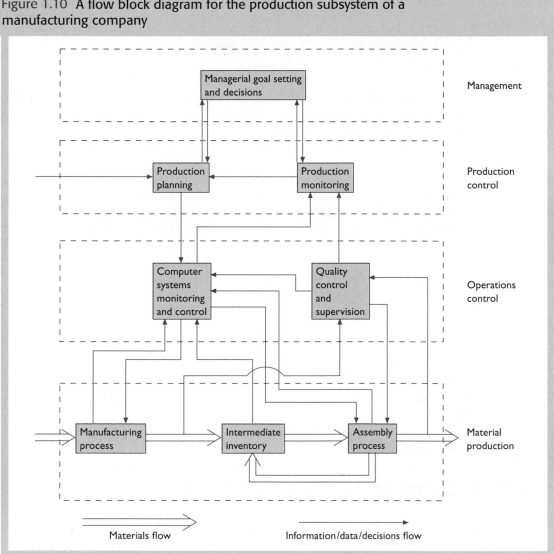

| Management |
| Production control |
| Operations control |
| Material production |

blocks and the flows of inputs and outputs by directed lines (arrows). The diagram shows the subsystems from the level 1 perspective of Figure 1.8.

Each of these subsystems can be decomposed into further subsystems. Figure 1.10 shows the flow block diagram for the production subsystem. There are four subsystems – material production, operations control, production control and the management subsystems. Each of these is further broken down. For instance, material production contains manufacturing processing, intermediate inventory and product assembly. Two types of input/output flow are distinguished – materials flow and information/data/ decisions flow. Apart from the material production, the other subsystems correspond to information processing and provision at the three levels of decision making and control – strategic, tactical and operational – covered in Section 1.2.3.

There are no hard-and-fast rules to be followed in systems decomposition into sub-systems or in the diagrammatic techniques used. The only rule is that if their use increases understanding of the system and aids communication of this knowledge then the technique is acceptable; otherwise, it is pointless.

Mini case 1.2

FT

Financial systems

Japan's seven largest consumer finance companies are joining forces to head off moves by the regulator to introduce stricter money lending rules, which the industry says could damage the sector. Proposals to lower the legal cap on interest rates on consumer loans from 29.2% to a maximum of 20% 'would absolutely kill the industry, the consumer credit market and the economy in Japan', said an industry official.

'If rates are lowered, fewer people get credit, there is less spending in the economy and it becomes quite a vicious cycle', he said. The number of criminal cases related to black market loan providers increased dramatically from about 15,000 in 2000 to 300,000 in 2004, according to figures from the National Police Agency.

Industry officials are calling instead for greater clarity in Japan's money lending laws, a comprehensive credit information system and stricter registration requirements for lenders. For example, banks, credit cards and consumer finance companies all have separate information on customers which they do not share widely with each other.

Adapted from: **Japan lenders join forces to head off new rules**
Michiyo Nakamoto in Tokyo, FT.com, 29 March 2006

Questions

1. Describe the Japanese consumer finance sector in terms of systems and subsystems.

2. How might the proposed information system assist in the more effective running of the consumer finance sector?

3. Would you agree that the banks, credit card companies and consumer finance companies are characterized in the article as being closed systems?

1.4.3 Subsystems decoupling

Subsystems can be connected together via their inputs and outputs either directly or through intervening subsystems. The extent of the dependence of the subsystems on one another is known as the **degree of coupling**. Two subsystems are **highly coupled** if a change in the outputs of one causes a substantial change in the state of the other. Two subsystems are **highly decoupled** if changes in the outputs of either have little or no effect on the state of the other. Coupling is a matter of degree.

Figure 1.11 shows two subsystems that are highly coupled. The output of production is fed directly into sales and distribution, and the demands by sales for products are communicated to production. A change in production will have a direct impact on sales and distribution. For such tightly coupled subsystems to work in harmony it is essential that there is close communication between them.

One way to achieve decoupling is by the insertion of a **buffer** or **inventory** between the two subsystems, as in Figure 1.11(b). The effect of this is to protect the state of the sales and distribution subsystems from variations in the output of production. For

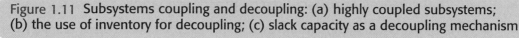

Figure 1.11 Subsystems coupling and decoupling: (a) highly coupled subsystems; (b) the use of inventory for decoupling; (c) slack capacity as a decoupling mechanism

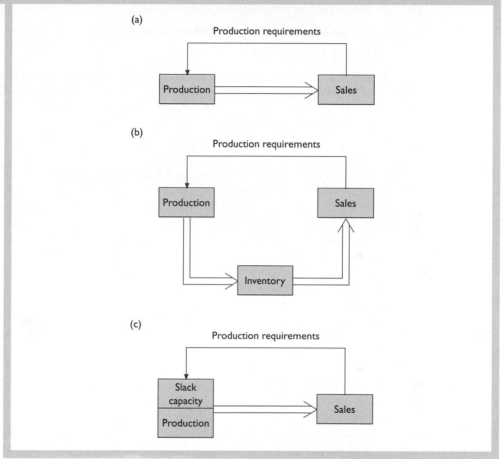

instance, production may come to a halt but sales need not change its activities, at least in the short term. Goods sold are made up from stock. Another way of achieving decoupling is to ensure that subsystems work with **slack capacity** that can be called upon. In Figure 1.11(c) the production system normally works at less than full capacity and can therefore accommodate a variation in the demand for the product from the sales and distribution subsystem. In each of the examples, the effect of decoupling leads to a greater stability.

Decoupling generally leads to systems stability. Business systems need internal stability to guarantee continued functioning and survival in the light of a changing economic, commercial and financial environment. This is not a free gain, as the mechanisms introduce inefficiency or extra cost. In the example, the cost was the carrying of buffer stock or the maintenance of slack production capacity. Nevertheless, a certain degree of stability through decoupling is usually thought desirable in any system and is often built in at the design stage.

1.4.4 Total systems approach versus piecemeal approaches

The total systems approach is based on the idea that all subsystems are related to one another and cannot be considered in isolation for:

1. the purpose of understanding the behaviour of the system as a whole;
2. the design of a new system.

In understanding systems, certain characteristics of individual subsystems only make sense in terms of serving overall systems goals. In a business system, this translates into the impossibility of making sense of functional subsystems activities except within the context of corporate objectives. The uncritical concentration on subsystems can lead to overall systems suboptimization, even though these parts taken individually appear to be performing optimally.

An example of this may be seen in Figure 1.12. Suppose that it is the corporate objective to minimize the total costs (production costs plus storage costs) of supplying a product to meet an externally given fluctuating sales demand. It seems reasonable to expect that if each subsystem functions at the minimum cost compatible with meeting the sales demand then the system as a whole should be optimized and working at minimum cost. Production minimizes its cost by having a constant run of 100 units per quarter, as shown in Figure 1.12(a). This avoids the machine set-up costs of different production runs for different volumes of output. The stock is maintained efficiently at a minimum average cost per unit. However, if the production subsystem can be made to perform suboptimally (with respect to cost minimization) by scheduling a fluctuating production, the extra cost incurred in the change of the production run levels (100 per change) is more than compensated for by the reduced cost of holding stock in the inventory subsystem. This is shown in Figure 1.12(b). Unless a total systems approach is taken, it is difficult to understand why the production subsystem is deliberately avoiding cost minimization in its scheduling.

This is an example that uses simplified figures. However, the general point is that it is not always in an organization's overall interests to adopt a piecemeal approach to subsystems and require each subsystem to function efficiently as measured by the same yardstick that is used to measure the system's performance as a whole. The move in organizations towards treating subsystems as financial cost or profit centres in order to remove internal inefficiency is in line with this piecemeal approach.

Another equally compelling reason for adopting the total systems approach is related to issues in systems design. A computerized business information system usually augments and sometimes, although increasingly rarely, replaces a manual information-processing system. The formal information in a manual system is conveyed in the form of documents flowing between subsystems. These are demarcated by the traditional functional specializations in the various departments of a business – accounts, purchasing, sales order processing, and so on. Concentration on the information inputs, outputs and processes within each of these subsystems independently of each other will generate a computerized information systems design that mirrors this functional decomposition. Given that all the processing will occur within the central resource of the computer there is no reason why this conventional decomposition should not be sacrificed to a more integrated design that takes into account the information system as a whole. In the later chapters on systems analysis and design, the approach taken is one that allows the development of integrated information systems.

Figure 1.12 Subsystems optimization versus systems optimization: (a) a case where each subsystem optimizes by minimizing subsystem cost, although the system as a whole suboptimizes on cost; (b) a case where the system as a whole optimizes on cost, even though the production subsystem is not optimal with respect to cost

(a)

	Production during period	Stock held at end of period	Sales during period
Period 0		30	
Period 1	100	60	70
Period 2	100	30	130
Period 3	100	60	70
Period 4	100	30	130
	400		400

Cost of production per item = 100 per unit
Cost of changing production level = 100 per change
Cost of holding stock = 10 per unit per period

Production costs = 100×400 = 40 000
Cost of changing production level = 0
Total production cost = 40 000

Total cost of holding stock = $10 \times (60 + 30 + 60 + 30)$ = 40 000 / 1 800
Total cost = 41 800

(b)

	Production during period	Stock held at end of period	Sales during period
Period 0		30	
Period 1	70	30	70
Period 2	130	30	130
Period 3	70	30	70
Period 4	130	30	130
	400		400

Cost of production per item = 100 per unit
Cost of changing production level = 100 per change
Cost of holding stock = 10 per unit per period

Production costs = 100×400 = 40 000
Cost of changing production level = 3×100 = 300
Total production cost = 40 300

Total cost of holding stock = $10 \times (30 + 30 + 30 + 30)$ = 40 300 / 1 200
Total cost = 41 500

1.4.5 Control

Systems have objectives. In order to ensure that the system's objectives are met, it is important that there is some control operating over the system's functioning. First, this may be needed in order to ensure that a system responds optimally to a change in its

Figure 1.13 A general model of feedback control

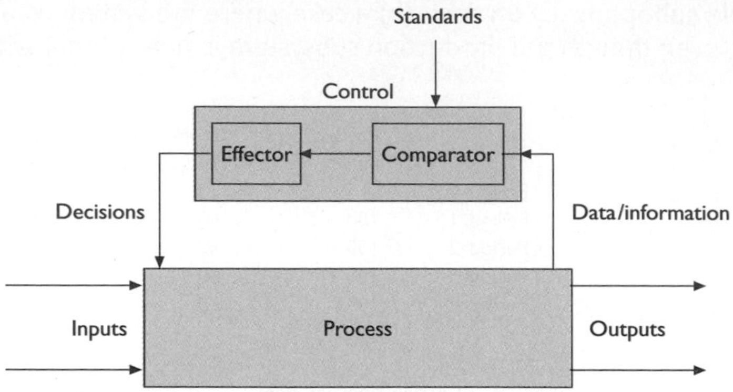

inputs or environment. For example, a change in the price of a raw material may lead to its replacement by a cheaper substitute, or a change in a competitor's price may result in a response to ensure a retained market share. Second, the internal functioning of the system may require controls to prevent or to remedy the effects of malfunctions or re-source degradation. For example, a labour strike or breakdown of equipment requires an internal response to ensure that systems objectives are not jeopardized.

Controls often work by gathering data on the state and outputs of the system, comparing this with the objectives of the system and taking some corrective measure if necessary. The general model is shown in Figure 1.13. Information on the state of the system or its outputs is collected and compared with some desired standard (**comparator**). The results of this comparison are sent to an element of control, which causes an appropriate decision to be sent to the system (**effector**). This changes the state of the system or its outputs. By continuously monitoring the system and changing it in the light of deviations from standards the system can be controlled to meet its objectives. This form of **feedback control** is common in business and industry. For example, in quality control the output of a process is sampled and its quality established. If this does not meet set standards some decision is made to alter the inputs or process involved. Many forms of regular reporting to management are examples of feedback control.

Feedback control may be automated by computerization. This is most widespread in production processes. More commonly, the computer is used to provide information to management, who then perform the control function and make the decisions. Advances in modern information technology and the increasing use of computer systems have cut the time lag in the provision of information for control purposes. The subject of control is covered extensively in Chapter 9.

1.5 Management information systems

The historical development of these systems is illustrated in Figure 1.14. During the mid-1950s, computers were first used commercially to carry out business data processing. These systems were limited to processing transactions. The most common application

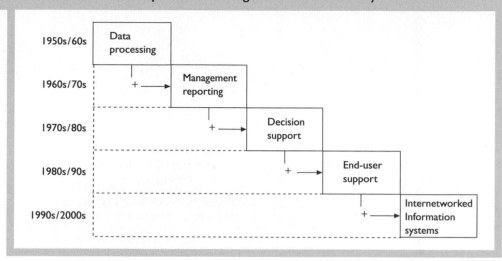

Figure 1.14 Historical development of management information systems

areas were payroll, high-volume billing (such as in the electricity industry) and simple ledger accounting activities. The results of this processing were stored. It soon became obvious that this wealth of stored transaction data could provide management with useful information. This information first needed to be extracted and processed to be digestible and useful to management. The early management information systems (MIS) were born when programs were written to do just this. These systems evolved to permit increasingly complex functions, such as *ad hoc* querying and reporting, and thereby support a wider range of decisions. Developments in the desktop computer and in distributed computing then moved the ability to manipulate and even to create these systems away from the centre of the organization and towards the users of these systems. More recently, the advances in Internet technology have seen systems being connected as and when required: across different business sites, between businesses, and between business and customers.

A **management information system** is, as its name suggests, any system that provides information for the management activities carried out within an organization. Nowadays the term is almost exclusively reserved for computerized systems. These consist of hardware and software that accept data and store, process and retrieve information. This information is selected and presented in a form suitable for managerial decision making and for the planning and monitoring of the organization's activities.

Today, no one would design a system for processing transactions without considering the way it could also be used to generate information. Figure 1.15 illustrates the reliance of the provision of information at strategic, managerial and operational levels on the transaction-processing base.

The increase in the power of computing technology witnessed over the last few decades, together with its decreasing cost, has meant that computers are used more and more by business organizations to carry out routine data processing. Over this period there has also been a change in management thinking to accept the importance of the fast, effective provision of targeted information for management planning and control.

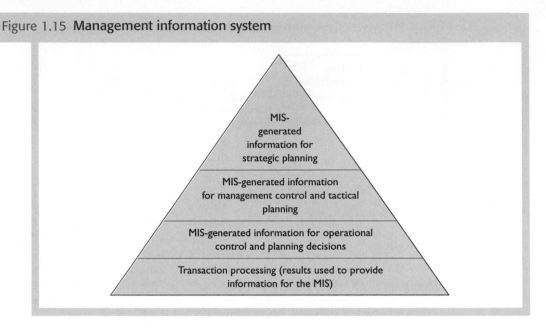

Figure 1.15 **Management information system**

The combined effect of these two factors has led to an increased growth in management information systems. Specifically, the reasons for this are:

- **Cost:** Once data has been entered for transaction-processing purposes it is within the computer system for the provision of information. The marginal cost of using it to generate information for many different purposes is now low.

- **Speed:** Information can be generated quickly. Even complex reports and statistics on the functioning of a business may take only minutes to prepare if in a standard format. This cuts down the time that management is required to wait for reports once they have been requested. It also means that information provided is up to date and decisions should be more effective.

- **Interaction:** Many modern management information systems provide interactive facilities so that users may request information to be produced on-line as and when it is needed. This allows end users to be selective about information extracted from the MIS.

- **Flexibility:** As well as being faced with a predictable set of decisions for which information is required, for example budgeting and performance reporting, management is also faced with new problems. A modern MIS will have some inbuilt flexibility enabling the manager to decide what information is to be produced.

Alternative terminology

This section has introduced the term 'management information system' as an all-encompassing designation for systems that assist managers of a business in making decisions. However, some authors use the term 'management information system' to define a smaller subset of the systems described above. This alternative terminology is shown in Figure 1.16.

Figure 1.16 Business information support systems (alternative terminology)

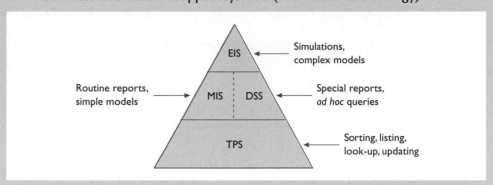

Under this classification, the highest-level information systems are termed **executive information systems (EIS)**. These are the systems used by senior management to assist in strategic decision making. Typical examples of their use are in medium- to long-term forecasting and budgeting. The middle layer of systems, used for tactical planning, is divided into two categories: those systems that facilitate routine summarizing and reporting, here called **management information systems (MIS)**, and those that allow *ad hoc* queries and analytical reporting, called **decision support systems (DSS)**. Examples of the use of the former would be in short- to medium-term forecasting and budgeting and in inventory control. Examples of the latter would be in analysis of sales, pricing and costing, and in the scheduling of production. The lowest layer is then similarly defined as **transaction processing systems (TPS)**. Typically, this includes such systems as payroll, order tracking, machine control and employee records. Where this classification is used, it is normal to describe the complete set of layers as computer-based information systems, management support systems or business information support systems. All of these layers of systems are elaborated in this book, but under the single, more generic definition of **management information systems**.

Mini case 1.3

Financial information systems

The London Stock Exchange yesterday reported a sharp jump in first-half profits and revenues, saying the surge reflected a permanent change to the way technology has altered the business of share trading. Clara Furse, chief executive, said she believed the rise in trading volumes via the LSE's electronic order book was sustainable and it reflected 'the modernisation of the fund management business'.

Electronic trading through Direct Market Access systems on traders' desktops now constituted 40% of all trading volume on the LSE, she said. Trading volumes had jumped sharply since introduction of a high-speed information system last October and a similar jump 'is possible, if not likely' by the end of June 2007 when the LSE's new trading platform, TradeElect, comes on stream. That platform is 10 times faster than the current one and will allow trades to be completed in less than 10 milliseconds.

Pre-tax profits for the six months to 30 September rose from £29.4m to £76.7m, reflecting in part a secular change in equities trading facilitated by the roll-out of new technology.

Adapted from: **Electronic trading sparks a surge in LSE's profits**
Norma Cohen, *Financial Times*, 9 November 2006

Questions

1. Which aspect of management information systems is being described here?
2. To what extent could this system be utilized to assist in the decision-making process?

1.5.1 Database

Essential to the idea of a management information system is the ability to retrieve data and use it for the production of targeted information for different purposes. Much data will be stored as the result of transaction-processing operations. It is important that this data is seen as a central resource for the entire management information system and not tied to the application that produced it.

For example, sales transaction data used to update the sales ledger will be stored after the updating process. This data should be available for other purposes. It can be used to provide reports on sales personnel performance as part of the personnel management function. Alternatively, it can be fed into models that use data and information from other sources to forecast cash flows and aid cash management.

In order to achieve the objective of common availability, the data needs to be managed as a central resource. The software that creates this database and handles access to it is called a **database management system**. This ensures that data is controlled, consistent and available to provide information.

Figure 1.17 illustrates this position. Within the organization, materials, energy and labour power are accepted as inputs and processed to provide outputs. Accompanying this will be data recording the transactions and movements involved. This will take the form of records of transactions that the company has with its environment. For example, the sale of a good, the sending of a purchase order to a supplier or the supply of a good will all be accompanied by a record of the transactions involved. Also, records of transactions between the various departments in the organization will be generated. An example from a manual system is the requisition of a part from stores for production. This is recorded on a requisition form. Resource use within the organization will also be recorded. Once again, in a manual system the use of individual employee time will be recorded on a worksheet.

The transaction data processing element of Figure 1.17 shows the acceptance of data inputs both from the environment and from internal materials processing within the organization. Transaction outputs are also generated. These may leave the organization, such as an invoice, or be stored in the database, such as the invoice details. This transaction processing is carried out within the computer system.

The database serves as a permanent store for the results of transaction processing, as a temporary store during processing and as a store for the records of the transactions themselves. Interaction between the programs controlling the data processing and the database is handled by the database management system software. This 'protects' the

Figure 1.17 The provision of information from a database

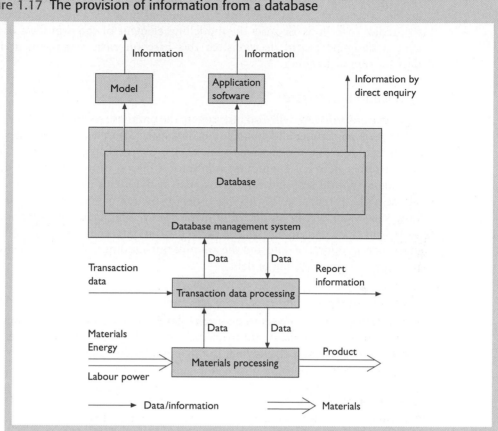

database from direct contact with the applications programs. These carry out such functions as stock control, payroll processing and sales ledger updating. It also maintains consistency of data in the database.

Once stored, this data is available for the production of information to management in its decision making and control activities. As shown in Figure 1.17, this information may be supplied through a model, may be generated by applications software working on data within the database or may be obtained by direct enquiry using facilities provided with the database management system. Examples of these methods are now explained.

Models

Transaction data on sales and receipts of payments will be processed and stored on the database. This can be extracted along with data on purchases, payment for purchases, wages, the current bank balance and other data that involves cash flows in or out of the organization. The data is then fed into a model. The model predicts the cash flow position of the company over the next six months on a month-by-month basis. This predictive model will also need data that will not be in the database. Data on inflation rates and growth in market sizes fall into this category. This example illustrates the integrating nature of the database. The original data was used in transaction processing for disparate purposes but has now been brought together and used to predict cash flow. Because the modelling element of the provision of the information is designed to aid decisions, in this case on cash management, it is called a **decision support system**.

Applications software

Applications software will also interrogate the database to produce reports for management decision making and control. For example, from the customer sales accounts it is useful management information to know how the total customer debt is aged. If half of the customer debt has been outstanding for a period of more than 60 days, say, then management will respond differently than if one-tenth of the customer debt is over 60 days old. A report on the ageing of debt provides management with information on how successful it is in its debtor control policy. The ageing information will not be stored on the database but will be derived from data held there. Specifically, for each customer account, the date and the amount outstanding on each invoice will be needed to provide a global ageing of debt.

Direct enquiry

Management may also wish to query the database to extract information from it selectively. An example, once again from customer sales accounts, would be to request the names and balances of all customers with an unpaid balance greater than a given figure.

1.5.2 Management information systems as a collection of subsystems

Although Figure 1.17 shows the *ways* in which information may be produced from the corporate database, it does not illustrate either the levels of management activity for which the data is provided or the functional subsystems of the organization served by the MIS. Figure 1.18(a) superimposes this on the data-processing base. The management information system supplies information for strategic, management (tactical) and operational decision making to all subsystems within the organization. This information provides an essential part of the feedback control mechanism in these areas and is necessary for the realization of subsystem objectives. Figure 1.18(b) shows how one functional area of the business might operate a number of subsystems. For example, the production department might have separate systems to address inventory management, computer-aided design (CAD), process control and knowledge management systems for office automation such as document management systems.

In the early days of MIS development, it was envisaged that a total systems approach would be taken towards the design of a highly integrated management information system. The reality of MIS development has demonstrated that MIS tend to evolve over time. It is too complex to design the unified system as an initial project. Also, the information needed by different subsystems is markedly disparate and the information required is calculated from differing bases. This has resulted in the development of individual information subsystems that are only loosely connected. The MIS should perhaps better be regarded as a collection of information subsystems, ideally sharing a corporate database. Each subsystem adapts and is tailored to the needs of the functional subsystem that it serves (Dearden, 1972).

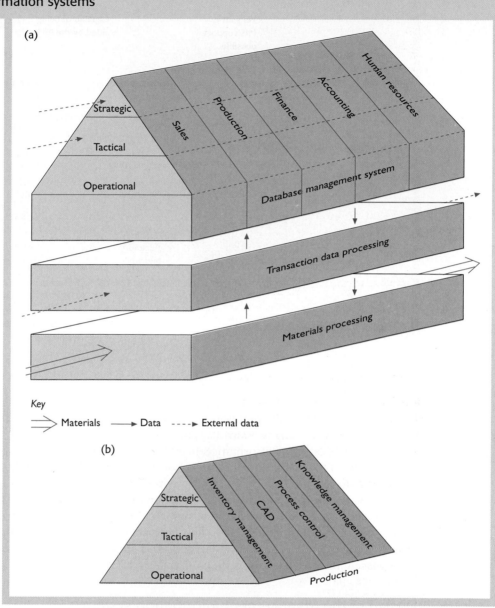

Figure 1.18 The relation between the data-processing and management information systems

1.5.3 Management information systems and decisions

By providing relevant information, management information systems aid the making of decisions. Where these decisions involve planning, current data is used for predictive purposes. This is often associated with using a model to generate future estimates from existing data. This model is used to test the impact of altering the values of parameters, analysing the effects of alternative plans and testing the sensitivity of predictions to change. Often the model is handled by the user in an interactive way. These decision

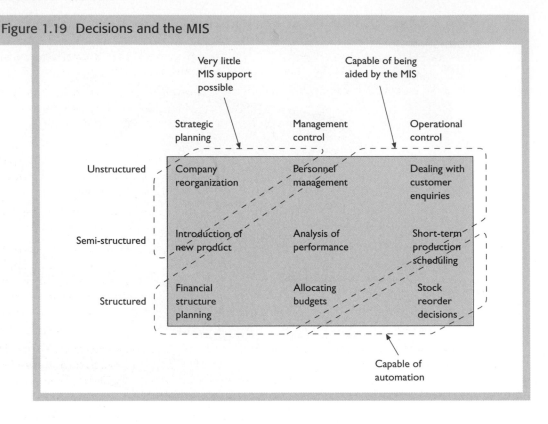

Figure 1.19 Decisions and the MIS

support systems, as they are known, are an important class of MIS applications, which involve more than just the representation of current information in ways suitable for decisions. In contrast, many control applications require much less – the selection, summary and presentation of information in a manner suitable for exercising control.

Previously (Table 1.2), the structure of decisions was outlined against the different levels of management activities. Those activities of a highly structured operational nature can be replaced by automated computer-based decision making. There is also an area of activities at the strategic unstructured level that require information that is largely external and often subjective. This lies outside the area of relevance for the MIS. However, there is a large band of decisions and activities that can be aided, although not replaced, by the MIS. This is shown in Figure 1.19.

1.5.4 Design of the management information system

The design of the management information system, like the design of any system, needs a methodical approach. A detailed explanation of the stages involved in the analysis and design of information systems is given in subsequent chapters. Here it will be sufficient to note special attributes of information that must be taken into account when designing an information system for management.

■ **Relevance:** The information that is generated by the MIS must be relevant to the tasks for which it is provided. The emphasis of the present chapter has been on stressing the importance of information in decision making. An analysis of the decisions taken is required to understand what information is or is not relevant. Information is relevant to a decision if its content potentially affects the decision taken. This is too easily forgotten, and information is provided on the grounds that it might be useful. This is often an excuse for not having carried out a proper decision analysis.

- **Accuracy:** Information should be as accurate as is required for the decision to be taken. Inaccuracy within limits may be perfectly acceptable, especially as increasing the accuracy of information will either increase the cost of its provision or slow its generation, or both.

- **Timeliness:** Information must be presented to the user during the time-span within which it is useful. Late information is not useful. Sometimes accuracy must be sacrificed in order to provide information within the optimum time.

- **Target:** The information must be directed to the correct recipient – that is, the person who takes the decisions for which the information is relevant.

- **Format:** The way in which the information is presented to the user will affect its effectiveness. Traditional attention to clear report formats can now be supplemented by the possibility of producing graphical and chart output. The use of colour and more sophisticated graphics opens up further possibilities in designing output formats. The flexibility of presentation opens the possibility of output designed to match the cognitive style of the recipient.

- **Interactive nature:** Some information is best provided on an interactive basis. This is because further information needs to be called up only if shown to be necessary by current information. To provide all information initially that might be relevant to a decision would be to deluge the decision taker and reduce the effectiveness of the decision process.

- **Control:** Some information may be sensitive or may be of value to competitors. Steps should be taken to ensure that secure procedures surround the MIS.

Dos and don'ts in MIS design

Ackoff (1967), in a now legendary article, stressed some common myths governing MIS projects. These observations are as relevant today as they were over 40 years ago. These myths have a familiar ring to them:

> *'If only I had more information I would be able to take better decisions'*

says the manager. The reality is often different. It is not that more information needs to be provided but less, and this should be more targeted. Relevant information is being lost in the swamp of large amounts of irrelevant information provided by a poorly designed MIS.

> *'The best persons to ask in order to establish what information is needed for decisions are the decision makers themselves.'*

This is not necessarily the case. The proper starting point is an analysis of the decision. Decision makers will generally attempt a wide specification of information requirements ('if it might be useful let's ask for it').

> *'Management needs to be supplied with accurate, timely, relevant information for its activities – it is unnecessary for it to know how it is produced.'*

In many areas, particularly in management accountancy, what appears to be the same information will have different implications depending on how it is compiled. The management accountant needs not only the information but also knowledge of the way it is produced.

'*If information is more freely available then departments can coordinate their activities more closely.*'

It should be remembered that departments in an organization may also be in competition with one another. This is especially true if they are profit centres or are attempting to gain as large a slice as possible of the organization's finite resources. Information about one another's activities may mean that departments behave in a way that is dysfunctional to the organization as a whole.

Mini case 1.4

FT

MIS and data quality

British official statistics have never fully recovered from the Rayner report. Derek Rayner suggested that the purpose of government information was to serve the needs of government. His experience was drawn from Marks & Spencer, the retail company where he had been managing director, and the model in his mind was a management information system. But ministers are not managers and their needs are often for propaganda rather than facts.

Accurate public information is a prerequisite of democracy. Statistics may be misused in contexts other than those intended. The value of health services increases as incomes rise and it can be argued that this increases the value of health output even if outcomes and procedures are unchanged. This statistical adjustment provides no basis whatever for claims that the National Health Service is more efficient. But the assertion grabs a headline, and it is only much later that pedantic journalists and academics can discover what is actually going on.

Such misrepresentations are now common. Decentralization of responsibility for the production of official statistics, a product of the Rayner years, has created a two-tier system. Statistics produced by the Office for National Statistics, which operates to internationally agreed criteria, are of higher quality than those produced by departments. Loss of confidence in official statistics is common to the public at large and among professional users, who recognize specific instances of abuse.

Adapted from: **A better way to restore faith in official statistics**
John Kay, *Financial Times*, 25 July 2006

Questions

1. Apply the principles of the value of information and the quality of data that were introduced earlier in the chapter to the types of information discussed in the article.

2. If a management information system is introduced to assist the users of government statistics what factors should be considered in its design?

Approaches to management information system design

Although most designers of information systems for management would subscribe to these dos and don'ts and take account of the special attributes of information for decision making described above, there still remains much scope for differing approaches in the design of management information systems.

Here, five approaches towards the development of a corporate MIS are identified. A brief explanation of each of these approaches and their limitations will indicate the minefield of disagreements that still exist on MIS design (Rockart, 1979).

1. The **by-product** approach to the development of an MIS is perhaps the earliest used. The emphasis is on developing a computerized system to deal with all the paperwork that was previously handled within a manual system. Payroll, accounts receivable and accounts payable, stock control, billing and so on are all computerized. Only passing attention is paid to the information needs of management. However, there is a recognition that information is used by management in its activities and that reports can be provided as a by-product of data-processing activities. Little or no analysis of requirements is undertaken. Information produced by the MIS is generally in the form of voluminous reports from which those that need information find it impossible to disentangle what is relevant.

2. The **null** approach is a reaction against the shortcomings of the by-product approach. As its name suggests, the null approach lays little emphasis on the production of formal information for management by means of an MIS. It views the activities undertaken, particularly by top management, as being dynamic and ever-changing. Under these conditions, the production of formal information by an MIS according to static requirements is entirely inappropriate. Supporters of this view also find support in the work of Mintzberg (1973), who showed that as much as 80% of a chief executive's time was spent in verbal communication rather than in absorbing information provided in formal reports. While this view has much to recommend it, one should not forget that the needs of lower management are more clearly defined and are more likely to be properly served by an MIS. Second, the advent of modern interactive systems with user-friendly query and report-generation facilities makes the production of information according to dynamically changing requirements much easier.

3. The **key variable** approach assumes that certain attributes of an organization are crucial for assessing its performance, taking decisions and planning. Examples of such variables might be total cash available, the profit-to-earnings ratio of each plant or the turnover rate of stock. The key variables in an organization are identified and the MIS is designed to provide reports on the values of these variables.

    A variation to the straight reporting of all variables is **exception reporting**. Here the value of a variable is only reported if it lies outside some predetermined 'normal' range. The idea of variance reporting and analysis is familiar to the accountant. Indeed, the emphasis of such systems always tends to favour financial and accounting data at the expense of other information. This is unsurprising given the accountant's propensity for assessing in terms of rates and ratios. The main strength of this approach lies in its recognition that to be effective information must be provided selectively.

4. **Total study** processes concentrate on establishing a comparison between the information requirements of management and the information supply of the current management information system. The IBM business systems planning (BSP) methodology does this by relying on the results of interviewing a large number of managers to determine their key decisions, objectives and information needs. The results of this fact gathering are displayed in matrix form for easy handling and visual understandability. An attempt is made at gaining an overall understanding of the organization's information needs and identifying just where the current system is falling

down. A plan for filling the gaps is then formulated. The total study process is comprehensive and can be useful in identifying shortcomings. However, in common with many total approaches, it is extremely expensive on manpower and the vast amounts of data collected are not easily amenable to analysis. There is also a significant possibility that in attempts at imposing structure on the network of accumulated facts unacceptable biases may occur.

5. The **critical success factor** (CSF) approach is based on the assumption that an organization has certain goals and that specific factors are crucial in achieving these goals. For instance, the general goals of a company in the automobile industry might be seen in terms of maximizing earnings per share, the market share and the return on investment as well as the goal of ensuring the success of new product lines. In order to achieve these goals, the critical factors for success are automobile styling, tight control of manufacturing cost and an efficient dealer network.

As well as general goals and critical success factors for a sector, such as the automobile sector, individual companies will have differing additional goals. These in turn will determine critical success factors based on such influences as geographical position, the past history of the company, local competitors, and so on. These factors are determined by interviews with relevant top managers. By focusing attention on the critical success factors, management highlights those areas where it is crucial to have good management information. Information subsystems can then be designed to serve these critical factors.

The main applicability of this approach is in the design of systems for the provision of control information to monitor the state of the critical success factors. It is less effective at designing MIS for planning. CSF is an active approach to the design of management information systems rather than the passive acceptance of reported information based on tradition and collected historical data. The CSF approach is therefore genuinely information- rather than data-led. Its chief importance is the recognition that the purpose of providing information is to serve corporate goals.

It should be clear from the foregoing that there is no universally accepted approach to the design of an MIS. Nor should it be believed that the few approaches covered above are exhaustive of those available. There are many different methods, each with strengths, weaknesses and areas of applicability. What is becoming quite clear though is that technical issues in the design of a management information system are of secondary importance. The primary aim in design is to establish information needs and requirements. Without success in this area the MIS will be a failure. This is not a simple task, however. It is an area in which the specialist in organizational behaviour, the management scientist and the psychologist as well as the systems analyst can make valuable contributions.

1.5.5 Production of the management information system

It is quite possible for the resources of the IT department of an organization to be devoted to the design, production and implementation of the management information system. In many ways, this appears to be a logical approach as the expertise and knowledge of the organization are readily available. Although this may be the best option in some situations, the trend, particularly for small and medium-sized enterprises, is increasingly towards contracting these services out or purchasing an off-the-shelf solution. Over the last two decades, a large industry has developed in the production of various management information systems. Software vendors and business analysts have built up a range of services and products; some are generic in their application, but others are aimed at very specific sectors of business. Examples of the latter can be found in medicine and healthcare.

By using a third party to provide the MIS, the organization is purchasing the expertise of the software vendor or analysts and combining it with their own business knowledge. A partnership can then be forged to develop the system to meet the requirements of the business.

1.6   Informal and formal information

Decision control and planning in an organization will be based on available information. If this is produced by standard procedures, is objective and is generally regarded as relevant to a decision the information is known as **formal information**. As well as following organizational procedures in its production, formal information is generally processed from data by known rules and presented in a standard format (see Figure 1.20). The data from which it is produced is usually quantitative and appears on formal documents in the organization. For example, formal information on actual average material costs of production will be generated from document records containing quantitative details of materials purchased and units produced. Formal information is an important component of the total information available to management. Because of its standard representation and its processing by known rules it is easy to generate using a computer system.

Informal information is also used extensively by management in its activities (Land and Kennedy-McGregor, 1987). This is often subjective and passed by word of mouth, and it involves hunches, opinions, guesstimates and rumour. It generally involves explanatory and/or evaluative information. It is most likely to be qualitative in nature. Although an important determinant of decisions, it is less likely to be used in their

Figure 1.20 Formal and informal information

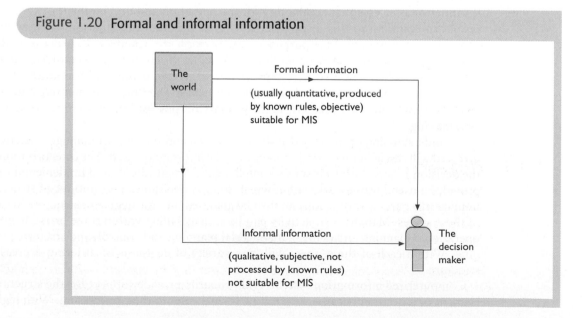

justification. For instance, a decision over job promotion from a junior to a more senior managerial post will be influenced by a variety of information. The candidate's formal qualifications, and the costs and revenues associated with the department over which the candidate has current control, are examples of formal information. The knowledge that the candidate is developing a dependency on alcohol, that the success of the candidate's current department is largely due to an efficient administrator or a competent deputy, are factors that will affect the outcome of the promotion decision. This informal information may even be quite public within the organization. More down-to-earth examples abound. For example, a formal computerized information system will give details of variances from budgets but no explanation as to why these have occurred. This information is precisely what is needed to remedy the situation. Empirical studies suggest that retention of and reliance on a large degree of informal information handling is associated with the more successful organizations (Earl and Hopwood, 1980).

The important point is that although informal information may be subjective, qualitative and not generated by standard procedures or conveyed by usual information channels, it can still be an essential component of effective decision making. Where the managerial activity relies heavily on person-to-person contact, as with top management (Mintzberg, 1973), informal information and its sources are crucial to decisions. By its nature, informal information cannot be readily processed or transmitted by a computer system. There is a great danger that in designing a computerized MIS the role of this other component will be ignored. In particular, where a computerized management information system is installed and much information retrieval and transmission is now handled through terminals, face-to-face contact between individuals will diminish. As a side effect, this will cut down the informal information flows and may reduce the effectiveness of decision making – just the outcome that the MIS was designed to avoid.

Summary

Information is an essential commodity for the operation and development of a modern business organization. It is distinguished from data in that information has been processed in order to serve some purpose in the business environment. In order to understand the nature of management information, it is important to understand the purposes for which it is provided. Information is used in planning, in monitoring and control of business activities and in making decisions. The first two, planning and control, themselves involve decisions, so the primary purpose of information is to aid decision making.

An understanding of the way decisions are taken and the level of managerial activity involved will cast light on general properties of the information used. The categorization of the decision process into four stages – intelligence, design, choice and implementation – provides a useful framework within which to view decisions. The amount of structure implicit in a particular decision can then be analysed into the degree of structure in each of these stages. Management activity can be seen as falling within three broad bands – operational planning and control, managerial planning and control, and strategic planning. Within each of these, there will be a variety of decisions of differing degrees of structure.

Computerized information systems will primarily provide support for the structured element of a decision because they follow formal rules in their processing. With highly structured decisions, such as in operational control, the computer may replace the decision maker rather than provide information for decision support. As one moves 'up' through the levels of management the types of decision change. At higher levels, there is an emphasis on the need for information that is supplied from sources external to the organization, is highly aggregated, uncertain and forward-looking, as well as being less rule-bound. The nature of this information makes it unlikely that computerized information systems relying on internally generated information will be of much value.

The estimation of the value of information is a difficult area. In some cases, a quantitative measure may be placed on the provision of speedier information, as in debtor control, or in the reduction of uncertainty. However, there are intangible benefits. It is difficult, if not impossible, to analyse the contribution of more effective information to a better decision, or to isolate the impact of greater information availability to customers on their purchases. It is a great mistake to ignore the intangible, non-measurable benefits in assessing the overall benefit to the firm of a proposed information system.

The provision of information in a business needs to be looked at in a systematic way. A useful perspective from which to operate is to view the organization as a system and apply systems concepts to the design of its information system. The general characteristics of systems were covered in the chapter. It was emphasized that in order to facilitate understanding of the business it is helpful to decompose the total system into its components. These subsystems and their relations to one another can be shown by means of a hierarchy chart. Flow block diagrams provide an alternative method of representation illustrating the flows between subsystems.

Although a system can be understood by analysis of its component subsystems, it should not be forgotten that this piecemeal approach to analysis may mask systemic properties that apply to the system as a whole. For example, subsystem optimization may occur at the expense of system suboptimization. The concept of control if viewed from a systems perspective is particularly important in understanding the role of the information system within the organization.

Management information systems are computerized systems that provide information for managerial decision making. These systems rely on extracting and processing data from a commonly shared corporate database that stores the results of transaction processing. Information may be provided via a forecasting model, as the result of the activity of a specially designed applications program or package, or by direct enquiry using powerful database query languages (see Chapter 8).

Designing an integrated, total management information system for an organization is a complex task and one that may lead to a final product that falls short of expectations. Instead, the MIS is better regarded as a grouping of information subsystems that are designed (or evolve) more or less independently to meet the information needs of the subsystems they support. This collection of information subsystems is unified by the shared database. In the design of an MIS, the presentation of information, its timeliness, levels of accuracy and the person to whom the information is delivered must be taken into account as well as the information content. No single approach towards the design of an MIS is accepted as standard. The chapter outlined several approaches to illustrate the wide diversity of differences. The information systems requirements can be developed by the company itself or contracted out to a third party. Finally, informal and formal information were distinguished and the importance of the former to effective decision making stressed. No MIS should block the use of informal information, as this will impair the effectiveness of decision making.

The advent of cheap, powerful microcomputers has added a new dimension to the provision of information. Together with versatile packaged software, designed for use by non-specialists in computing, these have led to the mushrooming of alternative information centres. They may not rival the sophistication of the traditional MIS that is centrally controlled and developed, but their ability to respond to local information requirements has been both an attraction to their users and a threat to the power and importance of the centralized computing resource.

Review questions

1. Distinguish between *data* and *information*.

2. What are the differences between strategic, tactical and operational levels of management activities?

3. What are the major differences in the types of information needed for each level of management activity?

4. What influences affect the decision-making process of a decision maker?

5. What problems are there in assessing the value of information for decision making?

6. Outline the main features of a system.

7. What is a management information system?

8. Outline the ways that information may be processed from a database and presented to management.

9. How is the structure and level of management activity related to the level of support given by a management information system?

10. Give basic guidelines that should be followed in the development of a management information system.

11. Outline *five* approaches to management information system design and explain some of the advantages and disadvantages of each.

Exercises

1. Give examples of *four* business decisions and specify the information needed for each.

2. Outline a model of decision making and illustrate this with a business example.

3. What is the difference between a programmable and a non-programmable business decision? Give two examples of each from business.

4. Apply the basic systems model to an inventory system, explaining how each of the parts of the model is exemplified in the inventory system.

5. Define *subsystem decoupling*. Give three examples of how this may be achieved in a business system. In each case, state the advantages and disadvantages of the decoupling.

6. What advantages do modern computerized management information systems have compared with their manual predecessors?

7. What are the differences between *formal* and *informal* information? Give examples of each that you encounter in your college or work routines.

 8. How have technological developments affected the provision of information over the last decade?

9. What are the similarities and differences between the field of information systems and the field of management accounting?

10. 'The information needs of managers are varied and change quickly in today's dynamic business environment. The lack of flexibility in computer systems implies that if managers rely on these for the provision of information then the effectiveness of their decision making will be diminished.' Do you agree?

11. What criteria do you suggest to assess the success or failure of a management information system?

CASE STUDY 1

Data standards in information systems

Data are at the heart of all regulatory compliance. The way information is generated, stored and processed defines the activities of every organization and provides the evidence of good, or bad, governance. It is no surprise, therefore, that all the regulatory initiatives currently affecting businesses around the world place great emphasis on how data is managed.

High-quality data are required for reporting under a wide range of regulations – from the general International Financial Reporting Standard (IFRS) and US Sarbanes-Oxley Act to specific financial sector regulations such as the Basel II capital accord and the European Union's market in financial instruments directive (Mifid).

Clearly, transactional data are a priority because they are a direct representation of business activity. But increasingly regulatory authorities want to see other kinds of less formal data. Text data, email – and even voicemail – are on the list of items to be archived under some regulatory regimes.

The scale of data archiving is enormous. IDC, the research company, estimates businesses around the world generated 161 exabytes (an exabyte is a billion gigabytes) of data in 2006.* Not all data come under a compliance regime. But a significant proportion will. 'Merrill Lynch generates 85m instant messages every quarter. This means for compliance purposes it must store around 1bn messages over a period of three years', says Bill Lyons, chief executive officer of AXS-One, a US-based data archiving specialist. He says the regulators' growing demands for a rapid response means organizations must have ways to get at archived data quickly.

'A typical large financial institution will carry out 800 searches a year in support of compliance and litigation and we expect this to triple in the next few years', says Mr Lyons. 'If you don't have effective archiving it can be very costly to respond to the demand for searches. The way we approach archiving is to aim to achieve Google-like speeds on data archive searching.'

*www.emc.com/about/destination/digital_universe/

Other data management software vendors have responded to the demand and built features into their software to handle the requirements of compliance. Leading enterprise software vendors SAP and Oracle, for example, include compliance features in their products. Organizations must also deal with the problem of data quality – especially when they need to draw data together from different sources.

Informatica, a data integration specialist, says companies must ensure they have a clear infrastructure for data integration to ensure data quality. 'The chief financial officer wants to know that when he signs off reports for regulatory authorities, he is signing off high-quality data', says Tommy Drummond, vice-president of product marketing for Informatica's data quality services. 'Companies need to clean up consolidated data to meet their compliance obligations so they can make sure the regulator has confidence in the data', he says. M&S Money, an Informatica customer and a wholly-owned subsidiary of HSBC bank, was faced with a significant data 'cleansing' exercise when it was obliged to meet the Basel II regulations on risk management. But it also saw the improvements in data quality in a broader context – beyond simply meeting the rules. 'The main reason for our data quality drive was for Basel II', says Neil Hershaw, information management officer at M&S Money. 'We have to prove to the Financial Services Authority (FSA) that we have the right processes in place and our data are up to scratch. Although this was the main driver, we wanted to get the most out of the exercise and gain from having high data quality.'

The bank set up its information management office in 2005 to see how it could improve data quality ahead of the Basel II deadline. Although it had used an Oracle data warehouse for several years, there were concerns about data quality. 'This approach to data quality was new to us and we did not have the processes in place to ensure it', says Mr Hershaw. 'The problem in any company is that everyone assumes the data are OK because they only see them as a summation. It is not until you get down to the low level that you can see where the faults are. And you need software to plough through and carry out the checks.' Mr Hershaw says there is a range of checks that need to be applied to ensure data quality. These include general completeness and consistency checks in addition to more detailed checks, such as making sure a postcode matches an address or a birth date is in range. 'The Informatica data quality checking software we use enables us to code up our rules and check that the data conform. The software produces a scorecard to show us how accurate the data are and we can use this as a basis for making corrections', he says.

Mr Lyons of AXS-One says organizations go through three phases in building high-quality data archives: 'Typically they begin with the aim of improving operational efficiency. Then they move on to meet compliance rules. Finally they ask how they can reuse the data for management information.'

Adapted from: **A window on the life of a company**
Philip Manchester, *Financial Times*, 29 March 2007

Questions

1. Identify examples in the article which differentiate data from information. Suggest examples of processes might turn the data into information.

2. Research the three standards for data quality referred to above (IFRS, Sarbanes-Oxley Act, Basel II) and evaluate their contribution to ensuring quality in data and the uses to which it is put.

3. What is transactional data? Why does the article single out transactional data as a particular area for concern?

4. Define formal and informal information. Why does the article suggest it might it be more difficult to deal with the informal types such as email?

5. Apply the notion of system hierarchy to explain why an executive user of a management information system might not see problems that exist in the data stored at the lower levels.
6. What problems in low-level data does the article highlight? What steps can be taken to improve the quality of data stored?
7. Define the levels of management decision making. Find examples in the article where the data discussed applies to different levels of decision making.
8. How does the article inform the earlier sections concerning the approach to designing a management information system?

References

Ackoff R.L. (1967). Management misinformation systems. *Management Science*, **14**(4), B140–56

Anthony R.N. (1965). *Planning and Control Systems: A Framework for Analysis*. Cambridge, Mass.: Harvard University Press

Dearden J. (1972). MIS is a mirage. *Harvard Business Review*, January–February, 90–9

Earl M. and Hopwood A. (1980). From management information to information management. In *The Information Systems Environment*, Lucas H., Land F., Lincoln T. and Supper K. (eds), Amsterdam: North Holland

Gorry G.A. and Scott-Morton M.S. (1971). A framework for management information systems. *Sloan Management Review*, **13**(1), 55–70

Kilmann R.H. and Mitroff I.I. (1976). Quantitative versus qualitative analysis for management science: different forms for different psychological types. *TIMS Interfaces*, February

Land F.F. and Kennedy-McGregor M. (1987). Information and information systems: concepts and perspectives. In *Information Analysis: Selected Readings*, Galliers R.D. (ed.), Wokingham: Addison-Wesley

Mintzberg H. (1973). *The Nature of Managerial Work*. New York: Harper & Row

Rockart J.F. (1979). Chief executives define their own data needs. *Harvard Business Review*, March–April

Simon H.A. (1965). *The Shape of Automation for Men and Management*. New York: Harper & Row

Simon H.A. (1977). *The New Science of Management Decision*. Englewood Cliffs, NJ: Prentice Hall

Recommended reading

Dearden J. (1972). MIS is a mirage. *Harvard Business Review*, January–February, 90–9
   Worth reading for an alternative 'pessimistic' approach to the possibility of design of an integrated management information system.

Frenzel C. (2003). *Management of Information Technology*, 4th edn. Thompson Course Technology
   An extremely thorough book full of illustrations and adopting a very academic approach. The text is an excellent one; the sections on tactical and operational considerations, controlling information resources and preparing for IT advances are particularly worth reading.

Hussain D.S. and Hussain K.M. (1997). *Information Management: Organizations, Management, and Control of Computer Processing*. Butterworth-Heinemann

This is a straightforward, highly readable text suitable as an introduction for non-specialists at final-year undergraduate or postgraduate levels. The text is divided into four sections dealing with the structure of computing resources within the organization; the control of information processing, including quality control, privacy, security, performance evaluation and auditing; the management of processing, including standards and resistance to change; and future areas of information systems development, including global information management. Each chapter contains a list of exercises.

McNurlin B. and Sprague R. (2005). *Information Systems Management in Practice*, 6th edn. Prentice Hall

This covers the management of information technology in modern organizations. The book gives a thorough description of information and information systems in setting a context for a deeper analysis of knowledge management. It employs case studies of organizations' use of information and technologies.

Ward J. and Daniel E. (2005). *Benefits Management: Delivering Value from IS and IT Investments.* John Wiley and Sons Ltd

A theoretical and practical view on the benefits that can be gained from information systems developments. The book considers traditional and more innovative approaches and suggests how an understanding of change management can assist in successful project implementation.

Chapter 2

Strategy and information systems

Learning outcomes

On completion of this chapter, you should be able to:

- Appreciate the need for businesses and other organizations to plan strategically
- Differentiate between information systems planning and information technology planning
- Identify models for determining the effects of internal and external factors on business information systems development
- Analyse external factors and forces as a guide for the development of information systems strategy
- Describe stages in the development of an organization's information system and the process of moving effectively from one stage to the next
- Describe how information systems can provide competitive advantage for an organization and how information system needs can be identified.

Introduction

In Chapter 1, the central idea of a business information system was developed by initially exploring the concepts of 'system' and 'business information'. Any introduction or expansion of an information system in a business will require:

- the allocation of large resources;
- a recognition that the firm's activities will change as a result of the information system; and
- the intention to improve the organization's services or increase its profits.

Such important decisions should be taken in the light of the business strategy. The subject of this chapter is to expand on the relationship between strategy and information systems. Initially, the need for a business strategy is explained together with a suggested overview of the strategic business planning process. The way in which this necessitates an information systems strategy is covered. There are many frameworks within which information systems strategy can be viewed. One framework is outlined in the chapter, and its various components are explained. Each emphasizes a different perspective on the issues that a firm may wish to take into account when formulating strategy. They all have one feature in common though – they acknowledge the need for an information systems strategy to be determined by the business needs of the organization, not by the functions of available technology.

2.1 The need for a business strategy

A business will function on a day-to-day basis without the obvious need for a business strategy. Orders will be taken from customers, goods dispatched, invoices sent and payments from customers acknowledged. Where stock runs low, purchase orders will be drafted and sent, goods will be received, stock stored and inventory records updated, and when the invoices arrive from the suppliers these will be authorized for payment and payment made. Work will be scheduled and products manufactured. Payroll will produce payslips and instruct banks to make automated payment of wages and salaries at the end of the month. Sales reps' cars will be put into garages for maintenance, bills received, and so on. This is the day-to-day functioning of business.

A business, or any other organization, may continue to function in this way for some period of time without reference to any strategy. However, a business under these conditions is analogous to a ship under way without a destination or without reference to the environment in which it is voyaging.

There needs to be a strategy and strategic planning for a business for several reasons:

1. As was seen in Chapter 1, the individual departments in an organization (subsystems within a system) may function well in terms of their own objectives but still not serve the objectives of the organization. This is because of a lack of coordination between departments, because departments themselves have specific objectives counter to those of the organization, or because subsystems optimization may on occasion lead to total systems suboptimization. It is therefore important that there be an agreed and communicated set of objectives for the organization and a plan on how to achieve these.

2. The organization will on occasion need to make major resource allocations, especially for the purchase and development of new plant, property and machines. Information systems will need expensive hardware and will incur design costs. They will need large resource allocations. These allocations can only be made against an agreed direction for the organization – a strategy for the future.

3. The organization will have responsibilities to a number of different groups. Included among these would be the owners, whether it be the shareholders or the public, the employees, the customers and those that provide finance, such as banks. These parties will have a particular interest in the corporate strategy as their interests will be served or otherwise by the extent to which the strategy takes into account their interests and the success of the organization in meeting these interests.

2.2 Strategic business planning

There is no *one* accepted method that a business should adopt in its strategic planning. However, there are a number of different steps that would normally be taken in the development of a business strategy (see Figure 2.1).

Most large organizations will already have strategies currently formulated. These strategies are often for a future period of five years. This is a convenient time horizon. If it was longer, then future uncertainties would render the planning process for the later stages of little value; if it was shorter, then many developments could not be planned

Figure 2.1 Developing a business strategy

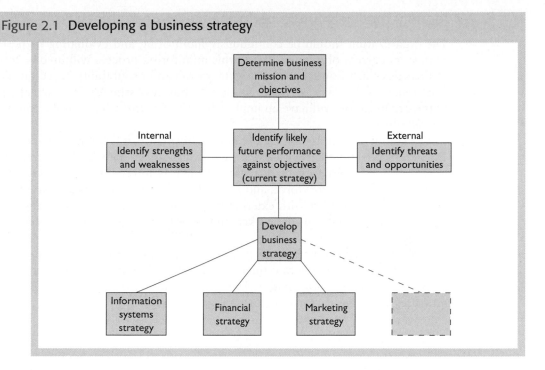

through to fruition. For some organizations, the planning horizon will need to be extended significantly – national defence and the nuclear industry are two such examples. In some very dynamic and fast-changing environments, a shorter period of say three years might be more appropriate – some high-technology industries might fall into this category.

The business strategy is not frozen into the operations of the business but is evaluated and redrafted from time to time. This often occurs on a yearly basis, when the strategy for the next five years will be decided. The strategic business planning process then yields a five-year rolling plan. Unless there are serious problems within the organization or it is undergoing major internal change, it is likely that changes to strategy will be incremental. The following sections expand on Figure 2.1.

2.2.1 Determine the business mission and objectives

The mission of the organization will be a general statement of its overall purpose and aims. It often consists of a number of individual aims. Examples might be (for a chemical company) 'to become a major supplier of agrochemicals to the farming sector through the research and development of new and more effective fertilizer and pest controls' or (for a chain of hi-fi shops) 'to expand the number of retail outlets and diversify into the sale of all electronic leisure goods'.

The objectives, both medium- and long-term, should support the organization's overall mission. Each objective should have a measurable performance indicator, which can be used to determine the success of the organization in meeting the objective. In the above, an objective could well be 'to increase the number of retail outlets by 35% within three years and the area of floor space devoted to sales by 50% within the same period'.

2.2.2 Identify the likely future performance against objectives

The organization should be continuously monitoring and evaluating its performance against its current objectives. Part of this monitoring process will involve forecasts of future sales, cash flows, materials requirements and profitability based on the current situation. In other words, when developing business strategy the current operations of the organization will have an implied future scenario, which can be compared with desired objectives.

As an input into the assessment of future performance, it is common to identify internal and external factors that will have a significant impact. This **SWOT** (strengths, weaknesses, opportunities, threats) **analysis** will identify internal strengths, such as a highly trained and flexible workforce, and internal weaknesses, such as a poor internal information system, together with external opportunities, such as the opening up of trade through a common European market, and external threats, such as low economic entry barriers to the industry.

Given the predictions and the identified strengths, weaknesses, opportunities and threats, it will be possible to estimate the extent of the gap between future objectives and forecast future performance. The business strategy should determine a series of measures and plans that will remove this gap.

2.2.3 Develop the business strategy

The business strategy will be the set of plans that the business will implement in order to achieve its stated objectives. These plans may involve new projects or the continued operation of existing activities.

Most businesses are modelled and managed in a functional way. Human resources, information systems, marketing, financial management and production are examples of common functions. The business strategy will have as components a human resource strategy, an information systems strategy, a marketing strategy, and so on. These strategies will support the business strategy and interact with one another. The information systems strategy is taking on a key role as more businesses rely increasingly heavily on their computerized information systems for all aspects of their business functions.

2.3 Business information systems strategy

The previous section identifies, in broad terms, the steps taken in strategic planning, but it provides no insight into what specific factors should be taken into account in business information strategy development. In particular, it does not give any framework within which to answer the questions as to which information systems should be developed and why. This section will be directed at these issues.

First, it is important to distinguish between a business information systems strategy and a business information technology strategy.

The **business information systems strategy** is focused on determining what information systems must be provided in order that the objectives of the business strategy can be realized. The concentration is therefore on determining information needs and ensuring that the information systems strategy aligns with the business strategy.

The **business information technology strategy** is focused on determining what technology and technological systems development are needed in order that the business information systems strategy can be realized. The concentration is therefore on how to provide the information, not on what information is required. The strategy will also cover how the information resource and information systems development is to be managed.

There is a close interaction between the information systems strategy and the information technology strategy. It is important, however, to make a distinction between them given that the information systems strategy should be led by the needs of the business, not by technology.

There has been a considerable debate as to how best to develop a strategy for information systems/information technology. The urgency of this debate has been fuelled by the speed with which information technology continues to change and by a recognition that information technology is being used less in a support function in the business but is increasingly integral to the business operations and development itself.

Many models have been put forward to guide the strategist in formulation. An important selection is explained in the rest of this section. They have different approaches and objectives and cover different aspects of the strategy formulation process. The framework in Figure 2.2 indicates that some models address the area of information systems strategy, whereas others can be seen as more relevant to information technology strategy. Within the former (information systems strategy), there is a division between those approaches that concentrate on internal aspects of the business compared with those that focus on areas within the environment of the organization. It should be noted that many of the models discussed in the following sections were developed as generic models of strategy that have since been adapted to provide models for the development of information systems strategy.

Figure 2.2 A framework for the interrelation of influences on information systems strategy and information technology strategy

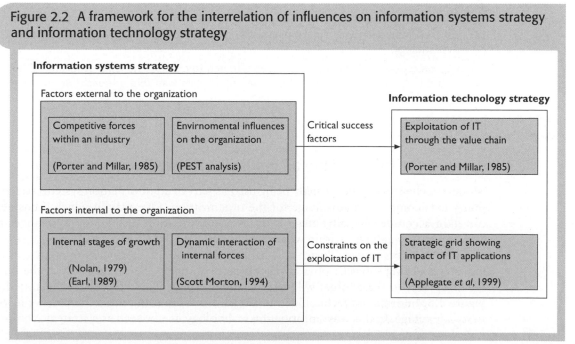

(Adapted from source material, Susan Gasson, the iSchool at Drexel University, USA)

Mini case 2.1

IT strategy

A dirty secret is sullying the reputation of the IT sector, and it is time for the industry to come clean. Every year customers are forced into spending hundreds of billions of dollars to integrate infrastructure and applications purchased from the vendor community. The 'technology highways' are littered with buzzword roadkill, with many of these projects never functioning properly or generating the expected competitive advantages, let alone a return on investment.

The cause of these failures is not hard to identify. The problem is that, all too often, CIOs have been seduced by vendors' latest buzzwords: connectivity, globalization, best of breed. Instead, they are left with projects that never fulfilled their promise.

Part of the difficulty is that the IT community, including vendors, consultants and systems integrators, encourages CIOs to invest in the latest systems. The losers are enterprise customers, who have little choice but to keep funding this inefficiency, with scant hope of achieving their business goals.

Customers need to abandon the best-of-breed approach, in which a company first acquires several leading, but separate applications and then tries to integrate them into its IT infrastructure. It is a nice concept in theory, but does not work in practice.

A more effective approach begins with a company's business model and then works out which applications make the most commercial sense. For vendors, this approach means offering sets of pre-integrated assets that are best matched to the customer's specific needs. Doing so will require vendors to focus on understanding each individual client's business rather than developing products.

Adapted from: **Vendors need new relationship with customers**
© Lou Eccleston, FT.com, 7 March 2006, with permission from author

Questions

1. Why is it important for an organization's information systems strategy to be led by the business strategy?

2. Why have organizations in the past been tempted to develop the IT infrastructure without regard to the business strategy? What are the dangers with this approach? Are there any benefits?

2.3.1 Competitive forces within an industry – the five forces model

Modern technology is increasingly being used as part of an information systems strategy that yields competitive advantage for the organization. One way in which a business can gain a **competitive advantage** is by using information technology to change the structure of the industry within which it operates.

The five forces model (Porter and Millar, 1985) views a business operating in an industry as being subject to five main competitive forces. The way in which the business responds to these forces will determine its success. These forces are illustrated in Figure 2.3. Information technology can aid a business in using these competitive forces to its advantage. In this way, information technology can be seen as a strategic competitive weapon.

Figure 2.3 **An industry and its competitive forces**

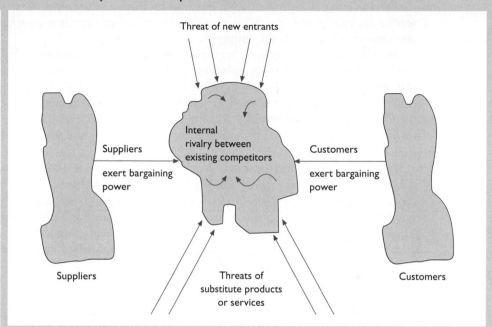

Suppliers

The suppliers provide the necessary inputs of raw materials, machinery and manufactured components for the firm's production process. The suppliers to a business can exert their bargaining power on that business by pushing up the prices of inputs supplied using the threat of taking their supply goods elsewhere to a competitor business in the same industry. It is in the interests of the business to make alternative rival businesses who would purchase the supplier's goods seem less attractive to the supplier.

One way of achieving this is by creating good relationships with the supplier by using **electronic data interchange (EDI)**. EDI requires that there is an electronic connection between the business and its suppliers. When supplies are to be ordered this is accomplished by sending structured electronic messages to the supplier firm. The supplier firm's computer decodes these messages and acts appropriately. The advantage of this for both partners is:

- reduced delivery times;
- reduced paperwork and associated labour costs; and
- increased accuracy of information.

For the business that is purchasing supplies, EDI can be part of its just-in-time approach to manufacturing. This yields benefits in terms of reduced warehousing costs.

Creating links with suppliers is becoming increasingly important in the manufacturing sector, especially between car manufacturers and the suppliers of component parts.

Customers

Customers can exert power over a business by threatening to purchase the product or service from a competitor. This power is large if there are few customers and many competitors who are able to supply the product or service.

One way in which a business may reduce the ability of a customer to move to another competitor is by introducing switching costs. These are defined as costs, financial or otherwise, that a customer would incur by switching to another supplier. One way of achieving switching costs is to allow the customer to have on-line ordering facilities for the business' service or product. It is important that customers gain a benefit from this or there is little incentive for them to put themselves in a potentially weak bargaining position.

For instance, with electronic banking the belief is that once a customer has established a familiarity with one system, gaining advantage from it, there will be a learning disincentive to switch to another. Another example is American Hospital Supplies. It has improved its competitive position by allowing on-line terminals into customer hospitals. These allowed the swift order/delivery of supplies by using less skilled personnel compared with more expensive purchase agents. Once established, it became very difficult for a hospital to change suppliers.

Recent developments in providing businesses with the information and processes necessary to understand and track customers' behaviour has been termed **customer relationship management (CRM)**. Analysis techniques and sophisticated software tools have been developed to exploit the potential information contained in databases of customer details and activity. CRM is often refined into customer profiling, developing categories of customer and attempting to predict their behaviour. One of the goals of CRM is to prevent **churn**, the gradual wastage of customers to competitors.

Substitute products

Substitute products or services are those that are within the industry but are differentiated in some way. There is always the danger that a business may lose a customer to the purchase of a substitute product from a rival business because that product meets the needs of the customer more closely. Information technology can prevent this happening in two ways. First, it can be used to introduce switching costs as stated above. Second, the technology may be used to provide differentiated products swiftly by the use of computer-aided design/computer-aided manufacturing (CAD/CAM). In this latter case, the business produces the substitute product itself.

New entrants

Within any industry there is always the threat that a new company might enter and attract some of the existing demand for the products of that industry. This will reduce the revenue and profit of the current competitors. The traditional response has been for mature businesses in an industry to develop barriers to entry. These have been:

- exploiting economies of scale in production;
- creating brand loyalty;
- creating legal barriers to entry – for example patents; and
- using effective production methods involving large capital outlays.

Information technology can assist a business in developing these barriers. In so far as information technology makes a firm more productive, for instance by reducing labour costs or by speeding up aspects of the production process, any firm attempting to enter the marketplace will be competitively disadvantaged without a similar investment in capital. If expensive CAD/CAM equipment is common for the production of differentiated products speedily then this will also act as a barrier to entry.

Competitor rivalry

Unless it is in a monopoly position, any business in an industry is subject to competition from other firms. This is perhaps the greatest competitive threat that the business experiences. Information technology can be used as part of the firm's competitive strategy against its rivals, as illustrated in the preceding sections. Close linkages with suppliers and customers produce competitive forces against rivals, as does the investment in technology allowing product differentiation and cost reductions.

In some cases, the investment in information technology will be necessary to pre-empt the competitiveness of other businesses. The major investment by the banks in automated teller machines is just one example of this.

Mini case 2.2

Business and IT strategies

Large corporations used to spend many years crafting and implementing an information technology strategy. Such projects could easily cost over $1bn and take five years or more to complete. The goal of such massive IT investments was to confer a competitive advantage that would vault them over, or keep them ahead of competitors. The problem is that there have been few examples of such expensive and long-term IT strategies succeeding. And the history books are littered with case studies of failed IT projects, forcing companies to scrap ambitious strategies after spending hundreds of millions of dollars.

Within the current climate of frozen technology budgets, talk of long-term IT strategies is placed firmly on the back burner. 'For an IT director, claiming there is a competitive advanatage from a technology investment is a career limiting move these days', says Paul Wiefels, co-founder of The Chasm Group, a leading technology strategy consulting company. But even when better times return, and IT spending growth resumes, the days of long-term strategic IT planning, and huge 'big bang' projects are unlikely to return.

'I don't know where my business will be in six months time, so there is nothing to be gained from long-term IT projects', notes Gaurav Dhillon, chief executive at Informatica, a leading business intelligence software company.

Adapted from: **The death of the IT strategy**
Tom Foremski, FT.com, 22 October 2006

Questions

1. What are the problems with developing a long-term IT strategy?

2. Does the author's reference to competitive advantage imply that it is becoming increasingly difficult to achieve a competitive advantage through IT expenditure?

2.3.2 Environmental influences on the organization – PEST analysis

Porter's five forces model (Porter, 1985) considers the industry sector within which the business operates. However, in formulating strategy there are other external factors that the strategist needs to take into account. This is the function of a PEST (political, economic, socio-cultural, technological) analysis.

The questions to be asked are:

Which environmental factors are currently affecting and are likely to affect the organization?

What is the relevant importance of these now and in the future?

Examples of the areas to be covered under each heading are given below:

- **Political/legal:** monopolies legislation, tax policy, employment law, environmental protection laws, regulations over international trade, government continuity and stability.
- **Economic:** inflation, unemployment, money supply, cost of parts and energy, economic growth trends, the business cycle – national and international.
- **Sociocultural:** population changes – age and geographical distribution, lifestyle changes, educational level, income distribution, attitudes to work/leisure/consumerism.
- **Technological:** new innovations and development, obsolescence, technology transfer, public/private investment in research.

At a minimal level, the PEST analysis can be regarded as no more than a checklist of items to attend to when drawing up strategy. However, it can also be used to identify key environmental factors. These are factors that will have a major long-term influence on strategy and need special attention. For instance, included in the key environmental factors for a hospital will be demographic trends (increased percentage of older citizens in the population and decreased percentage of those who are of working age), increases in technological support, government policy on funding and preventive medicine. These key factors are ones that will have significant impact on strategy and must be taken into account.

PEST analysis may also be used to identify long-term drivers of change. For instance, globalization of a business may be driven by globalization of technology, of information, of the market and of the labour force.

In general, a PEST analysis is used to focus on a range of environmental influences outside the organization and (perhaps) outside the industry that are important to longer-term change, and therefore strategy, but may be ignored in the day-to-day decisions of the business.

As has been seen in Chapter 1, where the characteristics of information needed for decision making were covered, the information needed for strategic decisions partly comes from outside the organization, is future-looking and may be highly uncertain. This is clearly true of some of the areas considered by the PEST analysis. This contributes towards the difficulty of the important task of drawing up strategy.

2.3.3 Internal stages of growth

The preceding two sections explain the way that factors external to the organization will need to be taken into account when developing an information systems strategy. However, factors internal to the organization will also need to be introduced into the strategy. The introduction, development and use of computing information systems cannot be achieved overnight. It requires the organization to undergo change and a learning process internally. This concerns not only the technological factors of information systems but also the planning, control, budgetary and user involvement aspects.

Over the last 30 years, several influential approaches have been formulated that look at the development of information systems in an organization as proceeding through several stages of growth. In the following sections, two of these models will be considered.

The Nolan stage model

The earliest of these models, developed by Nolan, explains the extent and type of information systems used in an organization as being determined by the maturity of growth of information systems within that organization.

It was Nolan's original thesis that all organizations went through four stages of growth. This was later refined by adding two intermediate growth stages. The six-stage growth model (Nolan, 1979) was used to identify which stage of growth characterized an organization's information systems maturity. This in turn had further implications for successful planning to proceed to the next level of growth. The model has been used as the basis in over 200 consultancy studies in the USA and has been incorporated into IBM's information systems planning (Nolan, 1984). Before considering any planning implications of the model, the stages will be briefly explained.

The Nolan stage model purports to explain the evolution of an information system within an organization by consideration of various stages of growth. The model is based on empirical research on information systems in a wide range of organizations in the 1970s. Expenditure on IT increases with the stages (see Figure 2.4).

Figure 2.4 **The six-stage Nolan model**

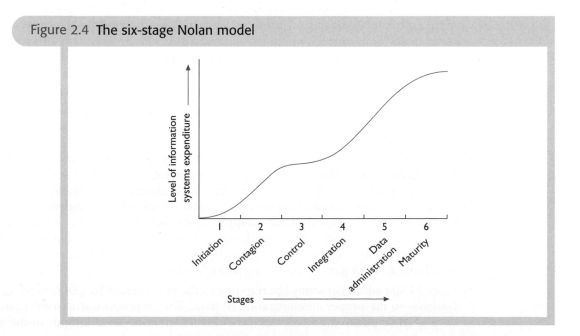

Within each stage of growth, four major growth processes must be planned, managed and coordinated:

1. **Applications portfolio:** The set of applications that the information systems must support – for example financial planning, order processing, on-line customer enquiries.

2. **DP organization:** The orientation of the data processing – for example as centralized technology-driven, as management of data as a resource.

3. **DP planning and control:** for example degree of control, formalization of planning process, management of projects, extent of strategic planning.

4. **User awareness:** The extent to which users are aware of and involved with the technology.

The stages have different characteristics (see Figure 2.4).

1. **Stage 1 Initiation:** The computer system is used for low-level transaction processing. Typically high-volume data processing of accounting, payroll and billing data characterize this stage. There is little planning of information systems. Users are largely unaware of the technology. New applications are developed using traditional languages (such as COBOL). There is little systematic methodology in systems analysis and design.

2. **Stage 2 Contagion:** The awareness of the possibilities of IT increases among users, but there is little real understanding of the benefits or limitations. Users become enthusiastic and require more applications development. IT is generally treated as an overhead within the organization and there is little check on user requests for more applications. Budgetary control over IT expenditure and general managerial control over the development of the information system are low. Technical problems with the development of programs appear. An increasing proportion of the programming effort is taken up in maintenance of systems. This is a period of unplanned growth.

3. **Stage 3 Control:** As continuing problems occur with the unbridled development of projects there is a growing awareness of the need to manage the information systems function. The data processing department is reorganized. The DP manager becomes more accountable, having to justify expenditure and activities in the same way as other major departments within the organization. The proliferation of projects is controlled by imposing charges on user departments for project development and the use of computer services. Users see little progress in the development of information systems. Pent-up demand and frustration occur in user departments.

4. **Stage 4 Integration:** Having achieved the consolidation of Stage 3, the organizational data-processing function takes on a new direction. It becomes more oriented towards information provision. Concurrent with this and facilitating it, there is the introduction of interactive terminals in user departments, the development of a database and the introduction of data communications technologies. User departments, which have been significantly controlled in Stage 3 by budgetary and organizational controls, are now able to satisfy the pent-up demand for information support. There is a significant growth in the demand for applications and a consequent large increase in supply and expenditure to meet this demand. As the rapid growth occurs the reliance on computer-based controls becomes ineffective. In particular, redundancy of data and duplication of data become a significant problem.

5. **Stage 5 Data administration:** The response to the problems of Stage 4 is to introduce controls on the proper administration of data. The emphasis shifts from regarding data as the input to a process that produces information as an output to the view

that data is a resource in an organization. As such, it must be properly planned and managed. This stage is characterized by the development of an integrated database serving organizational needs. Applications are developed relying on access to the database. Users become more accountable for the integrity and correct use of the information resource.

6. **Stage 6 Maturity:** Stage 6 typifies the mature organization. The information system is integral to the functioning of the organization. The applications portfolio closely mirrors organizational activities. The data structure becomes a data model for the organization. There is a recognition of the strategic importance of information. Planning of the information system is coordinated and comprehensive. The manager of the information system takes on the same importance in the organizational hierarchy as the director of finance or the director of human resources.

The Nolan model – implications for strategic planning

The Nolan stage model was originally intended to be a descriptive/analytic model that gave an evolutionary explanation for information systems development within an organization. It identified a pattern of growth that an organization needed to go through in order to achieve maturity. Each stage involved a learning process. It was not possible to skip a stage in the growth process. As such, the model became widely accepted. On the Nolan analysis, most organizations will be at Stage 4 or Stage 5.

However, the model has also come to be used as part of a planning process. Applied in this way, the organization identifies the stage it is currently occupying. This has implications for what has to be achieved in order to progress to the next stage. Planning can and should be achieved, it is argued, in the areas of the applications portfolio, the technology used, the planning and control structures, and the level of user awareness and involvement. Managers should attend to planning, which will speed the process of progression to the next stage and the accompanying organizational learning.

The Nolan model – critique

The model is based on empirical research in the 1970s. It cannot therefore incorporate recognition of the impact of more recent technologies. In particular, its concentration on database technology ignores the fact that:

■ the growth of desktop computers has significantly increased the extent to which users have been able to use information technology and to become autonomous of the computer centre;

■ there have been important developments in the area of communications and networks, especially local area networks linking desktop computers and other technologies together; and

■ new software development tools and decision support tools have shifted the emphasis to the user as development agent.

Despite these limitations, the Nolan stage model still provides a way of viewing the development of information systems in an organization by recognizing:

■ that growth of information systems in an organization must be accompanied by an organizational learning process;

■ that there is an important interplay between the stimulation of growth involving the presence of slack resources together with the need for control;

Figure 2.5 Earl's model of multiple learning curves

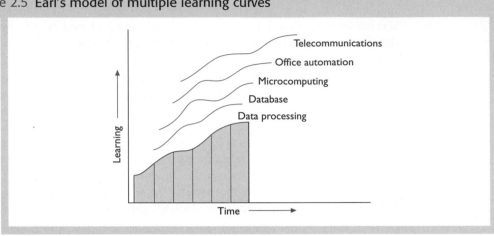

(Adapted from Galliers and Sutherland, 1991)

- that there is a shift of emphasis between the users and the computer centre in the process of growth; and
- that there is a move from concentration on processor technology to data management.

The Earl model

Earl (1989), along with others (e.g. Hirscheim *et al.*, 1988; Galliers and Sutherland, 1991), takes seriously the idea of maturity through stages of growth. For Earl, it is of particular importance to note that stages of growth apply to different technologies. The S-curve represents cycles of new technological developments where there is a sudden increase in understanding leading to a new plateau; this process of further developments and improvements and a higher plateau is a perpetual feature. This pattern is reflected for each technology, with the relationship existing between the degree of organizational learning, the technology and time (see Figure 2.5). It is also acknowledged that different parts of the organization may be at different points in the stages of growth.

Earl's model concentrates not on the interplay between expenditure and control but rather on the task and objectives of planning at each stage. The view taken by Earl is that the early focus in information systems (IS) development is around the extent of IT coverage and the attempt to satisfy user demands. As the organization develops along the learning curve the orientation of planning changes. Senior managers recognize the need for information systems development to link to business objectives and so take a major role in the planning process. During the final stages of growth the planning of information systems takes on a strategic perspective, with planning being carried out by teams consisting of senior management, users and information systems staff (see Table 2.1).

2.3.4 Dynamic interaction of internal forces

Nolan and Earl were interested in the various internal stages of growth through which organizations progress in the use of information technology, together with the implications of this for strategic planning. The current section takes a different perspective in that it concentrates on internal organizational forces and how these must be acknowledged in the derivation of a business information systems strategy.

Table 2.1 Earl's stage planning model (Galliers and Sutherland, 1991)

| Factor | Stages | | | | | |
	I	II	III	IV	V	VI
Task	Meeting demands	IS/IT audit	Business support	Detailed planning	Strategic advantage	Business–IT strategy linkage
Objective	Provide service	Limit demand	Agree priorities	Balance IS portfolio	Pursue opportunities	Integrate strategies
Driving force	IS reaction	IS led	Senior management led	User/IS partnership	IS/executive led: user involvement	Strategic coalitions
Methodological emphasis	*Ad hoc*	Bottom-up survey	Top-down analysis	Two-way prototyping	Environmental scanning	Multiple methods
Context	User/IS inexperience	Inadequate IS resources	Inadequate business/IS plans	Complexity apparent	IS for competitive advantage	Maturity, collaboration
Focus	IS department		Organization-wide			Environment

It has long been recognized that there is an internal organizational interaction between people, the tasks they perform, the technology they use to perform these tasks and the structure of the organization in which they work. This derives from organizational psychology and has influenced strategy formulation and, among other areas, approaches to the analysis and design of information systems (see Section 17.5.2 on socio-technical analysis and design).

Following this theme, an organization may be viewed as being subject to five internal forces in a state of dynamic equilibrium (as well as being subject to external influences and forces). This is illustrated in Figure 2.6. It is the central goal of the organization's

Figure 2.6 The dynamic interaction of internal forces

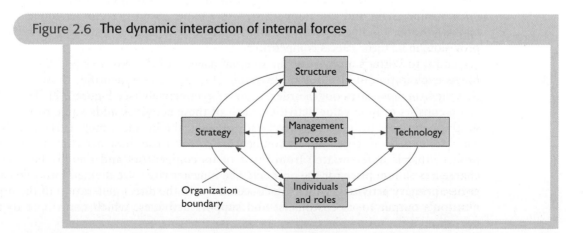

management to control these forces and their interaction over time in order that the organization may meet its business objectives and its mission. Scott Morton (1994) takes this model as the basis for research into the likely impacts that changes in IT will have on organizations, and to provide theories of management on how these changes may be steered to the benefit of the organizations concerned.

1. **Technology** will continue to change. The effect of this will be to cut down 'distance' within the organization as geographical separation is rendered less important. This will be aided through the development of telecommunications and will be evidenced by new applications such as e-mail, intranets, video-conferencing and shared data resources. The organizational memory and access to it will be improved through more effective classification of data and its storage.

2. **Individuals and their roles** will change as information technology provides support for tasks and increases interconnection within the organization. This will require significant investment in training and the reclassification of roles. The nature of jobs will change as IT facilitates some roles, makes some redundant and has no effect on others.

3. The **structure** of the organization will change as roles vary. The greater interconnection brought about by information technology will lead to integration at the functional level.

4. **Management processes** will be assisted by the provision of easy access to fast, flexible, virtually costless, decision-relevant internal information. This will enable new approaches to operational planning and control within the organization.

5. The key to effective planning and to the benefits of new information systems enabled by information technology lies in the proper use of **strategy**. This will ensure that information systems/information technology developments are aligned with the business strategy.

2.3.5 Exploitation of IT through the value chain

Continuing developments in information technology, together with decreasing costs, have enabled businesses to exploit new opportunities to change the nature of competition. In a series of publications (Porter, 1980, 1985; Porter and Millar, 1985), Michael Porter has developed a model of a business organization and its associated industry by focusing on the value chain and the competitive forces experienced (five forces model). This allows an understanding of the way competition affects strategy and the way information provision, in its turn, affects competition.

Central to Porter's analysis of the internal aspects of the business and the strategy for its exploitation of IT is the value chain. The **value chain** identifies those activities that the firm must carry out in order to function effectively (see Figure 2.7). The value chain consists of nine **value activities**. Each of these activities adds value to the final product. In order to be competitively advantaged, the business must carry out these activities at a lower cost than its competitors or must use these activities to create a product that is differentiated from those of its competitors and thereby be able to charge a premium price for the product. The nine activities are divided into two categories: **primary activities**, which are concerned with the direct generation of the organization's output to its customers; and **support activities**, which contribute to the operation of the primary activities.

Figure 2.7 The value chain

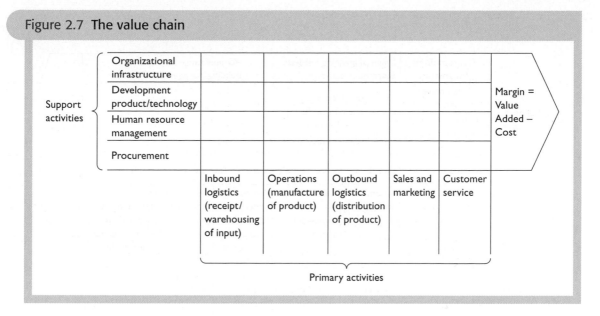

- **Primary activities**
  - *inbound logistics*: activities that bring inputs into the organization, such as receipt of goods, warehousing, inventory control;
  - *operations*: activities that transform the product into its final form, whether it be physical good or service;
  - *outbound logistics*: activities that dispatch products and distribute them to clients;
  - *marketing and sales*: activities concerned with locating and attracting customers for the purchase of the product – for example advertising;
  - *service*: activities that provide service and support to customers – for example maintenance, installation.
- **Support activities**
  - *firm infrastructure:* activities that support the whole value chain – for example general management, financial planning;
  - *human resource management:* activities concerned with training, recruitment and personnel resource planning;
  - *technology development:* activities that identify and develop ways in which machines and other kinds of technology can assist the firm's activities;
  - *procurement:* activities that locate sources of input and purchase these inputs.

As well as having a physical component, every value activity creates and uses information. The competitive advantage of the organization is enhanced by reducing costs in each activity as compared with its competitors. Information technology is used to reduce the cost of the information component of each activity. For instance, inbound logistics activities use information technology to provide information on goods received and use this to update inventory records. Financial planning, an infrastructure activity, will use information technology to collect information provided by many of the firm's activities to generate forecasts on future performance. Information technology may also be used

Figure 2.8 Information technology in the value chain

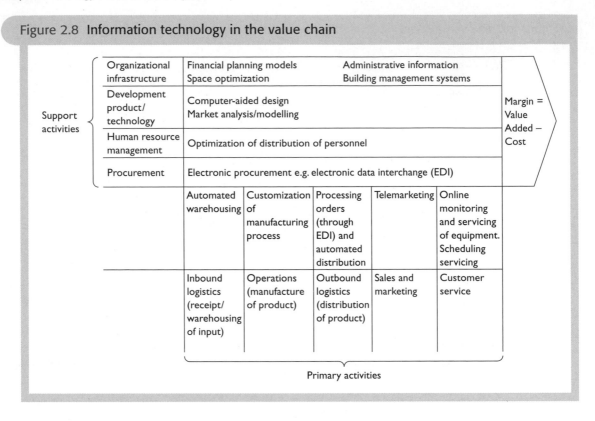

to increase product differentiation for specific customer needs. For instance, operations can use information technology to control the production process to generate tailor-made output for customers.

Where previously the organization relied on the manual production of information, it is now more common for information technology to permeate its entire value chain (see Figure 2.8). The greater the extent to which this reduces costs or enables product differentiation the greater the competitive advantage conferred on the business.

The organization's value chain is composed of a set of interdependent activities that are linked to one another. These **linkages** need to be coordinated in order to ensure that the activities are carried out in the most effective way. Information is necessary to manage these linkages. One way that this may occur is in **just-in-time (JIT) manufacturing**. JIT is an approach to production that requires the output of each stage of the production process to be fed into the following stage without undergoing an intermediate storage stage of indefinite length. The benefits of JIT are that it removes intermediate inventory storage costs for personnel and space and prevents the organization's working capital being tied up in goods waiting in the production process. JIT can also be extended outside the organization to include the purchase of inputs that are delivered just in time for the manufacturing process, which in turn produces an output just in time to meet the specific needs of a customer. **Automated billing systems** or **electronic data interchange (EDI)** can be used for the external linkages. The application of JIT can be viewed as an increase in the degree of systems coupling, as described in Section 1.4.3. The goal is to reduce the necessity for the inventory illustrated in Figure 1.11 and introduce more effective linkages between the systems. For JIT to work the effective management of these linkages is imperative, and it is here that information technology can provide the necessary information – accurately and on time. Hence cost reductions in the organization's value activities are achieved and the business can gain a competitive advantage.

In summary, information technology is at the basis of information systems in business, which increase the competitive advantage of that business over its competitors by:

- reducing the cost of the information component of value activities;
- allowing product differentiation; and
- providing information for the effective management of linkages.

The importance of this approach is that it views information not merely as a support for the tasks that a business undertakes but rather as permeating the entire set of business activities. As such, its correct provision can give the organization a strategic competitive advantage over its rivals in the industry.

2.3.6 The strategic grid

The strategic grid (Applegate, McFarlan and McKenny, 1999) assists the organization to determine in which of four categories it finds itself in with respect to the impact of IT and its information systems (see Figure 2.9).

The grid plots the extent to which the **existing** applications portfolio has a strategic impact against the likely strategic impact of the **planned** applications development. The four possible resulting positions are:

1. **Support:** The role of the information system is to support the transaction-processing requirements of the organization. Information technology is utilized to bring about cost reduction, and information is produced as a by-product of the process.

2. **Factory:** The current information systems are an integral part of the strategic plan of the organization. Few strategic developments are planned, and the focus of IT activity is on improving existing systems.

3. **Turnaround:** This is a transitional phase. Organizations move from the 'support' category to this as a result of internal and external pressures. Internal pressures result from the confidence of management in the support systems together with the

Figure 2.9 The strategic grid

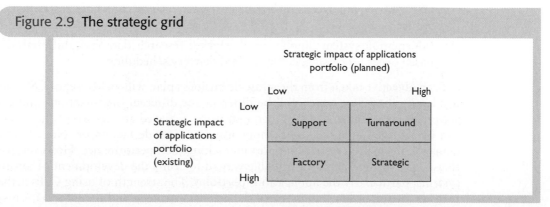

(Adapted from Applegate *et al*, 1999)

recognition of the strategic benefits of information technology as a competitive weapon. The external pressures come from improving technology acting as an enabler for development together with the increasing use of information technology by competitor firms in the same industry. If the firm continues with strategic innovation it will enter the 'strategic' category, otherwise it will revert to the 'factory' category.

4. **Strategic:** This category requires a continuing development of information systems through the exploitation of information technology at a strategic level. It can only be accomplished with the commitment of senior management and the recognition of the integral part played by the information system within the entire fabric of the firm's activities.

These categories aid managers in identifying the role and importance of information technology in their business. It plots 'where we are now' rather than 'where we want to go' or 'how we get there'. This is not unimportant, since each of the categories implies a strategy for the management of the information system. The 'support' and 'factory' positions are essentially static. They concern the more effective and efficient use of the existing applications portfolio and as such do not require an extensive senior management involvement. The 'turnaround' and 'strategic' categories imply a dynamic strategy that must, if it is to be successful, involve senior management in an active way in the implementation of strategy. An organization moving from one category to another should be prepared to adopt the appropriate involvement of senior management.

2.3.7 Critical success factors

The critical success factor (CSF) approach was developed initially by John Rockart (Rockart, 1979). Critical success factors are those limited areas of a firm's operations that if satisfactory will ensure that the objectives of the business are achieved. They are thus critical to the competitive performance of the organization. In order to ensure that the critical success factors are satisfactory, it is important to have appropriate information identifying their performance. This is a guide to which information systems should be developed, namely those that give information on the critical success factors, and the consequent implications for the information technology strategy.

For example, consider the case of a mail order supplier of clothes:

Objective: To increase market share by 5% per annum.

CSFs: Effective advertising; faster customer order processing; faster distribution service.

Information systems applications: Market research database and analysis; web-based order processing; computerized delivery scheduling.

Each objective taken from the strategic business plan will yield a set of CSFs. In order to identify the CSFs, which will be different for different organizations and different sectors, it is recommended that a consensus be achieved among senior managers. This can be achieved in special workshops using an outside facilitator. Not all CSFs will demand information systems support in tracking their performance. However, for those that do the method acts as a valuable way of focusing the development of information systems, particularly the applications portfolio. The strength of using CSFs is that they provide the important link between the business strategy and the information systems strategy, with the consequent impact on the information technology strategy.

The CSF approach has since been extended (Henderson *et al.*, 1987). The extended approach recognizes that critical success factors determine three distinct areas. First, each critical success factor remains critically based on only certain assumptions, and information is required on these assumptions. Second, the performance of each critical success factor must be monitored. This requires information (as explained above). Finally, each critical success factor will entail decisions that can be aided by information systems providing decision support. These three areas determine the information systems development.

2.4 Information systems strategy today

This section considers some of the developments of recent years that have challenged the accepted tenets of business and IS strategy.

2.4.1 Business strategy and IT strategy

The debate over business strategy and IT strategy has in the past focused mainly on the need for the former to precede and inform the latter. The business strategy has been perceived as the driver, while the IT strategy has guided the identification of resources and been the enabler. As information systems have become embedded into the operation of companies it has become clear that an IT strategy is a fundamental and integrated component of the overall business strategy.

The development of the Internet and electronic business has largely challenged this perceived wisdom. It has become evident over the last few years that developments in IT can be a driver for business strategy. For organizations in the Internet age, new threats and opportunities have emerged. Fundamental questions have been asked about the nature of the business, the appropriateness of business models and the structure of the organization. In these circumstances, organizations have been obliged to revisit their business strategies and reconsider the IT requirements.

The traditional approach has been one of alignment, i.e. bringing the IT strategy into line with the business strategy. Many see the future more in terms of integration rather than alignment. Creating a business strategy that recognizes the electronic business world also accepts that IT can be an input to as well as an output from the strategy formulation process. Changes in IT strategy can lead to new opportunities for business development.

A further factor is the pace of change in the business world. To reflect this rapid change, an almost continuous reassessment of IT and business strategy is needed. The traditional setting of IT strategy to meet business objectives does not recognize the rapid real-time responses necessary in the modern economy.

One school of thought divides IT investment into two pools: the mainstream and the innovative. The mainstream IT investment represents the traditional approach to developing and then implementing a well-constructed strategy. Innovative IT investment is the equivalent of the military 'rapid response unit', anticipating developments and being flexible enough to adapt to an environment or shape a new environment. As projects become embedded and established they move from the innovative to the mainstream pool. Thus, the integration model of strategy clearly has resonance with the innovative pool and the alignment model of strategy with the mainstream.

2.4.2 Enterprise resource planning (ERP)

Enterprise resource planning (ERP) systems are computer-based business management systems which integrate all aspects of a business's functions – for example, planning, manufacturing, inventory, sales, marketing, personnel and accounting.

ERP systems were developed in the late 1990s. ERP grew out of the manufacturer resource planning (MRP) of the 1980s which sought to integrate manufacturing and business functions. The effective planning of resources for a manufacturing company involves the integration of sales, operations, production scheduling, materials requirement planning and inventory with financial reports. ERP takes this a stage further in extension to all businesses, and integrates the remaining functions using relational database and object-oriented approaches to software.

The driver for the development of ERP was the recognition by organizations that they were disadvantaged in a global marketplace if their total information system consisted of different departmental functions being supported by different non-communicating computer systems. This led to many systems being involved in the handling, say, of a customer's order, as it went through the stages of placing, manufacturing, dispatch and invoicing. Moreover, merged corporations often still held independent systems for each of the components involved in the merger. The resulting set of systems could not be accessed easily to provide overall high-level business information needed for strategic development of the entire corporation.

The above ideas and concerns were not new. However, the trigger for the expansion of ERP systems came with the need to deal with the millennium (Y2K) bug. This led many organizations to consider replacing their existing legacy systems with new systems and to capitalize on the integrative opportunities offered by ERP. The later development of the World Wide Web and the possibility of greater on-line interactivity with customers further stimulated the search for an integrative approach.

The purchase of an ERP system often led to a reconsideration of the structure of the organization and the way it carried out its processes. In some cases this was beneficial, but quite often the exact nature of the purchased off-the-shelf ERP system placed constraints on the way the organization should be structured, and it was not clear that this was optimal.

In summary, the advantages of ERP leading to a single system were:

- one software vendor to deal with;
- reduced maintenance and other ongoing costs;
- a unifying and integrating strategy for the organization; and
- greater comparability between systems within the organization.

However, many systems have not lived up to their (promised) potential and have resulted in high costs, lengthy delivery times and disappointing functionality. In summary:

- Systems required high initial costs and development or tailoring, requiring long lead times.
- The software required the business to realign itself (rather than the business changing itself as a result of a more extensive business process engineering).
- The software was unable to respond to changes in the business.

The expenditure on ERP systems is beginning to decline. It leaves a small number of large ERP vendor companies which have grown with, or reoriented themselves to, enterprise resource planning systems. By far the largest of these is the German supplier SAP, with a claimed 33,200 customers in more than 120 countries.

2.4.3 Business process re-engineering

In the early 1990s, much attention was given to **business process re-engineering (BPR)**. This strategy demands a fundamental rethinking of how business processes are executed. It aims to bring about dramatic improvements by redesigning core activities such as production or sales order processing.

The origins of BPR are in the failures of organizations beset with rigid functional structures. Innovation and flexibility are often not encouraged in a strongly demarcated environment. BPR involves the consideration of particular core business processes and analysing them from start to finish. Existing structures such as departmental roles or responsibilities are ignored in an attempt to identify the key features of the business process. For example, a purchase might be followed from initial customer interest, through enquiry, order, delivery, settlement and after-sales service. Many different departments and personnel might be involved in the entire business process. By analysing the process like this, it might be possible to see why, for example, orders are delayed, delivery is made to incorrect locations or after-sales service does not meet expectations. Individuals are often too close to the process or have their own vested interests and agendas, which impede the effective completion of the process.

The evaluation of BPR has been varied. The early BPR projects took place in the difficult atmosphere of 'downsizing' in the early 1990s. The lessons of implementation were often learned 'the hard way', and the resulting effect on companies, and more so their employees, left bitter memories for many.

The critics of BPR point to its very high failure rate, with only about 30% of BPR projects clearly delivering the expected results. Their case is backed up by numerous examples of companies that effectively re-engineered themselves into liquidation. The strategy is clearly one of high risk. Fundamental change is rarely going to be readily accepted.

The proponents of BPR would say that the need to change is often inevitable. Leaner, fitter organizations, they claim, can only be produced through fundamental review and change, and failure to do so could lead to a more rapid and pronounced slide towards failure. They also point out that the critics of BPR have often characterized its use as mere 'downsizing', implying a straightforward shedding of staff and breaking up of business units. Supporters of BPR claim that it involves a much more philosophical review of the business.

Recently, the language of re-engineering has become more tempered, and many companies are considering business process improvements. This implies a more gradual and incremental strategy of looking at core processes, but perhaps just one at a time, thereby minimizing the disruption to the organization as a whole.

2.4.4 Outsourcing

The first business information systems tended to be developed and supported using in-house expertise. Project teams were set up to establish the needs and requirements and to specify the solutions. Consultants were often used to facilitate this process but the ownership was usually clearly located with the initiating organization. As the system was implemented, systems support and user support was provided by IT or computer services staff working for a department with its own line management structure. This model still prevails, particularly in many larger companies.

Over a period of time the concept of outsourcing has gained credence. Under this strategy a separate budget is established to finance the information systems requirements and then tenders are invited for the provision of the required services. The costs, risks and the associated research and development implications are transferred to the outsourcing agent thereby freeing the initiating organization to concentrate on its own area of business expertise. Specialist IT providers can reduce the cost of these services due to economies gained through specializing in this one activity. Recently there has been an increasing trend in outsourcing provision to economies such as India and the Far East where skill levels are high but wages are lower than in the West. Both routine systems maintenance and new project developments are increasingly being outsourced, adopting this strategy.

There are several reasons for adopting this approach:

- Businesses will not necessarily have the technical expertise to develop and support systems.
- In all but the largest organizations there may not be a sufficient IT requirement to justify or to retain the best technical and support staff.
- Outsource providers can specialize in their field and gain extensive sophisticated knowledge which an individual business in a non-computing-related sector could never achieve.
- Unlike an in-company IT department, outsourced service providers can seek economies, such as contracting staff overseas, to carry out functions at a reduced cost.

There are, however, some disadvantages:

- There is an inevitable loss of immediate control over the outsourced service.
- Although the initial contracting process might establish a lower cost solution, many organizations retain the services of the outsourcing company for long periods, vesting the outsourcer with an invaluable, almost unique understanding of the organization. This renders difficult any termination of the contract. In this situation the cost saving can be lost.
- There may be ethical issues concerning the employment contracts of workers in low-pay economies.

A number of services can be outsourced. Some examples include:

- system development, particularly coding software from a specification;
- system maintenance, such as hardware support, helpdesk provision;
- data entry and data conversion;
- document management such as scanning, OCR, OMR (discussed in the next chapter);
- website design and web hosting;
- back-office operations, including call centres.

One way that organizations can outsource their software requirements is to make use of an **application service provider (ASP)**. These are third-party businesses that manage software systems and services. Unlike a software vendor, an ASP will usually maintain a central access point to their services and will distribute their software over a wide area network, often using the Internet. Costs to the customer can be reduced as the expense of, for example, purchasing a mainframe computer, or an enterprise-level database solution such as Oracle is passed on to the ASP, which can distribute it over its customer base. The charge can be made on a per-usage basis or can be by subscription. ASPs might specialize in a particular sector of the economy, such as local government or health care, or might focus on clients by size, such as high-end enterprise solutions or pre-packaged mass-volume solutions. One of the most widely used applications is that of web hosting where the ASP provides expertise in the service along with web servers and other networking hardware, software, high bandwidth, backup and maintenance services.

Mini case 2.3

FT

Outsourcing

When Hurricane Katrina ravaged the US Gulf coast two years ago, among the first outsiders to have an inkling of the extent of the disaster were a group of computer engineers in Bangalore. Employees of IBM were managing computer networks for clients in the US from the Indian city as the storm wiped out systems half the world away. Since that event, one of several that helped to underline the value of its Indian outsourcing operation, the world's largest technology services company has rapidly built up its presence in the subcontinent.

The strategy is not isolated to IBM. As India emerges as the undisputed low-cost hub for global outsourcing, all of the leading western information technology services companies are setting up operations in the country on an unprecedented scale.

For India, the outcome of this struggle will be critical. The IT outsourcing and IT-enabled services sector has become an important driver of the country's economy. India's home-grown computer services outsourcing companies are able to prepare western clients' IT systems at a fraction of the cost of their global peers by drawing heavily on locals in their mid-20s whose salaries, while rising, are still well below those of their overseas rivals.

The western companies report that their Indian rivals are still largely confined to the middle to lower end of the business including writing software for banks, providing IT support for foreign retail chains and managing foreign computer networks. They have also moved further into 'business process outsourcing', an area ranging from the handling of truck leasing for US logistics companies to writing legal briefs for foreign law firms.

However, the Indians are barely present in business strategy consulting, the industry's most lucrative work, in which consultancies will help a retailer such as Wal-Mart to set up a supply chain management system or a telecommunications company to roll out a billing system.

Adapted from: **Western IT consultancies take the fight to India**
Joe Leahy, *Financial Times*, 5 June 2007

Questions

1. What benefits do companies obtain from outsourcing overseas?

2. What advantages are there to the hosting country from encouraging outsourcing?

3. What ethical implications are raised from this business strategy?

Summary

There is a general recognition that businesses must plan strategically in order to ensure that individual operating units act in a coordinated way to support the business objectives of the organization, that those objectives are realizable given the internal resources within the business and the external environment, and that current and future resource allocation is directed to the realization of these corporate objectives. Although there is no one accepted method of strategic planning, central themes are commonly accepted. Specifically, there must be a determination of business objectives, an identification of future performance against these objectives and the development of a plan to close any identified gap.

Businesses are commonly viewed as being composed of various functions. Each of these will require information in order to plan, operate and monitor performance. The function of the provision of information is thus key to an organization's success. The development of an information systems strategy to support this function recognizes the priority of information systems planning over information technology planning. The latter supports the former.

There are many frameworks within which one can develop an information systems strategy. The one provided in this chapter distinguishes the information systems strategy from the information technology strategy and within the former recognizes both the influence of factors external to the organization and those internal to it.

Factors external to the firm include the forces exerted on it, depending on the structure of the industry within which it operates. These competitive forces may be exerted by suppliers, customers, existing competitors or new entrants, or through differentiated products. An analysis of these forces can provide a guide to information systems strategy. A PEST analysis takes into account other political, economic, sociocultural and technological influences.

Emphasizing internal factors, the work of Nolan suggests that organizations undergo a series of discrete stages of development in their evolution. By identifying the current stage, an organization can plan the most effective and swift route to the next. Although this research was based largely on the evolution of mainframe systems, there are striking similarities with the development of microcomputers and local area networks. This approach has been extended by Earl. As well as the internal evolution of the information system within the organization and its connection with technological development, it is important to recognize that the technology will have an impact on the work of individuals and the roles they fulfil. Management control may be significantly affected, along with the internal structure of the organization. This must be taken into account in the formulation of strategy.

The work of Porter and Millar views the firm as being composed of a linked value chain consisting of nine primary and supporting activities. If an organization is to be competitive then each of these must function at a cost advantage over similar functions of its competitors or help to produce a differentiated product. The way in which information technology can be used to support these activities and coordinate their linkages, thereby gaining competitive advantage, was examined. The strategic grid of McFarlan and McKenny identifies the strategic impact of existing computer-supported applications as compared with planned applications. The firm broadly falls into one of four categories – support, factory, turnaround or strategic. Different information systems strategies are suggested depending on which category best fits an organization currently and which best fits its likely development.

Critical successful factor approaches view an organization as being crucially dependent on certain factors to meet its objectives. In order to keep the organization on its planned course in reaching these objectives, information on the workings of the factors needs to be supplied by the information system. In this way, the strategic information system needs of an organization can be identified and information technology planned to support them.

This chapter looks at a selection of the more influential approaches to information systems strategic planning. Other approaches, for example the information engineering approach, attempt to provide a methodology for the complete planning and development process from strategic information systems through to the implementation of designed systems. The emphasis of this chapter has been that business information needs should determine strategy, not the characteristics of the various technologies. Recently, some authors have challenged this view, citing developments in the Internet and e-commerce as evidence of technology driving business strategy.

Review questions

1. Why do businesses and other organizations have to plan strategically? What factors affect the timescale of the strategic plan?

2. How does information systems planning differ from information technology planning?

3. Outline the main characteristics of the following models and frameworks for analysis of strategy:
   (a) The five forces model
   (b) PEST analysis
   (c) Nolan's stage model
   (d) The Earl model
   (e) Internal forces model
   (f) The value chain
   (g) The strategic grid
   (h) Critical success factors.

Exercises

1. Consider the business, organization or university in which you work. Does it have:
   (a) a strategic plan?
   (b) process for developing and reviewing this strategy?
   (c) an information systems strategic plan?
   (d) a process for developing and reviewing the information systems strategy?

2. Explain and apply the *five forces* model to:
   (a) a bank
   (b) a holiday travel company.

3. By considering the business, organization or university in which you work, apply the Porter value chain analysis. To what extent is it appropriate? To what extent are information systems

used in supporting the activities and linkages? To what extent could information systems be further used?

4. Analyse the applicability of the Nolan stage model to your organization.

5. How does the Nolan stage model differ from the Earl model, and what are the likely implications for planning?

6. What are the objectives of the organization in which you work? What are the factors critical to the success of meeting these objectives? To what extent do computerized information systems play a role in the provision of information on these factors?

7. Outline factors along the lines of a PEST analysis specifically related to:
   (a) a bank
   (b) a university
   (c) a motor manufacturer.

CASE STUDY 2

Strategic planning

Andy Ferguson faced a daunting situation in 2003 when he moved up from commercial director to chief executive at the retail opticians, Dollond & Aitchison. The oldest retail chain on the UK's high streets, with 255 years of dedicated service and the Royal Warrant to its name, the 'opticians's optician' was in danger of losing sight of its customers.

The company's electronic point of sale system (Epos), installed in each of its 400 branches was old and inflexible. Written in COBOL, it had been expensively revamped in 1998 to solve the problem of the 'millennium bug' rather than run the risk of installing new and untried software.

The central supply chain and financial software, based on a package from the specialist US software house JDA, had already been fine-tuned a thousand times to match D&A's way of working and had reached the point where it could not be further upgraded. And the ancient IBM engines at the heart of the company's information systems were sorely in need of replacement.

Mr Ferguson's immediate response was to ask the price of a modern Epos system and new hardware: 'The costs were astronomical for a company like ours', he recalls.

So a different approach was required. Mr Ferguson, now 47, an approachable, energetic Scot who describes himself as 'a retailer through and through', had a number of advantages in tackling the issue. First, although no technologist – he resists laptop computers and BlackBerrys strenuously – his previous retailing experience had given him a broad appreciation of what information technology could be expected to achieve – and its limitations.

As operations director and then business unit director in an earlier career with Safeway supermarkets he had learned how powerful information could be in helping to provide customer service – if it could be analysed and harnessed: Most companies then had a plethora of information they were unable to do anything with. 'Safeway had just introduced its loyalty card. As a business director I was on the receiving end of a stream of data trying to link individual transactions to individual customers. It was physically impossible to cope with the volume and weight of information. I was excited by the prospect but unable really to harness the information', he says, arguing that in the UK perhaps only Tesco, through its joint venture with Dunhumby, has succeeded in making good use of customer data.

Mr Ferguson's second advantage was that around the time he became chief executive the company appointed Paul Willows, an internal candidate, to the post of information systems director. This was after some years during which a succession of IS directors had failed to make much of an impact on the company's problem. Mr Willows, who is still IS director, is a computer sciences graduate and has experience of the opticians business with Vision Express and other retailers. And, critically, at D&A he is a full board member.

The two sat down to plan the future. The board had decided that in a market dominated by price it would focus on customer service as its core proposition. The implication was that Mr Ferguson would have to find ways for branch staff to get their hands on the information held in 9m customer records in the database – information, as Mr Ferguson says, that most retailers would kill for: names, addresses, ages, all the raw material to draw up demographic profiles: 'We could see huge advantages in being able to segment our customers in new and different ways. The really exciting thing would be if we could get the information to our stores ahead of the customer coming in. Then their experience would be massively enhanced.'

D&A already had a reputation for technological innovation. Realizing that people often resent buying glasses and choose frames badly, it pioneered a digital imaging system allowing customers to view themselves in a variety of frames – long before digital cameras became popular. Mr Willows, with Mr Ferguson's backing, developed the idea of a system providing both central services and store support that could be accessed by any store via a browser: essentially a company intranet on a large scale.

Mr Ferguson was enthusiastic: 'I've got the information but I can't get my hands on it in one place. This offered a real-time single view. It sounded pretty good, but was it feasible technically and what would be the costs and benefits?' The company decided it needed large enterprise software to ensure the system would be future-proof and settled on SAP, the market-leading German group. D&A's parent and shareholder, the big optical group De Rigo of Italy, had installed SAP software for finance and sales and was pleased with the result. D&A's sister company in Spain had similar requirements to its own.

Mr Ferguson could see benefits in installing single company-wide software rather than tacking Epos separately on to a central IT system. There would be better quality of information and better customer segmentation. SAP also included features that would cut down on wastage by allowing frame, lens and prescription data to be matched before the glasses were manufactured.

At a likely cost of £10m, D&A and De Rigo were convinced. As luck would have it, SAP's UK implementation partner Ciber Novasoft had just completed a similar application for the do-it-yourself chain, B&Q. The project is now nine months old and the first elements are going live. The central system switches over in October and the store roll-out is planned to start in December.

Mr Ferguson says it is going well: 'We have a crisis every second day, things are taking longer than we anticipated and the number of people we've had to release from their day jobs to work on the project is absolutely phenomenal. The good news is that all the functionality we expected we have got, and the operational teams are delighted with what they can see emerging.'

It is early days to call the D&A project a success but the indicators look hopeful. These include an IS director combining computer and business skills, with a place on the board and briefing the chief executive weekly, and a chief executive who knows what he wants from his IS systems and who champions their development.

'Without doing that, I cannot see an organisation being able to do something of this scale. If it's clear that it's coming from the top, then everybody's at one with it', he says.

Adapted from: **Keeping a close eye on the customer**
Alan Cane, *Financial Times*, 30 May 2007

Questions

1. In what ways does this case study outline the need for businesses and other organizations to plan strategically?

2. Identify areas in the case study that differentiate between information systems planning and information technology planning.

3. What were the internal and external factors and forces on the business information system development described?

4. Describe how the proposed information systems might provide competitive advantage for the organization.

5. What critical success factors are identified in this project development?

References

Applegate L., McFarlan F.W. and McKenny J.L. (1999). *Corporate Information Systems Management: Text and Cases*, 5th edn. New York: Irwin/McGraw-Hill

Earl M. (1989). *Management Strategies for Information Management*. Hemel Hempstead: Prentice Hall

Galliers R.D. and Sutherland A.R. (1991). Information systems management and strategy formulation: the 'stages of growth' model revisited. *Journal of Information Systems*, 1, 2, 89–114
    This article explains the most important stages of growth models together with critiques. It also develops the authors' own variant.

Henderson J., Rockart J. and Sifonis J. (1987). Integrating management support systems into strategic information systems planning. *Journal of Management Information Systems*, 4(1), 5–24

Hirscheim R., Earl M., Feeny D. and Lockett M. (1988). An exploration into the management of the information systems function. In *Proceedings Information Technology Management for Productivity and Strategic Advantage*, IFIP Conference, March 1988

Nolan R.L. (1979). Managing the crisis in data processing. *Harvard Business Review*, March–April, 115–26

Nolan R. (1984). Managing the advanced stages of computer technology: key research issues. In *The Information Systems Research Challenge*, McFarlan F.W. (ed.), pp. 195–214. Boston: Harvard Business School Press

Porter M.E. (1980). *Competitive Strategy*. New York: Free Press

Porter M.E. (1985). *Competitive Advantage*. New York: Free Press

Porter M.E. and Millar V.E. (1985). How information gives you competitive advantage. *Harvard Business Review*, July–August, 149–60

Rockart J. (1979). Chief executives define their own data needs. *Harvard Business Review*, March–April, 81–92

Scott Morton, M.S. (ed.) (1994). *Information Technology and the Corporation of the 1990s*. Oxford: Oxford University Press

Recommended reading

Clarke S. (2006). *Information Systems Strategic Management.* Taylor & Francis Ltd

This text provides critical approaches to strategic aspects of information. It focuses on management and business aspects rather than technical implementations. It is appropriate for the general reader or MBA-level students.

Frenzel C.W. (2003). *Management of Information Technology*, 4th edn. Thompson Course Technology

A comprehensive book covering the development of IT strategy and IT planning. The book adopts a distinctive flavour by considering alternatives to traditional approaches and change management.

Galliers R.D. and Leidner D.E. (2003). *Strategic Information Management*, 3rd edn. Butterworth-Heinemann

Many of the leading academics in the area have contributed chapters on information systems and management to this book which is aimed at the MBA market. Information systems strategy and planning, and the relation between business strategy and information systems strategy is covered, as is its relation to the organizational environment.

Grindley K. (1995). *Managing IT at Board Level: The Hidden Agenda*, 2nd edn. Financial Times Prentice Hall

This is a readable, 'punchy' non-technical coverage of how management is coping/not coping with the problems of IT. It contains references to many practical examples.

Johnson G., Scholes K. and Whittington R. (2008). *Exploring Corporate Strategy*, 8th edn. Prentice Hall

This is a standard text on strategic analysis, choice and implementation. It is aimed at students on BA business studies and MBAs. It covers many of the major themes on strategic choice together with examples, exercises and case studies and has a European orientation, although some US cases are covered. Although it is not specifically aimed at IT, there is much of relevance to the strategic use of IT. There is also an accompanying 'text and cases' book.

Mohan Babu K. (2006). *Offshoring IT Services: A Framework for Managing Outsourced Projects.* Tata McGraw-Hill: India

This book provides a practical, managerial perpective on outsourcing IT services. It contains interviews and case studies, and provides suggested frameworks for managers who are considering offshore outsourcing.

McNurlin B.C. and Sprague R.H., Jr (2005). *Information Systems Management in Practice*, 7th edn. Prentice Hall

A standard comprehensive text covering the strategy and management of all aspects of information systems. Each chapter has exercises and discussion questions.

Mintzberg H., Quinn J.B. and Ghoshal S. (2003). *The Strategy Process.* Prentice Hall

Although not particularly directed at information systems or information technology, this major text has a very clear explanation of the entire strategy formulation process. It is readable, with many well-worked case studies. The length of the book, over 1000 pages, makes it a comprehensive reference.

Robson W. (1997) *Strategic Management and Information Systems: An Integrated Approach*, 2nd edn. Pitman

This is a seminal comprehensive text covering all aspects of information systems strategy and the management of information systems. It covers strategic management, management of information systems and risk management of corporate information systems. It is also useful as a reference text.

Sahay S., Nicholson B. and Krishna S. (2004). *Global IT Outsourcing: Software Development across Borders.* Cambridge University Press

This traces the management of software development across international boundaries by using case studies from North America, Europe and Asia. The latter chapters analyse the challenges facing the management of global software alliances.

Ward J. and Peppard J. (2002). *Strategic Planning for Information Systems, 3rd edn.* John Wiley & Sons.

A very well-written account of the effect that information systems have had on organizations, in particular focusing on their strategic development. The book discusses tools, techniques and management frameworks and emphasizes the importance of information systems in implementing a strategic plan.

Chapter 3

Business information technology

On completion of this chapter, you should be able to:

- Describe how computers and computer technology are used in the provision of business information
- Place current technology within a historical context
- Define the functional components of a computer
- Compare devices and media for the input and output of data
- Explain methods and techniques for data capture and select appropriate devices for particular situations
- Cite current issues in the design of processors
- Describe the different categories of software
- Differentiate between applications packages and specially commissioned software and make recommendations as to the suitability of each
- List commonly used programming languages and outline techniques used to translate them into machine-understandable format.

Introduction

In Chapter 1 the areas of information, systems and business information systems were approached from the perspective of information provision for business needs and in particular for decision support. Little emphasis was placed on the role of technology. In order to understand how computers can be used in the provision of business information, and their scope and limitations, it is important to have a basic understanding of the technological concepts. This chapter achieves this by first placing current technology within the historical context of its evolution over the last 50 years. The functional components of a computer are then explained, together with the way each function is performed by various types of hardware. The concept of a program is central to understanding the provision of computer-generated information. Various categories of programming language, including fourth-generation and scripting languages and their role in end-user systems development, are compared. Finally, organizations have a choice between applications packages and specially commissioned software. The advantages of each are outlined.

3.1 Historical development of computing technology

Electronic computers are a comparatively modern invention, although their manual predecessors go back several centuries. The mathematicians Pascal and Leibnitz developed some of the first primitive calculating machines in the seventeenth century. It was not until the mid-nineteenth century, however, that Charles Babbage designed his 'analytical engine'. This was a mechanical device incorporating a punched card input, memory, calculation section, automatic output and, importantly, a series of instructions that would control its operation.

3.1.1 The first generation

Progress in electronics allowed the first *electronic* computer to be built in the early 1940s. This was centred around the electronic valve. The valve is a device about the size of a small domestic electric light bulb. The valve is responsible for regulating and amplifying flows of electricity.

The first computers were seen mainly as pieces of research or military equipment, but by the mid-1950s the possibility of using computers for business data processing was realized. In 1954 the first commercial computers were produced. They were used for simple repetitive tasks that, until then, had been labour-intensive. Examples were payroll, billing and simple accounts processing. All the earliest computers were based on the valve. Unfortunately, valves are unreliable, consume a great deal of power, generate much unwanted heat and are large, expensive and slow in operation. In short, the development of the computer was limited by the operating characteristics of the electronics from which it was built.

3.1.2 The second generation

The reason for the increased interest and use of computers in the late 1950s and early 1960s was the development of the **second generation** of computers. These were based around the new technology of the solid-state transistor. Compared with the valve, the transistor:

- is faster in operation;
- is more reliable;
- uses less power;
- is smaller in physical size (about the size of the head of a match);
- generates less heat;
- costs less.

Not only had the hardware technology improved, so had the software. Instead of writing programs using instructions coded in 1s and 0s (or simple mnemonic translations of these instructions), programs were now written in specialized languages such as COBOL. This increased the productivity of programmers and enabled them to write more sophisticated software for business data processing.

3.1.3 The third generation

The miniaturization of transistors and their integration on circuit boards ushered in the next generation of computers. During the 1960s and early 1970s the cost of computers dropped. This was accompanied by an increase in their power. Smaller computers were now being built, and a number of suppliers entered the market specializing in these **minicomputers**. Businesses were beginning to use computers for a larger variety of purposes than previously. They were used not only for transaction processing but also for the provision of information for managerial decision making – MIS had been born. Computing equipment was now becoming cheap enough for medium-sized companies to purchase their own computing facilities. The technology of disk storage was also improving, becoming cheaper and more reliable, and providing larger storage capacities and faster access.

3.1.4 The fourth generation

The fourth generation of computers was stimulated by the dramatic developments in microchip technology. A **microchip** is a flake of silicon, smaller than a fingernail, on which millions of transistors have been etched in a mass-production process. Once again, compared with the previous technology the microchip was very much faster, cheaper, more reliable and smaller. As well as carrying out calculations, computers need to have a memory from which data and the program can be quickly retrieved. Microchips could also be used as the hardware for this fast-access memory storage. Developed in the 1970s, microchips became used in computers in the middle to late years of the decade. Firms such as Intel and Motorola have established leading positions in the worldwide production of microchips.

One of the major impacts of the microchip was that it at last became feasible to build small, cheap **microcomputers**. This potential was first exploited commercially by Apple Computers and later by IBM, which entered the market in the early 1980s and rapidly established an industry standard with the IBM PC. Increasing numbers of suppliers copied this architecture and these so-called 'clones' have become the typical personal computer (PC) or desktop computer seen today. There are two further categories, or **platforms**, of microcomputer: the Apple Macintosh (Mac) and the workstation.

The Mac has a fundamentally different and unique philosophy in terms of ease of use and extensibility. It has a different architecture and employs a different operating system. Designers and publishers often have a particular affinity for the Mac.

The workstation, such as the Sun SparcStation, is a high-powered microcomputer often employed in engineering and computer graphics environments.

Although many software packages are available for all three microcomputer platforms, they need to be programmed specifically for the operating system used by that platform.

More recent developments include highly portable computers such as a **laptop**, or **notebook** and **tablet PCs**. The performance of these machines approximates that of their more bulky desktop brothers but because they are small enough to be carried in a briefcase, they bring genuine portability to business computing.

The most recent examples of miniaturization are the hand-held devices. The **palmtop** computer has a small LCD screen and a pen for data entry. The processor is similar to that of a low-specification microcomputer and has several megabytes of RAM (see Section 3.2.7). A range of packages such as word processors and spreadsheets are available, and information can be exchanged with a desktop computer. Palmtops are sometimes referred to as **PDAs** (personal digital assistants). The miniaturization of technology has allowed mobile telephones to incorporate most of these features. Internet access, global positioning software and video capture are now possible on the most recent generation of mobile telephones.

For businesses, the development of the desktop computer has had a major impact on the way computers are used. Medium-sized and large organizations usually still have a larger computer (minicomputer or mainframe computer) for their major data-processing and management information provision. This installation will require a computer centre of trained technical staff to operate the company's information resource. However, the presence of cheap desktop computers has enabled individual departments and sections to purchase their own equipment. They typically use this for word processing, spreadsheet modelling, small database applications, electronic filing and managing multimedia content. Because desktop computers are so cheap, they can be purchased using departmental budgets without seeking central approval. This has a number of effects. First, the resulting greater autonomy and control possessed by the department is likely to stimulate computer use. Second, the power of the central computing resource is diminished. Traditional computer centres often view the mushrooming of desktop computers with alarm. This is based on a fear of a lack of standardization of hardware and software throughout the organization. Finally, there may also be a duplication of data and applications development effort on the part of staff in separate localities unless coordination is achieved.

The proliferation of local desktop computers in large organizations has been an impact of the development of the microchip. Businesses are able to use desktop computers in their day-to-day transaction processing, office work and decision support. A very large number of small businesses can afford to computerize their standard business functions. This has been stimulated by the production of cheap software that is easy to use by personnel who have not had formal technical computer training.

The explosion of desktop computers reflects the breakdown in **Grosch's law**. This states that the computing power of a computer is proportional to the square of its cost. In other words, it was always more cost-efficient for an organization requiring computing power to purchase a large (and therefore centralized machine) than several smaller desktop computers or minicomputers.

The power of the desktop computer has been further enhanced by the development of **local area networks**. These link various pieces of hardware, including desktop computers, together in order to communicate with each other and to share resources.

The rapid increase in performance and decrease in price can be seen by consulting Table 3.1. No other form of technology can boast such rapid performance and price developments. If a luxury motor car of the 1940s, for example a Rolls-Royce, had demonstrated changes on the same scale it would cost about a pound sterling, travel at one thousand million miles per hour at ten million miles to the gallon of fuel. It would also be the size of a matchbox yet, paradoxically, have ten thousand times the luggage capacity of the 1940s' Rolls-Royce!

3.2 Hardware

The terms 'hardware', 'software' and 'firmware' occur frequently in any literature concerned with computers. It is important at the outset to have some understanding of their meanings:

Table 3.1 An indicative summary of the effects of technological advance on the performance of computers

Date	Generation	Technology	Number of Instructions executed per second	Storage capacity (number of characters)	Cost (for a typical large computer)	Average time between breakdowns
1950s	1	Valve	1,000	10,000	£5m	Hours
1960s	2	Transistor	100,000	100,000	£2m	Hundreds of hours
1970s	3	Integrated transistor circuit board	10,000,000	10,000,000	£4m+	Thousands of hours
1980s	4	Micro-integrated circuit (microchip)	1,000,000,000	1,000,000,000	£2m+	Years
1990s			5,000,000,000	100,000,000,000	£1m+	Years
2000s			50,000,000,000	50,000,000,000	£100,000	Years

- **Hardware** is the physical components in a computer system. Circuits, keyboards, disk drives, disks and printers are all examples of pieces of hardware.

- **Software** is a set of instructions, written in a specialized language, the execution of which controls the operation of the computer. Programs are examples of software.

- **Firmware** is the permanent storage of program instructions in hardware. It is usually used to refer to a set of instructions that is permanently encoded on a microchip. The term 'firmware' is used because it is the inseparable combination of hardware and software.

3.2.1 Functional components of a computer system

A computer system is a system that accepts data as input and produces information as output. Information, as will be recalled from Chapter 1, is data that has been processed to serve some purpose. In producing this, the intermediate products of this process may be stored. The process of transformation of inputs into outputs is carried out by electronic circuitry. The process is controlled by a sequence of instructions – the program – that is stored in the computer.

Computer systems fit the common systems model explained in Chapter 1. Figure 3.1 illustrates the basic organization of a computer system.

1. **Input:** The purpose of the input component of a computer system is:
   (a) to accept data in the required form;
   (b) to convert this data to a machine-understandable form;
   (c) to transmit this data to the central processing unit.

Examples of input devices to be explained later are keyboards, magnetic ink character readers, bar-code readers, optical character readers and the mouse.

Figure 3.1 Functional components of a computer system

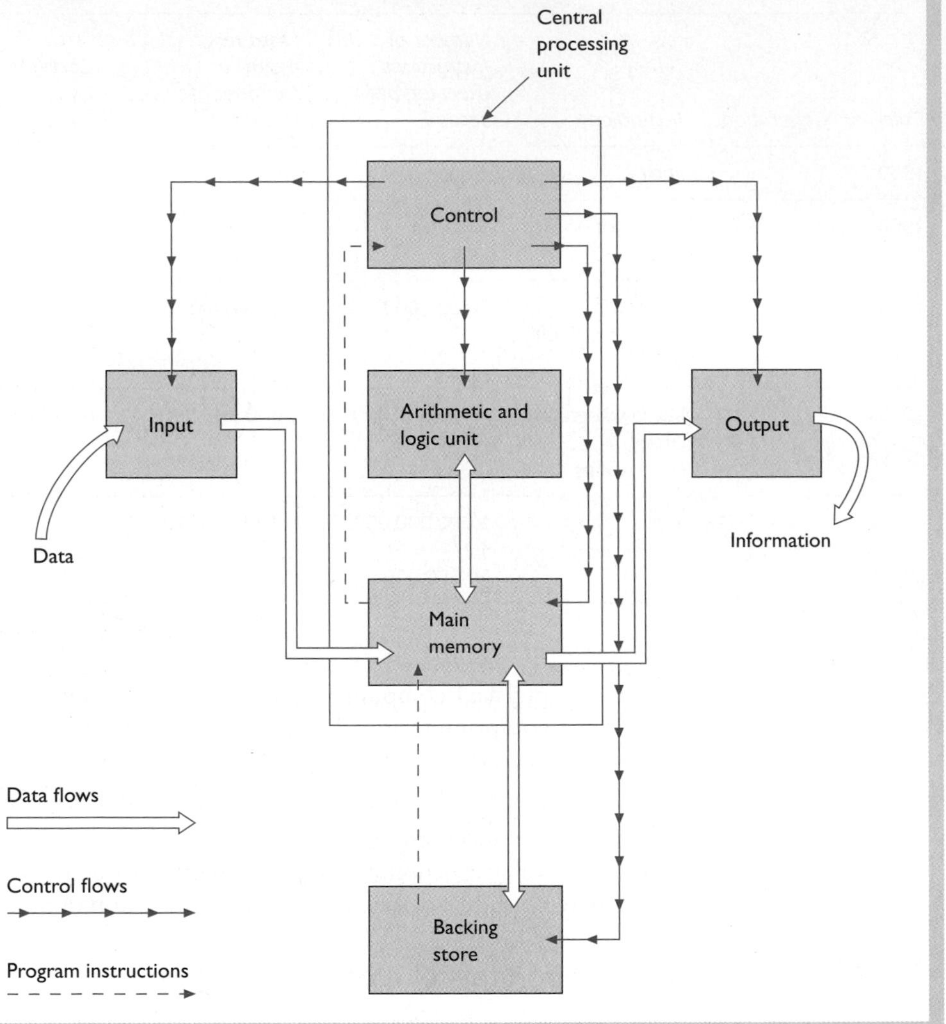

Central processing unit

Control

Input

Data

Arithmetic and logic unit

Output

Information

Main memory

Data flows

Control flows

Program instructions

Backing store

2. **Central processing unit (CPU):** This is made up of three components: the control unit, the arithmetic and logic unit, and the main memory.

   (a) The purpose of the **control unit** is:
   - to decode and execute the program instructions one by one;
   - to control and coordinate data movements within the CPU and between the CPU and the other components of the computer system.

   (b) The purpose of the **arithmetic and logic unit (ALU)** is:
   - to carry out arithmetic operations – for example, to add two numbers together;
   - to carry out logical operations – for example, to compare two numbers to establish which is the larger.

(c) The purpose of the **main memory** (synonyms – fast memory, immediate access memory, core store, direct access memory) is:
- to store programs during their execution;
- to store data that is being used by the current program;
- to store the operating system (this is an important program in the control of the computer; details are covered in a later section of the chapter).

Currently, the main form of hardware for carrying out the functions of the central processing unit is based on the microchip.

3. **Secondary storage (backing store):** The purpose of secondary storage is:

(a) to maintain a permanent record of data and programs when not being used by the CPU;

(b) to maintain a store for the program and data currently being used if the main memory is not large enough to accommodate the entire program and data;

(c) to maintain a copy for security purposes of data held in the main memory;

(d) to act as a secondary input/output device when the input is in magnetic form or the output is required in magnetic form.

Examples of secondary store hardware to be covered later are magnetic and optical disk devices, magnetic tape machines, and tape streamers.

4. **Output:** The purpose of the output component of a computer system is:

(a) to accept information/data from the CPU;

(b) to convert this information/data into the required output form.

Examples of output devices are printers, monitors, machines for producing computer output on microfilm and voice synthesizers.

In the next sections, each of these functional components is treated in some detail. In particular, the various ways in which each may be physically realized in a modern computer system are explained and evaluated.

3.2.2 Input devices, media and data capture methods

The purposes of input devices are:

■ to accept data in the required form;

■ to convert this data to a machine-understandable form; and

■ to transmit this data to the central processing unit.

Keyboard

The most common keyboard device used is the QWERTY keyboard. Keyboard data entry is almost invariably accompanied by a monitor or screen on which the characters input to the keyboard are displayed. Using a keyboard for data entry is common to a wide range of applications. They fall into three main categories:

1. The entry of data from a source document such as an invoice or an order. Controls must ensure that all the data is copied correctly and completely. Data entry controls are covered in the later chapter on controls.

2. Interactive use of the computer by a user. Here there is no source document but the user is inputting commands or queries into the computer system.

3. The entry of text data, as in word processing.

Advantages: Keyboard data entry has a number of advantages over other forms of data input:

- There is a low initial cost for purchase of the equipment.
- The method is extremely flexible as it relies heavily on the person entering the data. People are flexible.

Disadvantages: There are also a number of disadvantages:

- For efficient use, training of personnel is needed.
- It is a slow form of data entry. People are slow.
- It is costly in operation as it relies on people. People are expensive to employ compared with the capital cost of equipment.
- Unless there are adequate controls, using a keyboard will lead to high error rates. People are error-prone.

Where data is input by keyboard, invariably a **mouse** is used as a supporting device. The movement of the mouse controls the positioning of a pointer (often an arrow) on the monitor. The pointer can be moved to a position on the screen to select an item such as a menu option or position a cursor, such as the text insertion marker (called a caret) in a word processor. Alternatively, in graphics applications the movement can be used to trace out lines and draw and colour shapes. On a laptop, the function of a mouse is often implemented using a touch-sensitive pad and accompanying buttons.

Multimedia input devices

- **Digital camera:** A digital camera is similar in appearance to a normal camera and captures still images. Rather than using photographic film, the images are stored in memory inside the camera and later transferred to a computer. An advantage of the digital camera is that pictures of poor quality can immediately be deleted and replaced.
- **Webcam:** A webcam is similar to a digital camera in that it digitally captures images. Webcams are low-cost devices that are connected to a desktop computer system and usually placed on top of the monitor. Images are not usually stored but are communicated in real time using a local network connection or the Internet to another computer user.
- **Video capture:** Moving images, from either a digital video camera, a television transmission source or a prerecorded video disk or cassette, can be input directly into a computer with a video capture card installed. These images can then be edited or enhanced in a variety of ways and then either stored or output for immediate display.
- **Scanner:** A scanner is a desktop device used to capture a document image. The document is placed on a glass plate and an image is optically captured by passing a bright light across the source document. The image is converted into a digital bit-map, an array of 1s and 0s, and transmitted to a computer, where it can be stored in memory and later edited, if required, and saved. A particular application of scanning is in optical character recognition, which is described below.
- **Voice data entry:** Voice data entry consists of the reception of speech data by a microphone, the conversion of the data into electronic signals, the recognition of the data and its final conversion into textual form.

Currently, voice data entry systems are already used in telephone-based information provision and order-processing systems. Software for the acceptance of speech that is then turned into text has become more readily available. These programs run on standard PCs and interface with standard word-processing packages. In order to work effectively the user must undertake a period of training on the computer – training, that is, of the computer in order to allow it to recognize the particular voice patterns of the user. This typically takes a few hours. Accuracy rates of 95% with speech input at over 100 words per minute are claimed as standard at the current level of development.

The main advantage of voice data entry then lies in the possibility of remote interrogation of computers for information and the preparation of text documents by unskilled personnel rather than in high-volume business data entry.

Optical character readers

Optical character recognition (OCR) entails the reading of preprinted characters on documents. These documents are passed through an optical character reader, which optically detects the characters on the document and converts them to code, which is sent to the CPU.

Many large public utilities, such as gas, electricity and water, use OCR, as do the major credit card companies. The method is for the billing company to prepare a turnaround document with billing details and an attached counterfoil for payment. The customer returns the counterfoil with their payment. As well as details of the required payment being printed on the counterfoil, a special section is reserved for the characters that are to be optically read. This section is generally at the bottom of the counterfoil and appears below a printed warning such as 'do not write or mark below this line'. The characters will give the account number of the bill receiver together with other details. These may include the postal area, the type of customer, the amount of the bill and other management information.

A number of standard character fonts are capable of being read by commercial optical character readers. OCR-A is a standard American font that is used by about three-quarters of US applications. OCR-B is a standard British font. Examples of these fonts are shown in Figure 3.2.

Figure 3.2 Examples of optical character fonts: (a) OCR-A; (b) OCR-B

(a)

ABCDEFGHIJKLMNOPQRST
UVWXYZ
1234567890 . ¬ ; : &

(b)

abcdefghijklmnopqrstuvwxyz
ABCDEFGHIJKLMNOPQRSTUVWXYZ
1234567890 .,;:&!?

The characters may be preprinted on the documents using a standard printing technique such as litho. However, it is more usual for the character data to be produced using a computer-driven printer. Optical character readers have now been produced that will read carefully produced handwritten numbers and letters. This extends the use of OCR beyond the limitations of turnaround documents, as data can be entered by hand between the stages of document production and document reading. A common application of this form of data input is in hand-held PDAs. Many of these devices allow the user to write characters with a stylus into a particular area of the screen. These are converted immediately into printable characters and redisplayed on the text entry portion of the screen.

OCR has a number of advantages and disadvantages over keyboard entry.

Advantages: The advantages of OCR as opposed to keyboard entry are:

■ It is cheap in operation for high-volume activities, such as billing, which can include preprinted characters.

■ It has low error rates.

■ It is fast. Up to 500 characters per second can be read.

■ The fonts are easily readable by people (unlike magnetic character fonts).

Disadvantages: There are two main disadvantages:

■ The equipment is expensive to purchase.

■ It is easy to corrupt the characters; this can often be achieved by small pieces of dirt or smudges.

Mini case 3.1

FT

Optical character recognition

When I began my drive for a cleaner desktop in the mid-1990s, the first thing I did was to install a business card scanner called CardScan Executive from Corex Systems. It allowed me to capture and organize the data from my business cards in digital form. The latest version includes an updated, sleek desktop colour scanner and a Windows-based software bundle that combines optical character recognition software, optimized for the great variety of business cards, and an easy-to-use contact management database.

Scanning a business card takes three seconds. Then the OCR software gets to work interpreting the image and putting each component – name, address, phone number and so on – into the right database field. It does not get it right every time but the software is adept at interpreting even the most complex business cards. And it beats manually entering business card data.

CardScan is an excellent tool for anyone who collects a lot of business cards and needs an integrated contact database. It may even move users such as me a step closer to having an organized, if not paper-free, desktop.

Adapted from: **Business card scanners bring order to desktop in disarray**
Paul Taylor, FT.com, 26 October 2006

Questions

1. What are the advantages of using the CardScan device?

2. Why might the device not work for 100% of all cards?

Figure 3.3 Examples of magnetic ink character fonts: (a) E13B; (b) CMC7

(a)

0 1 2 3 4 5 6 7 8 9 ⑊ ⑆ ⑉ ⑈ ⑇

(b)

A B C D E F G H I J K L M N O P Q R S
T U V W X Y Z
1 2 3 4 5 6 7 8 9 0

Magnetic ink character readers

Magnetic ink character recognition (MICR) is a method of data entry widely used in the banking system for customers' cheques. Each cheque has identifying information (cheque number, account code and bank sort code) printed in magnetic ink in the lower left-hand corner. On depositing a cheque at the bank, the following process takes place. It is passed to an employee, who prints the amount of the cheque using a special machine; this appears on the right-hand side of the cheque. The cheque is then passed under a magnet, which magnetizes the iron oxide particles in the ink. It is finally sent through another machine, which detects the centres of magnetization and converts these into the codes for each character, representing the amount of the cheque.

The style of typeface, called the **font**, used by the British banking system is E13B. Another internationally recognized standard font is CMC7. This has characters as well as numbers and is used by the Post Office in its postal order system. Examples of both fonts are shown in Figure 3.3.

A cheque is an example of a **turnaround document**. This is defined as a document that is:

- machine-produced
- machine-readable
- readable by human beings.

Because of their machine-readability, turnaround documents allow the fast entry of data with low error rates.

Advantages: The advantages of MICR as opposed to keyboard entry are:

- It is cheap in operation for high-volume activities such as cheque processing.
- It has very low error rates. This is of crucial importance in the banking system.
- The magnetic characters are resistant to corruption by the folding of cheques or smudges of dirt.
- It is fast – for example, up to 1000 characters per second can be read.

Disadvantages: There are two main disadvantages:

- The equipment is expensive to purchase.
- The fonts are not easily readable; this limits the use of the method to applications where this is unimportant.

Both MICR and OCR suffer from the same limitation in that they are inflexible methods of data entry. Keyboard entry allows a large amount of 'intelligent preprocessing' by persons before data entry. This implies flexibility in the interpretation of handwritten data entered on documents between their production and final data entry of their contents.

Bar-code readers

Bar-codes are now familiar as part of the printed packaging on supermarket products. A bar-code consists of a series of thick and thin black bars divided by thick and thin spaces printed on a light-coloured background. These bars correspond to digits, which are also printed underneath the bar-code.

There are two common systems of bar-codes. The earlier Universal Product Code (UPC) is used in the United States. In Europe, the standard is the European Article Number (EAN). EAN consists of 13 digits, represented by 26 lines. The digits have a standard interpretation. Two digits indicate the country of origin of the product, five digits indicate the manufacturer, five digits indicate the product, and the remaining digit is used for checking that the other digits have been read correctly by the device reading the bar-code. Figure 3.4 shows a bar-code.

The bar-code is machine-read either by passing a 'light pen' over it in either direction or by passing the bar-code over a reader machine. The second method is more flexible as the bar-code can be passed over at any angle as long as the code is pointing towards the sensitive screen of the machine. The latter type of machine is common in supermarkets.

Bar-codes are suitable for data input where it is important to maintain a record of the movements of material goods. This occurs at the point of sale in a supermarket, at a library loan desk and in stock control systems.

As mentioned previously, a common use for bar-codes is at checkout points in supermarkets and other retail outlets. The bar-code is read at the point of sale and so such a system is known as a **point-of-sale (POS)** system. The way these systems typically work is that the code for the product, having been identified by the bar-code reader, is sent to the computer. There, the relevant record for the product is retrieved. The product price and a short description of the product are then sent back electronically to the point of sale, where the details are printed on the till slip. At the same time, the computer records of the quantity of the item held are decreased by one unit.

Figure 3.4 A bar-code – EAN standard

5 000243 925103

Advantages: The advantages of a bar-code point-of-sales system over the more traditional manually controlled checkout till are:

- Better management information: management has up-to-date information on stock levels and can thus sensibly plan purchases and avoid stockouts. The records of sales are also date- and time-stamped. This enables analysis of sales data to identify fast- and slow-moving items and peaks and troughs in the sales of items. It is also important to be able to have information on consumer patterns of expenditure. It may affect shelving policy if it is discovered that purchases of smoked salmon are often accompanied by white wine, whereas peanuts are associated with bottles of beer.

- Better customer service: there are lower error rates than for manual checkout tills. This is because operators have little scope for incorrect data entry. Itemized bills provide customers with the ability to check their purchases against till slips. Certain types of checkout fraud are also rendered impossible with the system.

- Easier implementation of price changes and special offers: because prices are held in computer records, a change of price merely requires a single data change in the item record and a replacement of the price card in the shop display. Individual pricing of items is no longer necessary (but see *Disadvantages*). Offers such as 'three for the price of two' can be easily implemented and detected at the till.

- Staff training time to use the systems is minimal.

Disadvantages: The two main disadvantages are:

- The necessary equipment is expensive to purchase and install.

- Unless there is an adequate manual backup system, a breakdown will immediately stop the retail sales of the organization. A typical manual backup is for a human readable version of the information to accompany the bar-code; this can be entered into the system using a keyboard.

Optical mark readers

Optical mark recognition (OMR) is a common form of high-volume data entry where the application requires the selection of a data item from various alternatives. In its most common form it consists of a printed document on which the various options are displayed, together with a box, or field, for each. To select an option, the person entering data puts a mark in the relevant box. Part of a typical document is shown in Figure 3.5.

Once marked, the document is passed through an optical mark reader. This machine optically scans the boxes and determines those in which a mark has been made – a 1 corresponds to a mark and a 0 to the absence of a mark. The computer, which has been preprogrammed with the meanings of the boxes, then interprets the binary code sent from the optical mark reader.

Typical applications are market research surveys, multiple-choice examination questions, time sheets for the entry of start and stop times for employees, and order forms for the selection of stock.

Advantages: OMR has a number of advantages over keyboard entry, MICR and OCR:

- Data can be entered on to a document not only by data entry personnel at the data entry stage but also by other people at any stage between the production of the document and its reading. This is a distinct advantage over OCR and MICR, which have a basic 'data out equals data in' limitation.

Figure 3.5 Part of a typical document suitable for OMR

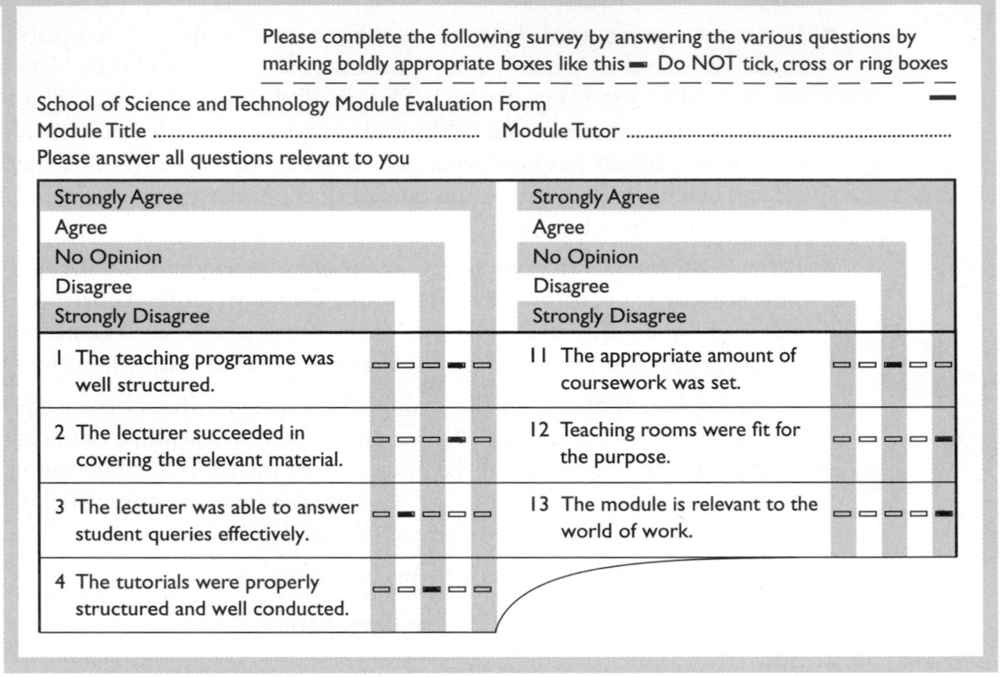

Please complete the following survey by answering the various questions by
marking boldly appropriate boxes like this ▬ Do NOT tick, cross or ring boxes

School of Science and Technology Module Evaluation Form
Module Title .... Module Tutor ....
Please answer all questions relevant to you

Strongly Agree		Strongly Agree	
Agree		Agree	
No Opinion		No Opinion	
Disagree		Disagree	
Strongly Disagree		Strongly Disagree	
1 The teaching programme was well structured.	□ □ □ ▬ □	11 The appropriate amount of coursework was set.	□ □ ▬ □ □
2 The lecturer succeeded in covering the relevant material.	□ □ □ ▬ □	12 Teaching rooms were fit for the purpose.	□ □ □ □ ▬
3 The lecturer was able to answer student queries effectively.	□ ▬ □ □ □	13 The module is relevant to the world of work.	□ □ □ □ ▬
4 The tutorials were properly structured and well conducted.	□ □ ▬ □ □		

- No knowledge or skill is necessary to enter data on to the document other than the ability to read and make the appropriate mark. This is to be compared with skills needed to operate a keyboard.
- It is less susceptible to erroneous machine reading than an OCR document.
- It is cheap and fast in operation compared with keyboard entry.

Disadvantages: There are also a number of disadvantages:

- There is a high initial cost for the purchase of the equipment.
- Its use is limited to those applications where selection from a few presented alternatives is required. It is therefore not appropriate for applications where character data is required. For instance, to enter a person's surname consisting of up to 15 characters would need 15 rows, each with 26 options for selection. Not only would this use much document space, it would not be easy to enter the data.
- It is not suitable where the printed documents need to be changed frequently as a result of flexible data requirements. Each document change necessitates the reprogramming of the optical mark reader.

Remote data entry using network technology

Increasingly, customers and businesses are being encouraged to make requests and enquiries or to place orders by establishing a data communications channel and, for example, completing an electronic form held on a web page. In other cases, electronic invoices are produced, which also cut the cost of handling paper and data entry.

Web page forms have similar advantages to their paper counterparts in that they direct the user to fill in data in a predefined and structured format. In addition, the accuracy of the data can be checked. For example, important fields can be made mandatory and thus cannot be left blank. Validation checks, where required, can be performed on key items of data. The data on the form is then uploaded to the host computer and can be input directly into their system.

Advantages: Remote data entry has several advantages:

- Data can be entered at the convenience of the user of the system, for example when the receiver is closed for business.
- The validation checks ensure that data is provided in a format that can be readily accepted.
- It is a cheap and fast method to accept data as the user is carrying out the inputting tasks.
- It removes the need to produce an input document.

Disadvantages: There are also disadvantages:

- There is a high initial cost in creating the website and pages to allow the data entry to be performed.
- The system requires a level of both computing equipment and expertise of the user. This minimum specification will be changing over time.
- Participants must have on-line access to place or process an order.

Swipe cards

These are in the form of plastic cards incorporating a magnetic stripe that contains identifying information. The magnetic stripe can be read by a machine, which converts this into code to be sent to the main body of the computer. They are most commonly used as identification for cash-dispensing machines or point-of-sales systems for credit card sales.

Smart cards

The smart card contains information encoded in a microchip built into the structure of the card. They are harder than swipe cards to copy, can contain much information and can be programmed to self-destruct if incorrect identifying information is keyed into the machine reading them. The use of smart cards has increased dramatically in recent years with the introduction of 'chip and pin' credit cards. These authenticate a purchase by a combination of data obtained from the remote system and from the data stored on the card itself.

Touch screen

A touch screen enables the selection of an item from a screen display by pointing to it with a finger, or touching with a stylus. It is used in some business applications such as stock dealing and in information kiosks, and is a common form of data input for hand-held devices such as PDAs.

Magnetic tapes and disks, optical disks and memory cards

These are often regarded as input and output media utilizing corresponding devices, such as disk drives, as input and output devices. In a sense this is true. For example, a road map can be purchased on a memory card and inserted into a PDA for use. However, here these media and devices are regarded as secondary, not because of their importance but rather because data held on them must previously have been entered through one of the other entry methods or be the output of computer processing. They are discussed in the next section.

3.2.3 Factors involved in the selection of data entry devices, media and methods

The data entry methods mentioned earlier have different characteristics and therefore will be appropriate for different types of data entry application. The main features that determine the data entry method are as follows:

- **The type of application:** This is perhaps the most important factor. Some applications allow turnaround documents to be used, while others do not. Some applications need only allow selections from a limited range of choices, which would suggest OMR, while others require the addition of a wide variety of data. Interrogation generally requires data entry personnel to interact with the computer, so a keyboard is required. It is impossible to specify in advance the range of applications, together with the most suitable data entry method and devices. Each application needs to be matched against the characteristics of the data entry methods before a choice can be made.

- **Costs:** In particular the difference between operating costs and initial costs. Most methods that are low in initial costs, such as keyboard entry, are high in operating costs, and vice versa.

- **Speed and volume of input:** Some methods are only applicable to high-volume applications.

- **Error tolerance:** All errors are undesirable, but in some applications it is more crucial to prevent their occurrence than in others. The banking sector, for instance, places a high priority on preventing error. There are many controls that minimize erroneous data entry. These are covered extensively in Chapter 9 on control. For the purposes of this chapter, it is worthy of note that those data entry methods that involve less human skill, such as MICR, are less prone to error than, for example, keyboard entry.

Over the last two decades, the cost of processing hardware has dropped considerably. The costs of producing software are also likely to diminish over the coming years. With the increasing power of computers to process data and the increasing demands of management for information based on this data, the importance of cutting data entry costs will be emphasized. It is likely that automated compared with manual data entry will continue to increase in the future.

3.2.4 Secondary storage devices

The purpose of secondary storage is:

- to maintain a permanent record of data and programs when not being used by the CPU;

- to maintain a store for the program and data currently being used if the main memory is not large enough to accommodate the entire program and data;

- to maintain a copy for security purposes of data held in the main memory; and
- to act as a secondary input/output device when the input is in electronically readable form or the output is required to be stored in electronic form.

All computers need permanent secondary storage facilities because the main memory store within the central processing unit is limited in size, and in the event of a power failure or the machine being switched off the contents of this main memory disappear.

The factors to be looked at when considering secondary storage technology are:

- **Speed of data retrieval:** Given a data retrieval instruction executed in the CPU, the quicker the desired data can be loaded into the main memory the better.

- **Storage capacity:** The larger the amount of data stored and accessible to the storage device the better.

- **Cost of storage:** This is usually measured in terms of the cost to store one byte of data (one byte – eight bits – of space is sufficient to store one character).

- **Robustness and portability of the storage medium:** The more secure the data storage medium is against corruption or 'crashes' the better.

Storage devices are often classified according to the type of access to data permitted by them. In general, there are **sequential-access storage devices** and **direct-access storage devices**. The difference between the two is that with the former, access to data begins at a given point on the storage medium, usually the beginning, and the entire storage medium is searched in sequence until the target data item is found. With direct-access storage devices, the location of the required data item can be identified. The target data item can then be retrieved from this location or addressed without the need to retrieve data stored physically prior to it; in other words, access is direct. Generally, all direct-access storage devices also allow sequential retrieval if required.

From a business information and business data processing perspective, these differences in access lead to differences in suitability for business applications. In particular, sequential-access storage devices are suitable for only those applications that require sequential processing. Here would be included routine data-processing operations such as the billing of customers, the production of customer statements and the production of payrolls. Many applications, including all those concerned with the selective retrieval and presentation of information for decision making, require direct access and thus direct-access storage media and devices. The increased use of computers for decision support, forward planning and management control has led to the increased use of direct-access storage devices as the more important form of secondary storage. Where the store of corporate data is centralized and held for access by many applications, then it is imperative to have direct-access storage.

This is not a text on the more detailed aspects of hardware. However, it is important to understand the basic principles underlying modern storage devices. Without this knowledge it is difficult to appreciate why the types of business activity impose restrictions on the forms of appropriate storage. The following are common types of storage media.

Optical disks

Optical disk technology consists of encoding data on a disk that is covered with a transparent plastic coating. The data can then be read by means of laser light focused with great accuracy on to the spinning disk; this is illustrated in Figure 3.6.

Figure 3.6 Reading data from a CD-ROM

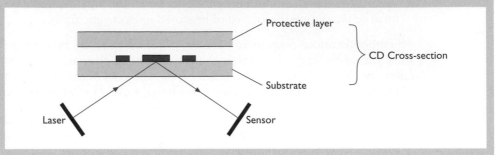

The storage capacity of such disks is huge: for a 12cm disk it can exceed 17 gigabytes. The trend is towards increasing this capacity. Because the disks are protected by a transparent plastic cover and there is no danger of the optical head coming into accidental contact (head crash) with the surface of the disk, optical systems are very robust.

There are three main types of optical system. **CD-ROM** was the first to be developed. The data is stored as a series of microscopic pits, which are burned into the surface of the disk. These disks are capable of read-only access but have very large storage capacities. The read rate of CD-ROMs has increased rapidly over the last few years – CD-ROM drives with read-in rates of over 50 times early read-in rates are now common. The costs of production of CD-ROMs is small for large production runs, and the cost of CD-ROM drives has dropped from several thousands of dollars to less than 50 dollars. CD-ROMs have three main uses:

1. **Software provision:** Most software is too large to be stored on floppy disks, and it is now usual that purchased software is provided on CD-ROM. This has paralleled the trend for the inclusion of CD-ROM devices in modern business PCs.

2. **Multimedia provision:** Modern PCs have the software and hardware capacity to display graphics, audio and video, as well as text. The storage capacity needed for the data for these is very large. CD-ROMs can meet this requirement. This ability has led to the development of multimedia disks, which intersperse text with graphics, audio and visual output. This is particularly common with the multi-billion dollar business of computer games. Also, businesses often produce marketing materials on CD-ROM for easy distribution.

3. **Mass storage of reference material:** Where reference material seldom changes, CD-ROM is ideal for cheap, easy-to-handle storage. Examples are accounting data of UK companies, telephone directories and permanent components details of manufactured products. Text archives of newspapers and academic journals are now commonly provided on CD-ROM for easy access in libraries.

A second type of optical system is the **WORM disk** (write once, read many times). These disks are often referred to as CD-recordable, or CD-R. This system allows data to be written once to any part of the disk. The data is written on to the disk by burning into a layer of sensitive dye. Once written, the data cannot be altered, although it can be read many times. WORM disk systems are thus more flexible than CD-ROMs for business purposes. The inability to remove data once encoded opens up the possibility for the permanent archiving of transactions. This is of importance from an accounting perspective in that a complete history of a business transaction's life is held permanently on record. Known as the **audit trail**, it can be used to establish the authenticity of accounting balances.

Finally, there is the full **read/write optical disk**. These are often referred to as CD-rewritable, or CD-RW. These provide mass, flexible, direct-access secondary storage at a low cost per byte of information stored. The material used in the recording layer of the disk adopts different properties depending on the temperature applied to it. These changeable states allow the recorded data to be amended by heating those parts of the disk to a different temperature. Optical disks are rivalling magnetic media in larger systems as the main form of secondary storage.

The latest technology in optical storage is the **DVD** (digital video disk, or digital versatile disk). These disks have the general appearance of traditional CDs but can contain a much larger volume of data. This is achieved by using a more precise laser, a narrower track width and smaller pits to store the 1s and 0s; the difference between the density of data stored on CDs and DVDs is illustrated in Figure 3.7.

In addition, a disk can be read from both surfaces and, by refocusing the laser beam, data can be read from more than one layer on each surface. This, combined with improved algorithms for error detection and data compression, allows up to 17 gigabytes (Gb) of data to be stored on a single DVD. Popular applications of DVD are for video and audio data, such as feature films and interactive training packages. The large potential storage capacity makes DVDs an attractive alternative for all forms of commercial data storage, and for large software suites that would otherwise require several CDs. Inevitably, the development path of DVD is mirroring that of the CD in that WORM and erasable DVDs have become commercially available.

Figure 3.7 Storage of 1s and 0s on optical media

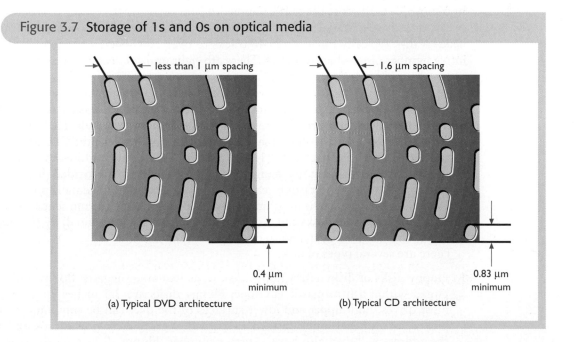

less than 1 μm spacing

1.6 μm spacing

0.4 μm
minimum

0.83 μm
minimum

(a) Typical DVD architecture

(b) Typical CD architecture

Figure 3.8 A typical magnetic disk

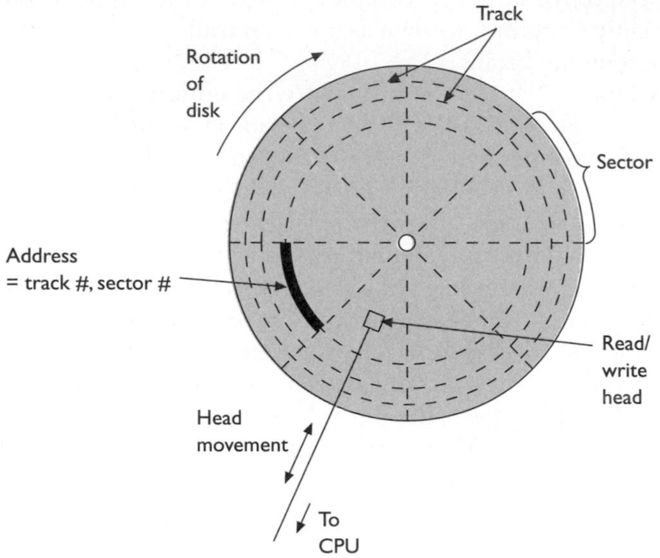

Magnetic disks

A magnetic disk has a magnetizable surface on which data is stored in concentric rings called **tracks** (Figure 3.8). These tracks are not visible to the eye. Each track is accessed by a movable read/write head. The number of concentric tracks on a disk is determined by the disk drive manufacturer and the program controlling the movement of the disk head. A disk typically ranges from 40 tracks to over 200. The disk is divided logically into a number of pie-shaped sectors. There are eight or more sectors on each disk. Once again, the number is determined by software.

The combination of a track number (track #) and a sector number (sector #) is called an **address**. The read/write head can be sent directly to an address by rotation of the disk and movement of the read/write head over the radius of the disk. The content of an entire address is the smallest unit that can be transferred between the CPU and the disk in one operation. The fact that (1) the disk is divided into addresses and (2) the read/write head can be sent to a designated address means that provided the address of a piece of data is known or can be calculated, direct access to the data is possible. This characteristic of a disk is the most important in distinguishing it from sequential media such as magnetic tape. Disks can also be read sequentially if required, by first reading one track and then the next, and so on.

There are several types of disk:

1. **Floppy disks** or **diskettes:** A floppy disk is, as its name suggests, floppy and is contained within a firm plastic envelope. Floppy disks are 3.5 inches in diameter. In most drives, both upper and lower surfaces of the disk can be simultaneously employed for storage (double-headed disk drive). As well as having a track and sector the address will then also have a surface number. Floppy disks typically store 1.44

megabytes (Mb) as standard. They can easily be inserted and removed from their drives and are portable. Floppy disks rotate at about five revolutions per second and so access to an address takes less than a second.

2. **Hard disk:** In order to increase the storage capacity of a disk and decrease its access time it is necessary to use different technology. Hard disks are inflexible magnetic disks sealed within their own drives. This provides an environment protected from dust. They can rotate at faster speeds than floppy disks and rather than the read/write head being in contact with the surface of the disk it floats just above it.

   Hard disks have significantly larger storage capacity than floppy disks, with access speeds significantly faster. Hard disks that can store over 200 gigabytes of data are common, with the trend being towards larger storage capacities. Hard disks provide the fundamental secondary storage in desktop and laptop computers.

3. **Exchangeable disk packs:** Larger computers use exchangeable packs of hard disks. These are usually 14 inches in diameter and come in packs of up to 10 disks, which are double-sided except for the two outer surfaces. The disks are read by means of a movable arm with read/write heads for each surface (see Figure 3.9). Tracks that are directly above and below one another on the disk pack are said to constitute a **cylinder**. A large mainframe system may have many disk drives and so can have massive direct-access secondary storage.

The trend in hardware is towards developing disk technology that is cheaper, has greater capacity and faster access times, and is more robust. Ultimately, however, the storage efficiency and access speeds for magnetic disk systems are limited by the moving mechanical parts, in particular the read/write head, and by the density with which data can be packed on to the magnetizable medium. These limitations put magnetic storage devices at a significant disadvantage compared with optical disk technology.

Figure 3.9 An exchangeable disk pack

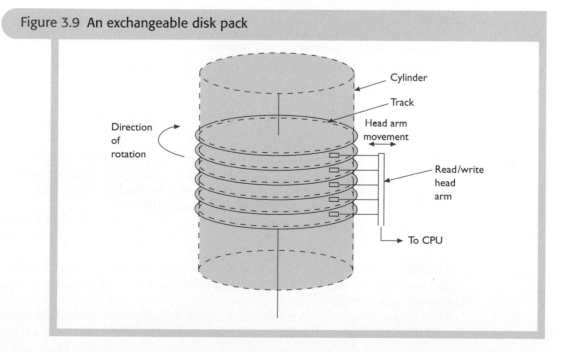

Mini case 3.2

Hard drive storage

As we enter the era of 1 terabyte (1000 gigabyte) drives, consumers and non-technical professionals such as photographers face a challenge that is growing too fast to cope with. So I was intrigued when a Californian start-up called Data Robotics (www.drobo.com) entered the fray with new technology and a product called the Drobo, which was launched this week. Its developers claim that the device, which looks like a shiny black shoebox, makes expanding storage simple and provides sophisticated automated data protection and unrivalled expansion flexibility without the need for complex configuration or management.

Setting up is super-simple, with no need for software or screw-drivers. The device simply plugs into a spare USB (universal serial bus) socket on either a PC or Mac. Users need to buy at least one hard drive, preferably two or more, to get started.

However many drives a Drobo finds in its bays, it treats them as a single large virtual drive, which makes it easy to find data on any of the physical drives. When you need to add capacity, you simply add another disk drive (of any capacity) into the slot indicated by Drobo. If there is already a drive there, you replace it with a higher capacity drive. You do not even have to power down the device. Drobo supports 'hot swapping' one drive with another without loss of data.

Perhaps most important, a Drobo automatically configures itself for data protection. If a drive fails, the device automatically moves unprotected data to protected space on remaining disks. It also incorporates self-healing concepts. It senses when a drive becomes corrupted and pre-emptively moves data, and it can survive power outages without data loss.

Adapted from: **Robot that redefines space**
Paul Taylor, *Financial Times*, 8 June 2007

Questions

1. What are the general features of hard disk drives that make them such a widely popular secondary storage medium?

2. What additional functions and benefits does the 'Drobo' provide for the users of hard disk drives?

RAID

Reliability and speed of data transfer are two essential aspects for effective hard disk drive utilization. Where two or more disk drives can be combined it is possible to address either or both of these concerns by creating a Redundant Array of Independent (or Inexpensive) Disks, commonly abbreviated to RAID.

To increase reliability, copies of data are written across several disks. This disk mirroring means that in the event of one disk failure, files can easily be restored from their mirror copy.

To increase reliability further, check bits (see later section on parity checks) can be added to the data so that in the event of data corruption it may be possible to repair the corrupted item without user intervention.

To increase performance, individual files can be split into blocks which are then spread over a number of disks. This is known as striping. When accessing a file, it may be possible to read the disks containing the required information in parallel, thereby reducing the overall disk access time.

A number of RAID levels have been established, allowing users to choose the level of reliability and speed which is most appropriate for their application. See Figures 3.10 and 3.11.

Magnetic tape

Standard magnetic tape stores data in the form of **records** (Figure 3.12). Several records are collected together and stored in a **block**. Between these blocks of data there are parts of the tape on which no data is stored. These are called **interblock gaps.** The

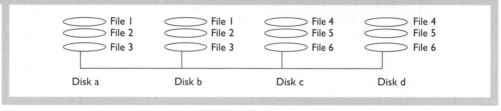

Figure 3.10 **RAID Level 2.** Six files (numbered 1 to 6) are stored, each with a mirror copy (file 1 on both disk a and disk b, file 5 on both disk c and disk d etc.). Data reliability is improved as in the event of an error in data transfer the mirror copy can be used to restore the file. Data access times may be improved as disks can be read in parallel allowing multiple reads on the same file from different source disks

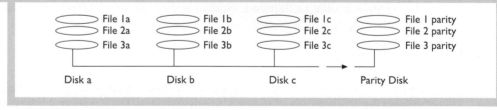

Figure 3.11 **RAID Level 3.** Three files (1, 2 and 3) are written in stripes across four hard disks (a, b, c and a disk for parity checking). Data reliability is improved as the parity bits can identify, and in some cases correct, errors in data transfer. Data access times are improved as disks can be read in parallel making data from the various stripes more readily available when required

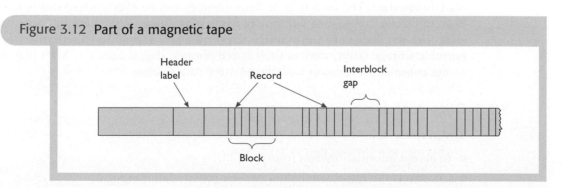

Figure 3.12 Part of a magnetic tape

Figure 3.13 A reel-to-reel tape drive

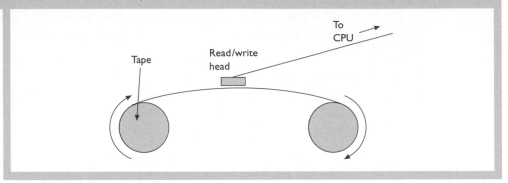

header label gives information such as the name of the tape, the name of the program that is used to update it and the last date of update.

Data is transferred between the tape and the CPU by means of a tape drive (Figure 3.13). This device passes the tape from reel to reel over a read/write head, which either reads the data into the CPU or writes data from the CPU on to the tape. In order to allow the tape-reading device to rest while the computer processes data previously read, the tape machine always stops on an interblock gap. The block is the smallest unit of data that can be read into the machine at one time.

Tape drives are used on larger machines for high-volume transaction processing. To update a payroll file requires at least three tapes and tape drives – one to read the current pay details for each employee, one to read the time-sheet data for the current period and one to write the updated details on to the new tape.

Although the use of tapes has been diminishing over the last few years, they are still employed for some sequential processes as mentioned earlier. Their cheapness and portability makes them ideal as a security backup and archiving medium. Copies of data held on other storage media may be made on tape for transport to a secure location. This is known as **dumping**. Special devices known as **tape streamers** facilitate the fast copying of data on to tape for security reasons.

Flash memory

Flash memory, or flash RAM, is a non-volatile form of storage. In a computer, flash memory is used to hold the essential control code which is required to start the booting-up process. This information occasionally needs to be updated, such as when new hardware is installed. The data held in flash memory can be overwritten; this is normally done in blocks, contrasting with the individual byte-level addressing in normal RAM.

Recent developments have made flash memory a popular alternative form of portable storage. Many devices such as cell phones, digital cameras, MP3 players and games consoles make use of flash memory for data storage.

3.2.5 Output devices

The purpose of the output component of a computer system is:

- to accept information/data from the CPU;
- to convert this information/data into the required output form.

Broadly speaking, there are two important categories of output. **Soft copy** is output that does not persist over time. Examples are the visual output from a monitor or speech from a synthesizer. **Hard copy** provides a permanent version of output and includes printing on to paper.

Monitor

Monitors are a common form of output device because they provide a fast output of information that is practically costless and does not yield vast amounts of waste product such as paper. Applications are of course limited to those where no permanent record of output is required.

Modern monitor screens are colour and high-resolution, allowing a fine-grain representation of the output. This is not only important for the display of graphics but is also essential for operators who may spend many hours each day studying screen output. Screens are designed to be minimally tiring to those using them. As well as being high-resolution, modern monitors provide steady, non-flickering images on anti-glare screens. The earlier monitors, based on cathode-ray tube (CRT) technology have been superseded by liquid crystal display (LCD) output. The quality rivals that of the CRT screen, and it has the advantage that the screen is flat. This is particularly important for machines with a high degree of portability, such as notebooks and palm devices. The development of flat-screen technology has been one of the key factors in enabling portable computer technology. Modern flat screens occupy a much smaller space (sometimes referred to as its footprint) than the CRT screen. The highest quality screens use thin film transistor (TFT) technology to generate the output.

Voice output synthesizer

Voice output from computers is becoming increasingly popular. It is chiefly employed where visual output is undesirable, such as satellite navigation systems in cars, or unhelpful, such as systems developed for the visually impaired. Voice output is also used extensively in telephone answering systems where callers are guided through a series of menu options. Prerecorded digits and words can be conjoined on an *ad hoc* basis to make dates, times or simple phrases.

Printers

Printed output persists and so is important for permanent records. Printed output is also portable and can, for instance, be posted to customers. The main disadvantage of printed output is its bulk and the expense of paper involved. The benefits of permanent, readable records and portability must be offset against these shortcomings. There are a large range of types of printer, all offering a different mix of:

- speed;
- quality of output;
- range of print fonts;
- graphics abilities;
- cost of purchase;
- cost of operation;
- associated noise levels.

The choice of printer will be dependent on how each meets the desired mix of these features.

It is not the purpose here to cover the technology of printers in detail. The interested reader is directed to the references at the end of the chapter. Rather, the main categories are outlined, together with their most general characteristics.

Laser printers

Laser printers generate a page at a time. Using the light of the laser, the page image is directed on to a rotating drum. This leaves an image area, which attracts ink through which the drum is rolled. The image is then transferred to paper. Page printers for large computers can produce output of high quality at 300 pages a minute and cost around $1m. Smaller laser printers aimed more at the desktop PC market cost less than $200 and produce a page about every 3 to 6 seconds.

Serial printers

Serial printers produce one character at a time. The two most common types are the inkjet and the dot-matrix printer.

Inkjet printers eject a stream of special ink through a fine nozzle to form the characters. These are 'painted' on to the paper. Inkjet printers provide good-quality output. They can also provide a variety of typefaces and produce diagrams, logos and other graphical output using either monochrome or multicoloured output. Inkjet printers are relatively quiet in operation. Typical speeds for an inkjet would be approximately 10 pages a minute. Improvements in technology have made inkjet printers a serious rival to laser printers for certain office purposes, particularly low-volume colour printing.

The **dot-matrix printer** has a movable print head, which consists of a matrix of pins. For example, a head may contain 252 pins in a matrix of 18×14. In printing, the set of pins corresponding to the shape of the character to be printed is impacted on to the ribbon, which then leaves an inked image on the page. Dot-matrix printers print at a range of speeds – 400 characters per second would be typical. Dot-matrix printers have largely been replaced by laser printers for business use and by inkjet printers for home use. The most common use for dot-matrix output now is in the production of documents such as receipts, where carbonized copies are produced for both the customer and the business.

Other less common types of printer include **thermal printers**, which burn away a coating on special paper to leave a visible character. Some credit card receipts are produced using thermal printers.

Output to optical disk, magnetic disk, tape and memory cards

Rather than producing an output that is directly understandable visually or aurally, it is possible to produce output on a magnetic medium such as disk or tape, an optical medium or a portable memory card. This is done if the output is being generated for eventual input into another computer system. Alternatively, it may be used where the disk or tape is employed at a later stage or at a different geographical location to supply output information based on one or other of the other output media.

Output on disk or tape is popular as a persisting medium because it is very cheap and fast to produce. The tape or disk itself is highly portable, requires little storage space and is even capable of being sent through the post. The obvious drawback of this output method is the need to possess a computer to understand its magnetic or optical contents.

3.2.6 Factors involved in the selection of output device and medium

The following features must be taken into account:

- **The type of application:** This is crucial when considering output. It is important to establish whether permanent copy is required or not, and whether the output is to be distributed or not, and whether receivers have access to special machinery such as microfiche readers or computers.

- **Costs:** Initial costs for the output devices vary enormously. The chief components of running costs will involve sundries such as paper, film ribbons, and so on. Depreciation and maintenance must be allowed for those output devices that involve mechanical parts.

- **Speed and volume of output:** Estimates must be made of the requirements under this heading and suitable devices chosen that match them.

- **Quality of output:** Internal documents generally require less high-quality output than external documentation used for clients or marketing purposes.

- **Storage of output:** Bulky output cannot be stored and retrieved easily.

- **Environmental considerations:** This is particularly important for output devices that would normally be located in an office. Many printers produce noise, which causes stress and other complaints. Manufacturers have responded to this need by emphasizing quietness, where applicable, to their advertising and naming of products.

Although aspects of technology have been emphasized in this section, it should never be forgotten that the first, and most important, consideration with respect to output is its content and format. Unless attention is paid to the selection of relevant information and its proper presentation at the right time and at the desired level of detail the output will be of little use. This area is covered in the chapters on systems analysis and design.

3.2.7 Central processing unit

The central processing unit is often described as the 'nerve centre' of the computer. It is a term that has been defined in many different ways. These include:

- a conceptual view of the functional units individually called the control unit, the ALU, the main memory and the register set (all defined below);

- the 'processor', i.e. the control unit and the ALU but not including the main memory;

- a proprietary chip such as one of the Intel Pentium series of processor chips;

- the entire base unit case containing fans, disk drives, chips, cables etc. (as in 'I keep my CPU on the floor rather than on my desk').

In this text, the first definition has been adopted. A general outline of the component parts of the CPU is now given (see Figure 3.14).

Main memory

Synonyms are fast memory, immediate-access memory, random-access memory, direct-access memory and primary storage. The purpose of the main memory is:

- to store programs during their execution;

- to store data that is being used by the current program; and

- to store the operating system.

Figure 3.14 The components of the central processing unit

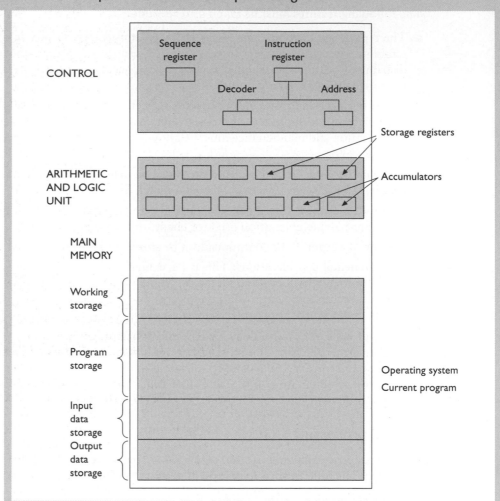

Main memory nowadays is exclusively based on silicon microchip storage. The unit of storage is the byte, and the declining costs per byte of store can be seen in Figure 3.15. Memory space is divided into separate storage locations. Each storage location is assigned an **address** and holds a certain number of bits of information. According to the architecture of the system, a fixed number of bytes (each byte containing eight bits) are held at each location. It is common to refer to a '64-bit computer' where data is stored in locations each of eight bytes (i.e. 64-bits). The contents of these locations can be directly recovered using the address of the location. The contents of other addresses do not have to be searched in order to retrieve a piece of data from a given address. Because the time taken to recover the contents of an address is independent of the address, main storage is called **random-access memory** or **RAM**.

The contents of RAM disappear when the power supply is disconnected, so RAM is said to be **volatile**. Another important feature of RAM is that not only can data be read

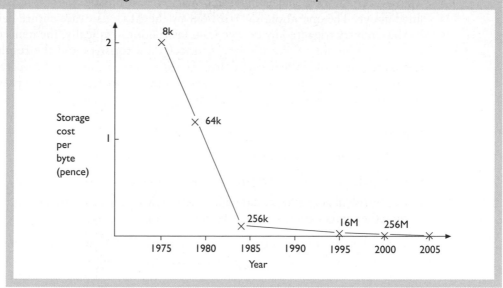

Figure 3.15 The declining costs of silicon-based microchips

that is copied from a memory location but data can also be written to that memory location. In doing this, it erases any previous contents.

As shown in Figure 3.14, main memory is divided into several areas depending on the function that is served.

One part of the memory is used to store the current program being executed. In a large computer there may be many 'current' programs, which are programs somewhere between their initiation and completion. The operating system, or a large part of it, is also stored in main memory. The functions of an operating system are covered in a later section in this chapter. Other parts of the primary storage are reserved for holding input data coming from either an input device or secondary storage, for holding output data that is to be transferred to an output device or secondary storage, or for holding working data that is being swapped in and out of the arithmetic and logic unit.

A typical size for main memory in a modern business desktop computer is 4 gigabytes. Each couple of years sees the doubling of average desktop computer RAM. For a mainframe, the primary store will run into many gigabytes.

Computers also have **read-only memory (ROM)**. ROM, as its name suggests, will not allow the data stored in its memory locations to be written to or changed. The data is permanent, even when the electrical power is removed. ROM is used to store the initial instructions in a computer's start-up routine. ROM is also used for the storage of **microprograms**. These are series of instructions that carry out commonly used routines.

Arithmetic and logic unit

The purpose of the arithmetic and logic unit (ALU) is:

- to carry out arithmetic operations – for example, to add two numbers together;
- to carry out logical operations – for example, to compare two numbers to establish which is the larger.

The arithmetic and logic unit consists of electronic circuits made with transistors. Many program instructions involve a logical or arithmetic operation of the type outlined above. The operation is carried out by the ALU, its exact nature being governed by the circuitry triggered by the program instruction. Typically, the items of data being operated upon are stored in special-purpose **data registers** and the result placed in a special register called the **accumulator**. Any specific outcomes of the operation, such as an overflow caused by a calculation result that is too large to be represented in the registers, are stored in a register called the **processor status register**.

Control

The purpose of the control unit is:

- to decode and execute the program instructions one by one;
- to control and coordinate data movements within the CPU and between the CPU and the other components of the computer system.

Inside the control unit are important registers dealing with the execution of a program. One register, called the **sequence register**, contains the address of the current instruction being executed. The **instruction register** contains the current instruction being executed. There are two parts to this instruction. The **operator** stipulates the type of instruction, such as **ADD**, **GET**, **MULTIPLY**. This is decoded by circuitry in the decoder. The **operand** contains the address or addresses of the data items on which the instruction must work. Having carried out the program instruction, the contents of the instruction register are incremented, and this provides the address of the next instruction to be executed.

Data must be moved around the computer. An example is the need to print the output of a program where the output is currently held in main memory. The CPU works by carrying out many millions of instructions every second. In contrast, the printer may print only a 100 characters a second. In order to make efficient use of computing resources, this speed difference must not be allowed to tie up the fast CPU while waiting for the slow printer to finish its task. What happens is that the CPU instructs the printer to produce output, and while it is doing this the CPU can carry out other activities. When the output device has completed its task it **interrupts** the operation of the CPU, which then continues to service the device. Handling these interrupts is a function of the control unit.

3.2.8 Current issues involved in CPU design

The control unit and arithmetic and logic unit are together called the **processor**. These two components are generally held on one silicon micro-integrated circuit (microchip). The immediate-access memory is held as several microchips, which are accessible to the processor. Each memory chip typically holds up to 512 megabytes of memory, depending on its type. Technological developments of the CPU concentrate on three major areas:

1. speeding up the operation of the CPU, so that programs run more quickly;
2. making larger amounts of cheaper RAM available to the processor, so that a larger number of more complex programs may be held entirely in main memory during execution. This saves the lengthy task of loading parts of programs in and out of secondary storage and main memory during a program run;
3. adding additional processor capability as seen in **multi-core processors**.

In order to achieve these objectives, several development strategies are adopted by microchip manufacturers and designers.

1. The speed of the CPU is partly determined by the **clock cycle time**. There is a clock in the CPU, and operations can only occur in time with the beat of this clock. If the clock is speeded up then more operations can occur per second. This is one strategy – to design microchips capable of operating with faster clock speeds. Clock speeds are measured in terms of the number of operations per second and are commonly expressed in terms of **megahertz**. One megahertz (MHz) is equivalent to one million operations per second. A business desktop computer might be expected to operate at over 1000 MHz.

2. Increasing clock speed is not the only possibility. All processors are designed to be able to decode and execute a determinate number of types of instruction. This is known as the **instruction set**. It is well known that a majority of these instructions are rarely used. Microchips can be designed to operate more quickly if the set of instructions is reduced to those that are most basic and commonly used. If one of the more rarely used instructions is needed it can be carried out by combining some of the more basic instructions. These microchips are known as **RISC** (reduced instruction set computer) chips.

3. The ALU and control unit are designed to carry out each operation with a chunk of data of a standard size. This is known as the **word** length. The earliest microchips worked with a word length of 8 bits, or one **byte**. If this is increased, then clearly the computer will be able to process more data in each operation. Word sizes of 32 bits and 64 bits are now common in business desktop computers. Mainframe computers have traditionally used longer word lengths compared to PCs. The trend is to develop processors that handle longer words.

4. Data is transferred between main memory and the processor frequently. The processor will be slowed in its functioning if it has to wait for long periods for the transfer of the data needed for an operation. Data is transferred in parallel along data lines. For an early 8-bit processor (word length equals 8 bits) there were eight data lines in and eight data lines out of the processor. Clearly, one byte of data could be transferred in one operation. This coincides with the word length. Modern processors can transfer several bytes of data in each operation.

5. The speeds of operation of processors and memory chips are so fast now that, relatively speaking, a major delay occurs because of the time the electrical signal takes to move from the memory to the processor. One way to shorten this period is to decrease the distance of the processor from the memory. This is achieved by building some memory on to the processor chip. This memory is called **cache memory**.

6. The single processor is based on the von Neumann model of the computer. In an application, although some of the tasks must be carried out in sequence, many can be performed in parallel with one another, provided that the results of these tasks are delivered at the right times. There is considerable research and development interest in **parallel processing** using several processors, each working in parallel with the others. This can increase the rate at which the computer can carry out tasks. Modern multi-core processors take advantage of the frequent need for a processor to handle multiple threads of activity. For example a large-scale virus scan can be undertaken on one core while the use continues to watch a video stream on another unaware of the intensive processing being undertaken simultaneously in the background.

7. All the developments mentioned so far are directed at increasing the speed of processing. There is also a need to increase the amount of RAM available to the processor. This cannot be achieved simply by plugging in more RAM microchips. Each RAM location needs to be separately addressable. Memory address lines fulfil this function. If there are 20 memory address lines associated with a processor, then a maximum of 2^{20} bytes or 1 Mb of memory can be addressed directly. Modern desktop computers may have over 4 Gb of RAM and processors are able to address increasingly large amounts of memory.

8. At the leading edge of developments, new technologies based on laser-light switching and biochemically based processors are being investigated. These are currently in an early stage of research.

3.3 Software

'Software' is the general term for instructions that control the operation of the computer. This section deals with the basic sorts of software and the various languages in which it may be written.

3.3.1 The concept of a program

In order to be able to serve any useful purpose, the operation of the computer must be controlled by a program. A **program** is a set of instructions, written in a specialized language, the electronic execution of which controls the operation of the computer to serve some purpose.

Software is the general name given to programs or parts of programs. There are two types of software. **Systems software** carries out functions that are generally required in order to ensure the smooth and efficient operation of the computer. Examples are the operating system (explained later), a program for copying the contents of one disk to another or a file reorganization program. **Applications software** performs functions associated with the various needs of the business (as distinct from the needs of the computer). Examples are programs that carry out accounting tasks such as sales, purchase and nominal ledger processing, a modelling program for forecasting sales figures, or a word-processing program.

Programs are stored in immediate-access memory while being run. The instructions are executed in sequence starting from the first instruction. They are loaded one at a time from immediate-access memory into the control unit of the CPU, where they are decoded and executed. Broadly speaking, there are four types of instruction:

1. **Data movement instructions**, when executed, cause data to be moved around the computer. The movement may be between the CPU and the input, output or backing store, or within the CPU itself.

2. **Arithmetic and logic instructions** lead to the transformation of data in the ALU.

3. **Program branching instructions** alter the sequential execution of the program. An unconditional branch instruction leads to the execution of a specified next instruction rather than the instruction immediately after the one being currently executed. This is achieved by putting the address of the desired instruction in the sequence register in the control unit. Conditional branch instructions lead to a change in execution

order only if a specified logical condition is met: for example, if $x > 19$ then branch to instruction 1200.

4. **Start, stop and declaration** instructions commence the execution of the program, terminate the execution of the program and make declarations, respectively: for example, that a certain area of memory is to be known by a particular name.

3.3.2 Applications packages and programs

When faced with the need to obtain software for its business information, decision support or data-processing systems, an organization may either commission specially written software or purchase a standard applications package.

An **applications package** is a piece of software designed to carry out a standard business function. It is usually produced by a computer manufacturer or software house intending to sell many copies of the package to different organizations. Purchasers of the package do not own the copyright and will usually have clearly specified limited rights to make copies or alterations. Applications packages are common in the following business areas: all accounting, payroll and stock control functions, word processing, electronic spreadsheets, critical path analysis, financial modelling, and statistical analysis, being described as 'off the shelf' or 'shrink-wrapped'.

In contrast, **specially commissioned software** is designed and written for the *specific* business needs of an organization. It may be written 'in house', if the organization is large enough to have a computer centre with a team of programmers, or it may be produced by a third-party software house. In either case, the commissioning organization usually owns the copyright. The software can be written in a high-level language, such as C++. The specification of the business needs of an organization and the translation of these into program specifications is often preceded by a considerable period of analysis and design. Specially commissioned programs are often described as being 'tailor-made'.

There are several benefits and limitations associated with purchasing applications packages as compared with commissioned software.

Benefits

In summary, the benefits are:

- **Cost:** Applications packages are intended for sale to many purchasers, therefore the research and development costs of the software are spread among many organizations. This lowers the cost to purchasers. For instance, a quality accounts package for a desktop computer may cost £2000 and for a mainframe £20,000. This compares favourably with the costs of specially commissioned software, which would be many times greater.

- From the supplier's point of view, when enough packages have been sold to break even with production costs, the profit margin on each additional copy sold is immense. For instance, on a £500 desktop computer-based package, after subtracting the costs of the disk and manual, it is not uncommon for there to be £490 gross profit. However, if there are few sales the software house can suffer a very large loss.

- **Speed of implementation:** A package can generally be purchased and installed on the hardware very quickly compared with a specially commissioned program, which requires much time to write and debug.

- **Tried and tested:** A successful package has been tried and tested by many previous purchasers. This means not only that various errors that may have occurred in earlier versions will have been remedied but also, more importantly, that the package will be one that is known to satisfy the general business function for which it was intended. However, a tried and tested package will not be 'state of the art' software but will reflect what was new several years ago.

- **New versions:** New, improved versions of a successful package are brought out from time to time. These updated versions are often made available to existing customers at a lower rate. This is one way the customers are assured that their software follows what the market is currently offering. From the supplier's point of view, it encourages 'brand loyalty'.

- **Documentation:** Packages often have clear, professionally produced documentation. This is a marketing point for the software house. It also prevents customers encountering difficulties that would otherwise involve the software house in answering time-consuming enquiries. Specially commissioned programs generally do not have such good documentation.

- **Portability:** Packages may be portable from one type of computer to another. As important is the portability of the user interface. For instance, a company that currently uses a particular word-processing package on a certain type of hardware may wish to change its hardware. If it can purchase another version of the package on the new hardware that presents the same screens and uses the same files it will not have to re-train its staff or convert files.

Although these reasons are persuasive in opting for packaged software, there are some limitations.

Limitations

In summary, these are:

- **Lack of satisfaction of user requirements:** This is the most important drawback of purchasing a package. A large business is likely to have specialized information and data-processing requirements. It is common that no package fits these needs exactly. Large businesses can afford to commission software. The situation is different for small organizations. However, their needs are simpler, and it is more likely that a package can be found that suits them. Also, they are often not able to afford the high costs involved in writing programs.

- **Efficiency:** In order to appeal to as wide a market as possible packages build in flexibility (for example, many report options) and redundancy (for example, the ability to handle many accounts). For the purchaser, much of this may not be needed and will cause the package to run less efficiently on the computer.

- **Compatibility with existing software:** It is unlikely that packages will be compatible with existing specially commissioned software. If interfacing is required it is usually necessary for further software to be commissioned.

The desktop computer market is more heavily package-based than the mainframe market. From the demand side, this is because there are more desktop computers, and in particular more small businesses with desktop computers, than larger computers. Small organizations are forced for cost reasons to purchase packages to meet their software needs. On the supply side, the desktop computer market presents more opportunities for very high volumes of sales of package-based software.

The price of the standard business desktop computer has dropped over the years. This can be largely explained by the decrease in hardware costs; the numbers of machines has expanded and so, therefore, has the market for software.

As the number of business desktop computers has increased, package software suppliers have produced more specialized packages. For instance, as well as many standard accounting packages for small businesses, there are now specialist packages for the general professions such as solicitors, insurance brokers and general practitioners, and for the more unusual needs of veterinary surgeons, funeral directors and others. As business desktop computers become more powerful in the future and competition between software houses more intense, the packages themselves are likely to become more sophisticated.

Office suites

Early applications packages in the desktop computer marketplace usually competed by product rather than by vendor. Each product type was promoted highlighting the unique features compared with its rivals. This often resulted in companies selecting their word-processing package, spreadsheet and database from different vendors to exploit these differences. More recently the trend has been towards package integration, with vendors putting together suites of packages for a range of business solutions. The emphasis is towards consistency in user interface, in features and functions and in file formats. Customers have usually selected the product of one vendor to gain the benefits of this consistency.

A typical suite such as Microsoft Office will comprise a word processor, spreadsheet and database, a presentation and graphics package, an e-mail package and possibly other items such as accounting software. The consistency is reinforced by the interconnections between the packages. For example, a spreadsheet can be embedded inside a word-processed document, and a database can be converted into a spreadsheet. A graphical image can be scanned in using a scanner, edited in a graphics package and then placed on to a slide as part of a presentation. The integration provides a valuable additional level of functionality while maintaining the loyalty of the customer across the range of packages.

Usually, the word processor is designed to integrate fully with the communications software, allowing a document to be e-mailed or faxed to another user from within the package. A spelling checker, which once found its home only in a word processor, is now a fully integrated part of the other packages.

3.3.3 Operating systems

An operating system is a piece of systems software that handles some of the housekeeping routines necessary for the smooth and efficient operation of the computer. Its relation to hardware, users and applications programs is shown in Figure 3.16. The operating system is loaded into main memory and run when the power is supplied to the computer. It is usually held initially on disk and is loaded by means of a short ROM-based 'bootstrap' program. The operating system has many functions. The main ones are:

■ **Handling input/output:** All applications programs require interchange of data between the CPU and input/output devices. This could be controlled by instructions

Figure 3.16 The relation between the operating system, users and hardware

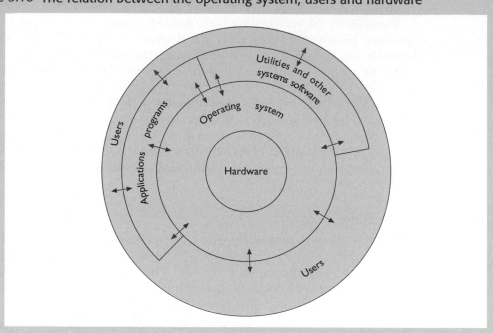

within the applications program, but as, say, sending output to a printer is common to most programs it makes more sense to produce the controlling instructions once and make the code available as part of the operating system, to be called upon as necessary.

- **Backing store management:** Data and programs need to be loaded into and out of main memory from time to time. It is important that this be done without overwriting existing files and in such a way that later retrieval is possible.

- **Main memory management:** Similarly, main memory must be allocated to programs and data in such a way that they do not overwrite one another. If the program is too large to fit into main memory, then the relevant parts are **paged** into and out of main memory. It 'appears' to the applications program that the computer has an indefinitely large **virtual** memory.

- **Handling job scheduling, multiprogramming and multiprocessing:** To meet the processing requirements of a business organization needing many 'jobs' performed by its hardware, it is necessary to prioritize these jobs and ensure that the CPU acts on them according to this priority. **Job scheduling** is controlled by the operating system. To make more efficient use of the hardware it is often necessary to run more than one program simultaneously so that the fast CPU can carry out operations on one program while waiting for a slow output device to handle the output from another program. The programs are not strictly simultaneous but rather interleaved in their execution. The operating system ensures this efficient **multiprogramming**. In larger computers with more than one central processor the activities of the processors need to be coordinated. The operating system controls this **multiprocessing**.

Mainframe manufacturers either produce their own operating systems in house or commission a software company to do this. With desktop computers, the main operating systems are produced by Microsoft and Apple. The former produces the set of operating systems for the PC, while the latter produces an operating system for its own Apple computers. Microsoft produced the operating systems MS-DOS for the early PCs. These primitive operating systems have now been superseded by the Windows set of operating systems.

Developments within the Windows set of operating systems include the ability to hold, run and pass data between many programs simultaneously within the CPU and to display this with sophisticated screen graphics. Windows ensures that the same graphical interface is consistent from one application to the next. It is possible to pass text, data, spreadsheet model output, graphs and images from one application to another. For instance, the output of a spreadsheet can be pasted into a word-processed document. Essential to this approach is the idea that the interface presented to the human being should be more than the ability to type in text commands at a prompt. Rather, the use of **windows, icons, menus and a pointing device (WIMP)** increases the ability of the user to interact with the machine (see Figure 3.17). The **graphical user interface (GUI)** has become a standard feature in most software applications.

Another development in operating systems is the UNIX range. UNIX is a multiuser operating system containing many features useful for program development. It comes in several versions and runs on a range of microcomputers, minicomputers and mainframe computers. The original intention was that software developed in a UNIX environment on one type of machine would be transportable to another. This is not now as straightforward as the original intention assumed, with different 'dialects' of UNIX being developed for different machines.

Figure 3.17 An example of a Windows Vista interface

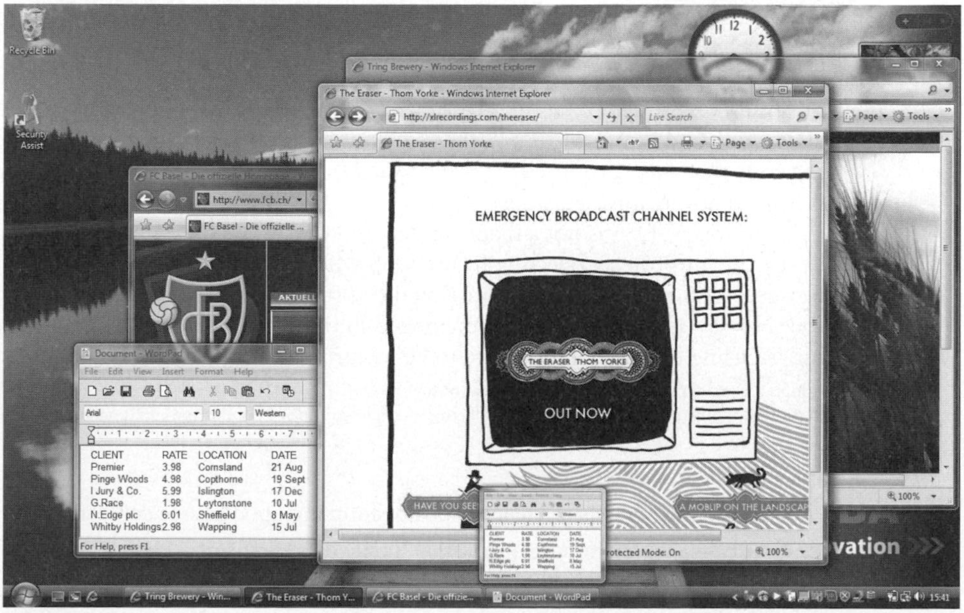

Source: www.xlrecordings.com

More recently, the Linux operating system has been developed as a virtually costless alternative to UNIX. A number of interested programmers have combined in the project to produce and distribute the code for the system. A popular application for Linux is to provide the systems software for web servers, which require a robust multitasking environment for their operation. Linux and the many applications designed for the Linux environment are referred to as **open source software**. This is because the code is made freely available for developers to inspect, amend and recompile.

Mini case 3.3

FT

Open source software

OSS can give businesses the ability to create standardized working practices and tailored business ecosystem models that allow industry vertical markets to collaborate in a way that hasn't been possible before. The quality of open source efforts has certainly increased and it is no longer perceived as a radical idea, but a trend and a method of software development that has produced good work and has sometimes surpassed its commercial alternative in terms of robustness.

The basic idea behind OSS is very simple. Programmers can read, redistribute, and modify the source code for a piece of software in an 'open' environment. The software can therefore evolve rapidly, and more people can use it as a 'standard'. As more people use the code, it becomes richer and evolves to become the choice for even more people to use. If you're used to the slow pace of conventional software development with limited numbers of developers, the speed of development and the deployment of capabilities across the Internet that OSS can support is astonishing. For these reasons OSS is likely to become the normal approach for many web services offerings.

The quality of OSS is usually very high, as the creation process applies strong peer pressure. Many professional programmers work in their own time on OSS code, where they feel freed from constraints of commercial management structures that demand 'good enough' results or even compromises. There is a serious code of conduct that OSS programmers adhere to around truth, and to the production of quality, that leads to acclaim for good work, as well as the kudos of seeing their name forever associated with the code they have produced. This perpetual linkage is a strong incentive to make sure it is a good advert for their skills!

In summary, OSS is not a magic bullet, and cannot be used for every type of software development project. Selecting to use OSS where the conditions are right will prove to be successful not only in the functionality provision but in the cost and time benefits too. However, it still needs to be managed in the same way as any other project, including licensing terms, and may have to be integrated with existing software.

Adapted from: **Open source software – friend or foe**
© Andy Mulholland, with permission (text factually correct at time of publication). FT.com, 10 November 2003

Questions

1. What are the benefits to organizations of adopting open source software?

2. An IT manager might have a view that 'I only buy Microsoft – I know where they are when things go wrong.' Evaluate this strategy.

3.3.4 Programming languages

A program is always written in a specialized language. There are a number of categories of language, each exhibiting different characteristics.

Machine code

Each CPU has its own particular basic set of instructions; a CPU can only 'understand' an instruction if it is taken from this set of instructions. These instructions, known as machine code, consist of strings of 1s and 0s. A typical instruction might be 0110 1010 0110 1011. The first programs were written in machine code in the 1940s. Writing in machine code is extremely difficult. Not only must the programmer think in terms of 1s and 0s when writing code, it is almost impossible to understand code once written. This leads to further difficulties if the program does not perform as intended – that is, has a **bug**. Programs are rarely written in machine code nowadays; where low-level coding is needed, assembly language is used.

Assembly language

Assembly language overcomes some of the difficulties of programming in machine code. The instructions use mnemonics such as 'ADD' or 'STO' (store) instead of binary. A typical instruction might be 'ADD R1,R2,R4' – add the contents of registers 1 and 2 and put the result in register 4. References to memory locations are replaced by reference to named memory areas. The use of binary to represent numbers is replaced by decimal or hexadecimal (a number system having a base of 16). Groups of instructions that are to be repeated many times in a program can be defined and named. These are called **macros**.

These differences mean that programming with assembly language is much easier than with machine code. Assembly languages were developed very early in the history of the electronic computer. Once written, an assembly language program needs to be translated into a machine code program. This is achieved by an **assembler** program. This straightforward program takes the original **source program** and translates it instruction by instruction to become the final machine code **object program** capable of being run on the computer.

Assembly languages are an improvement on machine code in terms of the ease of program production, but they do have some drawbacks:

■ Each different type of processor has a different set of instructions and a different assembly language. Assembly language programs are therefore not portable from one type of machine to another.

■ The assembly language is machine oriented. Reference is made to registers in the ALU and memory locations. In writing an applications program, a programmer would prefer to concentrate on the task to be coded rather than physical aspects of the machine on which the program is to be finally run.

■ Because each task must be specified in detail, programming is very time-consuming. Assembly languages are context free; they do not provide specific instructions for writing programs in particular problem domains such as business or scientific situations.

The main advantage of programs written in assembly language, as distinct from programs written in high-level languages covered in the next section, is that operations can be specified in detail, making the most efficient use of the machine. This leads to the production of programs that run quickly on the computer. Assembly language programming is used for systems software, where high-speed program execution is required.

High-level languages

High-level languages were developed to increase the productivity of programmers. These languages are task rather than machine oriented. This means that instructions in them are more suited to the types of application on which the programmer is employed than to the machines on which the programs will finally run.

Different types of application have spawned different types of high-level language. Well-known languages include:

- **C and C++:** The C programming language has always been popular with experienced programmers. It allows for the construction of very terse code that can, if required, control the machine at a very low level. By accessing registers and memory locations directly, programs can be highly optimized for speed of execution. Code is arranged into functions, with each function performing a logically cohesive task. There is a clear specification of what data is allowed to flow between functions. The aim is to ensure that programs once written are easily understandable, testable and amendable. C++ is a development of the C language. It provides additional programming constructs and structures that allow for the creation of object oriented programs. A further development on C++ that is gaining popularity is Microsoft's C# (C sharp). This includes aspects of C++ and Java, which is described next.

- **Java:** The growth in the Internet and developments in web page construction have led to a sudden increase in interest in the Java programming language. Java has a similar set of instructions to C++ and a number of additional features that make it well suited to developing programs for Internet computing and the development of web services. Alternatively, small blocks of code called **Java applets** can be stored on web servers. When a client requests a web page containing applets, the applet code is transferred to the client and run inside the client's web browser.

- **Ada:** The Ada programming language is named after Ada Augusta, daughter of Lord Byron. It is sponsored by the US Department of Defense for use in military applications.

- **PROLOG:** PROLOG is a language specifically designed for writing programs that require reasoning as distinct from record processing, text handling or number crunching. It is therefore often used in artificial intelligence applications. Unlike other languages previously covered, which are all based on writing code for procedures to carry out tasks, PROLOG is designed to be able to declare states from which implications are then derived. PROLOG and another popular artificial intelligence language, LISP, are playing a large role in the development of future intelligent business applications.

- **COBOL** (*CO*mmon *B*usiness *O*riented *L*anguage): COBOL was developed in 1960/61 as a general-purpose business data-processing language. It is particularly suitable for processing large numbers of records. COBOL was a widely used commercial language. It conforms to standards set by ANSI (American National Standards Institute) and CODASYL (*CO*nference of *DA*ta *SY*stems Languages). Although versions do exist for desktop computers, COBOL is used most extensively for business applications running on minicomputers and mainframes.

- **FORTRAN** (*FOR*mula *TRAN*slator): FORTRAN is a language developed in the 1950s specifically for the purposes of scientific and mathematical work. It is rich in its ability to handle formulae.

- **BASIC** (*B*eginners *A*ll-Purpose *S*ymbolic *I*nstruction *C*ode): BASIC was developed in 1963 at Dartmouth College as a language that could be learned and understood very quickly by students. It is now embedded in Microsoft's Visual Basic programming environment.

The languages discussed constitute a selection of some of the more important high-level languages in current use. There are many more. There are several advantages to using high-level languages compared with low-level assembly languages:

- It should be clear from the descriptions that high-level languages are task oriented, and there are different types of language for different types of programming requirement. This increases programmer productivity.

- High-level languages also increase programmer productivity because each high-level instruction will eventually be relatively straightforward to learn, often using expressions that are near English. Some, such as BASIC, are so straightforward that simple programs may be written after an afternoon's study of the language. Training times for programmers are reduced and programming requires less qualified personnel.

- Programs written in high-level languages should be portable from one type of machine to another. In practice, this is unlikely because of differences in dialects. However, changes that are necessary are often minor.

In order for a source program in a high-level language to run on a computer it needs to be translated into a machine code object program. This translation may be by **interpreting** or **compiling**. In each case, the translation is carried out by software. When a program is interpreted, as each line is translated into object code it is immediately executed. In contrast, when a program is compiled a compiler program translates the entire source program into object code. The object program can then be executed.

Once compiled object code is produced, it can be used again and again without the need for the source program. Applications software producers prefer to release their packages as compiled code. Compiled code is difficult to understand and so is difficult to alter. This prevents unauthorized tampering with programs. In contrast, no permanent object code is produced when a source program is interpreted. Moreover, the interpreted program will run less quickly than the compiled version. This is because of the necessity for the translation as well as the execution of instructions each time the program is run. Interpreting is popular in the writing of programs because there is no need to compile the entire program each time an alteration is made to it.

Compared with assembly language programs, high-level language programs, whether interpreted or compiled, always run more slowly. This is partly because inefficiencies occur in the process of compiling or interpreting, even though optimization procedures are used. It is also partly because the machine-independent nature of high-level languages prevents programmers using their knowledge of the internal structure of the CPU to increase run-time efficiency. These shortcomings are not enough to deter the use of high-level languages in business applications, where the increases in programmer productivity and the other advantages outweigh the run-time considerations.

Although it is difficult to derive an agreed standard against which programmer productivity can be measured, it is generally recognized that significant advances have been brought about over the last 30 years by the use of high-level languages. It is also generally accepted that with modern, cheap and powerful computers, together with the increasingly sophisticated programs required by business, these productivity increases are insufficient to meet the extra demand placed on software production. There are three separate but interrelated problems:

1. **High costs of software production:** High-level languages have reduced costs by increasing programmer productivity, reducing the training required for programmers and increasing the reliability of programs. However, as hardware costs drop, the cost of software production as a proportion of a company's total expenditure on its information system has been increasing over time. The production of versatile software packages to carry out standard business functions has gone some way towards reducing this cost burden. But for an organization that has special needs there is no alternative to commissioning purpose-designed software.

2. **Need to produce systems quickly:** Traditional high-level language programming is still a lengthy business. It cannot be easily speeded up by employing more programmers on the project. The man-month attitude to programming ('if it takes four programmers six months it will take twenty-four programmers one month') has been shown to be a myth. Project control and communication problems between programmers increase rapidly with the number of programmers. Modern project control and the use of structured techniques in programming have gone some way towards diminishing this problem, especially with larger systems. However, small systems are often needed quickly to meet fast-changing requirements, so some alternative to conventional programming must be found.

3. **Need to produce systems that meet user requirements:** The history of business information systems has many examples of systems that are technically efficient but do not serve the needs of users and so are underused or misused. Because traditional programming involves a long and expensive development by programming experts, much emphasis has gone into methods and techniques that ensure the correct identification of user needs. Another approach is to develop quick, cheap versions or prototypes of systems that users can test for their adequacy before revision and improvement. An extension of this is to develop languages so straightforward and powerful that users themselves can develop their own systems. **End-user computing**, as it is known, requires a different sort of programming language. This need is met in part by scripting languages.

Fourth-generation languages

The term fourth-generation language is applied to a set of languages that operate at a higher level than the third-generation languages described above. In an attempt to improve the software development process and reduce incidence of bugs in computer programmes, these languages typically provide a set of higher-level commands where each command would be the equivalent of multiple commands in a third-generation language. Although this simplifies the initial generation of correct code, it may result in programmes that are slower to execute or that are harder to maintain. The most successful of these languages is the **Structured Query Language** (SQL) which is built into most database development tools like Oracle and Microsoft Access. It is the standard language for creating, modifying and accessing data stored in relation databases. It has been used for the prototyping and, in many cases, the subsequent development of a very large number of data-processing applications.

Table 3.2 The generations of languages

Generation	Typical languages	Capabilities
1st	Machine code	Machine oriented, each language specific to a processor type, programs not portable
2nd	Symbolic assembly language	Easier to use than machine code, although still machine oriented, each language specific to a processor type, programs not portable
3rd	For example, COBOL, C, BASIC, LISP	Procedurally oriented, task oriented, increase in programmer productivity over 2GL, portable programs
4th	SQL, Scripting languages	Designed for fast development, end-user oriented applications, generally portable

Scripting languages

Scripting languages attempt to overcome the shortcomings of the previous generations of languages (see Table 3.2). Scripting langues provide programmers with powerful tools and also allow end users to construct their own systems. A number of features, though, are common to many scripting languages:

- They are usually interpreted rather than compiled. The source code is preserved and converted to machine code each time the programme is run.

- They are often associated with an application package. The scripting language allows the user to tailor the application to carry out user-defined actions.

- The use of these very high-level instructions reduces the total number of instructions needed in the development of the system compared with conventional code.

Scripting emerged from the need for the administrators of computer systems to group together sequences of instructions or tasks that could be submitted to be executed as a batch. Most operating systems provide such a facility; examples of the resulting languages are JCL (Job Control Language) and shell scripts.

The ability to create simple scripts has led to the addition of the facility to a number of applications. Examples include:

ActionScript: Increased interaction can be introduced into systems built with Adobe Flash or Coldfusion by including scripts written in Actionscript.

Lingo: The Macromedia Developer suite allows animations to be crafted using the Lingo scripting language.

QuakeC: The computer game Quake includes a scripting language QuakeC, based on the C programming language to allow gamers to modify the game.

One of the widest used examples of a scripting language is **Javascript**. The popularity of this language arises from its linkage with the development of client-side web systems development. Although there is a weak connection with the Java programming language, Javascript uses a simpler set of commands and is more forgiving to the novice users. It allows developers and end users alike to develop and implement applications at little cost as the interpretation of the source code is usually carried out by a standard web browser.

It should be clear from these features that a scripting language is not a conventional language in the sense that say C++ or Java is. The speed, cheapness and ease with which applications can be developed has had impacts in two main areas.

First, the traditional development process for a new system need not be followed. This traditional process involves the progression of a project from its feasibility study through the stages of analysis, detailed specification and implementation. Because the time and costs involved in implementation are great, it is important to ensure that an adequate and final design to meet users' needs is achieved during the specification stage. This linear development process, or rather how a structured analysis and design methodology is appropriate to it, is covered extensively in later chapters. Scripting languages allow the speedy and cheap development of applications software.

Second, scripting languages have been developed specifically with the intention of **end-user applications development** in mind. One of the problems of the traditional approach to programming to meet user requirements is that these requirements must be translated into a form suitable for a programmer to be able to write a program. It would ease any communication difficulties if users could translate their information requirements directly into the satisfaction of those needs by programs.

In summary, the main advantages of scripting languages are:

- It is possible to develop new applications quickly and cheaply.
- It is possible to maintain and update applications quickly and cheaply.
- Scripting languages are designed for end-user applications development and so remove the need for a separate body of experts (programmers) in applications development.

From the foregoing, it might be wondered whether scripting languages spell the end of conventional programming for business systems. This is unlikely, not least because there is a large investment in current programs and programming skills involving third-generation languages. These will need continual maintenance and updating. There are, however, other drawbacks and limitations to scripting languages:

- Although scripting languages provide a fast development time for software, the eventual code generated executes slower and requires more processing power than applications written in third-generation languages such as Java.
- The use of scripting languages particularly by end users can lead to lack of standardization of systems development in an organization because centralized standard setting and control tends to be diminished.

Summary

The last five decades have seen the rapid improvement and extensive use of the computer in business data processing and information provision. Successive generations of computers have incorporated technological advances enabling faster, cheaper and more reliable processing. The development of the microchip, as well as improving performance and decreasing the size of computers, has added a new dimension to business computing with the cheap, powerful desktop computer. This has not only extended the user types to include businesses of all sizes but has also enabled a 'leap to freedom' for users in larger organizations from the control of the centralized computer centre.

As a basis for appreciating the ways in which technology can support business information requirements and decision making, it is important to have a background understanding of the hardware and software aspects of technology. In this chapter, the functional components of a computer system and the ways these are implemented with hardware were explained. This was linked in the case of input devices to their suitability for various applications.

Hardware improvements have increased the demand for sophisticated software. Basic software was also examined in the chapter. In particular, the functions of an operating system were covered. Modern operating systems use graphical interfaces and exchange text, data and images between applications. High-level languages, procedurally based around the types of task for which they were suitable, were designed to increase programmer productivity and program reliability to meet this demand. Structured high-level languages are to be viewed within the context of a structured methodology of systems analysis and design. Small organizations, or those with standard business functions, can avoid the cost of specially commissioning software by purchasing applications packages. These have many advantages. The increasing sale of desktop computers has led to a substantial market for packaged software that is particularly user-friendly.

Review questions

1. What specific advantages did advances in electronics provide for the development of computer systems?

2. What are the factors that influence the selection of data capture method, input method, input devices and media for an application?

3. Explain the distinction between *hardware*, *software* and *firmware*.

4. What characteristics of a business application make it appropriate for computerization?

5. Explain why high-level languages have superseded assembly languages in the production of applications software.

6. How do scripting languages differ from other high-level languages and what benefits do they offer over traditional languages?

7. What are the advantages of adopting a package approach to the acquisition of software?

8. Give *four* reasons why packaged software is more common for the microcomputer market than for the mainframe market.

9. Outline the functions of an operating system.

Exercises

1. Why has there been a movement towards the use of desktop computers in large organizations rather than relying wholly on centralized mainframe resources staffed by experienced and highly trained personnel?

2. Why is it not feasible to include a code for the price of a product in the bar-code associated with its packaging?

3. A large TV rental company has high-street branches throughout the UK. Customers typically sign contracts for TV and video rental. Payment is monthly. The majority of customers pay by direct debit through the banking system. However, a significant minority pay at the high-street branches each month. Customer account records are held on a mainframe computer at the head office and require regular updating with customer payment details. Suggest two suitable methods of data capture and input for those customers paying at branch offices. Comment on the advantages and disadvantages of your proposals.

4. It is often claimed that programmer productivity has increased over the years. How would you measure programmer productivity?

CASE STUDY 3

Mobile phones as input/output devices

Ubiquitous and well entrenched as mobile phones may be, some potential uses have yet to catch on in a big way. Such is the case with mobile check-in at airports. A passenger survey at the end of last year by the International Air Transport Association (Iata) found only 2% of respondents had checked in via an SMS (text message) on their mobile phones. But that number looks certain to rise as more airlines introduce mobile check-in – those that already have are as enthusiastic about the service as are their passengers. 'To have your boarding pass on your mobile should be something that really excites the customer', says Patrice Ouellette, Air Canada's director of customer service platform, e-commerce.

Last June the airline launched mobile check-in for customers on domestic flights without baggage. Between one and 24 hours before departure, passengers can enter basic details about themselves and their flight into their mobile phones, then print out their boarding pass from a self-service kiosk at the airport. In the next few weeks, Air Canada plans to start pilot testing an 'E-Boarding passes' service, in which 2D barcodes would be sent directly to mobile devices of customers checking in at Montreal for domestic flights. The customers participating in the pilot would scan their device at airport security and proceed to the gate. Elsewhere, mobile check-in has inevitably established a foothold in countries where mobile users have been keen to try innovative or experimental services, pushing the devices beyond simple calling and texting. Finland and Japan are two good examples.

In October 2004 Finnair claimed a first in international air travel when it launched SMS check-in for frequent fliers. Customer feedback has been extremely positive, it says, reflecting the fact that the airline takes a proactive approach – it sends a text message and the customer needs only to reply. On average, says Finnair, about 75% of customers that receive a message go ahead with the SMS check-in. The system has become the third self-service channel, along with Internet and kiosk check-in, and is now comparable in popularity, with usage falling only when there is less business travelling.

In Japan, mobile phones can be used as part of Japan Airlines' 'Touch and Go' system, which was developed in-house for use on domestic routes, and introduced in February 2005. The system allows IC (integrated circuit) cardholders to board domestic flights without a physical ticket or boarding pass. From three days before departure and up to one hour before the flight, passengers can make or change a seat selection and check in via their computer or mobile phone. All relevant data for the booking are recorded automatically on the IC card, which can then be touched or swiped at machines in front of the airport security checkpoints and then at the boarding gate. The number of Touch and Go users has been steadily increasing since the system was introduced, says Ko Yoshida, JAL's vice-president for domestic marketing planning, and has already run into millions. Users tend to be individual business travellers.

At rival airline ANA, check-in via computer or mobile phone has been possible for two years for domestic flights, and if the phone has an RF (radio frequency) chip it can be used to pick up a boarding pass from a self-service kiosk at the airport. Last August, the airline introduced an enhancement known as Skip, allowing passengers who have paid for their tickets and reserved their seats – using their computer, mobile phone or at a travel agent – to skip check-in. One touch of their RF chip-enabled mobile phone, credit card, ANA Mileage Club or 2D barcode to a sensor at security prints a receipt with the customer's seat number. Another sensor at the gate lets customers on board and a boarding pass is then printed for final seat number verification. Skip is used by 10,000–15,000 customers a day.

Individual airlines have taken the initiative on these developments and are pushing for an industry standard that would help widen the usage of mobile check-in. Iata says this is a major activity for its barcoded boarding pass (BCBP) team this year – currently North America, the European Union and Japan each have a preferred 2D barcode to use on mobile phones for ticketing and other applications, and the challenge will be to agree one global standard. There are other obstacles, too. The biggest challenge, says Finnair, is the airport authorities' requirements for paper boarding passes at the airport service points. 'In Finland, the airport authorities and customs have accepted our text message confirmation as proof of travel', says the airline. 'At most of the airports in the world that is not the case'. Air Canada, meanwhile, is working with Canadian authorities on its Montreal 'E-Boarding passes' pilot. Talks with authorities about starting the pilot on a limited basis in June were successful, and then further implementation would be subject to the results of the test and continued working with authorities.

Finnair notes other provisos. Mobile devices must contain the required features by default, removing the need for customers to install software. Secondly, multimedia message service (MMS) provides a method to deliver a 2D barcode to a customer but mobile operators need to readjust their pricing policy, says the airline. It says roaming pricing, in particular, can be 'a real killer'.

Adapted from: **Airport check-in: Board your flight by mobile phone**
Andrew Baxter, *Financial Times*, 14 May 2007

Questions

1. The traditional airport check-in requires the traveller to visit a desk where an airline operator enters details into the ticketing system and produces a hard-copy boarding pass. List the peripheral devices that would typically be used to conduct this process.

2. Data concerning the booked journeys needs to be stored persistently. Compare two different secondary storage media indicating which would be the most appropriate for this function.

3. Using the case study, describe how the mobile phone can replace the traditional input and output devices used for checking in and producing a boarding pass. What advantages are there to the traveller and to the airline? What disadvantages are there to each?

4. One version of the process described in the case study produces a bar-code to be displayed on the screen of the mobile phone. How does a computer decode the information stored in a bar-code?

5. Evaluate the possibility of using the kind of technology outlined in the case study for these applications: purchasing theatre and cinema tickets; paying for car parking, bridge and road tolls and inner city congestion charging; other travel documents such as bus or train tickets. How does this compare with smart card technology?

Recommended reading

Chalk B.S., Carter A.T. and Hind W.R. (2004). *Computer Organisation and Architecture: An Introduction*, 2nd edn. Palgrave Macmillan

This is a concise introduction to the way computers work. It explains with straightforward detail the various hardware components, the way they are organized and interconnected, and the way that programs can be executed upon them. It is suitable as a more detailed introduction for those seeking a greater understanding of hardware.

Englander I. (2008). *The Architecture of Computer Hardware and Systems Software*, 4th edn. Wiley

An extremely comprehensive approach to the subject illustrated with numerous examples.

Hennessy J.L. and Patterson D.A. (2003). *Computer Architecture: A Quantitative Approach*, 3rd edn. Kaufmann Academic Press

This is a highly detailed text for students who wish to extend their knowledge of computer architecture well beyond the current text. It adopts a quantitative approach to all aspects of computer systems architecture. It uses illustrations of design from consumer electronics, multimedia and web technologies, and high performance computers, as well as a standard coverage of microprocessors. It is aimed at the computer science student.

Ritchie C. (2003). *Operating Systems Incorporating UNIX and Windows*, 4th edn. Continuum

This is a clearly written and straightforward text intended to give an overview of operating systems with specific reference to UNIX and Windows. The book is aimed at those doing a diploma or degree in computer science. The earlier chapters provide a clear introduction to operating systems accessible to those studying more generally.

Stallings W. (2005). *Computer Organization and Architecture*, 7th edn. Macmillan

This is a detailed text presenting the structure and functions of a computer in much greater depth than the current chapter. It is more than an introductory text. The 2003 edition includes a section devoted to RISC technology.

Chapter 4

Distributed systems, networks and the organization

Learning outcomes

On completion of this chapter, you should be able to:

- Define a distributed system
- Analyse the organizational benefits and drawbacks of distributed systems
- Appraise the degree of distribution in a system in terms of processing power and data
- Describe basic techniques used to transmit signals across networks
- Compare and evaluate techniques for creating communications channels across networks
- Describe topologies for local area networks
- Outline the OSI model and cite issues relating to standards in networking
- Discuss EDI communications between organizations and evaluate the benefits of EDI.

Introduction

Major developments over the last 30 years have been achieved in information technology. It is not uncommon to view this purely as the advent and development of computer systems. However, this ignores the significant impact that improvements and innovations in telecommunications have had as an enabling technology for information systems.

This chapter begins with a consideration of the way in which centralized and distributed systems can be seen as alternatives for handling information provision. The impact of a distributed system on the organization, its benefits and its acceptability, are analysed. In order properly to appreciate issues in networks and distributed computing it is necessary to have at least a basic understanding of the underlying technology. The 'language of networks' is explained, various types of public and local area networks are examined, and the way that issues concerning standards bedevil the full integration of systems is covered. The Internet and the World Wide Web are important enough to merit chapters on their own (Chapters 5 and 6, respectively), although concepts key to their understanding are covered in this chapter. Finally, the impact of electronic data interchange (EDI) and its effect on the competitive position of the firm in the marketplace is assessed.

4.1 Networks and distributed systems

In the last two decades, many organizations have adopted the policy of installing several geographically distinct computers within their organizations and linking these using telecommunications. The computers may be desktop computers linked together locally in one site or even one office. Or it might be the linking of minicomputers or mainframe computers across large geographical distances. As well as these traditional network connections, the growth of the Internet has introduced a simple and relatively inexpensive way for users to establish connections between computers. The issues involved in this distribution of computing power and the linking networks are the subject of this section.

It used to be believed that computing benefited from economies of scale. The previous chapter introduced **Grosch's law**; this stated that the computational and data-processing power of a computer increases with the square of its cost. It therefore made financial sense for an organization to centralize its computer systems in order to get the most power for its money. Under centralization, an organization that is located on several geographically distant sites would then incur a large communications cost. Terminals at each site needed to interchange data constantly with the centralized central processing unit.

With the development of much cheaper computing hardware and, in particular, the development of the microchip, Grosch's law has broken down. There are no longer the same economies of scale to be gained by centralization. Local computers can carry out local processing needs, and the need to communicate between different sites in an organization is reduced to those occasions where data held at one location is needed at another. This is called **distributed computing**.

An example of a distributed system is shown in Figure 4.1. A tyre and car battery manufacturer purchases materials and produces goods for sale throughout the country.

Figure 4.1 An example of functions in a hierarchical distributed system

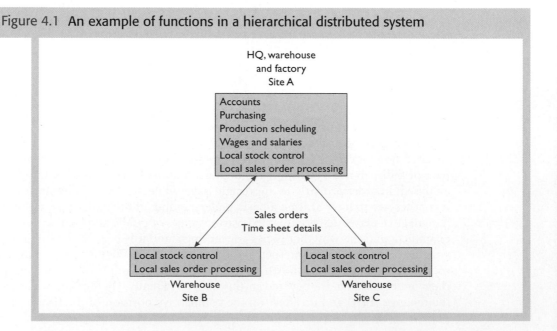

The headquarters, factory and a warehouse are located at one site. In order to cut distribution costs and satisfy retail orders quickly, the organization maintains two other warehouses in different parts of the country to which the manufactured goods are distributed for storage prior to sale. The headquarters' mainframe computer takes care of centralized accounting, purchasing, production scheduling, wages and salaries, local stock control and local sales order processing. Each of the two warehouses has a small minicomputer to handle its own local stock control and local sales order processing. These two minicomputers are connected to the mainframe computer so that an enquiry can be made to the other warehouses for products not held in the local warehouse that are needed for local retail outlets.

Most of the stock control enquiries and updates will therefore be on the locally held data stores. On the occasions when the local warehouse cannot satisfy a customer demand, the data held at the other warehouses is interrogated via the telecommunications links. As the accounting is carried out centrally, although the sales order processing is local, it is necessary to ensure that sales order and delivery details are exchanged between the local computers and the mainframe. As this is not required immediately on a sale the data can be transferred at the end of each day in one operation. Although accounting, wages and salaries are handled centrally in this organization, an organization with a different structure might grant greater independence to its branches. These functions would then be the responsibility of each site, and headquarters would receive consolidated accounting reports.

Compare this with a centralized system, as shown in Figure 4.2. Here all the functions are carried out centrally at headquarters. Each time there is a need to access the data store or carry out any processing the interaction between the local sites and headquarters will involve a telecommunications link – even though the processing of data

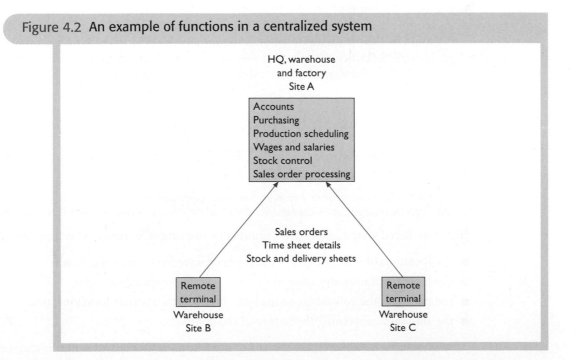

Figure 4.2 An example of functions in a centralized system

HQ, warehouse
and factory
Site A

Accounts
Purchasing
Production scheduling
Wages and salaries
Stock control
Sales order processing

Sales orders
Time sheet details
Stock and delivery sheets

Remote
terminal

Remote
terminal

Warehouse
Site B

Warehouse
Site C

only concerns stock held at the local site. This involves a heavy telecommunications cost. Moreover, unless the links involve high-speed connections the response times in the interaction will be slow. At the headquarters, the mainframe will need to be able to accept transactions from many sites and will need to give over some of its processing time to the maintenance and servicing of queues. This problem will be larger the greater the number of sites and the greater the traffic. In this scenario, it is unlikely that computer personnel will reside at each of the sites. It would be more common to have a centralized team at the headquarters responsible for applications development and the day-to-day running of computer operations. It is easy for users at the local sites to feel isolated – particularly if help is required or difficulties are encountered with the operation of the system. As can be seen from the two treatments of essentially the same set of functions, a distributed approach has much to commend it.

However, it would be simplistic to suggest that there were only two possible approaches – distributed or centralized. In the above case there is a hybrid. In the 'distributed' example certain functions are in fact centralized: the distribution of the stock control system, particularly that component dealing with the update of stock data relating to another warehouse held at another site, involves considerable technical complexity as the database itself is distributed. A variation on this is to hold copies centrally of the stock data on each of the sites. Downloading to each site of all the stock data on all of the sites occurs early in the morning. Local processing of data on stock held locally occurs during the day. However, information on stocks at other warehouses is obtained by interrogating the early morning copies received locally. These may be out of date – but only by a maximum of 24 hours. Requests for stock from other sites together with the end-of-day copy of the local stock data are transferred to the central mainframe at the end of the day. The central mainframe carries out overnight processing and produces up-to-date stock data for each site, which is downloaded the following morning. This escapes the complexity of requiring a truly distributed database at the expense of forfeiting the immediate update of all stock transactions.

It should be clear from the above that the simple idea of distributed versus centralized does not apply. Rather the question that is addressed nowadays is to what extent and how should the organization decentralize its functions and data?

4.2 The idea of a distributed system

The term **distributed system** has been used to cover many varieties of computer system. A computer system is said to be distributed if:

> it consists of hardware located in at least two geographically distinct sites, connected electronically by telecommunications, where processing/data storage occurs at more than one site.

In a distributed system, there are a number of important features to be considered:

- the locations of processing and the types of interaction between them;
- the location of data storage and the way data is presented to users;
- the nature of the communications links between the various locations; and
- the standards governing the nature of the communication.

These are introduced here and covered in more technical detail later in this chapter.

1. **Distributed processing** can occur in several ways. At the simplest level (and hardly justifying the term 'distributed processing'), individual computers may carry out their own processing but send messages to one another in an electronic mailing system. A more integrated connection occurs with **cooperative processing**, where processing is handled by two cooperating geographically distinct processors. One processor sends the output of its processing to another for completion. The situation becomes more complex if the operating systems of both machines are different. **Cooperative operating systems** are then needed as well.

2. **Distributed databases** occur when data is not held at one central site but is held at various locations. Broadly, this can happen in one of two ways. 'Master' data may be held at a designated site and copies downloaded via telecommunications to other sites to be held locally. When data is needed at a site it consults its own copy of the master data. With such systems it is usually not permissible for a site to change its locally held copy of data relating to another site, otherwise the various copies of the data held throughout the organization would become inconsistent. If data changes are to be made, data is uploaded to the master database, which is then updated, possibly overnight. New copies of the database are sent to all sites the following morning.

   However, truly distributed databases distribute the data over several sites without duplication. Any user wishing to access the data does so and the data is recovered from the database at the relevant site using database and communications software. As far as the user is concerned it is transparent as to where the data is held. In both cases of distributing data, common data definitions and standardization of data operations are crucial.

3. The **nature of the communications links** between the various locations concerns the topology of the network and the technology of its implementation. The ways in which sites may be connected – their topology – are shown in Figure 4.3. Different topologies serve different purposes. For example, the hierarchical topology often characterizes the arrangement in organizations that have a centralized mainframe (the top) connected through a **wide area network** to minicomputers at local sites, which in turn have PCs connected to them. The ring and bus topologies are common methods of connection for groups of PCs that need to communicate with one another and with other devices. These **local area networks** are treated more extensively later in the chapter. Finally, many systems may be connected together, yielding hybrid topologies. As well as the topology, the nature of the hardware – cabling and network cards in machines – and software controlling communications are major determinants of network characteristics.

4. The **standards** governing the way in which devices 'talk' to one another and the principles governing the way in which users can communicate are currently being specified through internationally agreed standards such as the **Open Systems Interconnection (OSI)**, treated later in the chapter.

4.3 Organizational benefits of distributed systems

Distributed systems were first introduced in the 1970s and have become increasingly common ever since. This is partly because of technological advances in telecommunications, distributed databases and communications software, and partly because of the recognition of the benefits conferred on an organization by the use of such systems.

Figure 4.3 Various network topologies: (a) hierarchical; (b) star; (c) ring; (d) bus; (e) hybrid

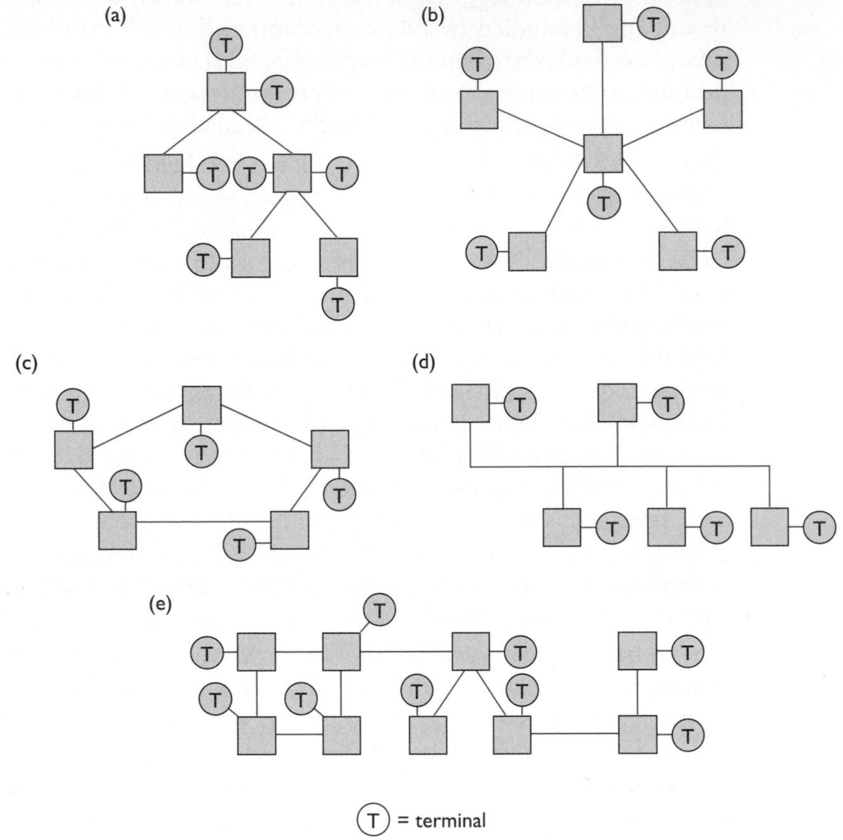

(a) (b) (c) (d) (e)

(T) = terminal

This is one area in which IT developments have responded to user needs as well as being driven by them.

Organizational benefits are as follows:

- **Increased user satisfaction:** As stated above, users can feel remote from the computer centre, its expert staff and the development of applications if geographically separated from the source of the computing power. User needs are often not taken into account, and assistance may be slow or at 'arm's length' through the computer terminal. Local computer centres serving local needs solve this problem by ensuring that users have greater autonomy. However, from a central organizational perspective, it is important that dispersed sites be connected to one another and the centre. This is not only for reasons of data sharing but also to ensure that, although autonomy may be welcomed, local sites act congruently with corporate goals. Distributed systems ensure that data transfer and connectivity with the centre occur while encouraging local autonomy and user satisfaction.

- **Flexibility of systems development:** An organization that is growing can add to its computer power incrementally in a distributed system by the purchase, installation and connection of new nodes to the network as the needs arise. With a centralized system, flexibility is reduced by the inability to grow incrementally. Growth typically involves the overloading of the current system, which is then replaced by a more powerful computer. If further growth is planned this will need to be taken into account by building in redundant computing power in the current system to cope with future growth in requirements. This is expensive.

- **Lower telecommunications costs:** In a distributed system, it is usual for most of the local computing to take place locally. The network is accessed only when data or processing is required elsewhere. Telecommunications costs are reduced compared with a centralized system, which requires transmission of local transactions for central processing.

- **Failsoft:** With a centralized system, if a breakdown occurs in the computer all computing functions in the organization come to a halt. This is an unacceptable state of affairs. Backup facilities, such as a duplicated computer or reciprocal agreements with other companies to use their computers in times of breakdown, are expensive and often not satisfactory. However, with a distributed system breakdowns will be limited to one computer at a time. The remaining machines in the network can continue to function and perhaps also take over some of the work of the failed node. What can be achieved depends on the particular network topology and the communications software.

- **Transborder data flows:** Many multinational corporations maintain separate computer systems in each country in which they operate. These are connected via networks. Only limited transborder data flows may be allowed by legislation. Thus it is important to ensure local processing while retaining the possibility of transnational data flows. Data protection legislation on the holding and processing of personal data (data on persons) is often different in different countries, and this is particularly restrictive on transnational data flows.

- **Response times:** Centralized systems can, at peak loading, give poor response time for users.

Persuasive though these organizational benefits may seem, there are potential drawbacks and costs associated with distributed systems. These should be taken into account when assessing the overall systems strategy:

- **Loss of centralized standard setting and control:** In a distributed system, where processing, data storage and computing staff are located at many sites, it is common for local practices to evolve, local alterations and 'patches' to software to be carried out to meet specific user needs, and local adjustment to data representation and storage characteristics to occur. All these can lead to non-standardization across the organization and to difficulties in data communications and security.

- **Complex networking software is needed:** This controls data communications.

- **Possibility of replicated common data at several sites:** If the same portion of data is used by all sites it is common for the data to be held as copies at each of the several sites rather than be held once and accessed through the network when needed. This cuts down data communications costs and increases response times. However, it may lead to inconsistencies if the data is updated or changed.

- **Loss of career paths for computer centre personnel:** A large centralized computer centre provides more opportunities for staff development and promotion.

Distributing staff leads to smaller numbers of personnel at each site. A move towards decentralization will also require changes in work practices and significant staff retraining for some employees.

Mini case 4.1

FT

Distributed systems

The endurance of legacy code highlights the surprise comeback of the computers on which they run: mainframes. These big, proprietary computers were considered doomed when in the 1990s distributed computing and client/server models promised cheaper hardware and cheaper operating systems, such as Linux and Windows.

Happily for IBM, which dominates the mainframe market, reports of the mainframe's death proved premature and its business has enjoyed a broad resurgence since 2000. Branching out into lower-end mainframe models and supporting Linux has undoubtedly helped. Bob Hoey, worldwide VP for System z9 Series sales at IBM, says that many customers find that the lower initial costs of a distributed system are outweighed by higher staffing costs required to maintain a group of single-application servers. At the same time, the ageing legacy workforce is 'one of the biggest concerns from customers worldwide', says Mr Hoey.

IBM is also tackling education. In 2004 it launched a five-year programme aimed at getting 20,000 people trained in mainframe administration, and recently embarked on another programme to simplify mainframe administration. It aims to cut the training time for mainframe proficiency from two years to six months.

Adapted from: **Programs written in old code pose business problem**
Kate Mackenzie, *Financial Times*, 22 November 2006

Questions

1. What are the advantages of a distributed system built around mainframe computers rather than single application servers and networks of PCs?

2. How might the training requirements and career progressions differ between these alternative approaches to distributed systems?

4.4 Organizational levels and distributed systems

It is not usual in a distributed system for each node to be directly connected to each other node. Nor is it common, if data is to be distributed, that it is spread over all nodes in the distributed network. It is more likely that the structure for the distributed system reflects the organizational structure it is meant to serve.

A typical organization structure is shown in Figure 4.4. This is a traditional hierarchical structure, which exemplifies many large industrial and service organizations. There is a headquarters for the organization. The organization has several local plants or sites that carry out many of the functions of the organization itself at a local level. Examples are the functional departments of production, stock control and order processing. In each functional department, there are work groups reflecting groupings of employees that perform much the same function in that department – an example might be customer enquiry handling in a sales order-processing department. Finally, there are

Figure 4.4 Typical hierarchical organizational structure

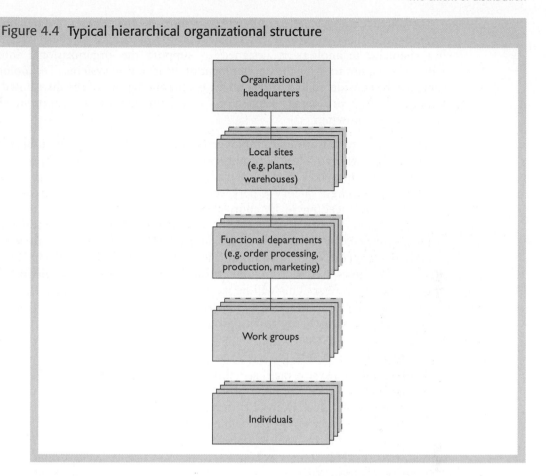

the individual employees, who are the simplest 'processing unit' (i.e. unit that may require a computer for support) in the organization.

Where there are distributed systems in an organization, one possible architecture for the distribution is to ensure that where data is distributed and computers are networked this occurs at the level reflecting the organizational structure. For example, within one work group the network ensures that connections and data needed by that group are spread over the entire group. The various levels will also be connected together and if required will effect data transfers.

The larger the organization the more likely it is to have large numbers of personal computers, minicomputers and mainframe computers. In this case, it is also more important that the distributed architecture is planned to reflect the needs of the organization.

4.5 The extent of distribution

In the early 1980s, one of the uppermost questions in the minds of those involved in long-term strategic planning of information systems was whether to employ distributed systems or whether to rely on centralized mainframes. The issue has now shifted to decisions on the extent to which the organization should embark on distributing its information systems for future information provision.

There are technological determinants governing the distribution of data and computers, especially those to do with communications. However, as has been stressed in earlier chapters, technology is designed to support the organizational information requirements, not to drive the development of information systems. Technological factors must be considered in deciding on the extent and nature of the distributed systems, but other features are equally significant. Central among the other important characteristics are the following:

- **The corporate culture and employee behaviour:** Managerial assumptions about human behaviour will have implications for the amount of control that is exercised over employee activities. A traditional model characterizes attitudes in two distinct groupings. Theory X perspectives hold employees as inherently unwilling to work and needing to be controlled by incentives and discipline in order to ensure that their activities align with organizational goals. In contrast, Theory Y perspectives hold employees as self-motivated and willing to ensure that their activities are congruent with organizational objectives. In an organization where Theory X views are the dominant culture there will be an unwillingness to relinquish central power. This will be mirrored in a hierarchical organizational structure and a pressure towards centralization of information systems, where standards and control are easier to implement. The local autonomy that accompanies distributed systems fits a managerial strategy of decentralization of control within a Theory Y culture.

- **The location of decision making:** Closely linked to the points raised above is the issue of who makes the key decisions. The further decision making is decentralized in an organization the more likely it is that the resources follow. Decentralization of resources and decisions over their commitment with respect to information technology is most compatible with a distributed system.

- **Interdependent activities:** Where one type of activity is very closely related to another it is more likely that the processing associated with both will occur in one location. Distribution of processing between two activities tends to lead to a lack of connectivity, which should only be allowed if the activities are themselves not connected.

- **Homogeneous activities:** In some cases, activities may be independent of one another but there is a case for centralized planning of distributed systems. For example, franchises may involve local franchisees in carrying out completely independent activities from each other. Yet their operations are so homogeneous that it makes sense that each has the same type of system. This can be achieved only if there is centralized planning and control over the development and purchase of the information systems.

4.5.1 Client–server computing

Most modern information systems are constructed following the client–server model of computing. This involves using desktop computers as the clients, which make requests for data or applications. The requests are passed to servers, which are the centralized stores of data and applications. Computer processing power is spread throughout the organization; some is available centrally at the servers, some is available locally at the clients. Clients and servers can run on the same or on different machines, use different languages and operate on different platforms. Typically, there will be a number of servers, each dedicated to a particular task. Examples are:

- file servers;
- application servers;
- database servers;
- print servers;
- mail servers.

An example of an application of client–server computing is that of a corporate e-mail system. Normally, e-mail is distributed via a designated computer called a mail server. Employees of an organization will be assigned an e-mail account, and any mail sent to that account is held on the mail server. In order to read the mail the client will need to run a mail application on their local computer; this collects the mail from the server and makes it available to the user. There is no permanent connection or shared application between the client and the mail server. Any compliant mail application can be used by the client to carry out this task.

The major advantage of the client–server approach is that the sharing of resources between clients and servers can be balanced to suit their particular environment. Typically, the server, a more powerful computer, will store both the data and the applications that can be run to update and interrogate the data. In certain situations, however, it may be desirable to locate more of the data at the client computer. Similarly, it is also possible to store the applications locally. In the example of the e-mail system, the client mail software might be stored on the local disk drive of the client or may be downloaded from the server then executed locally.

A typical decision for the designers of client–server systems might be as follows. A database holds a very large number of records. A client computer user wants to make a number of requests interrogating the data store. Should the entire file of records be copied to the client to allow fast searching by software at the client end? Or should the searching be carried out by the server and only the results passed to the client? Similarly, should an entire set of records matching the search criteria be copied to the client to allow fast access to the results at the client end? Or should the searching be carried out by the server and the matching records be passed to the client one at a time as they are perused?

Clearly, there are several factors which influence the balancing of resources between client and server:

1. **System performance:** Generally, applications will execute faster if stored locally. Similarly, data can be interrogated more quickly if located locally.

2. **Consistency:** Applications and data can be more easily maintained if held centrally. Upgrades to applications and updates to data can be made more easily if held at the server and distributed as required.

3. **Bandwidth:** The capability of the network must be such that it can support the volume of network traffic between clients and servers.

4. **Volume of data/size of application:** It may not be possible to hold some massive databases locally. Similarly, programs that are too large for local storage will need to be stored centrally.

Clients are categorized as **thick clients** or **thin clients** according to the extent to which applications and data are held and executed locally. A thick client will undertake a larger

Figure 4.5 Models of client–server computing: (a) two-tier with thick client; (b) three-tier model with thin clients

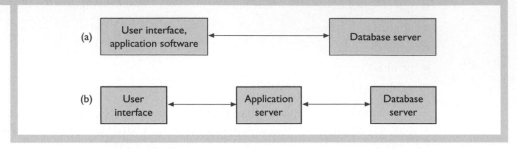

proportion of activity. Figure 4.5(a) shows a two-tier model of client–server computing where the application logic is held and executed by a thick client. In the three-tier model, seen in Figure 4.5(b), there is a separation into three activities: formatting and presenting results, the logic for querying and interrogating, and storage of data. In this model, a thin client might be responsible for only the input and output of data.

An extreme example of a thin client is the **Net PC**. These are low-cost computers designed to have minimal memory and disk storage; they are dependent on servers for most applications and data.

4.6 The distribution of data

In a distributed system it is likely that, as well as processing occurring at many sites linked by telecommunications, data will also be distributed. This can happen in a number of ways. These reflect the extent to which the organization wishes to relinquish control over its data as well as over technological issues.

1. A centralized repository of data may be downloaded each day to local nodes in a network. This typically happens when these nodes are separated geographically by large distances. The downloaded data can then be interrogated locally. During the day, transactions occur at local sites, which require update of the central data store. The transaction details may be transferred to the central site for processing immediately or held and uploaded at the end of the day. In either case, a new copy of the central repository is downloaded the following morning.

   The effect of this approach is to cut down on expensive enquiry traffic between the local sites and the central store of data. The disadvantage is that the information is up to 24 hours out of date. Whether this is acceptable or not will depend on the nature of the application.

   For instance, it is likely to be permissible in a situation where data on stock at local sites was held centrally and downloaded each morning provided that the number of update transactions was relatively small compared with the number of enquiries, and ample buffer stocks were held. In this case, the savings on telecommunications costs would compensate for the loss of immediate accuracy of the data. However, if the ratio of update transactions to the number of enquiries is high and the stock holdings are volatile with little buffer stock being held, then this method will be not appropriate.

This approach to distributing data is little more than a fast electronic version of printing out the database each day and sending the hard copy to the local sites.

2. A variation on the above, which overcomes some of the problems concerning lack of immediacy, is to download data from a centralized repository each day but allow update transactions to be made on records held locally and applying to local events immediately the transactions occur. The local data is uploaded at the end of the day along with other transactions in order to update the central data store. If most update transactions apply to local data then this method will yield high accuracy of data.

3. In order to ensure full immediacy of data but at the same time distribute it to gain the benefits of local data storage and processing, a fully distributed database must be used. Each piece of data is stored at one or other of the nodes in the network either with or without duplication. Distributed database and communications software ensures that when users interrogate or update the data it is transparent to them where the data physically resides.

Mini case 4.2

Distributed vs centralized data storage

Sabah is a Malaysian state, located on the island of Borneo. The Sabah Credit Corporation (SCC) is a financial institution fully owned by the State Government and under the portfolio of the State Ministry of Finance. Its mission is to encourage economic development through the strategic issuing of loans. Its main premises are in Kota Kinabalu, the capital, and there are several regional offices in towns across the state.

The Corporation is divided into two divisions, administration/finance and operational. The latter oversees the evaluation process for arranging loans in a range of situations: agricultural loans, bridging finance, hire purchase loans etc. The Corporation is supported by a Management Information System; this provides support for a range of decision-making activities at the operational, management and strategic levels. The MIS has evolved with the Corporation. Within the system a number of subsystems cater for functional areas such as personnel, property management, training and legal issues. These complement the core system activity of recording customer details and repayments and have been progressively added and augmented over time.

The borrower system records all transaction activity, including customer repayment details. Customers can check this information by logging onto a password-protected website. Managers can use the system to obtain reports on core indicators such as cumulative profits, liabilities and tax paid.

All data is held in electronic files at the head office. Regional offices use network connections to the head office to access or update the data. Although customers may deal with a regional office for making payments, obtaining advice etc. the records are stored at the head office and can only be obtained through the network communications channel to those centrally held files. It would be possible for data to be held at local branches but it would make reconciliation and reporting for the whole corporation far more difficult. By keeping multiple copies of the same data there is always the danger of inconsistency when one copy is updated.

Further details about the Sabah Credit Corporation can be found at http://www.sabah-credit.com.my ▶

> **Questions**
>
> 1. Data is held centrally. What advantages does this provide for the corporation?
> 2. An alternative model would be for data to be distributed throughout the regional branches. What benefits does this alternative model bring? Why do you think that this approach has not been adopted?

4.7 Networks and communications

The development of computer technology and applications software has been accompanied by a corresponding growth in telecommunications and the need to link computers together. Earlier sections have demonstrated the reasons for the distribution of data and computing power and the benefits it confers. The remaining sections investigate the technologies and standards governing the connections.

In the early years of data processing, corporate computing power was concentrated in the organization's mainframe computer. Where remote sites needed access to the computer, this was usually achieved through the public telephone network. A link was established between the dumb terminal and the central computer. The nature of the interaction between the two was controlled entirely by the centralized mainframe in a **master–slave** manner. If the amount of data to be exchanged was high and spread throughout the day (as compared with short bursts) it was cheaper to lease a direct line from the relevant telephone company. This also had the advantage that the connection carried a less distorted signal and was subject to less interference. Signal distortion and interference were lower because the connection between the terminal and the computer did not form part of a temporarily connected circuit through a number of telephone switching exchanges. With leased lines, data communication speeds were thus able to be higher.

Over time, the increased need to provide more extensive computing support for an organization – often at many sites – put a significant burden on the ability of the telecommunications network to carry the volume of data at costs the organization was willing to bear. The advent of local minicomputers for local processing was part of a solution to this problem. These would be linked together via the telecommunications network to form a distributed network. Another part of the solution was the introduction of more effective and cheaper means of transmitting a message from A to B across the public network – the use of digital transmission, packet switching and new types of physical link (see below).

Even within one site the explosion of demand by users for computing power, both caused by and enabled by the growth of user-friendly personal computers and applications packages, produced a requirement for communications between them that could not easily be satisfied by channelling all traffic through the site mainframe or minicomputer. Local area networks were designed to provide the necessary communications.

What had been experienced a decade earlier in the 1970s was a drive to distribute computing over many sites in an organization connected by a network of communications. In the 1980s this was repeated in a microcosm and experienced as the need to distribute computing within one site connected by a local network. There were differences, especially the fact that in networking between sites a third party – the telecommunications company or data carrier – was involved, but many of the issues and pressures had a familiar ring to them.

The arrival and massive uptake of use of the Internet has made distribution of data and systems a very cheap and easily implemented alterative. The introduction of digital telephone exchanges and improvements in the quality of communication channels have allowed businesses to implement a range of distributed systems that were either not possible or prohibitively expensive previously. These matters are dealt with in later chapters.

The evolution of distributed computing has been, and still is, bedevilled by the problem of standards. Standards are needed because different types of machine are used to send messages to one another across different types of network. Nowadays, this may also involve machines running under different operating systems cooperating with one another to carry out work. Standards problems are particularly noticeable in the area of communications across the public network. The public carriers have often appeared to regard themselves, particularly in the early years, as electronic postal services – their purpose was to ensure that a neatly packaged message was transmitted reliably, swiftly and cheaply between a sender and receiver. The concept was neutral as to whether the package consisted of an electronic message rather than one written on paper. Nowadays, the need is for computers not only to connect with one another but also to work with one another. This has led to the development of standards to avoid the proliferation of confusion in communications.

4.7.1 Communications – the basics

Communication involves the transmission of a **message** from a **sender** to a **receiver**. The physical line over which communication is established is known as the **communications channel**.

Where it is possible to send data simultaneously in both directions between two devices the type of communication is called **full duplex**. If transmission is possible between both devices, but not simultaneously, then the communication is called **half duplex**. The remaining case, where transmission is possible in one direction only, is known as **simplex** communication.

Transmission signals

Data in a computer is encoded digitally. The two discrete states correspond to 0 and 1 – the two values for the binary digit. This is transmitted in the computer by means of a digital signal where, for instance, 0 corresponds to a low voltage and 1 corresponds to a high voltage (see Figure 4.6(a)).

Transmission through the public telecommunications network has in the past been through communications channels that were designed for carrying voice (voice-grade channels). This involved the sending and receiving of analogue carrier signals (Figure 4.6(b)). In order to ensure that 0s and 1s could be communicated across voice-grade lines the carrier signal needed to be varied. Transmitting digital signals between one computer and another across the public telephone network required a device to modulate and demodulate the carrier signal at either end. The use of a **modem** (*m*odulate–*dem*odulate) device is illustrated in Figure 4.7. The modem is a device that is either housed inside the computer's covering or is plugged into the computer.

Figure 4.6 Data transmission by signals: (a) digital transmission; (b) analogue carrier signal

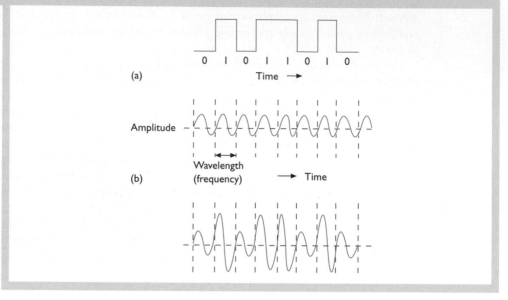

Figure 4.7 A modem link

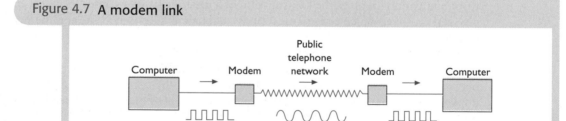

Bandwidth

The **bandwidth** of a communications channel is the range of electrical or electromagnetic frequencies that can be used for the signal transmission.

In a **baseband** channel, the entire channel is given over to the transmission of a digital signal. Baseband channels may have high transmission speeds – for example, transmission of data at up to 10 megabits per second over a limited range (a few kilometres). With baseband communication, only one signal may be transmitted at a time.

A **broadband** channel uses different ranges of frequencies carrying different signals at the same time. Each range of frequencies is modulated to represent the digital signal. In this case, the physical link will be carrying many messages simultaneously – the larger the bandwidth the greater the number of signals.

FT

Mini case 4.3

Broadband

The number of broadband subscribers in Asia is expected to double in the next four years to 216m, according to a report highlighting the growth of the Asia-Pacific broadband and pay-TV industries. Household penetration of broadband, currently at 13% in the region, is expected to reach 24% by 2012 and 31% by 2015, with China reaching 40% and India 11%.

'In 2006, Asia's pay-TV and broadband industries generated turnover in excess of $44bn, which represented 0.4% of GDP', said the report's author, Vivek Couto, director of content and research in Hong Kong at Media Partners Asia, a consultancy. 'This has the potential to grow exponentially.' The report, *Asia Pacific Pay-TV and Broadband Markets 2007*, tracks the growth of broadcasting and broadband services over a number of distribution networks, from cable to satellite, fixed-line and wireless networks, in 16 markets.

It found that total pay-TV subscribers in Asia were 255m last year, a number that is expected to increase to 381m in five years and 446m by 2015. By 2015, 55% of Asian homes will be watching pay-TV compared with 40% now, the report said.

Adapted from: **Asia set to double its broadband customers by 2012**
Joe Leahy, *Financial Times*, 18 April 2007

Questions

1. Why is bandwidth a key issue in determining the effectiveness of broadband communications?

2. What issues are raised by the article in respect to future demands on broadband Internet connection?

Parallel and serial transmission

Information is transmitted from sender to receiver translated into one of the major bit-coding schemes (usually ASCII). In **serial transmission**, the data is sent in a continuous stream with one bit followed by the next. **Parallel transmission** involves all the bits in a character being transmitted simultaneously along parallel transmission lines. Serial transmission is therefore slower, but parallel transmission requires many physical channels. Voice transmission over the public telephone network is usually via a twisted pair of wires and is serial. High-speed connections between computers and computers, or computers and peripherals such as printers, are nowadays usually via parallel transmission. Recent improvements in serial transmission, for example Universal Serial Bus (USB), have ensured that serial transmission remains a realistic alternative method of transmission.

Transmission media

The physical medium over which signals are transmitted is an important determinant of the speed, reliability and number of messages that can be sent simultaneously.

Twisted pair

A twisted pair consists of two insulated wires twisted around one another. One wire is for the send signal and the other for the return. It is common for twisted pairs to be

Figure 4.8 Alternative forms of cabling: (a) twisted pair; (b) coaxial cable; (c) optical fibre

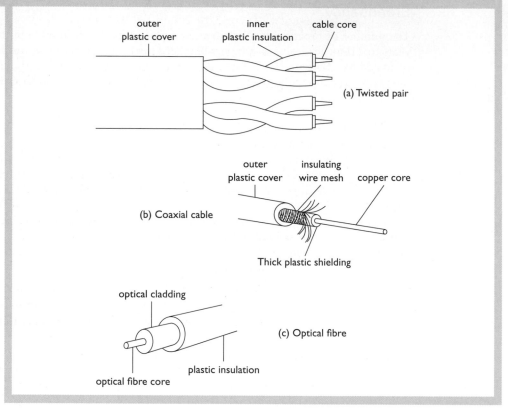

twisted with one another in a spiral configuration to improve the reliability of the signal (see Figure 4.8(a)). The individual wires and/or the whole cable can be shielded by insulation. This is the typical telephone cable, where each pair is a dedicated line for a private household. Typical data transfer rates are up to 10 megabits per second. The popular standard for connecting a desktop computer to a local area network is a generic telecommunications cabling system known as CAT5 ('CAT' being an abbreviation of category). This uses unshielded twisted-pair (UTP) wiring, normally terminated by a telephone-style jack plug. CAT5 allows data transmission at speeds up to 100 megabits per second with a bandwidth of 100 MHz.

Coaxial cable

Coaxial cable is made up of a central wire insulated and surrounded by a further conducting wire. This in turn is surrounded by insulation (see Figure 4.8(b)). Coaxial cable is used for the transmission of TV signals and for provision of domestic and business Internet services. The cable can conduct large quantities of data – up to 200 megabits per second – with very low error rates.

Fibre optics

An optical fibre cable consists of thin strands of glass, each about the thickness of a human hair. Messages are transmitted via a pulsating laser beam that is sent down the centre of the fibre. The light beam is reflected internally by the outer cladding around the fibre (see Figure 4.8(c)). The bandwidth of fibre optic transmission is large – for instance, one optical fibre can transmit half a million telephone calls simultaneously. The data transmission rates are several hundred megabits per second. Fibre optic cabling is becoming commonplace for the transmission of public data, with common carriers beginning to install fibre optic systems for the transmission of voice, data, text and images. It is also being used for the transmission of data within a single organization in local area networks. Typical data transfer rates are up to 10 gigabits per second.

Fibre optics has the following advantages:

- high capacity for message transmission;
- insensitive to electrical or electromagnetic interference;
- as cheap and easy to install as coaxial cable;
- low error rates;
- low power consumption;
- secure against illicit interception (as this requires physical breaking of the cladding, which results in signal breakdown).

Microwaves

Data can be transmitted using waves from the electromagnetic spectrum. Whereas fibre optics uses light in the visible wavelengths, microwave transmission uses radio signals of short wavelength. Microwaves may be used for satellite transmission or terrestrial links. Typical data transfer rates are up to 100 megabits per second.

With a **satellite link**, a microwave beam on which the data has been modulated is transmitted from a ground station to a satellite. The satellite remains in a constant position with respect to the Earth (geostationary orbit). The beam is then retransmitted to the destination receiver. Geostationary satellites typically orbit about 22,000 miles above the Earth's surface to enable them to synchronize with the Earth's rotation. The microwave channel has a very high bandwidth and may handle more than 1000 high-capacity data links. Microwave satellite transmission can relay both analogue and digital signals. Unlike a beam of light, the microwave beam is not interrupted by cloud or affected by adverse weather conditions. It has a reliable straight-line transmission distance of approximately 30 miles at the Earth's surface. As most of the transmission to and from a satellite is through empty space, this is sufficient.

Mini case 4.4

Global positioning systems

Galileo, the European Union's putative rival to the US Global Positioning System is one of the most intriguing technologies to come along since the Internet. GPS may appear merely a useful tool to get to the right place in your car, or fighter jet. GPS tells the navigation device in your car where it is by triangulating signals from several satellites. This is plotted on a map by services such as TomTom and Mapquest, and a voice tells you to turn right or left. It also has obvious commercial applications: a computer can dispatch the closest taxi and tell a customer when it is about to arrive more efficiently than a human being, for example.

But the most interesting consumer services, combining the Internet, social networking and GPS navigation, are only just starting to emerge. Once you have a GPS chip in your mobile phone, that opens up a whole world of software applications and services based on you and other people – in particular your friends and family – being able to pinpoint where you are. For example if someone gets lost on a cross-country trek, or even abducted – it can save lives.

Less ominously, GPS will also make social networking and other Internet-based services come to life. This makes it easy to find a nearby pizzeria, Starbucks or book-store and get walking directions to it. You can also let friends know where you are and give them directions to the location, or check who else is on the way to a party. For the Facebook, MySpace and Google Maps generation, that kind of thing that could easily become addictive.

Adapted from: **Europe should reach for the sky**
John Gapper, *Financial Times*, 28 May 2007

Questions

1. Describe the technology that makes GPS applications possible.
2. How might this technology affect businesses involved in activities such as delivery and transportation? What might be the effects on efficiency, service provision and employment?

Terrestrial microwave links are used when line-of-sight data transmission is needed over short distances (less than 30 miles) and it is inconvenient or impossible to lay cabling. This may occur because of physical difficulties such as ravines or rivers, or because high-bit-rate links are needed between buildings in sight of one another and where cabling cannot easily be laid.

Wireless technology

Much interest has been generated recently in facilitating wireless connections to both internal (private) and external (publicly available) networks. Both business and home users are benefiting from the ability to connect a laptop, PDA or other portable device to their existing network which itself may be wired or wireless. This adds great flexibility in the positioning of devices and in the ease of connectivity. In addition, mobile users are now able to access **wireless hotspots**; these are publicized locations which provide wireless access to the Internet via a service provider. The service provider offers connectivity and recoups costs through advertising and other services.

The main wireless protocol used is a standard known as 802.11g. This employs radio frequencies to effect a connection. Line of sight between connecting devices is not required but the signal does degenerate with obstructions and with increasing distance. One implementation of this standard is **Wi-Fi**. Using this, data transfer rates of up to 54 Mbps (Mega bits per second) are possible.

Another radio wave technology gaining popularity is **Bluetooth**. This is a short-range radio technology standard. Unlike Wi-Fi it does not support TCP/IP and wireless LAN applications very well. It is more commonly used for connecting PDAs, mobile phones and PCs across short distances for short intervals. Typical data transfer speeds are around 2 Mbps.

4.7.2 Public transmission links

The transmission between one device and another across common or public places is carried out in each country by one or more organizations licensed by the government of that country to provide these communication services. These are known as **common carriers**. Examples of common carriers are the telecommunications giants AT&T in the USA and British Telecom and NTL in the UK.

Leasing

Where a large volume of data traffic is to be exchanged between two sites, an organization may decide to lease a line from the common carrier. This is a physical link between the two sites that is dedicated solely to the leasing organization. Leasing a line has the advantage that the physical link does not require temporary circuit connections to be established between various telephone exchanges. These temporary circuit connections make the signal much more open to distortion and interference and result in generally lower transmission speeds. In cases where there are large amounts of data to be exchanged, leasing is also a much cheaper alternative than establishing 'dial-up' links. However, if a large number of nodes need linking over long distances then costs generally prohibit intersite leasing. Because the data travels across a permanent physical channel any network made up of such links is called a **non-switched network**.

Public switched telephone network

In cases where a channel connection is made for a temporary period during the time of the data exchange but is then discontinued after exchange the connection is known as switched. Devices that can be connected in this way are said to be part of a **switched network**. In the case of the public switched telephone network (PSTN), the exchange of data between two sites requires establishing a temporary voice-grade circuit link through the public network of exchanges (see Figure 4.9). As soon as the required data has been exchanged the circuit is broken. This is known as a **circuit-switched network**.

The advantage of this type of connection is that the public switched telephone network allows data exchange between any two points that are connected to the telephone system. This gives great versatility. The disadvantages are that transmission speeds are

Figure 4.9 Circuit-switched telecommunications network

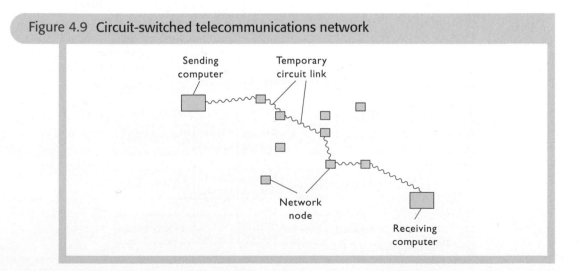

low, distortion and interference probabilities are high, and costs are high for long periods of connection. Transmission speeds are being increased and the period taken to establish the connection (dial-up time) is being decreased by the introduction of digital networks (see below). Finally, with a circuit-switched network the circuit link is dedicated to the sender–receiver connection until broken. It may be the case that during much of this time there is no traffic in either direction and the circuit is 'waiting' for data exchange. The physical links between the exchanges making up the circuit are nevertheless 'tied up' and cannot be used for other purposes. This is an inefficient use of the network.

Packet-switched network

With a **packet-switched network** a message to be sent from a sender to a receiver is split into a number of self-contained packets a few hundred bytes (characters) long by a packet assembler/disassembler (PAD). These packets are routed through the network by being passed from node to node. Each packet may follow a different route through the network. At each node, the packet is stored temporarily before being forwarded to the next node in the network. Once it has reached the destination in the correct order the message is reassembled by a PAD (see Figure 4.10).

The sender and receiver are oblivious of the assembling/disassembling process and of the routing. It appears to them that a dedicated circuit is established between them. Because no actual circuit link exists, the connection is known as a **virtual circuit**.

Figure 4.10 Packet-switched telecommunications network

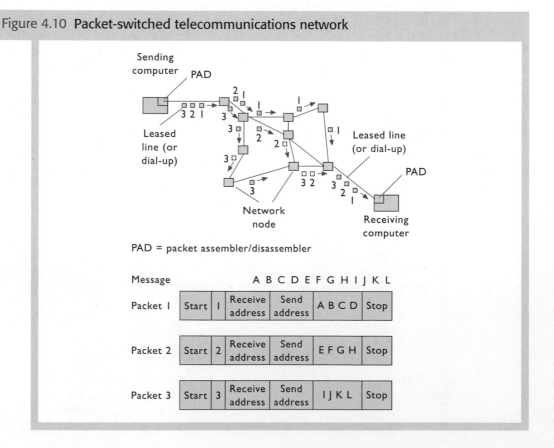

PAD = packet assembler/disassembler

The route for each packet through the network is computer-determined to ensure that the network is being used most effectively. Clearly, many messages broken into packets will be passing through the system simultaneously. Another advantage of packet switching is that data exchanges between two devices along the virtual circuit may involve considerable periods of waiting between a receiver receiving a message and sending out a reply. Because no physical circuit link exists continuously, valuable network transmission potential is not being wasted.

Many countries have now installed public packet-switched networks. International packet-switched network data transmission is possible between countries that have developed their own systems, provided that they follow certain standards in the way they represent data. A commonly used standard is known as **X25**.

Integrated services digital network

Most public telecommunications systems are being upgraded to be integrated services digital networks (ISDNs). All switching, networking and transmission is then by means of digitized signals.

In order to ensure that compatibility will exist between different national systems and that equipment can be connected to the system, an ISDN standard exists. The basic transmission speed for this system is 64 kilobits per second. A typical domestic user with basic access would have two transmission channels at this speed plus a control channel at 16 kilobits per second. Businesses are offered primary access with 24 channels, each running at 64 kilobits per second (one channel being used for control purposes). This is a substantial improvement over typical speeds for voice-grade lines, which are up to 9.6 kilobits per second.

Under an ISDN, transmission of voice, data, text and images will be fully digital. This will allow faster transmission speeds and much faster dial-up times for circuit connection (milliseconds compared with seconds).

ADSL and cable

Asymmetric Digital Subscriber Line

The potential for sending data over traditional copper telephone lines has been further expanded by the introduction of Asymmetric Digital Subscriber Line (ADSL). By employing a special ADSL modem, this technology supports data transfer of up to 9 Mbps when receiving data and up to 640 Kbps for sending data (hence the asymmetry in the title).

Cable connection

Even greater bandwidth can be exploited where coaxial cable is available. A cable modem connected to the lines also used for transmission of cable television provides very fast access to the Internet. Data transmission speeds of 8 Mbps are possible.

Although extremely popular, there are limitations to this approach. One problem is the availability of a cable connection. Until now this has been limited to urban areas of the more developed economies. In addition, the asymmetry issue persists; the TV infrastructure is primarily intended to transmit in one direction.

4.7.3 Local transmission links

Local area networks

As well as having minicomputer or mainframe computer facilities, most large and medium-sized organizations will also possess a large number of desktop computers, printers and other information technology. In order to be productive, it is essential for desktop computers to be able to communicate with one another, communicate with the organization's larger computers, share scarce resources such as printers or communicate with the outside world.

In order to achieve this a **local area network (LAN)** may be used. A LAN consists of:

- high-speed cable, such as twisted pair cable, connecting the various devices;
- a network card for each device that is connected to the network, which is a printed circuit board that manages the transmission of data across the interface between the device and the network cabling;
- network software, such as Novell Netware or Windows Server 2003, that manages data transmission around the network cabling.

A LAN is owned by a single organization and does not run outside the confines of that organization. It allows the following types of facility:

- downloading of data from the corporate database held on a mainframe computer for local processing – for example in spreadsheet models;
- communication of the personal computer with the 'outside world' and other networks via a **gateway** with the public telephone network;
- access to the Internet;
- use of a centralized shared data and program store held on a **file server**, which is a high-capacity disk storage device that is attached to the network;
- sharing of scarce resources by many users connected on the network;
- the use of electronic mail to send messages, memos and electronic letters to other nodes on the network;
- use of electronic calendar and diary facilities to schedule meetings.

The use of a file server reduces the need for, and therefore the cost of, a large hard disk for each computer on the network. Separate parts of the file server can be allocated for use by each node on the network. Programs for common use are stored on the file server rather than on individual hard disks. Smaller organizations that do not have a mainframe normally use a file server as a shared database. For instance, most of the major accounting packages for small businesses have a multi-user version to allow this (see Figure 4.11).

LANs vary in their topologies and in their transmission speeds. Examples of typical topologies are shown in Figure 4.12. Because LANs are non-switched networks the communications links are shared by all devices. Many devices may wish to transmit on the network simultaneously – the devices are in contention for the services of the network. As it is impossible for two devices to share the network literally at the same time, techniques have been devised to handle the situation. Two are examined here.

Carrier-sense multiple-access collision detection (CSMA/CD)

This is used on bus and tree networks. When a message is being transmitted from one node to another all nodes read the message and do not transmit while it is on the line. Only when no messages are on the network can a node initiate a transmission. If two nodes attempt to transmit simultaneously the collision is detected, the transmission is blocked and the nodes are forced to wait for a random time interval before retransmitting.

Figure 4.11 Devices connected to a local area network

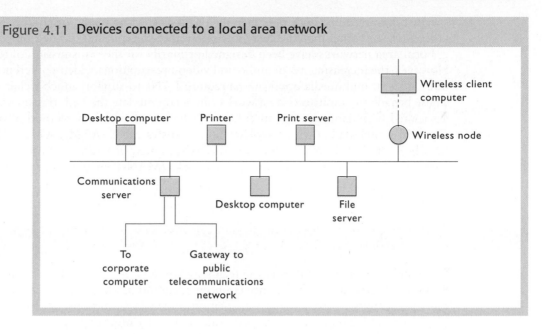

Figure 4.12 LAN topologies

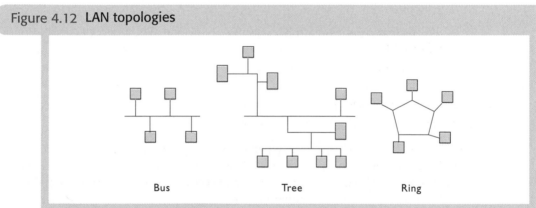

Bus   Tree   Ring

Ethernet is a commonly used type of LAN that employs CSMA/CD. The standard derives from its introduction by the Xerox Corporation. Ethernet systems are tree configurations using coaxial cable. Several hundred devices may be connected in one LAN.

Token passing

This can be used in ring or bus networks. If a device wishes to transmit on the network it removes a transmitted token before sending its message. After transmission the device retransmits the token. If the token is not available, it means that the network is being used and the device needs to wait until the token is retransmitted.

The **Cambridge ring** type of network is one using token passing. In it there is a continuously circulating packet of binary digits. If a sender node wishes to transmit, it alters the contents of the packet (takes the token) and puts the message on to the network combined with the address of the node to which the message is to be sent. When it has finished transmitting and has received acknowledgment that the data transfer was successful, the sending node puts the token back in the ring ready for another sender to take. No nodes other than the current token holder can transmit on the ring.

Local area networks have been designed primarily for the transmission of text data. However, the increasing use of audio and video presentations, video-conferencing, and more general multimedia applications require LANs to support much richer services. These **broadband multiservice networks** can accommodate the high transmission rates associated with data, speech and video. This has involved a new method of transmission and switching known as **asynchronous transfer mode (ATM)**. ATM LANs have now been developed to accommodate this. Also, a new generation of ATM wide area networks, known as **metropolitan area networks (MANs)**, have been produced to link ATM-based LANs.

4.8 Standards

Users and purchasers of information technology would like to be able to connect different technologies easily. These, once connected, should be able to cooperate in carrying out applications by exchanging information and, where appropriate, by sharing the workload of the application between many devices. Unfortunately, too often the following problems arise:

- The technologies cannot physically be connected. The devices just will not 'plug in'.
- Once the devices are connected the information passed from one device to another is packaged and formatted in a way that is not 'recognized' as information by the receiving device.
- Once recognized as information, the information cannot be 'understood' with respect to the applications software of the receiver.

These problems are increasingly being resolved by the take-up of 'plug and play' hardware technology, which automates the installation process, and by the use of 'hot plugging' where devices can be connected and recognized without restarting the computer.

4.8.1 The scope of the problem

The problem identified above is not an easy one to solve. There are several reasons for this:

1. The range of the different types of device that handle information and the many media through which the information is channelled would require a significant effort in global standardization to ensure compatibility. There are, for instance, keyboards, processing units, printers, fax machines, telephones, monitors, optical scanners, voice recognition devices and bar-code readers. Different media include coaxial cable, optical fibres, twisted pairs of wires, and microwave and infrared links.

2. Considering one type of product or transmission medium from the above, there will be many suppliers, each of whom may develop their product in what they regard as the most appropriate way. There is no guarantee that each supplier will regard the possibility of substitution of a rival's product as a benefit.

3. Even with one type of product and one supplier it may not always be possible to carry out full interconnection. Products develop over time and respond to the market environment. All companies attempt to standardize interconnections between their products as this encourages brand loyalty. However, advances in technology and the need to respond to competitor developments may on occasion preclude this. The problem is to try to develop the technology so that it looks backwards, forwards and sideways (to competitors) at the same time.

4. As well as competition between suppliers selling the same types of product, there is also rivalry between sectors. In particular, there has been rivalry between the suppliers of mainframe computer technology and the suppliers of telecommunications services (the public carriers).

In summary, everyone can realize the usefulness to the user of having the highest possible degree of interconnectedness and interworking between products. However, the independent interests of the suppliers, the need to develop and change to improve technology, and the diversity of the product field place severe difficulties on obtaining agreements on standards. This is most obvious in the area of network communications.

There are several standards-setting bodies that have influence over the development of new technology. The **International Standards Organization (ISO)** has developed a model for standard setting for devices engaged in communication across a network. This is known as the **Open Systems Interconnection (OSI)** reference model.

4.8.2 The Open Systems Interconnection model

The OSI model is intended to be a reference model for the development of protocols. It views exchange of information between two devices operating across a network from a number of levels of abstraction. These are known as **layers**. The seven-layer model is shown in Figure 4.13. The various layers correspond to different functions that must be carried out to ensure smooth and cooperative interconnection:

1. **Physical layer:** Standards for this layer govern the transmission of electrical signals between devices. Specifications would include the physical media, and the shape and size of plugs and sockets.

Figure 4.13 **The seven-layer OSI model**

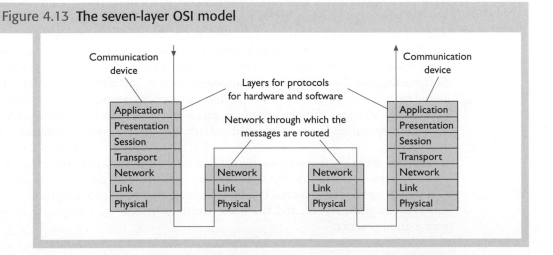

2. **Link layer:** This ensures that bits carried across the physical network have an agreed structure. Specification of packet structure and error detection and correction occur in this layer.

3. **Network layer:** This ensures that packets find their way across the network. Specifications for ways of handling address identification and routing are made here.

4. **Transport layer:** Specification of the way that multiplexing occurs and of the way that packets are assembled and disassembled is handled at the transport layer. This layer is responsible for ensuring that reliable two-way communication is established.

5. **Session layer:** This ensures that the two-way communication, once established, is co-ordinated between the communicating devices, and that protocols for information exchange are agreed.

6. **Presentation layer:** Specifications here deal with the way that data is encrypted and the way that data is formatted for processing or display in the receiving device.

7. **Applications layer:** This ensures that the information is in the right format for recognition and processing by the receiving application.

It may at first sight seem to be unnecessarily complicated to assume that each of these layers is involved in effective communication and that therefore there need to be standards at each layer. However, if a simple case of postal communication is considered it will be clear how some of these layers are already implemented in a familiar application. It is only a short step to realizing that the added complexity of electronic communication yields the need for extra layers.

Imagine that a manager at one organization wishes to order goods from another organization. The manager will need to know the name of the supplying organization and the sorts of information that are required to place an order (item to be ordered, quantity, and so on). This is accepted as standard information for the application of 'making an order' (applications level). The order needs to be presented in a way that can be understood by the receiver. This is written in English, although it need not be for foreign orders (presentation layer). At a lower level, to ensure that the order message is routed through the system properly, a recognized address for the carrying network, i.e. postal service, must be added. The standard agreed here is usually the post code or ZIP code (network layer). The order message, just like any other message through the system, has to be packaged in a way that the carrier network can handle. The standards agreed here involve encoding the message on paper, placing it inside an envelope and writing the address on the outside of the envelope (link layer). Finally, it is agreed that the letter will be taken to a post box, from which it will be physically picked up and carried through the system. Here the order message is treated just like any other (physical layer). Because the postal example does not require two-way interaction, the session and transport layers are missing. There is a certain artificiality in the example, but the point should be clear that the placing of an order for goods via the postal service can be viewed from various layers in which standards have to be agreed if communication is to be effective.

The OSI model was intentionally defined in a loose and all-embracing language in order to capture the full richness and variety of distributed applications. Although the OSI model was widely received by most vendors, it failed to provide sufficient detail for universal implementation and has been maintained more as a reference model to describe good practice.

4.9 Electronic data interchange

Electronic data interchange (EDI) can be defined as:

the transfer of electronic data from one organization's computer system to another's, the data being structured in a commonly agreed format so that it is directly usable by the receiving organization's computer system.

What distinguishes EDI from other electronic communications between organizations, such as fax, electronic mail, telephone and telex, is that in these latter cases the information is intended for consumption by a human being, who needs to understand it before any action can be taken. With EDI, the received electronic data can be processed immediately by the receiver's computer system without the need for human interpretation and translation before action.

4.9.1 An example

To see how EDI can be used in the context of significant in-house automation, consider the following example. It is important for many manufacturing companies that assemble final products to be assured of the supply of components from their stock. When the stock of a particular kind of component runs low the manufacturer orders replacements from the supplier. The supplier then dispatches these and invoices later.

The whole process can take a long time, particularly if the manufacturer's purchasing department needs to draw up a paper order that is posted to the supplier. At the supplier's end, this needs to be processed by the accounts and dispatch departments. The production of paperwork by the manufacturer and the supplier, together with the transfer of this between organizations, can lead to costly delays and errors. It may be necessary for the manufacturing company to maintain larger stocks to take account of the lead time in ordering. This in itself will be a cost. If the supplier is also low on stock of the component, it may take several days for the manufacturer to be notified. This scenario can occur even if both organizations are fully computerized as far as their own internal transaction processing is concerned.

In the context of full automation and EDI, this situation could be handled in the following way. As soon as the manufacturer's component stocks fall below a minimum level, a computer-based list of possible suppliers is consulted and the most appropriate chosen. An electronic order is generated on the manufacturer's computer system. This is then transmitted to the supplier's computer system (EDI), where it is matched electronically against stock records of the item held. A stock decrement is effected, and an instruction to dispatch the goods with full delivery details is sent to the supplier's dispatch department. An electronic acknowledgement of order satisfaction is transmitted to the manufacturer, along with an electronic invoice, which will await receipt of the goods before payment is made.

In the above EDI-automated version, there need be no paperwork exchanged at all. Human beings need only limited involvement – for instance, in the loading and distribution of the goods, or in the authorization of the placing of the purchase order by the manufacturer and agreement to satisfy the order by the supplier. These human authorizations can be by entry into the computer system, although it would be possible to automate the process of authorization entirely as well. The advantages for both companies are:

- the speed with which the order is satisfied;
- the lack of paperwork involved;
- the low cost of processing the transaction, as the involvement of costly human labour on both sides is minimal; and
- the lack of human error.

There may be further organizational advantages if the trading relationship between the two companies is altered. This point will be expanded fully later in the chapter.

4.9.2 EDI – the method

EDI may be introduced where a group of organizations wish to ensure that electronic transactions are passed between one another. One of the earliest EDI groups was set up to allow international airlines to process bookings electronically worldwide (IATA). SWIFT (Society for Worldwide International Financial Transfers) is another EDI group. This handles the transmission and processing of international financial transactions between banks.

EDI groups require EDI services in order to effect the data exchanges. These are often provided by a third-party organization. The service provided by the third party is more than merely the transmission of the data. It is customary for added facilities, especially mailbox facilities, to be offered. An electronic mailbox for a client is an electronic storage location for messages or data that are sent to the client by other organizations. The client (addressee) can read the data or messages, which are usually held on an identified area of the service provider's disk space. By providing these services the third party adds value to the data transmission and is thus said to run a **value-added network**.

A typical configuration for EDI transfer is illustrated in Figure 4.14. The message produced by the sender's applications software is translated into the agreed EDI format and placed on the network by the network access software. This electronic data is sent to the mailbox facility of the EDI service provider. Here it is stored until retrieved by the receiver organization using the retriever's network access software. The received electronic data, in the agreed format, is then translated by software into a form directly usable by the receiver's applications programs.

It is clear that a group of organizations needs to agree on standards for message representation and communication in order to take part successfully in EDI. For instance, the banks agreed on standards for SWIFT. It is becoming more common, though, for groups to come together to agree international standards for EDI. This has prompted the United Nations to set up a standards body for the commercial application of EDI. This group – UN/EDIFACT (United Nations/EDI for Administration, Commerce and Transport) – has produced a set of standards, known as EDIFACT, for the electronic transmission of data in relation to commerce in goods and services.

4.9.3 The benefits of EDI

Some of the benefits of EDI are clear from the examples in previous sections. In particular, EDI ensures that:

- The speed with which an interorganizational transaction is processed is minimized.
- The paperwork involved in transaction processing is eliminated.

Figure 4.14 EDI network

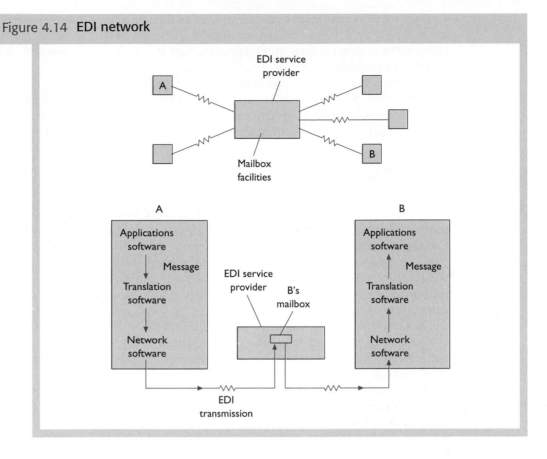

- The costs of transaction processing are reduced, as much of the need for human interpretation and processing is removed.
- Reduced human involvement reduces error.

These are benefits experienced by both sender and receiver in an EDI relationship. Of course there is a cost – the cost of purchase and installation of the technology. However, there are more strategic advantages associated with the introduction of EDI.

First, by increasing the speed of processing of transactions between an organization and its suppliers and between an organization and its customers it enables the supply chain to the customer to provide a faster service. This gives the companies in the supply chain a competitive advantage over other companies in the same sector.

Second, the speed of response to requests for component parts in the manufacturing process enables all participants in the supply chain to reduce their holding of buffer stocks. This reduces the need to tie up a company's assets in unproductive materials and is compatible with the organization of production on 'just-in-time' principles. The whole chain, therefore, gains a competitive advantage within the industry sector.

Finally, it is in the interests of an organization to 'tie in' both many suppliers and many customers through EDI. For example, a motor car production manufacturer will gain a significant competitive advantage by linking in many suppliers of substitutable component parts through EDI. While EDI benefits each supplier for the reasons stated above, its own position of dominance over the manufacturer in these circumstances is weakened by other suppliers participating in EDI. Similarly, it is in the interests of the supplier to link up with as many manufacturers through EDI as possible. The supplier's competitive position is then strengthened because it is no longer dependent on one customer manufacturer.

From the above it can be seen that the presence of EDI in the supply chain increases the competitive advantage of that chain over others in the sector. But, depending on the exact nature of the supplier–customer relationship, individual organizations in the chain may have their competitive advantage weakened or strengthened by EDI.

4.10   The effects of the Internet on business

The whole topic of the Internet and the World Wide Web is developed in subsequent chapters. However, at this point it is important to acknowledge the massive changes that the Internet has brought about in businesses and in the way that business is carried out. The proliferation of computing power through business and home users has provided many more opportunities for interchange of information and for business transactions to be carried out. Using the five forces model introduced earlier it is clear that competitive advantage can be gained through the successful development of a company website. Relations with suppliers (often referred to as business-to-business or B2B) can be greatly enhanced. Similarly, new opportunities for reducing the costs of goods and services to customers are introduced (reflected in the business-to-customer or B2C relationship).

The technology of the Internet can also be applied within the confines of an organization. An **intranet** of locally devised and accessed pages distributed over the company's own local area network can improve information sharing and communications within the organization. All these topics are dealt with in more detail in following chapters.

Summary

The last decade has witnessed a dramatic increase in the extent of use of distributed systems. Distributed computing may be defined as occurring when hardware located at two or more geographically distinct sites is connected electronically by telecommunications so that processing/data storage may occur at more than one location. The network may involve many organizations or the connection of several remote sites within one organization. These wide area networks use transmission services provided by licensed third parties known as common carriers.

The benefits of distributed systems include increased user satisfaction and autonomy – users do not need to rely on a remote computer centre for the satisfaction of their needs. Telecommunications costs are lower, as local processing will not involve expensive remote links. Distributed computing also allows for flexible systems development in that computing power can be expanded incrementally to meet demand. Although there are substantial advantages, an organization needs to be aware that unbridled distribution may lead to problems of standard setting and loss of control. If data is distributed then duplication of data may lead to inconsistency.

Although technological features will be operative in determining the extent of the use of distributed systems, it is important to remember that other features are also significant. In particular, the corporate culture and location of decision making need to be compatible with distribution, which, by its nature, involves devolution of resources and power. The type of activities undertaken by the organization must also be considered – distribution is more likely to be recommended the less dependent computerized activities are on each other.

There are several ways in which data may be treated in a distributed system. These range from electronic downloading of copies of data to various sites, to the development of a fully distributed database system with minimal duplication of data. Although there are still problems in distributing data, advances in software and telecommunications make this an increasingly attractive option for organizations.

In order to understand issues related to the implementation of distributed computing and the influence of networks, a basic understanding of technical issues is required. Transmission of data will be achieved through digital or analogue signalling, will involve parallel/serial and synchronous/asynchronous transmission, and may involve the use of high-bandwidth techniques and multiplexing. Media used are likely to be twisted-pair or coaxial cable, although, increasingly, fibre optics is being employed.

Transmission through the public network has traditionally required the leasing of special lines or the use of the public switched telephone network. Packet-switched networks and integrated services digital network transmission systems are also now in operation. These latter provide faster, more reliable services suitable for the transmission of large quantities of data and enabling the integrated transmission of image, data, voice and text.

Local links are usually via local area networks. These optimize the use of scarce resources. They are compatible with the implementation of a client–server approach in the satisfaction of user needs. Local area networks usually exhibit tree, bus or ring structures. They are used to provide commonly shared program and data files, printer services, communications with the corporate mainframe or the public networks, electronic mail, calendaring, and other facilities. Different topologies have different approaches to contention handling.

One of the major factors inhibiting the progress of networks and distributed computing is the difficulty in agreeing standards. The reasons for this largely reside in the variety of products and the commercial structure of the supplier market. Early attempts to set standards include SNA from IBM. Currently, an important influence on standard setting is the Open Systems Interconnection reference model for standards. This identifies seven layers as requiring standards for full distributed cooperation.

Electronic data interchange (EDI) is one area where developments in telecommunications and networking are having an impact beyond that of merely passing messages between computer systems. EDI is understood as the exchange of formatted data capable of immediate computer processing. Various benefits derive from EDI, including cost saving and speedy processing of transactions. In particular, though, EDI affects the nature of the trading relationships between organizations in a sector and, by way of influencing the supply chain, can considerably enhance the competitive advantage of a company.

Review questions

1. What important features need to be taken into account when considering introducing a distributed system?

2. What costs and benefits can an organization expect from using a distributed system for its information provision?

157

3. What benefits are likely to be gained by an organization if it uses a local area network to connect its separate computing devices?

4. Under what circumstances would it be desirable to distribute data and under what circumstances would it be desirable to centralize it?

5. What are the advantages and disadvantages of using a leased line compared with the public circuit-switched telecommunications network? Under what circumstances would it be recommended?

6. How do packet-switched networks differ from circuit-switched networks?

7. Explain the difference between *frequency modulation* and *amplitude modulation*.

Exercises

1. The same features that led to the advent of distributed computing and wide area networks between sites operated a decade later to provide the need for local area networks. Discuss.

2. What is meant by saying that the structure for a distributed system mirrors the organizational structure it is required to serve – and why should it?

3. Why has it been so difficult to obtain agreements on standards for interconnecting devices through networks?

4. What is EDI?

5. How can the effects of EDI be analysed within the terms of Porter's competitive advantage and competitive strategy approach?

6. Consider a large organization with which you are familiar (e.g. your college, your employer organization, your bank).
   (a) To what extent does the distributed structure of its information systems mirror its organizational structure?
   (b) How important have organizational characteristics such as corporate culture been in determining the extent of distribution?

7. ABC Co. is a medium-sized company manufacturing and installing office furniture. Manufacturing and installation are located in seven sites spread throughout the UK. Each site also runs its own sales team, which promotes and sells ABC office furniture by providing a concept design service for organizations wishing to refurbish their offices. Currently, all computerized information provision and transaction processing is by way of ABC's mainframe computer located in London. Local sites possess terminals connected to the mainframe by public telecommunications. Local site managers are arguing for more autonomy in responding to the needs of local customers. They claim that the central computer services, for which they are charged internally, provide poor and non-targeted information. As a group, individual site managers have put a case for abandoning the company's central mainframe system – which is due for review with respect to significant upgrading – and replacing this with local minicomputers that would communicate, if necessary, through the public carrier system. All functions appertaining to the local sites would be processed locally. Advise the managing director on this issue.

8. A large regional college is extending its network and IT infrastructure to support all its academic and administrative functions. Currently, the network infrastructure is used for internal personnel, payroll, accounting, student registration, administrative and financial functions. Academically, it is used by students following computing and engineering courses. It is the long-term intention of the college to ensure that all staff have a PC connected into the college network and that all students have IT skills training, especially in the use of word-processing and spreadsheet packages. Laboratories are gradually being upgraded under the direction of the computer centre. For some years, the Computer Science and Engineering Departments have been unhappy with much of the service provided by the computer centre. These departments have already implemented their own laboratories of desktop computers separately, cabled and networked for students on their courses. Staff in these departments have also been networked using a physically separate cabling system, as the respective department heads believe that with computing students there is a danger that their knowledge will allow them unauthorized access to staff data traffic. The college principal is concerned that there is an absence of strategic planning and control and is unhappy about the current situation. Advise the college principal on a course of action.

CASE STUDY 4

Networked storage

Arrojo Studio is known in New York's SoHo as a place the fashionable go for a sharp haircut. Founder Nick Arrojo is known further afield for his British wit: he is one of the stylists on US TV channel TLC's 'What Not to Wear'. But behind the scenes, setting styles brings challenges. Photo shoots, advertising, a range of hair products and a planned expansion of the salon's New York base are all placing an extra load on the business's IT, and especially its storage needs.

In the next few weeks Arrojo will take delivery of a new storage system in the shape of an Apple Xserve Raid, to provide shared storage and disk-based back-up to the company's 20 computers and Macintosh server. Currently, staff back up their data to external Firewire drives, with server back-up to tape. But with growth in mind, IT consultant Dominic Antiszko thinks this is no longer sufficient.

'With photographers creating at least 20MB files and up to 2000 pictures per shoot, they will fill up a 60GB drive', Mr Antiszko says. 'Even DVDs are not a solution. We have muddled along so far with decent-sized hard drives in our Macs but we are getting to the point where we want to centralise all our files and images'.

The investment should make managing the company's growing network easier too: if a staff member's computer fails, Antiszko will be able to restore their data from the server system. Documents and digital imaging are also displaying a voracious appetite for storage at law firm Wragge & Co. The practice, with two UK offices and branches in Hong Kong and Brussels, employs 1100 people, placing it among larger, mid-market companies. The firm was, however, an early adopter of technology more often associated with enterprises.

Four years ago Wragge installed a storage area network, based largely on Dell hardware. The San, which now runs to 4 terabytes of data, originally supported 80 servers. But one benefit of the San, according to IT director Nigel Blackwood, has been consolidating data storage. That allowed the firm to use virtualization (maximizing server use) to halve the number of servers, despite a growing workload.

▶

With law firms making more and more use of electronic documents, Mr Blackwood expects to double the size of Wragge's San in the coming year. This means a significant investment, but Mr Blackwood believes it will pay for itself in several ways, from faster access to documents, to reducing the space Wragge needs for storing paper files. 'More and more of our business is done electronically, so we have to look at how we manage that information in electronic rather than paper formats', says Mr Blackwood.

Small and mid-sized firms such as Wragge and Arrojo are moving towards modular or networked storage, in place of relying on the hard drives built into their PCs and servers. Companies are doing this for a number of reasons, including easier back-up and recovery, compliance demands and the need to handle large volumes of data efficiently.

Networked storage, for example can be significantly more efficient than in-built storage, because it allows IT managers to 'pool' resources across servers and applications. 'We had quite a few servers where about 50% of the disc space was unused', says Mr Blackwood at Wragge. 'That might not matter if you have just a few servers, but it does if you have 20 or 30.'

Eric Sheppard, European storage program manager at IDC, the industry analysts, agrees there is a migration from internal storage to networked storage both among enterprises and small and medium-sized businesses. He says: 'We are seeing 1.8% growth in the total storage market but 14 to 20% growth in networked storage.'

This trend looks set to continue, as smaller companies look towards networked storage both to hold their day-to-day data and, increasingly, as their main form of back-up. Research company IDC says that 86% of companies with 50 to 1000 employees already use discs rather than tape for at least some of their back-up. Cheaper, more efficient and larger drives will continue to make disk-based back-ups an attractive option. Some fast-growing businesses might skip tape-based back-up systems altogether, and move straight to low-cost, network-attached storage servers or, if their needs justify it, a small storage area network.

Developments such as iSCSI – which uses conventional Ethernet connections rather than expensive fibre optics for Sans – are further driving down costs. 'An Ethernet switch costs a few hundred dollars but an equivalent fibre-channel switch might be $5,000. That is a difference in price for an SMB, and we are seeing a significant swing to iSCSI', says Praveen Asthana, global director of storage and networking at Dell.

But regardless of the technology, smaller companies are increasingly finding that they need more storage, and more reliable storage, in order to support changes in the way they do business. 'More and more of the work we are doing is being stored, delivered and managed in electronic files', says Mr Blackwood at Wragge. 'It is not good enough for IT to say we don't have the storage to accommodate it. We have to provide it.'

Adapted from: **Storage needs met by networks**
Stephen Pritchard, *Financial Times*, 28 February 2007

Questions

1. What advantages does a distributed system provide?

2. Why do hairdressers have an increasing need for high-volume storage devices?

3. Compare and contrast the process of backing up files on individual external hard drives with a centralized server storage system.

4. The case study briefly mentions server back-up and archive issues. Propose a server back-up strategy for the two businesses discussed if they are to adopt a networked storage system. Why is such a strategy important?

Recommended reading

Cole M. (2002). *Introduction to Telecommunications: Voice, Data and the Internet*. Prentice Hall
A very readable introduction to telecommunications topics. The book has a technical focus and is very well illustrated.

Gutierrez J. (2006). *Business Data Communications and Networking*. IGI Global
A comprehensive coverage of networking and communications issues focusing on the business context. Particular attention is devoted to wireless and mobile technologies and to the issues of network security.

Hodson P. (2002). *Local Area Networks*. Letts Educational
The text is restricted to LANs and interconnections with wide area networks. Although not assuming any initial knowledge the text takes the reader into technical areas of LANs and communications. It is designed for the student and has many exercises and self-help questions.

Peng Z.-R. and Tsou M.-H. (2003). *Internet GIS: Distributed Geographic Information Services for the Internet and Wireless Networks*. Wiley
This provides the background to basic network architecture and then moves on to explore how geographical information systems have become a popular feature of the Internet. The book combines theory with applications and also discusses the importance of standards in network developments.

Peterson L. (2007). *Computer Networks: A Systems Approach*, 3rd edn. Academic Press
A thorough coverage of networks with an interesting chapter on congestion control, resource allocation and network security.

Stallings W. (2006). *Data and Computer Communications*. Prentice Hall
This provides an encyclopaedic coverage of the topic. Includes end of chapter review questions.

Chapter 5

The Internet and the World Wide Web

Introduction

Over the last three decades, the Internet has developed from a useful facility for the exchange of academic, scientific and military information to become a major force in information exchange globally. This explosion has been driven by the increased use of personal computers in the workplace and at home, and by the involvement of business on the Internet as a way of reaching trading partners and customers. This chapter sets the foundation for understanding how the Internet can assist businesses in reaching their objectives. It is important that the reader understands the background and basis of the Internet and its facilities. The earlier sections address this. The most important contribution to business activity (along with e-mail) is the World Wide Web. The latter part of the chapter introduces the World Wide Web as an easy-to-use and consistent interface to the Internet. Finally, intranets and extranets are introduced and the rationale for their use by an organization is outlined.

5.1 The evolution of the Internet

In order to understand the basis of the Internet, it is instructive to cover the history of its evolution.

During 1956, the United States set up the Advanced Research Projects Agency (ARPA) to assist it to gain increased military competitive advantage and to stimulate advances in science and technology. In the late 1960s, the US Department of Defense set up the **ARPANET** group to develop a secure network between computers. This was to develop stable methods by which computers could be connected to one another for military and scientific purposes. It had long been recognized that with the increasing reliance of the US military on computers and computer control of its defence systems it was imperative to ensure that in a 'hostile environment' when parts of a network were not working (or were destroyed) the remaining network should continue to function. Thus from the early days it was assumed that networks were unlikely to be stable but still had to function effectively. The connecting network between such computers became known as the ARPANET. In 1972, ARPANET connection was demonstrated between 40 geographically dispersed machines in the United States. By 1973, the UK had become connected to the ARPANET. During the 1970s, various facilities that are used today were developed initially for the ARPANET. These are covered later in the chapter and include e-mail, USENET (an electronic bulletin board) and various methods for transferring electronic files across the network.

For computers to communicate effectively across a network they need to ensure that they transmit and receive information in a standard way. These transmission standards are called protocols. During the 1980s, the International Standards Organization (ISO) was in the process of developing a comprehensive layered approach towards all computer communication through the development of the Open Systems Interconnection (OSI), which was covered in Chapter 4. However, progress was not fast enough for ARPANET members, and in 1982 the development of the transmission control protocol (TCP) and the Internet protocol (IP) established the standard for computer network transmission across the ARPANET and became the foundation of the Internet communication standards.

During the 1980s, local area networks (LANs) were being installed in businesses and other organizations for internal communication based around PCs. Organizations desired these internal networks to be connected to the ARPANET, which now had a much wider function that its original military/scientific objectives. In the UK, **JANET** (Joint Academic Network) was set up in 1984 to provide connections between universities, and scientific and major government organizations. Internal networks in each of these organizations had connections to JANET. JANET itself was linked to ARPANET.

One of the important new US networks commissioned by the National Science Foundation (**NSFNET**) involved the development of five supercomputers located at five major universities. These were to be connected together, and each was to be the centre of a regional network with links through the telephone network to local schools and colleges. The philosophy was to provide universal educational connection to the network. This network was to be connected to ARPANET. But as the number of networks had risen so had ARPANET bureaucracy, and it had become increasingly difficult to deal with the greater requirements on it. The NSFNET rapidly became more important, and connections to it rose rapidly in the United States. The late 1980s saw the serious commercial interest of the telephone companies in the interconnection of computers. The American telecommunications company MCI took over the management of the telephone connections within NSFNET. In 1989, the electronic mail provider CompuServe linked up with what was now becoming known as the Internet by a connection through Ohio State University. ARPANET had ceased to exist by 1990.

The Internet as it was known by the late 1980s was a collection of networks that could communicate with each other running under TCP/IP. Its use was still largely confined to educational, government and scientific organizations. Two developments led to the explosive growth of the Internet in the 1990s. The first was the rapid increase in the ownership of PCs, both privately and in businesses. This was most obvious in the United States but was a worldwide phenomenon. PCs were becoming cheaper and much more powerful. Modems, the devices needed to connect the PC through the telephone network, were becoming much faster in operation, thus allowing the possibility of graphics and sound being communicated to the PC as well as text. The other major development was the design and development of the **World Wide Web**. This was introduced in 1990. It allows users to retrieve information in text and graphic form easily from the Internet. Extensive use is made of **hypertext** and links to information held on other computers. These links make information readily available, and navigation around the Internet is easy. The World Wide Web is covered later in this chapter.

By 1992, over one million users had become connected to the Internet and the World Wide Web via linked networks. In 1993, The White House, the UK government, the United Nations and the World Bank all went online with the provision of information on the World Wide Web. Throughout 1993 and 1994 business use of the World Wide Web grew, credit card transactions were established over the Internet, and television commercials increasingly made reference to websites. During 1995, sophisticated software **browsers** were developed (in particular Netscape Navigator and Microsoft's Internet Explorer). These enabled advanced use of the World Wide Web to distribute and view video and sound as well as text and graphics. Developments in operating systems such as Windows XP and the free availability of the browser software made access even easier. Connection to the Internet, particularly for private use, was further accelerated as the number of Internet service providers (ISPs) increased and the cost of service fell. The introduction of broadband Internet connection has had a massive impact on both business and home usage. Rapid transfer of data, easy transfer of large files and 24-hours-a-day connection are all possible. It has also moved the charging model towards a flat rate subscription and away from a per-use basis. Membership and use have continued to grow at an exponential rate. By 2007, estimates have shown that there are over 500 million Internet hosts (measured by counting domain names such as 'mywebsite.com') hosting many billions of web pages in total. The Internet and the World Wide Web have now become established globally as a major source of information and entertainment for businesses and private individuals.

Mini case 5.1

Broadband

The development of 'Broadband Britain' – a nation with one of the highest rates of fast Internet connectivity in Europe – is one in which ministers and regulators take pride. The UK leads the Group of Seven industrialized nations in broadband availability, and another 3m people adopted broadband last year. Half of UK adults now have broadband, a seven-fold increase in just four years.

But it risks becoming a victim of its success as networks struggle to cope with the surge in traffic, particularly for new bandwidth-hungry services. The danger is not simply that YouTube video clips will take longer to download, but – with broadband 'the key enabling infrastructure of the global knowledge economy' – that innovation will also slow down. At first glance, the timing for such a warning seems odd. Average broadband connection speeds more than doubled last year to 3.8mbps and over the next five years download speeds will increase to up to 24mbps. However, a significant minority of users will see no real improvement in their broadband access speeds from the new network because one of the key determinants of download speed is consumers' proximity to BT's phone exchanges. The greater the length of copper wire between homes and exchanges, the slower the speed. Even 24mbps will not be fast enough for some users by 2012, the BSG warns. BT admits that a family trying to watch two live football matches simultaneously will push the capability of 24mbps broadband to its limit.

In Germany, Deutsche Telekom is spending €3bn to run fibreoptic cable from its exchanges to the street-side cabinets that in turn lead to people's homes. From next year it will offer download speeds of up to 50mbps in 50 cities. The debate is whether companies that rely on their customers being able to access their content on fast connections, such as Google or media companies, should share the cost.

Adapted from: **Report warns of broadband complacency**
Andrew Edgecliffe-Johnson and Andrew Parker, *Financial Times*, 16 April 2007

Questions

1. What problems does the article illustrate in broadband uptake?

2. What measures can broadband users and communications providers take to improve connection speeds?

3. The article suggests that content providers should share the costs of improved infrastructure. What would be the implications for businesses and for the wider community?

5.2 How the Internet works

5.2.1 Connection to the Internet

A computer may be connected to the Internet and transmit and receive information from the Internet in a number of ways:

1. If the computer is part of a local area network then it is quite likely that the computer will be connected through that network to a gateway, which will itself be linked to another network. This is linked to other networks, and so on. It is usual for the link to the first network to be a leased (as distinct from a dial-up) line. The links to other networks will also be via non-dial-up links.

2. Another method of connection is to utilize an **Internet service provider (ISP)**. An ISP is usually a commercial organization that provides access to the Internet for a private user or a small business. The ISP has high-speed machines and a fast link into the Internet. Connection might be established by dialling a number to create a link using a normal telephone connection. More usually, a modem connected to a telecommunications socket provides a constant broadband connection to the Internet; ready when required. The cost of the provision varies according to the service provided. The user might be charged a monthly subscription rental and, for a dial-up connection, may also pay a usage charge while connected. At the other end of the spectrum, a so-called free service ISP might make no charges at all, leaving the user with just

Figure 5.1 Connections and the Internet

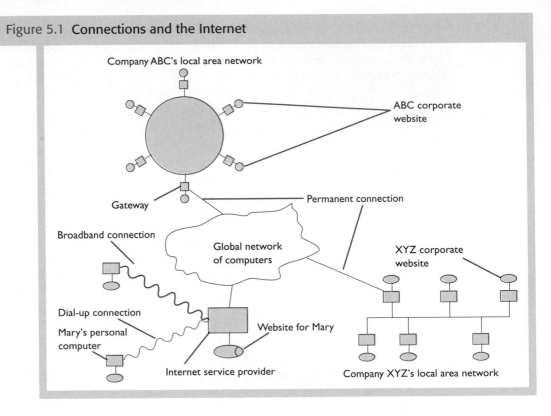

the cost of the phone call to the service provider. The level of service is normally reflected in the charges levied. The ISP, as well as providing access to the Internet, will usually provide news and other information services, e-mail and often an amount of space on a server which can facilitate the management of a small website for the subscriber.

Figure 5.1 shows how different users of the Internet might effect the necessary connections to communicate with other Internet users. Two companies, ABC and XYZ, each have a local area network. From a computer attached to the ring network in company ABC it will be possible to access pages from the ABC corporate website and send internal e-mail messages. Similarly, users of the bus network in company XYZ will also have access to their own internal e-mail system and web pages stored on their corporate web servers. Each of the companies has a computer identified as providing a gateway to the global Internet. If company users want to make a connection to an external computer user, e.g. to view pages hosted on an external web server, the gateway computer provides the interface through which that connection can be set up. Mary, a home computer user, can use Internet services, such as e-mail, and has a broadband connection provided by her Internet service provider. The ISP then acts as her gateway to the Internet. Many ISPs provide space for private users to create their own website, and these pages will become part of the globally accessible World Wide Web. Employees working at companies ABC and XYZ and Mary from her home computer can all now communicate with each other, whether it be exchanging e-mails, transferring files between computers or viewing designated web pages.

5.2.2 Addresses and domain names

Each computer attached to the Internet is given an address. This consists of a 32-bit number. Conventionally, this is expressed as a sequence of four decimal numbers, for example 128.146.16.5. Each number is less than 256. For ease of understanding to humans these host computers are known by more meaningful names. For example, *Sales.TringBabySupplies.co.uk*. The name gives information as well as being a formal address. It can be read as the computer server identified as *Sales* (the Sales Department) located at the Tring Baby Supplies Shop (*TringBabySupplies*) which is an business site (*co*) located in the United Kingdom (*uk*). It is convention that each country has an identifier, although it is also convention that the United States does not use a national identifier.

The host computer names are translated into the relevant 32-bit addresses by means of the domain name system (DNS). This is a worldwide hierarchical system of assigning names. Each name is allocated by a name server. This server is responsible for allocating all names within its domain. For example, a domain might be non-governmental organizations. This authority is derived from the next higher level. There is a set of two-letter domains that correspond to the highest domain in each country on the Internet. For example, *uk* stands for the United Kingdom and *ch* represents Switzerland. Within each country, the domains are broken down into lower-level domains. For example, Table 5.1 illustrates the original high-level domains in the United States.

Table 5.1 High-level domains in the United States

Domain	Area
Com	commercial organization
Edu	educational organization
Gov	governmental organization
Mil	military organization
Org	non-governmental organization
Net	network resource

Mini case 5.2

Domain names

One year after its official launch, the Internet domain name .eu has drawn more than 2.5m registrations, making it one of the fastest growing top-level domain names on the web. The .eu address is available to all companies and organizations located in the European Union, and to all citizens in the bloc's 27 member states. It was created thanks to an agreement by EU governments more than seven years ago, and is intended to complement the more established national top-level domain names (TLDs) such as .uk for Britain or .de for Germany as well as international TLDs such as .com or .org.

The European Commission said a string of well-known companies and organizations had adopted the .eu domain, including Air France, the airline; Dexia, the financial services group; Aldi, the retailer; Versace, the fashion label, and Greenpeace, the environmental

▶

pressure group. However, most groups continue to use international domains such as .org or .com or their national TLD in parallel.

The new domain has proved especially popular with groups created by cross-border mergers – such as Dexia, the Franco-Belgian group – and with companies registered outside their home country for regulatory reasons. Cyprus, a popular destination for company registrations, boasted the seventh-highest number of .eu domain names. 'Now that the initial flush of registrations has passed, there is an increasing trend towards using .eu domains immediately they have been registered as opposed to simply registering them as a precautionary measure and letting them lie dormant', the Commission reported.

Adapted from: **Use of .eu domain name grows rapidly**
Tobias Buck, *Financial Times*, 12 April 2007

Questions

1. What factors might influence whether a business or organization might adopt a .eu domain?

2. Why might companies register a .eu domain but leave it dormant?

The worldwide growth in the number of users of the Internet has been exponential. There are many ways of quantifying this growth: it could be measured in terms of the number of users of the Internet, the number of computers connected to the Internet, the geographical zones where Internet access is possible, the number of websites, and so on. The graphs in Figure 5.2 chart the growth of the Internet in terms of the number of hosts (where a host is defined as a machine with its own IP address) and the number of domains (where a domain is defined as a registered domain name). Although the exponential nature of the growth is evident, there are signs that the rate of increase in the number of hosts is beginning to fall, possibly providing evidence of a plateau of saturation.

5.2.3 Connection through the Internet

Network connection concepts were introduced in the previous chapter, and the reader is referred to that chapter for a more extended coverage than here. Connection between one computer on the Internet and another computer on the Internet is not like the connection of one telephone to another via a circuit link through the public-switched telephone network. In the case of a phone link, a circuit connection is established through the network at dial-up and exists for as long as the telephone call exists.

In the case of an Internet connection, the information that passes between one computer and another is divided into packets, with different packets taking different routes through the network. There is thus only a virtual circuit connection. This process is known as **packet switching** and was illustrated in Figure 4.11.

In order to ensure that information proceeds from the transmitter computer to the correct receiver computer, and that the information that is received in different packets is assembled in the correct order at the receiving computer, two important standards (protocols) are used.

The **Internet protocol (IP)** ensures that a packet of data arrives at the correct address (the destination computer) after transfer through the Internet. As the packet passes through the Internet, onward transmission from one network to another is handled by computers known as **routers**.

Figure 5.2 Growth in use of the Internet: (a) hosts; (b) websites

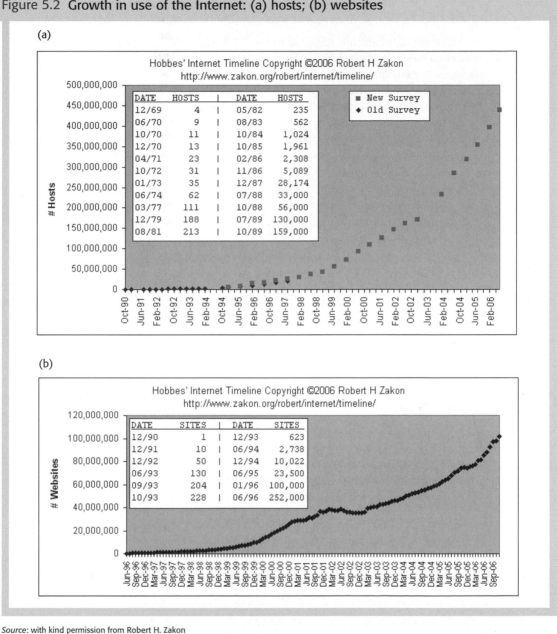

Source: with kind permission from Robert H. Zakon

Because a packet of data contains the equivalent of only about 1500 characters, it is usual for the information sent between one computer and another to be divided into several packets. Ensuring that these packets arrive at the correct address is the job of the Internet protocol. However, having arrived:

- the information held in the packets needs to be reassembled in the correct order;
- the receiving computer must determine whether the data has been altered in error during transmission; and

■ the receiving computer must be able to request the sending computer to resend any packets not received or determined to have been received in an altered state.

All of the information required to do this is inserted into each packet along with the information to be transmitted. The standard protocol that determines how this is done is known as **transmission control protocol (TCP)**. The combination of IP and TCP occurs so regularly that it is known as **TCP/IP**. Most operating systems (e.g. Microsoft Windows) contain software to handle these protocols.

Figure 5.3(a) shows a snapshot in time of the route taken by packets of data transmitted from the University of Lincoln in the UK to an information website in Sabah, East Malaysia. The packets can be seen travelling through London, the USA and onwards to Malaysia using a combination of satellite and land line connections.

The connection and route taken has been tracked using a software package called NeoTrace. Although the user of the system might assume that a direct route is followed, the enlargement in Figure 5.3(b) shows that a more idiosyncratic path is taken, particularly at the earlier stages.

Figure 5.3(c) shows a more complete trace and identifies 19 nodes that are involved in the data transfer. A more complete picture emerges, with the data being sent from a laptop computer in Lincoln through various cities in the UK until reaching a relay station in Southwark, London. From there (node 10) the time intervals increase dramatically, representing the switch from wired cables to satellite transmission. The message is then passed across North America and on to South East Asia and its destination in Kota Kinabalu, Sabah.

The process is dynamic and, if repeated, would produce a different trace with different time intervals. At the moment when this image was captured the longest time interval between nodes was 495 milliseconds (approximately half a second), with the total time to make the trace between the sender in the UK and the recipient in Malaysia being approximately two and a half seconds.

If all the data that is being sent can be fitted into one packet, an alternative protocol known as the **user datagram protocol** (UDP) may be used. It has the advantage of being less complex and swifter in operation than TCP.

Some users will be using a telephone connection and modem for the first part of the connection into the Internet. For example, an employee might connect to the Internet from home or while travelling on business through the employee's organization's local area network. The first part of the connection will often be made using a protocol known as **point-to-point protocol** (PPP). This protocol allows a computer to use a modem and telephone line to establish TCP/IP connection to the Internet.

5.3   What the Internet offers

Connection to the Internet makes available a number of facilities that are useful to business and private users (who may also be customers of businesses). Some of these are more important than others. For business, undoubtedly the two most important are e-mail and the World Wide Web. The full range of facilities are covered in the current section, although the World Wide Web is mentioned only briefly as it is covered extensively later. The application of the Internet to business is covered in the next chapter.

Figure 5.3 (a) A virtual network connection (produced by NeoTrace); (b) Nodes used to establish the network connection; (c) NeoTrace Version 3.25 – trial trace results

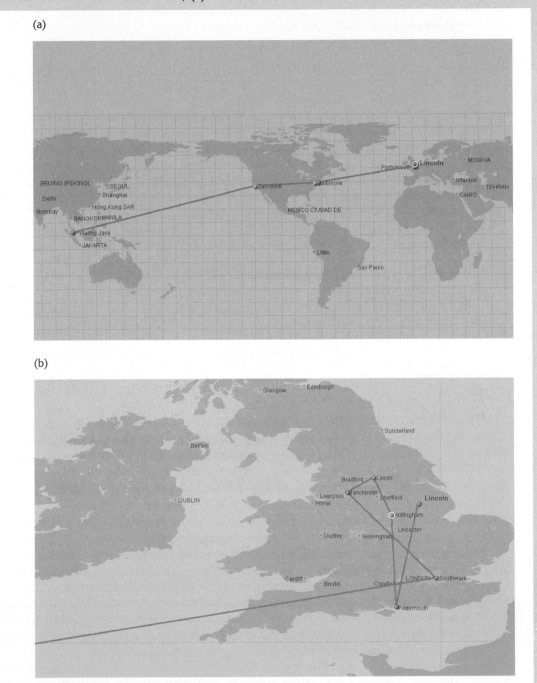

(a)

(b)

Figure 5.3 (cont'd)

(c)
NeoTrace Version 3.25 - TRIAL Trace Results
Target: www.sabah-credit.com.my
Nodes: 19

Node	IP Address	Location	Time (ms)	Node Name
1	123.321.11.11	Lincoln	0	LAPTOP
2	10.175.231.254	Unknown	24	
3	80.4.47.181	Portsmouth	26	nott-t2cam1-a-ge-wan52-135.inet.ntl.com
4	80.1.79.61	Nottingham	86	not-t2core-a-pos41.inet.ntl.com
5	62.253.188.33	Leeds	26	lee-bb-a-so-200-0.inet.ntl.com
6	62.253.187.186	Leeds	25	lee-bb-b-ae0-0.inet.ntl.com
7	62.253.185.193	Manchester	34	man-bb-a-so-700-0.inet.ntl.com
8	62.253.187.178	Manchester	34	man-bb-b-ae0-0.inet.ntl.com
9	213.206.159.245	Southwark	46	sl-gw11-lon-8-0.sprintlink.net
10	213.206.128.58	Southwark	39	sl-bb21-lon-11-0.sprintlink.net
11	144.232.19.69	39.617N, 74.383W	272	sl-bb21-tuk-10-0.sprintlink.net
12	144.232.20.132	39.617N, 74.383W	101	sl-bb20-tuk-15-0.sprintlink.net
13	144.232.20.122	Baltimore	215	sl-bb21-rly-14-3.sprintlink.net
14	144.232.7.254	Baltimore	276	sl-bb22-rly-13-0.sprintlink.net
15	144.232.20.186	San Jose	269	sl-bb22-sj-10-0.sprintlink.net
16	144.232.3.210	San Jose	276	sl-bb25-sj-12-0.sprintlink.net
17	144.232.3.114	San Jose	279	sl-gw8-sj-10-0.sprintlink.net
18	144.228.110.130	San Jose	495	sl-telec3-1-0.sprintlink.net
19	210.187.19.36	Petaling Jaya	----	www.sabah-credit.com.my
		Total	2523	

Source: McAffee www.mcaffee.com

5.3.1 E-mail

Electronic mail (**e-mail**) is the sending of an electronic message or memo from one person to another. The messages are sent and received through the use of e-mail software running on a computer.

In local area networks, e-mail software enables users within a company to send and receive messages to and from one another over the network. These packages work by reserving part of the hard disk of a file server on the network for each person. Each user has an individual address, which corresponds to the disk storage location. This is known as the user's **mailbox**. Messages sent to the person are stored electronically prior to (and after) being read in the mailbox. Users can access their mailbox through the normal procedure of identifying themselves by logging on to their network account and then running the e-mail software. Alternatively, employees may be able to access their mailbox from a remote (off-site) location. Generally, e-mail packages are user-friendly and have a large number of facilities for users such as filing messages, constructing distribution lists and linking to a calendar for diary-based activities.

Private users of e-mail have a mailbox located at their Internet service provider (ISP). The user sends and reads their e-mail by connecting to the mailbox, which is maintained by the ISP.

An e-mail message typically consists of a header and text (see Figure 5.4). The address consists of both the address of a host machine (the part after @ in the example) and the address of the person's mailbox at the host machine (the part before @ in the example).

Figure 5.4 **The format of an e-mail message**

To:	receivername@receiveraddress	*inserted by sender*
From:	g.a.curtis@uel.ac.uk	*inserted automatically by sender's package*
Organization:	University of East London	*inserted automatically by sender's package*
Date:	12 July 2008	*inserted automatically by sender's package*
cc:	copyreceivername@copyreceiveraddress	*inserted by sender*
Reply to:	g.a.curtis@uel.ac.uk	*inserted automatically by sender's package (usually the same as From address)*
The message text is inserted here and can be of any length.		*inserted by sender*

When the message is sent over the Internet, it is sent by the **store and forward** method. This means that during its progress from sender to receiver the message is not continuously in electronic transit but may be stored at a computer(s) on the Internet prior to being forwarded on the next part of its journey. This implies that e-mail transmission over the Internet is not instantaneous. Messages may take a few seconds to several hours.

The use of e-mail provides several advantages (and disadvantages) over the telephone and the postal system. These comparisons are outlined in Table 5.2. E-mail is increasingly used in organizations in preference to paper-based memos because:

- it is faster to transmit (almost instantaneous);
- it is more convenient and environmentally friendly (no paper);
- there is an automatic record of when the e-mail is read; and
- it is possible to send the same e-mail to a number of recipients for no extra effort.

The use of e-mail over the Internet is also increasing. It is preferred to the postal system because:

- it is faster than post (and unlike telephone messages time differences are unimportant);
- it is more convenient and environmentally friendly (no paper); and
- it is possible to send the same e-mail to a number of recipients for no extra effort.

Table 5.2 **A comparison of e-mail, post and telephone**

	E-mail	*Post/memo*	*Telephone*
Speed	fast	slow	instant
Security	moderate	high	low
Interactivity	moderate	low	high
Formality	moderate	high	low
As record	moderate	high	low
Multiple recipients	possible (cheap)	possible (costly)	limited

Typically, e-mail packages provide several facilities:

1. **Notification of receipt/reading:** On receipt/reading of the e-mail the receiver's package automatically replies with an acknowledgement. It is often useful to know if a recipient has received and (particularly) read a message.

2. **Mailing and distribution lists:** The e-mail package enables a user to build up several lists of e-mail addresses, which can be called up and inserted with one key stroke, for example all departmental heads, or all client contact names.

3. **Forward or reply:** A message may be forwarded or replied to. Typically, this can be accompanied by the reader's comments (editing) and be with or without the original text.

4. **File attachments:** Files, for example word-processed document files and spreadsheets, can be attached to messages and loaded into receiver software.

5. **Folders:** Received messages can be automatically stored in different electronic folders.

6. **Filters:** Filter facilities allow mail to be selectively read and stored depending on whether the messages meet some rule (filter rule) specified by the user. It might be the case that mail from a certain organization is filtered out to a particular folder, or only mail with certain key words in the headings is read.

An example of a typical interface provided by an e-mail package is shown in Figure 5.5.

Figure 5.5 An example of a screen from an e-mail package

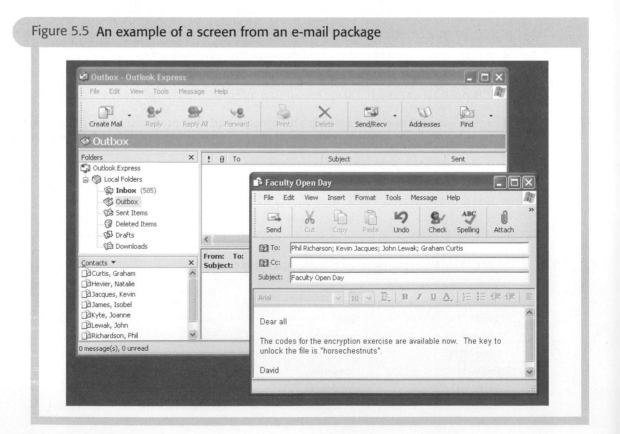

In order that different e-mail packages can send and receive information other than standard ASCII text e-mail messages to one another it is important that there be a standard way of representing the structure of these messages. This standard is called **MIME** (multipurpose Internet mail extension). As well as specifying the structure of the messages, the MIME standard also specifies how video, graphics and audio files can be sent as attachments to e-mail messages along with standard ASCII text. The MIME standard ensures that non-text files are converted into text – although the resulting text is not readable. Also, as well as specifying the type of file being sent, the MIME standard specifies the method that needs to be used by the recipient in order to convert the file to its original form. If two different e-mail packages can be used to send and receive non-text files to one another according to the MIME standard, these packages are said to be MIME compliant.

It is clear that e-mail is now an essential means of communication. This is especially so within a business, where e-mail together with intranets (covered in a later section) are rapidly replacing paper-based communications in an organization.

5.3.2 The World Wide Web

The **World Wide Web** has dramatically increased the accessibility of information on the Internet and the private and commercial use of the Internet. The World Wide Web, together with software that enables a user to browse, ensures that text, graphic, video and audio information is available globally in a standard manner. The Web is treated extensively in the following sections (5.4 and onwards) of this chapter.

5.3.3 Remote Connection

In an organization, a PC located on the organization's local area network will be able to run the organization's application programs in one of two ways. The program may be run off the hard disk on the PC, or it may be run over the LAN from a server. The PC is effectively acting as a terminal and as a client to the server. This client–server relationship was explained in Chapter 4. A similar relationship can exist between two computers over the Internet. A client computer can remotely log on to a server computer across the Internet.

Businesses may wish to allow access by Remote Connection for specified clients or for their own employees when they are remotely located (for example a travelling sales person, or an employee working from home). Applications such as Microsoft's Remote Desktop Connection allow a home or other remote-based computer to be used to connect to the company systems allowing that user to see a virtual version of the desktop screen that is normally presented when logging in on-site. The access that an organization allows to its own computer system is usually the subject of a high level of security restriction and password control.

The system will inevitably run a little slower because of the delays in communications transmission but the advantages in having access to files, emails and other applications are huge.

5.3.4 TELNET

Remote Connection is based on an earlier technology known as Telnet. Using Telnet a client computer can remotely log on to a server computer across the Internet. This allows access to files and applications that are stored on the server.

5.3.5 File transfer protocol (FTP)

Rather than logging on to a remote computer and using that computer's software to access and run applications, it may be desirable to obtain a copy of a file that can then be stored on the client's computer for later use. In order that this can be achieved over the Internet a protocol – **file transfer protocol (FTP)** – is used. As with Remote Connection and Telnet, there may be security levels allowing access to files only by a login account and a password. Some organizations may allow open access for transfer of files, for example public service or research organizations. FTP is a popular method of transferring web pages that have been developed on a local computer across to the website that will host them and is located on a remote system.

5.3.6 Instant messaging

Instant messaging (IM) is a rapid and simple way for two online users to communicate, normally by using text. Although the concept is similar to e-mail, IM provides a far more immediate transmission and simplifies the process where an extended exchange of messages takes place. As cell phone text message services have moved into the mainstream, IM has gained the interest of businesses who have realized commercial potential from using the technology.

5.3.7 Internet telephony

The Internet provides an alternative to traditional telephone services. With appropriate software and hardware installed on their systems, Internet users can make telephone or videophone calls, send faxes and leave voice mail or paging messages. The sound and picture quality might be lower than that achieved with a permanent circuit connection, but the cost is that of the normal Internet service provision (which regardless of the location of the participants could be just that of a local or free call).

5.3.8 Electronic conferencing

Tools for electronic conferencing provide a further medium of communication and facilitate collaborative working. Members of work groups can meet to share ideas in real time even though geographically dispersed. A number of alternative models exist:

- **Voice-conferencing:** This technology replaces the traditional method of using conference telephones to realize a meeting. Participants use the Internet telephony described above combined with browser-based software such as Microsoft's NetMeeting or Netscape's Conference to conduct a meeting.
- **Data-conferencing:** A browser package or specialized software tool is used collectively by participants to display, edit and revise text documents or graphical images in a technique known as whiteboarding.
- **Video-conferencing:** Groupware software packages called electronic meeting systems (EMS) can be used to offer the full range of voice, data and interactive video to provide a comprehensive virtual meeting. Document editing, whiteboard facilities and voice input are enhanced by the addition of video images of the participants and other audio or visual data content. Where conferences are dispersed over a number of sites, the term 'teleconferencing' is often used to describe this activity.

5.3.9 Collaborative work management tools

Many tools exist to help groups to accomplish a task or manage an activity. These tools include project management and resource scheduling software, calendar and diary systems, and work flow systems. The generic description of these tools is that of group support systems (GSS). The proliferation of networked computing has made all these tools far more accessible in a more distributed environment. They are evaluated further in Chapter 7.

5.4 The World Wide Web

In 1989, CERN (the European Laboratory for Particle Physics in Switzerland) proposed the development of the World Wide Web (now commonly known as the Web) in order to enable high-energy physicists across the world to collaborate through the easy provision and accessibility of information. Through CERN, the National Center for Supercomputing Applications (NCSA) at the University of Illinois, USA, soon became involved. Certain key features of the Web rapidly became established. Broadly speaking, these are:

- a standard way of providing information on web pages stored electronically on a host computer – this would include text, formatting, graphics, audio and video;
- the use of hyperlinks to direct a web page reader to other web pages on the same website or to a different website; and
- easy-to-use software that would enable users to transfer quickly between pages on a website or between different websites at the click of a mouse.

In 1993, the NCSA released a web browser program, **Mosaic,** which allowed easy and powerful access to the Web. At the time there were only about 50 websites worldwide. The facilities offered by Mosaic and particularly by its successor software browser, **Netscape Navigator,** led to an explosion in the development of websites and the accessing of these by users. (The author of Mosaic, Marc Andreeson, left NCSA to author the Netscape browser.) There are now over 20 million websites across the world. In order to understand the World Wide Web it is important to understand the basics of hypertext, browsers and the way websites are addressed.

5.4.1 The World Wide Web – basics

Hypertext and hypertext markup language

The concept of **hypertext** goes back to the 1940s. The idea is that when reading a piece of text, at certain points terms may need greater explanation, or related information may be helpful to the reader. Where this happens the reader should be able to call up directly the explanation or related information via a link within the text. Of course, these explanations are text and may themselves contain terms that need further explanation. These will be linked to other explanations, and so on. This system is known as hypertext.

Pages stored electronically on the Web have these hypertext links within them so that readers of a web page may click on a link and proceed along it to another web page (possibly at another website). In order to do this, the structure of the web page and its related links are designed in a special language called **hypertext markup language** (HTML). An example of a page specified in HTML is given as Figure 5.6. It leads to the

Figure 5.6 An example of a page (for the Red Cross Museum) written in HTML

```
<HTML>
<!-- Lotus-Domino (Release 5.0.5 - September 22, 2000 on Windows NT/Intel) -->
<HEAD>
<META NAME="description" CONTENT= "International Committee of the Red Cross (ICRC) -
Comité international de la Croix-Rouge (CICR)"><META NAME="keywords" CONTENT=
"International Committee of the Red Cross,Comite international de la Croix-Rouge,Comite
internacional de la Cruz Roja,ICRC,CICR,Red Cross,Croix-Rouge,Cruz Roja,International Red
Cross,Croix-Rouge internationale,Humanitarian action,Action humanitaire,International Humanitarian
Law,Droit international humanitaire,Geneva Conventions,Conventions de Geneve,Convenios de
Ginebra,War,Guerre,Guerra,Armed conflict,Conflit arme,Relief,Secours,Detention"><TITLE>International
Committee of the Red Cross (ICRC) - Home</TITLE>
</SCRIPT><SCRIPT LANGUAGE="JavaScript">

image = new makeArray(4);
image[1]="/WEBGRAPH.NSF/Graphics/home_1a.jpg/$FILE/home_1a.jpg";
image[2]="/WEBGRAPH.NSF/Graphics/home_1b.jpg/$FILE/home_1b.jpg";
image[3]="/WEBGRAPH.NSF/Graphics/home_1c.jpg/$FILE/home_1c.jpg";
image[4]="/WEBGRAPH.NSF/Graphics/home_1d.jpg/$FILE/home_1d.jpg";

</SCRIPT>
</HEAD>
<BODY bgColor=#ffffff><!DOCTYPE HTML PUBLIC "-//W3C//DTD HTML 4.0 Transitional//EN">
<DIV align=center>
    <TABLE width=740 border=0>
      <TBODY>
      <TR bgcolor="#FFFFFF">
        <TD colSpan=5 valign="top" align="center" bgcolor="#FFFFFF"> <font face="Arial, Helvetica,
sans-serif" color="#666666" size="6">International
          Committee of the Red Cross</font>
          <table width="100%" border="0" align="center" bordercolor="#666666" cellspacing="12">
            <tr>
              <td align="center" bgcolor="#e0e0e0"><A HREF=/eng><IMG
SRC=/WEBGRAPH.NSF/Graphics/eng.gif/$FILE/eng.gif BORDER=0 ALT = "English Home
page"></A></td>
              <td align="center" bgcolor="#e0e0e0"><A HREF=/fre><IMG
SRC=/WEBGRAPH.NSF/Graphics/fre.gif/$FILE/fre.gif BORDER=0 ALT = "Page d'accueil
Français"></A></td>
              <td align="center" bgcolor="#e0e0e0"><A HREF=/spa><IMG
SRC=/WEBGRAPH.NSF/Graphics/spa.gif/$FILE/spa.gif BORDER=0 ALT = "Home Español"></A></td>
              <td align="center" bgcolor="#e0e0e0"><A HREF=/ara><IMG
SRC=/WEBGRAPH.NSF/Graphics/ara_g.gif/$FILE/ara_g.gif BORDER=0 ALT = "Home Arabic">
</a></td>
            </tr>
          </table>
        </TD></TR>
<tr>
      <td width="159" cellpadding="1"><SCRIPT LANGUAGE="JavaScript">document.write("<IMG
SRC="+imagealeatoire() +" width=159 height=108>");</SCRIPT></td>
      <td width="159" cellpadding="1"><SCRIPT LANGUAGE="JavaScript">document.write("<IMG
SRC="+imagealeatoire1() +" width=159 height=108>");</SCRIPT></td>
      <td width="100" cellpadding="1"><img
src="/WEBGRAPH.NSF/Graphics/logo_lang.gif/$FILE/logo_lang.gif" width="100" height="108"></td>
      <td width="159" cellpadding="1"><SCRIPT LANGUAGE="JavaScript">document.write("<IMG
SRC="+imagealeatoire2() +" width=159 height=108>");</SCRIPT></td>
      <td width="159" cellpadding="1"><SCRIPT LANGUAGE="JavaScript">document.write("<IMG
```

Figure 5.6 (cont'd)

```
SRC="+imagealeatoire3() +" width=159 height=108>");</SCRIPT></td>
      </tr>
    <TR>
      <TD width=159> </TD>
      <TD width=159> </TD>
      <TD width=100> </TD>
      <TD width=159> </TD>
      <TD width=159> </TD></TR>
    <TR>
      <TD colSpan=2>
        <BLOCKQUOTE><!-- ENGLISH TEXT -->
          <P><FONT face="Arial, Helvetica, sans-serif"><B><FONT
        size=-2>International Committee of the Red Cross<BR>
            </FONT></B></FONT><A

href="/HOME.NSF/060a34982cae624ec12566fe00326312/125ffe2d4c7f68acc1256ae300394f6e?Open
Document"><FONT face="Arial, Helvetica, sans-serif"><B><FONT
        size=-2><font color="#003399">The mission of the ICRC</font><FONT
        color=#ff0000> </FONT></font></b></font></A></P>
          <!-- FRENCH TEXT -->
          <P><FONT size=-2><B><FONT face="Arial, Helvetica, sans-serif"><BR>
          Comit&eacute; international de la Croix-Rouge<BR>
            </FONT></B></FONT><A

href="/HOME.NSF/060a34982cae624ec12566fe00326312/b0b420c039178308c1256ae30043e89d?Open
Document"><FONT size=-2><B><FONT face="Arial, Helvetica, sans-serif"><font color="#003399">La
            mission du CICR</font></font></b></font></A></P>
          <!-- SPANISH TEXT -->
          <P><FONT size=-2><B><FONT face="Arial, Helvetica, sans-serif"><BR>
          Comit&eacute; Internacional de la Cruz Roja<BR>
            </FONT></B></FONT><A

href="/HOME.NSF/060a34982cae624ec12566fe00326312/8b8b90a08361b20dc1256ae300476983?Open
Document"><FONT size=-2><B><FONT face="Arial, Helvetica, sans-serif"><font
color="#003399">La misi&oacute;n del CICR</font></font></b></font></A></P>
          </BLOCKQUOTE></TD>
        <TD colSpan=3><img src="/WEBGRAPH.NSF/Graphics/keywords_15-07-
03.gif/$FILE/keywords_15-07-03.gif" width="400" height="145"
align="top"></TD></TR></TBODY></TABLE>
           </DIV>
  </BODY>
</HTML>
```

(Red Cross Museum)

page (as viewed through a browser) for the International Committee of the Red Cross, as shown in Figure 5.7.

Later versions of HTML allow for the specification of forms that the viewer of the web page may fill in and send back to the site on which the page is located. This facility allows interactivity over the Web. Once interactivity is fully and securely established it is possible to buy and sell merchandise. For example, the seller's products are displayed on a website. The user views this catalogue and, if wishing to purchase, fills in a form giving credit card details and address. The use of the Web dispenses with the need for the business to provide a physical shop front.

Figure 5.7 The page for the Red Cross Museum (see HTML version, Figure 5.6) as it appears through a web browser

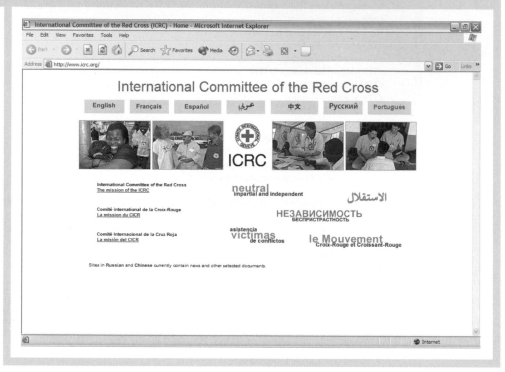

HTML is very easy to learn and easy to use, but it is not particularly flexible. It is one particular application of the more encompassing SGML or standardized general markup language. SGML is a meta-language, i.e. a language for defining other languages, of which HTML is just one. SGML can be used to create virtually any document type; examples include clinical records of patients, musical notation and even, it is claimed, transcriptions of ancient Irish manuscripts. SGML is very powerful and consequently very complex to use. As a result, a subset of SGML called the extensible markup language (XML) has been developed and has become very popular. XML can be used to define a wider range of document types than HTML, which is used only to create web pages, but it has a syntax that is more limited and hence more comprehensible than full SGML. Figure 5.8 shows the relationships between these markup languages. The solid boxes indicate the languages and their subsets, and the dashed boxes indicate the documents that can be produced.

HTML is far easier to learn and use than the high-level languages discussed previously in Chapter 3. However, its use is sufficiently complex and time-consuming that a number of packages have been developed to generate the HTML code automatically for web page developers. Packages such as Microsoft's FrontPage and SoftQuad Software's HotMetal Pro allow a designer to create a web page graphically from palettes of predefined background styles, images and controls. The HTML produced can then be stored and executed directly or can be edited 'manually' in a normal text editor to make minor alterations. Many word-processing packages also have a facility for saving a document as a web page. The package attempts to preserve the appearance of the document by generating HTML code that mimics the style of the original.

Figure 5.8 Markup languages

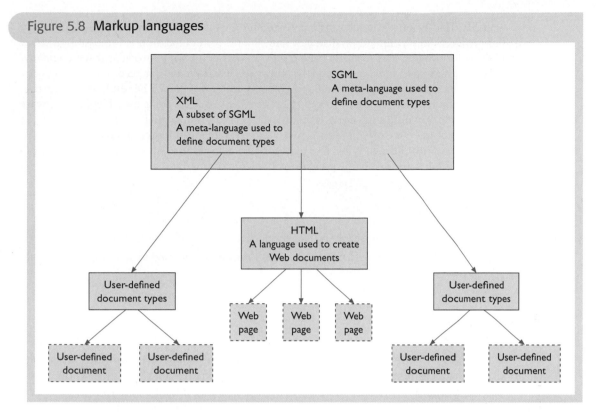

Mini case 5.3

XML and systems integration

The City of Chicago spent five years updating its IT systems. It bought an enterprise resource planning system, a revenue management system, a customer relationship management system and a host of other software packages designed to speed the work of city government.

Everything worked well until city managers started asking for information that required dialogue between two or more systems. Building links between systems required weeks of work by $200-an-hour programmers. The average cost of linking two systems was $100,000. To Chris O'Brien, a former management consultant who is now the city's chief information officer, this seemed hopelessly inefficient: 'What's the point of having all that data if you can't bring it together in a way that the average manager can use?' he says.

In Chicago, Mr O'Brien and his team have taken their first tentative steps towards a more flexible world by creating a dozen or so modular services. Each has standard interfaces and can be used by any of the city's systems. For example, the city's website includes a facility for paying parking tickets online, supported by software that checks the amount you owe, charges your credit card and routes the money to the appropriate municipal bank account. The programmers first had to decide how much of the software could be reused in different contexts and how much was specific to its existing function.

Once this was accomplished, the reusable part was wrapped in a layer of Extensible Markup Language (XML), an industry-standard system of tags and labels that can be understood by any computer system. In addition, while XML in theory provides a lingua franca that any computer system can understand, communication is impossible without shared meaning. This means agreeing on standard definitions throughout the company. When a service is asked to look up the 'list price' of an item does it need to be net of tax or gross? Inclusive or exclusive of shipping? Good until what date? The result is a service that can be used by any of the city's computer systems. Instead of writing near-identical software every time they need a payments engine, developers can simply plug into the service over the city's computer network. 'It took us two weeks to build and it has been reused at least seven times,' says Mr O'Brien. When new applications can be built easily by business process specialists, what is the role of the programmer, the systems architect or even the CIO?

Adapted from: **Building blocks for the future**
Simon London, FT.com, 26 January 2005

Questions

1. What problems were created by the introduction of the new IT systems in Chicago?

2. What is XML? How does it differ from HTML? How was XML used to solve the systems integration problems discussed above?

Web browsers

A **browser** is a software package that runs on the user's (client's) computer. It is able to display the contents of a web page (for example written in HTML) held on another (server) computer. In order to achieve this, the browser must be able to retrieve the contents of the page over the Internet. To make sure that this is carried out a standard for data transfer called the **hypertext transfer protocol (HTTP)** is used.

The most popular browsers include Microsoft's Internet Explorer, Firefox and Safari. An example of a web page viewed through a browser is given in Figure 5.9.

Browsers typically provide useful features to enable the Web user to retrieve the desired information as easily as possible. These may include:

■ **bookmarks:** these enable the Web address of a web page to be stored and called up again later – particularly useful if the same site is visited often;

■ **history:** this provides the user with a list of websites visited in a session – useful as it is often necessary to go back to a previously visited site;

■ **e-mail:** most browsers incorporate an e-mail facility;

■ **file/print:** this facility allows the user to store the web page(s) as a file, or print it out, which may be either as seen through the browser or as source HTML;

■ **find:** find enables a user to search through a web page(s) in order to locate the position of a word or phrase;

■ **format options:** these provide a range of colour, typeface and other possibilities affecting the presentation of the web page.

Uniform resource locator

Each page on the Web is on a website, which is itself located on a computer attached to the Internet. As has been explained earlier, each computer attached to the Internet has an address. The **uniform resource locator** (**URL**; note that some people call this the universal resource locator) identifies the location of a resource on the Web (type of

Figure 5.9 **The United Nations home page (as seen through Internet Explorer)**

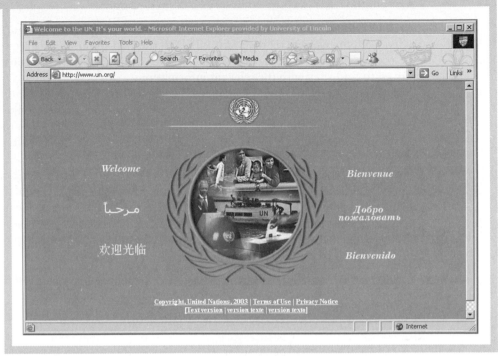

resource, site and position or path to the resource at the site). It is useful to think of the URL as the web page address.

The current format for URLs is:

scheme://path

The scheme identifies which protocol is to be used to retrieve the resource and is normally followed by a colon (:). The protocol normally used for web documents is HTTP. The path is taken to be a host identifier, conventionally preceded by a double forward slash (//). The remainder of the path usually gives the location within the host. This is often hierarchical, each stage being separated by a single forward slash (/). An example is given below:

http://www.un.org/overview/origin.html

This states that information may be retrieved using the HTTP at the website with the address *www.un.org*. Within that website, the page retrieved is a subpage, called *origin.html*, of the main page, *overview*.

Pages are usually organized as tree structures, with the top node known as the **home page**.

Web search engines

In order to display information from a website it is necessary to:

1. achieve connection to the Internet (either through an Internet service provider or through a local area network located at one's employer or university);

2. load web browser software;

3. input the URL (website address) of a desired resource.

The HTTP working through the web browser then displays text, graphics, audio or video from the website on the user's screen. If the URL is not known, for example when the user wants to search the Web for a particular topic, a web search engine can be employed to find sites with the relevant information.

There are several web search engines. Examples are Alta Vista, Yahoo! and Google. The **web search engine** is a program that, when running, makes connection to many thousands of websites a day, retrieving and indexing web pages from these sites. Web search engines will have visited and indexed millions of web pages. This index will be stored at the website associated with the search engine. A user accesses the website at which the search engine is located and enters, via a form on the screen, a word or words (known as the search string) of search interest. The web search engine then displays at the user's terminal the URLs of all sites at which the search string is located. The search string may be sophisticated, indicating that two or more words must be present (AND), or any of them could be (OR), or some words should not be present (NOT). An example of a search string might be:

Jackson AND president AND NOT (Michael OR music OR five)

A typical search engine page is shown in Figure 5.10.

Figure 5.10 **An example of an enquiry in a search engine**

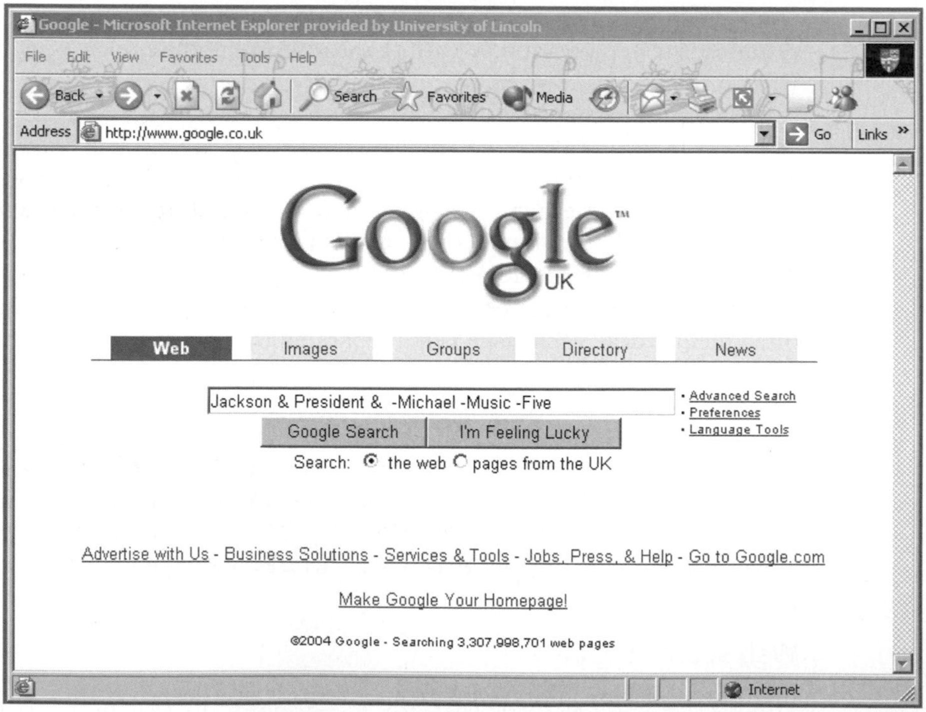

(Courtesy of Google Inc.)

Recent developments in web search engines have included simplified panels into which the search criteria can be entered ('include all of these words . . .', 'include any of these words . . .', 'exclude these words . . .', etc.). Also, the results of an enquiry are being presented in ever more innovative ways, classifying the findings and suggesting further places to look if more information is required. Providers of search engines have also found it advantageous to distribute miniature versions of their search engine interface that can displayed constantly as a toolbar in a host browser application.

Mini case 5.4

Search engines

Google has become embedded in users' web behaviour, but in some areas, such as desktop search, the company has arguably been outflanked. Most established search engines rely heavily on indexing web pages based on keywords. The results are variable. Keyword-based search tools in particular generally do not cope well with ordinary questions.

Hakia, funded by a consortium of European venture capital companies, is running a trial service and is due to launch commercially this year – one of the first of many expected 'semantic web' companies. Hakia claims that it 'understands' questions and performs 'meaning-based searches'. I found it produced good and often extremely comprehensive results to relatively complex questions, although not always better than Google. It provides search examples, but to get a feel for it you need to use it for a while. It may not replace Google, but Hakia could appeal to those researching knowledge-intensive subjects such as medicine, law, finance, science and literature.

Some search services are focusing on market segments. For example, if you are looking for a particular video clip, **Blinkx** (www.blinkx.com) delivers unrivalled results. Blinkx has already indexed more than 7m hours of audio, video, viral and television content. Another, **Retrivo** (www.retrivo.com), aims to make it easier for users to research, install, use and fix consumer electronics products. **Kosmix** (www.kosmix.com) helps conduct deep searches in categories such as health, travel, finance and US politics.

Like next generation semantic search services, these specialized search tools prove that, while Google may be the king of search, there is still room for innovative start-ups and niche search companies.

Adapted from: **New tools to vie with Google**
Paul Taylor, *Financial Times*, 30 May 2007

Questions

1. Do you consider that there is a market for specialized search engines to coexist with the major players in the sector?

2. How easy or desirable is it for the market leaders to attempt to absorb these competitors into their organization to enhance their own product and standing?

Plug-ins

Plug-ins are small programs that are 'loaded into' a larger program in order to add some function. The plug-in may be produced by a third party organization different from the publisher of the larger program. Web browsers may have plug-ins associated with them that allow them to carry out extra functions. The following are examples of plug-ins for browsers that extend their functionality:

- **Internet telephone tools:** These allow telephone conversations to be made over the Internet. These usually incorporate facilities such as audio-conferencing, a telephone answering machine and the ability for all participants to view common graphics on the screen as well as participating in discussion.

- **Interactive 3D viewers:** These **virtual reality modelling language (VRML)** viewers allow 3D to be viewed over the Internet, with the possibility of navigation through the scenes depicted.

- **Audio and video viewers:** Audio and video viewers are plug-ins that allow the user to view/hear video/audio files transferred over the Internet. Most of these allow viewing to occur before the data transfer has been completed.

- **Streaming audio and video viewers:** These allow the viewer to have online viewing of audio or video as it is streamed to the user's browser software through the Internet. Thus live events may be viewed as they occur.

Browser software has developed very rapidly, and the various offerings of the Internet listed in Section 5.3 have gradually been incorporated as standard elements in a web browser. Today's plug-in often becomes tomorrow's standard feature.

Java

Java, which was introduced Chapter 3, is an object oriented programming language similar to C++ that can be used to produce machine-independent portable software. Programs written in Java can be downloaded over the Internet and run immediately on the user's computer. Small Java programs, known as **applets,** may be embedded in HTML in a web page. This may be downloaded across the Internet with the web page and the program executed from within the user's browser program. Security is maintained as the executed program cannot have access to the user's resources such as files, printers and other computers on the same network. In theory, this should prevent the infection of the receiving computer by a virus. An applet loaded over the Internet may only create a link to the host computer from which it was downloaded. The execution of applets allows web browsers to have more interactive areas and thus extends their functions.

5.4.2 Organizational control of the Internet

There is no organizational control over the Internet. However, there are a number of organizations with influence. First, there are the businesses that are providers of either hardware or major software items used on the Internet. These operate a de facto steering direction via the products they produce. However, three organizations are recognized as having authority over coordination of developments on the Internet. The **Internet Engineering Task Force (IETF)** is a large, loosely connected group of designers, researchers and vendors who influence the development of the standards governing the architecture of the Internet. They achieve this through setting up working groups. The IETF is chartered by the **Internet Society (ISOC),** which is a professional member organization of Internet experts that oversees policy and practice. The Internet Society also charters the **World Wide Web Consortium (W3C),** which is a consortium of voluntary member organizations that funds developments on the Web. There is much common membership between the IETF and the W3C.

5.4.3 The World Wide Web and business opportunities

As has been mentioned earlier, the ease of accessing documents over the World Wide Web together with the rapid increase in personal computers has been a major factor in the burgeoning use of the Internet for business. This is discussed more fully in the next chapter.

5.4.4 The Semantic Web

The first usage of the World Wide Web saw presentation of content in a human readable, largely textual format which was subsequently enhanced to include graphical and multimedia content and the processing of transactions. More recently, Web content has been enriched to allow it to be read not only by humans but also by software agents. These agents can glean further information from the machine readable content allowing it to be shared and integrated more easily.

A key element to the development of the Semantic Web is the **Resource Development Framework** (RDF). Information can be modelled using an RDF specification which can capture particular traits or aspects. Whereas a simple Web page representing a catalogue of stock might use HTML to contain the item descriptions and where they should be positioned on the page, RDF can associate a price with each item allowing a software agent to search the page and extract the relevant information. To associate items with their traits RDF uses 'object–attribute–value' triples. These are considered in more detail when the topic of knowledge representation is covered later in Chapter 18.

A further technology that is facilitating the development of the Semantic Web is the **Web Ontology Language** (usually abbreviated to OWL as an easier mnemonic). This allows for descriptions of classes and their instances and properties in a machine readable format that can be exchanged across the Web. It is a development on RDF and provides more sophisticated mechanisms for capturing the semantics of web content.

5.5 The Internet and copyright

Copyright law has historically developed to ensure that an author had the exclusive right to copy his or her work and distribute those copies to the public. The author could also assign this right to others. Copyright law was originally designed for the printed word but has been adapted to deal with broadcasting, software and satellite television.

Copyright protects the expression of an idea – not the idea itself. It comes into existence when the expression is fixed on some medium, such as paper or disk. In some countries it may be essential to register the material as copyright. Generally, copyright applies to classes of work – for example, literary, sound recordings, films. The **Berne Convention** is an international treaty to which approximately 160 member countries belong. An infringement of copyright in any one of these countries of work produced by a foreign national from one of the others is protected in the country as though the infringement were of locally produced material within the country. In this way, the level of protection in each of the countries is standardized for home or foreign publications. In countries not signatory to the Berne Convention, the infringement of copyright needs to be enforced in the country of the alleged infringement and is dependent on the law of that country and not of the country in which it originated.

Copyright applies to the Internet. In UK law, for instance, copying, even if only temporarily into RAM in order to display on screen, is a potential infringement of copyright. It is not necessary for the material to be printed or stored to disk. Since the only way of accessing material on the Internet involves the temporary storage of material in RAM in the recipient machine, it seems to imply that a copyright holder, in placing material on the Internet, authorizes this level of copying. However, the law is at present unclear on this. It is therefore advisable for businesses to establish copyright in much the same way as for printed material, by seeking permission, rather than assuming that the presence on the Internet grants copying permission. There is another important issue. Material on the Internet may already be in infringement of copyright and be held and distributed without the permission of the author. Finally, it is common for businesses to hold copies of popular websites on their own servers to prevent excessive employee use of Internet connection. **Mirror sites**, as these are called, are also held in different countries in order to cut down international Internet traffic. It is quite clear that unless permission has been granted these will infringe copyright.

For any business intending to copy works from the Internet it is safest to seek permission to copy, to distribute the work and to authorize others to do so. This applies to text, graphics, video and audio and, in some cases, synchronization of audio and video and graphics.

5.6 The Internet and financial transactions

In the early days of the Web it quickly became clear to businesses that the Internet would be not only a vehicle for dispersing information but also a shop front for the sale of goods and services. This would entail commercial transactions being conducted electronically. As a result, 'cybercash' has now become an accepted way of payment over the Internet and particularly over the World Wide Web. It is likely that with increased use of the Web the use of cybercash will become more common. There will be many more transactions. Also, there will be a large increase in the number of small transactions – for example, attachment to a news service based on time connected. With a large volume of small transactions the cost of processing the transaction becomes important and needs to be minimized.

Three forms of electronic payment or electronic cash substitute are currently being used.

1. **Electronic credit card transactions:** This form of payment had already become acceptable prior to the Internet with card swipe and electronic transfer from points of sale. Equally, the quotation of a credit card number over the phone will often secure purchase of goods and services. In this respect, the Internet poses little that is new. The credit card number and other verifying information will be input and the transfer of liability for payment of goods will move from the purchaser to the credit card company, which will then take over responsibility for the transfer of funds to the seller and recovery of money at the end of the month as part of a consolidated bill from the purchaser. No real issues arise that are new – although security (see below) will continue to be a concern. The seller will still be able to gain information concerning the purchaser and purchaser's credit card number, so anonymity of purchasers will not be guaranteed. The costs of processing the transaction are still high relative to the purchase of goods through electronic cash.

2. **Electronic cash or e-cash:** With electronic cash a sum of e-cash is purchased from a 'money merchant' and is held electronically in an account. When a purchaser of a good makes a purchase then the merchant is informed electronically and the e-cash

is transferred from the purchaser's account to the seller's account at the merchant (or the seller's account at some other merchant who accepts the e-cash). The entire transaction is conducted electronically over the Internet. The anonymity of the purchaser (and of the seller) can be maintained. This form of payment requires the acceptance of e-cash, which has no intrinsic value, by both purchaser and seller. In some ways this mirrors 'paper money'. Paper money has no intrinsic value and only works as a medium of exchange because it is backed by the government and is difficult to reproduce (counterfeit). E-cash will work only if there is confidence in its exchange value, and this will be unlikely unless there is confidence in the organization 'backing' it. It is likely that well-established major financial institutions will need to be involved with e-cash before it becomes readily acceptable. There are security issues (see below) but also the need for confidence in the accuracy of the software that handles the accounting aspects. E-cash has one major advantage in that the transaction cost is minimal. Governments will need to take a regulatory interest in e-cash, since it is easy to see how repetitive and transnational flows of e-cash could be used for money laundering and tax evasion purposes. A common use of e-cash is in the settlement of internet-based consumer transactions such as the use of the Paypal service as a means of payment for goods purchased from an e-commerce website.

3. **Electronic cash substitutes:** Air miles, supermarket points and other forms of non-cash rewards are becoming increasingly prevalent. These may be earned by a purchase on the Internet, recorded electronically and redeemed electronically for goods, air tickets, etc. These, therefore, become e-cash substitutes.

Electronic payment generates two different types of major security issue. First, all transactions over the Internet require the transmission of electronic data. The data is publicly accessible. This may be a credit card number, e-cash or an electronic cash substitute. The normal way to prevent this information being identified and copied for fraudulent purposes is to encrypt it. It is also important that no corruption of the information occurs, and this will need to be handled by devices such as error-checking codes.

The second major security issue surrounds the businesses that operate on the Internet. Businesses may appear to be providing legitimate investment opportunities, for example, but actually deceive the would-be investor into parting with money. There has always been a problem with unscrupulous companies, but what gives rise to additional concerns with the Internet are:

- it is largely unregulated;
- it crosses international boundaries;
- the business is not tied to some place that the purchaser/investor can visit that is relatively stable, such as a building; and
- the credibility of the company is largely dependent on the web page presentation.

These concerns over security are not seen as preventing the use of the Web for commercial transactions but rather viewed as problem areas that should and will be addressed.

5.7 Intranets and extranets

The software and technology used by an organization to develop web pages and to access them over the Internet is equally suitable for the development and access of web pages designed purely for consumption by employees and clients of that organization.

This system is known as an **intranet**. It is a privately accessible network, constructed using Internet technology and tools. Businesses quickly recognized that the richness of media (text, graphics, audio, video) for presenting information on the Web, and the use of hyperlinks to other web pages, was ideal for the development of an organization-wide information system. This has now been extended to cover direct access from outside of the organization.

Businesses are using intranets for the internal display of:

- company manuals covering employment and other procedures;
- easily updatable internal news and information services;
- company catalogues; and
- project notice boards (to which project participants can add information and comments to be seen by all).

Intranets are replacing historical paper-based information systems because they are both cheaper and more easily updatable. Software specifically aimed at supporting intranet functions is now readily available.

5.7.1 Intranet construction

An intranet is created by using the normal network infrastructure existing in an organization. The standard features of Internet applications are used: software such as web browsers, web protocols such as TCP/IP and HTML hypermedia documents. The use of the intranet is limited to those in the company who are given access rights. The adoption of the same standards as those used for Internet-delivered systems and the World Wide Web means that the applications created are available throughout the organization on a variety of hardware platforms, and the look and feel is that of any other Internet-based application.

Public access to an intranet is prevented by channelling all external connection through a **firewall**. This is normally a dedicated computer or computers running specialized security software. The packets of data that arrive are inspected and depending on the contents of the address information are either accepted and passed on or rejected.

5.7.2 Intranet usage

Intranets have a variety of business uses, which fall largely into two categories: those involving the management and running of the business; and those relating to communications and group working. The business applications of the intranet include systems such as stock control, order processing, which might interface with existing core data, and enterprise-wide applications. The communications applications relate to the range of collaborative and group-based applications discussed earlier.

Intranets have potential applications for most functional areas of a business. Accounting and finance staff might use the local intranet to perform *ad hoc* queries on financial data, to access standard summary reports or to produce consolidated reports taken from different legacy systems.

Sales and marketing staff might use the intranet to track and manage the activities of their sales force. Latest promotions, price details or information about customers can also be made readily available.

The personnel department might display details about financial packages available to the staff, or advertise current vacancies. It could also use the intranet to inform staff about training opportunities or forthcoming staff events.

5.7.3 Extranets

Intranets have become such a valuable and integral part of information systems that many organizations have seen the benefits in widening their availability and access to users who are located outside the scope of the local area network. When access to an intranet is extended outside the organization, the resulting system is referred to as an **extranet**. The connection to the organization's intranet can either be by secure leased line, creating a **virtual private network**, or by using the less secure Internet. In the latter case, the security is enforced by the firewall and by using access codes, passwords and data encryption. In addition to providing employees with an external method of accessing the company intranet, an extranet can be used to forge strategic links with trading partners and customers. They provide a medium for collaborative ventures such as product development.

Information systems strategy is moving increasingly towards the development of integrated systems that provide fast and effective methods of communication, support for decision making and ways of sharing information and working collaboratively. Extranets fit into that strategy by widening the scope of the in-company systems to include a selected subset of all Internet users. As the success, or even just the survival, of businesses becomes increasingly dependent on their ability to communicate effectively between employees and with other partners, it is clear that extranets will have a decisive role to play in that success.

Summary

The Internet has evolved over the last decade from being a small set of interconnected networks for the exchange of scientific information to a highly sophisticated set of publicly accessible networks for the global provision of information and services to business and private individuals. The key to this development has been the agreement of protocols for information exchange (TCP/IP) and the exponential growth in the use of technologically advanced microcomputers in business and for personal use. E-mail is now a recognized method of cheap, fast, secure information transmission either across a local area network or globally across the Internet. Other facilities provided by the Internet are Telnet, enabling remote login to host computers over the Internet, and file transfer protocol for the transmission of all forms of files. Newsgroups and Internet relay chat allow the development of particular areas of interest globally over the Internet – the latter in interactive real time. Access to stored information held on remote computers has been enabled by the Internet and a number of applications have, over time, progressively simplified access to this information. However, the most significant development came in the 1990s with the growth of the World Wide Web.

The World Wide Web allows pages to be written and stored in hypertext markup language (HTML) in such a way that they can be accessed over the Internet using hypertext transmission protocols (HTTP). What is particularly important is the ability to use hypertext links to other websites or pages for greater amplification of information obtained. The World Wide Web protocols also allow graphics, audio and video information to be stored and retrieved as well as text. The development of web browser software, especially Netscape Navigator and Internet Explorer, has enabled inexperienced users to retrieve and display information easily. The ability for users to find information has been increased by the development of web search engines, which index millions of web pages. Software plug-ins have enhanced the presentation of information.

Recently, there has been very rapid development in both intranets and extranets. Intranets use the technology of the Internet internally within an organization to present corporate data and to host applications to employees. The extranet extends an organization's intranet by giving access to a restricted group of users who are based outside the company. This extends the scope of the intranet and provides further opportunities to work collaboratively with partners and to distribute more widely the access to data and applications.

Review questions

1. Explain the following terms:

   Hypertext   browser
   Internet service provider   domain name
   TCP/IP   routers
   point-to-point protocol   file transfer protocol
   HTML   XML
   HTTP   URL
   search engine   intranet and extranet

2. Explain the difference between the Internet, intranets and extranets.

Exercises

1. Which factors drive and which factors limit the growth of the use of the Internet for business?

2. Compare and evaluate the three markup languages SGML, HTML and XML in terms of ease of use, flexibility and comprehensibility.

3. Define what is meant by 'electronic cash' and discuss the extent to which it may become the de facto trading currency of the Internet.

4. Should the Internet be regulated, and if so by whom and how?

5. To what extent is e-mail leading to a more paperless office, given that many e-mail users print their e-mails on to paper?

6. 'Searching for something on the Web is like looking for a needle in a haystack. Even hunting through the search results of a query can be like looking for a needle in a haystack.' What tools and techniques are available to aid web searches? How can they be made even more efficient?

CASE STUDY 5

Google

Over a period of about ten years Google has fought off all competitors to become the leading search engine. Although the product today is one of the most sophisticated software systems, its initial success came from the simplicity of the user interface that was uncluttered and intuitive. The home page is attractive both to novice users, who like the lack of complexity, and also to experts, who are often focused on a particular task and are unconcerned about related issues. The product has grown in popularity due to the speed and effectiveness of its searching and query processing algorithms coupled with its importance as a contributor to business solutions.

How it works

There are three key processes to the Google system: fetching the Web content stored on pages across the web; indexing the content; processing the user queries to present those results that are most likely to be relevant and interesting.

Fetching the content

Google operates a web crawler called Googlebot: this is implemented through a vast array of computers that constantly send requests to websites across the Web to retrieve pages.

Figure 5.11 Proactively adding a URL to be found in subsequent Google searches

(Courtesy of Google Inc.)

Many of these computers are not particularly powerful, but the parallel nature of their constant requests provides the speed necessary to cover the Web. In order not to swamp individual websites, Googlebot operates a strategy of limiting its requests. In addition to its constant automated searches Googlebot will accept a request from a user to have their website URL added to its searches. This will lead to the site being found proactively rather than by a chance event.

Any links contained in a located page are added to lists for subsequent searches. This iterative searching of links leading to further links is known as 'deep crawling'. The scale of the Web is so huge that some remote locations may only be revisited around once a month. To make the crawling as efficient as possible the time between returning to a site is dictated by the frequency that the page changes. A rapidly updating news site might be revisited several times a day; these are known as 'fresh crawls'.

Indexing the content

Google's massive index files are constructed from the content fetched by Googlebot. To make searching more effective, very short items such as punctuation, multiple spaces, single digits and short words like *of*, *on* and *the* are stripped out. Like an index at the back of a book the index files contain one occurrence of each text item found and a set of links that record the URLs where that word had been found. Text is then all converted to lower case.

Processing the query

Most users' interface to Google is through the Query text box on the Google home page. When a user enters a query (for example a search for a two-word expression), the query processor consults with the index. This gives access to every page where there exists an occurrence of these words. In order to prioritize the results of the search Google employs a method of ranking pages known as PageRank™. The ranking given to each page influences how high on the list of results it will appear. The effectiveness of this algorithm is a major factor in user satisfaction with the search engine. Unsurprisingly, more than 100 factors contribute to the results in Google's PageRank algorithm. Pages are each attributed an 'importance' value, partly derived by the location of the page (e.g. do other 'important' pages link to it) and the popularity of the page (e.g. how many other links point to this page). For a particular query, this ranking will then be further adjusted to take account of the position of the search words on that page.

As well as calculating the rank for a page, Google applies certain machine learning techniques to improve its searching. For example, alternative spellings for the search terms may yield a higher rank than that already obtained, prompting a 'Did you mean . . .' message for the user and a set of alternative results.

The business opportunity

It is clearly in the interests of content providers to have their pages awarded high PageRank values so that they appear at the top of search results. One way that **cannot** be done is by payment to Google. The PageRank is purely derived from the application of the patented algorithm. Although it is possible to affect factors such as the date the page was uploaded to the hosting website, the frequency that it has been updated etc., these factors are weighted and combined alongside so many others that it is extremely difficult to artificially affect a page ranking either significantly or for a sustained period.

Content providers who are interested in using Google for marketing purposes are offered a range of services to allow their business a greater presence when search results are returned. For example:

Google Adwords

When the results of a search are returned, a lists of related advertisers sometimes appears in a pane on the right-hand side of the screen. These links are free to place but are charged out on a 'per click' basis. Businesses provide a set of keywords that relate to their product and a URL that users can follow by clicking on the link that Google displays. The placer of the Adword suggests a cost per click amount and a maximum monthly budget. They can also indicate a geographic region to be targeted. Google then uses an algorithm to decide whether to display the Adword and where to rank it compared to other Adwords.

Google Adsense

Businesses that host a website can insert Google advertisements on their web pages. Using a sophisticated matching algorithm, only adverts relevant to the website are selected and these can be further filtered by the hosting site to exclude inappropriate content or competitor advertisements. The system is paid for on a cost per click basis.

Google Websearch

The technology/power of the Google search engine can be brought to a website by pasting the Google search box onto a web page. Users of a website can then conduct a Google search without leaving the host page.

Google Search Applicance

For large organizations it may be beneficial to replicate the entire Google search, index and query process locally so that only their own Web content is indexed and returned in queries. To facilitate this, Google provides a combined hardware and software solution; a device is installed into one host system that subjects all the pages on the organization's web servers to a Googlebot web crawl. The material is indexed and pages are ranked by the local device. Local queries submitted to a Google Websearch now only generate results based on local Web content.

Question

1. Develop a proposal for a medium-sized company of your choice for a marketing campaign that is based on using Google for advertising and sales.

Recommended reading

Crystal D. (2006). *Language and the Internet.* Cambridge University Press

This book examines the Internet as a cultural rather than technological phenomenon. The author adopts a linguistic perspective in analysing the world of chat rooms, e-mail and other virtual environments.

Keogh J. (2001). *The Essential Guide to Networking.* Prentice Hall

A comprehensive coverage of LANs, WANs, the Internet, intranets and extranets, and interesting sections on Internet security, privacy and reliability. The book is written in a non-technical style and is easy to read.

Kou W. (2003). *Payment Technologies for E-Commerce*. Springer

A thorough coverage of different methods of electronic payment such as smart card systems, payment agents and digital cash.

Newcomer E. and Lomow G. (2004). *Understanding SOA with Web Services*. Addison-Wesley

This book describes and evaluates web services in a way that is accessible to both managers and technicians. Topics include the planning and implementation of XML web services and service oriented architecture.

Sterne J. (2002). *Web Metrics: Proven Methods for Measuring Web Site Success*. John Wiley & Sons.

This book provides a range of techniques for measuring the success of a website. It includes a number of interesting examples and applications.

Chapter 6

Electronic commerce and business

Learning outcomes

On completion of this chapter you should be able to:

- Define and identify key features of e-commerce
- Identify the drivers for and barriers to e-commerce
- Evaluate the extent to which e-commerce maps on to traditional trade cycles
- Describe and review a broad range of business models for e-commerce business activity
- Discuss the issues in creating a business website
- Assess potential developments in web technology.

Introduction

The move into the Internet age is both driving and being helped by significant changes in the information systems that support the commercial activity. Just as the early data-processing era was supplanted by the management information systems generation of the last 30 years, so the Internet era is building upon and replacing the MIS age. The accessibility of data and information and the relative ease of establishing channels of communication have fundamentally changed the expectations of decision makers in companies, and of all participants in the supply chain from manufacturers through suppliers to customers. The supporting information systems tend to be collaborative rather than stand-alone, distributed rather than centralized, networked globally rather than locally.

The coming together of business activities and Internet technology has fundamentally changed the environment and structure of business. This is evidenced in many ways. For example:

- The marketplace for all vendors has become potentially global.
- Execution and settlement of transactions can easily be automated for small as well as large organizations.
- The trading model has moved from 'normal business opening hours' to a 24 hours a day, seven days a week trading model.
- The interconnections throughout the supply chain are being reconfigured.

Conducting business over the Internet can be a very different experience to commercial activities that take place in more traditional environments. This chapter focuses on the implications of e-commerce for business.

6.1 A brief introduction to e-commerce

E-commerce is certainly not a new phenomenon. Electronic data interchange has been available for over 25 years and has had a number of very successful applications in that time. The range of EDI applications includes such diverse activities as the issuing of student examination results from central examining boards to schools and the registering of investors who are interested in purchasing new issues of shares in companies. However, the major concentration of EDI activity has been in heavy manufacturing industries and in high-volume and routine restocking.

In the last 10 years there has been explosive growth in e-commerce developments. The reducing cost and complexity involved in establishing electronic connectivity is clearly a prime factor in this growth. In addition, the Internet has opened the door to different ways of trading; it supports the traditional system-to-system trading seen in EDI but also allows for computer-mediated trading between otherwise unconnected companies, and between companies and individuals.

The development of websites

There are many advantages to an organization in developing a website. These include:

- **Reduction in cost of advertising:** Organizations, particularly those selling products or services, rely on providing information and advertising to a marketplace in order to attract new customers and retain existing ones. The cost of this is considerable, especially if achieved through the media – newspapers, magazines, television, radio, advertising hoardings. Alternatively, mailshots may also be used. These are also very expensive unless target mail groups are tightly defined. However, running a website is comparatively cheap. Computer hardware, the design of the site and maintenance seldom take a start-up cost of more than a few thousand pounds or dollars. Once running, the website provides 24-hour access daily across the world. Nowadays, the content of advertising on the web is sophisticated in relation to that provided a few years ago. The move towards regarding the design of website material to be the province of the creative rather than the computing media has ensured that the approaches towards advertising commonly seen on television are now becoming more prevalent on the Web.

- **Cheaper and easier provision of information:** Some organizations, particularly public services, provide information. These traditionally have been by way of paper-based publications or through recorded telephone messages. Putting such reports on a website to provide electronic access offers a cheaper way to disperse information for the host organization and a faster and more convenient method of access for the public (at least the public with access to the Internet). Governments, and non-government organizations that are not commercial, now provide extensive information services on the Web.

- **Ease of update:** An organization can easily update its product range, list of services, list of prices or any other information if provided on a web page. This compares with the costly resending of catalogues and other paper-based information through the postal system.

- **Lack of need to maintain a shop front:** When viewing an organization's supply of information, or list of products and services, the web user does not need to enter the organization's premises – there is no need therefore for the organization to maintain a costly shop front. Indeed, the view of the organization is largely determined by the impression given by its web pages, unless the organization is a household name. For a business this is important as it can overcome the limitations of capital investment in the provision of expensive buildings to impress clients. Importantly for the business, the web user has little idea whether they are dealing with a large multinational or a small business. In this way, the small business can compete with the large. From the perspective of the customer, however, it is difficult to make judgements about the status of the business behind the web page.

■ **The ease of crossing geographical boundaries:** Because the Internet provides global access the business has a worldwide audience through its web pages. If the business is selling a product, provided that postal or shipping services are reliable, even a small business is able to market and sell its products globally. If the product is information, this can easily be dispensed electronically.

■ **The absence of the middleman:** A business that needs a distributor and a retailer to ensure its goods are sold and delivered to a customer can now dispense with these middlemen. Direct marketing to the customer is possible. It should, however, be pointed out that in many cases retailers provide a service over and above that of merely being point of sale. Advice and other services may also be provided. But if the customer is in need of no such help, then the shop front becomes superfluous.

Multi-channel commerce

For most existing businesses the issue is not about e-commerce being a new or alternative way of conducting business but about providing an additional complementary avenue for trade. The challenge here is to align the electronic business with existing channels, such as the traditional so-called bricks and mortar business, tele-sales, catalogue business, and so on. This requires a strategic approach that looks holistically at the business and fits e-commerce into the overall structure of the organization. Recent evidence suggests that the most successful e-commerce ventures are those with a traditional business background or infrastructure; these multi-channel organizations are sometimes called 'clicks and mortar' businesses.

6.2   E-commerce – key features

E-commerce can be defined as

> *any exchange of information or business transaction that is facilitated by the use of information and communications technologies.*

Although the popular perception of e-commerce is that of individuals buying goods and services over the Internet, the parties involved are more likely to be small and large companies and public authorities or other not-for-profit organizations rather than home computer users. The variety of systems used to facilitate e-commerce is huge, and it is helpful to attempt to categorize them. Whiteley (2000) classifies e-commerce systems as falling into one of three categories:

1. **Electronic markets:** These are information sources that can be used to search for a particular service or product. Rail travel operators might provide timetables of services, details about seat types and other services, and various ticket options. In such an electronic market, customers can examine the alternatives and make comparisons

between the services and prices offered before making a purchasing decision. In addition, the Internet allows for the provision of other information services, such as after-sales service, technical support and the sharing of expertise.

2. **Electronic data interchange:** Companies, in their regular dealings with other trading partners, such as suppliers and retail outlets, might establish electronic communications to process the volume of transactions carried out. These lines of communication might be permanent, using leased telephone connections, or established temporarily for the duration of the transactions, using the Internet to establish the connection. EDI provides a standard protocol for encoding this data exchange.

3. **Internet commerce:** This category of e-commerce incorporates the popular image of home computer users making purchases over the Internet. In fact it includes a much broader range of trading. In Internet commerce, goods and services are advertised and individual transactions are executed. The participants might both be businesses, leading to a business-to-business (B2B) transaction, or might involve a private individual, in which case the transaction is described as business-to-customer (B2C).

6.3 Conducting business over the Internet

Trading over the Internet creates challenges and opportunities. As has already been stated, business can be conducted at any time of the day. Markets become globally accessible, whether on the opposite side of the world or, possibly just as important, in the locality of the company itself. Small operators discover new-found access to large companies, and vice versa. In addition, e-commerce pays no attention to time differences between countries.

In many market sectors, the introduction of e-commerce has changed the nature of the business itself. In the music distribution and software industries, the medium adopted for creating and storing the product has evolved progressively using advances in the hardware (from tapes through CDs to DVDs). Now the distribution of the product is being revolutionized with Internet releases and online product updates.

The features that make a product more likely to be able to be sold over the Internet are:

- browsing over a range of products where touch prior to purchase is not needed;
- no advice is needed from the seller;
- the desired choice is known unambiguously by a title or specification;
- the range of products is large (and difficult to accommodate under one shop front);
- the products can be dispatched easily (ideally non-bulky, high-price products);
- there would not be differences in the quality of the product between one seller and another.

The economic comparison of retailing through a shop front and through the Internet is given for a typical outlet in Figure 6.1.

The expansion of e-commerce brings about associated benefits. The participants become members of virtual communities in ways that are not possible through traditional trading. Marketplaces have become more open and trading activities more diverse. In addition, e-commerce allows businesses to gain competitive advantage in a number of ways:

- **Price competitiveness:** Reduced transaction costs in automated ordering and invoicing systems can lead to lower prices.

Figure 6.1 A comparison of Internet and traditional retailing margins

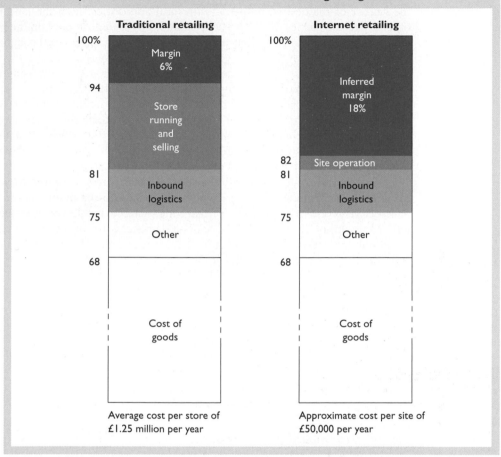

Source: Authors' own work based on figures presented by Hoskyns Gemini

- **Timeliness:** Faster ordering, delivery and invoicing can reduce the time to market for suppliers.
- **Knowledge of market:** Trading electronically provides additional methods for companies to acquire knowledge of the market in which they operate. Customer information and profiling can improve the trading relationship and lead to new marketing opportunities.

Mini case 6.1

Legal services

The provision of legal services over the Internet is becoming increasingly widespread. Examples include the writing of wills, support for the purchase and sale of property, and online quotations.

Traditionally, in the UK, the buyer of a property instructs a solicitor to act on their behalf. If the client also has a property to sell the same solicitor will often take on this additional role. The solicitor acts on behalf of their client by liaising with the solicitor of the vendor of the desired property, with local authorities, with the land registry and other interested parties. They also collect and hold the deposit paid on the property and ensure that the exchange of contracts occurs smoothly and moves through to the completion of a sale.

Fidler and Pepper are a UK-based partnership of solicitors comprising six partners and fifty staff distributed over three offices in the Nottinghamshire area. They have been operating a website (www.fidler.co.uk) since 1995 that offers a range of services to clients, including an online matter progress report to inform their clients about the latest developments in the sale and purchase of their properties. The system also preserves confidentiality by assigning a unique case number to each property purchase or sale and by using a system of passwords to prevent unauthorized access.

'The system has made a huge difference', says Mat Slade, the partner responsible for conveyancing. 'From the client's viewpoint there is up-to-the-minute notification about all issues. The system cuts out those frustrating switchboard delays and telephone transfers. More importantly, it gives 24-hours-a-day access to information that previously could only be obtained by speaking to a solicitor and thereby incurring additional expense. It also makes us accountable to the client in that if any piece of work hasn't been done the client will see that it hasn't been done on the online reports.'

'From a company perspective', said Slade, 'it provides an internal tracking system across our intranet whereby we can trace and monitor work flow and, if necessary, share work loads between us. Another useful advantage is the reduction in low-priority phone calls from clients which, although well intentioned, could slow down progress.'

The latest improvements to the system include a facility to communicate case matters on the website to clients using the mobile phone short message service (SMS). Slade says: 'With over 50% of the population having mobile phones we believe that this is a huge step forward in providing clients with up-to-date information at what is a very stressful time. As soon as an important step is progressed on a file, for example exchange of contracts or the local search is received, a short text message is automatically sent to the client's mobile phone telling them what has happened.'

'We definitely believe we have gained a competitive advantage from using the system', added Slade. 'Solicitors are notoriously slow at adopting new technology. Our client base has opened up, taking us from being essentially a regional service to becoming an international operation.'

Questions

1. Outline the advantages of web-based support for legal services.
2. In a customer-focused environment such as this, could the Internet eventually replace the personal contact traditionally offered by solicitors?

6.3.1 The drivers for using the Internet for business

A number of factors are promoting the adoption of e-commerce:

- **Cost:** For a business, the entry costs for participating in e-commerce are relatively low. Systems can be designed and implemented and a web presence can be established relatively cheaply. The systems therefore offer a potentially fast return on the investment.

- **Flexibility:** Organizations can select the appropriate level of participation from simple access to the Internet through the creation of a Web presence to full-blown transaction-handling systems. The systems can be developed incrementally to add this additional functionality.

- **Protecting investment:** In the Internet world, many common and open standards are employed. The switching costs incurred when a business selects an alternative system are, as a result, relatively low.

- **Connectivity and communications opportunities:** Buying into Internet technology brings an accompanying range of opportunities, such as creating a local intranet or establishing video-conferencing links.

- **Low risk:** A critical mass of e-commerce participants already exists, and the technology, although constantly developing, is well understood. In addition, there are many government initiatives aimed at promoting e-commerce, and there is a significant level of activity in educational institutions to provide additional backup.

- **Improved customer service:** Although essentially a medium that promotes relationships at a distance, the Internet does also provide opportunities for businesses to work more closely with customers. For example, many techniques of directed, or focused, marketing are made easier when trading over the Internet.

- **Globalization:** The competitive pressures on businesses are increasingly of an international dimension. The Internet provides an easier and lower cost route for companies to participate in global business activity.

Mini case 6.2

E-commerce and globalization

Blue Nile, an online seller of diamonds and jewellery, is to become one of the first 'pure play'* US retailers to cross the Atlantic, in a move that reflects the growing interest of such companies in international expansion.

The potential of international sales for US retailers has been demonstrated by Amazon, the world's largest retailing website. Amazon's sites in the UK, Japan, Germany, China and France accounted for 46% of the company's $3bn sales in its first quarter, and rose faster than North American sales.

Scott Silverman, executive director of Shop.org, an association whose membership is made up of US e-commerce retailers, said he had seen evidence of growing interest in international markets as his members became more confident. 'Companies such as Blue Nile that have been around for six or seven years are pretty big. They are seeing some signs that 50% per year growth cannot continue, so international expansions seem to be an increasingly attractive option for them', he said.

At the same time, UK underwear retailer Figleaves.com and the Italian fashion site Yoox have established US offshoots. Jim Okamura, partner at JC Williams retail consultancy, noted that online-led international expansion is being explored by US chains that have started to reach the limits of market growth at home. 'It's not for everyone, but we've definitely seen a growing interest in international expansion strategies that

*'pure play' is where a company specializes in one particular product or service area to obtain a brand identity and large market share in that area.

▶

use an e-commerce platform as an initial entry point', he said, citing efforts by JC Penney and Victoria's Secret to develop online sales in Canada.

Blue Nile says its operation will be in Ireland and involve 'only a handful of employees', with site technology handled from the US. So far, it has sold goods worth about $3.3m to UK customers using a trial site with products priced in dollars.

Adapted from: **Blue Nile uses website to extend across the Atlantic**
Jonathan Birchall in New York, 14 May 2007

Questions

1. What motivates businesses to expand into new international markets?
2. To what extent does e-commerce make international expansion a more realistic proposition?

6.3.2 Barriers to entry

Despite the many drivers persuading businesses to venture into e-commerce activities, there are nonetheless several concerns that might induce caution.

- **Uncertainty over business models:** The technology has developed at such a pace that businesses have had little time to reflect on the most appropriate structures to facilitate e-commerce. This concern could lead to a reluctance of some businesses to commit themselves to e-commerce solutions. Business models are discussed further in Section 6.5.

- **Telecommunications costs:** In many geographical areas, particularly outside the USA, the cost of telephone communications is a significant factor. This situation is changing rapidly, as local calls in particular are becoming much cheaper, if not completely free, in many countries. The cost of leased lines, while an expensive option for smaller enterprises, is also becoming less prohibitive.

- **Bandwidth:** The multimedia content of the traffic on the Internet can create bottlenecks and slow down other forms of Internet access. The managers of many organizations fear that providing a facility for employees to access online sports updates and events, radio and TV broadcasts on their PCs might interfere with the normal running of the business. Continuing improvements in hardware, software and network infrastructure, along with the increasing uptake of broadband connectivity, are helping to alleviate the effects of increasing volumes of data transfer requests.

- **Security:** Several notable breaches of security have caused organizations to be cautious about implementing e-commerce solutions. Major problems have been caused by recent violations of confidentiality such as the customers of Internet banks being shown the account details of other customers, by virus attacks, and by unauthorized intrusion (e.g. Microsoft source code being stolen).

- **Lack of clear standards:** Although the Internet operates on largely open standards some tensions remain, for example the battle between Netscape and Microsoft to produce the de facto web browser.

- **Law and legal frameworks:** The global Internet environment poses many questions over legal issues, particularly when disputes occur. Trading may cross national boundaries, and the appropriate contract law must be employed. This can be difficult to establish where customer, vendor and web server are all located in different countries.

- **Preparedness:** Many businesses foresee the 'crest of the wave' effect of participating in e-commerce and are cautious about entering this global marketplace until completely prepared (for example, Fedex competitors).

6.4 Trade cycles and e-commerce

This section considers the three modes of e-commerce identified in Section 6.2 and investigates how they map on to more traditional business trade cycles.

6.4.1 E-commerce and traditional trade cycles

Business transactions have traditionally fallen into one of three so-called trade cycles. These cycles reflect the participants, the frequency of the transactions and the nature of the transactions involved.

Repeat trade cycles

This pattern of trading is characterized by companies that are closely linked in the supply chain. A typical example might be a manufacturer selling components to an assembly plant, or a regional warehouse supplying stocks to a supermarket. Often the restocking follows the just-in-time approach of maintaining minimal stock levels. In repeat trade cycles, orders are placed at regular intervals, invoicing is carried out periodically, and settlement is often automated.

Transactions that feature in repeat trade cycles are most suited to an EDI e-commerce solution. The placing of orders, raising and issuing of invoices and transfer of funds electronically (represented by the shaded area in Figure 6.2) can all be carried out using EDI technology. Once the initial negotiations have established the specification of product or service and price, the trading cycle iterates around the execution and settlement phases. Changes to the initial contract are shown by the feedback loop to the pre-sale phase. Once renegotiated, the business falls back into a new iteration of execution and settlement.

Irregular invoiced transactions

This form of trade is normally characterized by business-to-business transactions. One company might search for the best price or trading arrangements from a number of competing suppliers before placing an order. Settlement is often achieved through an

Figure 6.2 Repeat trade cycles

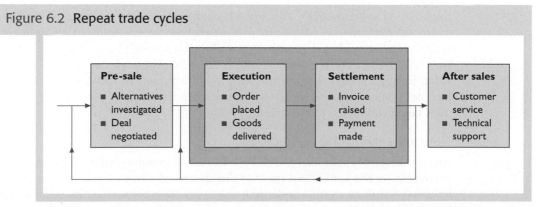

Source: FT.com

Figure 6.3 Irregular invoiced transactions

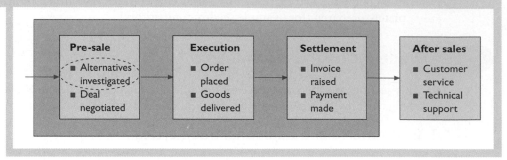

invoice relating to the particular order placed, and payment is made at a later date. An example of this sort of trade is an estate agent locating a property on behalf of a customer, based on a set of criteria.

The search described above reflects the category of e-commerce that was classified as electronic markets. An estate agent might use a property management system to compare details such as location, number of bedrooms and price. The focus of the interaction is usually only on the investigation (highlighted in Figure 6.3), although in other situations, such as a travel agent locating a particular journey, it may follow the transaction through to payment. The e-commerce trade cycle in the former case is unlikely to cover all stages of the transaction, as the estate agent is acting only as an intermediary. The settlement and after-sales components are more likely to be dealt with by traditional business methods.

Irregular cash transactions

The third type of trade cycle is that of irregular cash transactions. This equates to a one-off purchase of a service or product by an individual or a company. The settlement is normally made at the point of sale. The term 'cash' is therefore misleading, as payment may be by a variety of methods, such as a credit card. However, the principle is that mechanics of payment are established and commenced.

The best-understood aspect of e-commerce is that of individual 'home shoppers' purchasing goods and services over the Internet. However, the model does also apply to business-to-business transactions. As with the previous example, the Internet-based component may only comprise the search for and investigation of alternative products (highlighted in Figure 6.4). This again is characteristic of the electronic market classification of e-commerce. More often, however, the search leads to an online purchase with settlement and execution being combined into one phase and, in the case of software and music, delivery may be instantaneous. After-sales service may also be provided through access to a website with e-mail contact. In this case, the full activity of Internet commerce occurs with the entire transaction from pre-sale through to after-sales being conducted electronically.

New variants on the trade cycles

An e-commerce solution provides additional business opportunities and creates variations on the traditional trade cycles described above. Customers participating in irregular transactions may undertake only a pre-sales enquiry or use only the after-sales facilities such as 'frequently asked questions'.

Figure 6.4 Irregular cash transactions

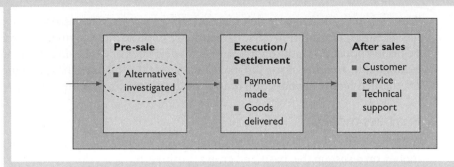

Once the lines of communication between participants in e-commerce have been established, it is possible to distribute a company newsletter or marketing mailshot. In other situations, it may be desirable to implement an order and delivery tracking service.

6.4.2 Porter's five forces model and e-commerce

The model of competitive forces introduced in Chapter 2 can usefully be applied to the e-commerce marketplace.

Threat of new entrants

Competitors considering adopting e-commerce may not need to match the IT infrastructure of the existing players. Indeed, because of the rapid development of new technology, it may be possible to bypass existing technology completely and establish a new 'leading edge' by employing fresh ideas. This has been the case in the rise of Internet bookshops and banking.

Threat of substitution

E-commerce solutions may lead to the introduction of substitute products. An example is seen in the introduction of alternative methods of product delivery, not always through legitimate channels, such as in the software, books and recorded music businesses.

Bargaining power of buyers

The role of intermediaries may be reduced where e-commerce is adopted. An example of this is seen in airline ticketing, once the preserve of specialized agencies. The introduction of cheap online flight ticketing has segmented the market. Increased information to customers poses similar threats to suppliers who may have faced much less intense competition in traditional markets.

Bargaining power of suppliers

As has been stated previously, the adoption of e-commerce may be a requirement of the suppliers. This is the case in some industries where EDI is a precondition to engaging in trade.

Competition with rivals

E-commerce solutions can reduce transaction costs, reduce stockholding, increase the reliability of supply and help to differentiate the company's product or service.

6.5 E-commerce business models

There are many different models for conducting business. The introduction of e-commerce has brought a revolution in some markets, with accompanying new business models being introduced. Traditional business models coexist alongside these new models for e-commerce. In other cases, the traditional model for business has been modified but not overhauled by the introduction of new electronic trading relationships.

Business models

A business model is the theoretical design for an organization that describes how it makes money on a sustainable basis and grows. Business models take on many forms, including:

- straightforward industry classifications, such as heavy industry, service sector;
- methods of trading, such as shop, supermarket, auction;
- structural definitions, such as functional responsibilities, 'everyone does everything'.

The following section introduces a number of business models for conducting e-commerce. These models are summarized in Table 6.1.

6.5.1 E-shops

An e-shop is a virtual store front that sells products and services online. Orders are placed and payments made. The logistics of delivery are usually accomplished by traditional methods, although some electronic products can be downloaded directly. Examples of electronic delivery can be seen at the site for recorded music company SonicNet (www.sonicnet.com), and the image and photographic services provider Photodisc (www.photodisc.com). An example of a business-to-consumer e-shop is shown in Figure 6.5. Toys'Я'Us, the children's toy retailer, offer a range of items which customers can order and have delivered to their home. An example of a business-to-business e-shop is shown in Figure 6.6. Ladybird is a brand label for children's clothing and distributes its products via a network of franchised retail businesses.

Table 6.1 Business models for electronic commerce

Type	Features	Examples
E-shop	Business-to-business	www.cisco.com
	Business-to-customer	www.amazon.com
E-mall	Diverse range of products and services	www.emall.com
E-procurement	Supply chain operations on the Internet	www.sap.com
E-auction	Electronic bidding for goods and services	www.ebay.co.uk
Specialist services	Online provision of goods and services	www.mcafee.com
Market segmenters	Differentiated markets	www.comet.co.uk
Content providers	Information services	www.ft.com
Internet infrastructure	Trust services, electronic payments	www.verisign.com

Figure 6.5 A business-to-consumer website

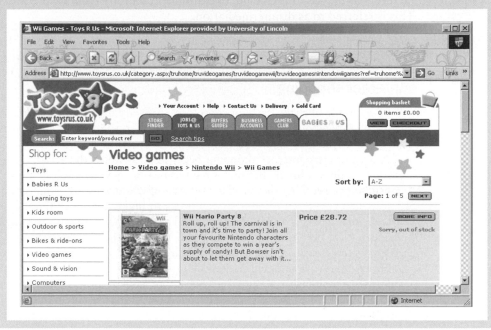

Figure 6.6 A business-to-business website

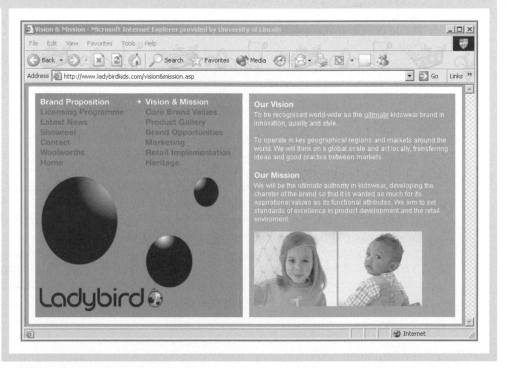

Source: with permission from Woolworths

E-shops are a convenient way of effecting direct sales to customers; they allow manufacturers to bypass intermediate operators and thereby reduce costs and delivery times. This is referred to as disintermediation.

Mini case 6.3

FT

Internet shopping

With a couple of clicks, fashion consumers can snap up a pair of Chloé 'as seen on the catwalk' three-strap cream heels for £335 from Net-a-Porter, or a belted trench coat 'in the style of Kate Moss' for £50 from Asos.

A decade after Internet shopping began to transform the retail experience, selling clothing online is finally becoming big business as new technology makes it easier for consumers to see what they are buying without recourse to a changing room.

Retailers have been using new web tricks to make buying clothing easier. Exclusive brands such as Gucci and Burberry, as well as more mainstream stores such as Marks & Spencer, have been using zoom and rotate tools on their websites to make it easier for shoppers to get a good look at what they are buying.

However, the US research showed that the conversion rates from browse to buy were still low, remaining at about 3%, with about half of all customers abandoning their transactions before they were complete. Natalie Massenet, the founder and chairman of upmarket online boutique Net-a-porter.com, said: 'More and more next-generation fashion consumers are growing up on the internet.'

Adapted from: **Online tricks turn browsers to sales clicks**
Elizabeth Rigby, *Financial Times*, 18 May 2007

Questions

1. If many Internet transactions are abandoned before they are completed why do companies persist with developing e-commerce shop fronts?

2. What are the challenges for clothing and shoe retailers in developing e-commerce sites? How do web designers improve the on-line shopping experience?

6.5.2 E-malls

The retailing model of a shopping mall, a conglomeration of different shops situated in a convenient location, is mirrored in e-commerce by the development of electronic malls or e-malls. The e-mall provides a common interface to the range of participants. This amalgamation of different businesses produces a virtual community with associated benefits such as shared costs and mutual advertising.

The iMegaMall e-mall, shown in Figure 6.7, is an electronic marketplace offering a wide range of products and services.

Another type of e-mall development comes about where an individual e-business diversifies to the extent that it presents itself as a virtual shopping arcade. E-companies such as Lastminute.com present customers with a wide range of products and services, all hosted from a single website providing a common interface.

6.5.3 E-procurement

Procurement is the whole process of obtaining services, supplies and equipment from identifying a business need through to fulfilment of contract. With the continuing

Figure 6.7 An e-mall website

trend in globalization of business the management of the supply chain has become an increasingly complex activity. An operation that has traditionally been controlled by specialists has now been largely automated. The ease of establishing connections using the Internet and web browsers rather than a costly infrastructure of dedicated private networks enables suppliers to open up their catalogues and product ranges at significantly reduced costs. The provision of information to customers thereby improves, and alternative methods of tender specification become possible. In addition, delivery times are reduced, leading to lower stockholding and further cost savings.

Mini case 6.4

FT

E-procurement

The predominant message from the history of e-procurement is that there has to be something in it for both buyers and suppliers. Too often, suppliers have been put off by initiatives they perceive to be 'buyer-led', and vice versa.

Recent developments are well illustrated at the St Mary's National Health Service Trust in London, one of a group of hospital trusts introducing the Zanzibar e-procurement system. Andrew Holden, its finance director, says improved flows of information

▶

about prices should now prevent any individual health trust being 'picked off' by suppliers. On the other hand, he notes, a fully electronic system in which an online order is 'flipped over' to become an invoice means suppliers can be paid much more quickly. And while suppliers may, within a year or two, have to use Zanzibar to sell to St Mary's, those with catalogues adopted by the system can look forward to bigger markets as Zanzibar develops critical mass within buying organizations.

Until recently, progress has been stymied by a mismatch in technology. It could be either side's technological immaturity to blame, but in the UK health service, at least, the problems have been on the buyers' side.

Janice Kite, UK e-business manager at Johnson & Johnson Medical Devices, part of the US healthcare company, visited an NHS customer in 2001 who did not even have an e-mail account or a personal computer. She says J&J still receives a high volume of NHS orders by fax or e-mail. 'For us, that isn't electronic – it still has to be pulled out and keyed into our system', she says. But things have improved significantly, and last year J&J saw its NHS-related transactions double in number, albeit from a small base, on Global Healthcare Exchange (GHX), one of the few surviving dotcoms offering e-procurement and marketplace services to the NHS. Another crucial issue, says Ms Kite, is ensuring that catalogue information within a system such as GHX is kept up to date and consistent: 'You can have all the technology in place, but if the data are not aligned and up to date, then you will get failures.'

Adapted from: **E-procurement: History proves the greatest teacher**
Andrew Baxter, *Financial Times*, 11 July 2007

Questions

1. Using the models of the supply chain described in Chapter 2 analyse the effect of e-procurement on both the purchasers and the suppliers of healthcare products and services.

2. To what extent might e-procurement address the issues raised in the article of purchasers getting 'picked off', or suppliers dealing with inconsistencies in data and systems?

6.5.4 E-auctions

The e-auction business model is based on the traditional auction concept of a bidding mechanism where the customer making the highest offer secures the purchase. The multimedia nature of e-auctions allows the supplier to make a more attractive presentation of the product offered. Figure 6.8 shows the popular eBay auction website. This is the longest running and most successful of the web-based electronic auction sites.

Highly interactive e-auctions can operate like clearing houses, where the prices of goods fluctuate in real time as the stocks vary. Revenue for the auctioneer is derived from transaction fees and from associated advertising. The potential global audience for an e-auction makes the sale of low-cost, small-margin items a more viable proposition. Business-to-business auctions may offer additional services, for example guaranteed payment for the seller or a warranty for the buyer. As described before, membership of an e-auction leads to the development of a virtual community, with accompanying benefits for all participants.

An alternative model for the e-auction is for a number of buyers to make a communal bid for an item. As more buyers are persuaded to participate in the purchase, the web company can strike a better deal and thereby reduce the price. An example of an e-auctioneer is LetsBuyIt.com.

Figure 6.8 A web auction site

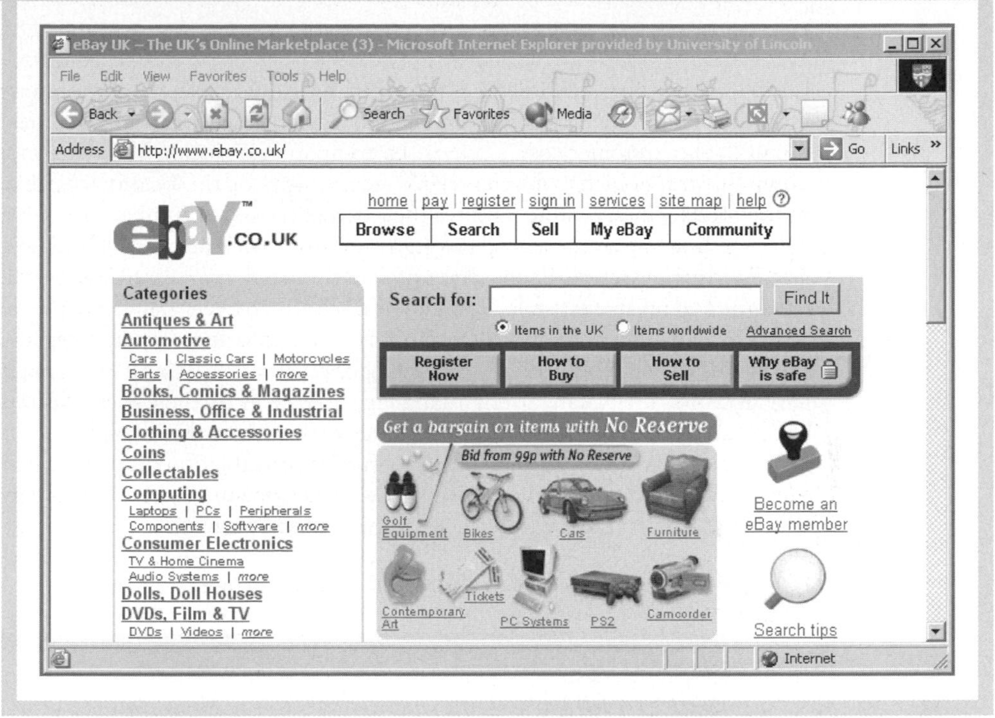

Source: eBay

A novel twist to the concept of an auction is the **reverse auction**, where buyers submit their proposed price to multiple suppliers in an attempt to secure the best deal. An example of a reverse auction specialist is Priceline.com, which offers a range of products such as airline tickets, cars and hotel rooms. The customer supplies key information (in the case of airline tickets the dates, cities and desired price), along with a credit card number. Priceline locates possible matches from a range of suppliers and, if successful, books the ticket at up to the price desired and charges the credit card automatically. The customer has to be flexible and is not allowed to be too prescriptive about times of travel or particular hotels in a given city.

In addition to the models above, there are an increasing number of more innovative business models for e-commerce.

6.5.5 Specialist service providers

Many companies engaged in e-commerce specialize in a particular market function. An example is the provision of logistics support, where Federal Express is a leading player (www.fedex.com), and in postal services, where the UK Royal Mail offers a range of delivery and tracking facilities. Another example of specialist services is the online computer support offered by companies such as NortonWeb (www.nortonweb.com). This service provides software updates, technical support and tools to tune and enhance the performance of a personal computer.

Mini case 6.5

Parcel-tracking services

The parcel-tracking sector of the commercial World Wide Web was the first sector to reach maturity. The largest courier services in the world provide tracking facilities for their customers at no customer cost. Each of the companies claims to be saving money as it cuts down the staff needed to answer telephone enquiries on the location of packages. In order to use the facilities, customers enter their parcel reference number through a form on the company's web page as viewed through a standard web browser. The carrier's computer system is then searched and the latest information on the parcel retrieved – when and where it was picked up, its current location, or, if it has already been delivered, the time of delivery and the receiver's name will be displayed. The main courier companies register hundreds of thousands of 'hits' on their web tracking pages each week. The service is expanding.

Companies are placing foreign-language interfaces on their sites. It is now possible to arrange pickup of parcels over the Internet with each of these carriers.

The stimulus has come from the pre-emptive introduction of the first tracking service. Once one provider had offered this service it became imperative for all others to follow suit. An example tracking interface can be seen in Figure 6.9.

Figure 6.9 **An example of a shipment tracking page**

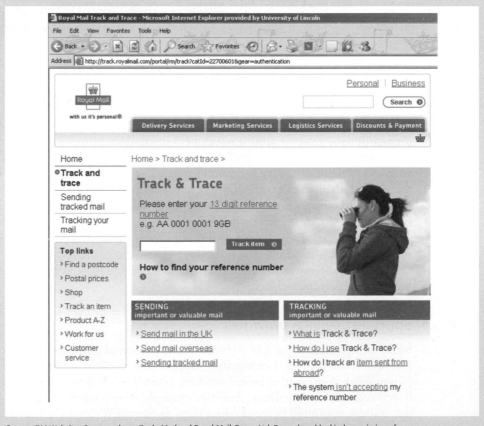

Source: RM Websites Screengrab are Trade Marks of Royal Mail Group Ltd. Reproduced by kind permission of Royal Mail Group Ltd. All Rights Reserved.

> ### Question
> What advantages do you think have accrued to these companies by offering tracking services to their customers?

6.5.6 Market segmenters

The immediate and accessible nature of electronic business has enabled some large companies to engage in market fragmentation in ways that would not otherwise have been possible. Recently, the major airlines identified electronic markets as a way of offering the same product, an airline ticket, at a lower price to certain sectors of the market. By creating e-businesses to handle these cut-price sales they successfully separated these alternative markets from traditional business customers, who continued to purchase tickets at a higher price through more conventional channels. Similarly, retailers of consumer durables and electronic goods have had great success in creating online stores as an alternative to the conventional high street or retail park store.

6.5.7 Content providers

The developments in digital storage media, particularly optical media, have led to the creation of e-businesses whose function is purely to maintain electronic archives. Newspapers have traditionally been archived in paper and microfiche formats. Now dedicated websites such as FT.com maintain archives of news reports and press releases and provide search facilities to extract the desired content. Other content providers are creating a niche as information specialists. Search engines such as Altavista provide an increasing range of search facilities and post-search links and services to enrich the information provided.

6.5.8 Internet infrastructure providers

Electronic commerce requires its own infrastructure. E-businesses are being created to fulfil those facilitating roles. Examples can be seen in companies that offer trust services, which provide facilities to enable secure transactions and communications. These companies provide certified authority that the service provided is reliable and secure. One such company is Verisign (www.verisign.com), which offers facilities to make secure a website, intranet or extranet to enable secure payments and to protect program code from being tampered with or corrupted.

6.5.9 Push and pull marketing strategies

A number of the business models above feature highly interactive participation. A key marketing decision for an e-business is to decide whether a proactive strategy to marketing will be adopted. The passive activity of customers or clients accessing and downloading pages from the Internet is termed **pull marketing**. The information is made available by suppliers, and customers search for and request, or pull, the pages from the server. Once a supplier has stored details about its customers, it could then develop a more active strategy of distributing information. This is known as **push marketing**. Particular benefits can be gained when push marketing is targeted at selected users.

However, much of the activity in push technology is of a broadcast nature, with suppliers sending streams of information relating to recent developments such as price changes or new products. The information can be broadcast globally or sent to a select group of interested individuals. The recipients can receive the information in many different ways:

■ For general release of product information, e-mails can be composed and distributed to those identified.

■ Details of software upgrades, such as the latest version of a web browser, can be transmitted when the user logs on for a new session.

■ If the user runs special software in the background on their computer it becomes possible for the information to be transmitted in real time, for example across a scrolling banner or as an update on a screen saver.

Often a mixed approach is employed where there is an initial (customer) pull followed by subsequent (supplier) push of information. An example of this mixed marketing approach can be seen in the use of **RSS** (Really Simple Syndications) feeds. Once a user has subscribed to an RSS feed, the content provider will publish material to the feed; typically this will be material that is updated frequently. The user must be running a feed reader (sometimes called an aggregator). The reader performs regular checks to see if new material is available and, if updates are detected, the material is transmitted from the host server.

6.6 The development and management of a business website

As has been explained earlier, a business may choose to develop and maintain a website for a number of reasons. Most commonly, these are (some of) the following:

■ to advertise services and products;

■ to sell services and products;

■ to promote the corporate image;

■ to provide information (especially public services).

Three main areas must be considered in the development and maintenance of a corporate website. These are **connection**, **publication policy** and **presentation of materials**.

Connection

Strictly speaking, a business could develop a website purely for access by its own employees through its own local area network (LAN). It might wish to create an intranet like this in order to provide a better and more cost-effective internal information service. The remaining sections on publication policy and presentation of materials apply to this, although the observations on connection do not.

However, it is more common for a business to use a website for public access. In order for the website to be publicly accessed over the Internet it must be permanently connected to the Internet. This can be achieved by the organization connecting its own host computer (or LAN) containing its website pages on a permanent connection to the Internet, either through ISDN lines or through connection to one of the established wide area networks. An alternative is to allow a third-party organization to handle the provision of the access to the business website by placing the business website pages on that organization's computer systems. This is common for smaller businesses, which may wish to use the disk space and web access service provided by Internet service providers (such as CompuServe or America On Line). This still requires the business to design and maintain its own web pages, which is partly a technical and partly an editorial/ creative operation. Nowadays, third-party organizations are providing services to business that involve not only the provision of public access websites for the business but also the development and maintenance of the content of the website.

A final factor taken into consideration by a business in deciding on the method of connection of its website to the World Wide Web is the security aspect. If the public-access website is held by a third-party organization then it is impossible for unauthorized access to be made to the business's own computer systems – at least by way of the World Wide Web. However, update and maintenance of the website contents are not as easy or immediate as when the website is under the direct control of the business itself. On the other hand, if a business runs its own website on its own host computer/local area network it incurs a risk of unauthorized access and must take precautions to ensure that security is maintained.

Generally speaking, large businesses will prefer to run their own websites and incur the costs of extra computers, permanent connection to the Internet and the need for security. They do this for the convenience of maintaining easy control over the content and update of the website, together with the ability to allow a high volume of public access. Small businesses may have neither the finances nor the trained personnel to do this; nor would the volume of public access justify that level of expenditure. These small businesses are likely to opt for a third-party provision.

In all cases where possible, it is desirable to have a web address that is meaningfully connected to the organization, then those wishing web access will be able to intelligently guess the address. For example, the web address of CNN is *www.cnn.com*, not *www.cablenetworknews.com*.

Publication policy

Once an organization has decided to develop its website it will need a policy governing the publication of material. This should cover the following areas:

- **Objectives of the website:** It is usual to state clearly the objectives of the website. This acts as guidance to the overall development.
- **Responsibility:** The policy must specify those with responsibility for the development and maintenance of:
  - the pages;
  - the information;
  - the computer support.

In a large organization many departments may have the right to provide material for pages governing their activities. The policy must be clear on this matter, and the individuals with responsibilities must be identified. The more centralized, hierarchical and authoritarian the organization the less responsibility and authority will be devolved to departments. It is instructive to observe that organizations such as universities, for which individual autonomy is an important cultural aspect, often allow staff and students the right to develop personal web pages with little or no control over their content – save the requirement to remain within the confines of the law.

- **Public relations and consistency of presentation:** It is usual for a policy to lay down guidelines for the level of consistency that must be contained within the presentation of each one of its pages. This may cover fonts, the way graphics are presented, layout and the presence of the corporate logo. The pages are what the organization presents to the world, and it is imperative that the correct corporate image be conveyed. It is therefore likely that the appearance of the home page (the first page to be accessed at the top of the hierarchy) and subsequent pages may have their style and content closely specified by the corporate public relations department.

- **Accuracy:** The organization will have a view on the need for the maintenance of accuracy of information on its website. It is likely that those with the responsibility for the provision and maintenance of the information will also have the responsibility for accuracy.

- **Security:** As has been mentioned above, security aspects over unauthorized access from outside the organization need to be established. It is also important that within the organization those with rights and responsibilities for page development and maintenance have procedures developed that allow them appropriate access, while those that do not have such rights and responsibilities are denied access.

- **Audit:** It is important that the organization checks whether its publication policy, as outlined above, is being observed and so will specify the internal audit (procedures for checking) on this.

Presentation of materials

In the early days of the Web, the material presented on a website was:

- largely text;
- aimed at the provision of factual information;
- written in source HTML;
- populated largely with static (unchanging) content
- developed by programming/technical personnel.

More recently, there has been a shift in orientation, and now material for a website is likely to be:

- a mixture of text, graphics and often audio/visual content using plug-ins;
- aimed partly at the provision of a corporate image and advertising objective;
- developed using a mixture of high-level web development tools;
- changing dynamically with real-time information feeds and context-dependent content
- developed by end users or those specifically charged with website development.

The contents of the website of today are more likely to be the province of the advertising and publicity and public relations departments of an organization than of the computing department. This shift in emphasis acknowledges the role of websites in the corporate image and as part of the business interface with the organization's marketplace. The development of high-level tools for the design of web pages has removed the focus of the developer from programming aspects to end presentation issues. These tools will generate HTML and XML code as their output.

Decisions on website development and approach are now considered to be of strategic importance to the organization in the presentation of itself to its market. Once developed, it is important that the business website be accessed. This will only be the case if the website address is known. There are a number of ways in which the web address may be publicly available:

- by inclusion of the web address in TV and other media advertising;
- by selection of a web address that is self-explanatory – for example, *www.ibm.co*;
- by advertising the web address on other websites using hypertext links;
- by inclusion in the catalogues of large indexing websites such as Yahoo! or Lycos.

Web presence

An organization contemplating an involvement in e-commerce must consider which type of Web presence is most appropriate. A simple Web presence might have no interactive component and just consist of a website hosting pages of information; the communication with the company in this case might be by conventional methods. The site could be developed further to include a facility for the client to e-mail the company. At a more involved level of Web presence still, clients would use the website to place orders for goods and services. This can be enhanced by the inclusion of the settlement stage, where either the method of payment is established or, more usually, payment is actually made. For some electronic products, delivery might also be carried out through the website.

Increasing sophistication in Web presence might lead to the provision of online and real-time information relating to items in stock or latest prices. Alternative methods of customer contact such as regular or ad hoc marketing mailshots can also be incorporated.

Website awareness

In the above cases, the customer needs to know of the fact that the business or organization in question has a website and that the business is a seller of a product or service that is desired by the customer. This is handled in a number of ways:

- The business will conventionally advertise on television or in the press and place the website address on the advertisement.
- The business will ensure that the home page contains key words that make it easy for a searcher to use a web search index produced by a search engine.
- The organization will attempt to have its link placed on another website so that visitors to that website may click on a hyperlink to the organization's website.

The last method is important and can be achieved in different ways:

- **Reciprocal arrangements:** The organization may have a reciprocal arrangement with another so that both websites cross-link.
- **Web communities:** The organization may be part of a group or community that provides a website for a particular interest area (see below on web communities).
- **Commercial advertisement:** The organization may pay to have an advertisement and hyperlink on a frequently visited website. For example, web search indexes are visited by millions of clients per day. If a company has a corporate logo and link advertised

on the web search site then only one-tenth of one per cent of readers need to click on the hyperlink to ensure that thousands of potential customers are in touch with that company's products or services.

The business trend is to make more extensive use of websites for the provision of information and the exercise of business operations. This will be fuelled by improvements in telecommunications, the increasing proportion of the population owning PCs and the economics of the Internet as a medium for information provision.

Website metrics

A range of tools are available to web managers to evaluate the success of their websites. These primarily divide into those that evaluate the usability of the website and those that record and analyse actual usage. Typical measures of usability include:

- optimal path analysis;
- page impression analysis;
- acceptance testing;
- accessibility evaluation.

Typical tools that measure and analyse usage include those that:

- count hits and track visitor paths and return visits;
- optimize performance in both web page delivery and web server activity;
- audit site activity and analyse visitor behaviour;
- measure search engine performance and keyword ranking.

6.7 Trends in e-commerce

Although e-commerce has now been established for some time, the models for electronic business are still fairly immature and the underpinning technology is constantly evolving. However, some trends are already discernible.

6.7.1 Structural developments

There appear to be two strands of divergent development in the more innovative e-business models. The first is a move to greater integration in business activity, the second a specialization into business services and functions.

The increase in integration can be evidenced by the reinforcement of linkages along the supply chain. This is demonstrated by specific arrangements such as EDI and in the integration of transaction support in the electronic sales functions.

The specialization into business services is seen in the growth of third-party arrangements such as trusted services and electronic transaction settlement.

6.7.2 The reliance on advertising

The business plans of many e-businesses are framed with a built-in reliance on advertising revenue. In recent years, the advertising revenue generated by these dot.coms has been less than was originally predicted. Alternative sources of revenue can be found in subscription or transaction fees, but these in turn lead to strategic implications for the organization.

6.7.3 Maintaining competitive advantage

A constant desire of companies is to sustain any competitive advantage gained, particularly where the company has been first to market with a new technology. The first mover takes the risk of testing the market and also incurs the higher development costs associated with the pioneering technology. However, they do take the initiative upon launching the product. The challenge is then to maintain that advantage. This can be accomplished, for example, by associating the brand image with the new development, as was achieved initially by the FedEx parcel-tracking system and by Amazon.com booksellers. The advantage can be further reinforced by enhancing the website and augmenting the range of services that it provides.

It is far harder to achieve this degree of competitive advantage with EDI. Here it is relatively easy for competitors to establish the systems required and imitate the first mover. With EDI, it is more a case of producing a competitive disadvantage for those not following the first mover.

6.7.4 Intelligence on the Web

Intelligent agents

It is becoming increasingly common for software products to exhibit a degree of 'intelligence' in their activities. Familiar desktop artefacts include organizers that suggest layout changes while text is entered, spelling correctors and other 'wizards' that suggest the best time to carry out system maintenance such as defragmenting the hard disk of a PC. The intelligence comes from an ability to learn from and adapt to the environment in which the software is operating. The software might, for example, monitor the user's responses and incorporate that newly acquired knowledge into future suggestions to the user.

Electronic business can provide many opportunities for the use of intelligent agents. Customers are often persuaded to take up membership or become a registered user of a Web-based facility. Having stored these details, the business can build up a profile of customers and their behaviour and use the information for targeted marketing activities. An online bookseller might use an intelligent agent to store information about previous choices and make suggestions about future purchases, or notify users when selected new books become available.

Bots

A **bot** (a shortened form of the word '*robot*') is a piece of software that trawls through vast numbers of websites searching for particular items of data and gathers the results into massive data stores. They are commonly used by sites that offer shoppers comparative price information. The bot searches in much the same way as an individual uses a search engine, but it issues the query repeatedly in a relentless search through sites on the Web. An example is the bot used by Bidders Edge, which targets e-auction sites, collecting product price information. The bot is not always a welcome visitor to a website.

Apart from using up valuable processing power and bandwidth, it can instantaneously rank the price of a product against that of competing brands. Although this information is in the public domain, once gathered by a bot it can be made much more readily available to the public at large. A further possible concern to suppliers is that once posted in a comparative format, the information might rapidly become out of date, giving customers a misleading impression. A number of sites attempt to detect and block an incoming bot and attempt thereby to restrict access to the information to private individuals. There have also been legal actions taken, such as that brought by eBay against Bidders Edge, to attempt to deny access to sites by bots.

Another application of bots is in the creation of animated advertising banners. As the average take-up rate on most banner advertisements is less than 1%, companies are looking for innovative ways to increase user participation. Companies such as Artificial Life have developed Banner Bots, which allow natural-language conversations with users. They are intended to enhance an advertiser's online presence by entertaining, educating or leading users where they want to go by responding to questions instantaneously. These bots are also valuable market research tools that store and analyse conversation logs between consumers and the bots.

One of the more innovative uses of bots is in providing a virtual human interface. The interactive division of the Press Association in Britain has developed Ananova, a virtual newscaster who acts as the front end of the PA's online news services. Other human-like incarnations include Eve, the customer service advocate of eGain of Sunnyvale, California, and German retailer net-tissimo.com, whose bot is an exclamation mark dressed in a tuxedo!

Summary

Businesses have been swift to realize the opportunities provided by the Web and have developed websites in order to:

- advertise services and products;
- sell services and products;
- promote corporate images;
- provide information (especially public services).

As the various mini case studies indicated, advantages in using the Web include a reduction in the cost of advertising, cheaper and easier provision of information, the lack of a need to maintain a shop front, the ease of crossing geographical boundaries, and the absence of the middleman. Issues, including the security of electronic communications, particularly commercial transactions, will need to be tackled before the Internet becomes a stable environment for business operations.

It is likely that the use of the Internet and the Web will continue to grow in importance for business as new applications are exploited and the number of people able to access the Internet increases. The activities of e-commerce can be classified into the three areas of electronic markets, EDI and Internet commerce. These activities are embodied in the traditional business trade cycles: EDI represents an example of a repeat trade cycle; electronic marketplaces are extensively used in the pre-sale phase of irregular transactions; and full Internet commerce takes place in irregular transactions, particularly where there is cash settlement.

A number of business models for conducting electronic business have emerged. The most commonly found are:

- e-shop (business-to-business and business-to-consumer);
- e-mail;
- e-procurement;
- e-auction.

In addition, there are companies providing specialist online services, information archives or tools for developing Internet infrastructure.

Trends in e-commerce are likely to include greater integration into business activity, with stronger linkages through the supply chain and a specialization into business services and functions such as trusted services and electronic transaction settlement.

Review questions

1. Provide a definition of e-commerce.

2. In what ways does e-commerce allow businesses to gain competitive advantage?

3. What factors encourage participation in e-commerce? What are the barriers to entry for businesses?

4. List *eight* business models for e-commerce. Give an example of the type of business that might adopt each model.

5. Give *two* examples of intelligence as seen in Web-based business activity.

Exercises

1. Using Porter's value chain and five forces model (Chapter 2), analyse the strategic impact of the use of the World Wide Web for the following business areas:
   - food and grocery retail
   - courier parcel tracking
   - property agency
   - banking
   - equity and stock trading
   - news and publishing.

2. Provide three different definitions of e-commerce, giving a justification for each.

3. How would a business identify the cost-effectiveness of its website?

4. Search the World Wide Web for a range of different business websites and analyse these with a view to answering the following:
   - What are the objectives for the business of the website?
   - How effective has the business been in meeting these objectives?
   - Which features of the website should be added to or removed?

5. To what extent do traditional business trade cycle models help us to understand the way in which e-commerce is carried out?

6. 'If the Internet is a lawless frontier, then the service providers are the new marshals in town' (Spar and Bussgang, 1996). Is this the case?

CASE STUDY 6

E-commerce

Since the nation first discovered the joys of Internet shopping 12 years ago, Britons have spent more than £100bn online. Consumers swapping the mall for the mouse in ever greater numbers pushed sales past that milestone this month, fuelled by a very strong April performance. A total of £3.47bn worth of goods were purchased online – an eye-catching 55% rise on the previous year.

James Roper, chief executive of the Interactive Media in Retail Group, the industry body which tracks Internet sales, pointed out that more and more goods had become available online. The IMRG's figures include spending on travel, which is still the largest category of consumer spending, accounting for about £7bn of spending last year, followed by electrical goods at £5bn. Clothing sales are also increasing rapidly, mirroring trends in the US, where online sales in that sector recently overtook computer sales for the first time.

People are using the Web to buy increasingly expensive items. Just a few years ago, the average Internet transaction was a book or CD costing about £15. Today, a breed of sophisticated and web-savvy shopper thinks nothing of buying big ticket items such as sofas and fridges online.

The spread of high-speed broadband has proved a magic bullet. About half of UK adults are now estimated to have a broadband connection in their homes, many of them with speeds of more than 1 megabit a second. Back in 1995, as the Internet made its first tentative inroads into people's lives, just 2m homes in the UK had any kind of connection – in most cases very slow 14.4 kilobit-a-second modems.

The IMRG expects Internet sales in the UK to rise to £42bn this year, a 39% increase over 2006. It predicts sales will reach £78bn, accounting for 20% of retail sales, by 2010. And with a sizeable minority of retailers yet to embrace the Internet at all, the sector has huge room to grow. According to a survey earlier this year by Microsoft, only 56 of the UK's 100 largest retailers had a website which allowed consumers to shop online.

The UK punches well above its weight internationally, accounting for about 6% of the world's £250bn a year online shopping market, and about a third of all European online retail. In contrast, consumers in the US are expected to spend about £88.4bn online this year. Much of the growth in UK Internet sales has come at the expense of – rather than in addition to – high street sales, however. 'A lot of it is cannibalization', said Mr Roper. 'The high street is not growing much.'

While online sales are increasing at rates of about 40 to 50% year on year, overall retail sales for the three months to the end of March grew just 4.5% from a year earlier. Many of the UK's largest internet retailers, such as Argos, Tesco and John Lewis, have a hybrid, 'clicks and mortar' model, in which they sell both online and in stores. Schemes – such as Argos' 'click and collect' – which allow consumers to order online but collect in store have proved a hit.

However, there are a number of thriving stores that exist solely on the Internet, especially specialists, such as Figleaves.com the lingerie retailer and Firebox.com which specializes in gadgets. In some sectors, such as electrical goods, fierce online competition is driving retailers to abandon the high street. Last year, Dixons announced plans to start trading solely online. Keen Internet pricing and high rents made a high street presence untenable. Whether others will follow this route is still unclear. 'It is too early to say which model will be dominant on the internet', said Mr Roper. 'Retailers are barely beginning to scratch the surface yet.'

Adapted from: **Internet shopping tops £100bn**
Maija Palmer, *Financial Times*, 18 May 2007

Questions

1. What technological factors have facilitated the massive growth in Internet shopping?

2. Describe the various business models that companies can adopt in pursuing e-commerce markets. Which models are discussed in the case study? What aspects of the business make these models particularly appropriate?

3. The case study implies that much e-commerce is simply diverting consumers from traditional to online shopping. If the market volume is unchanged, why do businesses pursue e-commerce alternatives? Use analytical tools and models such as those introduced in Chapter 2 to support your answers.

4. Describe the barriers to the successful development of e-commerce. For each barrier, evaluate the extent to which the businesses described in the case study might be affected.

5. The development of an effective website is crucial to the success of an Internet-hosted business. Using the different businesses described in the case study, identify features that should be considered in the development of their website and their web presence.

References and recommended reading

Barnes S. (2007). *E-Commerce and V-Business*. Butterworth-Heinemann
    This book takes a business-focused look at Internet trade, virtual organizations and disintermediation.

Benyon-Davies P. (2004). *E-Business*. Palgrave Macmillan.
    This text takes an international view of e-commerce and e-business issues with many case studies and other illustrations. The book is written with a number of learning aids to reinforce the content.

Boon M. (2001). *Managing Interactively: Executing Business Strategy, Improving Communication and Creating a Knowledge-Sharing Culture*. McGraw-Hill
    This book looks at informing and engaging people, sharing knowledge and practical strategies for 'smart' communication.

Bressler S. and Grantham C. (2000). *Communities of Commerce*. McGraw-Hill
    This book contains a collection of case studies and looks at the business climate of Internet communities and the effect of putting a community online.

David W.S. and Benamati J. (2006). *E-Commerce Basics: Technology Foundations and E-Business Applications*. Addison-Wesley, Pearson
    This is a comprehensive introduction to all aspects of e-commerce. Later chapters also cover cybercrime, cyberterrorism, security and ethical issues. Chapters contain summaries, review questions and exercises.

Fellenstein C. and Wood R. (2000). *Exploring E-Commerce: Global E-Commerce and E-Societies*. Prentice Hall

This text focuses on many issues, including the management of the supply chain, e-societies, e-governments and techniques for anticipating customers' needs.

Lawrence E. *et al.* (2003). *Internet Commerce: Digital Models for Business*, 3rd edn. John Wiley & Sons.

An excellent book packed full of examples, illustrations, mini cases and case studies that takes a business-focused look at e-commerce. As well as the expected chapters on business models and technology basics, it also includes sections on taxation, legal and ethical issues.

Liautaud B. and Hammond M. (2001). *E-Business Intelligence: Turning Information into Knowledge into Profit*. McGraw-Hill

This book looks at the new enterprise business intelligence, information governance, customer care and the supply chain.

Lucas H.C. Jr. (2003). *Strategies for Electronic Commerce and the Internet*. MIT Press

This is an accessible book intended for those with a business background who wish to learn about strategy, business models and the Internet. It provides a good introduction to business models and shows how these are used in strategies adopted in the introduction of Internet business by established organizations and by new businesses.

McCue S. (2006) *Farce to Force: Building Profitable E-Commerce Strategies*. South-Western Educational.

A very readable text providing a range of examples of business models and e-commerce strategies that have achieved varying degrees of success. The book provides helpful advice for constructing e-commerce websites and describes hardware, software and social aspects for successful e-commerce design.

Raisch W.D. (2001). *The E-Marketplace: Strategies for Success in B2B E-Commerce*. McGraw-Hill

A readable book covering business models, the dynamics of the e-marketplace, community and commerce strategies, and value trust networks.

Spar D. and Bussgang J.J. (1996). Ruling the Net. *Harvard Business Review*, May–June

A thought-provoking paper comparing the use of the Internet to the lawless frontiers of the Wild West. The authors highlight the contrast between the lack of a legal framework for the Internet, making e-commerce unpredictable and unstable, and the tremendous opportunities for business.

Sterne J. (2002). *Web Metrics: Proven Methods for Measuring Web Site Success*. John Wiley & Sons.

The book presents an encyclopaedic range of approaches for the measurement and evaluation of web pages and sites.

Timmers P. (2000). *Electronic Commerce: Strategies and Models for Business-to-Business Trading*. Wiley

This well-written book provides an excellent coverage of the subject, with numerous examples and illustrations.

Turban E., King D., Lee J. and Viehland D. (2006). *Electronic Commerce: A Managerial Perspective*. Prentice Hall, Pearson

This is the fourth edition of an established undergraduate text and contains new material on launching successful online businesses, an extended coverage of the digital economy, e-marketing, e-supply chains and market mechanisms. There are role-playing exercises, summary and discussion questions at chapter ends.

Whiteley D. (2000). *E-Commerce: Strategy, Technologies and Applications*. McGraw-Hill

A good all-round overview of electronic commerce written with a business focus. The book contains a large amount of material relating to EDI.

Chapter 7

Business intelligence

Learning outcomes

On completion of this chapter, you should be able to:

- Discuss the drivers for business intelligence
- Describe tools and techniques that can provide business intelligence
- Describe business intelligence that can be derived through analysis of organizational data, through management of human factors and through analysis of business performance
- Evaluate the role of decision support and describe a range of tools, including spreadsheets and digital dashboards, that offer support for decision making
- Explain the concept of a data warehouse and describe techniques for extracting data from a data warehouse
- Describe data mining and give examples of how data mining techniques can benefit business operation
- Characterize the contribution that customer relationship management can make to effective business operation
- Discuss the development of end-user computing and evaluate its contribution to applications development
- Evaluate the importance of human–computer interaction in business information systems.

Introduction

In Chapter 1, information, decisions and the use of information in decision making were examined. This was achieved without recourse to discussion of any technology involved. Earlier chapters have introduced aspects of technology. This chapter covers how technology can provide business intelligence which in turn supports decision making in systems for planning, control and management. The chapter analyses the characteristics and classes of business intelligence including decision support systems, group decision support systems, data warehousing, data mining and customer relationship management.

The influence of modern technology and, in particular, the role of fourth-generation languages, spreadsheets, expert systems tools and model generators in the development of business intelligence are emphasized. The role of end users in the specification and development of applications, especially decision support systems, is introduced. The phenomenon of end-user computing, its benefits and its challenge to management, are examined. Prototyping as a method of developing decision support systems within the context of end-user computing is explained. The focus on decision support and end-user computing has emphasized the need for a theory of the role of the user in the total system. Approaches to this area in the context of human–computer interaction are covered.

7.1 The increasing focus on business intelligence

In Chapter 1 the rapid growth of the information age was outlined. Subsequent chapters highlighted the development of technology that can store ever-increasing amounts of data and process that data increasingly quickly to provide information. In addition, the developing means of communication have made transmission of data easier and therefore rendered the resulting information more readily available to organizations and their customers.

By processing data to produce information an organization can potentially gain a better understanding both of how it is functioning internally and also of the external environment in which it is operating. A better understanding of these two factors can improve the efficiency and competitiveness of a business. This is captured by the term **business intelligence**. It can defined as

> 'the result of applying tools and techniques to the data and information available within and without an organization to facilitate a better understanding of both its environment and its operation and thereby improve the decision-making process'.

Business intelligence can be thought of as an umbrella term for a collection of approaches. These include the support of the decision-making process but also go further in analysing the operations and functioning of the organization. It can be thought of as *information about information* – in other words, taking the known facts and records available and further processing and interrogating them to discover new information. For instance, records which yield patterns of customer purchases might be associated with the sales personnel profiles of those sales persons who generate these, together with various sales incentive schemes, to produce a much more effective putting together of customers, sales persons and incentive schemes. This crosses over into the area commonly described as **knowledge management**. The data already available to the organization is processed to produce information which in turn is further analysed to produce new knowledge. Knowledge management covers the production and sharing of the intellectual assets that might be derived from utilizing business intelligence tools and techniques. Knowledge-based systems are discussed briefly later in this chapter and then in more detail in Chapter 18.

7.1.1 Key features of business intelligence

Internal and external inputs

Management information systems, as previously introduced and defined, can in some cases focus only on internal inputs, such as the transaction data resulting from sales to customers or the stock levels held in warehouses. Although business intelligence will utilize this raw data it will also draw from sources that are external to the organization whether derived from competitor activity, governmental sources, supplier or customer activity or behaviour and so on.

Structured and unstructured data

Intelligence can be found from a wider range of sources than the formal and structured outputs of business transactions. Business intelligence might derive from the content or destination of e-mails, logs of browsing activity on websites, content of web pages and so on.

Improved support for creating business strategy

As previously described, the determination of business missions and objectives is crucially founded upon detailed and accurate information. Business intelligence can improve the basis for the development of business strategy.

Gaining competitive advantage

By understanding more about itself, its competitors and the environment in which it operates, an organization can utilize the intelligence in order to gain a competitive advantage.

Improving support for decision making

In models of decision making that have previously been introduced, the first stage was *intelligence*. This provided the basis from which the *design*, *choice* and *implementation* stages could follow. Business intelligence can not only provide the raw data to inform this process but might, for example, provide examples of similar decisions in the past or the decisions that have been made by competitors.

Increasing the use of performance indicators

In many areas of operation, organizations are increasingly applying and then evaluating their performance against targets. This is particularly the case in the non-profit-making sectors such as local authorities and health provision (which cannot use only profit or financial targets). To introduce pressures similar to those in the commercial sectors, targets are set and metrics employed to assess the success in achieving those targets. Business intelligence tools and techniques can assist an organization in taking appropriate actions to ensure it meets specific targets and to assess the degree of success in achieving the target.

External drivers

Businesses are increasingly required to operate in more transparent ways. Public scrutiny, endorsed by legislation concerned with freedom of information, discrimination, equality in employment processes etc. requires that organizations can make statements about their own performance in terms of these factors. Business intelligence tools and techniques can provide knowledge and the level of understanding necessary to operate in this more transparent environment.

Business intelligence focuses on three key aspects, namely **analysing data and information**, **analysing human behaviour** and **analysing the performance and processes of the business**. These three aspects are looked at in greater detail in the next sections.

7.2 Business intelligence from analysing data and information

There are a number of tools and techniques for generating business intelligence. These include

- Decision support systems
- Group decision support
- Document management systems
- Digital dashboards
- Online analytical processing (OLAP)
- Data warehousing
- Data mining.

These are each looked at in greater detail in the following sections.

7.2.1 Decision support systems

Although the term **decision support system (DSS)** is a general one used to cover virtually any computerized system that aids decision making in business, most DSSs share certain features.

DSS support decisions

One of the important characteristics of a decision support system is that it is intended to *support* rather than replace decisions. The Gorry and Scott Morton framework relating the structure of a decision to the level of managerial activity involved in the decision was covered in Chapter 1. Computerized systems can replace the human decision maker in structured decisions but are of little help in completely unstructured situations. There is, for instance, a large group of decisions taken by personnel in business organizations that have a structured computational and data transformation element to them as well as an unstructured non-rule-governed component. It is just these decisions that can be aided but not replaced by decision support systems.

Examples of semi-structured decisions are: planning a mix of investments for a portfolio; looking at the financial implications of various ways of financing a short-term cash flow deficit; consideration of alternative production and pricing policies; assessing the impact of potential future changes in exogenous variables such as interest rates; analysis of the creditworthiness of corporate clients; and assessing the likely impacts of departmental reorganization.

DSSs involve flexible interactive access to data

Decision support systems are designed with an understanding of the requirements of the decision makers and the decision-making process in mind. This has implications, two of the most important being:

1. **The need for interactive support:** Typically, many of the semi-structured decisions for which DSSs are relevant involve the decision maker in asking questions that

require immediate answers. As a result of this, further interrogation is made. Examples are:

- **what if** – as in 'what would be the effects on profits if we were to be subject to a 5% material cost rise?'
- **goal seeking** – as in 'what would be the required mix in the liquidation of short-term and medium-term assets to reduce a projected cash deficit to zero over the next six months (the goal)?'
- **optimization** – as in 'how do we ensure optimum utilization of our machines?'

2. **Flexible access to data:** Many semi-structured decisions are only possible if the decision maker has immediate access to ad hoc data-retrieval and report-generation facilities. For internal decisions this generally means that access by powerful query languages to existing data held in a corporate database is required.

Modern decision support systems meet these requirements by ensuring easy and quick availability of access to decision makers. This can be supplied by PCs placed on the desks of managers. The use of local area networks of PCs and the connections between these networks and mainframes, coupled with increasingly easy access to the Internet, have enabled easier data access to decision makers.

The use of spreadsheets, database management systems and other modelling packages has provided the necessary modelling and data-retrieval facilities. The standardized web page interface to the Internet and local intranets has further simplified the problems surrounding presentation of information to decision makers. Although data may be collected from a range of different systems and sources, the acceptance of a standard document structure for the Web simplifies the presentation of this information.

DSSs are fragmented

In Chapter 1 we saw that the totally integrated corporate management information system designed as a single project is extremely unlikely to be successful. Information systems are more likely to be loose federations of subsystems evolving separately to serve the information needs of the individual functional subsystems of the organization. This pattern is also exhibited with decision support, where the trend is towards development of models to provide support for individual decisions or types of decision. No attempt is made to develop global comprehensive decision support models for entire organizations.

DSS development involves end users

This is reinforced by the involvement of end-user decision takers in the development of models for computerized support. Nowhere is this more pronounced than in the use of local PCs and spreadsheet modelling. The purchase of PCs and the development of models are often carried out independently of any knowledge or aid from the central computer department. The use of fourth-generation languages in general has increased the influence of end users over decision support design.

In summary, the trend in modern decision support systems is towards end-user involvement in the development of simple fragmented models targeted to aid, rather than replace, the kinds of decision to be made. Easy and flexible interactive access to data and modelling facilities is as likely to be provided by PCs and networks as by the more traditional large central computers.

Types of decision support system

Decision support systems can be divided into a number of categories, depending on the type of processing of data and information involved and the type of decision made.

1. **Data retrieval and analysis for decision support:** These systems rely on interaction with an existing database:

   (a) **Simple entry and enquiry systems:** These support decisions by providing immediate interrogation of a database for specific enquiries. Examples are stock enquiry systems, airline booking systems and account enquiry systems. They are used to aid operational decisions – for instance, whether to reorder stock.

   (b) **Data analysis systems:** These provide summaries and selected reports of data held on the database. An example is a system to provide information on the rate at which sales orders are being satisfied.

   (c) **Accounting information systems:** These are very similar to the last category as accounting information is provided as an analysis of accounting transaction data. However, because accountants commonly need the same types of report – for example, aged analysis of debtors, summary balance sheets, cash reports, profit and loss reports – and such information is prepared according to professional accounting standards, much of this information is supplied by accounting applications packages.

2. **Computational support for structured decisions:** These involve using existing general data held on a database and computation together with details of individual cases to arrive at information for a decision. An example would be a motor insurance quotation system. This accepts data on an individual, searches a database of insurance companies' terms and computes a set of calculated premiums, which optimize on some group of variables such as low cost, maximum protected bonus or minimum excess.

3. **Decision support involving modelling:** These systems rely on the use of existing data from a database or user input data, which might be hypothetical. Using this data, its consequences are calculated using a model. The model reflects relationships that the decision taker believes to hold between the variables relevant for a decision.

   (a) Spreadsheet models are used to represent accounting relationships between numerical accounting data. They are used to take the tedium out of budget preparation and forecasting. The sensitivity of the organization to changes in the values of accounting data is then easy to estimate by hypothetical 'what if' changes.

   (b) Probabilistic models incorporate elements of probabilistic reasoning and risk analysis in their modelling calculations.

   (c) Optimization modelling involves mathematical computation of optimization or goal seeking based on constraints.

Many decision support systems in this category exhibit all three characteristics.

The development of decision support systems

The development of a decision support system is determined by the types of information and the facilities needed for making the decision. In this sense, DSS development is decision-led. Because an intimate knowledge of the decision-making process is needed it is important that end users – that is, the decision makers – are involved in the process of design. They may carry out the development and design themselves, as is common with spreadsheet modelling, or it may be undertaken by analysts and programmers.

Decision support systems are developed using programming languages or produced by packages specifically incorporating decision support development tools. These methods will now be considered. In all approaches, it is generally considered advisable to develop prototypes initially.

The use of very high-level languages

Conventional high-level languages such as C++ and Java can be used to develop decision support systems. They are extremely flexible. However, decision support systems using these languages involve a lengthy analysis and design phase. They are not suitable for prototyping. It is now not common to use them, especially as technical efficiency considerations, which may be important with transaction-processing systems, are not so important for decision support.

Fourth-generation or very high-level languages are more appropriate. They are particularly useful as they are generally database oriented. This is important for those systems that rely on data retrieval and analysis for decision support. An example of a prominent fourth-generation language is SQL, which can be used on many relational database systems, such as IBM's DB2 and ORACLE. The advantages of using them are that:

- applications development is more rapid;
- many are end-user oriented; and
- they are more likely to be declarative rather than procedural.

The use of spreadsheets

Of all the computerized productivity tools made available to the decision maker in business organizations over the last two decades, the electronic spreadsheet is among the most powerful, widely employed and user-friendly.

Spreadsheets are a particularly suitable tool for the accountant, although they may be used for many general business modelling tasks. A popular area is the development of cash flow forecasts. A firm's cash flow position can be crucially affected by changes in average debtor or creditor periods, in the pattern of expected future costs and sales, and the charge incurred in remaining in overdraft, which is particularly sensitive to interest rate changes. Model building and 'what if' analysis enable the accountant to keep an up-to-date and changing view of the firm's current and future cash flow position without the laborious need to recalculate in the light of unexpected changes.

To understand the idea of a spreadsheet, imagine a large sheet of paper divided into many rows and columns. Through the keyboard the user may enter text, a number or a formula into each cell; a cell is the 'box' at the intersection of every row and column. Spreadsheet software running on a computer provides a computerized equivalent of this grid-like worksheet. The entry in each cell is made by moving a cursor to the required cell and entering the data. The cell entry is displayed on the screen. For example, in Column S, Row 35 the text **SALES** or the number 100.23 might be entered. Or again the formula (**COLUMN B ROW 23** + **COLUMN C ROW 14**) × 2 might be added. In the last case, the resulting number calculated from the formula would be displayed on the screen in the cell position. Any cells referred to in a formula may themselves contain numbers or other formulae. Cells may be linked together in this way.

Figure 7.1 The output of a spreadsheet for profit forecasting

	1	2	3	4	5	6	7
1	DVD players TYPES DVD-A and DVD-B						
2	6 months projections from January						
3							
4	SALES	Jan	Feb	March	April	May	June
5	units DVD-A	43	43	44	44	45	45
6	units DVD-B	121	109	98	88	79	71
7							
8	price DVD-A	123	121	118	116	113	111
9	price DVD-B	278	306	336	370	407	448
10							
11	sales revenue DVD-A	5289	5235	5182	5129	5076	5025
12	sales revenue DVD-B	33638	33302	32969	32639	32313	31989
13		--------	--------	--------	--------	--------	--------
14	TOTAL	38927	38537	38150	37768	37389	37014
15							
16	COSTS						
17	labour DVD-A	1075	1086	1097	1108	1119	1130
18	labour DVD-B	5203	4683	4214	3793	3414	3072
19							
20	materials DVD-A	2795	2823	2851	2880	2908	2938
21	materials DVD-B	21296	19166	17250	15525	13972	12575
22		--------	--------	--------	--------	--------	--------
23	TOTAL	30369	27758	25412	23305	21413	19715
24							
25	GROSS PROFIT	8558	10779	12738	14463	15976	17299
26							
27	TABLES	Jan price per unit	Price growth	January sales	Sales growth	Material cost per unit	Labour cost per unit
28							
29	DVD-A	123	0.98	43	1.01	65	25
30	DVD-B	278	1.1	121	0.9	176	43

The example in Figure 7.1 concerns the projected sales, sales income and costs for two types of DVD disc player, DVD-a and DVD-b. Figure 7.1 would be displayed on the screen. Figure 7.2 shows the logic behind the model from rows 4–30 and columns A–C as it would be entered at the keyboard. Text is clearly shown as enclosed by quotation marks. The separation of data in rows 29 and 30 from the logic of the model makes it easy to carry out 'what if' analysis. Suppose that the managing director of the company wanted to know the impact of an increase in material cost of components for the DVD-a model of DVD player. After the estimated figure has been entered in row 29 column F the spreadsheet program will automatically recalculate all cells that are affected by the change. The managing director can carry out as many 'what ifs' as required.

As well as standard arithmetic functions, most spreadsheets have the ability to calculate financial ratios such as internal rates of return and net present value, along with common statistical functions such as standard deviation.

A feature of many spreadsheet packages is that the individual spreadsheet models may be linked together so that figures in one spreadsheet can be fed into another. For instance, the cost side of the production of DVD players would be modelled by the production department. The responsibility for developing the sales forecasting part of the model in

Figure 7.2 The logic part of the model in Figure 7.1

	A	B	C
4	"SALES"	"Jan"	"Feb"
5	"units DVD-a"	D29	B5*E29
6	"units DVD-b"	D30	B6*E30
7			
8	"price DVD-a"	B29	B8*C29
9	"price DVD-b"	B30	B9*C30
10			
11	"sales revenue DVD-a"	B5*B8	C5*C8
12	"sales revenue DVD-b"	B6*B9	C6*C9
13		"----------------"	"----------------"
14	"TOTAL"	B11+B12	C11+C12
15			
16	"COSTS"		
17	"labour DVD-a"	G29*B5	G29*C5
18	"labour DVD-b"	G30*B5	G30*C5
19			
20	"materials DVD-a"	F29*B5	F29*C5
21	"materials DVD-b"	F30*B5	F30*C5
22		"----------------"	"----------------"
23	"TOTAL"	SUM(B20:B21)	SUM(C20:C21)
24			
25	"GROSS PROFIT"	B14–B23	C14–C23
26			
27	"TABLES"	"Jan price"	"Price"
28		"per unit"	"Growth"
29	"DVD-a"	123	0.98
30	"DVD-b"	278	1.1

Figure 7.1 might lie with the sales department. Selected parts of each of these separate spreadsheets, saved on disk, can then be linked to a third spreadsheet, which produces the projected profit/loss forecast for the next six months. Changes, or 'what ifs', in the subsidiary spreadsheets feed through to the main spreadsheet by way of the linking.

Because spreadsheet packages represent information to the user in rows and columns, they are particularly suitable for tasks that require report production. They can therefore be used to produce profit and loss, balance sheets and other reports. Most modern spreadsheets also provide the facility to present information in other forms, such as charts, diagrams and graphs.

Spreadsheet packages also enable the development of models that interact and extract data stored in a database. This is important where future rolling projections based on current rolling figures are needed.

Modern spreadsheet packages incorporate their own very high-level programming languages. Although limited, these enable the user to write various application programs that interact with the spreadsheet model or that control the interaction of the spreadsheet with the user.

The use of spreadsheets as an interactive modelling tool is limited by the matrix nature of the model representation and data input. Only applications that are high in number handling as distinct from text handling are suitable for spreadsheet applications.

There are other drawbacks to the use of spreadsheets. Spreadsheet model design, although capable of being carried out by end users, is time-consuming. Unless much 'what if' investigation is to be carried out or the same relationships used again and again it may be quicker and more flexible to use pen and paper. Spreadsheet package developers are conscious of this limitation and are constantly adding new facilities to speed up complex model building. It is also now becoming obvious that spreadsheet model development cannot be carried out in an ad hoc manner if reliable, testable and amendable models are to be built. It is necessary to follow good modelling practice.

Another limitation of spreadsheets is in their ability to display only a small part of the spreadsheet at a time on the screen. Package manufacturers have attempted to overcome this by the provision of **windows**. Windows show several selected rectangular sections of the spreadsheet simultaneously on different parts of the screen. A facility is often provided to split a window into two panes, allowing the user to freeze one pane, for example a section containing the headings, and manipulate the other.

Despite these limitations, spreadsheet packages will continue to be used widely in business, especially accounting and decision making, not least because models can be built using them by those without technical computing skills.

Spreadsheet design

Spreadsheets may be very large, containing several different sheets, each comprising several hundred rows and columns. Data may be entered directly on to the sheet or into a 'form' that encapsulates the contents of a single row of the sheet. The results may be displayed on the sheet in numerical form or may be converted into a textual equivalent, a graphical representation or a summary report. In all these cases, the development and presentation of a spreadsheet should be in accordance with a systematic method. If this is not done, individuals may have difficulty in using the spreadsheet – data entry, report and logic functions may not be clearly distinguished. Also, the process of building the spreadsheet can, as with software, yield errors, and these must be capable of discovery and identification before rectification.

A well-designed and robust spreadsheet should distinguish clearly the data input, working formulae and output aspects of a spreadsheet model. Other areas should be reserved for general information for the user and for the reporting of error conditions. The main areas can be developed in a diagonal formation on a single sheet (see Figure 7.3(a)), or on separate sheets within a workbook (see Figure 7.3(b)), to ensure that operations on complete rows or columns do not affect the contents or display of entries in other main areas. Spreadsheets have the facility to protect cells or blocks of cells. This prevents the contents of the cell being altered without first disabling the protection. Once a model has been designed, all cells except for data input cells are protected as a precaution against inadvertent alteration. The five main areas are:

1. **User information:** When the spreadsheet is loaded the user should automatically be placed in this area of the spreadsheet. The information area gives essential information about the purpose and limitations of the spreadsheet. Users may not be designers. If so, their knowledge of the spreadsheet may be minimal and this area is essential.

2. **Data input:** Users should only be able to alter the contents of the spreadsheet by inputting data in this area. The data input area contains no formulae. It is the only area of the spreadsheet not covered by protection. It may be implemented by using data entry forms. Data validation checks and routines may be included to ensure, for example, that the items entered are within specified ranges, types or prescribed lists.

Figure 7.3 The five main areas of spreadsheet design

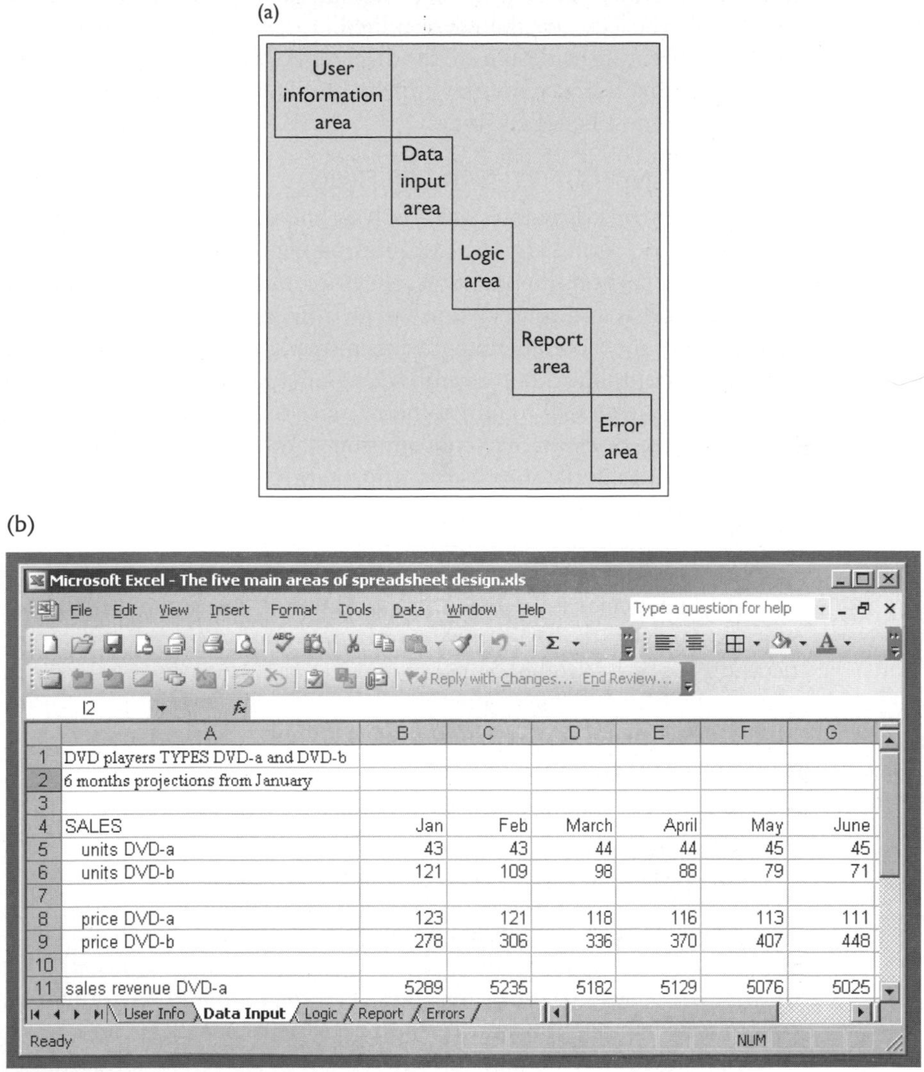

(a)

(b)

Source: Financial Times

3. **Logic:** This area contains the formulae to carry out the calculations of the spreadsheet. It should contain no data.

4. **Report:** The output of the logic area is taken and displayed in the correct format. This may include graphical display. The design of the report area is based on considerations of the optimum way to present information for user needs.

5. **Error:** Spreadsheets contain some functions that are suitable for error checking. Others can be built into the design of the spreadsheet. For instance, certain data inputs may require a set of percentages to be entered, which should total 100. A simple check and display of error in the error section is an aid to data input.

A spreadsheet is a decision support tool. In order that decisions may be supported properly, the output of the spreadsheet should present information in the most helpful way. It is therefore good practice to design the report area first. The data requirements and finally the logic are then determined.

Good spreadsheet design methods ensure that the model performs operations correctly and that users, who may not be builders, are presented with information organized in the most beneficial way.

The use of expert system tools and shells

Systems involving data retrieval, analysis and computation do not exhaust the range of systems for decision support. Decision makers often seek advice from human experts before taking action. For example, the doctor seeks additional expertise from a specialist for diagnosis and prescription for an ailment with which the doctor is not familiar. The accountant recommending a business plan for a client will seek specialist advice from a tax consultant. Before embarking on a major contract with another company, a business executive will require expert advice on that company's financial health.

All of these cases involve consultation with an expert prior to decision taking. The expert provides decision-relevant information not purely by analysis or computation but by applying the facts of a particular case to a body of knowledge possessed internally by that expert.

Expert systems are computer systems that mimic the expert in being effective consultants in a particular knowledge area or domain. In common with experts they can provide explanation for their advice and conclusions. They are distinguished from other decision support systems by possessing general knowledge in a specific domain of expertise. This knowledge is often represented in the form of interconnected rules. An example of a rule from a system designed to aid a bank manager on whether to grant a loan to a client might be:

If the client is a home owner then establish:

1. the amount of the mortgage;
2. whether there have been any payment defaults.

Many similar rules would be incorporated into such a system. The aim of the system would be to provide a recommendation, based on the bank's standard lending policy, on whether to lend to the client, the size of the loan and any other conditions attaching to it. It is decision support rather than decision replacing because it is just one of the factors that the bank manager would take into account. There may be other circumstances, not covered by the system, that the bank manager finds relevant. Using discretion, the manager could 'overrule' the advice of the expert system.

Expert systems are used where *reasoning*, as distinct from computation, is important in providing advice. These systems are particularly suitable for handling vague and uncertain reasoning under situations of incomplete information and data. This is also an important characteristic of an expert.

Not all expert systems are used for decision support. Other uses include training personnel, archiving important knowledge in an organization and aiding a person in a complex procedure such as registration of a company under the Data Protection Act. Their use in all these spheres is increasing and will continue to increase over the coming decade. Expert system decision support for business will be an important area of artificial intelligence.

Expert systems can be developed in a conventional programming language such as C++ or using a language more suited to artificial intelligence such as PROLOG or LISP.

These approaches, though flexible, are time-consuming and costly. Expert systems can be built using **expert system shells**. In essence, these are expert systems from which all domain-specific knowledge has been removed. All that is left is the shell, comprising the user interface, the programmed reasoning strategies and a knowledge entry module through which the expert's knowledge is initially input into the system for later reference. Expert system shells allow speedy prototyping of expert systems – often by end users. There are a large number of shells on the market for use with PCs, minicomputers and mainframe computers. Examples are CLIPS, Leonardo and XPertRule.

Shells that are used to prototype decision support systems suffer many limitations. The chief one is that they are not very flexible in the ways that they allow knowledge to be represented and the ways in which reasoning can be carried out. **Expert system tools** provide a middle ground of increased flexibility over shells while avoiding the time-consuming and costly design of an expert system using conventional languages. Among other features, these tools provide:

- control over ways of representing knowledge;
- control over the reasoning strategies adopted by the expert system;
- the ability to use interactive graphics in the development of the system; and
- the ability to customize the user interface.

Expert system tools are suitable for a prototyping approach to the development of expert decision support systems. They are often sophisticated and require extensive training to use. They are not associated with 'casual' end-user development, as for instance spreadsheets are.

Examples of commercial expert system tools are KEE, ART and Goldworks. Expert systems are covered in more detail in Chapter 18.

The use of model generators

Spreadsheet packages are designed primarily for use with PCs. Although their facilities are now extended to include graphical presentation and they have their own languages, often called macro languages, they are still based around the concept of the grid-like worksheet. Model generators are more extensive packages, often mainframe-based, that enable speedy development of a wide range of models using interactive design techniques.

All packages provide model generation facilities. Individual packages differ in the additional features offered, but the following are common:

- sophisticated report generation facilities;
- capacity to carry out complex statistical analysis;
- capacity to carry out time series analysis, linear programming and solutions to linear equations;
- Monte Carlo risk analysis simulation;
- sensitivity analysis;
- sophisticated financial and mathematical functions;
- consolidation of different models;
- interaction with a database.

Model generators incorporate many of the features of very high-level languages, spreadsheet packages and statistical packages. Because of the complexity in the range of features offered, they are not suitable for use by casual end-users.

7.2.2 Group decision support

The decision support systems considered so far have been concerned with computerized support for an individual taking a decision characterized as semi-structured or unstructured. Many decisions taken in an organization will be taken not by a single individual but as a result of group deliberations. **Group decision support systems (GDSS)** provide computer-based support for group decisions.

Groups typically consist of fewer than 20 people, who arrive at decisions through communication. The communication serves to share information and facilitate the decision-making process. The decision may be taken by vote but is more often by negotiation, consensus or preference ranking.

Three types of computer-based support are available:

1. **Decision networks:** This type allows participants to communicate through networks with each other or with a central database. Applications software may use commonly shared models to provide support. The commonest implementation is using a local area network and PCs. The technology filters out many of the typical group dynamics of a participative meeting.

2. **Decision room:** Participants are located in one place – the decision room. The purpose of this is to enhance participant interaction and decision making by computerized support within a fixed period of time using a facilitator. Specific computer-based tools are provided (see below).

3. **Tele/computer conferencing:** If groups are composed of members or subgroups that are geographically dispersed, tele/computer conferencing provides for interactive connection between two or more decision rooms. This interaction will involve transmission of computerized and audiovisual information.

Whereas decision networks can be viewed as the use of local area networks, for decision making involving groups the decision room is an entirely new development.

The decision room is used by an organization to create an environment in which groups may enhance their decisions. The decision-making process is guided by a **facilitator,** who is usually not from within the organization but a trained professional in group dynamics brought in for the decision-making sessions. There will also usually be a computer controller, whose responsibility it is to maintain computer communications and software support within the room.

The decision room (an example of which can be seen in Figure 7.4) consists of a table with networked workstations for the participants and workstations for the facilitator and controller. The screen of any node of the network can be projected on to the wall screen. The facilitator can also ensure that, if required, any participant's screen can replace some or all of the other nodes for demonstration or interactive purposes. Breakout rooms, used for smaller discussions, are also equipped with similar networked machines. A combination of overhead projector, flipchart, photocopier and other presentation devices is also provided.

The software may take many forms but will always consist of tools that aid group decision making, are easy to use and are interactive. Examples of software (as well as spreadsheet and statistical/graphical packages) are:

■ **Brainstorming:** Brainstorming software may be used at any stage of the proceedings but is particularly valuable in the early stages, when members of the group need to think and converse freely on issues. A problem or statement can be entered for

Figure 7.4 A typical layout for a decision room

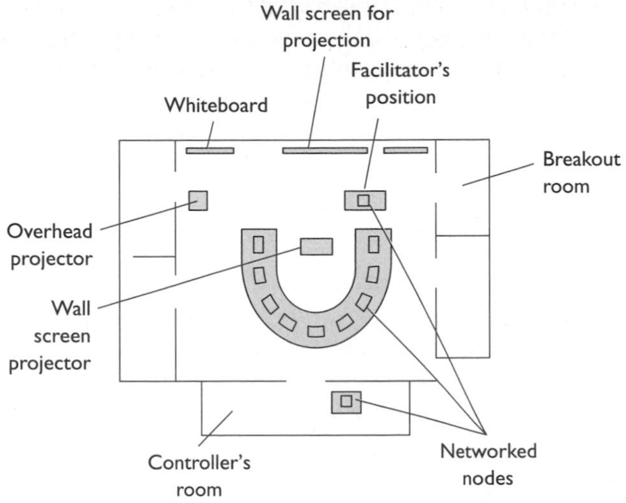

Source: Financial Times

comment. This will appear on all screens. Each individual may then produce comments, which are consolidated and displayed anonymously. The tool increases creativity and lateral thinking.

■ **Voting:** It is frequently important to obtain a swift view on the acceptability of proposals from a group perspective before proceeding. Voting software enables this to happen. It is not merely restricted to yes/no but will also enable different formats for expressing preferences, including multiple choice and 1–5 scales.

■ **Policy formation:** Software can aid policy formation by allowing decision makers to identify connections and relations between issues and communicate this to all present for comment.

The software will be used as part of a methodology followed by the facilitator in arriving at decisions. Much work is still to be done in the area of development of tools to support decision rooms.

Decision rooms are expensive to equip, and all but the largest organizations would find it difficult to justify the expenditure, particularly as the use of the decision room is not regarded as an everyday occurrence. It is becoming more common for establishments, especially academic institutions, to hire out these facilities to organizations when needed.

It is difficult to analyse the effectiveness of these group decision support systems, although it appears that they are most likely to be beneficial (and to be regarded as beneficial by participants) for larger group sizes (eight and above). Participants are aware of the need to impose some structure on groups of this size and welcome the direction given by the decision room and the facilitator.

Recently, a number of businesses have been making use of web-based facilities that have emerged from social networking activities to support group decision making. Two particular approaches have been adopted:

1. **Blogs:** A blog (the term is a portmanteau of 'web log') allows a facility for the user, or blogger, to record an online journal. In a group decision support environment this

can be used collaboratively by setting access rights and making the contents available to relevant individuals. The resource can drastically cut down the volume of irrelevant email that often characterizes group projects.

2. **Wikis:** A wiki is a collaboratively constructed web resource, typically a web page on a company intranet or portal. Participants in a wiki can add additional content and hyperlinks to develop and augment the resource. This device can cut down the need for face-to-face meetings and can eliminate the need for extensive use of email distribution lists and the resulting traffic.

7.2.3 Document management systems

Managers, in making decisions, need information. Prior to the common use of computerized information systems, this information was typically held in the form of documents or derived from these – data on source documents, summarized documents, intelligence reports and so on. These documents were held in manual filing systems and the filing systems could grow large in size. Sophisticated filing systems, involving indexing, needed to be developed in order that the right documents could be assembled to aid any given decision.

The advent of computers, and particularly large and cheap means of electronic storage on disk, enabled such documents to be stored electronically. Initially this was by scanning the documents and holding images on file. These were then indexed and could be retrieved electronically. This enabled remote and fast access to information. Later, optical character recognition enabled many documents to be converted to electronic characters on scanning. This had advantages in that indexing and retrieval of these documents could be based on content. The latest developmental stage is to omit the use of paper in the production of the stored document. The documents themselves are produced electronically and stored electronically. The documents may go through several stages in production with different personnel (with different functions) inputting data at various stages. This also fits very neatly with the idea of an electronic office.

A **document management system (DMS)** is a computer-based system involving procedures and software for the storage, retrieval, tracking and management of electronic documents or scanned paper documents. The system will typically have a number of functions

Features of a document management system

1. **Hardware:** The system is usually maintained on a server with the document management software controlling access for users over an intranet.

2. **Input:** Documents may be input through batch scanning of input documents. Incoming documents may be in a range of formats and sizes and modern systems will cope with these. Intelligent data capture involves optical character recognition of some or all of the input data, especially that associated with key identifiers for the organization, e.g. patient number for a hospital, customer number for a business. These will be linked to other records held. Copies of output documents will be stored electronically (as input) for records management. As electronic documents are created and passed from person to person (function to function) these will be stored and tracked. This is particularly important for documents which go through various stages of authoring and approval. On any of the above methods metadata on the documents may be input and stored – such as author names, dates produced or key words for search.

3. **Retrieval:** Documents may be retrieved flexibly. This may involve searches on multiple key words (which may be incomplete) and using Boolean constructs such as and/or. Depending on the system and documents used this may involve content as well as predefined indexes and key words.

4. **Integration and sharing:** Documents which are held electronically may be produced by, updated by or read by other software applications. In order to carry out this degree of sharing by different applications (often produced by different software companies) the use of open standards for the format of such documents is used.

5. **Security:** Document management systems provide for enhanced security of documents. These are now not stored on an open folder system on shared drives with the minimal security of folder passwords. Systems allow for a range of permissions for different users for different classes of documents. For example, one class of users may be able to read instances of a type of document, another may be able to update and another also create and delete these instances.

6. **Versioning:** Documents may go though various updates over time yet it is important to maintain older versions – often for legal purposes. Document management systems provide sophisticated versioning capability.

Benefits of a document management system

- Reduced physical storage space (over a manual system).
- Flexible retrieval in terms of targeted search, speed of retrieval and availability across the organization.
- Managed availability of documentation distribution – different entitlements for different users for different classes of documentation can easily be specified.
- Improved security of access (and consequent management of access to ensure compliance with data legislation).
- Enhanced internal communication and operations.
- Ability to implement workflow for the production and approval of documents.

As well as these advantages, document management systems will increase the competitive edge of an organization by improving customer satisfaction and internal operations.

Increasingly document management systems are using output directed to the Web to be read by web browsers with key input also being achieved through a web interface. With this comes the ability to manipulate the format so that it appears in the most appropriate way for different users. The content has to be managed rather than the document. The emphasis is moving to **content management systems** to manage the content of the documentation rather than its format – the latter being a function of its view on the Web.

7.2.4 Digital dashboards

In a previous era, when transport was the horse-drawn carriage, the dashboard was the piece of wood placed in a carriage in order to prevent the wheels splashing the driver. With the advent of the horseless carriage, i.e. the motor car, the name was retained for the piece of wood between the driver and the engine. This housed a series of dials and lights which illustrated key performance indicators for the driver concerning the functioning of the car. For instance, gauges indicated petrol remaining, speed, oil pressure, battery charge and cooling water temperature. Things have changed for the motor car although the concept of the key performance indicator still remains and modern dashboards for motor cars still indicate measures of key performance in various ways, often augmented by warning lights or sounds when these indicators 'go critical'.

The idea of providing information from various sources to a decision maker is not new. However, Microsoft was one of the early pioneers of the concept of the digital dashboard (also known as the **executive dashboard** or **enterprise dashboard**) in the 1990s as part of an internal project to allow senior executives to monitor the performance of the company on a daily basis. The idea was that, just as with the motor car dashboard, the status of key variables for the company would be shown together on one screen. This would provide a snapshot of company performance and enable more informed decision making.

A digital dashboard may provide information on the screen in a variety of ways using visual displays such as tables, graphs, charts and maps as well as gauges and traffic lights. These display the values of key variables in the organization. Many dashboards also offer the ability to 'drill down' to gain further detail. They often will sense real-time information to give an accurate snapshot of the required key variables. A recent survey (Hurwitz & Associates, 2005) of IT companies in the USA showed that 60% had implemented dashboards with 40% intending to do so over the following 18 months. Those surveyed indicated that the average number of different sources needed to make a decision ranged between six and ten. These could be displayed on the dashboard. An example of a digital dashboard is shown in Figure 7.5.

Figure 7.5 An example of a digital dashboard

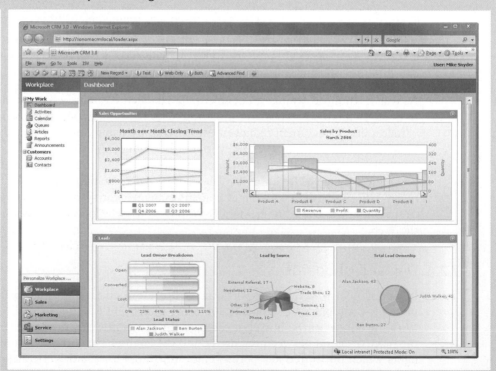

Mini case 7.1

Digital dashboards

Until very recently, performance management at Derby City Council involved keying information from dozens of sources into a Microsoft Access database. This then formed the basis for reports on individual sectors or lines of activity. John Cornall, assistant IT director at the council, recalls 'a massive data collection exercise, where as soon as we had reported on one quarter, we had to start out all over again on the next quarter'. But central government was becoming more preoccupied with performance targets, and Mr Cornall and his colleagues had to find a way to meet a host of external key performance indicators that had been introduced to monitor local government performance.

Over the past four years, Local Public Service Agreements have been introduced for local authorities, such as Derby. These stipulated performance targets that were tied to funding. The idea is that issues of public concern, such as the removal of abandoned vehicles and underachievement in schools, are treated as priorities. Hitting LPSA targets entails applying complex formulas in order to prove that the local authority has really changed services for the better. The result was the introduction of a performance management system.

'The beauty of it is that we can have all of our existing data input but also take a step backwards and capture more from our systems. It is very, very simple. Each performance indicator compares items numerically and we then monitor that against a full year, or quarterly target.' Known as 'Performance Eye' at the council, the system has just completed its first full quarter.

Derby has veered as far away from spreadsheet-based IT as possible with Performance Eye, relying instead on an extremely visual front end. 'It is very graphical; you see a digital dashboard with red, amber or green colours in bar charts and graphs to indicate just how the council is performing in a particular area against its targets', explains Mr Cornall. The previous system resulted in lots of hard copy littered with tables and figures. 'We had taken the Access database to the absolute limits of what it could do', he adds, 'and it did not capture the essence of performance management. Performance Eye highlights what needs improving and triggers a demand for an action plan to rectify things. It then treats that plan as a key performance indicator and monitors it. We intend to open it up over the Internet so council tax payers can see the performance management dashboard themselves.'

Adapted from: **Performance for the public**
Michael Dempsey, FT.com, 6 October 2004

Questions

1. What is the City Council in the article attempting to achieve by the introduction of digital dashboards?

2. To what extent is this an exercise in fragmentation or unification of decision support systems?

7.2.5 Online analytical processing (OLAP)

Many traditional databases are involved in recording day-to-day operational activities of the business. This activity is termed online transaction processing (OLTP) and is typical of information systems such as airline bookings and banking systems. Typical features of these systems are that:

- they need extensive data control and availability;
- they have high multi-user throughput;
- they require a fast response; and
- they are normally used by clerical users rather than managers.

Once an OLTP system has been established, it is possible to use the data that it generates to aid decision making. Reports and summaries can be drawn from the operational data to inform the decision-making process. This mode of working is described as online analytical processing (OLAP). The characteristics are:

- it involves trend analysis and forecasting;
- it uses summarized historical data (from operational databases);
- it entails complex queries, often building very large tables;
- it is read-intensive;
- the decisions it informs are strategic, so response is time-critical; and
- the users are managers/analysts.

A major problem with performing OLAP queries is that these compete with OLTP systems for resources, leading to poor response times. A solution is to extract and summarize the data in a data warehouse.

Mini case 7.2

FT

Online analytical processing

It might sound like a type of Scandinavian folk dance, but Olap is an acronym for online analytical processing, a valuable type of software that helps users analyse data stored in a database.

Transforming information from raw data into a wide variety of multidimensional representations, Olap tools are to data what a gourmet chef is to the humble risotto. Olap tools can do clever tricks, performing feats such as trend analysis over sequential time periods, slicing subsets of data for on-screen viewing and creating summary-level models across the different dimensions and hierarchies of a database. Users can explore their data from a historical point of view and use 'what-if' data model scenarios to project ahead into the future.

So how do these Olap tools work?

While the souped-up data are generally accessed through a simple web interface, the brains behind the operation is the Olap server, a high-capacity, multi-user data manipulation engine specially designed to operate on multidimensional data structures.

Sitting between a client and a database management system, the Olap server understands how data is organized in the database and has special functions for analysing the data. This can be done in a variety of ways, which can affect response times.

Adapted from: **Olap**
© Chloe Veltman, with permission. FT.com, 29 October 2003

7.2.6 Data warehousing

A **data warehouse** is a massive independent business database system that is populated with data that has been extracted from a range of sources. The data can be collected on both a current and a historical basis and can come from both internal and external sources. The data is held separately from its origin and is used to help to improve the decision-making process. Any data that might be of relevance and interest to the decision makers of the business can be included in the warehouse.

Data warehouse architecture

A data warehouse is a collection of subject-oriented data integrated from various operational databases and other external sources. It is usually accessed by end users employing graphical analysis tools and tends to offer read-only access. A diagram showing the use of a typical data warehouse is provided in Figure 7.6.

As the data has been taken off-line and placed into the warehouse, the query functions no longer take valuable system resources from the processing of day-to-day transactions. A corollary of this is that once created, the data warehouse becomes instantly out of date. A policy of updating the warehouse at appropriate intervals must therefore be established.

In some situations it may be appropriate to partition or copy a subset of the data warehouse into a smaller, self-contained collection of data. These smaller versions of data warehouses are often termed **data marts**. The separation of data might be carried out on a departmental or subject-related basis. A data mart can offer improvements in speed of access and search times by localizing the data, but it introduces yet more potential for inconsistencies. Data marts often provide the source data for online analytical processing and for decision support systems.

The stages in creating and maintaining a data warehouse are normally as follows:

1. **Data extraction:** Data is collected from a range of sources using gateways, e.g. the open database connectivity (ODBC) protocol, and incorporated into the warehouse.
2. **Data cleaning:** Where possible, missing fields are completed, and inconsistencies are reduced or eliminated. For example, data containing the sex of an individual might be stored as 'm/f', 'male/female', '0/1' or even 'true/false'. Data cleaning will ensure that all fields are stored in a consistent format, e.g. 'm/f'.
3. **Data loading:** The data is summarized and aggregated with the existing warehouse data.
4. **Optimization:** Indices are built to improve data access times.

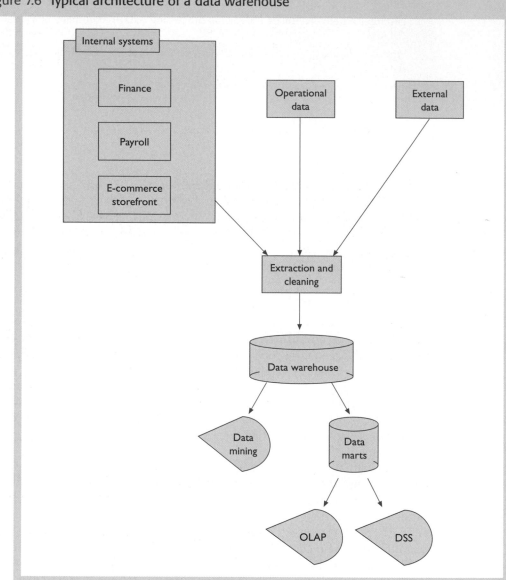

Figure 7.6 Typical architecture of a data warehouse

Searching the warehouse

Data tends to have a multidimensional structure. A typical example might be information regarding sales of a particular product over different locations over a period of time sold by different sales representatives. A range of techniques exists to allow the data to be presented in different formats.

Pivoting

Different managers might want different views of this data. A sales team manager might want data summarized by sales representatives over time. A product manager might want to see summaries of production across different regions.

The ability to switch between different perspectives on the same data is known as pivoting. Figure 7.7(a) shows an extract of data illustrating sales of different insurance policies by a team of agents working in different geographical areas. Figure 7.7(b) shows chronologically how each agent has performed, subtotalled where appropriate by region. Figure 7.7(c) shows the effect of pivoting the same data again, this time summarizing the figures by agent and policy type.

Figure 7.7 Pivoting data to provide different perspectives

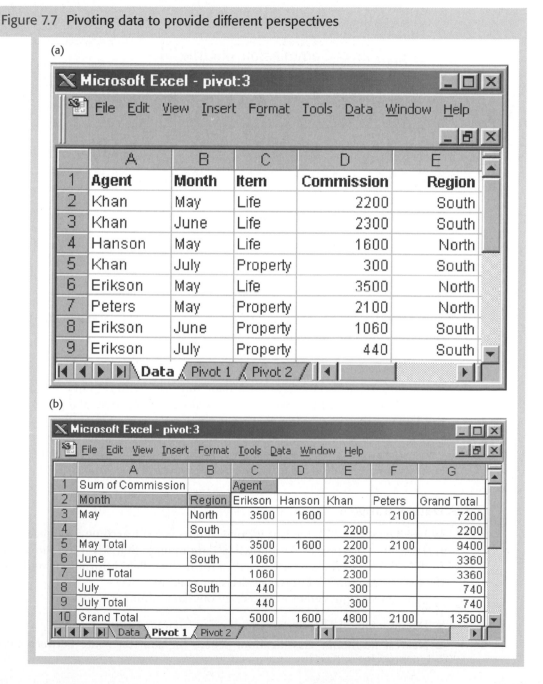

(a)

(b)

Figure 7.7 (cont'd)

(c)

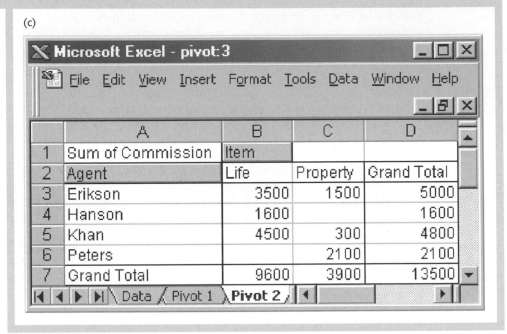

Roll-up and drill-down

The level of detail required from the data warehouse will vary according to context: precise figures can be obtained by drilling down into the data; a higher-level summary can be obtained by rolling up the data.

Slice and dice

The ability to partition a view of the data and work with that in isolation is known as slice and dice. Like drill-down, it allows a more focused view of a particular section of the data warehouse to be obtained.

A data warehouse is an extremely sophisticated piece of software and consequently is very expensive to create and maintain. Although the potential benefits are great, the costs can prove prohibitive for smaller organizations.

7.2.7 Data mining

Where data is held in large sets, it can be interrogated searching for trends, patterns and relationships. This process is known as data mining. Statistical techniques are applied to the contents of the data set to search for this 'hidden' information and the resulting discoveries can further inform the decision-making process.

Typical techniques employed to carry out data mining include:

- **Decision tables:** This topic is discussed in Chapter 12.
- **Nearest neighbour classification:** Where the shortest route between two items is calculated.

- **Neural networks:** Where processors often acting in parallel mimic the operation of the human brain by applying rules to local data sets.
- **Rule induction – using if–then rules:** This topic is discussed in Chapter 18.
- **K-means clustering:** This entails partitioning an aggregate set of data into logical groups.

A typical use of data mining might be as follows. A business might require sales representatives to travel across a number of geographical areas. The data concerning the details of a sale, the time of sale, location of sale, volume sold etc. for each salesperson would be stored. Mining the data might reveal that certain sales representatives are more or less productive at certain times in the year or in certain geographic regions of the country. It could also show that certain products sell particularly well independently of the person involved or that there are seasonal trends affecting the sales. These patterns might not be apparent from a cursory glance at the raw data but may be revealed using the statistical techniques outlined above. The results of data mining such as this might lead to strategic changes in the operation of the business in an attempt to gain a competitive advantage.

Often the results of data mining are presented visually to facilitate data analysis. A scatter chart, for example, plotting the age of victims of crime against the age of their alleged assailants, might reveal patterns which would assist detectives in building a profile of a typical suspect of such crime.

7.3 Business intelligence from analysing human behaviour

There are a number of tools and techniques that consider human behaviour as the basis for generating business intelligence. These include customer relationship management and human resource management systems. These are each looked at in greater detail in the following sections.

7.3.1 Customer relationship management systems

Businesses depend on customers to buy products and services and pay for them. These revenues finance the ongoing survival of the business – pay its staff salaries, maintain the premises, pay its suppliers etc. It is therefore important to ensure that the customer is the focus of significant effort on the part of the business for its survival. Other organizations may be funded in different ways – for example partly or wholly by government from taxpayers' revenues. These will also have customers who may or may not pay for the services provided – for example, university students, hospital patients. In these cases the focus is increasingly also on the 'customer' as organizations use 'customer satisfaction' as one of the measures of achievement. **Customer relationship management (CRM)** is a philosophy which puts the customer as the central focus of the organization and seeks to manage that relationship in the way most beneficial to the organization. Software is employed in order to achieve this. **Customer relationship management systems** are applications which seek to:

- provide information on existing customers to the sales force to enable the organization to increase customer profitability (sales);

- identify and target new markets for the creation of new customers (marketing);
- provide a range of services to customers to enhance their satisfaction and the effectiveness of the organization in meeting their needs (customer service);
- manage relationships with partner organizations.

Implementation of customer relationship management systems

The decision to implement a customer relationship management system is a business decision and like any such decision it will have to be justified on a cost (software, development and training) versus a benefit (increased revenue, profit, and customer satisfaction) basis. In order to ensure the success of any implementation it is important that the organization has a prior culture of customer focus. There are several large suites of application software available on the market (for example the Oracle Siebel or the SAP systems) as well as smaller packages for smaller or niche businesses. In implementing a CRM system a business may:

- **Develop bespoke applications software:** This is only available for larger businesses with systems development departments or with the finance to purchase the software development from outside. The approach will generate the best fit for the organization but at substantial cost and often considerable development time.
- **Purchase applications software:** This will be the cheapest and quickest solution. However, it is unlikely that the purchased solution will entirely fit the current operations of the business. The business may of course use this development opportunity to redesign its business processes.
- **Tailor standard applications software systems:** This approach may be taken by all sizes of business. In essence it involves the purchase (or rental) of proprietary CRM systems and then employing a third party (usually the organization producing the software) to tailor the package to the needs of the business.

More aspects of these general approaches to applications are covered in Chapter 3.

Components of customer relationship management systems

These will vary from business to business and from one proprietary system to another. There are themes and functions which are commonly covered. These are sales, marketing and customer service (see above).

Sales

The aim is to increase profitability by focusing sales staff attention on the most profitable existing customers and provide information on these customers in order to increase sales. To achieve this some (or all) of the following will be provided by the CRM:

- sales account information giving past records, and current contact information for customers;
- product information which can be aligned to customers' requirements;
- the generation and tracking of quotations;
- generation and management of orders;

- controlled access facilities to other departments (finance, delivery etc.);
- sales analysis facilities.

One of the measures of success of a CRM system, and particularly of its sales side, is the amount of customer churn. The **churn rate** is a measure of the number of customers a business is losing, i.e. stopping purchase of its products or services. Businesses with high churn rates are usually in decline or in danger.

Marketing

It is not sufficient for a business to rely on existing customers and their traditional sales patterns. It must generate different additional sales to existing customer and generate new and profitable customers. Three marketing concepts are important:

- **Cross-selling of other products:** this is when complementary products to an existing sale are made. For instance, a used car company may sell various kinds of repair warranties with its cars, or a travel agent may sell travel insurance with its holidays.
- **Upselling of products:** this is where a higher value product or service is sold to a customer to replace a lower value product or service previously purchased. For instance, hire car companies may routinely offer more luxurious models at special rates. Credit card companies target 'good' customers for higher priced accounts offering premium services.
- **Bundling:** this is where a range of products is sold where the cost of the bundle is less than the some of its parts. Thus the customer who wishes to purchase broadband, phone, digital TV and mobile phone services will be attracted by a provider who can bundle these services together at special rates.

In order to achieve this it must be able to analyse markets and target the appropriate market directly. A CRM will be able to:

- analyse existing customer data for patterns;
- accept and analyse incoming data for prospective customers. This may be purchased from third party sources;
- assist in the design of new products for customers;
- provide operational support for the identification and follow-up of leads;
- provide operational support for the generation of targeted marketing campaigns (such as direct mail, e-mail and phone);
- capitalize on the opportunities of cross-selling, upselling and bundling.

Customer service

Customers may contact the business with a wide variety of requests. These could include the generation of a sale, the status of a current order or payment, account information, product information, help services, or technical support. It is common for there to be one point of contact and then the customer is routed through the relevant departments. CRM modules assist in the recording of information, including that supplied by the customer, and the passing of this *en route* to ensure that information, once supplied by the customer, is not requested again. This builds up a profile of the request and leads to more effective handling of the customer. Consequent customer satisfaction will promote loyalty. Software also handles the increasing use of mailboxes for incoming e-mail requests. In summary, CRM supports the handling of customer service thereby assisting the operation of call centres and help desks by:

- routing inbound customer service communications;
- managing service orders and contracts;
- managing complaints and returns;
- managing warranties;
- providing help desk support;
- providing service analysis facilities.

Mini case 7.3

Managing undesirable customers

The cost of customer acquisition in many industries can be high, but some large retailers are investing in computer systems to help them get rid of customers. These systems identify 'devils' – unwanted customers who cost the retailers money.

'In all retail businesses there is a segment of customers which is unprofitable, and often this is far larger than expected', said Tony Stockil, chief executive of retail consultancy Javelin Group. 'This varies by industry, and in some cases this segment may be as large as 20% of the entire customer base.'

Devil consumers' behaviour ranges from the legal to the fraudulent. At one end of the scale are devils who only visit a store to buy loss leaders. At the other end are criminals who carry out scams such as buying an item to get a valid receipt, then stealing the same item and returning it for a refund using the original receipt.

Other devil activities include wardrobing – the practice of buying an expensive item of clothing such as a cocktail dress, wearing it for one night with the labels tucked out of sight, and returning it the next day for a refund; pack attacks – damaging the packaging of an article on display in the hope of buying it later at a discount; and excessive returning, which may involve buying the same item of clothing in many different sizes and colours with the intention of returning all but one item after a few days.

To combat this, some American retailers are turning to a data warehouse service, operated by a California-based company called The Return Exchange, to identify customers carrying out wardrobing or fraudulent returns. Every time a return is made, relevant transaction data and customer identity information from a driver licence or other ID card is sent to The Return Exchange where it is stored in its database. By analysing large samples of customer returns data, the company helps retailers recognize the mark of a devil: specific patterns of returns behaviour that indicate excessive returning or return fraud.

When a customer takes an item to a store to return it, that customer's previous return history at that store – which includes the number, frequency and value of returns that have previously been made – is examined to see if it matches the profile of a devil. If so, the retailer can decide whether the customer should be given a warning or refused a return. Devil customers who are consistently refused returns are thus forced either to change their habits and become profitable customers, or take their unprofitable custom elsewhere.

Adapted from: **How to get rid of 'devil customers'**
Paul Rubens, 13 June 2007

Questions

1. What aspects of undesirable behaviour are the customer relationship management systems in the article addressing?
2. What facilities do CRM systems offer for dealing with undesirable customers?

Partner relationship management

A business may also work through partner organizations rather than directly with end-point customers. This for instance would happen when a manufacturing company relies on third party outlets to sell its products and handle much of the direct contact with customers. The relationships with the partner organizations (having many of the properties of a customer) need management in order that the business can maintain its profitability and effectiveness. After all, the perception and success of its product in the market will be influenced by the performance of these partner organizations. CRM systems often have modules which manage partner relationships. Typically these will:

- manage partner account and contract information;
- manage orders and sales though the partner organization;
- provide information on products to the partners;
- forecast and analyse sales though the partner channel.

The main functions of CRM applications are summarized in Figure 7.8.

Figure 7.8 Customer Relationship Management Systems

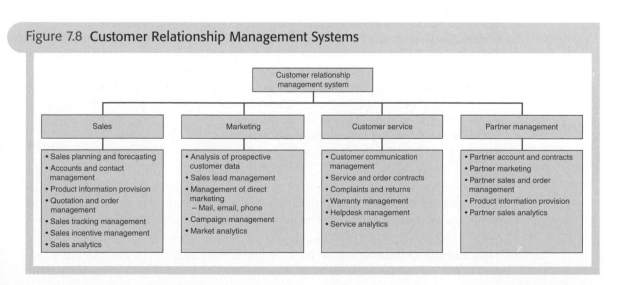

Business benefits of customer relationship management

CRM leads to a strengthened relationship with existing customers. In particular increased sales and profitability are based on:

- better timing based on analysis of past sales;
- better identification of needs of a customer based on past sales;
- cross-selling, upselling and bundling of new products;
- improved handling of the order/delivery life cycle;
- managed incentivization of the sales force;
- enhanced customer satisfaction through improved helpdesk responses;
- reduced cost in supporting and servicing customers in a more effective way.

CRM leads to new customer sales through:

- general market analysis of external data;
- targeted marketing through identification of customers and their needs from data on potential customers;
- managed support for campaigns, e-marketing, direct mail and telemarketing.

7.3.2 Human resource management systems

Customers are important to an organization – hence the rise of applications software to support various aspects of the customer relationship, together with the later integration of these supported functions into customer relationship management systems. Another highly important component of any organization is its people or, as it is often known, its human capital or human resource. The human resource of an organization needs to be managed as does any resource in order to achieve organizational goals – in a business some of these will generally include profit.

Functions of a human resource management system

A modern integrated **human resource management (HRM) system** will cover the following functions:

1. **Personnel records maintenance:** Central to any HRM system is the storage of information on the personnel of the organization. Such information will include obvious details: name, address, position held, start date, salary, and so on. Also included will be other information such as references, disciplinary record, together with details required for internal and external reporting. As examples of the latter, organizations are under legal requirements to collate statistics and report on gender, ethnicity, disability etc. The module will also assign different rights to individuals (through their functions) to create, edit, view and destroy records.

2. **Payroll:** Payroll is fundamental to any HRM system. The payroll module will calculate and ensure payroll is delivered on time. Information will be taken from the database accessed by other modules (e.g. time and labour data, incentive management) and will be subject to standard rules for automatically assigning pay, tax, and other benefits and deductions. The payroll module will also produce standard pay and tax reports.

3. **Time and labour data management:** Time and labour data can be automatically captured and tracked through input systems. As well as being a source for the payroll

module, the output will also be used within the organizational accounting process, e.g. to calculate labour input from various sources into the manufacture of a product – this is important for management accounting purposes.

4. **Benefits management:** This module allows the organization to manage the involvement of the employee in benefit schemes. These may include health benefits, corporate discount schemes and various profit participation schemes (such as share options).

5. **Incentive management:** This allows the organization to relate sales incentives to business objectives. The module will calculate, allocate and accumulate incentive credits for individual sales force personnel. The module will often interact with the relevant module in the sales module of the customer relationship management systems dealing with incentivization.

6. **Recruitment:** This part of the HRM systems will manage the recruitment life cycle. This involves assistance in advertising, screening, selecting, interview and hiring of applicants. The modules will provide analytics for assessing various search locations.

7. **Staff training and development:** This will keep track of training and development within the organization related to the skills and qualifications of the employees. It will also provide facilities to assess the effectiveness of training. Some modules will go further and manage the learning process itself, providing online training facilities for staff.

8. **Workforce scheduling:** The workforce scheduling component manages the time allocation of employees to ensure that the workforce meets both customer service and cost objectives.

9. **Human resource business intelligence:** This provides accurate, timely, comprehensive on-line information on all the human resource processes. This intelligence assists the decision maker in managing the HR processes. For example support may be provided for analysis of competence gaps between employees and their jobs, comparison of the values of HR key performance indicators against goals, analysis of salary and trends, statistical analysis of workforce types (e.g. by gender, ethnicity), analysis of the effectiveness of recruiting.

The movement is to remove the burden on the HR department in using some of the functions of the human resource management systems and allow users the ability to access certain functions through a common user interface over the organizational intranet. Modern human resource management systems allow this. It is known as **self-service human resources.** For example, an employee may update personal details such as address, bank accounts, but of course not salary details. Sickness reporting may be entered directly by departmental administrators. The authorization and recording of leave may be through the employee inputting a request to be authorized by their line manager. Managers may be able to regrade staff or perform departmental transfers of staff. These self-service activities not only remove the burden on the HR department but are faster and more efficient. They further empower the employee and manager whilst providing the necessary electronic update of organizational records.

Benefits of using human resource management systems

The use of human resource management systems brings a wide variety of benefits, both quantifiable and non-quantifiable, to the organization. These benefits are to be seen against the cost of development, implementation, training and maintenance of the system. Benefits include:

- Improved quality and availability of information on human resources to the organization. This is both on an individual basis and also on a summaried basis for support of effective decision making.

- A reduced administrative load on the HR department. Some of the previous responsibilities of the HR department are supported or automated (most obviously payroll but also recruitment). Other responsibilities are devolved to user departments, e.g. sickness reporting.

- Increased speed of availability of HR information together with the ability to select information in flexible way.

- Improved services to employee – for example the ability to view their own details, incentive accumulations or tax history.

- The production of HR metrics for performance improvement.

- The production of HR statistics for legal requirements of the award of industry kite marks (such as Investors in People in the UK).

- More effective management of employees' time.

- Provision of departmental effectiveness measures aiding the overall reduction of costs and increase in profitability.

7.4 Business intelligence from analysing performance and processes

There are a number of tools and techniques that consider the business activity as the basis for generating business intelligence. These include business process re-engineering, executive information systems, supply chain management, finance and budgeting tools, scorecarding, service oriented architecture, and Web services. Some of these have already been covered in earlier chapters; the latter three are dealt with in greater detail in the following sections.

7.4.1 Scorecarding

Scorecarding is concerned with communications, goals, and strategy. It is an approach that attempts to keep the activity and tactics of a team in alignment with the business strategy. By using scorecarding it is hoped that the vision of the company will permeate through the various activities, clarifying the targets and measuring performance. Figure 7.9 shows a typical business intelligence tool. The scorecard is shown in the centre table just above the charts. Activities can be viewed by status, owner or in a strategy map showing a matching fit with corporate strategy. Activities can be assigned benchmark figures and threshold values and can be used for impact analysis and to produce cause-and-effect diagrams.

Scorecarding is a development of the Balanced Scorecard system devised by Robert S. Kaplan and David Norton (2006). This was devised to provide businesses with a clear indication of what they should be measuring to 'balance' the financial aspect of their

Figure 7.9 A typical business intelligence tool

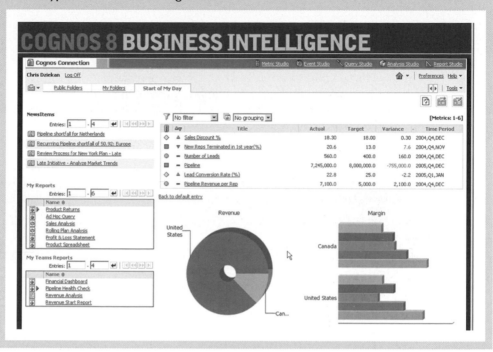

Source: www.cognos.com

operation. It is intended to make clear and realize the business strategy. It provides feedback on internal and external processes and outcomes, thereby contributing to business intelligence. Figure 7.10 shows a typical diagrammatical representation of the Balanced Scorecard approach.

7.4.2 Service oriented architecture

Service oriented architecture (SOA) is an approach to systems development that builds (or orchestrates) software from existing services. Unlike modular programming and object oriented development that operate at a relatively low level of granularity, SOA utilizes pre-written services: building blocks that are based on much larger and more complete applications. By combining third party intercommunicating services with each other or with services produced in-house, the desired functionality of a new system can be developed. Typically each building block will take on one of the following responsibilities:

- **A service provider.** This is the publisher of the service. This element will need to make clear the visibility of the service, its interface, how it can be purchased or obtained etc.
- **A service broker.** This acts as a registry of services. This element will publicize the availability of the service and match requestors with providers.
- **A service requestor.** This element seeks available services from the broker.

Figure 7.10 The balanced scorecard model

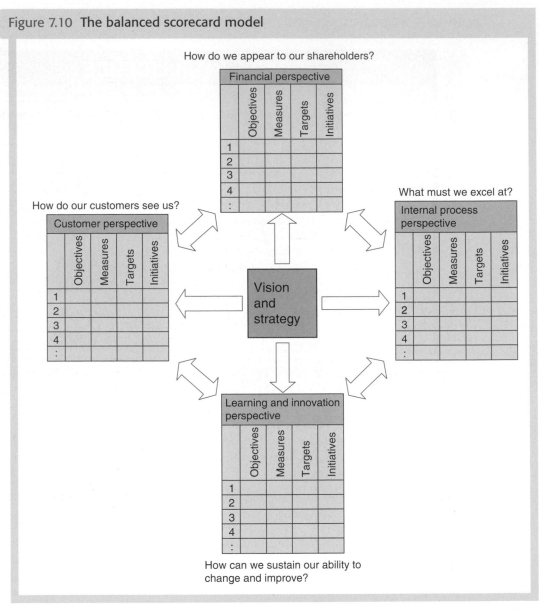

(Adapted. Reprinted by permission of Harvard Business School Press. From *The Balanced Scorecard: Translating Strategy into Action,* by Kaplan, R. S. and Norton, D. P., Boston, MA 1996. Copyright ©1996 by the Harvard Business School Publishing Corporation; all rights reserved.)

Although the use of SOA has implications for systems development in general and end-user computing in particular, in the context of business intelligence it can be used to unlock otherwise unavailable resources. For example, systems developed using COBOL in a mainframe environment can be make accessible by creating a **wrapper**, a service that provides a managed interface to the legacy system.

Mini case 7.4

Service-oriented architecture

A company's geographical dispersal can cause problems for IT, but British American Tobacco (BAT) is implementing a service-oriented architecture (SOA) to gain a consistent platform for its global systems, without constraining local regions which retain significant autonomy.

With more than 300 brands, BAT covers 180 markets with 87 factories in 66 countries, and building IT infrastructure is an ongoing task. Kevin Poulter, application technology manager with worldwide responsibility for application infrastructure and technology components, says BAT was disillusioned with 'traditional' methods. 'Momentum in our organization has come from people finding integration expensive and difficult', he says. 'The approaches we were using were too expensive and too slow.'

The company has just reached the stage of implementing services using Skyway Software's development environment. Infrastructure components deployed include Blue Titan Software for registering and managing services and Cast Iron Systems' Cast Iron Application Router as an integration tool for creating services.

BAT's determination to implement a consistent infrastructure upfront has created an excellent platform for the future, and the company can now apply SOA to business solutions on a broader basis. He aims to create a growing registry of software services that the business units can utilize and build on. 'Demand will come from local and global projects and their business requirements, not the central strategy team', he says.

Mr Poulter believes SOA is an inevitable technology that all companies will eventually embrace. He sees BAT's move to SOA as the first steps to an 'infrastructure of the future', providing stronger integration between system level, application layers and business processes.

Adapted from: **BAT steps up to new platform**
© William Knight, 26 January 2005, *Financial Times*

Questions

1. Define the term service-oriented architecture. What benefits can a company such as the one in the article derive from SOA solutions?

2. How does this method of systems development compare to more traditional approaches? How does it relate to the topic of end-user computing?

7.4.3 Web services

The World Wide Web Consortium defines a web service as 'a software system designed to support interoperable Machine to Machine interaction over a network'. In general this is implemented as servers and clients that, using the service-oriented architecture protocol (SOAP) standard, communicate through messages created in XML.

An example of use might be where a retailer wants to perform a credit check on a new customer. A web service might allow a request to be sent to a credit agency without requiring any knowledge of the system employed by the web service provider.

Web services are a key feature of the development of Web 2.0, the second generation of websites that emphasize interaction and collaboration in usage. A recent development in this area is the mashup. This is the bringing together of a number of elements of content into a single location. For example a sales analysis of a particular geographic location might combine data from the corporate database with a local map uploaded as a service.

7.5   End-user computing

End-user computing generally refers to a situation in which the target users of an information and decision support system are involved extensively in the specification, development and use of the system and its applications.

This is to be contrasted with the more traditional approach, where analysis, design and development of computer systems are carried out by a team of analysts and programmers affiliated to a centralized computer department. In this case, the final users of the system are likely to be involved at only two stages. First, they may be required at the early stages of specification for interview to establish the nature of the activity to be computerized, together with the information required. Their next involvement is likely to be at the stage where the system is tested.

In end-user computing, those that use the system will be expected to play a leading role in most, if not all, of the following:

- the identification of the need for a system or application;
- the specification of the type of system and/or software to satisfy that need;
- the purchase/resourcing of the hardware/software;
- the development of the application according to corporate standards;
- the use of the application for business purposes;
- the management of security/backup for the application.

7.5.1 The rise of end-user computing

The growth of end-user computing began in the late 1970s, and is now seen as an important component of the strategy of many organizations for their information and decision support provision. The trend was stimulated by demand considerations and facilitated by supply developments.

First, the backlog of computer applications developments that accumulated in many organizations meant that users were becoming increasingly frustrated with the computer centre. When applications were finally delivered they were often over budget and disappointing in that they did not meet user expectations. Although end-user computing was not the only response to this situation (another was the design of more appropriate methodologies for systems analysis and design), it can be seen as one of the reactions to problems with the traditional approach to information systems development and management – problems that had been building up throughout the previous decade.

Second, the introduction of microcomputers placed computing power within the reach of departmental budget holders and users of information systems. The rapid increase in the power of microcomputers, together with the decrease in costs, was supplemented by the production of software specifically designed for the end user. End-users wanted the autonomy provided by PCs. Software suppliers responded to this by designing programs serving end-user requirements. This in turn stimulated the growth of end-user computing.

Third, there was a general increase in computer literacy among business users. This was an essential prerequisite for the full growth of end-user computing. The improvement in computer literacy can be partly put down to the stimulus of the reasons mentioned above – the demand for more independence from the computer centre and the availability of the means of establishing that independence. However, it should be remembered that the growth in computing in universities and colleges was also turning out computer-literate graduates who were able to utilize computer support in their work.

7.5.2 Types of end-user computing

End-user computing as a category involves a range of individuals with differing types of skills, access to and relationships with the computer system. End-user computing may be at varying stages of maturity of development in different organizations. If end-user computing is going to be managed well in the organization then an understanding of the types of end user is essential so that proper training, control, resourcing and applications development can be undertaken, and an understanding of the stage of development will determine appropriate strategies for management of the process.

Categorization by skills of end users

One categorization, by Rockart and Flannery (1983), distinguishes end users in terms of the type of computer skills they possess and the way this interacts with the types of information the end user requires. There are six categories, and end users may 'progress' from one category to another. Each is distinguished by a different type of skill and information requirement. Recognition of this will aid end-user management.

1. **Non-programming end user:** This is the 'traditional' end user. In this category the user is not involved in the systems development process. The non-programming end user responds to prompts and menus on screens, inputs or extracts data. Typically, the user will have little understanding of the way the application is built. The data entry clerk, the shop assistant using computer-based checkout facilities and the airline reservation clerk are examples in this category. Improvements in the interfaces to the World Wide Web have greatly increased the number of non-programming end users. The ease of use of browser software and search engines has encouraged even those with very few IT skills to take advantage of the Internet.

2. **Command-level end user:** Users in this category have a greater understanding of the way the application is handled. Typically, individuals will be able to form database query commands or interact with the operating system using commands. This level of user is generally responsive to training if their systems-level knowledge is in need of upgrading.

3. **Programming-level end user:** This category refers not to the traditional programmer in the computer centre but to personnel usually working in one of the functional business departments, such as accounting, who have a deep understanding of the use of 4GLs or development tools in building applications. An example would be the management accountant who, with a thorough understanding of both spreadsheet software and management accounting, can develop spreadsheet models to support management accounting decisions.

4. **Functional support personnel:** Users in this category are technically skilled information systems developers located in functional departments within the organization. The difference between this category and the previous category is one of perception.

For example, accountants who develop models for decision support would primarily view themselves as accountants (programming end user), whereas computer-trained systems developers in an accounting department will need to know about accounting in order to develop systems. These latter personnel would nevertheless regard themselves as information systems professionals (functional support personnel).

5. **End-user support personnel:** End-user support personnel usually reside in the computer centre. They will be specialists in the technicalities of a range of applications development software packages. Their understanding, though, will be limited to the software aspects, not to an understanding of the business nature of the applications developed. They will provide support on development, from a technical point of view, choice of software and installation services.

6. **Data-processing programmers:** Although the term is slightly archaic now, this category of users is composed of highly trained computer centre personnel. The data-processing programmer is likely to be computer trained (not business trained) and to take creative decisions using the full power of the array of software available. This breadth and depth distinguishes the data-processing programmer from the programming-level end user.

As can be seen by examination of the different categories, there are a wide range of skills and approaches associated with end users. All categories represent end users in the sense of persons who use the computer system for business purposes or take part in the applications development process. However, the term 'end-user computing', as introduced at the start of this section, is restricted and generally understood to involve only categories 3 and 4 – programming-level end users and functional support personnel. The different categories in the Rockart and Flannery typology provide insights into what activities are appropriate for what types of personnel, what training must be provided in order to develop end users from one category to another, and how an organization might decide to spread its approach to applications development using 4GLs between different types of user. As with any categorization, its chief purpose is to enhance understanding and to differentiate what was previously undifferentiated.

Categorization by maturity of end-user computing

Chapter 2 dealt with the Nolan stage model for the evolution of information systems in an organization. Huff *et al.* (1988) have adapted this approach to consider the development of end-user computing specifically. As with the Nolan model the importance lies in identifying the stage of growth associated with the organization. This provides a guide to obtaining the most effective management strategy for the process of growth to the next stage of maturity. The model has five stages, in which the degree of integration of the applications is taken as the measure of maturity:

1. **Isolation:** Applications are developed in an individually uncoordinated way. There is no exchange of data between applications. The developments are more associated with learning than with enhancing productivity.

2. **Stand-alone:** Applications development takes place at a greater rate. These are still 'stand-alone' applications developed and used generally on personal computers. There is no exchange of data between applications. Individuals come to depend on their own applications development support to enhance their productivity. Data, if shared with other applications, is rekeyed in.

3. **Manual integration:** The next stage is where the need for significant exchanges of data is recognized. This may occur through the physical exchange of disks or through the downloading of files over a local area network. Issues of standards in hardware, software and communications become more important.

4. **Automated integration:** This stage differs from the previous one chiefly in that the trend towards automation of data exchange increases. Integration and the need to exchange data are now considered in applications development and design. End-user exchange of data still requires substantial knowledge of the location of data, and exchange is only effected by transfer commands.

5. **Distributed integration:** Here the physical location of data becomes transparent to the user. Network or other software handles the data supply. The application serving the end user may use data fully distributed across a network.

If organizations are to proceed in their growth towards maturity in end-user computing, then management must plan to move smoothly from one stage to the next. It is particularly important to emphasize standardization issues in order to achieve the integration necessary in the later stages.

7.5.3 The benefits of end-user computing

End-user computing confers many benefits on an organization. Among those most commonly identified are the following:

- End users are now able to satisfy their own requirements in many cases. This cuts the waiting period resulting from the backlog of applications awaiting development in the computer centre.

- Innovation and control over one's own information provision stimulated by end-user computing encourages autonomy and responsibility in users.

- End users are able to translate their information requirements into applications without the need to transfer these via an analyst/programmer, who will not in general be an expert in the application area. This reduces one of the main difficulties in systems development – designing a system that meets user requirements.

- End users are able to release analyst/programming staff for other uses. In particular, centralized resources such as the corporate database will not be developed or controlled by end users.

- End users are able to adapt their systems to their needs as they evolve.

7.5.4 The risks of end-user computing

Its liberating impact has undoubtedly been a major force in the growth of end-user computing. However, there are risks and pitfalls that can easily remove corporate advantages or create corporate problems. These may occur even if the benefits to the performance of the individual are realized. Many risks concern proliferation without standardization. Among these, the following are the most important:

- Quality assurance may be diminished in end-user applications development as compared with centralized systems analysis and design. Centralized control, combined with the knowledge that a lack of quality control would revisit the programmers and analysts at a later date, meant that quality issues have always been accorded a high priority in traditional computing centres. The potential anarchy, especially at the earlier stages of the growth to maturity of an organization's end-user computing, can yield problems. This may be revealed in a number of ways:

– poor development methodologies, which yield error-prone applications;

– incomplete testing;

– inadequate or non-existent development documentation and user manuals – both may make it difficult for anyone but the developer to use the system;

– inadequate access control, backup and archiving.

■ Computer centre analysts are used to making complete systems specifications. The end-user developer is far more likely to be interested in a swift development without the need to produce a complete specification. The familiarity that users have with their own requirements can be a drawback. The systems analyst may be able to provide insights with a more general questioning approach.

■ At the later stages of mature growth, when end-user applications involve the manipulation of shared data, the absence of controls on data may yield data integrity problems.

■ Unless there are mechanisms in place for directed growth, unrelated applications in different areas of the organization may be created that duplicate each other. Although this can create waste, it should be borne in mind that other benefits, such as the creation of user autonomy and responsibility, must be offset against this.

■ Costs of hardware and software need to be monitored. If the growth of end-user computing does not proceed in parallel with central policies on purchase standardization and bulk purchase discounts then the benefits will be jeopardized.

■ End-user applications are likely to service local needs and objectives. This is only beneficial to the organization if these are congruent with and support global corporate objectives.

■ There is a risk that users produce private and informal information systems that run counter to company policy or are against the law. Compliance with data protection legislation is one known area of difficulty.

7.5.5 End-user applications development and management

If the corporate benefits from end-user computing are to be realized then ultimately the organization must proceed to the final stages of the Huff model – that is, to distributed integration. This requires a responsible role to be taken both by the computer centre and by the end users themselves.

The role of the computer centre

■ **Standard setting:** Standards need to be set, monitored and maintained for end-user computing. These will apply to hardware, software, systems analysis and design, documentation, data structure definition, data communications, access, security, and the privacy of personal data. It is not an easy task for the computer centre to ensure that these standards are adhered to and at the same time create the necessary climate of autonomy within which end-user computing can flourish.

- **Communications and networks:** As well as maintaining standards for communications and networks, it is likely that the computer centre will be responsible for the provision and maintenance of a cross-organizational local area network. This is key to successful integrated end-user computing as well as bringing benefits such as electronic mail and the sharing of scarce resources.

- **Training:** The computer centre is usually responsible for training end users in the use of development packages. As well as providing end users with the necessary skills, this is also an important mechanism for developing a culture of following standards.

- **Data administration:** The computer centre will also be responsible for defining the corporate data structure so that it meets the needs of the organization, including those of end users.

- **Research:** End users will rely on the computer centre to be continually aware of developments in the software and hardware market. The mature computer centre is providing a research service to ensure that the needs of end users are satisfied.

The role of end users

- **Applications portfolio identification:** One of the benefits conferred by end-user computing is the autonomy granted to the development of applications meeting user requirements. However, this should not be done independently of corporate objectives; nor should it be done in isolation from similar or complementary developments in other departments. It may be the case that cross-departmental applications are implemented. This coordination facility is not easily established.

- **Applications development and implementation:** End-user departments are responsible for applications development. This must be in accordance with policies and standards set out by the computer centre.

- **Applications operation:** As the end user is responsible for the application, the end user is also responsible for security. This includes following procedures for secure access, backup and recovery. Once again, it is usual that standards in these areas will be set by the computer centre.

Influences on end-user computing development

Managerial approaches to end-user computing should be designed to create effects in accordance with the information systems strategy of the organization. The aims will always attempt to maximize the benefits and minimize the disadvantages of end-user computing. Two important influences on end-user computing need to be managed (Munro *et al.*, 1987):

1. the rate of expansion of end-user computing;
2. the level of control over end-user computing activities.

The rate of expansion is managed by (1) making hardware and software easier/more difficult to obtain; (2) making information easier/more difficult to obtain; and (3) imposing/relieving the end-user departments of the costs of end-user computing. The level of control over activities is managed by (1) more or less restrictive standards over the purchase of hardware/software; (2) the level of requirement of mainframe use compared with PC use for applications; and (3) restrictions on access to data.

Figure 7.11 The expansion/control matrix for end-user computing

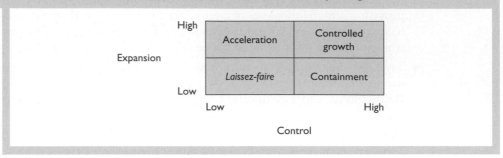

In general, the organization can manage the rate of expansion to yield a high or low rate of growth of end-user computing. Similarly, by using the above levers the organization can ensure a high or low level of control over end-user activities. The matrix of possibilities that this yields is shown in Figure 7.11. High expansion strategies are associated with forcing the growth of end-user computing in order to obtain its benefits. High control strategies are aimed at limiting the disadvantages of end-user computing, particularly those associated with lack of standards, duplication and waste. As can be seen, there are four broad possible mixes of strategy:

1. **Laissez-faire:** This is the 'no policy' situation. End-user computing is neither encouraged nor controlled. This state typifies the early stages of the organizational growth path – either the isolation or the stand-alone stage in the Huff growth model.

2. **Containment:** Here the organization concentrates its strategies on channelling any end-user activities. The growth of end-user computing is not organizationally encouraged by its policies, yet it is recognized that where such activities occur they must be controlled lest organizational disadvantages result.

3. **Acceleration:** The policies adopted by an organization wishing to 'kick start' end-user computing will stimulate growth of activity without emphasis being placed on control. An organization adopting policies within this quadrant will be risk-taking. This is unusual, as it is consonant with a planned diminution of computer centre control.

4. **Controlled growth:** Policies are in place to encourage expansion and at the same time to ensure a directed effort at the organizational level. This is a characteristic of a mature level of organizational end-computer development and activity. It corresponds to a situation in which the roles of the end users and of the computer centre as identified in the previous two sections are fully realized.

In summary, the essence of the analysis of Munro *et al.* is that there are just two dimensions to manage with respect to end-user computing: the rate of expansion and the level of control over activities. Depending on how these are managed, the organization's end-user computing will fall broadly into one of the four categories (although in reality these categories shade into one another).

Generic management strategies for end-user computing

Gerrity and Rockart (1986) defined four generic management strategies for end-user computing. These offer a different perspective on the management of end-user computing from that of Huff *et al.* in the previous section, although one that is not necessarily in conflict with it. The four generic strategies are examined below.

1. With the **monopolistic approach**, the computer centre attempts to block the development of end-user computing. This is not so much a strategy for management as a strategy for prevention. It can only succeed for a short time. The pressures, mentioned earlier, fuelling the growth of end-user computing eventually make this policy untenable. In particular, the combination of the backlog of applications waiting for development, the increasing computer literacy of end users and the decreasing cost/increasing power of desktop computers and software ensure that this policy ultimately fails.

2. The **laissez-faire approach** involves doing nothing to stimulate, prevent or interfere with the growth or control of end-user computing. Once again this is not so much a policy for the management of end-user computing as the absence of one. With laissez-faire, end-user computing may initially flourish, but the problems associated with lack of control soon start to arise. In particular, the inevitable lack of standards causes difficulties. In addition, the duplication of end-user effort, poor selection of inappropriate (and often expensive) hardware and software, and the lack of training make this an untenable generic policy in the long run.

3. The **information centre approach** offers both support and control. The computer centre designates specific groups of staff who are assigned to respond to the needs of end-user computing. These needs could be for training, package support and installation, analysis of needs, production of user support documentation, or applications development. The emphasis is on creating an organizational culture of support for end-user computing. The identified support groups are decentralized from the computer centre. However, because these groups are organizationally linked to the computer centre and are themselves computing professionals they will ensure that proper standards are maintained over the development and use of end-user applications. This is a common approach in many organizations. However, its very strength – the presence of computer professionals in a support role, thus ensuring standards – is also a weakness. The support personnel will still not have the requisite knowledge of the business activities they support.

4. In the **management of the free economy approach**, the relationship between the computer centre and the end users is altered. This approach recognizes the importance of providing end users the freedom to define their own needs while providing the skilled support necessary to guide development and ensure standards. The balance is achieved by following a number of guidelines:

   (a) A clear statement of the strategy for end-user computing is needed. This should be a senior management function, which must identify the role of end-user computing within the information systems strategy and the business strategy.

   (b) Balance between the responsibilities of the computer centre and of the end users must be clearly articulated.

   (c) The provision of end-user support should be by an information centre independent of the computer centre. In this way, end users will be assured of their autonomy.

   (d) Identification of a range of critical end-user applications must be made. These are then given a high organizational priority.

   (e) There is a continuing emphasis on improvement, growth and autonomy for end-user computing through the use of education.

The management of end-user computing is regarded as important, yet there is no received wisdom on the most appropriate strategy. For other views, see Galletta and Hufnagel (1992) and Clark (1992).

End-user applications development – prototyping

One method of developing an application is to carry out the process of development through a series of linear stages. In this approach, the computer centre is heavily involved at all times. The process can be summarized in the following way:

> A user department identifies a need satisfiable by a computerized system. The computer centre will investigate and provide a feasibility study and report. If this report and its cost implications are accepted by management then computer centre personnel carry out a detailed analysis of the data and activities and specify a systems design that will satisfy these. Upon acceptance of the design, the computer centre develops software, purchases and installs hardware, tests the system and finally hands it to the end users for ongoing use.

The previous paragraph summarizes a linear approach to systems development. Each stage of the project is completed before proceeding to the next. Clear specifications and reports are provided at each stage. The computer centre is responsible for managing and working on what may be a very large project, involving many staff, with a large budget, to be developed over a lengthy period. This approach is at odds with the type of end-user development examined in the preceding sections. In the linear approach, end users have no involvement at most stages in the development process. The linear approach has had numerous significant successes (and some failures!) in the design and delivery of large, well-defined systems. The approach is covered extensively in later chapters on structured process and data analysis, design and implementation. However, it may not be the best way forward for the development of decision support systems, where end-user knowledge and involvement are important and there are applications development tools and 4GLs. In this case, **prototyping**, involving end users, may be the most appropriate development method.

Prototyping is the approach where systems are developed swiftly, without having undergone a complete analysis and specification. The system that is developed is known as the **prototype**. The process relies on the prototype system itself being an aid to the specification – by consideration of the prototype and identification of its weaknesses an improved version can be developed. Prototyping also relies on the presence of software tools to produce prototypes quickly. Typically, users take part in the prototyping process either with or without the aid of the computer centre. The process is thus heavily user oriented. There are two types of prototype:

1. **Discardable prototypes:** In this situation, the prototype is produced and assessed as to its suitability in meeting user needs. An operational version of the system is then written, usually in a third-generation language such as C or Java, and is used for ongoing work. Discardable prototypes are developed when there is a need to produce a final version that is technically efficient in the way it uses computing power. This is most common if a large volume of data needs manipulation. The discardable prototype written in the 4GL may have been produced quickly and is unlikely to use code that is efficient. Other features, such as error-checking routines and security, will need to be added to the final operational system.

2. **Operational prototypes:** In the development of a system using prototyping, it is not uncommon for a first prototype written in a 4GL to be refined and replaced by a second. This in turn may undergo successive alterations until a final version that satisfies the user is good enough to become a working version. At the various stages of development and use the prototype is always thought of as being the current version open to change as needs arise. The approach is only possible through the use of fast systems-building tools and 4GLs. The process of development is one of iteration.

Advantages of prototyping

- By using prototyping, it is possible to obtain working versions of a system very quickly, often within days. This is particularly important where decision support systems are involved. With these systems, as dictated by the varying information needs of management in making decisions, the type of computer-based support needed may vary within a short period of time. It is not easy for linear methods, with their long lead times, to be so responsive.

- Often it is difficult to provide clear, detailed specifications for the requirements of a system. This may be because these requirements are not readily understood. With a linear approach, it is assumed that there is a clear understanding of both the current set of operations and those that need to be computerized. Unless this condition is met, developers may be forced into some type of prototyping, which can, among other advantages, be viewed as a systems specification method.

- Prototyping is end-user driven. It should therefore meet the requirements of end users. Involvement in the development of a system is one of the ways in which a user gains confidence and understanding of the system. This in turn increases the likelihood of a system being successful. Many of the benefits of end-user computing are realized with the prototyping approach to development.

- A system developed through operational prototyping is capable of easy adaptation.

Disadvantages of prototyping

- Because of prototyping's iterative nature, there is no clearly defined deliverable or completion deadline. This may give rise to considerable management concern. One of the guidelines of project management is to specify deliverables, deadlines and budgets. None of these clearly fits the prototyping approach.

- As has been stated above, the prototyping approach is aimed at obtaining speedily working systems meeting user requirements in terms of functionality. Code inefficiencies may be a drawback.

Prototyping is most appropriate in the following situations:

- The user finds it difficult to define the requirements of the system clearly.
- It is important to develop a system quickly – this is often the case with systems needed for decision support.
- User satisfaction, understanding and confidence are important considerations.
- Appropriate development tools are available.
- Users are committed to being involved with applications development.
- End-user autonomy is regarded as important.
- Low-volume transaction processing is involved.

Prototyping is least likely to be appropriate when:

- Appropriate development tools are not available and not understood by the users/computer centre.
- End users are unwilling to commit the necessary development time to prototype development.
- High-volume transaction processing is required.
- Technical efficiency in the use of computer-processing resources is a high priority.

Prototyping has become an increasingly important element in applications development. The nature of decision support systems and their relation to end-user computing has contributed to this growth. Prototyping is also an important component of approaches such as rapid applications development (RAD) using CASE tools. These are covered in Chapter 17.

7.5.6 Desktop applications and programming languages

At the time when the personal computer first became a significant factor in business computing there was a clear distinction between the programming environments available for developing software and the desktop packages employed in end-user computing. Programming was a separate activity leading to the development of unique products tailored to meet particular user requirements, whereas desktop applications such as spreadsheets and databases were largely purchased and used without modification.

The development of desktop applications

The arrival of desktop computing packages such as word processors, spreadsheets and databases put computing power onto the desktop. These packages eliminated the need for many areas of development that had traditionally been carried out through the use of high-level languages. Desktop computer users, however, still wanted the facility to tailor their systems to perform job-specific tasks. The early desktop applications usually included facilities to create **macros**; these are collections of instructions that can be recorded as a single named sequence of activities, then replayed to automate a particular task. Gradually, the macro facilities became more sophisticated and became more like programming languages in their own right.

Programming for a graphical user interface

The rapid growth of graphical user interfaces such as Windows as a standard environment for the desktop PC required extensions to high-level programming languages or the creation of new languages to build the new interfaces. The extensions to some languages, such as C++, resulted in a very complex range of programming tools and libraries, putting the development of Windows-like software clearly in the hands of experienced software developers only. Other programming environments, such as Microsoft's Visual Basic, provided a simple language and an easy-to-use set of tools, which made it possible for end users to construct desktop applications with potentially mission-critical importance. Several large organizations began to question traditional methods of systems development, which were proving to be costly and unreliable, and consider a move to applications development using these new end-user approaches. This is discussed in more detail in later chapters.

The merging of end-user packages and programming environments

The demand for more sophisticated tools to be provided in desktop applications has continued to grow. The traditional macro has not proved powerful enough to enable end users to produce the solutions they require. Software vendors have now, as a result, incorporated the power of the visual programming language into the desktop application. This allows users to enhance the built-in facilities of the application, whether word processor, spreadsheet or database, by building a front end or interface and some application logic to meet their own particular requirements.

This blurring of applications packages and programming environments is likely to continue as applications development for the Internet becomes a more prevalent programming activity. End users are now looking for their desktop packages to be 'Web-enabled' to allow, for example, access to database tables over the Internet. Similarly, programming languages that are used to create Web applications are constantly being enhanced to provide stronger integration with desktop applications. This strategy has been adopted in Microsoft's .NET approach.

7.6   Human–computer interaction

Early in the development of business information systems, it was realized that the way the screen or printed output was designed influenced the ease and accuracy with which users understood the information supplied by the computer. It was also recognized that input screen design was crucial to input performance and accuracy.

Attention was given to the design of the **man–machine interface** (**MMI**), as it was then called, in order to ensure maximum effectiveness of the information system. Concerns concentrated on presenting information that was necessary and sufficient to user needs and to present that information in the most uncluttered way. Determination of what information was necessary and sufficient was achieved through a careful analysis of the task for which the user needed the information. (The reader's attention is drawn to the section on input/output design in Chapter 15 for further coverage of related issues.)

It is now recognized that this approach is no longer sufficient, for the following reasons:

- The development of decision support systems has brought with it a recognition of the change of emphasis from information supplied in order to perform a task to information supplied in order to support a decision. As has been stressed earlier in the chapter, and in Chapter 1, the use of the computer for decision support involves not only an analysis of the decision but also the decision maker's cognitive style, the objectives of the decision and the organizational setting within which the decision is taken. The focus on screen design is no longer sufficient.

- The increase in end-user computing, particularly the involvement of end users in applications development, has meant that designers of development tools are required to take into account the background, skills and objectives of these end users. Without attention to this point, development tools could well turn out to be technically powerful but unusable.

- Developments in computing power and the sophistication of software, particularly dealing with graphics, have led to a range of pictorial screen possibilities. This has made possible a much richer set of methods of communication with the user. It is easier to take into account the vastly increased range of people using computers and the purposes for which they use them.

■ Failure of computers to achieve the business objectives for which they were designed has often been put down to user resistance and a failure to take into account user needs (as distinct from the information a user requires to perform a task). Several studies on the introduction of new technologies, including information technology, suggest that designers need to extend their focus beyond the narrow technical system to be designed. They should also take into account the interrelationship between the technical system, the tasks to be performed, the people involved in these and the organizational setting.

All of the above has shifted the emphasis from the man–machine interface as the focus of design to a consideration of the interaction of the human with the computer systems in an organizational setting. This is the study of **human–computer interaction (HCI)**.

The phrase 'human–computer interaction' appeared in the mid-1980s. There are many definitions. The following gives a picture of the scope of the term:

> Human–computer interaction is a discipline concerned with the design, evaluation and implementation of interactive computing systems for human use and with the study of the major phenomena surrounding them.

(ACM SIGCHI, 1992, p. 6)

It is important to realize that what distinguishes human–computer interaction is the last phrase – 'the study of the major phenomena surrounding them'. This goes far beyond the scope of input/output screen design.

The major features of human–computer interaction design for computerized information systems are:

■ The approach is user-centred. End users are involved as much as possible in the design process. Involvement may occur through users building systems with user-oriented development tools or by participation in the analysis and design process.

■ The approach integrates knowledge from a wide range of disciplines. The major influential disciplines in the area of human–computer interaction are shown in Figure 7.12.

■ Rather than the development of a system occurring in a linear fashion (analysis through design to implementation), the process of design involves iteration of various stages. Often this involves the building of prototypes, which can be used to test the efficiency of the human–computer interaction.

In order to account properly for the human in human–computer interaction design, it has been necessary to utilize a model of the human within the process.

7.6.1 The human information processor model

One of the most influential models derives from the area of cognitive psychology, in which the human is treated as an information processor. The human information processor model starts out from the basis that information enters via the senses through the processes of attention and perception. Decoding of information takes place and comparison of the internal representation of the information is made with the internal representations in the memory. A response is selected, executed and output. In the model, information is processed in a linear manner (see Figure 7.13). By concentrating on the

Figure 7.12 Influential disciplines on human–computer interaction

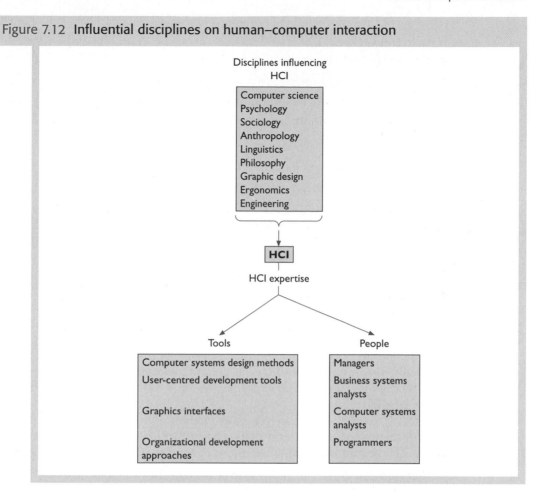

Disciplines influencing
HCI

Computer science
Psychology
Sociology
Anthropology
Linguistics
Philosophy
Graphic design
Ergonomics
Engineering

HCI

HCI expertise

Tools

Computer systems design methods
User-centred development tools

Graphics interfaces

Organizational development
approaches

People

Managers
Business systems
analysts
Computer systems
analysts
Programmers

Figure 7.13 The human information processor model

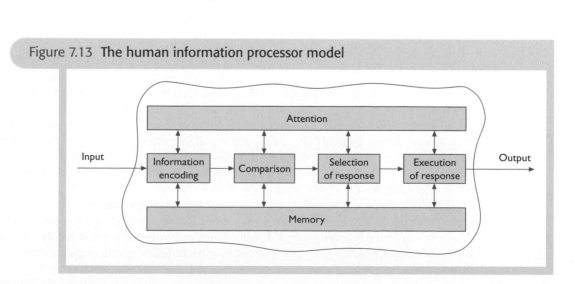

Attention

Input

Information
encoding

Comparison

Selection
of response

Execution
of response

Output

Memory

sequence of operations and their timing, a proper account can be taken of the human in human–computer interaction. Areas of general interest, among others, would be:

- how information is perceived and encoded;
- how information/knowledge is represented in memory;
- how comparisons are made;
- how information is stored and retrieved from memory;

and specifically on:

- how humans represent models of familiar objects to themselves;
- how users learn to use computer systems.

The human information processor model has been profoundly influenced by the development of computing itself. More sophisticated versions of the simplified model outlined here have included, for example, analogues of serial and parallel processing, and of buffer stores.

7.6.2 The distributed cognition approach

The human information processor model has recognized that the human is more than merely the provider of information to, and receiver of information from, the interface with a computer system. The user has a task to perform and will process information internally for the execution of this task. The basis of the approach assumes that an understanding of the internal processing in the mind of the user will enable the design of a better interactive system.

Later approaches to human–computer interaction recognize that the human information processor model is too limited. Its concentration on the individual, the computer and the task leaves out important dimensions of human–computer interaction. Specifically:

- Users do not carry out individual information-processing tasks in theoretical settings. Rather, the user performs part of a complex function involving many interrelated tasks for a purpose.
- This function occurs in a real organizational setting.
- Users interact with one another, particularly in teams.

Distributed cognition is an evolving theoretical framework for human–computer interaction that takes account of these points. The approach goes beyond the individual to viewing activities as involving the interaction of people, technology and tasks in an organizational setting (see Figure 7.14). The emphasis is on the study and design of functional systems that concentrate on the way information is transmitted and processed through the various components of the system in order to perform a function such as accounting control. The components will include computers and humans. This and similar approaches have influenced the development of systems design methodologies. See, for example, the socio-technical approach and soft systems analysis – both covered in Chapter 17.

Human–computer interaction involves concepts that pervade many aspects of the analysis, design and use of information systems. The reader is referred to other parts of this text, particularly input/output design, Windows interfaces, socio-technical design, soft systems analysis, knowledge representation techniques, group decision support and prototyping.

Figure 7.14 Human–computer interaction in an organizational setting

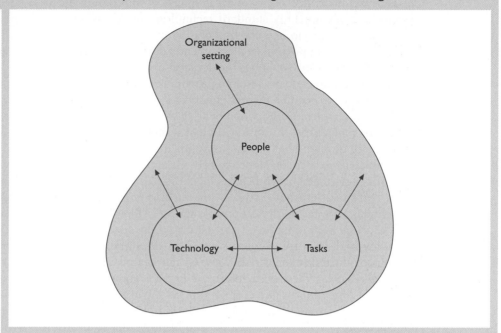

Summary

The last four decades has seen the rapid improvement and extensive use of the computer in business data processing and information provision. A number of tools and techniques have evolved or been developed which provide businesses and other organizations with the necessary intelligence to achieve corporate goals. This intelligence derives from external sources as well as from within the organization. The intelligence may be structured or unstructured. The emphasis has been on providing intelligence to report on performance indicators, to improve decision making and, overall, to gain competitive advantage. In providing this the focus has been on analysing information and data, analysing human behaviour and analysing performance and processes.

Decision support systems make use of many of these aspects of modern technology. They aid, rather than replace, decision making. They may involve the provision of business intelligence from the selection and analysis of data from a corporate database, the use of models for predicting outcomes, optimization techniques, or the application of details of particular cases to general rules in order to support decisions. Decision support systems allow flexible access to data and the interactive use of models. These systems supply information to managers for semistructured problems.

In the design of decision support systems, the emphasis is on stand-alone systems rather than the grand design of the total integrated decision support system. Because the development of a decision support system is driven by the type of decision-making process and the information needs of the decision, end users play a prominent role in design. Fourth-generation languages, spreadsheets, expert system shells and tools, and model generators are all used in decision support system (DSS) design.

Group decision support systems are a more recent development that takes account of the fact that many decisions are taken in group situations. The group decision support system involves not only standard technology for decision support but also specific software to aid group activities such as brainstorming, voting and policy formation. Group decision support takes place in carefully constructed environments with an experienced facilitator to enhance the decision process.

Document management systems, originally designed to index and manage scanned documents, have become increasingly useful as the technology has improved to allow scanning of characters and consequent keyword searching and indexing. The way forward is to replace the physical document with electronic documents which go through a process of development at various points in the organization. Digital dashboards are tools which have been developed to provide a visual indication within one screen of the state of key performance indicators in an organization to aid the decision maker to obtain a real-time snapshot picture of the functioning of the organization or its relevant departments. Online analytical processing (OLAP) systems have been developed which analyse a vast accumulation of internal organizational data, particularly with a view to providing high-level trend forecasting. This data might be stored in data warehouses which provide multidimensional views of aggregated data for different users or applications. Increasingly these warehouses are being searched or 'mined' in order to look for new and useful patterns and correlations for the organization.

Other business intelligence tools focus on human behaviour. Customer relationship management systems seek to analyse and improve the relationships of the organization with those that purchase its products and services. As well as providing information on existing customers and sales they identify and target new markets. These systems also offer a range of services to enhance customer satisfaction. Whereas customer relationship management systems predominantly look out of the organization, human resource management systems are more internally focused to aid the management of staff and to optimize their performance.

There are a number of tools that treat business activity and processes as a source of business intelligence. These include scorecarding, which is a method of ensuring that the various parts of the business are performing up to the standards required to achieve corporate goals. The Web is also being used to provide services to support business intelligence. This may range from the specific credit rating of a customer to a demographic analysis of a geographical location which will inform marketing and sales drives.

End-user computing has been fuelled by the need to develop systems, particularly those providing business intelligence, that speedily meet the needs of users. This has been facilitated by the presence of easy-to-use enabling software. 'End users' is a term covering a wide range of individuals, involving different types of skill and different information requirements. The growth of end-user computing progresses through several stages in an organization, depending on the level of integration of applications. At all stages, to be successful it is necessary to manage the process. The computer centre is expected to set standards and also to take on the role of the provision of training, education and technical support to end users in the development of their own systems. There are several different approaches to the management of end-user computing. One emphasizes the importance of managing the balance between control and expansion. Another concentrates on the role of end-user support and examines the information centre concept.

The traditional linear development process for systems, where progression is through a number of stages culminating in final implementation, may not be appropriate for the production of decision support systems. Prototyping is an alternative that is compatible with the need to develop systems quickly in situations where a clear specification is not available, when there is a need to involve users in development, and there is a desire to create adaptable responsive systems. Discardable prototyping is the approach that views the role of the prototype as the specification of the functionality of the desired system. The final version is written to ensure greater technical efficiency in computer processing. In operational prototyping, the prototype is successively and interactively refined until it becomes the final version. Prototyping has been made possible by the design of 4GLs and applications development tools.

Developments in business intelligence systems, the rise of end-user computing and prototyping have emphasized the need for a theory on the way in which the user interacts with computer systems. The study of human–computer interaction provides this. Approaches that look merely at input/output screen design have been superseded by those that regard the user as an information processor in performing a task (human information processor model). Later approaches have attempted to remedy the limitations of this approach by concentrating on the functions performed by users and technology in a real organizational setting.

Review questions

1. Business intelligence focuses on the three key categories of analysing data and information, analysing human behaviour and analysing the performance and processes of the business. Give examples of tools and techniques that relate to each of these categories.

2. Identify characteristics of a decision support system and explain how these distinguish decision support systems from the more general notion of an information system.

3. What classes of decision support system are there? Give examples of each.

4. What are the risks associated with end-user computing? How can they be reduced?

5. What is the difference between a *computer centre* and an *information centre*?

6. Describe the architecture of a typical data warehouse. What are the issues in maintaining a data warehouse?

7. Describe the techniques employed in data mining.

8. What are the main features and benefits of prototyping?

9. Distinguish between *input/output design* and *human–computer interaction design*.

Exercises

1. Identify the drivers that are encouraging interest in business intelligence. Evaluate three of the tools or techniques that contribute to providing business intelligence.

2. In Chapter 1, decision making was divided into four stages. The first three were intelligence, design and choice. By selecting an appropriate example, illustrate how decision support systems can be used in each of these stages.

3. Why are there many different types of aid and approach to the development of decision support systems?

4. What special advantages do spreadsheets confer over the use of pen and paper in accounting modelling?

5. Why is it important to have a facilitator in group decision making using a decision room?

6. What characteristics of group decision making distinguish it from individual decision making? How could these be supported by a GDSS?

7. By considering the classification of types of end user, identify the types of training and support needed for each.

8. Compare online transaction processing with online analytical processing. Explain how the competetition for system resources has in part led to the development of data warehouses. What other factors have encouraged the development of data warehouses?

9. Describe typical techniques for conducting searches on a data warehouse. Evaluate the use of a data warehouse compared to the more straightforward queries that can be carried out on data stores.

10. As a senior manager working in an organization that can best be described as adopting the monopolistic approach to end-user computing, what policies would you wish to see adopted in order to transform the management of end-user computing to a managed free-economy model?

11. You have been commissioned to conduct a third-party investigation into decision support systems as used in ABC Co. This has revealed that many departments are developing their own applications independently and without the knowledge of the computer centre. The computer centre has traditionally taken a very strong line against end-user computing and has been unwilling to provide support for end-user applications development. In the current situation, the proliferation of end-user decision support systems involves duplication of resources, data and applications. The culture of senior management is one of centralized control. How would you advise the company to proceed?

12. For each of the disciplines mentioned in Figure 7.11, discuss how these may be of use in HCI design.

13. Outline the main differences in approach between the human information processor model and the distributed cognition model to understanding human–computer interaction.

CASE STUDY 7

Business intelligence

Coming soon to an office near you: wikis for workers, mash-ups that make creative use of the different pools of data at your fingertips, and a host of other flexible new Internet-based tools to make working life more productive. At least, that is if you believe the latest hype coming out of the technology industry.

The 'Web 2.0' movement, first apparent in a wave of consumer applications that grew up on the Internet, has now spread, inevitably, to the world of corporate computing. This technology wave is all about creating low-cost applications on the fly to make communication and collaboration easier – but it also comes with some heavy marketing overkill.

'There's no limit to the technology industry's ability to hype new technologies', warns Russ Daniels, chief technology officer of Hewlett-Packard's software division. He adds, though: 'Enterprises are all about getting people to collaborate to do things they couldn't do on their own', so the potential benefits from this new technology certainly sound compelling.

Notoriously difficult to pin down, the 'Web 2.0' label is generally applied to three things. One is a family of 'social' software – the blogs, wikis (web pages that are open to a group of people to write on or edit) and other tools that have made it easier and cheaper to self-publish and collaborate on the Internet. This promises an escape from e-mail hell: rather than circulate endless e-mail attachments to groups of co-workers, why not cooperate on web-based applications?

A second use of the term is to describe a low-cost, rapid approach to software development. The most visible results are mash-ups, services created by combining data from different sources to create composite applications. Thanks to new standards-based technology (Web 2.0 draws heavily on the so-called web services standards), it is now easier to create these ad hoc.

Third, the phrase is used to describe new browser-based technologies, such as Ajax, that make Internet applications behave more like desktop-based software, creating a richer experience.

To a certain extent, these three ideas are linked. A better user experience for web-based applications makes it more likely they will be adopted as alternatives to PC-based software. With more information stored online, it becomes easier to combine applications and services and merge data for ad hoc mash-ups. This points to the broader force at work behind Web 2.0.

'We are past the point where the Internet has become the platform', says Tim O'Reilly, the technology commentator and publisher who is generally credited with coining the term 'Web 2.0'.

Software applications, he says, behave differently when they are born and live on the Internet. Interaction by the people who use these online applications creates network effects that add to the value of the software. 'Fundamentally, you write applications that get better the more people who use them', he says. Mr O'Reilly sums this up as: 'Live' applications driven by databases that are self-improving.' Applied to the corporate world, the idea is starting to be felt in two distinct ways.

One is a new generation of communication and collaboration tools that could enhance and, in some cases, replace the familiar instant messaging and e-mail that are now a standard part of office workers' lives.

Together with things such as RSS (a method of syndication that automatically 'pushes' newly published content to people who have expressed an interest in seeing it) and Internet search, this family of technologies could create an 'entirely different kind of information system' in the corporate world, says Ross Mayfield, founder of Socialtext, an early exponent of the idea of applying wikis to the workplace.

The second impact of Web 2.0 inside companies is a broader one, and points to a more open, rapid-fire approach to software development that raises deeper questions about how companies adapt technology to their business needs. For instance, creating composite applications by combining data from different sources on the fly could smooth the workings of complex supply chains, says Mr O'Reilly. If factories published data about

▶

their output levels, other companies could combine it with data of their own to present a clearer view of supply and demand.

If this sounds a lot like the vision of 'web services' that was first advanced in the late 1990s, that's because it is. The banner of web services for corporate use has been taken up most recently by proponents of 'service-oriented architecture', or SOA – systems that draw on reusable software components, or services, from different sources to create composite applications to solve particular business needs.

The products of these heavy-duty corporate systems sound very much like the mash-ups promoted by the Web 2.0 crowd. The difference, says Mr Daniels at HP, is that mash-ups and other lightweight Web 2.0 tools are available to the average office 'power users', the sort of workers who in the past have proved adept at stretching Excel spreadsheets for wider departmental uses.

Also, the ideas of some of the Web 2.0 evangelists look likely to produce a culture clash for both IT departments and corporate managers. The nature of the technology – dynamic applications that are always in the process of adaptation – runs counter to the way most IT departments operate. 'It is never finished, it is an ongoing process', says Mr O'Reilly – not the sort of message that will sit well with risk-averse CIOs more accustomed to testing new applications exhaustively before adoption.

To be effective, the sort of new technologies that go under the 'Web 2.0' banner also rely on a willingness to share data that in the past has sat in isolated silos. 'Understanding what data you can abstract and share among users is the fundamental Web 2.0 exercise', says Mr O'Reilly.

Adapted from: **Can mash-ups match up to business needs?**
Richard Waters, *Financial Times*, 24 January 2007

Questions

1. What are the new technologies that the article suggests are having such an impact? How do these technologies contribute to the development of business intelligence?

2. What effect do these new technologies have on collaborative working and on the accessibility of data?

3. Evaluate the effect that developments under the Web 2.0 banner have in terms of development of new information systems.

References

ACM SIGCHI (1992). *Curriculum for Human–Computer Interaction.* ACM Special Interest Group on Computer–Human Interaction. Curriculum Development Group, New York

Clark T. (1992). Corporate systems management: an overview and research perspective. *Communications of the ACM*, February, 60–75

Galletta D.F. and Hufnagel E.M. (1992). A model of end-user computing policy. *Information and Management*, 22(1), 1–18

Gerrity T.P. and Rockart J.F. (1986). End-user computing: are you a leader or a laggard? *Sloan Management Review*, 27(4), 25–34

Huff S.L., Munro M.C. and Martin B.H. (1988). Growth stages of end-user computing. *Communications of the ACM*, 31(5), 542–50

Hurwitz & Associates (2005). Dashboards – enabling insight and action. Research paper.

Kaplan R. S. and Norton D. (2006). *Alignment: How to Apply the Balanced Scorecard to Corporate Strategy*. Harvard Business School Press.

Munro M.C., Huff S.L. and Moore G. (1987). Expansion and control of end-user computing. *Journal of Management Information Systems*, **4**(3), 5–27

Rockart J. and Flannery L. (1983). The management of end-user computing. *Communications of the ACM*, **26**(10), 776–84

Recommended reading

Adelman S. *et al.* (2000). *Data Warehouse Project Management*. Addison-Wesley
A thorough text covering the goals and objectives and organizational and cultural issues involved in implementing a data warehouse.

Biere M. (2003) *Business Intelligence for the Enterprise*. Pearson Professional Education
This text provides an introductory outline and history of business intelligence. It then moves into more advanced elements of business intelligence solutions and treats corporate issues justifying investment

Chaffey D. (1998). *Groupware, Workflow and Intranets*. Digital
An interesting overview of the design issues in collaborative applications.

Delmater R. and Hancock M. (2001). *Data Mining Explained: A Manager's Guide to Customer-Centric Business Intelligence*. Digital Press
This is a book written for managers who have a technical orientation. It explains in an easy way how data mining will determine future customer relationship strategies. The book describes how to develop a data mining strategy and shows how data mining can be applied to specific vertical markets. There are a number of case studies of key industries such as retail, financial services, health care and telecommunications.

Dix A. *et al.* (2003). *Human Computer Interaction*. Prentice Hall
A very readable book investigating the usability of computer technology. The book takes a multidisciplinary approach. Many examples are provided, in particular from web applications.

Edwards J.S. and Finaly P.A. (1997). *Decision Making with Computers: The Spreadsheet and Beyond*. Pitman
Aimed at the reader with existing knowledge of the use of computers and spreadsheets, the book is intended to explain new decision-making techniques that will enable the most effective use to be made of the spreadsheet facilities. It also contains chapters on the methodology of good spreadsheet design. It is aimed at the business person rather than the computer scientist.

Galitz W. (2007). *The Essential Guide to User Interface Design: An Introduction to GUI Design Principles and Techniques*. John Wiley & Sons.
This describes the fundamentals of good interface design. The book covers a range of GUI applications, including design for the web.

Inmon W.H. (2005). *Building the Data Warehouse*, 4th edn. John Wiley & Sons.
The book covers, at an accessible level for students or managers, data warehousing techniques for customer sales and support, including data mining, exploration warehousing, and the integration of data warehousing with ERP systems. Future trends including capturing and analysing clickstream data for e-business are covered.

Isaacs E. (2002). *Designing from Both Sides of the Screen: A Dialogue Between a Designer and an Engineer*. Sams
This is equally relevant to software engineers and designers. It covers the principles of good interface design and provides many examples of good and bad practice. An extended case study provides the context for much of the theory.

Marakas G.M. (2003). *Decision Support Systems in the 21st Century*. Prentice Hall

This book covers decision support systems, modelling decision processes, group decision support, knowledge engineering, data warehouses and data mining. It also covers implementing and integrating decision support systems.

Mo A.M. (2003). *Advanced Topics in End User Computing*. Idea Group

This offers a more theoretical and in-depth approach to issues in end-user computing.

Preece J. (1998). *A Guide to Usability: Human Factors in Computing*. Addison-Wesley

This book provides a clear and concise account of the human factors in computing.

Regan E. and O'Connor B. (2006). *End User Information Systems: Implementing Individual and Work Group Technologies*. Prentice Hall

This is written in a style that would be easily accessible to both general managers and those involved in technical support. It covers help-desk management, office automation, and a vast range of end-user issues. It also provides techniques in managing projects in this area.

Shneiderman B. (2004). *Designing the User Interface*, 3rd edn. Addison-Wesley

This book provides a straightforward, thorough and relatively jargon-free exposition of the development of effective interactive software.

Thomsen E. (2002). *OLAP Solutions: Building Multidimensional Information Systems*. John Wiley & Sons.

An interesting text covering the technical aspects of data warehousing, data mining, and online analytical processing. Using case studies, it also attempts to explain how these tools and techniques can inform the decision-making process.

Turban E. *et al.* (2006). *Decision Support and Business Intelligence Systems*. Prentice Hall

This is a comprehensive textbook covering all aspects of DSS and expert systems from the perspective of a manager wishing to know about management support technologies. It has several case studies and chapter-end questions.

Chapter 8

File organization and databases for business information systems

Learning outcomes

On completion of this chapter, you should be able to:

■ Describe the physical and logical characteristics and structures of computer files and records

■ Compare and contrast file-based and database approaches to data management

■ Describe alternative approaches to data modelling and database design.

Introduction

This chapter covers the organization, storage of and access to business data held in files and databases. It introduces key concepts in the representation of data at both a logical and a physical level. The central ideas behind files and file access are explained. Files and file-based approaches to data storage are important, but they suffer from limitations. Database systems were developed as a response to these shortcomings. File-based and database approaches to data storage are compared. The central ideas underlying databases and database management systems are explained. As well as highlighting the facilities offered by database systems, the importance of data models is stressed. The analysis of an organization's data requirements, the development of a data model for that organization and database design techniques are left to Chapter 13 on data analysis and modelling, part of the sequence of chapters on systems analysis and design.

8.1   Files and file structures

The survival and successful growth of a business organization depends crucially on the data it keeps. Whether the business is computerized or not, much of this data will be held in files. A manufacturing company will keep files on its employees, customers, stock supplies, plant and many other items. These files will be updated by data on employee hours worked, customer sales and payments, and stock transactions. The files will be searched and sometimes sorted.

Figure 8.1 Producing a wage slip by consulting a manual file

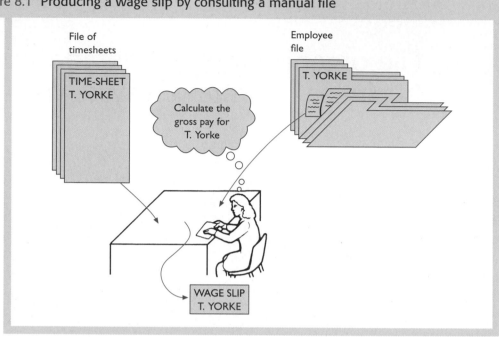

Simple concepts used in the operation of manual files are often a good guide to computerized data processing. Figure 8.1 is an illustration of the process of producing a wage slip. Time-sheet data on an employee is taken from a file. The relevant employee record is then found in the employee file. Data from this record is used to produce a wage slip, and the employee record is updated. Exactly the same description could be applied in a computer-based system. The only difference is that the files would be held on tape or disk and the process of producing a wage slip would be handled by a computer program.

Document files in manual systems contain records. For instance, an employee file will contain records on employees. These records are often collections of employee data prepared on preprinted company documentation. Other documents, old references and the like are kept in an individual employee's record. A cursory glance through document files may indicate that there is little organization in them.

By contrast, a **computer file** is more structured. It contains records of the same **record type** rather than a mixed collection of data held in different formats. An example of a simple employee file is shown in Figure 8.2(a). For each employee, data such as the employee # (# is the symbol that commonly abbreviates number), name, date of appointment, salary and sex are held. This data will be used in a number of activities, such as preparing the payroll and establishing the length of service of employees.

Each record is a collection of **data items** on each employee. These data items are also sometimes known as **field values**. For instance, in Figure 8.2(a) the field values are 1234, Yorke, Jones, 14500, etc. The **fields** themselves correspond to the types of data held on the employee and are *employee#, family name, first name, date of appointment, salary* and *sex*.

The record type (or structure as it is often called) is shown in Figure 8.2(b). Saying that a file contains records of the same record type means that all records in the employee

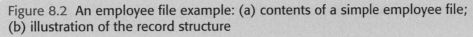

Figure 8.2 An employee file example: (a) contents of a simple employee file; (b) illustration of the record structure

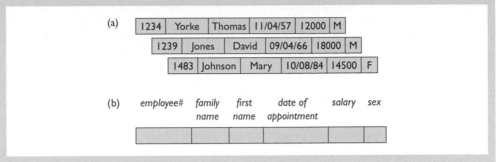

file exhibit that structure. It is important to realize that we know that Yorke is the family name of the employee and Thomas is the first name *not* because of our knowledge of typical family and first names but rather because of the positions of the data items in the record structure.

The distinction between data and the objects in the world on which the data is kept is important. It is necessary to keep this distinction in mind in order to understand some of the modelling ideas covered in Chapter 13 on data analysis and modelling. This is summarized in Figure 8.3.

The **key field** of a record type is an important concept. It is the field that uniquely identifies a record. The key field in the employee record would be *employee#*, because a value such as 1234 will occur in only *one* record. This is the reason that employers are given employee numbers – to identify them and their records. If there are two key fields in a record type, one is called the **primary key**. This is the one that is most likely to be used to pick out the record. For instance, in an employee record the National Insurance number of the employee would also be a key, but the *employee#* would be the primary key.

Obviously, the record structure in Figure 8.2(b) has too few fields to be realistic for an employee file. It is left as an exercise for the reader to list the fields that he or she would expect to find on an employee record type. Think of the processes for which a business might wish to use an employee record. The data needed for these will give a clear indication of which fields should exist.

Figure 8.3 The relation between the world and data

Example	World	Corresponds to	Data	Example
Thomas Yorke	Object	→	Record	1234 Yorke Thomas...
Employee	Object type	→	Record type	(employee#, family name ...)
Sex	Attribute	→	Field	sex
Male	Value of attribute	→	Field value or data item	M

8.2   Records and record structure

A simple record structure consists of a fixed number of fields of a fixed length. The record structure in Figure 8.2(a) is an example of this. A file comprised of records with this simple structure is often referred to as a **flat file** as it can be pictured as repeated rows of identically structured data. There are shortcomings associated with restrictions such as these. An important problem arises with the desire to have many occurrences of the same field in a record. For example, in an employee file it may be useful to hold not only the current position, date of appointment and salary but also the history of the employee with the organization. One way of achieving this is to have a fixed number of fields set aside for the past history. This may not be satisfactory. An employee may have held only one position with the firm, in which case several fields will be blank, or may have had more positions than can be accommodated by the number of repeated fields. In the latter case, only the most recent history of the employee can be held. The solution is to allow a field or group of fields to be repeated. Figure 8.4(a) gives an example of this. Note that the key is underlined and that the repeating group of fields is indicated by [field1, field2, . . .]*. The asterisk indicates repetition. The employee record shown is regarded as two-dimensional.

Figure 8.4 (a) A two-dimensional record structure; (b) a three-dimensional record structure

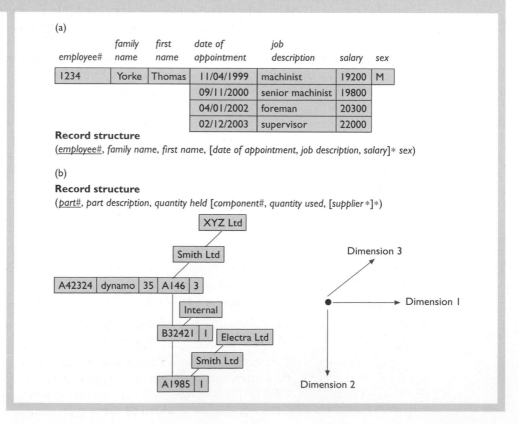

(a)

employee#	family name	first name	date of appointment	job description	salary	sex
1234	Yorke	Thomas	11/04/1999	machinist	19200	M
			09/11/2000	senior machinist	19800	
			04/01/2002	foreman	20300	
			02/12/2003	supervisor	22000	

Record structure

(employee#, family name, first name, [date of appointment, job description, salary]* sex)

(b)

Record structure

(part#, part description, quantity held [component#, quantity used, [supplier *]*)

A record structure can have repeating fields within repeating fields. For instance, a record of stock held by a manufacturing company may contain a variable number of fields for the components and for each component a variable number of fields for the suppliers. This is shown in Figure 8.4(b). It is called a three-dimensional record structure.

Record structures can be multidimensional, but details of the number of repeating groups and groups within groups must be held somewhere in the record. When programs are written to obtain information from these files the programmer's task is made considerably more complex. They now need to pay particular attention to the structure of the record as well as to the task for which the obtained data is to be used.

8.3 Physical and logical views of data

An important concept in data processing and systems analysis and design is the difference between a physical and a logical view of data. Broadly speaking, a **logical view** is concerned with the nature of the data or information as viewed independently from the physical details of storage or presentation. In contrast, a **physical view** involves physical aspects of the storage and presentation. The difference is important. A business computer systems analyst will be interested in the nature of the data stored and in what forms it needs to be retrieved. Exactly how this data is stored will be of less interest. Technical details on, say, disk sector division and blocking factors are not needed. The analyst is concerned with the use made of data in the functioning of the business. The technical systems analyst and the programmer, though, must pay attention to physical detail in order to design technically efficient storage and write programs that access data in stored files.

In the present context, the difference between a logical and a physical view of files and record structures can be summarized as follows.

8.3.1 Records

Physical and logical record structures

A logical view of a record structure consists of the names of the record fields, including repeating groups. A logical view of a record (logical record) is the set of data items filling that structure.

A physical view of a record structure shows how the logical view of the structure is implemented. The following, from Figure 8.2, illustrates physical details:

- The *employee#* consists of up to six characters preceded by leading blanks.
- The *family name* and the *first name* consist of characters, the two fields being divided by a *.
- The *salary* consists of a binary number 16 bits long.
- The *date* consists of eight characters representing the year/month/date in that order – for example, 6 February 2003 is represented as 20030206.

A **physical record** is the minimum chunk of data that is transferred between the storage medium and the CPU in the course of data processing. It is sometimes called a block. The physical record may contain many logical records or, if the logical records are large, several physical records may be spanned by one logical record.

Fixed-length and variable-length records

A decision to be taken at the physical level of record design is whether the record structure should be of a predetermined size – a fixed-length record – or whether it should be allowed to expand and contract to accommodate the size of the actual field items stored in it – a variable-length record.

A comparison of fixed- and variable-length records is shown in Figure 8.5. There are advantages and disadvantages to each.

If a variable-length record is used, it is apparent that the storage locations occupied are all gainfully employed, with the small addition of some markers to indicate the end of each field. Where a fixed-length structure is operated, the field lengths default to the size of the largest expected item. A large amount of storage space is thus potentially wasted using fixed-length records.

When a query is carried out a record must be located. If all records are of the same length, a simple arithmetic calculation (such as *record number × record length*) may

Figure 8.5 (a) Fixed-length records; (b) variable-length records

(a)

FORENAME	SURNAME	DEPARTMENT	SALARY
Linsey----------	Woodcock--------------	Quality Control------	-43000
Oliver---------	Smee------------------	Sales----------------	-24000
Myra----------	Cottesmore-------------	Marketing----------	-45000
Ajay-----------	Yousef-----------------	Finance-------------	-45000
Kosoladevi-------	Thirugnansampantamoorthy	Director------------	103000
Ukay-----------	Amponsah--------------	Production ---------	-64000

Each record shown occupies 55 characters of data storage. The six records require 330 (6 × 55) characters of data storage space. 151 of the characters (almost 50% of the file) are redundant space characters (represented by the – character to make them visible here).

(b)

Linsey*Woodcock*Quality Control*43000*Oliver*Smee*Sales*24000*Myra* *continued*

Cottesmore*Marketing*45000*Ajay*Yousef*Finance*45000*Kosoladevi* *continued*

Thirugnansampantamoorthy*Director*103000*Ukay*Amponsah*Production*64000*

Records are stored contiguously in the file using, in this example, markers represented by the * character to separate the fields. The total storage requirement is 203 characters (including the markers which occupy less than 13% of the file).

lead directly to the position of the required record in the file. Where the records have a variable-length structure a sequential search through all preceding records is required to reach the required record. Searching through a file comprised of variable-length records can therefore take much longer than for fixed-length records.

8.3.2 Files

A **logical** view of a file is the representation of the logical records together with the order in which they are represented for storage and retrieval purposes. For instance, an employee file might have its records arranged in ascending order of *employee#*, as they were in Figure 8.2.

A **physical** view of a file consists of the way in which the physical records are stored. For example, an employee file can be stored on several disks, with an index stored on a different disk from the disks on which the records are stored. The records can be stored physically adjacent to one another in ascending order of *employee#*. Once one track is filled, the next track inwards contains the next record. When records are deleted they may not be removed from the disk but merely marked with an *X* in the delete field of each physical record. These are all physical details of a file.

When programs are written, the programmer will need to be aware of some of the physical structure of the records and the way that the files may be spread across tracks. However, the analyst who is designing the file structure for a system need concentrate initially only on the logical aspects of the files to ensure that the data held is sufficient for the task for which it is required. Later, the analyst will decide on how the file is to be arranged physically. The distinction between logical and physical views is never as clear-cut in practice as has been suggested. Rather, there is a spectrum ranging from logical to physical on which a particular view will lie. As will be demonstrated in Chapters 10–16 on systems analysis and design, the distinction between logical and physical views of data, although difficult to grasp at first, is important because it runs right through the process of analysis and design.

8.4 Data storage – files, records and lists

There are many ways of categorizing files, but in data processing there is an important division of files in terms of their usage: files may be master, transaction or backup files.

1. A **master file** consists of records that contain standing data on entities that are of a permanent nature and are of importance for the successful operation of the business. For example, an employee master file holds the employee name, address and date of birth, all of which need little or no change, together with data on gross pay to date and tax paid to date, which would be regularly updated. Master files can be logically organized in a number of ways. For example, an employee master file may be in employee # sequence or with an index on employee name, or both.

2. A **transaction file** contains records, each of which relates to a single, usually dated, event or fact. These files are source data and are used to amend or update master files. For example, a timesheet transaction file contains records, each of which has data on the number of hours worked by a particular employee.

3. **Backup files** are copies of transaction files and master files held for security purposes.

Files may be physically stored on disk in the following ways:

- **Sequentially:** Records are physically ordered by some field such as employee number.
- **Randomly:** Records are stored at a physical address computed by an algorithm working on a field value such as the employee number.
- **Indexed:** Records are physically stored randomly with a sequentially ordered index field (e.g. by customer name) and a pointer to the physical location of each record.
- **Indexed-sequential:** Records are physically stored sequentially ordered by some field together with an index, which provides access by some, possibly other, field.

If files need only be processed sequentially, then they can be stored sequentially. The sequential update of an employee master file by timesheet data is an example. However, if individual records need to be accessed from time to time by some field, for example employee name, then one of the other storage methods must be used.

In the files considered so far, the individual records have not been connected to one another in any way. With a simple **list structure**, each record has one field in it that points to (has the address of) another record in the structure. Thus a list could be linked by pointer fields that point from one record to another in ascending order of customer name alphabetically. Insertion and deletion of records merely involves the readjustment of pointers. Sequential processing involves passing along the list. List structures may be extremely complex, with many pointer fields in each record, so that records can be accessed sequentially in many ways. Also, indexes may be attached to list structures to allow maximum flexibility in data access. If all the fields of a record that can take values have indexes, the file is said to be **fully inverted**.

Because pointer organizations allow data to be retrieved in flexible ways, list structures are among those used in databases. Access to the database and the insertion and deletion of records are controlled by specialized software called a database management system. This is covered extensively in later sections of this chapter.

8.5 File-based and database approaches to data storage

A central feature of a database approach is the recognition that data is an important resource of an organization. Data is not regarded merely as the input and output of the data-processing department but as a valuable asset that requires careful planning and management.

The database is a store of data that may be used for many applications in the organization. It must be designed to service these and future needs. In particular, it must allow extraction of information for management information requirements in as flexible a manner as is needed for management decision making. For this reason, the database is at the heart of a comprehensive and evolving management information system.

The main characteristics of a modern database are:

- It is an integrated store of shared data for servicing the requirements of many users and applications.
- It is structured in a manner that is logically meaningful to the organization. For example, if data was held both on employees and on the company projects on which they work, then in the database there would be a link between the data on each employee and the data on the projects on which they work.

■ There is minimal redundancy of data; this means that as far as possible the same item of data will not be repeated in the database.

Modern databases are usually held online on disk. Databases require careful design because they hold information that is structured for the organization. An important aspect of management is the use of software to handle all data access to the database. This software, the **database management system**, interfaces between users and user applications and the database itself, so enabling centralized control over the data. The main characteristics of a modern database management system (DBMS) are:

■ It is software that handles all read and write access by users and application programs to the database.

■ It is capable of presenting users with a view of that part of the database that is relevant to their needs.

■ It presents a logical view of data to users – details of how this data is stored and retrieved by the database management system software are hidden.

■ It ensures that the database is consistent.

■ It allows authorization of different users to access different parts of the database.

■ It allows the person in control of the database to define its structure.

■ It provides various facilities for monitoring and control of the database.

The differences between a file-based and database approach towards data can be seen in Figures 8.6 and 8.7. Three application programs are considered in this example. In Figure 8.6, the company runs a payroll program that uses a payroll master file for employee details. The data on this payroll file is the responsibility of the payroll department. The company also runs a program for handling various departmental administration routines to do with staffing and staff locations. This was developed later

---

Figure 8.6 An illustration of an application-led, file-based approach

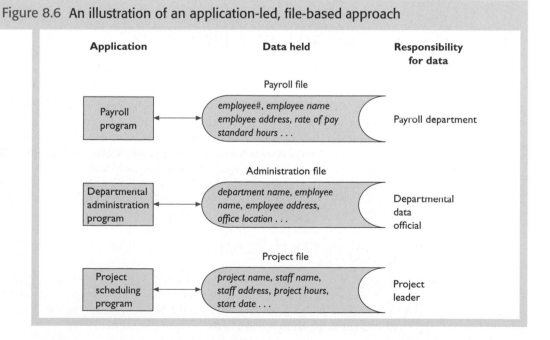

Application	Data held	Responsibility for data
	Payroll file	
Payroll program	employee#, employee name employee address, rate of pay standard hours . . .	Payroll department
	Administration file	
Departmental administration program	department name, employee name, employee address, office location . . .	Departmental data official
	Project file	
Project scheduling program	project name, staff name, staff address, project hours, start date . . .	Project leader

Figure 8.7 **An illustration of a database management system interfacing user programs and a database**

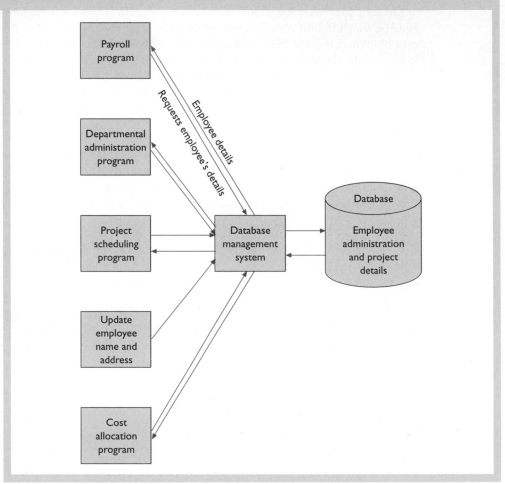

and has its associated file, the administration file. Each department has an official who is responsible for forwarding data changes for this file. The company also has a program to aid the scheduling of staff to the various projects on which they work. Ensuring that project details are up to date is the responsibility of each project leader. This example typifies characteristics of the file-based approach:

- Files are developed in a piecemeal fashion to service the data needs of an application and are associated with that application.
- The same data may be repeated on many files – for example, *employee address*.
- The same data may be held under different names – for example, *employee name* and *staff name*.
- The physical characteristics of storage of the same data on different files may be different.
- The responsibility for data is dispersed.

Two main problems arise with this approach. First, amendment of data is likely to lead to inconsistent data being held by the organization. In the example, if an employee changes his or her address, unless this is notified to all persons responsible for files on which this data is held, updates will be haphazard and inconsistency will result. Second, the retrieval of data for new applications is difficult. Suppose it is required to develop a program that allocates costs against projects (for pricing purposes) and allocates costs against departments (for internal budgeting and management accounting). All this data is present but is spread over three files and is not easily accessible. It may be difficult to retrieve as it is not stored in a manner convenient for this new application.

The central weakness of the application-led approach is that files are tied to applications, not to the objects or entities to which those files refer. Another way of viewing the position of the data needs of the organization in the example is to recognize that three types of entity are involved – EMPLOYEES, DEPARTMENTS and PROJECTS. Not only may details be held on these entities but there are also relations between them. EMPLOYEES *work* on PROJECTS and are *members* of DEPARTMENTS. These relationships are ignored in the file-based approach, only being recognized when needed for an application. Databases and database management systems manage to encode these relationships.

In Figure 8.7, the database approach overcomes the difficulties experienced by the applications-led, file-based approach by storing all the organizational data in an integrated manner, which is accessible to all applications. Access to this database is always through the database management system. This ensures that consistency is maintained if data is altered, such as an employee address. The DBMS also provides data in the form required for new applications – for example, a cost allocation program.

8.5.1 The advantages of using a database approach

- **Data redundancy is reduced:** In the application-led, file-based approach, data such as *employee name* may be unnecessarily duplicated in various files. This is a waste of storage space and can be reduced, if not entirely eliminated, in a database system.

- **Data consistency can be maintained:** A corollary of the elimination of redundancy is that update inconsistency is reduced. Some inconsistency may result unless care is taken in database design, because some duplication of data is not eliminated.

- **Independence of data and programs is possible:** In the file-based approach considered earlier in this chapter, the application programs are closely interdependent with the file structure. For example, the payroll programs will need to 'know' how the employee file is organized in order to access records. It makes a great deal of difference whether the file is organized sequentially by *employee#* or organized with an *employee#* index. At the level of the record, the order of the fields and the length of each will probably need to be 'known' by the program. It is not possible to change the file organization or change the record structure without changing the program or programs that access it. The program is dependent on the data.

In a database system, many programs will share the same data. It is not desirable to require each program to be changed when there is a change in the physical form of storage of data. (Changes in physical storage can be made for reasons of technical efficiency.) The database management system maintains the same view of the data to the accessing program no matter how the data may be reorganized physically on the disk.

- **A logical view is presented to the user or user programs:** Following from the last point, it is clear that the view of data presented to users or user programs must be independent of the physical storage details – it must be logical. Many database management systems allow different logical views of the same data to be presented to different users or programs. This is important as it frees programmers from a need to pay attention to the physical details of storage and allows them to concentrate on the applications to be coded. In the example covered earlier in this chapter, it is much easier for programmers to develop the cost allocation program if it is not necessary to consider the physical details of data retrieval. Programmers can concentrate on *how* to do a task, not on how to obtain the data to do it.

- **Applications development is enhanced because data sharing is possible:** The ability to use the database management system to retrieve data across the database in any required form once it has been stored opens up the range of applications for which the existing data can be used.

- **Standards can be enforced:** The fact that all access to data occurs via the database management system allows the individual responsible for this, the database administrator (DBA), to ensure that applications standards are followed in the representation of data.

- **Security is more easily implemented:** The DBA will control access to the database. The DBA can ensure that authorization codes for users are set restricting their access to only those parts of the database and for only the functions (read, write, copy) that are legitimate to their data purposes. Databases allow more effective control over access than the dispersal of responsibility associated with file-based systems. However, a breach of security may lead to a greater risk, as more data is accessible than with a traditional file-based system.

The advantages of a database approach can be summarized in that it leads to a system where:

- data management and control are more effective; and
- the ability to share data is increased.

8.5.2 Disadvantages of a database approach

Databases have become more common in recent years, but they still have limitations, and there are circumstances that might suggest a file-based environment is more appropriate.

- **Database design involves time and cost:** When an organization opts for a database approach it is necessary to pay considerable attention at the outset to the design of the database structure. This involves a study of the entities on which the organization wishes to hold data, the types of data to be held on these entities and the relationships and links between them. In comparison, a file-based approach leads to a piecemeal design of files for applications as they are required. This both simplifies design and spreads the cost over time as applications arise.

- **Database hardware and software costs need to be taken into account:** The database management system for a mainframe computer system is a complex piece of software costing many thousands of pounds. It is usual to use a standard package such as IDMS or ORACLE. As the entire database must be online all the time, it is also essential to purchase large amounts of disk storage.

- **Database access is slower than direct file access:** Recovery of data from a database using a DBMS involves another layer of software over and above an application program directly reading a file. The database may be physically implemented using large numbers of pointers, which will slow down access. These two considerations imply that database access is considerably slower than reading files.

Over time, disk technology has become cheaper and faster, which diminishes the importance of some of the disadvantages and partially explains why there is a drift towards business databases. In general, a file-based approach will seem more appropriate (as compared with a database) if:

- Different applications require different data.

- Fast, repetitive transaction processing in high volumes is to be undertaken.

- The application needs of the organization are unlikely to change over time.

- Information production is according to standard formats – little flexibility is required.

For these reasons, it is common to use file-based systems for accounting purposes, particularly financial accounting and book-keeping, where heavy transaction processing occurs. The flexible requirements of internal management accounting and the provision of information for tactical and operational management decisions are best served by database systems supplying data through management information systems.

Mini case 8.1   FT

Databases

When the winning horse passes the finishing post at today's Epsom Derby to claim a share of the £1.25m prize pot, Weatherbys' meticulous record keeping will be trusted to prove there has been no skulduggery. Buried in the archives at the company headquarters in Wellingborough, Northamptonshire is a document detailing the scandalous events of the 1844 Derby – 'the dirtiest on record'. On that occasion stewards used Weatherbys' pedigree records to expose the 'winner', Running Rein, as a fraud. The disqualified horse was really called Maccabaeus, a four-year-old – too old to enter the race.

'It was much easier to do that sort of thing in the old days', says Johnny Weatherby, modern-day chairman of the family-run firm, which has provided British horseracing with its central administration for more than two decades.

The Weatherby name has for generations been associated with its role updating and publishing 'The General Stud Book'. This calf skin-bound bible, a Wisden for the horse racing community, documents the pedigree of every thoroughbred in the UK. The company has published the stud book every year since Mr Weatherby's ancestor, James Weatherby, collated the first edition in 1791.

Under a contract with the British Horseracing Board the company books all race entries, levies entry fees and distributes prize money. It records a jockey's colours, a ▶

horse's ownership and collates racing cards, programmes and calendars. It also runs an auction system by which racecourses bid to host prized races. The resulting volume of data collected by the company is vast. More than 50 of Weatherbys' 360 employees are IT specialists who manage its large database. It also employs laboratory technicians in Ireland to analyse foals' DNA, to provide proof of bloodline. When a thoroughbred is born a vet must record the foal's physical characteristics, insert a microchip and take a blood sample. The data is collated by Weatherbys and added to its database.

Adapted from: **Weatherbys bloodline runs into banking**
Chris Bryant, *Financial Times*, 2 June 2007

Questions

1. Could information on race horses be stored in a simple file-based system?
2. What are the advantages and disadvantage to Weatherbys of using a database rather than a file-based system?
3. How can such a database prevent fraud in the racing business?

8.5.3 Database users

The corporate database is an important resource and may be needed by several types of user. These generally fall into one of three categories. Each has differing levels of understanding of the database and differing requirements.

The database administrator

The database administrator (DBA) is an experienced and senior member of the computer centre staff. The post requires involvement with different categories of user as well as extensive technical knowledge. The dependence of the organization on the smooth and effective management of its data resource ensures that the DBA's post is one of considerable responsibility. The DBA is typically involved in:

- assisting the development of the database during the analysis and design life cycle of the information system;
- achieving and maintaining an acceptable level of technical performance of the database;
- attaining a satisfactory level of security, including:
  - ensuring that authorization codes for database access are implemented according to the rules of the organization;
  - ensuring that backup and recovery facilities in case of database failure are adequate;
  - establishing integrity constraints within the database;
- monitoring use of the database from the point of view of accounting and the efficient utilization of the data resource;
- reorganizing the physical structure of the database when necessary;
- setting standards for documentation and data representation in the database;
- liaising with users of the database to ensure that their data requirements are satisfied;
- educating the organization on the use and availability of the database.

Applications programmers

Applications programmers are responsible for developing and maintaining programs for the functions required by the organization. Many of these programs will involve manipulation of data held in the database. Major programming languages contain instructions that enable calls to be made on the database via the database management system. This **data manipulation language** (DML) typically contains instructions governing the handling of data such as **STORE**, **RETRIEVE**, **MODIFY**, **DELETE** and **INSERT**. The programmer needs to know enough of the structure of the database to provide correct data-handling instructions in the host language.

Casual users

These are management and clerical personnel who make specific data enquiries of the database. This is an important group of users who are able to make *ad hoc* requests for information reports in a flexible way. They use simple query languages (see Section 8.5.4) to frame their requests. This group of users has been greatly liberated by the presence of online database systems. Previously, reports they required needed to be extracted in standard form and often produced at standard times. By being able to target their requests for information to what is relevant and obtaining speedy online responses, their decision making has become more effective.

8.5.4 Database utilities

In order to aid the DBA and other users in their tasks concerning the database, utility programs or modules are commonly used.

Query languages

Query languages are designed for casual users making enquiries of the database. Unlike data manipulation commands embedded in a host programming language such as COBOL, these languages can be used for *ad hoc* queries of the database. They are easy to understand and use and generally consist of near-English expressions. An example might be:

DISPLAY ALL EMPLOYEE.*employee-name* **FOR** EMPLOYEE.*employee-age* > 60

meaning 'display on the screen a list of employee names for all employees who are over 60 years old'.

It is easy to combine conditions in data enquiries. In the case of the employee/project/department example used earlier in this chapter, a typical request might be 'display all employee numbers and names for employees from any department located in London and working on more than two projects'. Such a request is easy to frame using a query language. It would be virtually impossible to extract such information from the file-based system. Examples of simple enquiries using actual query languages on databases are given in Section 8.7.

Data dictionaries

A data dictionary may be defined as a store of data about data. The data dictionary will keep information on the record types, field names and types, and other information on the structure of the database. Data dictionaries are useful for the development and maintenance of the database structure. Nowadays, data dictionaries are often part of the database itself.

Accounting and monitoring utilities

These are used by the DBA to determine the extent of use of the database by individuals, departments and other cost and use centres. This is useful information for charging the database to the various user departments.

Report generators

It is sometimes necessary to produce output data in a special format. This may be desirable for reasons of clarity or standardization in the company. Alternatively, there may be accepted and required formats for certain types of report. Common examples are balance sheets and profit and loss statements. Output data from a database is printed or displayed on the screen in a standard form. This is generally just a list of the data items produced by the database management system. Report generators are utilities that allow different formats to be defined for the data. They are generally powerful and easy to use.

Backup and recovery

In order to make sure that data is not lost irretrievably after a database failure it is common practice (from time to time) to dump or store the database on to a secure medium. Between these dumps, a record is automatically kept of every transaction that affects the database (insertion, deletion and modifications). This combination of the saved database plus the log file of these transactions allows the state of the database before failure to be recovered.

Concurrency control

Databases contain data that may be shared between many users or user applications. Sometimes there may be demands for concurrent sharing. An example is the simultaneous access to inventory data in a multi-access system by two different users. No problem arises if each demand is to read a record, but difficulties occur if both users attempt to modify the record at the same time. The database utility responsible for concurrent usage then 'locks' one user out until the modification by the other has been effected.

Physical reorganization

These aid the DBA with the efficient restructuring of the physical database when necessary. This restructuring is necessary as data modification, addition and deletion of records change the physical characteristics of the stored data, resulting in long access times or inefficient storage of data across many disks.

Mini case 8.2

FT

Databases

David Smith uses his actuarial background to apply a mathematical analysis – securing him a job at GAM. There are still many people running hedge funds who pride themselves on their ability to use contacts and golf club associates to secure access to some of the best hedge funds. But many more take an analytical approach, investing heavily in computer systems and researchers to look at the performance and underlying strategies of funds.

'When you think of what we actually do, we collect and interpret information', Mr Smith says. 'The more we can automate that the more methodical our interpretation can be and hence the more scalable we will become.' And automate it he has. GAM's latest set of databases, live for about a year, allow managers to drill down into each hedge fund's exposure to ensure the overall portfolio has the set exposure to each asset class, while examining volatility and performance for individual funds or asset types.

The new system grew out of Mr Smith's frustration at the difficulty of keeping up with the vast number of new funds being created. In February 2004 he took a momentous decision: he closed GAM's funds to new investments. 'The sales people went absolutely berserk', he recalls. 2004 saw the first year of underperformance.

The new system did not go down well with every hedge fund, either. Notoriously secretive, many funds refuse to disclose positions they have even to their investors – although GAM demands only data on allocations to classes of assets, such as commodities or equities, as a minimum.

But, after bedding down, the new system has paid off. Performance has returned and GAM, since sold to the Swiss bank Julius Baer, is again performing strongly.

Adapted from: **A maverick who used maths to make his clients a mint**
James Mackintosh, *Financial Times*, 4 June 2007

Questions

1. What facilities are provided by a database management system to a hedge fund manager?

2. To what extent do you think the use of a database was important in turning around the fortunes of the business referred to in the article?

8.6   A three-level architecture for databases

Some of the key reasons for the use of a database have been illustrated in terms of:

■ the separation of the data from the applications that use it;

■ the presentation of a logical view of the data independent of the physical details of storage; and

■ the restriction and presentation of only relevant data to users and application programs.

Central to the understanding of the way a database and DBMS works in achieving these aims is the concept of schemas and views. This is shown in Figure 8.8 (derived from the ANSI/SPARC Study Group's report in 1978).

In overview, the conceptual schema provides the logical view of the entire database, the external schemas provide 'tailored' views of the database for each application or user, and the internal schema provides information on the detailed aspects of data storage, which have little to do with the logical content of the data.

Figure 8.8 A three-level model of a database architecture

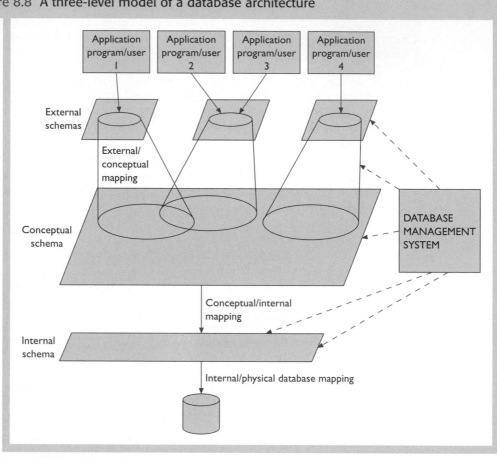

Source: Tsichritzis and Klug, 1978

Conceptual schema

The conceptual schema is the logical view of the entire database. Among other details it will contain a specification of:

- The types of data held on each entity of interest to the organization. For example, the following might be held on a supplier:
  - *supplier#*:numeric(6)
  - *supplier-name*:character(15)
  - *supplier-address*:character(30). . . .

This is similar to the specification of a record type.

- Any relationship between the entities. For example, suppliers *provide* products.
- Any restrictions on data – for example, *item-quantity* > 0.
- Authorization codes applicable to various items of data. For example, employee salary data may only be read by a user with authorization codes 5,6,9 and modified by a user with code 9.

The conceptual schema will be defined in a special language, the **data definition language** (DDL). This language is specific to the DBMS used. The schema can be regarded as derived from a model of the organization and should be designed with care as it is usual for its structure to remain relatively unchanged.

External schemas

An application program or user is uninterested in large sections of the database and is best presented with a view of the relevant sections. This is the external schema, and it exists in a subset of the conceptual schema. There may be a different external schema for each user of the database.

For instance, it is usual for a user to require only certain types of record and logical relationships between these. In these records, the user may need access to only a few selected fields in order to perform the specified user tasks. The external schema supplies just this window on the conceptual schema.

Internal schema

This describes how the database is implemented in terms of pointers, hashing functions, indexes, stored record sizes, and so on. It is concerned with storage details that are not part of a logical view of the database.

Mappings between schemas

As well as maintaining these views, the DBMS needs to keep a record of how each view is connected to (that is, maps to) each other. For instance, components of the internal schema will be represented at a logical level by components of the conceptual schema. It must be possible to reorganize the physical database without altering the logical content of the database (conceptual schema) or to alter the conceptual schema without altering the existing external schemas. The presence of mappings enables this.

For instance, it may be necessary to add extra fields to hold details on an employee's health where health details were not held before. This alteration to the conceptual (and internal) schema should not affect existing external schemas that have no need of this data. Again, it may be decided to reorganize the storage characteristics of the database for efficiency reasons. Although this may affect the internal schema, it should not affect either the conceptual or external schemas.

Models and schemas

This section has stated that the conceptual schema is derived from a model of the organization. It is important to be clear that a conceptual schema is defined in a data definition language that is particular to the DBMS used. Each DBMS imposes different restrictions on what can and cannot be defined. Some database management systems severely limit what can be specified within the conceptual schema for the benefit of providing fast data access times. Others are very flexible, at the expense of slow access speeds.

Most database management systems fall into one of four types, depending on what restrictions are imposed. These types correspond to four distinct models of data structures: network, hierarchical, relational and object oriented models.

- **Hierarchical model:** This was the first model to be developed. In this model data is organized hierarchically in a tree structure: a root node is connected to branches which in turn are connected to further branches with data stored at the leaf nodes.

This model is mainly associated with older, large-scale systems implemented on mainframe computers.

- **Network model:** The use of the term **network** in this context has no connotation of the interconnecting of computers; rather, it refers to the network of linkages between data items within files. A system of pointers is used to create the necessary structure in storing the data. This model is also mainly associated with older, large-scale implementations.

- **Object oriented model:** The increase in interest in object oriented systems has been accompanied by an increased interest in object stores – databases of objects. This is the newest of the four models and uptake is therefore much lower. Object orientation is discussed in greater detail in Chapter 16.

- **Relational model:** This is by far the most popular model in commercial database usage and as such the following section is devoted to explaining it in more detail.

8.7 Relational models

Relational data models draw heavily on the theoretical work carried out by E.F. Codd in the 1970s. Database management systems based around the relational model (such as ORACLE, SQLServer and MySQL) offer substantial advantages over the network and hierarchical approaches.

8.7.1 The model structure

In a relational model, data is stored in a **relation** (or table) as shown in Figure 8.9(a), the table for **EMPLOYEE**. It is important to distinguish between a relation, which is a term applying to a component of a relational model, and a relationship, which is a real-world association between objects. Muddling the two terms is a mistake. They have different meanings and, as will be shown later in this section, relationships can be represented by relations, although not all relations represent relationships.

Each table consists of a number of columns or **attributes**. In the example, *employee#*, *employee_name* and *employee_salary* are all attributes. Attributes take their values from a set of values of a common type known as the **domain** of the attribute. For example,

---

Figure 8.9 An example of a relation: (a) the relation as a table; (b) the relational structure

(a) EMPLOYEE

employee#	employee_name	employee_salary
134	Smith	12,000
146	Harvey	15,000
139	Jones	4,600
468	Mendez	14,000
201	Patel	9,000

(b) EMPLOYEE (*employee#*, *employee_name*, *employee_salary*)

employee_salary might have a domain consisting of integers greater than or equal to 0. Two different attributes may share the same domain.

A row of the table is also known as a **tuple**. No two rows in a table are allowed to be identical.

The number of attributes determines the degree of the relation. **EMPLOYEE** is a relation of degree 3. The number of rows or tuples is known as the **cardinality** of the relation.

An important relational concept is the **key attribute of a relation**, which is any attribute (or group of attributes) the value(s) of which uniquely identify a tuple of the relation.

A 'key attribute' is a semantic concept. This can be illustrated by considering the **EMPLOYEE** relation. A given value of *employee#* identifies exactly one row, if it identifies any at all. The same, however, appears to be true of *employee_name*. The difference is that there could be an occurrence in another row of the *employee_name* entry 'Smith' but there could not be another row with *employee#* '134'. Put another way, two employees might be named Smith, but it is not possible for two different employees to be numbered 134. Note that the key is underlined in the relational structure of Figure 8.9(b).

A formal definition of relation is:

> Given a collection of domains $D_1, D_2, \ldots D_n$ (not necessarily distinct), a relation, R, on these domains is a set of ordered n-tuples $\langle d_1, d_2, \ldots d_n \rangle$, where d_1 is a member of D_1, d_2 is a member of $D_2, \ldots d_n$ is a member of D_n.

This has two important formal implications. First, the order of rows in a relation is insignificant. The row corresponding to *employee#* = 139 in **EMPLOYEE** might have been at the top of the table. It would still have been the same relation.

Second, as the set is an ordered n-tuple the column ordering *is* significant. In the *EMPLOYEE* table, if *employee_salary* occurs between *employee#* and *employee_name* then it is a different relation. In practice, both of these pure conditions may not be followed in commercial relational database management systems. Different attribute order is often allowed, as users generally do not access a value in a row by its relative position but by the column name under which it falls. Some systems also allow an ordering among rows to be expressed, for example according to ascending *employee#*. Rows can then be retrieved in order.

The theoretical system, though, allows access to a tuple only by value and there is no implied index or ordering. The physical implementation in terms of indexes and pointers is unseen by the user.

The hierarchical, network and object oriented models represent relationships by links. The relational model represents a relationship by a relation or table. This is shown in Figure 8.10. The model in 8.10(b), together with the specification of the domain of each attribute, corresponds to a conceptual schema.

Remember that each employee belongs to just one department, whereas each department may have several employees. The key to the **DEPARTMENT** relation is *dept_name* and if this is added to the **EMPLOYEE** relation we can represent the fact that an employee is a member of a department. Loosely speaking, given an *employee#*, 139, the relevant **EMPLOYEE** tuple can be identified and the fact that the employee is in the production department established. Then from the **DEPARTMENT** table the relevant **DEPARTMENT** tuple containing the information on the department of production can be identified.

Figure 8.10 A relational model for EMPLOYEE/DEPARTMENTS/PROJECTS: (a) relations; (b) relational structure

(a)

EMPLOYEE

employee#	employee_name	employee_salary	dept_name
134	Smith	12,000	sales
146	Harvey	15,000	sales
139	Jones	4,600	production
468	Mendez	14,000	planning
201	Patel	9,000	production

DEPARTMENT

dept_name	dept_location
sales	floor 6
production	Tetherdown
planning	floor 5

PROJECT

project_name	budget
project A	45,000
project B	500,000
project D	9,400
project C	12,000

ASSIGNMENT

project_name	employee#	hours
project A	146	3.2
project B	134	9.0
project A	201	11.0
project C	146	4.9
project A	134	6.2
project B	146	6.1
project C	201	9.3

(b)

EMPLOYEE (*employee#*, employee_name, employee_salary, dept_name)

DEPARTMENT (*dept name*, dept_location)

PROJECT (*project name*, budget)

ASSIGNMENT (*project name, employee#*, hours)

Many employees are able to work on one project, and each project might have many employees assigned to it. This is shown by capturing the many-to-many relationship in a new relation, **ASSIGNMENT**. The unique key to this relation is not a single attribute but rather a combination of the key of **PROJECT**, *project_name*, and the key of **EMPLOYEE**, *employee#*. A key comprising a group of attributes in this way is termed a **combination key**. The field, *hours*, allows data on the number of hours that each employee works on each project to be stored.

In general, a $1:n$ relationship is represented in the relational model by inserting the key attribute of the entity on the n side of the relationship into the relation representing the entity on the 1 side of the relationship. A many-to-many relationship is represented by creating a new relation that has as its combination key the key attributes of each of the entities in the relationship.

It is important to be clear about the way the relational model is a data model of the world. The world can be viewed as being constructed of three types of component. There are entity types (types of objects), there are attributes of these objects, and there are relationships between the objects. The relational model represents an entity type by a relation or table and the attributes by columns of the table. An individual object with values of its attributes corresponds to a row in the table. A relationship between two objects is not modelled as a third type of component. Rather, the key attributes of each entity type are associated in a table that acts as proxy for the relationship. Relationships are not distinguished from entity types in the relational model. We only see the distinction because the table representing a relationship has a composite key, its components being the keys of the tables representing the entities in the relationship. There are only two distinct kinds of component in the relational model – tables (or relations) and values of attributes. In contrast, the network model straightforwardly represents entity types by record types, entities themselves by occurrences of these record types, relationships by links between the record types (CODASYL sets), and values of attributes of objects by data items in record occurrences.

Some of the advantages of relational systems are:

- Relational database models involve no non-logical concepts such as indexing, storage details or ordering, which occur in the network and hierarchical models.
- They require no non-logical access paths (via pointers, CODASYL sets or the like) to data items. These items are retrieved purely on the basis of the rules and conditions.
- The relational model is therefore a logical data model independent of storage considerations. It can be thought of as falling neatly into a conceptual schema level.
- Relational database systems allow large chunks of data to be processed in a single operation.

8.7.2 Conceptual, external and internal schemas

The relational equivalent of a conceptual schema is the set of relations defined in the relational model, together with specification of the domains of each attribute. In relational database management systems, these **base tables** have an independent existence.

At the internal schema level, each base table will probably correspond to a stored file and each row in the table to a record in the file. There may be many indexes associated with a given file. The conceptual view should not reveal these indexes (or if it does, data access should not be specifiable via them).

The equivalent of an external schema for a relational model is sometimes called a **view**. A particular view consists of presenting those attributes and tables needed for the specific purpose of a user. The contents of the view will be equivalent to a set of relations generated from the relations stored in the database. These relations may be either base table or relations capable of being generated from these by the relational operations described in Section 8.7.3.

8.7.3 Data manipulation

As well as independently existing relations (known as primary or base relations), which are stored, it may be necessary to generate new and temporary relations (known as **derived** relations) to answer user enquiries. The operations that may be legitimately performed on relations can be described using either relational algebra or relational calculus. The workings of both the algebra and the calculus have been extensively investigated from a mathematical perspective, and their properties are fully understood. All data manipulation is based on these, rather than the traversal of hierarchies or networks between records.

Three relational algebra operations, **SELECT**, **PROJECT** and **JOIN**, are illustrated. Each takes a relation (or number of relations) as its argument and produces a relation as its value.

1. **SELECT:** This produces a new relation consisting of a number of selected rows (tuples) from an existing relation. For example:

SELECT EMPLOYEE **WHERE** *employee_salary* > 13,000

gives the relation in Figure 8.11(a).

Figure 8.11 Examples of relational operators: (a) use of SELECT; (b) use of PROJECT; (c) use of JOIN; (d) use of nested operators

(a)

employee#	employee_name	employee_salary	dept_name
146	Harvey	15,000	sales
468	Mendez	14,000	planning

SELECT EMPLOYEE **WHERE** *employee_salary* > 13,000

(b)

employee_name	dept_name
Smith	sales
Harvey	sales
Jones	production
Mendez	planning
Patel	production

PROJECT EMPLOYEE **OVER** *employee_name, dept_name*

(c)

employee#	employee_name	employee_salary	dept_name	project_name	hours
134	Smith	12,000	sales	project B	9.0
134	Smith	12,000	sales	project A	6.2
146	Harvey	15,000	sales	project A	3.2
146	Harvey	15,000	sales	project C	4.9
146	Harvey	15,000	sales	project B	6.1
201	Patel	9,000	production	project A	11.0
201	Patel	9,000	production	project C	9.3

JOIN EMPLOYEE **AND** ASSIGNMENT **OVER** *employee#*

(d)

employee_name	project_name	hours
Smith	project B	9.0
Smith	project A	6.2
Harvey	project A	3.2
Harvey	project C	4.9
Harvey	project B	6.1

PROJECT (**SELECT** (**JOIN** EMPLOYEE **AND** ASSIGNMENT **OVER** *employee#*)
WHERE *dept_name = sales*) **OVER** *employee_name, project_name, hours*

2. **PROJECT:** This produces a new relation consisting of a number of selected columns (attributes) from an existing relation. For example:

> **PROJECT** EMPLOYEE **OVER** employee_name, dept_name

gives the relation in Figure 8.11(b).

3. **JOIN:** This produces a new relation from two existing relations joined over a common domain. It is best described algorithmically. First, take the first row from the first relation and compare the attribute value from the common domain with each value of the attribute from the common domain in the second relation. Wherever the two values are identical, form a row by concatenating the first row with the row from the second relation (striking out the repeat of the common attribute). Do this for each row in the first relation. For example:

> **JOIN** EMPLOYEE **AND** ASSIGNMENT **OVER** employee#

gives the relation in Figure 8.11(c).

It is possible to nest the operations. Suppose that a user wishes to establish the names, projects worked on and hours worked on these projects by staff in the sales department. This could be achieved by the following nested operations:

> **PROJECT** (**SELECT**(**JOIN** EMPLOYEE **AND** ASSIGNMENT **OVER** employee#)
> **WHERE** dept_name = sales) **OVER** employee_name, project_name, hours

By working from the innermost nesting outwards, the resulting relation can be constructed (see Figure 8.11(d)).

Relational algebra also uses other operations. There is a **DIVIDE** operation as well as the set theoretical operations corresponding to **UNION**, **INTERSECTION** and **DIFFERENCE**.

Relational algebra involves a procedural specification of how the final relation is to be constructed by defining intermediate relations to be produced. The relational calculus, in contrast, defines a relation in the form of a predicate. The calculus is a version of the predicate calculus applied to relational databases.

The relational algebra provides a formally precise way of extracting data. However, it is difficult to use to specify complex enquiries. It is not used itself to query a relational database or as a set of data manipulation procedures. Query languages and data manipulation languages derived from the algebra have been developed. These are straightforward to use and provide the ease and flexibility of enquiry that make relational databases powerful in the provision of information. IBM's SQL (structured query language) and QBE (query by example) are examples.

8.7.4 SQL

SQL is a relational data manipulation language developed by IBM initially for use with its relational database management system DB2. The language can be used for standalone queries or embedded in programs written in various languages. The language is simple enough that substantial parts may be employed by casual users for queries on the relational database. SQL has become the standard relational data manipulation language. Basic operations are covered below.

Projection

The project operation is implemented in SQL by the construction:

SELECT ⟨attribute 1, attribute 2 . . .⟩
    FROM ⟨relation⟩

The projection in Figure 8.11(b) would be framed as follows:

SELECT *employee_name, dept_name*
    FROM EMPLOYEE

This produces the result in the table in Figure 8.11(b). With SQL, it is possible to specify any desired order among the columns. A different command would have produced *dept_name* followed by *employee_name*. SQL projection differs from the logical projection operation in that duplicate tuples resulting from the projection would not be removed; in other words, the result of SQL projection is not strictly a relation.

Selection

Selection is achieved by adding a qualification to the **SELECT** command. Its construction is:

SELECT ⟨attribute 1 . . .⟩
    FROM ⟨relation⟩
    WHERE ⟨qualification⟩

The qualification is a Boolean construction using **AND**, **OR** or **NOT**. Using the **EMPLOYEE** relation in Figure 8.10, the following selection:

SELECT *employee_name, employee#*
    FROM EMPLOYEE
    WHERE *employee_salary* > 8,000
    AND (*dept_name* = Sales **OR** *dept_name* = Production)

would yield

SMITH	134
HARVEY	146
PATEL	201

Join

Join is achieved by specifying the two attributes (with common domain) over which the join is to be made. The construction is:

SELECT ⟨attribute 1 . . .⟩
    FROM ⟨relation 1, relation 2, . . .⟩
    WHERE ⟨attribute from relation 1 = attribute from relation 2 etc.⟩

If it is wished to select the names, project and hours worked on the projects by staff as shown in the **EMPLOYEE** and **ASSIGNMENT** relations in Figure 8.10, the join operation with the selection would be:

SELECT EMPLOYEE.*employee_name*, ASSIGNMENT.*project_name*, ASSIGNMENT.*hours*
    FROM EMPLOYEE, ASSIGNMENT
    WHERE EMPLOYEE.*employee#* = ASSIGNMENT.*employee#*

Figure 8.12 The result of the SQL **JOIN** command on **EMPLOYEE** and **ASSIGNMENT**

Smith	project B	9.0
Smith	project A	6.2
Harvey	project A	3.2
Harvey	project C	4.9
Harvey	project B	6.1
Patel	project A	11.0
Patel	project C	9.3

SELECT EMPLOYEE. *employee_name*, ASSIGNMENT. *project_name*, ASSIGNMENT.*hours*
FROM EMPLOYEE, ASSIGNMENT
WHERE EMPLOYEE. *employee*# = ASSIGNMENT. *employee*#

This command gives the display in Figure 8.12. SQL commands can be nested, and several relations can be 'searched' by using join qualifications with more than two relations. The following command lists employee names, the projects on which they work and the budgets of these projects using the relations in Figure 8.10:

SELECT EMPLOYEE.*employee_name*, ASSIGNMENT.*project_name*, PROJECT.*budget*
FROM EMPLOYEE, ASSIGNMENT, PROJECT
WHERE EMPLOYEE.*employee*# = ASSIGNMENT.*employee*
AND ASSIGNMENT.*project_name* = PROJECT.*project_name*

SQL allows nesting of the **SELECT–FROM–WHERE** construction, and it is often easier to conceptualize a query this way. For instance, the following query selects the names of employees working on a project for more than eight hours.

SELECT *employee_name*
FROM EMPLOYEE
WHERE employee# = **ANY** (**SELECT** *employee*# **FROM** ASSIGNMENT
WHERE *hours* > 8.0)

As well as searching, SQL allows deletion and insertion of rows using the **DELETE** and **INSERT** commands. These work using the same underlying principles as the constructions that apply to **SELECT**.

8.7.5 Query by example

Query by example (QBE) is a query technique for relational database systems that uses the idea of a table (relation) with which to frame the query. The language is designed to be used interactively with a VDU. The user selects the desired relation or relations and is then presented with a skeleton table. From the various fields shown the user can select the fields to be displayed in response to the query. Conditions are entered in the other fields as desired. Figure 8.13 is an example involving selection and projection from one relation. It specifies the retrieval of all employee names together with their department names where the employee earns more than £13,000 per year. More complex queries may involve several relations and complicated search conditions. QBE queries can be created that involve several relations and complex search conditions. The power of modern QBE facilities is approaching that of SQL; indeed,

Figure 8.13 A QBE query on EMPLOYEE

Query

EMPLOYEE	employee#	employee_name	employee_salary	dept_name
		P. Fred	> 13,000	P. Stores

Response

employee_name	dept_name
Harvey	sales
Mendez	planning

many systems allow QBE queries to be automatically converted to SQL for further editing and optimization.

8.7.6 Assessment of relational database models

The relational model, relational database management systems and relational languages have had a large impact on the development of sophisticated data resources. Their advantages are summarized below.

Advantages

- They provide a clear and conceptually straightforward representation of complex data relations.
- They allow powerful data manipulation and query languages to operate on them.
- The database is maintained in a table form, which is a 'natural' representation of data to business-oriented users.
- Query languages (such as QBE) can be developed to exploit this tabular form.
- Data is accessed by value and conditions, and the database can be accessed from any point (relation).
- Access paths are not seen (or usable) by the database users.
- The representation of the data is entirely logical, once again reinforcing the simplicity of representation from the point of view of users and application programmers.

Disadvantages

- The indexes used in implementation are often large and require heavy storage overheads.
- The operational speed of current commercial relational database systems can be slower than systems that have been designed and programmed using high-level languages and file handling routines. This makes them unsuitable for some very high-volume processing activities.

As disk storage capacities and disk access speeds rise, combined with the diminishing cost of disk storage, the flexible features of relational databases will ensure their long-term superiority in the marketplace.

8.8 Object oriented databases

The relational database described in detail in Section 8.7 has become an industry standard for much of the database development that occurs today. The recent attention on the object oriented model for information systems development has been reflected by interest in object oriented databases. Whereas a relational database stores data in relations as rows of tuples, an object oriented database stores collections of objects. This is explained further in the next section.

8.8.1 The object oriented perspective of information systems

The relational model views the world as entities, attributes and the relationships between them. The missing component in this model is the processing carried out on that data. Proponents of the object oriented model argue that to separate data and process in this way leads to a weakness in the design of systems. Indeed, it is using an unnecessarily artificial premise upon which to model the physical system. They would point out that real-world 'objects' are viewed and described in terms of what they do as well as what they are. Using this approach, an object such as a bank account is described using the attributes that describe its state (the account holder's name, the account number, the balance, etc.) as well as the activities that the object initiates or participates in (debiting and crediting the account, calculating interest accrued, etc). A bank account object would therefore contain both the account data and the operations that the account must carry out.

8.8.2 Object oriented database management systems

If the world is to be modelled as objects then a database management system is required that can store these objects. Object oriented databases fulfil this role. Each type of object is specified as a collection of data items and of functions that can be invoked. The actual instances of these objects can then be created and stored. Because the functions for every instance of a particular object type are identical, only a single copy of these functions is usually stored, with pointers to connect object instances to their functions. An example of an organization using an object oriented database is MedStar Health, a large community-based, not-for-profit health system in the Baltimore–Washington region of the United States. The system integrates a range of functions, including financial, clinical and administrative data. It employs ORACLE database technology and object oriented data models with online analytical processing.

Although only a small proportion of the database systems developed at present use an object oriented database management system, a view held by many is that this will grow rapidly as object modelling approaches gain a wider audience. Hybrid databases built on an integrated object–relational model are more likely to obtain commercial acceptance and are already gaining in popularity.

Mini case 8.3

Object oriented databases

During the past two decades of the software industry, the database vendors ruled the roost and Larry Ellison, founder and chief executive of Oracle, was the industry's chief rooster. But Mr Ellison has less to crow about these days. The database market is mature and global sales of new licences in 2002 dropped 6.9% to $6.6bn, according to Gartner Dataquest, the IT researcher.

'This is about the third or fourth time that the database has been declared dead, but the database is more important than ever', says Chuck Rowzat, executive vice-president of server technologies at Oracle. 'People come up with new types of data and models for how information is accessed.'

This drives innovation in database technology and creates new demand, he says. For example, in the late 1990s, the Internet created new market opportunities for storing web pages and other Internet data. Oracle responded with Oracle8, the predecessor to its current database, which was designed to support the Internet, network computing and 'richer' multimedia data types.

Oracle also included support for object-oriented development, thus answering those critics who argued that the relational database could not adapt to new types of data. In the 1990s, when object technologies were all the rage, a clutch of little-known vendors tried to create an alternative database industry around the object model. They failed to make much of an impression, although Versant, the best known, is still around and making sales. Manish Chandra, vice-president of marketing at Versant and a former Sybase engineer, argues that an object database is still the best choice for 'real world' data, such as GPS positioning signals or real-time data collected from the factory floor, but for mainstream commercial applications, a relational database is probably a better bet.

'There are still a few zealots who want to apply object technology to everything but we no longer try to compete with the relational database vendors', he says.

Adapted from: **Battle to make sense of it all**
Geoffrey Nairn, FT.com, 6 August 2003

Questions

1. What are the arguments for adopting an object database?
2. In what ways does the object model differ from the relational model?

Summary

Business organizations need to keep and process data for their survival. Data is held in master files about ongoing entities of interest to the business. Examples are customer, debtor, employee and stock files. Data used to update master files is stored in transaction files. Examples are sales, payments, receipts, time-sheet returns, credit notes and sales order files. The storage and access strategies for disk files go hand in hand. List structures offer the capability of sequential access while providing for fast record insertion and deletion. Inverted list structures place attribute values in indexes, and pointer fields are transferred from the records to the index. This opens the way for the retrieval of records based on properties of record fields other than the key field.

The database approach recognizes data as an important resource of the organization that is shared by many applications and so requires careful planning, management and control. Databases and database management systems have been developed to replace file-based systems of data storage. This is because, first, sophisticated file interrogation techniques have led to the need for automated data management and, second, business has demanded more flexible data retrieval and reporting facilities to meet the needs of managerial decision making.

File-based, application-led approaches to data storage often lead to problems. The duplication of data over many files, each being the responsibility of a different person or department, can lead to update difficulties and the presence of inconsistent data in the organization. The same data may also be represented in different storage formats in different files, and the files themselves may have different organization and access characteristics. The dependence of application programs on the files that serve them increases the difficulty of changing data storage structures without having to change the programs that access them.

The database approach, on the other hand, recognizes the importance of developing an integrated store of data structured in a meaningful manner for the organization. The database contains data stored with minimal redundancy and organized in a manner that is a logical reflection of the relationships between the entities on which data is held.

Database management systems are sophisticated software packages that maintain the database and present an interface to users and user programs that is independent of physical storage details. This logical presentation of the data facilitates user enquiries and applications program development – programmers need be concerned only with what data is required for an application, not with the physical aspects of how to retrieve it. The independence of the logical representation also allows physical reorganization of the database without the need for application program changes. Commercial database systems define the logical structure of the database using a data definition language (DDL) and allow data alterations through a data manipulation language (DML). Other facilities provided are data dictionaries, accounting utilities, concurrency control, backup, recovery and security features.

In understanding database systems, it is useful to identify three separate levels at which data may be represented:

1. the conceptual schema (an overall logical view of the database);
2. the external schema (a logical presentation of part of the database in the way most suitable to meet a user's requirements);
3. the internal schema (the representation of storage and access characteristics for the data).

Relational database management systems are table-based logical representations of data structures that allow simple and powerful data manipulation. The advantages of relational systems in terms of their representation and retrieval characteristics are to be set against their slow speed of operation. This makes them unsuitable for high-volume, transaction-based data processing.

The way that a data model is developed for an organization and the design of a database to incorporate this model is reserved for Chapter 13 on data analysis and modelling. The entity–relationship modelling approach will be used, and the techniques of normalization (often associated with the design of effective relational databases) will be explained there.

Review questions

1. Explain the following terms:

file	variable-length record
backup file	transaction file
record type	inverted list
file update	fully inverted file
record	master file
field	

2. Explain the difference between logical and physical files.

3. Define the following terms:

database	concurrent use of data	relational join operation
database management system	relation	database query language
	attribute	data dictionary
data independence	domain of an attribute	report generator
database administrator	key	internal schema
data redundancy	relational selection operation	conceptual schema
data sharing	relational projection operation	external schema

4. Explain the difference between a *data definition language* (DDL) and a *data manipulation language* (DML).

5. What limitations are there for the application-led, file-based approach, and how does the database approach overcome these?

6. What is the distinction between a conceptual schema and a data model?

Exercises

1. Explain the advantages and disadvantages of using a flat file as against a multidimensional file.

2. By considering a stock record, give an example of an entity, an attribute, a record, a field, a data item, a key and a repeating group.

3. Figure 8.14 shows an order form for the ABC Company.

   (a) Suggest a record structure suitable for keeping data on orders. Show any repeating fields and specify field sizes and types.

   (b) The order file is to be kept as a permanent record so that customers can make enquiries concerning the status of their order and its contents by providing the order number. The status possibilities for the order are 'received', 'awaiting stock', 'being processed', 'finished'. The file is also used in end-of-week batch processing of orders. Suggest a suitable file organization and provide a justification for your answer.

4. Using your knowledge of the way a typical business functions, suggest typical record structures for each of the following:

   1. employee record;
   2. stock record;

Figure 8.14 Order form for the ABC Company

```
ABC Company    _____        Delivery address _____
Order#         _____                         _____
Date           _____                         _____
Customer#      _____                         _____
Customer name  _____
Invoice address _____
               _____


Item#   Item description              Quantity    Price      Total
 __     _____        ____        ____       ____
 __     _____        ____        ____       ____
 __     _____        ____        ____       ____
 __     _____        ____        ____       ____
 __     _____        ____        ____       ____
                                                      Subtotal ____
              Discount ___%  Discount _____
                             Sales tax _____
                                                      Total ____
```

3. sales ledger customer record;
4. salesperson commission record.

5. A road haulage company is to introduce a computer-based system to handle customer bookings for the transfer of customer freight from one town to another. Each lorry will make a special journey from one town to another if the customer's freight consignment is sufficient to count as a full lorry load. Otherwise, different consignments are accumulated and transferred from the source town to the destination town on one of the freight company's standard journeys. It has been decided to implement the system as a series of files. The following have been suggested:

   (a) customer file;
   (b) consignment file;
   (c) journey file;
   (d) special journey file;
   (e) lorry file.

   The application must be able to accept and record consignment bookings, assign these consignments to journeys, ensure that invoicing for completed transport of consignments occurs and answer random queries from customers on expected delivery dates. You are required to specify record layouts for the various files.

6. 'There is no reason for an accountant, financier or any other business person involved with a computerized file-based information system to know about the storage organization of data in files and access methods to that data, only about the nature of the data.' Do you agree?

7. Explain the terms internal schema, external schema and conceptual schema. Illustrate your answer by reference to the project/employee/department example in Section 8.5.

8. Give an example of two relations and the result of applying a JOIN operation without specifying the common domain over which the join is to be made.

9. Using the information in Figure 8.15:

(a) What records would be displayed in response to the following queries?

(i) **SELECT** supplier_name
    FROM SUPPLIER
    WHERE supplier_city = "London"

(ii) **SELECT** warehouse#
     FROM STORAGE
     WHERE part# = "P2" **AND** quantity_held > 40

(iii) **SELECT** SUPPLIER.supplier_name, CONTRACT.part#
      FROM SUPPLIER, CONTRACT
      WHERE SUPPLIER.supplier# = CONTRACT.supplier#
          AND CONTRACT.quantity_supplied > 30

(iv) **SELECT** supplier_name
     FROM SUPPLIER
     WHERE supplier# = **ANY** (**SELECT** supplier#
                      FROM CONTRACT
                      WHERE part# = P1)

Figure 8.15 Example table structure and contents

SUPPLIER

supplier#	supplier_name	supplier_city
S1	Smith	London
S2	Jones	London
S3	Smith	Derby
S4	Patel	Kentucky
S6	Mendez	Bristol

PART

part#	part_name	price
P1	dynamo	20
P2	alternator	30
P3	carburettor	30
P7	dynamo	27

WAREHOUSE

warehouse#	w_city
W1	London
W2	London
W3	London
W4	Leeds

CONTRACT

part#	supplier#	quantity_supplied
P1	S1	43
P1	S2	49
P1	S3	58
P1	S6	14
P2	S1	5
P2	S6	134
P3	S1	19
P3	S2	19
P3	S3	14
P3	S4	21
P3	S6	31
P7	S6	34

STORAGE

part#	warehouse#	quantity_held
P1	W1	482
P1	W2	394
P1	W3	201
P2	W1	43
P2	W2	41
P2	W3	31
P2	W4	41
P3	W1	95
P3	W2	0
P3	W4	91
P7	W1	6
P7	W2	5
P7	W3	1
P7	W4	4

   (v) **SELECT** *supplier_name*
         FROM SUPPLIER
         WHERE *supplier#* = **ANY** (**SELECT** *supplier#*
                      FROM CONTRACT
                      WHERE *part#* = **ANY** (**SELECT** *part#*
                      FROM STORAGE
                      WHERE *warehouse#* = "W3"))

(b) Design relational database enquiries in an SQL-like language to:

   (i)   Determine the part #s of dynamos.

   (ii) Determine all supplier #s of suppliers who supply more than 40 units of part # P1.

   (iii) Determine all part #s and part names stored in either warehouse 1 or warehouse 2.

   (iv) Select all suppliers located in the same city as any warehouse.

   (v) Select all supplier names who supply parts in any warehouse not located in the same city as the supplier.

10. For the relations:

    BOOK (*book#, title, author, stack address*)
    BORROWER (*borrower#, borrower name, borrower address, borrower status*)
    LOAN (*loan#, borrower#, date, loan status*)

    specify SQL or relational algebra expressions to represent the following queries:

   (a) What are the titles of all books by Tolstoy?

   (b) What book titles were loaned on or before 1 April 2004?

   (c) List the borrower names and book titles for staff users (*borrower status* = staff) that have been borrowed since 11 August 2004 and are still on loan (*loan status* = on loan).

CASE STUDY 8

Relational databases

Opening a stack of circulars and credit card solicitations this weekend, my thoughts turned to the late Edgar F. Codd. The British mathematician, who died two years ago, was the father of 'relational' databases, today used by government agencies looking for signs of terrorist activity, retailers analysing weekly sales figures and credit card companies deciding whose mailboxes to stuff.

It is hardly an exaggeration to say that Ted Codd's invention changed the world. Until the early 1980s, when his ideas were widely adopted, data was mostly stored in 'hierarchical' databases that were both inflexible and difficult to interrogate without a PhD in computer science. The relational model, based on an easy-to-analyse system of rows and columns, made it possible to identify quickly, say, customers in California with two children and size 11 feet.

This led not only to the development of the direct marketing industry but also to many of the information technology tools we take for granted. Relational databases underpin enterprise resource planning systems, customer relationship management systems, supply chain management systems, executive dashboards and other faddish tools of the executive trade. Judging by the contents of my mailbox, however, very few companies are exploiting the real potential of relational databases. Most of the direct mail I receive is based on information that is inaccurate (I am not, and never have been, a supporter of the Oakland Raiders), out of date (my Honda Accord was written off more than a year ago) or incomplete (since when did British citizenship imply an interest in faux-royal carpet slippers?).

It seems unlikely that lack of investment is to blame. Companies spend billions of dollars each year on the hardware and software required to store, retrieve and analyse customer data. They collect names, addresses, transactions, telephone calls, website clicks and more besides. The world's largest commercial database (belonging to an unnamed corporation) now includes close to 3000bn records, a fivefold increase in two years, according to Winter Associates, a US consulting company that tracks these things.

Data integrity – or, rather, lack of integrity – is a problem that even the biggest IT budget cannot overcome. In a world where people move house, change car and swap spouse every few years, much of the information stored in corporate databases is unreliable. There are also human errors to contend with. Oh, for a quiet word with the hotel clerk who once tapped me into a reservation system as 'Mrs' – thereby triggering an avalanche of offers for cut-price pedicures.

Even if the information they hold is correct, few organizations seem to know how to use it. Most big corporations employ statistics savants whose job it is to glean 'insight' from mountains of raw data. But they are, for the most part, distanced from the real centres of corporate power. It is rare indeed to find a company that has made data analysis a source of genuine competitive advantage.

A small handful of retailers seem to have taken analytics to a high level. In the UK, Tesco has used its customer loyalty scheme to establish market leadership over rival grocers such as J. Sainsbury and Asda. In the US, Wal-Mart commands hushed reverence among data mining aficionados, although the world's largest retailer remains notably discreet about what data it collects and how it uses it.

Tom Davenport, professor of information technology and management at Babson College, Massachusetts, points to a number of common traits between these companies. First, data analysis is a corporate priority rather than a job left to business units. The chief cheerleader in most cases is none other than the CEO. Second, a substantial investment has been made in not only hardware and software but also hiring business analysts with a profound grasp of statistical methods. Capital One and Harrah's each employs a legion of pointy-headed statisticians. Data analysis is not delegated to amateurs with Excel spreadsheets. Third, while these companies are not afraid to attempt sophisticated predictions and modelling, they focus on just one or two aspects of the business where analytics might deliver real advantage. Thus Harrah's has concentrated on its loyalty scheme, with the aim of substantially increasing occupancy rates at its casino hotels. Wal-Mart seems to have focused less on customer data than on merchandising – getting the right goods on the shelves for any given day and location. These companies also know that analytics will not compensate for shortcomings in other aspects of the business. Witness the dismal financial performance of the US airline industry despite its massive collective investment in yield management and customer loyalty schemes. Similarly, knowing that fatigued dads tend to buy beer along with nappies – a triumph of what retailers call 'market basket analysis' – is fruitless if they prefer to visit the store next door. Codd, father of four children as well as an epoch-making advance in information technology, would surely have concurred.

Adapted from: **Faulty customer data and the faux-royal slipper syndrome**
Simon London, *Financial Times*, 7 December 2005

Questions

1. Define the three main data models that have been used in commercial database development.

2. What factors have led to the relational model becoming dominant?

3. The article compares the two-dimensional view of a table in a relational database with a spreadsheet. To what extent is this comparison valid? What are the implications of this for data analysis?

4. Relational databases were designed at a time when almost all data that needed to be stored was textual content and structured. Today much of the data that needs to be stored is multimedia and unstructured. What are the implications for database designers? What enhancements have been made to relational databases to address this changing requirement for content?

Recommended reading

Adelman S., Abai M. and Terpeluk L. (2005). *Data Strategy*. Addison-Wesley

This text considers the storage, management and use of data. It focuses on the dangers of adopting piecemeal approaches and presents strategies for data and databases that align more closely with business objectives.

Allen S. (2005). *Beginning Data Modeling and Relational Databases for Everyone*. 2nd edn. Springer-Verlag Berlin and Heidelberg GmbH & Co. KG

This book provides a straightforward approach to developing an effective logical model from which a relational database may be designed and implemented. All the key concepts are covered in the 17 chapters. The first three chapters introduce ideas of modelling and relational databases which are relevant here.

Benyon-Davies P. (2004). *Database Systems*, 3rd edn. Palgrave Macmillan

This updated text gives coverage of databases, database management systems and database development. Latter chapters cover trends in database technologies, especially concerning distributed and parallel processing, and chapters on data warehouses and data mining. Although this book goes beyond the needs of many business studies programmes, its clarity would render it useful.

Codd E.F. (1970). A relational model of data for large shared data banks. *Communications of the ACM* **13** (6): 377–387.

Connolly T. and Begg C. (2004). *Database Systems: A Practical Approach to Design, Implementation and Management*, 4th edn. Addison-Wesley

A comprehensive text covering databases, SQL, transaction management, data warehouses and data mining, and advanced concepts.

Date C.J. (1998). *Relational Database: Writings*. Addison Wesley Longman

Date C.J. (2003). *An Introduction to Database Systems*, reissued 8th edn. Longman Higher Education Division

A comprehensive classic textbook in this area. Although largely technical and written for the computer scientist, this provides a clear introduction to databases and data models.

McFadden F.R. *et al.* (2004). *Modern Database Management*, 7th International edn. Prentice Hall

This is a standard student text covering all aspects of database design and management. Each chapter has review questions, problems and exercises.

O'Neill P. and O'Neill E. (2004). *Databases Principles, Programming and Performance*, 2nd edn. Academic Press

A detailed text taking a technical approach to SQL, the object/relation model, transactions, distributed databases and indexing techniques.

Pratt P.J. and Adamski J.J. (2007). *Concepts of Database Management*, 6th edn. International Thomson Publishing

This is a detailed student text on databases. Also included are sections on data warehouses, and object oriented databases.

Tsichritzis D. and Klug A. (eds.) (1978). The ANSI/X3/SPARC DBMS framework: report of the study group on database management systems. *Information Systems*. Pergamon Press Ltd, Vol. 3: 173–191

Chapter 9

Information systems: control and responsibility

Learning outcomes

On completion of this chapter, you should be able to:

- Describe the controlling effect of feedback and feedforward in an information system
- Evaluate the preventive measures necessary to effect control in an information system
- Describe controls that can be applied to data in transmission
- Evaluate a range of organizational controls that should be considered in the design and operation of an information system
- Discuss the rights and responsibilities of individuals, organizations and society in the development, implementation and use of information systems
- Apply principles of data protection legislation.

Introduction

This chapter introduces the general principles behind control and security in systems. These are then applied to computerized information systems. The increasing dependence of business on the reliable, complete and accurate processing of data by computers, often without manual checks, indicates that controls must be planned and designed. This occurs before the development of computer systems and their surrounding manual procedures. Security and control should therefore be considered prior to systems design and certainly feature in the design process itself, not as afterthoughts. The increasing use of computers in the processing and transmission of confidential data and funds has also made computer systems attractive targets for fraud. The need to take steps to guard against this possibility has been a powerful stimulus to an emphasis on security in the process of systems analysis and design.

In the early part of this chapter, the basic concepts of control systems are developed by considering the general ideas behind feedback, feedforward and preventive controls. These are explained and applied to manual business systems. Controls over computerized information systems are introduced by identifying the various goals and levels of control that are applicable. Controls over data movement into, through and out of the computer system are covered, together with controls over the transmission of data between computers or through the public telecommunications network. Some of the ways that fraud may be prevented are by restricting access to the computer system or to the data in it, or by scrambling the data prior to storage or transmission so that it is useless to any unauthorized person. The methods of achieving these ends are also explained.

Computer systems always lie within and interface with a surrounding manual system. Not only should computer aspects of this combined socio-technical system be the subject of control but also the organizational and personnel elements. To aid security, it is important that the system be structured in a way that facilitates this. The way that functions are separated as a means of control is developed in later sections of this chapter. The reliability of controls and security procedures operating over a working transaction- and information-processing system can be established by means of an audit. Although auditing is a large area in itself, the overall strategy adopted and the aid given by computer-assisted tools in the auditing of computer-based systems is outlined. The chapter also considers the relationship between information systems, organizations and individuals. Issues such as crime, privacy and acceptability of behaviour raise questions of responsibility. Who should ensure that certain practices or activities are restrained or even prevented? Is it the duty of an individual, an organization or society as a whole? There may be a collective belief amongst members of a community that there is a social responsibility in resolving a particular problem. In other situations the responsibility may rest on an organization. In this case the resolution may be in corporate governance and how the organization manages its own affairs. Also, the form of action taken may vary greatly. Checks, controls and balances take many forms. They can be imposed by legislation, they can be adopted voluntarily by individuals or organizations or they can just become custom and practice with no formal agreement. Judgements of the courses of actions taken are ethical considerations. Once a framework of policies, rules and legislation is in place, the ethics of actions taken can be considered. One example given extended treatment is that of privacy, in particular as enshrined by data protection legislation. Data on persons is the subject of data protection legislation. This has implications both for security and for the design of systems holding data on persons. The reasons for the rise of this legislation and the general principles behind the Data Protection Act in the UK are explained, together with the effects of the legislation on personal data security and access.

Finally, the need for a methodology for the identification of risk and the design of controls is stressed. Controls are an integral part of systems design, which is covered in Chapter 14 on systems design and Chapter 15 on detailed design.

9.1 Control systems

Controls, if they are to be effective, must operate in a systematic way. This section considers the general principles behind control systems before applying these to business systems. Some controls work by sensing or predicting the state of a system, comparing that state with a desired standard and then carrying out some correcting action if the state does not meet favourably with the standard. Other controls prevent (or attempt to prevent) a system moving away from a desired state. They do this by preventing abnormal but possible occurrences that would have this effect.

Feedback and feedforward are examples of the first type of control. Preventive controls are examples of the second. Feedback and feedforward controls involve the collection and processing of data and so operate within the business information system. Preventive controls prevent inaccurate and unreliable data processing, damage to data-processing equipment and unauthorized access to data, and so too are within this environment.

It is one of the responsibilities of management to ensure that adequate and effective controls are present at all levels in a business organization. There is always a cost–benefit dimension to the existence of any control – it is insufficient to consider the control outside this context. All controls have some cost associated with their installation and also a probability/possibility that they will fail in their control function. On the benefit side, there is the prevention or correction of the undesired state of affairs. It may be possible to assign a money value to this benefit, but it is important to bear in mind that this undesired state of affairs might not have happened in the absence of the control (this is particularly true with preventive controls), so probability factors also have to be taken into account here. Cost–benefit considerations surrounding a strategy for control in a business are covered in a later section of this chapter, but it should be made clear from the outset that the major question surrounding a control is not 'does it work?' but 'is it cost–benefit effective?'

9.1.1 Feedback control systems

The general nature of a feedback control system is shown in Figure 9.1. It consists of:

- A **process,** which accepts inputs and converts these into outputs.
- A **sensor,** which monitors the state of the process.
- A **controller,** which accepts data from the sensor and accepts standards given externally. The controller then generates adjustments or decisions, which are fed into and affect the process.
- A **comparator** in the controller, which compares the sensed data with the standard and passes an indication of the deviation of the standard from the monitored data to the effector.
- An **effector** in the controller, which on the basis of the output of the comparator makes an adjustment to the output from the controller.

Figure 9.1 **Feedback control**

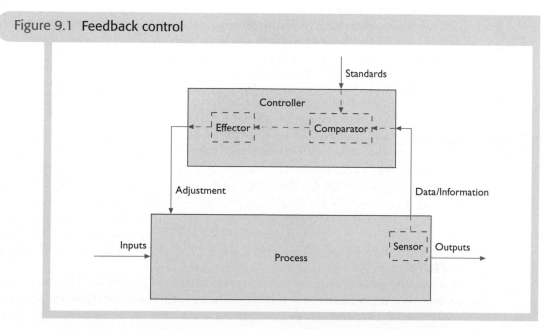

325

The example often given of a controller in a feedback control system is a thermostat. It accepts data about temperature from a sensor, compares it with a standard that is set by the householder and if the temperature is below or above this standard (by a certain amount) makes an adjustment to the boiler, turning it either on or off.

Feedback control enables a dynamic self-regulating system to function. Movements of the system from equilibrium lead to a self-correcting adjustment, implying that the combination of process and controller can be left over long periods of time and will continue to produce a guaranteed output that meets standards. Automated controller–process pairs are seldom encountered in business (although they often are in production engineering). However, it is common for a person to be the controller. That is, an individual will monitor a process, compare it against given standards and take the necessary action in adjustment. This is one of the roles of management.

In an organization, it is usual for control to be applied at several levels. The controller of a process at level 1 supplies information on the process and adjustments to a higher-level controller (who also receives information from other level 1 controllers). The information supplied may be an exceptional deviation of the process from the standard (exception reporting) or perhaps a summary (summary reporting). The higher-level controller can make adjustments to the functioning and structure of the system containing the level 1 controllers with their processes. The higher-level controller will also be given standards and will supply information to an even higher-level controller. The nesting of control may be many levels deep. At the highest level the controllers are given standards externally or they set their own. These levels of control correspond to levels of management. Above the lowest levels of control are the various layers of middle management. Top management responds to standards expected of it by external bodies, such as shareholders, as well as setting its own standards.

The study of feedback control is called **cybernetics**. Cybernetics ideas and principles have been applied to the study of management control of organizations (see for example Beer, 1994). Although real organizations are never so simple and clear-cut that they fit neatly into the feedback model, the idea of feedback provides a useful perspective on modelling management decision making and control.

In order to be useful, feedback controls, as well as satisfying the cost–benefit constraint, should also be designed in accordance with the following principles:

- Data and information fed to the controller should be simple and straightforward to understand. It must be designed to fit in with the intellectual capabilities of the controller, require no longer to digest than the time allowed for an adjustment to be made, and be directed to the task set for the controller. It is a common mistake for computerized systems that are responsible for generating this data to generate pages of reports that are quickly consigned to the rubbish bin.

    For example, a person in charge of debtor control (where the process is one of debtor-account book-keeping) may only need information on debtor accounts that have amounts outstanding over a set number of days, not information on all accounts. On these debtor accounts the controller probably initially needs only summary information, such as the amount of debt, its age profile and the average turnover with the debtor, but not the delivery address or a complete list of past invoices.

- Data and information fed to the controller should be timely. Two possibilities are regular reports on deviations from standards or immediate reports where corrective action must be taken quickly.

■ Each controller (manager) will have a sphere of responsibility and a scope for authority (ideally these should cover much the same area). It is important that the standards set and the data provided to the controller are restricted within these limitations. The manager is in the best position in the organization to understand the workings of the process and may often be expected to take some responsibility for the setting of realistic standards.

Standard cost systems – an example of feedback control

In management accounting the term **standard cost** refers to the budgeted cost incurred in the production of a unit of output. It will be made up of various components such as material, labour and power as well as overheads such as machine maintenance. During the production process the various costs of production are monitored and the **actual cost** per unit is established. This is compared with the standard cost and variances of the actual cost from the standard are calculated. There may be some labour variances attributable to the cost of labour or the amount of labour per unit of production. There may be variances on material or overheads, or some combination of both. On the basis of the variance analysis, various adjustments to the production process may be recommended. For instance, an adverse labour variance analysis might be adjusted by speeding up a production assembly line or increasing piece-rate benefits.

9.1.2 Feedforward control system

The general nature of a feedforward control system is shown in Figure 9.2. The chief difference from a feedback control system is that the monitored data on the current performance of the system is not used to compare this performance with a standard but is used to predict the future state of the system, which is then compared with the future standard set. To do this, a further component called a **predictor** is added to the controller. The predictor takes current data and uses a predictive model of the process to estimate the future

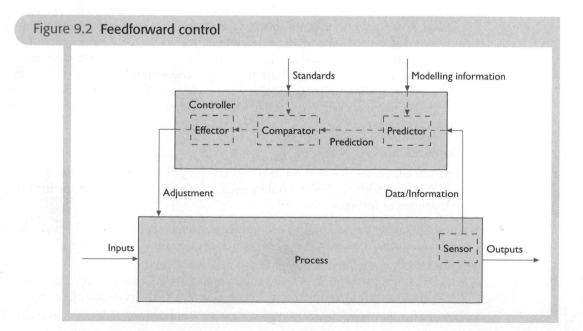

Figure 9.2 **Feedforward control**

state of the system. In carrying out the prediction it is likely that future estimates of variables occurring outside the process, but affecting it, will need to be input into the predictor. The prediction is then fed into the comparator and effector, which will make any necessary adjustment to ensure that the system meets future objectives. The success of feedforward control depends on the suitability of the model and modelling information.

Cash flow planning – an example of feedforward control

Most organizations like to keep their cash balances within certain limits. To stray outside these limits leads to excess funds that could be profitably employed, or to diminished funds, making the company vulnerable to a cash crisis.

The cash inflows and outflows of a company result from a number of factors. Inflows will generally be receipts from customers, investments and sales of assets. Among outflows will be payments to suppliers for purchases, wages and salaries, payments for overheads, payments of interest on loans, capital expenditures, tax payments and dividends. Inflows and outflows will be spread over periods of time, and the amounts and exact timing will be subject to uncertainty.

It is important that predictions (accurate within limits) are made so that adjustments can be implemented to ensure that the cash balances remain at the desired level. For instance, a predicted cash drop may be financed by a sale of securities held by the organization rather than by incurring a heavy bank overdraft with a punitive interest rate.

Feedforward systems are needed because time is required to implement the necessary adjustments, which need to be active rather than reactive. In this cash management example it is common nowadays to use computer-aided prediction either with spreadsheets or with financial logic-modelling packages. The predictions are passed to a senior manager or financial director, who takes the decision on the adjusting action.

9.1.3 Preventive control systems

Feedback and feedforward control work by a controller 'standing' outside a process and evaluating current or predicted deviations from a norm as a basis for taking adjusting action. Preventive controls, by contrast, reside within a process, their function being to prevent an undesired state of affairs occurring. Just as with the other types of control mechanism, preventive controls are an integral part of manual and computerized information systems. In business information systems, these controls are broadly aimed at protecting assets, often by ensuring that incorrect recording of assets does not occur and by preventing inaccurate processing of information. Preventive controls fall into a number of categories.

Documentation

Careful design of documentation will aid the prevention of unintentional errors in recording and processing. Several points need to be taken into account for the preparation of document formats:

- Source documentation requires enough data entry spaces on it to collect all the types of data required for the purposes for which the document is to be used.
- Transfer of data from one document to another should be minimized, as transcription errors are common. It is usual to use multipart documentation, which transfers the contents of the top copy through several layers by the pressure of the pen.
- Documents should be clearly headed with a document type and document description.

- Documents should be sequentially prenumbered. Provided that any 'waste' documents are retained, this allows a check on the completeness of document processing. It is aimed at preventing the accidental misplacing of documents and ensures that documents used for the generation of fraudulent transactions are retained for inspection.

- A document generally represents the recording of some transaction, such as an order for a set of items, and will undergo several processes in the course of carrying out the transaction requirements. It is important that wherever authorization for a step is required, the document has space for the authorization code or signature.

- The documentation needs to be stored in a manner that allows retrieval of the steps through which a transaction has passed. This may require storing copies of the document in different places accessed by different reference numbers, customer account numbers and dates. This is called an **audit trail**.

Procedures manual

As well as clearly designed forms, the accurate processing of a transaction document requires those responsible to carry out the organization's procedures correctly. These should be specified in a procedures manual. This will contain a written statement of the functions to be carried out by the various personnel in the execution of data processing. Document flowcharts (covered in Chapter 12 on process analysis and modelling) are an important aid to unambiguous specification. They indicate the path that is taken through the various departments and operations by a document and its copies until the document finally leaves the business organization or is stored.

The procedures manual, if followed, prevents inconsistent practices arising that govern the processing of transactions and other operations. Inconsistency leads to inaccurate or incomplete processing. The manual can also be used for staff training, further encouraging consistent practice in the organization.

Separation of functions

It is sound practice to separate the various functions that need to be performed in processing data. These different functions are the responsibility of different personnel in the organization. The separation is aimed at preventing fraud.

If a single member of staff were to be in charge of carrying out all the procedures connected with a transaction then it would be possible, and might be tempting, for that person to create fraudulent transactions. For instance, if a person were responsible for authorizing a cash payment, recording the payment and making the payment then it would be easy to carry out theft. When these functions are separated and placed in the hands of different individuals, fraud may still be tempting but will be less possible, as collusion between several persons is required. It is usual to separate the following functions:

- the custody of assets, such as cash, cheques and inventory;
- the recording function, such as preparing source documents, carrying out bookkeeping functions and preparing reconciliations; and
- the authorization of operations and transactions, such as cash payments, purchase orders and new customer credit limits.

These functions may also be carried out in different geographical locations (in different offices or even different sites). If documentation is passed from one department to another, the physical isolation of personnel provides further barriers to collusion.

Both functional and geographical separation are difficult to implement in a small business organization, as there may be so few staff that separation becomes impossible.

Personnel controls

A business relies on its personnel. Personnel must be selected and trained effectively to ensure that they are competent to carry out the tasks required of them.

Selection procedures should establish the qualification, experience and special talents required for the post being offered. Tests, interviews, the taking up of a reference and the checking of qualifications held will determine whether a candidate meets these requirements. The prevention of incompetent personnel being selected for tasks is an important control because once they are hired, the employment legislation in many countries makes it difficult to remove a member of staff even if that person's unsuitability for the job is subsequently discovered.

Training needs to be planned carefully to ensure that it delivers the necessary skills to staff, given their initial abilities and the tasks that they are to perform.

Supervision of staff in the workplace, as well as preventing fraud, also aids staff who are learning a new process by giving them the confidence that experience and authority are available to assist them with any difficulties that may arise.

Finally, it should never be forgotten that the personnel in an organization are people in their own right, with a wide range of interests, abilities, limitations, objectives and personality styles. If they are to work together successfully and happily, considerable ability needs to be displayed by management in preventing interpersonal differences and difficulties escalating and leading to disputes that affect the smooth running of the organization.

Physical controls

One way of avoiding illegal loss of assets such as cash is to exclude staff from unnecessary access to these assets. A range of physical controls may be used to prevent access – locks, safes, fences and stout doors are obvious methods. It may be equally important to prevent records being unnecessarily available to staff. Once again, physical controls may be used as a preventive measure. There are a range of natural hazards that affect a manual information system, hazards that can be guarded against. Fire controls, for instance, are an essential and often legally required feature of a business.

9.2 Controls over computerized information systems

If terminal operators never keyed in inaccurate data, if hardware never malfunctioned or disks never became corrupted, if there were no fires or floods, if computer operators never lost disks, if software always achieved what was intended, if people had no desire to embezzle or steal information, if employees harboured no grudges, if these or many other events never occurred, there would be no need for controls. However, they do happen and happen regularly, sometimes with devastating results.

The three types of control – feedforward, feedback and preventive – covered in Section 9.1 are applicable to manual information systems. The presence of a computer-based information system requires different controls. These fall within the same three-fold categorization, although in computer-based systems there is an emphasis on preventive controls.

Controls are present over many aspects of the computer system and its surrounding social (or non-technical) environment. They operate over data movement into, through and out of the computer to ensure correct, complete and reliable processing and storage. There are other controls present over staff, staff involvement with the computer, staff procedures, access to the computer and access to data. Further controls are effective in preventing deterioration or collapse of the entire computing function. This section starts by considering the aims and goals of control over computer systems and then covers these various areas of control.

9.2.1 Goals of control

Each control that operates over a computer system, its surrounding manual procedures and staffing has a specific goal or set of goals. These goals may be divided into categories. There are primary goals, which involve the prevention of undesired states of affairs, and there are secondary goals directed at some aspect of loss. If the primary goals are not achieved, other controls take over and provide some support. The various levels of control are:

1. **Deterrence and prevention:** At this level, the goal is to prevent erroneous data processing or to deter potential fraud. Many controls are designed to operate at this level.

2. **Detection:** If fraud or accidental error has occurred (that is, the primary goal has not been achieved), it is important that the fraud or error be detected so that matters may be corrected if possible. Indeed, the existence of detection often acts as a deterrent to fraud. Detection controls are particularly important in data communications, where noise on the communications channel can easily corrupt data.

3. **Minimization of loss:** Some controls are designed to minimize the extent of loss, financial or otherwise, occurring as a result of accident or intention. A backup file, for example, will ensure that master file failure involves a loss only from the time the backup was made.

4. **Recovery:** Recovery controls seek to establish the state of the system prior to the breach of control or mishap. For instance, a reciprocal arrangement with another company using a similar computer will ensure that the crucial data processing of a company can be carried out in the case of massive computer failure.

5. **Investigation:** Investigation is a form of control. An example is an internal audit. Nowadays, the facilitation of investigation is one of the design criteria generally applied to information systems development in business.

Controls are directed at:

1. **Malfunctions:** Hardware and software occasionally malfunction, but the most common cause is 'people malfunction'. People are always the weak link in any person--machine system as far the performance of specified tasks is concerned. They may be ill, underperform, be negligent, misread data, and so on. Unintentional errors are common unless prevented by a system of controls.

2. **Fraud:** Fraud occurs when the organization suffers an intentional financial loss as a result of illegitimate actions within the company. (Fraud might be regarded as the result of a moral malfunction!) Fraud may be of a number of types:

    (a) Intentionally inaccurate data processing and record keeping for the purpose of embezzlement is the most well-known kind of fraud. The advent of the computer means that all data processing (including fraudulent data processing) is carried out faster, more efficiently and in large volumes. Embezzlement may take the form of a 'one-off' illegitimate transfer of funds or may use the massive processing power of the computer to carry out transactions repeatedly, each involving a small sum of money.

There is a now-legendary fraud perpetrated by a bank's computer programmer, who patched a program subroutine for calculating interest payments to customer accounts so that odd halfpenny interest payments (which are not recorded in accounts) were transferred to his own account. A halfpenny is not a fortune, except when transferred thousands of times a day, every day.

(b) The computer is used for processing transactions that are not part of the organization's activities. It is not uncommon for staff to use computer facilities to word process private documents occasionally or to play adventure games when the time is available. At the other end of the scale, and more seriously, computer centre personnel have been known to run their own independent computer bureau from within the organization using large chunks of mainframe processing time, company software and their own time paid for by the organization.

(c) Illegitimate copying of data or program files for use outside the organization's activities may be considered a fraud. For instance, the transfer of company customer data to a competitor may cause financial loss.

3. **Intentional damage:** Computer centres have been the target for sabotage and vandalism. The angry employee who pours honey into the printer or plants a logic bomb in the software is an internal enemy. Increasingly, computer centres are aware of the possibility of external attack from pressure groups or individuals that step outside the law. A recent development has been the **denial of service** attack. By bombarding a system such as an authentication server or a web server with massively multiple requests, a malicious client can overwhelm the system. The stream of unwanted messages renders the system unavailable or even non-functional, thereby depriving intended users a normal level of service.

Mini case 9.1

FT

Denial of service

When it comes to dealing with denial of service (DoS) attacks, Adrian Asher is an expert. As head of security at online gaming company BetFair, he has successfully thwarted numerous attempts to bring down the company's website with the vast floods of bogus traffic associated with DoS attacks – but the cost of that achievement, he says, has been considerable.

'We've invested huge amounts in security and availability, in everything we need to ensure that uptime for our site is as close to 100% as possible', he says. 'We've got multiple levels of firewall, enormous amounts of network bandwidth and numerous highly specialized devices designed to alert us to, and protect us from, denial of service attacks.'

Mr Asher also has a 'huge' team of in-house security specialists at his disposal, who spend their working lives analysing Internet traffic, identifying deviations from the norm and dealing with them immediately. While he declines to say exactly how many people are in that team, he claims that it is bigger than IT security teams at some of the big banks he has worked at in the past.

Given that BetFair's site handles 5m bets each day and eager gamblers deposit around £2000 of funds on the site every minute, its enthusiasm for DoS protection is hardly surprising. Any period of downtime would cost the company dearly. But plenty of other organizations do not have the resources in-house to protect themselves so comprehensively, as evidenced in recent months by successful DoS attacks on the London Stock Exchange, the *Telegraph* newspaper and a host of commercial and government websites in Estonia.

Adapted from: **Diverting dangerous traffic**
© Jessica Twentyman. *Financial Times*, 11 July 2007. With permission from author.

Questions

1. What strategies have the company discussed in the article adopted to address the threat of a DoS attack?
2. Research DoS attacks further and propose alternative approaches that could be adopted.

4. **Unauthorized access:** Unauthorized access is generally a prelude to fraud or intentional damage and therefore needs to be prevented. It occurs when persons who are not entitled to access to the computer system or its communication facilities 'break in'. Hackers generally do this for fun, but there may be more sinister motives. Many internal company personnel as well as the public at large are in the category of those not entitled to use the computer system. Alternatively, unauthorized access may occur when a person who is entitled to access does so, but at illegitimate times or to part of the computer to which he or she is not entitled. For instance, company employees may access parts of the database for which they have no authorization.

5. **Natural disasters:** Included in this category are fires, earthquakes, floods, lightning and other disasters that may befall a computer installation. Each of these may be unlikely, but their effects would be serious and imply a large financial loss to the company. Power failures are rare nowadays in developed countries, but if there is a power cut and the temporary non-functioning of the computer is a serious loss then backup power supplies need to be provided. The same is true for communications facilities. There are a large number of special circumstances that might need to be taken into account. For instance, a large computer installation located near a naval radar and communications base had to be rebuilt inside a Faraday cage (a large, metal mesh surround inside which it is impossible to create an electromagnetic potential) to avoid interference.

6. **Malicious software:** A number of types of malicious software exist to create at best mischief but often to cause substantial damage to computer systems. The main types are as follows:

   ■ **Virus:** Computer viruses have become prevalent since the 1990s. A virus is computer code that has been inserted (without authorization) into a piece of software. Upon execution of the software, the virus is also executed. Its function may be innocuous, e.g. to flash a 'HELLO' message, or harmful, such as destroying files or corrupting disks. The virus may be resident in the software for a long period of time before being activated by an event, such as a specific electronic date inside the computer. Copying and distributing software on disks, memory sticks and over the Internet can spread viruses quickly. Recently, virus attacks have tended to be introduced from e-mails with infected attachments. These are often passed between unsuspecting users, who believe they are sharing a supposedly useful or interesting piece of software. The vulnerability of e-mail address books can be a factor in particularly virulent virus attacks where e-mails are forwarded to huge numbers of users without the knowledge of the sender.

■ **Trojan:** Like the mythical Trojan Horse, these malicious pieces of software appear to be of use or benefit but in fact contain a destructive payload. They often masquerade as being an enticing and innocent programme or hyperlink that the user unwittingly downloads or follows. Once loaded, the Trojan can then execute and wreak havoc on the host system. An example could be to breach security and open up a system to other users over the Internet.

■ **Worm:** These are self-replicating pieces of software. Often introduced to a system through an attachment to an email, a work will make numerous copies of itself. Unlike a virus that is transferred through a deliberate albeit misguided user action, a worm will usually attempt to reproduce itself without intervention. Often a worm will exploit network communications to make copies of itself, or will attempt to hijack an address book to send copies to other users. An example of the intent of a Worm might be progressively to use up computer resources with the end result of causing resource starvation and inducing system failure.

Organizations should protect themselves from these attacks by:

1. installing and regularly updating anti-virus software;
2. downloading the latest operating system and other software amendments (known as 'patches');
3. briefing their staff on appropriate courses of action such as not opening e-mails from untrusted sources.

Mini case 9.2

FT

Protecting corporate networks

Many mobile workers risk bringing their company's business to a standstill whenever they connect to the corporate network while away from the office. If virus scanners, firewalls and security patches on their computers are not up to date, they could unleash a virus or worm. The risks are growing as more people access corporate networks: 'Companies are increasingly providing suppliers and customers with access to their applications and data', says Rob Whiteley, an analyst at Forrester Research.

In response, there is an emerging set of technologies collectively known as network access control (NAC), developed by companies including networking equipment makers Cisco, Microsoft and an industry club called Trusted Computing Group. When an NAC system is installed on a company's network, any computer which attempts to connect – from outside or within the organization – is interrogated to ensure it complies with security requirements. If a computer is not running the latest security fixes or has not been scanned for viruses within 24 hours, for example, it can be restricted to a quarantined area from where it can download the required fixes or carry out a scan before being allowed on the network.

An NAC system also includes an authentication and authorization component which forces anyone wishing to connect to the network to verify who they are to keep intruders out. Authorized users are only given access to the applications and data for which they have specific permission. NAC systems can cost tens of thousands of pounds, and could cost millions to implement depending on scale and scope, but these sums could represent good value if they prevent a network outage.

Adapted from: **Mobile workers can be cleansed at the gate**
Paul Rubens, *Financial Times*, 11 July 2007

Questions

1. What different threats are posed by Viruses, Worms and Trojans?
2. Define the terms *virus scanner, firewall, security patch*.
3. What particular security problems are posed by mobile workers?
4. How does the NAC system attempt to address these threats?

9.2.2 Controls over data movement through the computer system

Erroneous data processing by a computer system is likely to be the result of incorrect data input. This is the major point at which the human interfaces with the machine, and it is here where important controls are placed.

Input controls

Many of the controls over data input require some processing power to implement. They could be classed as processing controls, but given that interactive data input with real-time correction is becoming very common it is convenient to group these together as controls over input.

Accuracy controls

1. **Format checks:** On entry, the item of data is checked against an expected picture or format. For instance, a product code may always consist of three letters, followed by a forward slash, followed by two digits and then three letters. The picture is AAA/99AAA.

2. **Limit checks:** A data item may be expected to fall within set limits. An employee's work hours for the week will lie between 0 and 100 hours, for example, or account numbers of customers lie between 1000 and 3000.

3. **Reasonableness checks:** These are sophisticated forms of limit check. An example might be a check on an electricity meter reading. The check might consist of subtracting the last reading recorded from the current reading and comparing this with the average usage for that quarter. If the reading differs by a given percentage then it is investigated before processing.

4. **Check-digit verification:** Account reference codes consisting of large numbers of digits are prone to transcription errors. Types of error include:
   (a) **Single-digit errors:** Where a single digit is transcribed incorrectly, for example 4968214 for 4966214. These account for approximately 86% of errors.
   (b) **Transposition errors:** Where two digits are exchanged, for example 4968214 for 4986214. These account for approximately 8% of errors.
   (c) **Other errors:** Such as double-digit errors and multiple transpositions. These comprise about 6% of errors.

In order to detect such errors, a check digit is added to the (account) code. The digit is calculated in such a way that the majority of transcription errors can be detected by comparing the check digit with the remainder of the (account) code. In principle, there is no limit to the percentage of errors that can be detected by the use of more and more check digits, but at some point the increasing cost of extra digits exceeds the diminishing marginal benefit of the error detection.

The modulus-11 check-digit system is simple and is in common use. The principle is as follows:

First, take the code for which a check digit is required and form the weighted total of the digits. The weight for the least significant digit is 2, the next least significant is 3. . . . If the number is 49628, then:

$$(4 \times 6) + (9 \times 5) + (6 \times 4) + (2 \times 3) + (8 \times 2) = 115$$

Second, subtract the total from the smallest multiple of 11 that is equal to or higher than the total. The remainder is the check digit. In the example:

$$121 - 115 = 6 (= \text{check digit})$$

(If the remainder is 10, it is common to use X as the check digit.) Thus the account number with the check digit is 496286.

Suppose that an error is made in transcribing this number during the course of manual data processing or on input into the computer. A quick calculation shows that the check digit does not match the rest of the (account) code. For example, the erroneous 492686 is checked as follows:

$$(4 \times 6) + (9 \times 5) + (2 \times 4) + (6 \times 3) + (8 \times 2) + (6 \times 1) = 117$$

117 should be divisible by 11. It is not, so the error has been detected.

The modulus-11 method will detect most errors. Because of its arithmetic nature, computers can carry out these checks quickly.

5. **Master-file checks:** With online real-time systems where interactive data entry is available, the master file associated with a transaction may be searched for confirming data. For example, a source document order form that is printed with both the customer code number and customer name may be handled by input of the customer number at the keyboard. The master file is searched (perhaps it is indexed on account reference number) and the name of the customer is displayed on the screen. This can be checked with the name on the source document. This type of check is very common in microcomputer-based accounting packages. Obviously, it is not possible with batch systems.

6. **Form design:** General principles of good form design were covered in Section 9.1.3. With respect to data input, the layout of source documentation from which data is taken should match the screen layout presented to the keyboard operator. This not only minimizes errors but also speeds data input. Data fields on source documents should be highlighted if they are to be input.

Completeness totals

To input data erroneously is one type of error. To leave out or lose data completely is another type of error against which controls are provided.

1. **Batch control totals:** The transactions are collected together in batches of say 50 transactions. A total of all the data values of some important field is made. For

example, if a batch of invoices is to be input, a total of all the invoice amounts might be calculated manually. This control total is then compared with a computer-generated control total after input of the batch of transactions. A difference indicates either a lost transaction or the input of an incorrect invoice total. The method is not fool-proof, as compensating errors are possible.

2. **Batch hash totals:** The idea is similar to control totals except that hash totals are a meaningless total prepared purely for control purposes. The total of all customer account numbers in a batch is meaningless but may be used for control by comparing it with the computer-generated hash total.

3. **Batch record totals:** A count is taken of the number of transactions and this is compared with the record count produced by the computer at the end of the batch.

4. **Sequence checks:** Documents may be pre-numbered sequentially before entry, and at a later stage the computer will perform a sequence check and display any missing numbers.

5. **Field-filling checks:** Within a transaction record there is a computer check to verify that the necessary fields have been filled with a data value. This is of particular use with complex documentation that requires only certain fields to be entered; the required fields are often determined by the values of other fields. (If sex = *female* and marital status = *married* or *divorced* then insert married name, otherwise leave blank.)

Recording controls

These enable records to be kept of errors and transaction details that are input into the system:

1. **Error log:** This is particularly important in batch entry and batch processing systems. Many of the accuracy checks discussed previously can only be carried out during run-time processing. It is important that a detected error does not bring the run to a halt. On discovery, the erroneous transaction is written to the error log. This is a file that can be examined at the end of processing. The errors can then be corrected or investigated with the relevant department before being re-input and processed.

2. **Transaction log:** The transaction log provides a record of all transactions entered into the system. As well as storing transaction details such as the transaction reference number, the date, the account number, the type of transaction, the amount and the debit and credit account references (for a sales ledger entry), the transaction will be 'stamped' with details of input. These typically include input time, input date, input day, terminal number and user number. It is usual for multi-access mainframe systems to provide this facility, especially when dealing with accounting transactions. The transaction log can form the basis of an audit trail and may be printed out for investigation during an audit. Alternatively, audit packages now have facilities that analyse transaction logs for the purpose of identifying possible fraud. Another reason for maintaining a transaction log is to keep a record of transaction input in case there is any computer failure. The log can be used for recovery of the data position of the system prior to the failure.

Storage controls

These controls ensure the accurate and continuing reliable storage of data. Data is a vital resource for an organization, and special care must be taken to ensure the integrity of the database or file system. The controls are particularly directed at mistaken erasure of files and the provision of backup and recovery facilities.

1. **Physical protection against erasure:** Floppy disks for microcomputers have a plastic lever, which is switched for read only (3.5-inch disks). Magnetic tape files have rings that may be inserted if the file is to be written to or erased. Read-only files have the ring removed.

2. **External labels:** These are attached to tape reels or disk packs to identify the contents.

3. **Magnetic labels:** These consist of magnetic machine-readable information encoded on the storage medium identifying its contents. File-header labels appear at the start of a file and identify the file by name and give the date of the last update and other information. This is checked by software prior to file updating. Trailer labels at the ends of files often contain control totals that are checked against those calculated during file processing.

4. **File backup routines:** Copies of important files are held for security purposes. As the process of providing backup often involves a computer operation in which one file is used to produce another, a fault in this process would have disastrous results if both the master and the backup were lost. The grandparent–parent–child method provides a measure of security against this mishap in the file-updating routine.

5. **Database backup routines:** The contents of a database held on a direct-access storage device such as magnetic disk are periodically dumped on to a backup file. This backup is often a tape, which is then stored together with the transaction log tape of all transactions occurring between the last and the current dump. If a database fault, such as a disk crash, happens afterwards, the state of the database can be recreated using the dumped database tape, the stored transaction (if a tape batch update is used) and the current log of transactions occurring between the dump and the crash point.

6. **Database concurrency controls:** In multi-access, multiprogramming systems using an online database environment, it is possible for two users/user programs to attempt to access the same part (record) of the database more or less simultaneously. Provided that both of these are read requests no problem arises. If one is a write request though, the database management system prevents access to the record by other users until the write action has been carried out. This not only ensures that two users do not, for instance, book the last remaining seat on a flight but also that all users of the database are presented with one consistent view of its contents.

7. **Cryptographic storage:** Data is commonly written to files in a way that uses standard coding (such as ASCII or EBCDIC). It can be interpreted easily by unauthorized readers gaining access to the file. If the data is confidential or sensitive then it may be scrambled prior to storage and descrambled on reading. This is particularly important where data files are sent by telecommunications. Then the hacker (unauthorized entrant) not only has to gain access to the link but also has to unscramble the code.

Processing controls

It was stated in Section 9.2.2 that many of the controls over input, and incidentally over storage, involve some element of processing. This is clear from the fact that all computer operations involve processing. However, some controls are processing-specific:

1. **Run-to-run controls:** The processing of a transaction file may involve several runs. For instance, an order-processing system might have a transaction file that is used to

update first a stock master file, then a sales ledger, followed by a general ledger. Various control totals may be passed from one run to the next as a check on completeness of processing.

2. **Hardware controls:** Some run-time errors are checked by circuitry. For instance, the value of a variable may be changed to zero during the execution of (part of) a program. An attempt to use this variable as a divisor (division by zero) may be detected by hardware. Other checks may involve data overflow, lost signs and checks on components. Dual circuits in the central processing unit (CPU) may duplicate computations. The outputs of each set of circuits are compared for discrepancy. This reduces the probability of processing errors.

Hardware should be designed to incorporate fault detection, avoidance and tolerance features. Duplicating central processing units, input/output channels and disk drives for comparing the results of data processing is one option. Another is to maintain redundant components, which are brought in when hardware failure occurs or during maintenance. A third option is to increase the tolerance of the system to hardware failure by having a common pool of resources such as CPUs and disk drives that meet the needs of tasks as required. If one of these fails operations can still continue, albeit somewhat degraded in performance, in the remainder.

Output controls

Output controls ensure that the results of data processing are accurate and complete and are directed to authorized recipients:

1. **Control totals:** As in input and processing control, totals are used to detect data loss or addition.

2. **Prenumbering:** Cheques, passbooks, stock certificates and other documentation of value on which output is produced should be prenumbered and accounted for.

3. **Authorization:** Negotiable documents will require authorization, and steps must be taken to ensure their safe transport from the computer centre to the relevant user department.

4. **Sensitive output:** Output that is regarded as confidential should be directed automatically to secure output devices in a location that is protected from personnel not entitled to view the output.

Data transmission controls

Data transmission occurs between the various local peripheral components of a computer system and the CPU and may, on a wider scale, also involve telecommunications links between a number of computers or peripherals and the central computing resource. These latter links are vulnerable to unauthorized access, giving rise to data loss, data alteration and eavesdropping. All communication is subject to data transmission errors resulting from electronic 'noise' interfering with the reliable transmission of 1s and 0s.

1. **Parity bit control:** Characters will be encoded as strings of bits according to some standard or other such as ASCII. A parity bit is added to the end of the bits representing a character. A protocol of **odd parity** means that the coded character, including the parity bit, must consist of an odd number of 1s. The set of bits is tested by hardware, and any failure to meet the control standard requires retransmission.

For its success as a detection control it relies on the corruption of data affecting an odd number of bits, otherwise the errors may be compensating. The vast majority of errors, however, entail corruption of a single data bit.

2. **Echo checks:** The message transmitted by the sender to the receiver is retransmitted by the receiver back to the sender. The echoed transmission is then compared with the first transmission. Any discrepancy indicates a data transmission error somewhere. Echo checks are common between the CPU and VDUs or printers.

3. **Control total:** At the end of a transmitted message, a set of control totals is placed that give information such as the total number of blocks or records sent. This is checked on receipt of the message.

Firewalls

A firewall is a layer of security, implemented through either hardware or software, that limits access to a system by filtering requests. Unlike other security systems that limit access by authenticating the user or giving different degrees of access to different categories of user, a firewall adopts a more indiscriminate approach, for example by refusing all requests of a certain type or emanating from a particular source. Depending on how the firewall settings have been implemented the request, with a warning message, might be passed on to the user to decide what action to take. Alternatively the message is simply refused and blocked.

At the organizational level a firewall will be implemented in hardware with one or more dedicated servers acting as the gateway to the system, refusing access to unauthorized requests. At the individual user level a firewall is often implemented in software through a constantly running programme on the user's computer that checks requests and only accepts those that meet certain criteria.

Firewalls are not only concerned with controlling external access: often within a networked system, certain areas will be placed behind internal firewalls to preserve integrity or address security issues.

Mini case 9.3

FT

The Great Firewall of China

With an estimated 137m people online and a Communist party that sees 'thought guidance' as a cornerstone of its power, China has become the greatest test of the ability of authoritarian regimes to tame the Internet. Beijing leaders, who have long practised censorship of the media, consider the Internet essential to a modern economy and as a potentially potent source of political threat.

To minimize the risk, Beijing has developed a multi-layered system of controls that starts with the 'Great Firewall', which blocks access to tens of thousands of websites judged inappropriate. Within China, the systems involve public and state security departments that monitor online activity.

The goal is not total control of content but to keep most websites to which ordinary Chinese can access within vaguely defined boundaries – and to maintain the ability to quickly identify and isolate individuals who appear to be threats.

Despite its scale and sophistication, the system is secret. Beijing officials generally admit to trying to block pornographic sites and to trying to suppress 'rumour-mongering'. The result is that while sophisticated users can usually gain access to any overseas online content, most people have little way of knowing the degree to which their Internet experience has been filtered.

Adapted from: **The Great Firewall of China**
Mure Dickie, *Financial Times*, 15 March 2007

Questions

1. How can a state use firewalls to control Internet traffic?
2. How possible or desirable do you consider it is to control Internet activity?

Internet communications controls

In response to concerns about the security of messages passed over the Internet, an enhanced version of the hypertext transfer protocol (HTTP) called **Secure-HTTP (S-HTTP)** has been developed. It uses encryption techniques to encode the data being transmitted and produces digital signatures. The technique is often used in conjunction with the **secure sockets layer (SSL)**. Rather than focusing on the individual message, SSL encrypts the entire communications channel. The joint use of these two protocols gives combined benefits in achieving security in data transfer.

9.2.3 Access controls

Access controls are usually aimed at preventing unauthorized (as distinct from accidental) access. The controls may seek to prevent persons who are authorized for access having unauthorized access to restricted data and programs, as well as preventing unauthorized persons gaining access to the system as a whole.

Controls over access to the computer system

Before a user is granted access to the system, that user needs to be identified and that identification authenticated in order to establish authorization. It is common for users to be given login codes or user identification codes. These are not regarded as particularly secret. The authentication of the identity is established by:

- a unique characteristic of the person, such as a voice print, fingerprint or retinal image;
- a security device unique to that person, such as an identity card; or
- a password.

Unique personal characteristics are currently infrequently used but will be employed with greater frequency in the future. Developments await technological advances, particularly in voice recognition and retinal imaging.

Security devices are commonly used where physical access control is important, such as entry into the various rooms of a computer centre.

Passwords are the most common form of authentication or identification. A password scheme requires the user to enter a string of characters, which the computer checks against its internal record of passwords associated with user identification. Generally, there is a facility for the user to change his or her password once logged into the system. The use of passwords appears to be a simple and effective access control, but there are limitations.

User-selected passwords are often easy to guess. The number of people who choose 'PASSWORD', 'ABC', the name of their husband, wife, child or dog is notorious. A recent report on computer security indicated that for a number of years the chairman of a large organization used 'CHAIRMAN' as his password. It is easy to see why these passwords are selected. Users are not interested in computer security but in the easiest legitimate access to the system in order to perform the tasks for which they require the computer. They may view passwords as a hindrance, albeit a necessary one, to carrying out their tasks rather than an essential component of the organization's security system.

System-generated passwords appear to be a possible solution, but these are difficult to remember and therefore likely to be written down, which provides further security problems. An alternative is to require individuals to change their passwords regularly and to prevent selection of a previously used password. This makes them less vulnerable (whether user-selected or system-generated) but more difficult to remember.

It is generally recognized that good password security depends on better education of users in the need for security rather than on more technologically sophisticated techniques.

Password details are encrypted in the computer and are never displayed on the screen. They should not be accessible even to senior computer centre personnel. Loss of a password should require a new user identification code to be issued, as well as a new password.

Although password controls are common they are not infallible, even with the most conscientious user. Short programs have been written that repeatedly attempt to log into a computer system. The program may be set to increment the tried password in a methodical fashion until a password fitting the login code is achieved. It is easy to prevent such clumsy attempts by automatic testing of the number of password trials associated with the login code. When a given number of unsuccessful attempts have been made in a period of time, no further login is possible under that code.

It is harder to prevent other equally simple but more elegant methods of password evasion. A simple terminal emulation program may be written and run. To the user sitting in front of the screen it appears that a perfectly normal request for a login code and password is being presented. On entering these details, they are recorded on a file for future consideration by the person attempting to gain unauthorized access. The user will not realize that this has been done, as the terminal emulation program will then display a simple error message or abort and pass the login code and password to the control of the legitimate procedure for handling login access. To prevent this deception, a system should always be shut down and restarted before use.

Control over access to data

Once legitimate (or unauthorized) access has been gained to the computer system the user should then be faced with other restrictions. Obviously, any system of control should not allow all users access to all files and programs. Generally, users are restricted to:

■ the execution of a limited number of programs;

■ access to a limited set of files or part of the corporate database;

■ access to only certain items in these files or database;

■ performing only limited operations on these areas of access. For instance, one user may be entitled to read and write to various records, another may be restricted to read only, and a third to read and copy.

In deciding on data access, two issues arise:

1. the policy to be adopted;
2. the mechanisms by which the policy is implemented.

Under 1, certain principles should be followed for a sound policy on security.

- Each user should be entitled to access data and perform operations in the computer system only to the extent needed to carry out that user's legitimate tasks. Put another way, access is restricted to the minimum compatible with the user's needs. For instance, a management accountant might be entitled to read stock records but not to write to them and to neither read nor write to employee records. Once again, a member of the department dealing with weekly wages may be entitled to read the employee records of only those who are waged (not salaried). For this policy to be carried out it is necessary to spend considerable time and effort determining for each user the nature of tasks that they perform and the range of data needed for these. As well as restricting authorized users, limitation also minimizes the damage that can be achieved through unauthorized access via the route taken by an authorized user.

- The simpler the control mechanism the more effective it is likely to be. Complex mechanisms are more difficult to maintain and less easily understood.

- It is often claimed that the design of the security mechanisms (although not their specific content) should not rely on secrecy for part of their effectiveness.

- Every data access request should be checked for authorization.

Under 2, the mechanisms by which the policy is implemented are known as **access-control mechanisms**. They come into force both at the level of the operating system and independently through the database management system. They may be represented in an access matrix, where the rows of the matrix are users or user groups and the columns are the objects over which access is controlled. The cell entries indicate the type of access allowed for the user–object combination. Figure 9.3 is an illustration of the ideas behind an access matrix for operating system controls and database control over records.

Operating system access controls

These may be organized in the form of hierarchies, where superior users have all the access of inferior users plus extra rights. Another approach is to associate with each object, such as a file, a list of users that are authorized to use it and the type of operation they may perform. The access control list for a file then corresponds to the non-emptying cell entries for a column in the matrix in Figure 9.3(a). Operating systems may store files in tree structures, where a user 'owns' a tree or part of a tree as their file space. It is common for that owner to have maximum rights over the tree or subtree, whereas non-owners have restricted rights as specified by the owner. A facility may also be available to set passwords over trees or subtrees, so further enhancing security.

Database management system access controls

These are more fine-grained in their selectivity than operating system access controls. They will restrict access not only to records but also to specified logical relationships between these records and individual fields within the records. The nature of the allowed operations will also be defined. Read, update, insert and delete are common. Unlike operating system access controls, database management system access controls may be

Figure 9.3 Examples of access matrices: (a) operating system access matrix; (b) database access matrix

(a) **Subject/ user**   **Object**

	File 1	File 2	File 3	File 4	Device 1	Device 2
A43801	Read		Execute			
A43802		Read/Write		Execute	Use	
A43803	Read	Read			Use	Use
A43804	Read		Execute		Use	

(b) **Subject/ user**   **Stock details**

	Stock ID	Description	Quantity held	Cost price	Sale price	Reorder level	Reorder placed
Management accountant	Read	Read	Read	Read	Read	Read	Read
Inventory control	Read	Read	Read/ Write		Read	Read	Read
Purchasing	Read	Read		Read	Read	Write	Write

data-dependent as well as data-independent. In some database environments, data items are selected by value; access can therefore be allowed on the basis of the values satisfying some condition. For example, a user may only be allowed to read an employee salary field if that employee salary is less than a specified amount. Database controls are selective, so they require a detailed study of each user's data requirements if the access is not to be too slack (ineffective controls) or too tight (impeding user tasks).

Cryptographic controls

Preventing unauthorized access to the computer system and then restricting the access of legitimate users to subsets of the file base or database may be regarded as insufficient control in the case of very confidential data. If a breach of security leads to data access then it is a further control to store the data in an encoded form so that it will be meaningless and worthless to the intruder. Cryptography is the science of coding and decoding for security purposes.

Encoding data, or encrypting it, is not only used as a secure storage form but is also particularly important in data transmission where communications channels are vulnerable to eavesdropping. Cryptography has always been important for military communications but has only recently been of commercial significance. This is a result of electronic funds transfer and the increasing use of networked computers in the transference of confidential business data.

The security process involves the conversion of the plain text message or data into cipher text by the use of an encryption algorithm and an encryption key. The opposite process, decryption, involves deciphering the cipher text by the use of an algorithm and decryption key to reproduce the plain text data or message. If the encryption and

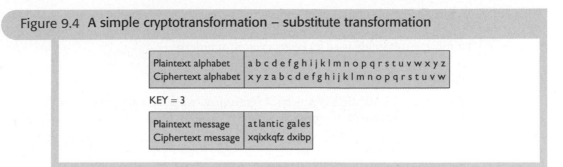

Figure 9.4 A simple cryptotransformation – substitute transformation

| Plaintext alphabet | a b c d e f g h i j k l m n o p q r s t u v w x y z |
| Ciphertext alphabet | x y z a b c d e f g h i j k l m n o p q r s t u v w |

KEY = 3

| Plaintext message | atlantic gales |
| Ciphertext message | xqixkqfz dxibp |

decryption keys are identical, the entire procedure is known as a **symmetric cryptoprocess**. Otherwise, it is said to be **asymmetric**.

A simple cryptotransformation of the kind used in junior school secret messages is shown in Figure 9.4. This is called a **substitute transformation**. In the case of encryption used for communication the key is transmitted over a highly secure data link from the message sender to the receiver. The cipher text can then be sent through a less secure channel, often at a much faster speed. If encrypted data is stored then the key is kept separate from the cipher text. The application of the key with the decryption algorithm (which can be public) enables decryption to produce the original plain text. Simple encryption algorithms and keys, such as those shown in Figure 9.4, which associate a unique character on a one-to-one basis with each character of the alphabet, are easy to 'crack'. A common method is to take the most commonly occurring cipher text character and associate it with 'e', which is the most commonly used letter in the alphabet in English prose. The next most common are then paired, and so on. More complex algorithms and keys ensure that plain text characters are coded differently depending on their position in the plain text.

The data encryption standard

The data encryption standard (DES) is a standard for non-military data. It requires splitting the plain text into 64-bit blocks. The encrypting algorithm requires the iteration of a certain transformation 16 times to produce a 64-bit cipher text block. This is performed on each 64-bit plain text block. The key used in the algorithm for both encryption and decryption consists of 64 bits (eight of which are parity bits). Once the key is possessed, both encryption and decryption are straightforward algorithmic processes, which may be carried out effectively and quickly by a computer.

The security of the system (data stored or message transmitted) now relies on the security of storage or the security of transmission of the key. This is an improvement, as security control now has to be maintained over a piece of data of 64 bits (the key) rather than several megabytes of stored or transmitted data. Obviously, the key itself should be made unpredictable, say by generating the 64 bits randomly.

Doubt has recently been cast on the DES. Using very fast computers, a large enough piece of cipher text and its corresponding plain text, all 2^{56} possible keys can be used to decrypt the cipher text. The result of each decryption can be compared with the given plain text and the correct key established. The time taken to carry out the exhaustive search would be a matter of hours rather than weeks, and if computing power continues to increase both the cost and time taken for such an analysis will drop considerably. It has been argued, though, that the principle behind the DES is sound and can be guaranteed against plausible advances in computing power by increasing the key to 128 bits (16 of which are parity bits). This would require an exhaustive search of 2^{112} keys and is becoming increasingly used as an encryption standard.

Public key cryptography

While the DES uses an asymmetric crypto-process, public key cryptography is an asymmetric crypto-system. It works as follows:

- The encryption and decryption algorithms are straightforward and public.
- A receiver has a code number, which may be public. This number is the product of two very large prime numbers (each in excess of 100 digits), which are known to the receiver but to no one else. It is impossible, because of the computational power needed, to determine these prime numbers from the public code. (The standard method of dividing the code by successively large prime numbers until a perfect divisor is found is too lengthy even with a high-powered computer.)
- The transmitter of a message selects an encryption key determined by the public receiver code number satisfying certain conditions, which are publicly known.
- As well as the cipher message, the receiver code and the encryption key are transmitted.
- It is impossible to 'back encrypt' the cipher text to reach the plain text using the encryption key.
- The decryption key can only be found by calculation using the encryption key together with the prime numbers whose product is the public code of the receiver. The system relies on the impossibility of discovering these primes from the public receiver code.

The system is very attractive, as different receivers can have different public codes, and transmitters can change encryption keys as often as is liked for security. The cipher text, the encryption keys and the receiver keys can be transmitted without jeopardizing public security. The strength of the system lies in the impossibility of determining the decryption key without the two large prime numbers. Recent research by mathematicians has come up with more efficient algorithms for determining whether a number is prime than the traditional sieve of Eratosthenes (to determine if a number is prime, divide it by each whole number less than or equal to its square root). It remains to be seen whether this will affect the security of the product of primes method of cryptography.

As data communication traffic increases in volume and the need to maintain secure data storage and transmission becomes more important it is likely that crypto-systems will become an integral part of data handling. Trends in data protection legislation, where data holders are legally obliged to take reasonable steps to ensure the privacy of personal data against unauthorized access, can only increase this movement.

Physical access controls

The access controls considered earlier in this section all assume that physical access to some aspect of the computer system, such as a terminal or data transmission channel, has been achieved and the task is to prevent the unauthorized intruder gaining further access. Physical access controls aim to prevent this initial state arising. They are particularly effective when the computer system is geographically centralized. The greater the dispersion of equipment and distribution of connected computing power the less effective they become. (It is easier to maintain control over equipment that is located in one big box [the computer centre] than when it is geographically dispersed in smaller boxes all connected by communication lines.) Currently, the trend is towards networks and decentralized computing; therefore, physical access controls play a less important role than previously in the prevention of unauthorized access. The following are some of the most common types of these controls:

■ **Magnetic cards:** Plastic cards with user identification encoded on magnetic strips on the card are a popular form of access control to equipment and to the rooms containing the equipment. The user runs the card through a magnetic strip reader, and the details are checked for authenticity. In some systems the user is also required to input a personal identification number. These systems are popular because they are cheap and also provide computer-based monitoring of access if the magnetic strip-reading equipment is connected to a computer. For instance, a computer centre may have a magnetic card reader on each door in the building. At any moment, the computer has a record of who is where in the building and how long they have been there. Moreover, the records of personnel movement may be retained on a file for future analysis if required.

■ **Smart cards:** Smart cards are the same size as magnetic cards (that is, credit card size) but contain information encoded on microchips built into the cards. They store more information and are harder to counterfeit than magnetic cards, but their cost of production is higher. They are used in a similar way to magnetic cards in access control.

■ **Closed-circuit video monitoring:** As for many other installations that require security controls, closed-circuit video can be used. It is expensive if manned operation is required but may be used as an unattended video record of computer centre occupants.

■ **Fingerprint or retina scan control:** Modern technology makes a number of biometric tests possible to control access. A reader or sensor can scan a fingerprint or a retina and match key features against a database. To preserve the privacy of the users of such a system, it is possible to store a minimal number of features that prevents unauthorized copying and subsequent reuse of the fingerprint or retinal scan.

■ **Radio frequency (RF) tagging:** Radio frequency identification is now an economically viable way of providing security. Already used in shops for stock protection and in cards that provide road toll and building access, a RF card or tag can be used to authenticate access.

Mini case 9.4

Retina scan

FT

Radio frequency identification (RFID) has found many uses: tags in shops, building access, pre-pay travel cards, toll booths on motorways, and in passports. It also looks as though it will become a key component in identity card systems.

RFID readers send out a signal that is picked up by the tag's antenna. The signal provides power for the chip to run processes and send a response back. This can be simple, such as triggering a shop security alarm, alerting staff that an unprocessed chip is leaving the store, or complex, perhaps allowing a gate to open and rewriting a cash value to the chip.

▶

Various organizations and groups are researching RFID technologies for use in passports. The real interest lies in how it is going to be used. Passport chips do not contain masses of personal data – yet. Maybe they never will. But they do store data used to recognize a biometric signature, such as a retina scan. This means the passport acts in much the same way as another secure token might.

The UK government's Iris (Iris Recognition Immigration System) scheme requires a passport holder to enter a booth, have their retina scanned and wave the passport in front of a reader. If both pieces of data match, the holder is deemed 'legitimate'.

Adapted from: **Broadcast your details with an RFID passport**
© Ken Munro. *Financial Times*, 28 February 2007. With permission from author.

Questions

1. What advantages are there to using biometric data in passwords?
2. What security implications are there to using RF technology in passports?

- **Guards and escorts:** Guards may be placed at entry points to the computer facility and act as administrators over other entry procedures and escorts for unfamiliar personnel or sensitive material.
- **Data transmission controls:** Data transmission lines throughout the computer centre should be securely embedded. It is particularly important if the lines pass out of the building, as they may with a local area network, that attention should be paid to preventing unauthorized tapping.

9.2.4 Organizational control

Up to now in this chapter, controls over data movement through the computer system and access to the system and the data in it have been considered. Many of these controls are technical and clear-cut in the sense that they require some kind of physical or electronic mechanism (for instance a computer) to implement, or they are straightforward procedures connected with these (such as the batching of transactions and calculation of a control total prior to data input). Other controls are more general and are best thought of as principles rather than clearly defined procedures or mechanisms. In particular, the way the information systems function is organized and managed and the way the work is allocated between different personnel will affect the overall accuracy and reliability of information processing. Also, if certain principles are followed in systems project development then the resulting information systems are less prone to failure – however failure may be interpreted. These areas are outlined in this section.

Organization of the information systems function

Over recent years the emphasis in business computer systems has shifted from the processing of data on a batch basis to the provision of information, often interactively within an integrated total information system consisting of the computer, computer centre personnel, users and tasks for which the information is provided. This move towards the information-based approach has, in some organizations, been accompanied by the partial decentralization of equipment and application processing as a result of the proliferation of microcomputers and microcomputer-based networks. This is particularly evident in the increasing use of the Internet. It is difficult to maintain the same

Figure 9.5 The organization of a generic information systems department

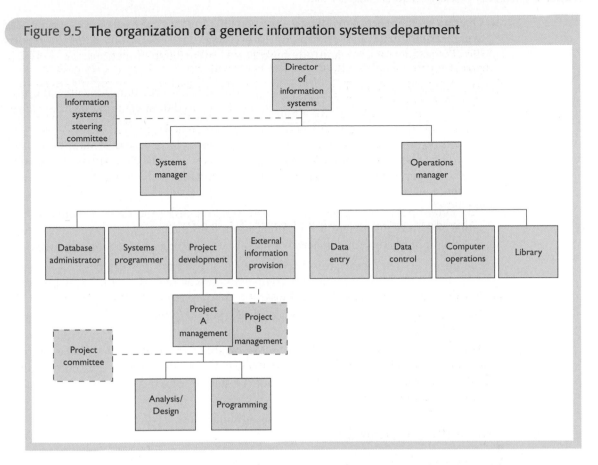

degree of control over microcomputer-based systems. Their easy access, their simple-to-use operating systems, and their removable CDs and floppy disks are both an attraction to users and a problem for the exercise of control. This section concentrates only on those information system functions carried out centrally in what was, and still often is, called the computer centre.

Figure 9.5 is a hierarchy chart of the typical divisions of responsibility in a generic information systems department. The functions are divided into the day-to-day data entry and processing and other activities such as the administration of the database and systems project development. The chart illustrates a project-centred approach, where programmers and analysts are assigned to development projects as they become current.

- **Director of information systems:** This person fulfils two roles. Externally to the computer centre, but within the organization, the director represents the information system at a senior managerial level (vice-president or director). He or she will be expected to play a part in deciding the overall goals and plans of the organization and in ensuring that the information system contributes to them. Internally, the director is responsible for the establishment of a structure and personnel base that will lead to a reliable and cost-efficient provision of information, not only currently but throughout the changing future of the organization. As well as a thorough understanding of technical issues concerning information systems, the director needs considerable managerial and administrative skills.

349

- **Operations manager:** This person is responsible for the day-to-day execution of the organization's data and information processing. The operations manager reports directly to the director and administers the subordinate functions, as shown in Figure 9.5.

- **Data entry:** Personnel in this role prepare and verify source data for entry and processing. They are also responsible for input of prepared data via input devices such as keyboards and optical character readers.

- **Data control:** Data control staff record and chart the progress of data-processing jobs. They also ensure that input control procedures are followed and are responsible for the preparation and checking of control totals for establishing the completeness of input and processing.

- **Computer operators:** The computer operators load disks and tapes, monitor and respond to console messages during processing, load printers with paper and remove the output hard copy, and generally service the day-to-day processing activities.

- **File librarian:** The librarian is responsible for storing offline files held on tape and disk. It is important that the librarian maintains a record of files and programs checked out to other personnel for use.

- **Systems manager:** This management responsibility is for the development of new projects and the maintenance of existing software and the database. Within project development, the systems manager is responsible for setting standards for systems design, programming and documentation, for overall planning and coordinating new applications, and for the allocation of staff resources (analysts and programmers) to projects.

- **Database administrator:** The database administrator ensures that the database is maintained in a secure manner and functions efficiently to the satisfaction of data requests from users and applications programs. He or she will be involved in amending the database conceptual schema and defining external schema in the course of new project developments. The role of the database administrator was covered more extensively in the chapter on databases.

- **Systems programmers:** This group ensures the effective functioning of the operating system and its associated utilities, compilers, database management system and software. They will give technical support to applications programmers on programs that require special interfacing with the operating system. The system programmers will carry out operating system enhancements as supplied by the computer manufacturers.

- **Project managers:** Each project will have a manager whose task it is to ensure that adequate detailed planning and administration of the project is carried out. This will involve setting points at which various 'deliverables' such as documentation (according to standards) or programs will be completed. The manager is also responsible for ensuring that development standards are adhered to, especially in program development and testing.

- **Systems analysts:** The analyst determines the information needs of the users and produces a system design in accordance with these. The process of systems analysis and design and the role of the analyst are considered extensively in the following chapters.

- **Programmers:** The programmers convert the process design by the analyst into programming code in a specified language.

- **External information provision:** Although much documentation in a computer centre is for internal consumption there are requirements externally within the organization for details on aspects of information provision. These may take the form of newsletters, user manuals for applications programs and presentations to other department of services offered by the centre.

Separation of functions and control of personnel

The separation of functions and control of personnel was considered from a general standpoint in the coverage of preventive controls presented in Section 9.1.3. Applied to the computer centre, functional separation is accomplished between four separate areas: computer operations, project development, the file and program library, and data entry and control.

The separation of analyst/programmer functions from those of day-to-day computer operations prevents programmers who make unauthorized changes to programs having the power to put those programs into operation. Conversely, access to programs and program documentation is restricted for operations staff to prevent a computer operator making unauthorized program changes then activating that program.

Programmers should have written instructions specifying program changes, and these changes should be fully documented. During systems development the program specifications supplied by analysts provide such documentation. At all times, it is inadvisable to allow programmers access to live data or current master files.

Computer operations staff should be closely supervised. Rotation of personnel in shifts and ensuring that at least two members of staff are always present in the computer room are steps that can be taken in centres with large numbers of staff.

A separate file library in which all access to program and data files requires authorization is a further control. Details of loans should be kept.

The separation of data entry from the function of data control provides a measure of security against fraudulent transactions generated on data input. There should, anyway, be independent controls (such as batch totals) created by departments originating transactions. These should be administered by data-control personnel as well as those controls emanating from within the computer centre. In data entry, it is common to separate the functions of master file amendments (such as insertion of a new customer) from transaction entry to prevent the creation of a fictitious customer and subsequent processing of fraudulent transactions.

Systems programmers are in a particularly powerful position, and it is important that they do not have unrestricted access to live data files and are not able to execute applications programs. One further safeguard is to ensure that applications programs documentation is not made available to them.

Such separation of duties is more difficult to maintain in a small organization, where it is common for one member of staff to fulfil several functions. Microcomputer-based systems are perhaps the extreme case where integration of functions is commonplace.

9.2.5 Contingency planning

In spite of all the controls that may be devised to support the reliable workings of the computer centre, hazards may arise that lead to breakdowns. Some, such as a lengthy power cut, can be safeguarded against and overcome by a backup power generator. Others, such as fires, floods, riots, earthquakes or sabotage, are more devastating. Many organizations have moved away from a decentralized manual approach to data processing with pieces of paper to using a centralized electronic computer. Although their activities now depend on computer support, the organization cannot afford to come to an immediate standstill in the face of computer failure.

The recent increase in distributed systems has diminished the consequences of failure. Even if one computer site suffers a disaster the others may take over much of its important activities in the short term. This assumes that network links have not been severed and that copies of the files and database at the breakdown site are maintained elsewhere so that they may be loaded into the network. It is uncommon to opt for distributed systems purely on the basis of this graceful degradation in their function (except perhaps for military systems operating in hostile environments). Rather, it should be seen as a useful feature of distributed data storage and processing.

Some form of contingency planning is needed in order to take care of the unexpected computer failure (even in the case of distributed systems). These plans should involve several areas:

- Copies of files and databases should be made regularly and stored at a distant location so that when computer operations are restored the original position of the organization can be recovered.

- Personnel need to be appointed (beforehand) to take managerial responsibility in the event of a disaster. They will need to be acquainted with procedures to be followed and with activities that are judged to be essential to the organization (as distinct from those that can be suspended). It is impossible to plan completely for all the unlikely disruptions that may arise, and the success of the contingency plan will depend on how these personnel adapt to the changed working conditions.

- Standby procedures and operations for the period of disruption will need to be arranged.

With respect to the standby plans, a number of approaches can be taken. Generally, those that cost more give a faster and higher level of support in the case of failure. They can be broken down into the following categories:

1. **Manual backup:** This is a short-term stopgap, which may be used before other standby assistance is brought in. If stock lists and accounts (particularly sales ledger) are printed at regular intervals then the trading of the organization may be maintained for several days. There will need to be special stationery for data entry that will enable input of transactions occurring during the disrupted period after computer support has been re-established.

2. **Hot-line support:** A company may offer hot-line support as a service on the basis of an annual fee. It usually works in the following manner. The company has a set of popular minicomputers or a mainframe and also has contracts with user organizations having similar equipment to take over their data-processing activities in the event of disaster. Generally, the servicing company will guarantee immediate support in the case of computer failure in the serviced organization, and the level of support will depend on prior arrangement (and the fee). In some cases, almost total support can be guaranteed and the computer users in the serviced organization will hardly notice the switch-over to operations at another site. Problems may arise in the unlikely event of a computer failure simultaneously occurring in more than one serviced organization. There may also be reservations about processing confidential data off-site.

3. **Company-owned backup facility:** This is a low-risk, high-cost way of meeting a computer failure. The entire system is duplicated at another site.

4. **Reciprocal agreement:** Two companies with the same equipment may agree to carry out each other's essential data processing in the case of failure. As well as possible security problems arising, it is unlikely that each of the organizations will have much spare computer capacity.

Survey reports have indicated that major accounting firms are concerned about the lack of computer contingency planning in British companies. Of computer disasters occurring over the five-year period surveyed, two-thirds were judged by the accountants to have been preventable, and of these, an inadequate backup facility was given as the major reason in over half the cases. Half of the accountants surveyed carried out checks and reported on disaster recovery procedures during the audit, but little interest was shown by clients. Of companies surveyed, four-fifths were inadequately protected against fire, and nearly all had no flood precautions and little or no protection against sabotage. All the current evidence points to little change having occurred since the 1990s. The combination of inadequate protection against unlikely computer failures together with poor or absent backup and recovery procedures is likely to turn a crisis into a disaster for most UK companies and underlines the need for adequate contingency planning.

9.2.6 Audits

The primary objectives of an **external audit** are to express an expert and independent opinion on the truth and fairness of the information contained in financial statements, and to ascertain and evaluate the reliability of the systems that produced this information. Secondary objectives include the investigation of fraud, errors and irregularities and the provision of advice on these and other matters to clients.

The primary objective of the **internal audit** is to evaluate controls against fraud and to maintain surveillance over the organization in order to detect fraudulent activity.

Both internal and external audits are a form of control. As well as improving preventive controls against unreliable processing, they also serve to deter fraud and detect errors once they have occurred.

An extensive coverage of auditing is beyond the scope of this book – only the basic strategies are covered and then applied to a computer-based system.

The approach to an internal audit

1. The auditor first needs to establish an understanding of the way the system functions. This will be achieved by consulting document flowcharts, procedures manuals and examples of documentation, by interviewing personnel and by observing the way that transactions are processed.

2. The next step is to document and evaluate the internal control that operates over the procedures and functioning of the system. Controls are divided into two categories. First, there are actual controls such as the provision of a check digit associated with an account code number or the preparation of a control total. The purpose of an actual control is to ensure that data is recorded and processed accurately. Second, there are higher-level controls designed to ensure that the actual controls work properly. These higher-level controls tend to conform to principles covered in Section 9.1. Examples are the separation of the custody of an asset from its recording, the supervision of personnel and the authorization of a transaction by a second person.

The controls are evaluated to decide whether 'in theory' they are adequate to meet the standards required of the system. The auditor may have a checklist against which the controls will be evaluated. For instance, the evaluation checklist dealing with company purchase orders might have the following questions:

(a) Can goods be purchased without authority?

(b) Can liabilities be incurred even though goods have not been received?

(c) Can invoices be wrongly allocated?

Each of these would be subdivided. For example:

(a) (i) What are the limits to a buyer's authority?

(a) (ii) Are unissued orders safeguarded against loss?

(a) (iii) Are purchase requisitions tied to their associated orders?

(a) (iv) Is purchasing segregated from receipt of goods, stock records and accounts payable?

3. The next stage is compliance testing. The performance of compliance tests is designed to provide the auditor with reasonable assurance that the controls established under 2 were functioning effectively throughout the period to which the audit is applied. For example, the auditor may check on compliance with the control over purchasing by:

(a) testing for evidence of a sequence check on purchase orders;

(b) testing for evidence of purchase order approval;

(c) testing for evidence of a sequence check on goods-received documentation;

(d) testing for evidence of authorization of changes to purchase ledger balances.

The evidence may be provided by examination of existing documentation and records, or re-performance of the way a transaction is handled, or again by interview and enquiry as to whether and how the controls are operated. The auditor may use statistical sampling techniques in research, and these lead to statistical confidence factors.

The auditor attempts, at this stage, to identify those areas of weakness in the system over which controls are ineffective or are not properly administered throughout the period.

4. The fourth stage is substantive testing. If empirical evidence established under 3 indicates that the controls may be relied on, little substantive testing is required. However, where the controls are weak it is necessary independently to verify that transactions have been processed properly and that account balances are correct. This is a lengthy and expensive process, and as the cost of the auditors is borne by the company it is in its interests to ensure that internal controls can be relied upon.

5. Finally, the auditor will produce an audit report, which may be qualified if material weaknesses have been discovered in the organization's system of control.

Auditing computer-based systems

The advent of the computer has meant that transaction recording and processing happen in part within the confines of a computer system. In order to testify to the satisfactory treatment of transactions, the auditor needs to take account of this new development. There are two approaches:

1. **Auditing around the computer:** The computer is treated as a 'black box'. The auditor examines the inputs and outputs and verifies that the outputs correspond to correct

procedures operating on the inputs. However, the auditor does not attempt to check the processes carried out on the data within the computer. This approach can only be adopted when relatively simple computer processing occurs. The greater the complexity of the system the more serious is the omission of being able to examine the intermediate steps in the processing of transactions.

2. **Auditing through the computer:** Not only are the processes and controls surrounding the computer subject to the audit but also the computer processing controls operating over this processing are investigated. In order to gain access to these, computer audit software will aid the task of the auditor. These packages typically contain:

- interactive enquiry facilities to interrogate files;
- facilities to analyse computer security logs for 'unusual' use of the computer system;
- the ability to compare source and object (compiled) program codes in order to detect dissimilarities;
- the facility to execute and observe the computer treatment of 'live transactions' by stepping through the processing as it occurs;
- the generation of test data;
- the generation of aids showing the logic of applications programs.
- The general strategy adopted in a computer-based audit will be similar to that outlined earlier in this section. The actual controls and the higher-level controls will be evaluated and then subjected to compliance testing and, if necessary, substantive testing before an audit report is produced.

The area covered in an audit will concentrate exactly on those controls covered in Section 9.2. Specifically, the auditor will need to establish the completeness and accuracy of transaction processing by considering:

- input control;
- storage control;
- processing controls;
- output controls;
- data transmission controls.

The auditor will also need to be satisfied that there are adequate controls over the prevention of unauthorized access to the computer and the data in it. The auditor's task will further involve a consideration of the separation of functions between staff involved in transaction processing and the computer system and that adequate supervision of personnel is maintained.

As more and more firms become computerized, the importance of computer-based audits and the pressure to audit through the computer grow. Auditing is not a straightforward task that can be completed by satisfying a checklist of questions. Rather, it involves experience and the ability to apply that knowledge to differing circumstances. No two information systems are the same. From the point of view of analysis and design of computer systems, audit considerations are becoming increasingly important. Nowadays, the design of an information system needs to take not only the information provision requirements and computer security into account but also the need to design the system so that auditing is facilitated.

9.3   Ethics, social responsibility and corporate governance

Information systems have affected many aspects of our society and of our everyday lives. Any new technology brings with it changes. Changes can be good or bad. Is the impact of computerized information systems good or bad? Such a question could be the topic of a book in itself. However, with respect to information technology and information systems, where there are choices and resulting changes, decisions have to be made and there will be ethical considerations involved. In particular:

- An individual's actions can be viewed as right or wrong.
- An organization can be regarded as acting ethically or unethically.
- A society will adopt policies and legislation which can be judged ethically in terms of their social impact and the impact on the individual.

A major determinant of the actions of individuals, and of the approach taken by an organization to ethical aspects of information systems, is delimited by state policies and legislation. Within this framework, though, there remains a range of actions over which the state remains silent but where ethical decisions remain.

9.3.1   Individual's actions

There are many theories of ethics governing what actions are right and wrong for an individual. Some of these are **prescriptive** and state how we should act – examples are below:

- *Act always according to some accepted moral principle or rule* (often used by religions with reference to absolutes on right and wrong given by a god or prophet or written in a Holy Book).
- Act towards another person in such a manner that you would find it acceptable if they acted towards you in a similar manner in similar circumstances (often associated with Christianity or theories which seek to gain objective support for a principle by abstracting away from the self-interest of the agent).
- *Act in such a manner that the consequences of your actions maximize general welfare or happiness* (utilitarianism – attributed to a range of philosophers and influential in bringing about social reform over the past two centuries).

Other theories of ethics are **descriptive** and seek to explain why societies believe certain courses of action are right or wrong.

For information systems (IS) professionals, working either as consultants or employed within an organization, the actions they perform can be regarded by themselves and others as right or wrong. The pressures on the individual from the organization, legislation, the need to serve society as a whole and his/her own personal goals can work in harmony reinforcing a course of action (see Figure 9.6).

However, sometimes these pressures can come into conflict. It is at this stage that a way of choosing the right way forward is needed. For instance, the need to achieve the corporate goal of keeping within budget for a project can clash with the IS professional's personal goal of ensuring a high standard of software through extensive testing. Or again, the requirements of keeping within data protection legislation may prohibit the use of personal data needed to assure some greater public good (e.g. the use of personal data to prevent terrorism). These dilemmas can be resolved by the individual themselves following

Figure 9.6 **Pressures on the IS professional**

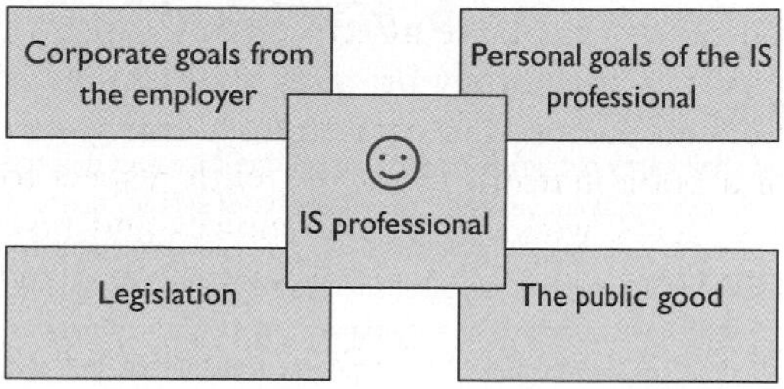

their own code of conduct and choosing what is morally right. The IS professional, though, is also a member of a profession and as such the profession will have its own code of conduct to inform practice.

In the UK the major professional body concerned with information systems is the **British Computer Society (BCS)**. A professional body typically restricts membership by ensuring that those eligible have attained a high standard of competence in the area of the profession. This is achieved by the body stipulating minimum entry qualifications which the proposed member must satisfy (often in the form of passing examinations set by the professional body itself). The professional status of the member is enhanced by membership (which also involves payment of a fee). The professional body also provides various services such as representation and staff development. In return for membership the member agrees to follow a code which governs their professional practice. Figure 9.7 contains summary extracts from the BCS code of conduct. All professions have codes of conduct. Similarly, the same profession will have a code of conduct in another country. In the USA the lead professional body for the IT professional is the **Association of Computing Machinery (ACM)**. There is much similarity between the codes of various professions in different countries.

9.3.2 Organizations and ethical policy

The managers and owners of businesses and other organizations are responsible for determining how the organization's affairs are managed; in effect determining how they behave. This is often referred to as **corporate governance**. Increasingly organizations are developing their own ethical policies. These go beyond information systems to, for example, the organization's responsibilities to its employees or its environment. With respect to information systems, areas which may be involved are the following.

Accountability

Both the quality of the information system developed and its operation can affect employees, customers and the public at large (as well as the profits of the corporation). The corporation itself may incur legal or moral liability for the effects of its system. It is good practice to put in place clear lines of responsibility for the development and operation of the information system. In this way the effects of actions can be attributed to identified individuals.

Figure 9.7 Summary extracts from the BCS Code of Conduct

British Computer Society (BCS) Code of Conduct

The Public Interest

1. You shall carry out work or study with due care and diligence in accordance with the employer or client's requirements, and the interests of system users. If your professional judgement is overruled, you shall indicate the likely risks and consequences.
2. In your professional role you shall have regard for the public health, safety and environment.
3. You shall have regard to the legitimate rights of third parties.
4. You shall ensure that within your professional field/s you have knowledge and understanding of relevant legislation, regulations and standards, and that you comply with such requirements.
5. You shall conduct your professional activities without discrimination against clients or colleagues.
6. You shall reject any offer of bribery or inducement.

Duty to Employer or Client

7. You shall avoid any situation that may give rise to a conflict of interest between you and your employer or client. You shall make full and immediate disclosure to them if any conflict is likely to occur or be seen by a third party as likely to occur.
8. You shall not disclose or authorise to be disclosed, or use for personal gain or to benefit a third party, confidential information except with the permission of your employer or client, or at the direction of a court of law.
9. You shall not misrepresent or withhold information on the performance of products, systems or services, or take advantage of the lack of relevant knowledge or inexperience of others.

Duty to the Profession

10. You shall uphold the reputation and good standing of the BCS in particular, and the profession in general, and shall seek to improve professional standards through participation in their development, use and enforcement.
11. You shall act with integrity in your relationships with all members of the BCS and with members of other professions with whom you work in a professional capacity.
12. You shall have due regard for the possible consequences of your statements on others. You shall not make any public statement in your professional capacity unless you are properly qualified and, where appropriate, authorised to do so. You shall not purport to represent the BCS unless authorised to do so.
13. You shall notify the Society if convicted of a criminal offence or upon becoming bankrupt or disqualified as Company Director.

Professional Competence and Integrity

14. You shall seek to upgrade your professional knowledge and skill, and shall maintain awareness of technological developments, procedures and standards which are relevant to your field, and encourage your subordinates to do likewise.
15. You shall not claim any level of competence that you do not possess. You shall only offer to do work or provide a service that is within your professional competence.
16. You shall observe the relevant BCS Codes of Practice and all other standards which, in your judgement, are relevant, and you shall encourage your colleagues to do likewise.
17. You shall accept professional responsibility for your work and for the work of colleagues who are defined in a given context as working under your supervision.

Quality of systems development and operation

This is related to the above and is of importance not only for commercial reasons but also because of the impact of information systems on individuals. The impact in moral terms of a customer who receives a late delivery is relatively small. However, when the impact is in a safety-critical system, such as an air traffic control system or a hospital records system, that impact could be large. It is generally accepted that organizations have an obligation in these areas over and above that 'forced' on them by legal liability. The organization should have in place systems and procedures for ensuring quality to complement accountability.

Privacy

Data protection acts (see later) outline the framework within which organizations should operate with respect to data on persons. Over and above this, the organization may wish to make explicit the way that data on individuals is going to be used. A good example involves the transmission of customer data to third parties for marketing purposes. Many organizations now are completely transparent on this and give each customer the right to state their wish to allow their personal details to be transmitted for marketing purposes – an **opt-in policy** (failure to act by the customer results in their data not being transmitted). Alternatively an **opt-out policy** may be adopted (failure to act by the customer results in their data being transmitted).

Staff development and retraining

The impact of information technology has reshaped the types of work involved within organizations. Frequently those with skills for previous jobs do not have the skills appropriate for the new technology. Many organizations have developed policies to provide the retraining necessary to enable employees to move internally. The drive to develop policies is not just the commercial consideration of 'fire and hire' as against the costs of retraining. Rather it reflects the fact that organizations regard themselves increasingly as having a moral obligation towards their workforce.

Use of IT and time

Organizations are making policy decisions on the use of their IT facilities by employees for non-work-related activities. The policy may cover, for example, the right of the employee to use e-mail for personal purposes, during or outside of work time. The content of the e-mail may also be subject to the policy (e.g. pornography) or whether the e-mail is being used for personal consultancy purposes. Issues concerning the owning of copyright on software produced by the employee either in or outside of work time but using the employer's technology will need to be clarified (often in their contract of employment).

9.3.3 Society issues and legislation

Many of the issues resulting from the impact of information technology have been experienced before with new technologies. What distinguishes the impact of information technology from previous technologies is the penetration of information technology into most aspects of our work and leisure and the power which it brings for processing information. When these impacts are regarded as undesirable, existing legislation may be able to control this. Increasingly though, extant legislation cannot be applied successfully to the characteristics of information technology and new laws need to be passed. This is an example of **social responsibility** – members of a community sharing a collective belief and deciding on the most appropriate actions for the benefit of the majority while protecting minorities and the disenfranchised.

Mini case 9.5

Identity theft

So-called 'phishing' attacks – involving fake email messages that try and fool Internet users into revealing their bank account and other private details – are growing. The number of phishing-related crimes in the UK soared from 1713 in 2005 to 14,156 last year. Similarly another scam called 'skimming', or card cloning, is also on the rise. This type of fraud rose 3% to £99.6m last year, representing nearly 25% of all UK card losses.

Skimming and cloning are becoming an international problem. Criminal gangs often export card details from the UK to countries such as the US where organized gangs use 'money mules' to carry out fraudulent transactions using counterfeit cards.

In an effort to combat identity theft and fraud, companies are beefing up their security systems, encrypting data and introducing new measures designed to reduce the risk if laptops, BlackBerry smartphones and other devices go missing. These include biometric security devices like fingerprint readers and supplement PIN and password-based security systems. In some cases companies are also adopting systems that enable them to delete data stored on a laptop hard drive or smartphone remotely, should the device be lost or stolen.

Security experts believe such measures are particularly important because, despite all the attention that external security breaches attract, the majority of cases involve 'insiders'.

Adapted from: **Phishing and skimming surge**
Paul Taylor, FT.com, 27 June 2007

Questions

1. Describe the methods of identity theft known as phishing and skimming. Why do they cause a problem for individuals and for institutions?

2. What measures can be taken to prevent identity theft? What are the implications that, according to the article, most cases involve 'insiders'?

Computer crime and abuse

The rise of IT and the Internet has led to different activities which, at best, are considered to be abuse and, at worst, so counter to individuals and society that legislation has been passed to make these activities illegal.

1. **Theft** through the use of computers was an early activity. It often centred on the movement of money or on false accounting. Now it has extended to data theft and software theft through copying.

2. **Hackers** are individuals who attempt to electronically enter a computer system, usually remotely via the Internet, when they have no authorization to do so. Such individuals may do this for 'fun' or the 'challenge', to damage the system's functionality in some way (e.g. destroying data, or transmitting a virus), or to perpetrate theft.

3. **Pornography** is now commonly distributed across the Internet. The ability to disguise the source of the receiving address for pornography has limited police activity in enforcement of legislation on obscene materials. Further legislation has been necessary to define what constitutes the transmission and holding of pornography since the medium is electronic signals.

4. **Spamming** is the automated sending of large quantities of unsolicited e-mails. This may be for marketing purposes (largely regarded as a nuisance by the recipients) or to jam or disrupt computer facilities, as these become increasingly devoted to the transmission and delivery of e-mails thus removing them from their legitimate processing purposes.

5. **Sniffing** is the electronic eavesdropping on electronic data transmissions. This may be of e-mails or of data which might be used for pecuniary gain, e.g. credit card details. Encryption of this data is increasingly used to ensure its security.

6. **Scams** attempt to prey upon the gullibility of the user to respond to a request or an offer. Examples include the religious website that offered 'a place with God for just $15' or the site that promised visitors they could 'get rich quick' but needed to provide their credit card details first. One of the most prolific email scams originated in Nigeria, although it is now more widely practised. This involved a huge fictitious sum of money that the potential victim of the scam could obtain by providing a smaller payment in advance to the fraudster. It is reported that this scam has extracted many billions of dollars since it first appeared.

7. **Identity theft** is the illegal use of the details of another person to obtain goods, services or the transfer of funds. The increase and the improvement in telecommunications technology and business have been mirrored by a growth in crime using the same technologies. By obtaining details such as name, address, passwords, bank account or credit card details, thieves can adopt the identity of another person to access. Two examples of identity theft are:

   - **Phishing,** where potential victims receive highly credible but fake requests, often by e-mail, from organizations that request confirmation of account details or passwords. The requests are often framed in similar style and content to the actual organization in an attempt to deceive the recipient of the e-mail that the request is real.

   - **Skimming,** where the details contained on the magnetic strip or the RF tag of a card are illegally copied. This is often achieved by luring the user to allow their card to be read through a device masquerading as a real card reader.

Countries are responding to these challenges with legislation. For example:

- Governments, whilst clamping down on sniffing, are enshrining their rights to eavesdrop in the national interest through legislation. The **Regulation of Investigatory Powers Act (2000)** in the UK allows the government mass surveillance of electronic communication and access to Internet activity through Internet service providers (ISPs). A bill was rapidly passed in the United States after the September 11 terrorist attacks allowing the FBI to make widespread usage of its e-mail sniffing software product, Carnivore.

- The **Computer Misuse Act (1990)** in the UK was passed to make illegal the unauthorized access to, or modification of, computer material. This has now been supplemented by the **Computer Misuse Amendment Bill (2002)** designed to prohibit denial of service attacks ('degradation, failure or other impairment of a computerized system').

However, it is often proving difficult to frame such legislation as the activity often spans several countries through web hosting and data transmission.

Intellectual property

Intellectual property is intangible property created by an individual or organization. Examples might be books, music or art, or ideas behind inventions. The intellectual property is often produced to make profit and considerable time, effort and funding can go into its production. In order to reward this investment the producer of intellectual property must be assured that others will not immediately take it over and reap profit from it, thereby denying the producer the reward. The two main ways of achieving this are via **copyright** and **patent.**

Copyright protects the expression or manifestation of an idea – not the idea itself. Copyright applies to a work automatically when it comes into existence. For example, when a book is written or software code is produced it becomes the copyright of the author. The author may license others to produce copies of the work or, indeed, may be required to transfer the copyright to an employer (if produced in the employer's employment and this is covered by the employment contract). Copyright prevents the copying of all or some of a work by others during the author's lifetime and beyond (different countries have different time periods). There are also international agreements protecting copyright. Software when produced is automatically copyright. However, this copyright will not prevent another from understanding the ideas behind the software and producing code to manifest the same idea.

Patent protects the idea behind an invention and the way it functions. It therefore powerfully protects the intellectual property of the author. However, it is not automatic – the patent right must be applied for. This can be a long process and to gain a patent the intellectual property must be considered to be original and non-obvious. Further, a patent granted in one country may not be acceptable in another. Therefore patents may be needed from many countries. Software is not usually patented.

Although covered by legislation (for example, **Copyright, Designs and Patents Act 1988**, UK, and **Computer Software Copyright Act 1980**, US), illegal copying of software is common and technologically usually simple. Organizations such as the global **Business Software Alliance**, with major software companies as members, bring group pressure to identify and act against illegal use of software through copyright fraud.

Liability and accountability

The new technology also throws up questions on liability and accountability for which older concepts may not be applicable. The following examples illustrate the ways in which old concepts are being challenged.

(a) It is usually accepted that public carriers are not liable for the content of what they carry. The postal service is not responsible for the fact that a package contains a faulty item or even a bomb. The telephone company is not responsible for the content of the conversation held using its services. However, difficulties in dealing with illegal pornography are leading governments to consider holding Internet service providers responsible in some ways for the services they provide – particularly for the content of websites the ISP provides.

(b) Similarly, copyright laws are being pressed by Napster and Gnutella-type network protocols which distribute copyright music, not by storing it or transmitting it, but rather by facilitating individuals who hold (illegally) the copyright material on their hard disks to distribute it freely across the network to those that demand it.

(c) Liability for the effects of the use of a computerized system is not always clear. For instance, an independent expert provides information to a software company to build an expert system which is sold to a client. In using the expert system incorrect advice is given which damages a customer. In such cases it is not always clear where liability lies.

Privacy

Information technology has significantly increased our capacity to store, transmit and analyse data held on individuals. In particular:

- Decrease in data storage costs together with improved data access times has enabled organizations to maintain detailed databases on individuals.
- The sophistication of data analysis techniques has enabled this data to be put to very different purposes from that for which it was originally collected.
- The massive increase in computing power together with declining costs has enabled these analysis techniques to be applied to large amalgamated databases.
- The increased used of networking (in particular the World Wide Web) has enabled the remote interrogation of data, the amalgamation of large databases and the near-instant recovery of the output.

These developments have enabled the bringing together of data on individuals from various sources. This is particularly useful in building **profiles** of individuals which can be sold to organizations with products to market. These profiles allow targeted marketing to occur. The data collected may be from credit card transactions (giving patterns of expenditure), point-of-sales systems in supermarkets (also giving more detailed expenditure patterns), to travel locations such as petrol stations or airports (giving geographical detail) as well as banking records, Internet transactions, telephone records and many more. Sophisticated technology such as **non-obvious relational awareness** software provides powerful data analysis techniques enabling the data to be prepared for marketing purposes.

All of these developments have enabled benefits but also allow for the possibility of practices which affect the privacy of the individual beyond their consent. In particular:

- Data on a person can be used for purposes different from that for which it was orig- *inally collected or agreed to by the supplier.*
- Data from different sources can be combined and analysed to build a profile of a person not previously envisaged.
- Inaccurate data held on individuals can be erroneously copied, transmitted and combined with other data and interrogated remotely across the globe in a swift and non-recoverable way.

For these reasons many countries have adopted data protection legislation. This puts restrictions on organizations as to how data on persons is collected, what this data can be used for, how long and securely personal data is to be maintained and procedures for ensuring accuracy of data. All involve the right of the person on whom the data is held (the data subject) to have access to the data held on them and to know for what purposes it will be used. The **Data Protection Acts (1984, 1998)** of the UK are an example and are covered in detail in the next section.

9.4 Data protection legislation

Data protection legislation has been enacted in many countries in the past 20 years in the wake of increased concern over data held on persons using powerful computer-based storage and processing technology. It is a generally recognized right that on the one hand individuals should have some protection surrounding the holding and use of data on them but on the other that individuals and organizations, including the state, also have rights to possess and use personal data to serve their purposes. Data protection legislation attempts to define this balance and to reconcile competing needs. The essence of the problem is to ensure privacy for individuals yet not restrict the legitimate workings of the state and other aspects of society.

Concern over data protection has increased as a result of the power of modern computers to process, store and transmit vast amounts of data cheaply and quickly. This sets them apart from their manual predecessors. Specifically:

- Large files of personal data can be interrogated easily, often using indexes on names, addresses, account numbers, and so on. Manual file access is more difficult.
- The speed of response to an interrogation is extremely fast in computer-based systems compared with their manual counterparts.
- Computer-based files can be interrogated from any part of the world (if telecommunications and outside access are provided).
- The presence of networking facilities means that entire files can be transmitted and duplicated anywhere in the world in a matter of seconds or at the most in minutes.
- It is technically possible to cross-reference and link disparate files to obtain 'personal profiles' on individuals.
- Individual records can be selected easily on the basis of sophisticated searches: for example, find all names and addresses of individuals owning a black Ford, living in the Greater Manchester area and with a criminal record.

In themselves, these characteristics of modern data storage and processing are not undesirable. However, they have certain implications. First, inaccurate (as well as accurate) data can be transmitted and duplicated quickly and efficiently. Second, remote data access, targeted data retrieval and the linking of files mean that data access ability in the wrong hands can lead to a severe misuse of power. Finally, there is a danger that data on private aspects of a person's life held for legitimate purposes may be spread and become widely accessible, intruding on that person's right to privacy.

These concerns have led to data protection legislation in many countries – Sweden (1973), USA (1974), West Germany (1977), Canada (1977), France (1978) and Norway (1978). However, it was not until 1984 that data protection laws were first enacted in the UK.

9.4.1 The Data Protection Act 1998

In the UK, personal data has been offered a degree of protection since the first Data Protection Act in 1984. The 1998 Act implements the EC Data Protection Directive (95/46/EC) and came into force on 1 March 2000. It increases the level of protection significantly. Importantly, it can apply to data that is:

- held on computers, or in computer-readable format;
- held manually (if held in a structured form);
- held as medical and educational records.

Many of the provisions of the Act refer only to personal data, i.e. that relating to an identifiable living person. There are further restrictions on sensitive data such as medical, sexual and criminal history, religious and political beliefs, racial origin, and trade union membership.

The 1998 Act introduces some new terminology into data protection legislation.

- **The Data Protection Commissioner:** The Data Protection Commissioner supervises the implementation of the Act, considers complaints concerning breaches of the data protection principles and has powers to act against offenders.
- **Data controller:** This is normally the company or business.
- **Data processor:** Any person (other than an employee of the data controller) who processes the data on behalf of the data controller.
- **Data subject:** A data subject is 'an individual who is the subject of personal data'. This could be a customer or client.

The eight data protection principles

The 1998 Act provides eight fundamental data protection principles. These go further than those under the 1984 Act and include the activities of obtaining and disclosing data, not just the activities related to data processing. The eight principles are:

1. Personal data shall be processed fairly and lawfully and, in particular, shall not be processed unless certain listed conditions are met. These conditions deal with how essential the processing of data is and emphasize that a data subject must consent to the data collection, or, in the case of sensitive personal data, must have given explicit consent.
2. Personal data shall be obtained only for specified lawful purposes and shall not be further processed.
3. Personal data shall be adequate, relevant and not excessive in relation to the purpose for which it is processed.
4. Personal data shall be accurate and, where necessary, kept up to date.
5. Personal data shall not be kept for longer than is necessary.
6. Personal data shall be processed in accordance with the rights of data subjects under the 1998 Act.
7. Appropriate measures shall be taken against unauthorized or unlawful processing of personal data and against accidental loss of or damage to personal data.
8. Personal data shall not be transferred to a country or territory outside the European Economic Area (EEA) unless that country or territory ensures an adequate level of protection for the rights and freedom of data subjects in relation to the processing of personal data.

The new rights of data subjects

Under the 1984 Act, data subjects had the right to know what data was held about them once the data had been collected. Under the 1998 Act, data subjects have the right to know not only what data and information about them has been collected but also

- to know the nature of the data being held;
- to know why and how it is to be processed;
- to know to whom it may be disclosed;
- to have copies of the data, subject to payment of a nominal fee (currently £10);
- to object to and prevent processing of the data if damage or distress would be caused;
- to claim compensation for damage caused by any breach of the Act.

Exemptions

The Data Protection Act 1998 provides a number of exemptions that apply to various sections in the Act. For example, in the interests of the state, such as issues of national security or the investigation of a crime, exceptions to the Act are possible. These exemptions are intended not to pose a threat to the privacy of the data subject.

Criticisms of the Act

In the early stages of its implementation, a number of concerns have been voiced:

- A data subject might not be aware of archived records relating to them that describe painful historical events. If these records are stored in a structured or computerized way they would need to be disclosed, causing possible distress to the data subject.

- Similarly, some archived records are known to contain some inaccuracies but are stored for reasons of historical importance. Archivists are concerned that data subjects might object to and block the storage of these inaccurate records, thereby destroying their value as a historical record.

- Data about a limited or public company is not caught by the 1998 Act. The Act applies only when an officer or employee of a company discloses data about him or herself, such as their name, e-mail address or other personal details.

9.5 Risk identification and controls

In Section 9.2 it was stressed that controls cannot be viewed in isolation from cost–benefit considerations. The decision to implement a certain control will have initial and operating costs, and these have to be set against the likely benefits. These benefits will include the expected saving resulting from prevention of the loss that would have occurred in the absence of the control. The possibility that the control, on occasion, may be insufficient to prevent the loss occurring must also be taken into account.

Two approaches to risk analysis can be identified. These are quantitative approaches, many of which use sophisticated modelling techniques to arrive at cost–benefit optimal mixes of controls, and **heuristic approaches**, which are more concerned with situations in which controls and failures of control are not easily structured or quantifiable.

9.5.1 A quantified approach to risk and controls

The method explained in this section (covered in Burch and Grudnitski, 1989) involves deriving a matrix in which the columns are types of hazard and the rows are types of

Figure 9.8 Part of a hazard-control matrix

	Errors and omissions	Lost data and documents	Computer failure	Unauthorized access	Fire	Fraud
Input controls	✓	✓		✓		✓
Processing controls	✓					✓
Output controls	✓	✓		✓		✓
Storage controls		✓				✓
Operating system controls				✓		✓
Records management	✓	✓			✓	
Accounting controls	✓	✓				✓
Contingency plan			✓		✓	
Physical security			✓	✓	✓	

control. A type of control might be effective against several different types of hazard. For instance, input controls are effective against inaccurate data input, incomplete data input (loss of documents) and fraud. Similarly, a type of hazard such as fraud may be prevented by different types of control – personnel controls, computer access controls, data access controls and the separation of organizational functions. Part of a hazard–control matrix is shown in Figure 9.8.

Having established the type of hazard that each type of control is effective against, it is necessary to assign numerical values to the following:

■ the loss value associated with each type of hazard; and

■ the probability over a given period of time that the hazard will occur.

The expected loss associated with the hazard can be computed by multiplying the loss value by the probability that the hazard will occur. For instance, if fire has an expected loss of £1,000,000 and the probability of its occurrence is 0.01 per year, then the expected loss is £10,000 per year. This calculation is repeated for each type of hazard and the total expected losses found. Suppose that they are equal to £55,000 in each year. This figure may then be used to justify the expenditure of £55,000 per annum on controls.

Of course, it will be pointed out that there are different types of fire, which are associated with different loss values and different probabilities. In essence, this does not affect the calculation as the expected losses for each type of fire may be calculated and the sum total for fire found. The further criticism that there may be a range of loss values occurring with differing probabilities associated with each type of fire can also be accommodated. However, there is a great danger that too much emphasis is placed on the numerical sophistication of the model when in reality accuracy is swamped by the guesswork accompanying estimation of the loss values and probabilities. It is often better to restrict the calculation to the average loss and the probability that this will occur. Even this may involve very rough estimations.

It is now necessary to establish the effect of the controls. For each control, numerical values are assigned to:

■ the installation cost of the control;

■ the operating cost of the control; and

■ the probability over a given period of time that the control will fail.

Each control will be effective against a number of hazards, and the total cost of control per annum is equal to the sum of the following three costs:

1. the installation cost (divided by the number of years over which this is to be spread);

2. the operating cost per annum;

3. the total of all expected losses associated with each hazard over which the control is applied, multiplied by the probability that the control will fail to prevent the respective hazard occurring.

This gives some measure of the net cost of the control, and as a rule of thumb if this is less than the expected loss associated with the hazards to which the control is applied then the control is justified.

The total impact of a range of controls can be found by summing the net costs of each control, together with the expected losses associated with hazards over which the set of controls is not applied. This assumes that the controls are mutually exclusive in the sense that no two controls apply to one type of hazard. The range of controls with the smallest cost value is the one that is most cost–benefit efficient, and this value gives a financial measure of the advantage of the range over the 'no control' situation, where the cost is £55,000.

Where the controls are not mutually exclusive, this needs to be taken into account as the loss associated with a failure of one control may be prevented by the action of another. The techniques are standard but the computation can become quite lengthy, and it is often possible to profit from computer-aided support.

Having determined and implemented the optimum mix of controls, these should be reviewed periodically as costs and probabilities change. In determining expenditure on these controls, management would also take into account the time–cost of money (by discounting or payback techniques) and also weigh the implementation of controls against alternative projects that are competing for the scarce resources of the organization.

Criticisms of the quantified approach

The method illustrated is an example of just one type of quantified approach to risk analysis. Others differ, but all concentrate on a mathematical modelling of losses, costs and probabilities. Some common criticisms are directed at all these types of approach.

First, it is agreed that the approaches do not help to determine which types of threat exist for an organization and which types of control would be effective. The quantified methods are useful only once this initial investigation has been carried out.

Second, quantitative approaches assume that figures can be assigned to expected losses and probabilities, whereas in practice this is not possible.

Both of these points have merit but should not be seen as invalidating quantitative approaches; rather, they indicate that they should be limited in scope. The first criticism shows that they are incomplete and are best regarded as part of a total approach.

The second criticism varies in strength depending on which hazards and which controls are considered straightforwardly quantifiable. For instance, research can determine the average number of errors and the resulting loss occurring in every 1000 account numbers entered via a computer keyboard. This can be used in the cost–benefit analysis. Other hazards such as fire may be estimated by consulting actuarial records (after all, insurance companies have to base their premiums on some cost–benefit analysis) or the local fire station may be able to identify particular fire hazards in a computer installation, enabling figures to be put on losses.

However, figures for some hazards, such as fraud, are notoriously difficult to estimate because they are specific to industry/company computer systems. Once important hazards and controls become impossible to quantify, the chance of a cost–benefit analysis applied to an overall system of controls vanishes and controls are justified on a piecemeal basis.

It is perhaps best to view quantitative risk analysis modelling as providing one channel of information among others relevant to managerial decisions on the nature and extent of controls.

9.5.2 Heuristic approaches

Strategies that attempt to assess risk based on experience and partial information using rules of thumb are known as 'heuristic'.

Perhaps the simplest heuristic technique is the checklist of areas that should be considered in reviewing a system of controls. This may be compiled from the experience of many practitioners and will incorporate what might be described as 'group knowledge'. The checklist may serve no more than to direct attention to the areas of possible weakness and indicate types of control that are effective.

Other approaches recognize that major computer-associated losses are caused by the accidental or deliberate actions of persons. It is important to clarify and assess the strengths and weaknesses of personnel at all levels of the organization associated with computer use. For instance, employees are known to work with greater accuracy and effectiveness in some working conditions rather than others; motivation and career prospects have effects on the likelihood of an employee perpetrating damage and fraud.

Previous incidents may also be a guide to future losses. Various scenarios can be sketched and discussed with computer personnel to assess the impact of these. Controls can then be identified and added to the scenarios, which are then reconsidered. This iterative process may be repeated many times. This type of approach can be extremely valuable in promoting communication and cooperation between those involved in considering the scenarios and so is regarded as part of an education process in the importance of controls.

Heuristic approaches are of assistance in those areas where quantitative techniques are weakest. It is becoming clear that risk identification and analysis, together with taking appropriate measures in control, are an increasingly important feature both in the operation of computerized information systems and in their design. As a result, methodologies are gradually evolving to aid this process.

Summary

The design, application and administration of controls is an integral part of the analysis and design of any information system. There are three main systems of control that can be applied to both manual and computerized information systems.

First, feedback control mechanisms monitor the state of a system and its output, compare these with a desired standard and make appropriate adjustments in the case of deviation. Feedforward control mechanisms use the current state of a system together with a model of the system to predict future states. If these do not meet systems objectives then appropriate action is taken to alter the state of the current system. Finally, preventive controls operate continuously, preventing an undesirable state of affairs arising.

Controls operate at various levels. They may deter or prevent errors occurring, detect errors that have occurred, minimize the loss associated with a failure, enable recovery or facilitate investigation. In a computerized system, they are directed at malfunctions in hardware and software, poor performance by personnel, fraud and various types of physical hazard.

Controls over data movement through the computer are particularly important in respect of transaction areas. The controls operate at key points over input, storage, processing, output and transmission of data.

Other controls, mainly aimed at fraud, prevent unauthorized access to the computer system and restrict access to files and parts of the database in it. Encryption is a way of encoding data so that in the case of a breach of security the data is meaningless.

The organizational structure of staff functions supporting the information system ensures not only that proper administration occurs but also that the separation and compartmentalization of functions lead to added security.

An important aspect of information systems development is to form a contingency plan that is put into operation during massive computer failure. This will make provision for new staff functions to deal with the emergency, the arrangement of standby or backup facilities and the eventual recovery of the information system.

Legal requirements to audit the financial accounting aspects of a computer system, as well as ongoing audits, act as a further control. They will not only identify the effectiveness of existing controls but may have a deterrent effect on fraud. Modern computer-based audits use software tools to aid the audit process. These enable auditing through the computer rather than limiting the audit to events around it and allow the examination of input and output documentation.

Issues of rights, responsibilities and behaviour are the subject of ethics. Individuals, organizations and society as a whole form views about the way that issues should be tackled. The outcome may vary greatly. In some cases legislation may be enacted, in others voluntary codes of conduct may be adopted. Where there is no clear 'right' or 'wrong' way to act, an ethical consideration and evaluation by those concerned can lead to the 'best' or 'most appropriate' course of action. For a professional working in the information systems domain a number of ethical dilemmas arise and it is essential that proper consideration is given to these issues.

Recent data protection legislation implies that steps must be taken to ensure that the design of an information system enables it to function in accordance with data protection principles. These include the need to take reasonable precautions over the security and accuracy of personal data as well as the facility to allow individuals to obtain personal data held on them by the system.

Managerial strategy on the implementation of a system of controls will always take into account cost–benefit considerations – the cost and effectiveness of controls versus the expected loss in their absence. Quantitative models may aid the process of risk analysis but are complementary to other approaches.

Review questions

1. Explain the ideas behind feedback control.

2. Explain the ideas behind feedforward control.

3. How do feedback and feedforward control differ?

4. How is functional separation used as a control in accounting systems? Illustrate your answer with several examples.

5. Explain the following checks and controls:

control total	master file check	transaction log
hash total	format check	concurrency control
sequence check	reasonableness check	run-to-run control
field filling check	limit check	parity bit
check digit	error log	echo check

6. Explain the difference between fault detection, fault avoidance and fault tolerance.

7. Differentiate between each of the following activities: spamming, scamming, sniffing.

8. Explain the difference between a symmetric and an asymmetric crypto-process.

9. Describe the responsibilities of the various members of staff supporting a large computerized information system. What aspects of the functions performed by each are control functions?

10. List five physical hazards that may affect a computer system and state physical controls that would prevent these or aid recovery in the event that they occur.

11. What questions should an auditor be asking in order to evaluate controls over a sales ledger system?

Exercises

1. Give an illustration of feedforward control in:

   (a) inventory planning
   (b) budgeting.

   What features of your example correspond to each of the components in the general feedforward model?

2. Give an illustration of feedback control in:

   (a) production
   (b) internal auditing
   (c) credit control.

   What features of your example correspond to each of the components in the general feedback model?

3. What is preventive control, and how does it differ from feedback and feedforward control?

4. (a) What categories of preventive control are there?

   (b) Give an illustration of each of these categories in the following areas of a business:
      - payroll
      - cash receipts
      - stores.

5. List and explain *five* levels of control.

6. Is there a clear distinction between input controls and processing controls?

7. Which of the following account codes (containing a check digit modulus-11 in the least significant position) is a legitimate account code?

   (a) 459364   (b) 36821   (c) 27   (d) 19843.

8. Why is it necessary for computer users to use both a login code and a secret password rather than just a secret password, which could serve as both identification and, because it is secret, authentication of identification as well?

9. Give *four* conditions that password authentication of identification should satisfy in order to ensure maximum security.

10. Give two examples of identity theft. What can be done to prevent identity theft occurring?

11. Describe the purpose of a firewall. What is the difference between a hardware firewall and a software firewall?

12. What characteristics should a secure access control policy exhibit?

13. Explain the difference between *substantive* and *compliance testing*.

14. 'It is insufficient to consider whether a control is justified purely on monetary cost–benefit grounds; it is equally important that it works.' What confusion is involved here?

15. 'We ensure that personal data held on the database is accessible only to authorized personnel by preventing other database users accessing personal data records by their key fields or other identifying fields such as name or address and preventing display of these fields.' Is this a secure personal data protection policy in the light of powerful query languages?

16. A bank has a centralized computer system with online terminal connections at each of its 300 branches. These terminals are operated by counter tellers. Each branch also has an automated online 'card point', which can be used by customers to withdraw cash, make deposits, request statements and pay bills to accounts directly. The bill account details must be notified in writing to the bank in advance. There is a personal identification number (PIN) code associated with each customer's card. For security purposes, this is known to the customer and no one else. The PIN needs to be entered for each 'card point' transaction. The

card may also be used over the counter at branch offices to carry out the same transactions as offered by the 'card point' machine, although the teller keys in all the details.

Identify preventive controls that should be present in such a system and specify the purpose of each control.

17. The computer-based audit cannot be regarded as independent, as:

    (a) the auditor is paid by the client,
    (b) the auditor relies on the client to supply information on the workings of the computer system.

    What steps can be taken to ensure auditor independence?

18. You have been appointed data protection officer for your company. It has a large number of microcomputers holding personal data used by many users. At present, no attempt has been made to satisfy the requirements of data protection legislation. Outline the steps that you would take in order to ensure that your organization complies with legislation.

19. 'The Data Protection Act 1998 poses a severe threat to the work of historical archivists.' Do you agree?

CASE STUDY 9

Security and control

The number of coordinated attacks by criminals aimed at bringing down corporate and e-commerce websites for blackmail purposes has increased sharply in recent years. IT security firm Symantec estimates that distributed denial of service (DDoS) attacks rose 51% in the past six months of 2005 and detected an average of 1402 attacks a day. Research by NOP adds that 13% of UK businesses were affected by DDoS attacks in 2005, at a cost of more than £558m.

Detective inspector Chris Simpson at London's Scotland Yard computer crime unit says he expects to see a further rise in attacks: 'The technology to launch such attacks is now in the public domain, or at least it is available to the technically proficient within the Internet community', he says. 'Inquisitive teenage hackers through to international crime gangs are increasingly able to buy DDoS tools over the Internet and crash websites by bombarding them with thousands of page requests. DDoS attacks may be launched for a number of reasons: it could be extortion, as recent attacks against financial institutions have demonstrated through to revenge or political reasons', says Mr Simpson.

But so far attacks have focused mainly on e-commerce sites that depend on the Internet as their sole revenue source. One industry hit hard by DDoS attacks is online gambling. In March 2004, at the time of the UK Cheltenham horse races, several online bookmakers were targeted, including William Hill, Paddy Power and Blue Square. Criminals took control of thousands of home computers, which had been surreptitiously infected by a computer virus. The compromised computers, or 'bots', were used to send thousands of page requests to betting websites in an attempt overwhelm servers and take their business offline.

The bookmakers were then contacted by extortionists: Blue Square, for example, was ordered to pay £7000 to cease the attacks. Similar attacks have since occurred in the US in the buildup to the Super Bowl. 'Online bookmakers are a clear target for this because they have a large flow of money and if they miss a sale, it's gone. You can't bet on the FA Cup the day afterwards', says Phillip Hallam-Baker, principal scientist at IT security firm VeriSign. 'Bots are being traded on Internet bulletin boards. They start off being used for high value stuff like phishing and spam, and then the absolute dregs are used as DDoS attack droids', he says.

But Elad Shaviv, head of Cisco's European security operations, says that while the majority of criminals are targeting companies who rely on the Internet for their survival, some gangs are launching DDoS attacks for political reasons. For example, in 2004 political 'hacktivists' distributed an e-mail virus called the Maslan-C worm. The e-mail tricked users into opening an attachment by claiming it contained pictures of a glamour model. While computer users were enjoying the images, hidden malware commandeered their computers and used them to launch an attack on Chechen separatist websites.

Criminals have become even more sophisticated in their approach recently. In February, online payment processing firm StormPay was hit by a ferocious attack which closed its business for two days. 'Attacks are coming from everywhere', says Mr Shaviv, who works with Internet hosting firms, such as Telecom Italia and AT&T, to mitigate the problem. He says that the main problem businesses face is trying to spot genuine customer requests from those sent by cybercriminals. 'There is no way to distinguish who really wants to do business with you. In the past, companies would just shut the door, but today you can filter traffic', he says.

Cisco, Juniper Networks and Prolexic, among others, are developing DDoS mitigation technology, which routes web page requests via a filter looking for anomalies and abnormal amounts of activity coming from one computer or location. Scotland Yard's Mr Simpson advocates the use of such systems but says, as such protection can be costly, the decision should be balanced against the perceived risk a company faces: 'If a significant percentage of your business is conducted online, then higher levels of investment are probably justified.'

But Dr Hallam-Baker at VeriSign believes 'prevention is better than cure', saying more needs to be done to stamp out the botnets being used to launch DDoS attacks. While better education of computer users and anti-virus software can reduce infection rates, Internet service providers should also do more to improve online security, he says.

By introducing 'reverse-firewall' technology into a computer's modem connection, which can detect and block abnormal Internet activity, problems could be greatly reduced, he says. 'As a casual Internet user you're only going to read a certain number of web pages, talk to a certain number of friends and send a number of e-mails during a day. If your computer is making more than, say, 10,000 outbound contact requests an hour, then this should be spotted', says Dr Hallam-Baker. 'Ultimately what you need to do is drain the pond. Until you get rid of all the botnets you won't get anywhere.'

Adapted from: **Websites face more attacks**
Daniel Thomas, FT.com, 30 May 2006

Questions

1. Define the following terms that are used in the case study. For each term provide an example of how it might affect the security of a business.

   - distributed denial of service
   - computer crime
   - hackers
   - computer virus

- phishing
- spam
- malware
- hacktivists
- Cybercriminals
- reverse-firewall

2. Why do different types of business face different threats from computer-based crime? For a named business of your choice, construct a security policy that attempts to minimize the threats posed by criminal activity. Your policy should consider physical and electronic threats. It should make reference to the advice of professional bodies such as the BCS.

References and recommended reading

Beer S. (1994). *Brain of the Firm*, 2nd edn. John Wiley & Sons.
This is an interesting, highly readable text, which applies cybernetic principles and control mechanisms as evolved in the human being, by analogy, to the management of an organization.

Burch J. and Grudnitski G. (1989). *Information Systems: Theory and Practice*, 5th edn. Wiley
This provides an excellent all-round coverage of IS topics with particularly good treatment of the management of risk.

Clark L.D. (2003). *Enterprise Security: The Manager's Defense Guide*. Addison-Wesley, Pearson Education
This easy-to-read book provides a comprehensive state-of-the-art coverage of e-business security. It considers recent attack strategies and offers techniques for combating attempts at data infiltration, data destruction and denial of service attacks. As well as explaining traditional security technologies, such as firewalls and virtual private networks, it shows how these can be integrated with risk management, vulnerability assessment, and intrusion detection to build a comprehensive security plan.

David W.S. and Benamati J. (2003). *E-Commerce Basics: Technology Foundations and E-Business Applications*. Addison-Wesley, Pearson
This is a comprehensive introduction to all aspects of e-commerce. Later chapters also cover cybercrime, cyberterrorism, security and ethical issues. Chapters contain summaries, review questions and exercises.

Furnell S. (2002). *Cybercrime: Vandalising the Information Society*. Addison-Wesley, Pearson
This is an entertaining and well-researched text in which an accessible analysis of cybercrime, including hacking, viruses and other forms of malicious software, is provided. The effects of these crimes on the wider society and organizations in which they take place is considered. Areas covered include the commercial and political evolution of the computer hacker, the likely future development of cybercrime and implications for responses to this from the legal system.

Maiwald E. (2004). *Fundamentals of Network Security*. McGraw-Hill
This is a comprehensive textbook introduction to computers and network security. It contains chapter-end quizzes, questions and lab projects. The text provides a basic understanding of best practice for security laws and standards that are necessary to build complete security systems.

Moynihan T. (2002). *Coping with IS/IT Risk Management*. Springer Verlag
The book looks at how experienced project managers deal with the development of IT systems. Several experienced managers are interviewed as to the way they handle projects. These are then analysed by other professionals. The book is aimed at software professionals but is useful to students to give a 'real life' approach to problems.

Pfleeger C. and Pfleeger S. (2006). *Security in Computing*, 4th edn. Prentice Hall

An extremely comprehensive coverage of all aspects of security. As well as considering technical matters the book addresses legal issues and the business case for security strategies.

Romney M.E., Steinbart P. and Cushing B.E. (2002). *Accounting Information Systems and Business Organizations*, 8th edn. Addison Wesley Longman

This book gives extensive coverage of control as applied to accounting systems for the non-technical reader.

Sherwood J., Clark A. and Lynas D. (2005). *Enterprise Security: The Manager's Defense Guide*. Addison-Wesley, Pearson Education

This easy-to-read book provides a comprehensive state-of-the-art coverage of e-business security. It considers recent attack strategies and offers techniques for combating attempts at data infiltration, data destruction and denial of service attacks. As well as explaining traditional security technologies, such as firewalls and virtual private networks, it shows how these can be integrated with risk management, vulnerability assessment, and intrusion detection to build a comprehensive security plan.

Singleton S. (1998). *Data Protection: The New Law*. Jordan Publishing

This book provides an excellent, highly summarized introduction to the principles behind data protection legislation and its implications for systems analysis and design.

Singleton T. and Hall J. (2003). *Information Systems Auditing and Assurance*. South Western College Publishing

A good coverage of the topics of auditing, assurance and internal control. The book considers computer operations, data management, electronic commerce systems, auditing revenue and expenditure, and it has an interesting section devoted to fraud and fraud detection.

Chapter 10

Information systems development: an overview

Learning outcomes

On completion of this chapter, you should be able to:

- Explain the need for systems analysis and design
- Explore the origin of new information systems projects and consider the participants involved
- Define the systems life cycle and describe the structured approach to information systems development.

Introduction

The purpose of this chapter is to introduce and give an overview of the process of systems analysis and design. The first section identifies the need for analysis and design. It is recognized that systems developments do not occur in isolation, and an overall systems strategy for the organization is required. The way that steering committees provide for this is explained. Various participants are involved in the process of analysis and design. The role of the analyst is highlighted in the earlier part of this chapter. The remainder of the chapter is given over to justifying the need for a methodology – in this case a structured approach – and explaining in general terms how this is applied to the life cycle. Details of the stages involved are explained in Chapters 11–15. Chapter 16 covers the alternative approach of object oriented analysis and design and Chapter 17 provides a comparison between different approaches to systems development.

10.1 The need for systems analysis and design

At first, the following might seem a plausible course of action by an organization when purchasing and installing a computer system. The first step is to identify the application areas. For instance, these might be accounting, budgeting and word processing. A search is then made of the computer literature in order to establish the names and reviews of accounting, spreadsheet and word-processing packages. A small group of likely candidates for each application is selected. These are then demonstrated by the dealers selling them and the package that best meets the needs of the users for each application is chosen. Compatible hardware is then purchased, often recommended by the dealer, and the equipment is installed. The software and the existing business data are loaded up and, hey presto! the organization has a working information system that meets the requirements of the users and delivers all the benefits associated with computerization.

This approach may work when a small business is in need of computer-assisted support for its standard procedures and when those needs are clearly identified. It is unlikely that it will be satisfactory for the development of a more complex system for a medium-sized or large organization. As a rule, the larger the organization the more complex and individual are the data-processing and information needs of that organization and the greater is the potential amount of funding available for a computer project. These organizations are most likely to develop their own system or pay specialist firms to do this for them. Their needs are individual and often initially unidentified. Custom designed systems are required.

For larger systems, the requirements of users must be identified and a suitable system designed and specified meeting those needs. This must take account of the hardware, the software and the data storage structure. The design must incorporate control and security features. It must also take account of predictable future needs. The hardware will be purchased and installed, the programs written and tested and existing data loaded into the data structure. Networking infrastructure may need to be installed and adequate security arrangements with external networks established. The system will be tested and necessary amendments made. Staff training will be organized. Finally, after the system is up and running, continued maintenance will be necessary. All of this requires many people with differing areas of expertise. The sums of money involved may be large, the time taken for completion many months or even years. It is essential that the project is planned and coordinated properly.

10.1.1 The need for an information systems strategy

During the past 40 years computerized data processing and information provision have changed vastly. Developments in technology have included the microprocessor, sophisticated telecommunications systems, networking and the Internet, new office automation equipment and the development of cheap, user-friendly packaged software. These changes have allowed cheap and powerful processing facilities to be open to all parts of an organization. Within the organization, the needs of users have evolved rapidly. In order to prevent anarchic chaos through the development of many independent internal information systems, it is necessary to provide some kind of control by way of a well-worked-out information systems strategy.

This strategy will aim to identify those business activities within the organization that are appropriate to computerized systems development. It will map out, in broad terms, a plan for the development of projects. The strategy will look closely at the size of the investment and consider which of the returns are appropriate and where they will come from. It will incorporate new developments in technology and future needs wherever possible. This strategy will also decide between a policy of centrally controlled development of projects and a strategy of local developments to meet local needs. This latter approach is likely to be applicable to large organizations that already have a philosophy of dispersed management control. A policy on internal charging for computer services needs to be established. For instance, is the running of the computer centre (or information centre) to be an organizational overhead or is it to be charged to user departments? If charging is agreed then on what basis? Can the service be contracted out to a third party? All these issues need to be incorporated in a systems strategy if the information systems development is to have any coherence.

Figure 10.1 Several projects running concurrently in an organization

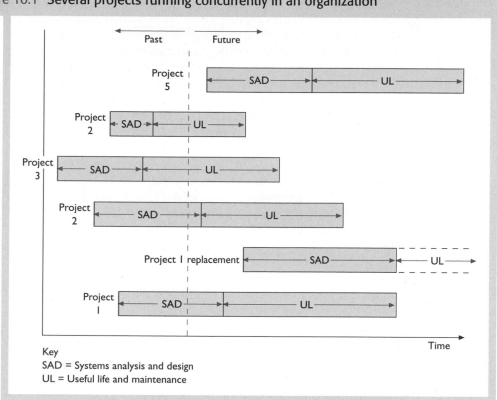

Key
SAD = Systems analysis and design
UL = Useful life and maintenance

A large organization will not have just one computer systems project running at any one time. Rather, several projects will be under way simultaneously. Each will have a different starting point in time and a different projected completion date and will probably be in a different area. These areas will not be completely independent – there will be some overlap and interaction. For instance, a project to develop an automated stock control system may be tied into a separate project dealing with e-commerce and secure payments. These projects need to be coordinated with one another as well as ensuring that each is internally well organized. Moreover, as a project may take a number of years before it comes online and its lifetime may be short, it is often necessary to start planning and designing its replacement before it finally becomes outdated or fails to meet the changing requirements made of it (see Figure 10.1). All of this indicates some need for overall project control and coordination as well as an information systems strategy.

10.1.2 Information systems steering committees

The responsibility for overall strategic planning and control of computer systems development will usually reside with a standing steering committee. This will not be a committee required to take detailed technical decisions. In fact, many of its members will have little technical knowledge or experience. It will be required to frame overall development strategies and allocate resources. Its aim is to ensure that the information

Figure 10.2 The relationship between the steering committee and project groups

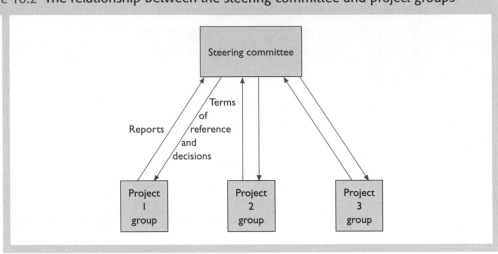

systems in the organization deliver an effective service compatible with cost efficiency. The purposes of the committee may lie within the following areas:

■ **To recommend an overall policy for information and data-processing systems development:** This will include such issues as whether or not to standardize on the computer equipment of one company, whether to go for a centralized or decentralized system, the method of charging for development and use of computer systems within the company, the policy on data protection legislation, and the resources available for information systems projects.

■ **To ensure that individual user department needs are being satisfied:** The information system should service the needs of the organization. The presence of individual user department managers or representatives ensures that user views are articulated.

■ **To initiate and monitor individual projects:** This will include specification of budgets, the scope and objectives of each project; setting up a project team for each project and determining its terms of reference; receiving progress reports and taking major decisions, for example stop/go on a project (see Figure 10.2).

■ **To coordinate individual projects:** Individual projects that will affect one another must be made aware of this in order to ensure harmonious development. It is also important that projects are not viewed independently but taken together as a strategy.

■ **To report 'upwards' to top management:** Management will need summary reports on project development and present and future costs.

■ **To be responsible for the appointment of senior personnel in the computer centre:** Job specifications and appointments will be decided at this managerial level.

Typically, the steering committee will meet regularly. It will be composed of managers of the departments that use the information systems, the head of the computer centre or its equivalent and other senior members of the computer centre, such as the chief analyst, and any other person that senior management judges necessary. One of the most important functions of the steering committee is to initiate and set the terms of reference for new projects.

10.1.3 Reasons for project initiation

Projects are initiated by the steering committee, but where does the idea for a new development come from? What causes a recognition of the need for computer systems development? There are a number of reasons, many of which can be related to Porter's models of competitive advantage introduced in Chapter 2. The following are among the most common:

1. **The current system cannot cope:** Many systems projects replace old systems. The previous system may have been a manual system or be based on a computer. Either way it may not have been able to cope with the demands on it. For instance, increases in the volume of transactions processed may have made the system so slow that it ceases to be efficient. Backlogs in orders may build up. Staff may be bogged down with excessive paperwork of a routine nature. Or a merger may lead to a change in organizational structure that renders the current system inappropriate.

2. **Cost savings:** One of the most common reasons for the earliest computerization projects was the replacement of time-consuming, and therefore expensive, manual, rule-governed, repetitive procedures by quick, cheap computer substitutes. This was most notable in the area of payroll and mass billing for the nationalized industries, where computer systems quickly and cheaply carried out the tasks of entire rooms of clerical workers. Nowadays, most savings in these areas have been made and this is rarely a reason for computerization.

3. **The provision of better internal information for decision making:** Management has recognized the ability of computers to supply fast, accurate, targeted information. If management decisions are analysed for their information requirements, information systems can be designed to enable more effective decisions to be taken.

4. **The provision of competitive customer services:** This may range from fast enquiry services and clear, itemized bills to customer-operated input/output equipment. Automatic cashpoint systems are in the latter category. Once one bank supplies this service they all must or else lose their customers.

5. **The opportunities provided by new technology:** Unlike cars, old computer systems are rarely scrapped because they wear out. It is possible though that outdated technology does not offer the same range of facilities as that currently being produced. Networks, improvements in storage devices and processing power, the development of micros with their cheap and end-user oriented packages and the widespread adoption and application of the Internet have in themselves opened new doors for the exploitation of the benefits of computerization.

6. **High-technology image:** Some companies feel that their image suffers unless they are seen to be using computers in their operations. These companies always display the technology in prominent areas, such as reception.

7. **Changes in legislation:** Changes in legislation such as data protection legislation may act as the trigger for new systems development. Other examples include significant alterations to taxation or changes to National Insurance legislation in the UK, or the basis for the preparation of company accounts.

8. **Balancing the portfolio of projects:** An organization may have a policy of spreading the risk inherent in new project developments. This may lead to a range of projects being undertaken, from those with low risk (and possibly low business impact) through to those with high risk (but potentially with business impact).

FT

Mini case 10.1

Shared services

Running a jail poses a particular set of management challenges. For that reason, prison governors have traditionally enjoyed a high degree of autonomy in how their prison is run. But prisons are not islands, and in the UK they are being encouraged to embrace best practices from the broader public sector, including the shared service centre.

Newport in Wales is home to the new shared services centre for Her Majesty's Prison Service (HMPS), which is responsible for the custody of 77,000 prisoners in 128 prisons in England and Wales. The centre went live in May 2006 using Oracle software. The project is being implemented gradually but when fully operational all the back-office functions for these jails will be performed by a team of 500 people in Newport.

'It's not just a new IT system', says Steve Hodgson, head of shared services at HMPS. 'There is a whole new process and that has a big impact on the roles of people.' The big attraction of the shared service centre concept is, of course, economies of scale. By centralizing back-office functions, HMPS hopes to reduce the cost of processing transactions by £17m a year.

That is the theory, but how is the project working out in practice? Surprisingly well, according to Mr Hodgson. Prior to opting for a shared services centre, HMPS had already decided to upgrade its IT systems in three separate projects covering human resources, financials and procurement systems.

It made sense to combine these projects and consolidate the IT systems into a single data centre at Newport instead of running separate 'instances' of the software in each prison, as was previously the case.

Adapted from: **Her Majesty's Prison Service**
Geoff Nairn, FT.com, 7 September 2006

Question

1. Which of the reasons for project initiation are evident in the shared services model adopted by HM Prison Service?

10.1.4 The participants in analysis and design

It is common for a computer systems project to be initiated because someone has recognized that a problem exists with the way that things are currently done. Alternatively, an opportunity is perceived that will lead to an improvement on the present system. In either case, the **users** of the existing system will play an important role. They can provide information on the current system. They will also be able to specify, in their own terms, the requirements of the new system.

Systems developers or **programmers** are responsible for turning those requirements into programs. They may either be writing code from scratch, using program generators, or applying system development tools such as CASE (defined and described in more detail later) or database management systems. When executed, these will control the operation of the computer, making it perform to serve the needs of users. However, the programmer will be a computer specialist and will see the problem in computer terms. He or she will be talking a different language from the users. There is a communication gap.

Figure 10.3 **The role of the analyst**

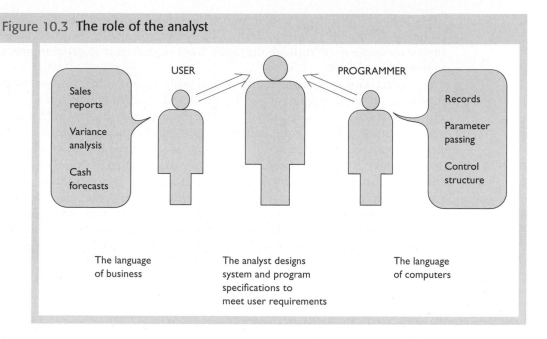

The language of business

The analyst designs system and program specifications to meet user requirements

The language of computers

This gap is filled by the **systems analyst** or **business analyst**. This person is able to understand and communicate with users to establish their requirements. The analyst will also have an expert knowledge of computers. He or she will reframe those requirements in terms that programmers can understand. Code can then be written. It is important that the analyst be a good communicator who can think in terms of the user's point of view as well as that of the programmer (see Figure 10.3).

This translation of requirements is not a straightforward process. It is not, for instance, like translation from German into English. It is more helpful to think of it along the lines of architecture and building. The client (user) states his or her understanding of what the building should look like and what functions it should perform (user statement of the requirements of the system). The architect (analyst) then takes these intentions and provides a general sketch of the building that will satisfy them (logical model of the intended system). Having agreed this with the client (user) the architect (analyst) then draws up a detailed blueprint of the design (detailed program specification) from which the builders (programmers) can work. Just as the architect's task is a skilled one requiring a knowledge of building materials, so the analyst needs a knowledge of computers.

The analyst's task is not restricted to providing specifications for the programmers. The analyst has a range of responsibilities:

1. The analyst is responsible for investigating and analysing the existing system as to its information use and requirements.
2. The analyst judges whether it is feasible to develop a computer system for the area.
3. The analyst designs the new system, specifying programs, hardware, data, structures and control and other procedures.
4. The analyst will be responsible for testing and overseeing the installation of the new system, generating documentation governing its functioning and evaluating its performance.

The analyst is likely to come from either a computer science or a business background. He or she will usually possess a degree and/or be professionally qualified. Sometimes an analyst may have risen 'through the ranks' from programmer to programmer/analyst to a full systems analyst.

As well as possessing significant technical skills in computing, the analyst must fully appreciate the environment and work practices of the area in which the computer system will be used. Knowledge and experience are necessary but not sufficient. The analyst must, above all, be a good communicator with business personnel as well as with technical staff. He or she must be able to handle diplomatically the conflicts of interest that inevitably arise in the course of a project. Managerial, particularly project management, skills are another essential asset as a project involves a complex interaction of many people from different backgrounds working on tasks that all have to be coordinated to produce an end product. The design process is not mechanical, and the analyst must demonstrate both considerable creativity and the ability to think laterally. Finally, analysts need to exude confidence and controlled enthusiasm. When things go wrong, it will be the analyst to whom people look as the person to sort out the problems and smooth the way forward.

10.2 The need for a structured approach to analysis and design

Suppose for a moment that information has been collected on the workings of an existing manual system, for example a payroll system (Figure 10.4). This is a simple system that accepts as inputs:

- transaction time-sheet data (such as *employee #*, *number of hours worked*, *date*);
- standing data on each employee (such as *employee #*, *hourly wage rate*, *tax code*);
- standard tax and National Insurance tables that give deductions for various levels of gross pay.

The time-sheet data is compiled on each employee by the manager of the department in which that employee works. The employee data is supplied by the personnel department and is held in the wages department on an employee master file.

Each week, the wages clerk works out the gross wages and deductions applicable to each employee by using the time-sheet details and performing calculations after consulting the employee master file and the tax and National Insurance tables. Some global totals for management, the Inland Revenue and others are also calculated.

Figure 10.4 A simple input/process/output diagram of a payroll system

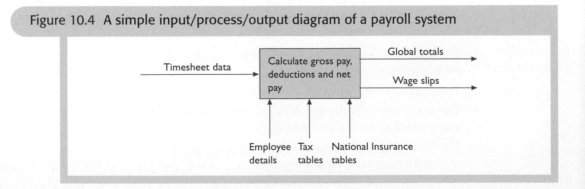

The systems analyst has a relatively straightforward task in analysing and designing a computer system that entirely mimics the workings of this manual system in terms of the data accepted, the processes occurring and the output produced. The computer system will have certain advantages over the manual system in terms of speed, reliability and operating costs, but the data processes, data inputs and outputs will all be similar. The analyst designs a computer master file for the employee record. This contains fields for storing exactly the same data as the manual master file. The analyst designs a data entry screen to look like the old timesheet. A program is specified that accepts timesheet data as input at the keyboard, reads the master file details on the employee, reads the two tables (now stored as files), computes the gross wage and the various deductions, writes this to a file for later printing of the wage slip and, if required, updates the employee master file with new information such as the gross pay to date.

Of course, things will not be quite this simple as the program will need to handle enquiries, produce end-of-year summaries of employees' pay and carry out a range of other tasks. However, given estimates of the average numbers of transactions processed and records maintained, standard documentation forms to record the manual system (document description forms would be an example), and standard forms to define the computer system (so that programmers have a clear specification of requirements to work from), analysis and design becomes a straightforward task. The technical expertise will lie in the selection and sizing of hardware.

The following points emerge from the example as described:

1. The computer system was expected to be a copy of the existing manual system. No evaluation or redesign of the system was expected. This enabled the analyst to proceed immediately from a *physical* description of the existing system to a *physical* design of the computer system. The physical description of the existing system involved the description of input and output documents used and their contents, together with the records held on employees and the types of data held in those records, and a description of the manual processes undertaken to prepare a payroll. The physical design included a specification of the computer file and record structure, the data entry screen format and the program specifications.

2. The system was not expected to change much over time. The data needed for payroll does not change in form and the procedures for calculation are constant.

3. The existing system was clearly understood by those working with it. It was easily defined as data needed for calculation and the calculations themselves are precise.

4. The processes did not need to have data made available to them from outside the payroll subsystem, and data within the subsystem was not used by processes elsewhere. In other words, the system is not a small part of a larger integrated system involving shared data.

5. Although simplicity is a relative term, as can be seen from the example, producing a payroll is not a complex process. One would not expect to have large teams of analysts and programmers devising the new system.

It is easy to understand how things can be more complicated by dropping some of the assumptions implicit in the example.

1. If it is assumed that a subsystem is to be designed that is an integrated part of a much larger system with which it shares data and processes, a straightforward piecemeal *physical* description of the existing system will not lead to an integrated new system.

This is because the existing geographical and departmental boundaries between subsystems will be translated into the new system. No attempt is made to 'step back' and view the system as a whole. Although individual subsystems will be designed optimally, the system as a whole may function suboptimally (see Figure 10.5).

Figure 10.5 Traditional analysis and design by way of a logical model: (a) traditional physical design process preserving subsystems relations; (b) design of an integrated system by means of a logical model

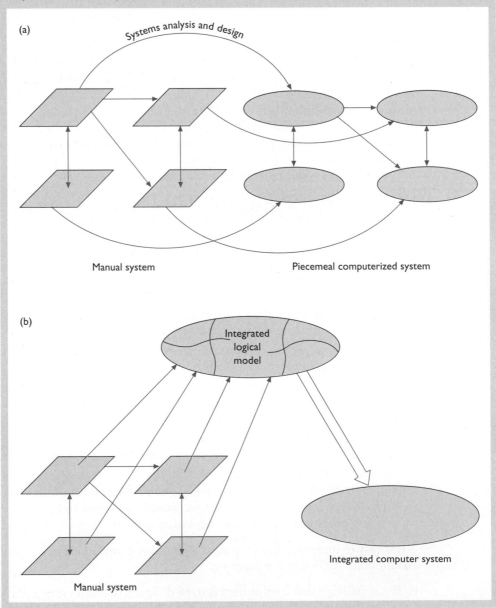

2. The existing area may be a part of a much larger intended system, which does not currently exist in its entirety. Redesign may be required because of new features that are added with computerization or simply because a new system provides the chance to evaluate and change an existing manual system that is not running efficiently.

3. The requirements made on the system may also change over time, and the structure of the data and processes may need amending. This adds further difficulty, as in designing the system not only do current practices need to be catered for but the design must also allow for change.

4. The added complexity may mean that large teams of analysts and programmers will be involved. This in itself brings problems, as these teams need organizing, monitoring and coordinating. Communication can easily break down between and within teams.

5. Users and management need to understand what the new system is offering before major investment in hardware and software is undertaken. It is important that communication tools are developed that aid this understanding. A physical specification of a system in terms of file structures and access methods, computing processing power in instructions per second, RAM size and so on will not be appropriate.

These considerations have led to different approaches to the analysis and design of information systems. Some focus on business processes, some focus on the management of information systems development projects, and others attempt to match social and technical aspects. A comparison of different approaches can be found in Chapter 17. Before that, the structured approach to the analysis and design of information systems is presented in detail.

10.2.1 A structured approach

The main features (see Figure 10.6) of this approach are:

1. (a) Once a physical description of the existing system has been obtained, the analyst's attention is turned to building a logical model of that system. This involves abstracting away from physical details to leave the bare-bones logic of the system. For instance:

    – The media on which data is stored are ignored. It is irrelevant to the logical model whether data is stored on manual record cards, scraps of paper, magnetic tape or anything else. Only the type of data is recorded in the logical model.

    – The organization of the data stores is ignored. For instance, it is irrelevant that the data stored on the manual record cards is stored in employee order with a side index based on name. Only the type of data held is found in the model.

    – Who or what carries out the data processes, or where they are carried out, is not relevant to the logical model. The fact that employee John Smith consults a price catalogue before pricing a customer order in the sales department is translated in the logical model as a process for pricing order details using price data from a data store. Geographical and physical boundaries are not shown in the logical model. Document flows between operations in departments become data flows between the processes that use the data.

Figure 10.6 A model of the process of analysis and design

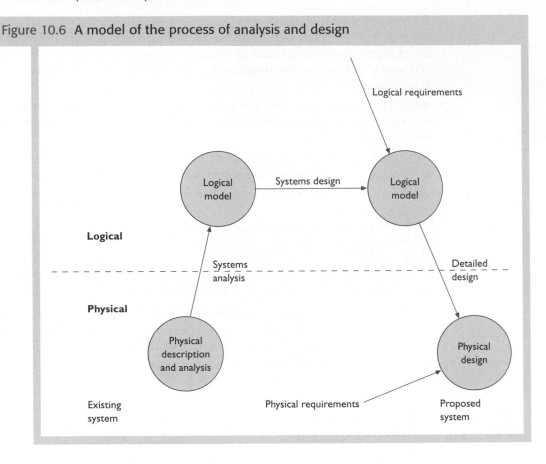

(b) Once this has been done, extra logical constraints and requirements are added as needed. A new system may now be designed at the logical level. The logical model of the designed system will aid in the physical design.

(c) The new physical system is now defined and incorporates any further physical constraints. It is only at this stage that the analyst is concerned with file sizes, storage media, processor types, allocation of disk space, construction of program code, and so on.

2. (a) Complex problems and functions are partitioned and then decomposed into their parts, which themselves are further partitioned and decomposed (process analysis). For instance, a complex process such as 'establish future product availability' can be broken down into the three subprocesses: 'establish current stock', 'establish future production' and 'establish existing commitment to allocate future product'.

(b) The basic entities in an organization are ascertained and the relations between them charted before looking in detail at the fine-grained level of what information is to be held on each (data analysis).

(c) This is a 'top-down' approach. In contrast, a 'bottom-up' approach starts by considering in detail the individual tasks and the data items needed for these.

The system is then built up from this basis. The latter approach is only effective in the case of relatively simple systems in which little redesign or alteration is needed.

3. Emphasis is placed on rigorous documentation and charting. This mirrors the *physical → logical → logical → physical* development discussed in this section. The documentation:

   (a) aids communication between analysts and users by concentrating on the logical aspects of a system rather than technical, physical features which may confuse the user;

   (b) encourages the design of (structured) programs that are straightforward to code, easy to test and (through their modular make-up) amenable to future alteration;

   (c) aids the organization and scheduling of teams of analysts and programmers for large projects;

   (d) enables effective design and representation of the database;

   (e) acts as permanent documentation of the system.

The need for a structured approach is most easily understood when describing the replacement of a manual system by a computerized system. The points made, however, also apply to the replacement or enhancement of an existing computerized system. This section provides a rationale for adopting a structured approach and outlines some of its main features. Section 10.3 traces an overview of the development process. Chapters 11–15 apply the structured approach in detail to these stages.

10.3 The life cycle of a system

In order to develop a computerized information system, it is necessary for the process of development to pass through a number of distinct stages. The various stages in the system's life cycle are shown in Figure 10.7. These stages are completed in sequence. The project cannot progress from one stage to the next until it has completed all the required work of that stage. In order to ensure that a stage is completed satisfactorily, some 'deliverable' is produced at the stage end. Generally, this is a piece of documentary evidence on the work carried out. Successful completion of the stage is judged by the documentation. This is known as the 'exit criterion' for the stage.

It is common for some of the tasks carried out during a stage of the process to be initially unsatisfactory. This should come to light when the exit criteria are considered. The relevant tasks will need to be redone before exit from the stage can be made. Although 'looping' within a stage is commonplace, once a stage has been left it should not be necessary to return to it from a later stage. This structure – a linear development by stages, with deliverables and exit criteria – enables the project to be controlled and managed. The benefits of this staged approach are:

■ Subdivision of a complex, lengthy project into discrete chunks of time makes the project more manageable and thereby promotes better project control.

■ Although different parts of a project may develop independently during a stage, the parts of the project are forced to reach the same point of development at the end of the stage. This promotes coordination between the various components of large projects.

Figure 10.7 **Stages in the life cycle of a systems project**

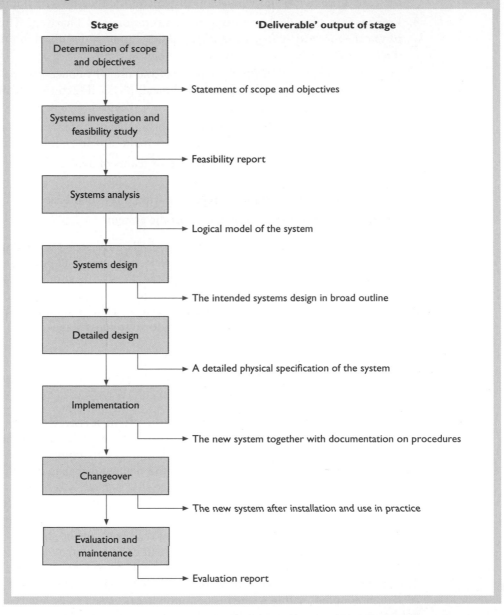

- The deliverables, being documentation, provide a historical trace of the development of the project. At the end of each stage, the output documentation provides an initial input into the subsequent stage.
- The document deliverables are designed to be communication tools between analysts, programmers, users and management. This promotes easy assessment of the nature of the work completed during the stage.

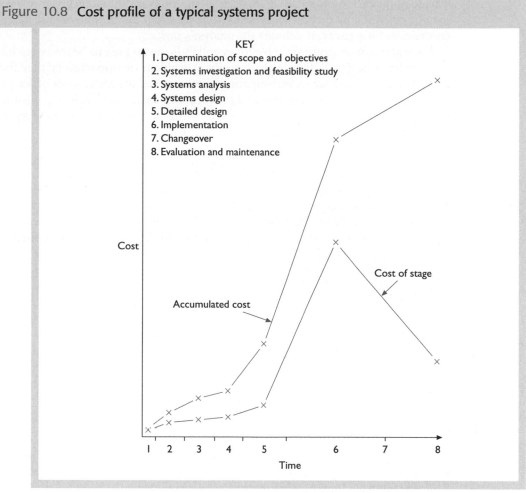

Figure 10.8 **Cost profile of a typical systems project**

KEY
1. Determination of scope and objectives
2. Systems investigation and feasibility study
3. Systems analysis
4. Systems design
5. Detailed design
6. Implementation
7. Changeover
8. Evaluation and maintenance

Cost

Accumulated cost

Cost of stage

Time

- The stages are designed to be 'natural' division points in the development of the project.
- The stages allow a creeping commitment to expenditure during the project. There is no need to spend large sums of money until the previous stages have been completed satisfactorily (see Figure 10.8).

The approach progresses from the physical aspects of the existing system (systems investigation) through logical analysis (systems analysis) and logical design (systems design) on to the physical aspects of the new system (detailed design, implementation and evaluation).

Stage 1 Determination of scope and objectives

Before an analyst can attempt to undertake a reasonable systems investigation, analysis and design, some indication must be given of the agreed overall scope of the project.

391

The documentation provided on this acts as the analyst's initial terms of reference. This may be provided by the steering committee or written by the analyst and agreed by the committee. Either way, it delimits the analyst's task.

The statement of scope and objectives will indicate an area to be investigated, such as sales order processing. It will also specify a problem or opportunity that the analyst should have in mind when investigating this area. For instance, sales order processing might be perceived to be too slow and the company fears that it is losing customers. The document should also specify a date by which the feasibility report (see stage 2) is to be produced and the budgeted cost allowable for this.

Stage 2 Systems investigation and feasibility study

The output of this stage is a report on the feasibility of a technical solution to the problems or opportunities mentioned in the statement of scope and objectives in stage 1. More than one solution may be suggested. The solution(s) will be presented in broad outline. An estimate of the costs, benefits and feasibility associated with each will be included. The purpose of the report is to provide evidence for the steering committee to decide whether it is worth going ahead with any of the suggestions. If the whole project is dropped at this stage, there will have been very little cost to date (sunk cost) (see Figure 10.8).

In order to establish the feasibility of a future technical system, it will be necessary for the analyst to investigate the current system and its work practices. This will provide evidence for the functions that the new system must perform even in the case of substantial redesign. The analyst will need to interview users and view existing documentation. The information collected during this stage will be useful for the next stage of the life cycle as well.

Stage 3 Systems analysis

Provided that the project has been given the 'go ahead' as a result of the feasibility study, the next task for the analyst is to build a logical model of the existing system. This will be based partly on information collected during the stage of systems investigation and partly on new information gathered from the existing system.

The purpose of this stage is to establish what has to be done in order to carry out the functioning of the existing system. This 'what has to be done' is not to be confused with what actually happens in the existing physical system. That is, it is not to be confused with who does what to which document before transferring it from one department to another, or who provides what information for whom on whose authorization. Rather, the central question to be asked is 'what, logically speaking, must be done in order to satisfy the objectives and functions of the system under investigation?' This will involve a decomposition of the functions of the system into their logical constituents and the production of a logical model of the processes and data flows necessary to perform these. This is called **process analysis**. The logical model will be illustrated by data flow diagrams and structured techniques for specifying algorithms. Incorporated into this model will be any additional logical requirements to be made of the new system. No decisions on the way the system will be physically realized should be apparent from this model.

The processes will be fed by data. This data will relate to entities of interest to the organization. These entities will stand in relation to one another. For instance, data will be held on employees and the departments in which they work. Thus work is a relationship between employees and departments. These entities and relationships are combined in a data model of the organization. This procedure is called **data analysis**.

The output of this stage will be a logical process model as revealed by data flow diagrams, together with the specification of the process algorithms, data dictionary and a data model. This output is reviewed by management and users. Agreement needs to be established as to whether the model is a reflection of the logic of the problem area.

Stage 4 Systems design

Once the analysis is complete, the analyst has a good idea of what is logically required of the new system. There will be a number of ways that this logical model can be incorporated into a physical design. For instance, are the data stores to be implemented as a series of files, or is there to be a database? If a database is the chosen route, should this be centralized or distributed? The data flow diagrams will reveal the processes and the data flows between them. How many of the processes are to be incorporated into a computer system, and how many are to remain manual? Of those to be computerized, which are to be run under batch processes and which interactively online? Is the computerized system to be centralized or distributed?

There will not be one correct answer to these questions. Rather, there will be a range of alternative designs. Each of these will have different implications for cost, security, ease of use, maintainability and efficiency. Some will yield more computerized facilities than others. Structured tools, such as data flow diagrams, enable these design alternatives to be clearly identified. They also allow the various options to be presented in a manner that requires little technical expertise in order to understand them.

The analyst will suggest two or three design alternatives to management, together with their implications. Management will then decide between them. Often these alternatives will reflect a low-, a medium- and a high-cost solution to the problem. The first will provide a system that is very basic. The second alternative will incorporate more facilities, while the third may go beyond this to illustrate the full potential of extensive computerization.

By the end of this stage, the attention of the analyst is turning away from purely logical considerations to the various ways, in general terms, that the logical model can be physically implemented. This stage ends with a choice between the alternatives presented to management.

Stage 5 Detailed design

The stage has passed beyond that when the analyst can look only at the logical requirements of a system or at broad-outline design solutions. Detailed physical specifications need to be made so that the system can be purchased/built and installed. A number of distinct areas must be considered:

1. Programs will need to be developed so that the computer can perform the various functions required of it. These programs will be coded by programmers, who need a clear statement of the task to be programmed, or created using application or code generators. Structured tools make possible clear specifications from which the program is written. They also enable the programs to be easily testable and amendable if necessary.

2. Hardware requirements must be specified that, together with the programs, will allow the computer system to perform its tasks efficiently. These requirements for computers, monitors, printers, network infrastructure and so on must be detailed enough to allow the purchasing department to obtain the items.

3. The structure of the database or system of files will also be specified.

4. A schedule for the implementation of the system will be derived at this stage. This will ensure that during implementation all the various activities are coordinated and come together at the right time.

These areas can be summarized as software, hardware, data storage and the schedule for implementation. Two other threads will run through consideration of these areas. The first is security. The system must be designed to ensure maximum reliability in secure, complete, accurate and continuous processing. The second is the user–machine interface. Unless this is designed with the characteristics of the tasks and the users in mind, it is unlikely that the system will be fully effective in meeting its objectives.

The systems specification is a highly detailed set of documents covering every aspect of the system. From this it is possible to estimate costs accurately. The specification is finally ratified by senior management or the steering committee. Once it is agreed, large sums of the project budget can be spent on major purchases and programmers' time.

Stage 6 Implementation

During implementation, the system as specified is physically created. The hardware is purchased and installed. The programs are written and tested individually. As programs often interact, they will also be tested together.

The database or file structure is created and historical data from the old system (manual or computer) is loaded. Staff are trained to use the new system. The procedures that will govern the operation of the new system are designed and documentation detailing these is then drafted. Particular attention will be paid to security features surrounding the conversion of existing files, whether manual or computer-based, to the new system.

The system is formally tested and accepted before changeover.

Stage 7 Changeover

Changeover is that time during which the old system is replaced by the newly designed computer system. This period may be short if, at the time the new system starts running, the old system is discarded immediately.

Alternative methods of changeover exist. The old system can be run in parallel with the new. Although expensive in labour costs, this method does have the advantage that if the new system fails there is a backup system to rely on. The old and the new systems can also be compared with one another for discrepancies in their performance and output. Another approach is to run a pilot scheme. This involves running a small version of the system before the full systems implementation is carried out. The way that the pilot system functions allows identification of any errors and shortcomings that will be encountered in the full system. These will be involved in the life cycle of a project. No matter how extensive the planning has been, no matter how rigorous the systems testing, there are always unexpected problems during the first few days or weeks of use of a new system. The problems should be minor if the preceding stages of the project have been carried out according to correct standards. These teething troubles may be technical, or thcy may result from the use of the system for the first time by inexperienced (although trained) company personnel.

A further approach is to 'phase in' the new system, allowing different functionality to be introduced in a staged fashion. This is usually a less risky and sometimes less costly method of changeover and can be viewed as being more tangible than a pilot scheme. The disadvantage is that a piecemeal approach might not lead to such a robust and coherent final product. There is inevitably a complex proliferation of legacy and new systems with which to contend.

After the system has 'settled down', the next phase of the life cycle is entered.

Stage 8 Evaluation and maintenance

By now, the system is running and in continuous use. It should be delivering the benefits for which it was designed and installed. Any initial problems in running will have been rectified. Throughout the remainder of the useful life of the system, it will have to be maintained if it is to provide a proper service.

The maintenance will involve hardware and software. It is customary to transfer the maintenance of the hardware to the manufacturer of the equipment or some specialist third-party organization. A maintenance contract stipulating conditions and charges for maintenance is usual. The software will need to be maintained as well. This will involve correcting errors in programs that become apparent after an extended period of use. Programs may also be altered to enable the machine to run with greater technical efficiency, but by far the greatest demand on programmers' time will be to amend and develop existing programs in the light of changes in the requirements of users. Structured techniques of design and programming allow these changes to be made easily.

It is customary to produce an evaluation report on the system after it has been functioning for some time. This will be drawn up after the system has settled into its normal daily functioning. The report will compare the actual system with the aims and objectives that it was designed to meet. Shortcomings will be identified. If these are easily rectified, then changes will be made during normal maintenance. More major changes may require more drastic surgery. Substantial redesign of parts of the system may be necessary. Alternatively, the changes can be incorporated into a future system.

10.4 The structured approach and the life cycle

Structured systems analysis and design both define various stages that should be undertaken in the development of a systems project. In the life cycle, the structured techniques and tools are used in analysis and design. Their benefits are realized throughout the project in terms of better project control and communication, and during the working life of the system in terms of its meeting user requirements and the ease with which it can be modified to take into account changes in these requirements.

The philosophy of the approach distinguishes it from other methods used in analysis and design. Central to this is the idea that a logical model of the system needs to be derived in order to be able to redesign and integrate complex systems. This is evident in the stages of systems analysis and design. The detailed tools are explained in Chapters 11–15, but they all follow from and through this central idea. Table 10.1 summarizes these as applied to the stages of the life cycle.

Table 10.1 Stages of the life cycle

Stages	Purpose	Comments
Determination of scope and objectives	To establish the nature of the problem, estimate its scope and plan feasibility study	
Systems investigation and feasibility study	To provide a report for management on the feasibility of a technical solution	Involves the analyst in investigation of the existing system and its documentation. Interviews used
Systems analysis	To provide a logical model of the data and processes of the system	Use of data flow diagrams, entity relationship models, structured English, logic flowcharts, data dictionaries
System design	To provide outline solutions to the problem	Automation boundaries indicated on data flow diagrams, suggestions offered on type of systems: for example, centralized *v.* distributed, file *v.* database. Cost estimates provided
Detailed design	To provide a detailed specification of the system from which it can be built	Programs specified using hierarchical input process output (HIPO) and pseudo-code, hardware and file/database structures defined, cost estimates, systems test plan and implementation schedule designed
Implementation	To provide a system built and tested according to specification	Code programs, obtain and install hardware, design operating procedures and documentation, security/audit considerations, test system, train staff, load existing data
Changeover	To provide a working system that has adequately replaced the old system	Direct, parallel, pilot or phased changeover
Evaluation and maintenance	To provide an evaluation of the extent to which the system meets its objectives. Provide continuing support	Report provided. Ongoing adaptation of software/hardware to rectify errors and meet changing user requirements

10.5 Alternative approaches to information systems development

Although the structured approach is the most widely understood and practised method of systems development, many alternative viewpoints exist. These range from differing perceptions of how progress is made through the stages of the life cycle through to fundamental differences in how systems should be modelled, such as the object oriented paradigm introduced in Chapter 16. A comparison of alternative models is provided in Chapter 17.

Summary

Organizations can best utilize the benefits from changing and improving modern information technology by designing a corporate information systems strategy. This will outline the areas and approach taken towards information systems in the organization. It will decide on the overall development plan, the resources available and the likely benefits. The information systems steering committee initiates and takes major decisions on individual projects. This committee is also responsible for coordinating project developments and monitoring their progress.

All but the smallest and simplest projects require a series of stages to be undertaken to develop them successfully. This set of stages is known as the systems project life cycle. It consists of defining the scope of the area of the project and arriving at a decision on its feasibility. A logical model of the existing system is developed taking into account the extra requirements of the new system. Various physical solutions to the task of computerization are outlined in broad detail, together with their costs and implications, during systems design. The design of the chosen solution is then developed and specified in greater physical detail. This specification acts as a blueprint from which the system is implemented. After implementation and changeover, benefits accrue to the organization during the system's working life. A post-implementation review of the success of the system in meeting its objectives provides useful information for maintenance and design of its eventual replacement.

In order to ensure that a successful development takes place, a structured approach to analysis and design is recommended. This involves the use of techniques and tools that reinforce the central idea of taking account of the logical requirements of a system before attending to the physical design. This avoids premature physical commitment to systems that would not satisfy user needs. Structured methods also facilitate the management of the project and the coordination of programmer teams and others involved in the development. Documentation ensures that communications between analyst, users and programmers are clear. The final system is likely to be one that is easily adaptable to the changing user requirements associated with any modern, evolving organization.

Review questions

1. Why is systems analysis and design essential for large systems whereas it may not be appropriate for a small system for a small organization?

2. Why is a systems or business analyst needed?

3. Outline the stages involved in a systems project. What is the purpose of each stage?

4. What is the purpose of a feasibility study?

5. Why is it important that the life cycle be divided into stages with deliverables to mark the exit from each stage?

6. What role does the information systems steering committee fulfil?

7. Why have an information systems strategy rather than developing new systems as and when they become needed?

Exercises

1. Under what circumstances is a piecemeal approach to developing a computer system appropriate and under what circumstances is it inappropriate?

2. What benefits are expected from adopting a structured approach to analysis and design?

3. What is wrong with taking early physical design decisions? Surely this would aid in an accurate early estimation of cost?

4. Outline a profile of a suitable person to appoint as a systems analyst.

5. 'It is important that a systems analyst have a strong technical background in computers rather than a background in general business practices.' What is to be said for and against this view?

6. 'User needs are often hard to identify prior to gaining experience from the running of a system. It is therefore a mistake to adopt the philosophy of designing the system to meet user needs. It is better to design and implement a "rough and ready" version of a system to see how users take to it. This can then be systematically amended to remove its shortcomings. The process of design becomes iterative rather than linear.' What is to be said for and against this view?

7. 'If the people who were going to use the computerized information systems were involved in decisions as to what kind of system was needed and how to design it then better information systems would be produced.' Do you think this is a desirable and realistic policy?

CASE STUDY 10

Information systems project development

Julian Granville, managing director of Boden, the catalogue clothing group, recalls the meeting at which it was decided to develop a website. One board member said a woman in her late 30s had no interest in computers: she would never use the Internet, she will ring up. 'The voice of IT on the board, which was effectively me, said "We have a budget of £5000. We'll give it a go". So we bought a website package for about £500, integrated it into our core system and almost instantly it was taking 10% of business.'

That was 1999. Today, the company, which is active in the UK and North America, does about 70% of its business via the web. Turnover is expected to be about £160m this year.

Mr Granville is young enough, at 39, to have programmed a BBC Microcomputer in Basic in his schooldays, versatile enough to have combined the roles of managing director and head of IT at Boden and big enough to admit that running a growing company and managing a problematic IT project simultaneously was not a good idea. 'I like computer systems, which is why I didn't let go sooner. There is sense in the managing director also being head of IT because you are responsible for both the business and the IT strategies. But there was the opportunity cost to the business of what I wasn't doing when the project was in trouble.'

The amiable, informal Mr Granville joined Johnnie Boden as finance director in 1995 when the company – then turning over about £2m a year – was in permanent crisis and running up large losses. He stopped the business going bankrupt, renegotiated terms with suppliers and kept the company's bankers happy. He was quickly promoted to managing director, while the entrepreneurial Johnnie Boden became chairman.

Between 1995 and 2000, the company experienced compound annual growth rates of 60 and 70%. There was little cash left over for capital expenditure. 'In IT terms, it was a matter of hanging on and making sure everything worked. We needed a telephone system, a core stock and sales system and something that would run our warehouses.'

Boden, in fact, like many young companies, was at the start of a process that would see it create a computer system that worked well enough but had been cobbled together with string and sealing wax and was therefore lacking flexibility and adaptability.

In 1999, the company recruited a head of IT – Robin Ailes – who Mr Granville describes as an individual of enormous energy and dedication to the business. 'Robin created the IT department. I didn't have a vision of what was required. I knew what the business needed but not what the IT department needed.' Mr Granville remained the voice of IT on the main board, however, a role he has only just relinquished.

The small and enthusiastic team that Mr Ailes built up proved more than proficient at developing applications to meet the needs of the fast-growing business. 'Between 2000 and 2004, we experienced slightly slower growth but IT became a real enabler of the business in that period. Whatever we wanted to do in taking the business forward, for example, launching in North America, the IT department had a fantastic "can-do" attitude', Mr Granville says. But their skill and enthusiasm carried the seeds of inflexibility which would lead to the decision to redevelop the entire system.

Mr Granville recalls Mr Ailes asking him how many separate databases he thought the company was supporting. He, as board director for IT, knew there were a lot and suggested there might be 60 or 70. The answer, in fact, was 900.

'If I look back and think what we did wrong, it was that we lacked a strategic vision of how it would all pull together. It was not multi-currency. It was not multi-country and it was written in COBOL. We had locked ourselves up by doing many different things, all in themselves quite clever, but not part of a coherent whole.'

So Mr Granville decided to build a modern system with up-to-date technology. The minicomputer was replaced with Dell servers running SQL databases and browser-based .net applications. The project cost about £3m and came in late and over budget.

The biggest problem was cultural. The small IT team had reflected the early days of Boden, when everybody mucked in together. With the big project, however, came professionalism. 'It's been painful because of the cultural change', Mr Granville says, recalling his relief on reading *The Mythical Man-Month*, Fred Brooks' iconoclastic essays on software development that showed that adding more developers to a late project delayed it further. 'This was a revelation. Scaling up from the small projects we had been doing was so difficult. Now we had 15 to 20 people not communicating very well.'

But the project went live on 1 January this year and has proved a success, with little disruption to the business – in itself, quite a feat.

Mr Granville believes he should have acted more rapidly in bringing in an expert with big project experience, but the benefit of having a knowledgeable, enthusiastic champion on the board almost certainly outweighed his lack of experience. Very few companies have managed a big systems transformation without pain, no matter how expert the project managers.

And Mr Dreyer, a Boden board member for nine years, can count on an unusually understanding managing director when the catalogue giant eyes its next big systems change.

Adapted from: **Enthusiasm and skill led to inflexibility**
Alan Cane, *Financial Times*, 18 April 2007

Questions

1. Does the case study confirm the need for an effective information strategy?
2. Many companies make use of steering committees to instigate systems developments. How were these developments initiated in Boden?
3. How does the traditional life cycle apply to the experiences of Boden?
4. The case study references the seminal *Mythical Man Month*, by Fred Brooks. Research this topic further to discover why sometimes productivity increases as teams are reduced in size.

Recommended reading

Avison D. and Fitzgerald G. (2007). *Information Systems Development: Methodologies, Techniques and Tools*, 4th revised edn. McGraw Hill

A leading text book that provides extensive coverage of the area. Practical examples are provided and contextualized through consideration of social and business factors.

Benyon-Davies P. (1999). *Information Systems Development*, 3rd edn. Macmillan Computer Science Series

A non-deterministic book covering a number of frameworks, tools, techniques and methodologies for the analysis and design of systems. The book includes an interesting chapter on project management for information systems.

Brooks F.P. Jr (1995). *The Mythical Man-Month: Essays on Software Engineering – Anniversary Issue*. Addison-Wesley

This is a twentieth anniversary publication of the important text published in 1975 – *The Mythical Man-Month*. This is a highly readable essay on software project management and how it can go wrong. The essays are based on the author's experience of project management for the IBM series 360 and the development of the massive operating system OS/360 for this. From it the author draws many morals on pitfalls to be avoided. Historically, the author was writing at a time when structured approaches to systems analysis and design were being developed to overcome such problems.

Schwalbe C. (2005). *Information Technology Project Management*. Thomson Learning

A very readable text that provides a clear introduction to project management in the context of IT developments. The book takes the reader through such issues as project scope, time, cost and risk. It also contains a guide to using Microsoft Project.

Whitten J.L. and Bentley L.D. (2007). *Introduction to Systems Analysis and Design*. McGraw-Hill Education, Europe

This provides a thorough overview to the process of systems analysis and design. Though not designed for those with no experience of computing, it is suitable for a student doing a first course in systems analysis and design. Coverage also includes object oriented design using UML.

Yeates D. and Cadle J. (2004). *Project Management for Information Systems*. FT Prentice Hall

A very readable text aimed at undergraduate students. It provides a clear introduction to project management in the context of information systems developments. The book takes the reader through such issues as project scope, time, cost and risk. It also considers why some projects fail.

Chapter 11

The systems project: early stages

Learning outcomes

On completion of this chapter, you should be able to:

■ Explain the need for an initial statement of the scope and objectives of an information systems project

■ Describe the techniques for gaining familiarity with an existing system or a new information system and documenting the findings

■ Explain the steps taken in developing a feasibility report and describe its likely contents

■ Compare different perspectives on project feasibility.

Introduction

This chapter deals with the early stages in the development of a computerized information system. The main channels of information open to the analyst for information gathering during systems investigation are explained, together with their weaknesses in the accurate provision of information. It is important that the analyst has a frame of reference through which to conduct the systems investigation. Here the systems model is used. During investigation the feasibility of a proposed system is assessed. The central ideas behind the economic, technical and operational feasibility of a system are explained, together with the difficulties encountered in arriving at an overall economic assessment of the project. The feasibility report and its role in project control and decision making are covered. During this chapter, a case study is introduced that is developed in Chapters 12–15 as the life cycle of the system unfolds.

11.1 Initial stages

The impetus to develop a computerized information system arises because someone somewhere has perceived a need or opportunity that can be satisfied by the introduction of modern information technology. Ideas for developments and enhancements to information systems might originate from many sources, but in a large organization with an information systems strategy and existing technology the focus is through the information systems steering committee. In a smaller organization, the idea will be introduced by, or at least channelled through, a senior member of management.

The reason for initiation of a computer systems project, as explained in the previous chapter, is likely to be a combination of a number of the following reasons:

- The current information system, whether manual or computer-based, cannot cope with the demands placed upon it.
- Significant cost savings are realizable by the cheap processing power of a computer.
- Management perceive a need for better internal information for decision making.
- Computerization will provide better services for the organization's customers.
- The advent of new types of technology opens up a range of available facilities that the organization wishes to exploit.
- The organization wishes to promote a high-technology image, possibly as part of a much wider-ranging marketing strategy or a venture into e-commerce.
- Changes in legislation require systems redesign.

11.1.1 The case study

Throughout this and subsequent chapters on the systems life cycle (Chapters 12–16), it is helpful in understanding the stages, tools and techniques if they are explained by way of a case study. Unlike previous case studies in the book, this one is presented as part of the text rather than at the end of the chapter. The case study used here concerns a company called Kismet Ltd. Kismet purchases electrical goods from a range of suppliers and manufacturers and distributes these goods to retail trade outlets.

Case studies are a useful vehicle for understanding the process of systems analysis and design, but they will never be a substitute for learning through the actual *practice* of analysis and design. The most important respect in which any case study is limited is that it preselects information to be presented to the reader and presents this in a neatly summarized and organized way. In reality, the analyst would be subject to a large amount of (often unconnected) information collected from various interviews, existing works standards manuals, samples of transaction documents, auditors' reports, and so on.

Only a part of the Kismet organization is covered here. In Chapter 1, it was seen that it is often convenient to view a business as being made up of several subsystems, each of which is determined by the function it fulfils. Examples are the sales, manufacturing, storage, purchasing, accounting, planning and control subsystems. This study provides a slice through three of these. It deals with the basic processing of orders from customers, the generation of invoices and the provision of some management information.

Kismet case study 11.1

Kismet supplies a range of hi-fi, TV, radio and video goods to retail outlets throughout the country. The goods are supplied by manufacturers, who each supply a variety of types of equipment. Currently, Kismet has over 40 suppliers, who supply a total of over 500 different item types. The number of suppliers is expected to remain fairly constant during the foreseeable future, although the range of types of equipment may alter considerably. Kismet has approximately 1200 live customers and receives on average about 300 orders per day, each one averaging ten items requested.

Kismet employs about 150 people in a number of departments:

- *Sales order department*: Accepts and processes customer orders.
- *Credit control department*: Responsible for customer credit checks.
- *Stores department*: Responsible for stock control.
- *Invoicing department*: Responsible for customer invoicing.
- *Accounts department*: Handles general accounting requirements and the provision of reports.
- *Packing and dispatch department*: Responsible for goods inward and goods outward.
- *Purchasing department*: Responsible for placing orders with suppliers.
- *Sales and marketing department*: Deals with advertising and establishing new outlets.
- *Payroll department*: Prepares Kismet's payroll.
- *Maintenance department*: Responsible for general maintenance and also for maintenance of Kismet's fleet of vans.
- *General administration*: Handles administration not specifically covered elsewhere.

Kismet was started 30 years ago by Harold Kismet and has grown rapidly in the last five years with the increased consumer use of home media centres, digital music players and the whole range of modern electronic leisure equipment. Josephine Kismet (Harold's daughter) has pioneered this development, with a subsequent 300% increase in trade in the last three years. However, problems are beginning to emerge. Kismet's domination of the north-east of the country and its expansion into the north-west is being threatened by a serious rival, Hardy Ltd. This company was set up nine months previously with a large injection of capital. Hardy provides a website offering customers a range of electronic leisure equipment and the opportunity to place a credit card order. Also, and this is most serious for Kismet, Hardy is now moving into the area of supplying retail outlets, in direct competition with Kismet.

The management of Kismet has been conscious for some time of slowness in satisfying the orders received from retail outlets. These orders are taking an increasing time to process. This has been further exacerbated by the expansion of Kismet over the last three years. The entirely manual system that Kismet uses has not been able to cope adequately with the increase of trade, even though more staff have been employed. Hardy is able to offer a superior service because of its modern computerized data-processing and information systems, which give it a significant edge over Kismet.

Harold Kismet has long resisted his daughter's representations to computerize the business. This is partly because of loyalty to his older employees, who have been with Kismet since its foundation. He fears that they, like him, would be unable to make the transition to computerization. Also, he is conscious of the demise of his best friend's business, which rapidly moved from being a flourishing enterprise to bankruptcy as the result of a completely mismanaged and inappropriate introduction of a computer system.

The recent rise of Hardy and his own impending retirement have forced Harold Kismet to reconsider the possibility of computerization. He has subsequently given responsibility for the project to his daughter. Although knowing little about computers, the daughter realizes the potential and sees this as a necessary requirement if Kismet is to stave off the threat from Hardy and to expand further (possibly into satellite TV and personal computers).

Harold Kismet has called in a systems analyst with whom he wishes to discuss the problems and opportunities.

11.2 Statement of scope and objectives

It is important to 'get the project off the ground' in the right way. It would be a mistake to call in the systems analyst, provide a verbal indication of what is needed and let the analyst 'get on with it'. Very often it is not clear at the outset what the task of the analyst is to be – it is clear neither to the analyst nor to the steering committee nor to management.

A common approach that avoids this pitfall is that the analyst is required to provide a written statement of the scope and objectives of the project. It works like this. The analyst is given a rough indication, often verbally, of the problem or opportunity as perceived by the project initiator. The analyst then looks into the problem and the system within which it is located. The purpose is to come up with a written statement of what the analyst perceives to be the problems to which the systems project is addressed, its scope and objectives and some very rough estimate of the costs. This document will act as a starting point from which the analyst will investigate further and eventually produce a feasibility report.

The statement will not be the result of much investigation on the part of the analyst. Indeed, it is important that only a small amount of time, and therefore cost, is incurred before the analyst and management have an agreed understanding, however broadly specified, of the project. The investigation may take only a day or two.

Kismet case study 11.2

With respect to Kismet, the analyst spends some time with the new managing director Josephine Kismet and then tours the company for the remainder of the day, where he talks to a number of personnel. After this, the analyst produces the statement of scope and objectives (see Figure 11.1). This is to be taken as the initially agreed scope of the project. At this stage, the analyst will not feel tied to any of the figures except the requirement to provide a feasibility report within two weeks at a cost of around £5000.

Figure 11.1 A statement of scope and objectives

Statement of scope and objectives

Project name: Sales order processing – Kismet Ltd date: dd/mm/yy

Current problems:

The following problems have been identified:

1. The sales catalogue of prices and products used to price customer orders is often out of date. In particular, new items are not catalogued immediately and items that are now no longer stocked still appear. The problem is located in the time-consuming nature of the manual preparation of the catalogue from the inventory records.

2. Customer enquiries are sometimes difficult to deal with as records of orders are not stored in a form that is easily accessible.

3. Orders that cannot be immediately satisfied from current stock – that is, back orders – are not processed consistently.

4. Owing to the large number of documents flowing through the system, the time taken to process an order may be days, even if all the goods are held in the warehouse.

5. Data in the system is generally stored in a way that makes it difficult for management to retrieve useful information. For instance, regular reports are time-consuming to produce and are often late, rendering them ineffective for control purposes or to aid medium-term strategies.

Objectives:

To investigate initially the feasibility for computerization of the sales order processing, invoicing and stock systems.

Constraints:

The entire project is to be budgeted for completion within six months at a cost of approximately £500,000.

Plan of action:

Investigate fully the existing sales order processing, stock and invoicing systems. Investigate the feasibility of a computerized system as a solution to the current problems.
Outline in general terms the recommended system(s) with costs.
Produce a report on this feasibility within two weeks with a budget of £5,000.

11.3 Systems investigation

The analyst must now become thoroughly familiar with the existing system. In particular, the analyst has to determine:

- the objectives of the existing system;
- how the existing system works;
- any legal, government or other regulations that might affect the operation of the system – for example, the Data Protection Act in the UK;
- the economic and organizational environment within which the system lies and in particular any changes that are likely to occur.

Why should the analyst pay much attention to the workings of the existing system, because, after all, is this system not deficient or else why would there be a need to replace it? There are a number of observations to make. First, although it is assumed that the problem is one that is amenable to a computerized solution, this has not yet been established. It may turn out that a change in existing manual procedures or organizational structure is the best way of solving the problem. This will only come to light after investigation of the existing system. Of course, analysts may be blind to such alternatives. Analysts are trained to look for technical solutions. They may also have a vested commercial interest in a computerized solution, so it is easy for them to miss alternative solutions. There is, though, a second reason for extensively studying the existing system. This will give the analyst a thorough understanding of the nature of the activities to be incorporated into the final computerized system. No matter how weak the existing system is, it must function at some level of effectiveness. This will provide a rich source of information from which the analyst can work.

11.3.1 The analyst's channels of information

The analyst needs to obtain information about the existing system and its environment. There are five main sources that the analyst can use:

1. interviews;
2. documentation;
3. observation;
4. questionnaires;
5. measuring.

Interviews

This is the most important way in which an analyst will obtain information. Setting up interviews with key personnel at all levels in the organization ensures a rich and complete view of what is happening. Interviewing is more of an art than a mechanical technique. It improves with experience. There are, however, several guidelines that are recognized as being essential to successful interviewing.

First, the analyst must have a clear purpose for each interview undertaken. This should be specified by the analyst as part of the preparation for the interview. It is not enough to define the purpose as 'attempting to find out more about such-and-such an area'. This will lead to a rambling interview. Rather, the analyst should establish the missing information that the interview is meant to supply. The analyst should prepare thoroughly for the interview by becoming familiar with technical terms that are likely to be used by the interviewees and with their positions and general responsibilities. The analyst should also outline a list of questions to be asked during the interview.

During the interview, the analyst should:

■ Explain at the beginning the purpose of the interview. This gives the interviewee a framework of reference for answering questions.

■ Attempt to put the interviewee at ease.

■ Go through the questions that were prepared. General questions should be asked first, followed by more specific questions on each topic area. The analyst should always listen carefully to replies and be able to follow up answers with questions that were not in the original list. The analyst must always bear in mind the purpose of the interview and discourage time-wasting digressions.

- Never criticize the interviewee. The analyst is merely seeking information.
- Not enter into a discussion of the various merits or weaknesses of other personnel in the organization.
- Summarize points made by the interviewee at suitable stages in the interview.
- Explain the purpose of note taking or a tape recorder if used.
- Keep the interview short; generally 20 minutes or half an hour is sufficient.
- Summarize the main points of the interview at the end.
- Book a following interview, if required, with the interviewee at the end of the interview.

No checklist of guidelines is adequate to become a good interviewer, but the list given should enable any serious pitfalls to be avoided.

Problems with the interview as a channel of information

The interview, although the most valuable tool for information gathering for the analyst, is limited in that:

- The interviewee may refuse to cooperate with the interviewer through fear of job deskilling, redundancy or the inability to cope with the new technology as a result of computerization. This may take the form of a direct refusal to take part (unlikely), being vague in replies, or, by omission, continuing to let the analyst believe what the interviewee knows to be false.
- The interviewee may feel that they should tell the analyst how the tasks that they carry out *should* be performed rather than how they actually *are* performed. It is common for people to cut corners, not follow works procedures, adopt alternative practices. All of these may be more efficient than the officially recommended practice, but it is difficult for the interviewee to be honest in this area.
- Clerical workers do tasks. They generally do not have to describe them and may not be articulate in doing so. Indeed, many managers might have some difficulty in articulating their decision-making processes.
- The analyst cannot avoid filtering all that the interviewee says through the analyst's model of the world. The analyst's background and preconceptions may interfere with the process of communication. One of the distinguishing marks of good interviewers is the ability to think themselves quickly into the interviewee's frame of mind. This almost therapeutic skill is not one that is usually developed through training in computing.

Documentation

Most business organizations, particularly large ones, have documentation that is of help to the analyst in understanding the way they work:

- Instruction manuals and procedures manuals provide a statement of the way that tasks are to be performed.

- Document blanks that are filled in by personnel in the organization and then passed between departments or stored for reference give the analyst an indication of the formal data flows and data stores.

- Job descriptions define the responsibilities of personnel.

- Statements of company policy provide information on overall objectives and likely changes.

- Publicity and information booklets for external bodies provide a useful overview of the way that a company works.

The problem with using documentation is that there is often a great deal of it, particularly in large organizations. The analyst has to read extensively in order to gather a small amount of useful information. Unlike interviews, where the analyst can direct the information that is provided by targeted questions, documents cannot be so easily probed. Finally, documentation may be out of date, and the analyst has little way of knowing this. The last thing to be changed when a clerical procedure is altered is usually the documentation governing it. Despite these weaknesses, documentation is a useful channel for information gathering.

Observation

Observation of employees performing activities in the area of investigation is another source of information for the analyst. Observation has the edge over the other methods of information gathering in that it is direct. The analyst wishes to understand the way that the existing system functions. Interviews provide reports from people of what they do, subject to all the distorting influences stated. Documents are an indication of what employees should be doing, which is not necessarily what they are doing. Only by observation does the analyst see directly how activities are performed.

However, there are some notable drawbacks:

- It is extremely time-consuming for the analyst.

- When observed, people tend to behave differently from when their behaviour is unobserved – the 'Hawthorn effect' – thus devaluing the information obtained.

- Observation, unlike interviewing, does not reveal the beliefs and attitudes of the people involved.

However, observation is an important source for the analyst on informal information flows between individuals. These are often essential for the efficient execution of activities. They may not be obvious from interviews and would not appear in documentation.

Questionnaires

Questionnaires are of only limited use in obtaining information for the purposes of investigating an existing system (as opposed to market research, where they are essential). This is because:

- It is difficult to avoid misunderstandings on the part of respondents as they cannot gain clarification of a question on the questionnaire if it is judged to be vague or confusing.

- Questionnaires that are simple provide little information; questionnaires that are more ambitious are likely to be misunderstood.

- Response rates to questionnaires are often low.

- To set a good questionnaire, the analyst often has to have more information about the system under investigation than the questionnaire could hope to provide in the first place.

Certain limited situations may make a questionnaire suitable. These usually occur when the number of people involved makes interviewing prohibitively expensive, the questions are generally simple, a low response rate is satisfactory, and the questionnaire is used to confirm evidence collected elsewhere.

In designing questionnaires, it is important to:

- Keep questions simple, unambiguous and unbiased.

- Use multiple-choice questions rather than ask for comments. This makes the questionnaire both easier to answer and easier to analyse.

- Have a clear idea of the information that is required from the questionnaire.

- Make sure that the questions are aimed at the level of intellect and particular interests of the respondents.

- Avoid branching: for example, 'if your answer to question 8 was "yes" then go to question 23 otherwise go to question 19'.

- Make clear the deadline date by which the questionnaire is to be returned and enclose an addressed and prepaid envelope.

Measuring

Sometimes it is important to have statistical information about the workings of the existing system. The total number of sales ledger accounts and the activity of each will be of interest to the analyst who is looking at the possible computerization of an accounting system. The statistical spread as well as the gross figures may be relevant. For instance, with a sales order-processing system not only may the average number of sales orders processed in a day be of use to the analyst but the pattern of these orders throughout the day and throughout the week may also be of significance. Are there peaks and troughs, or is it a constant flow?

11.3.2 Approaching the investigation

Although the foregoing channels provide the analyst with information, it is necessary to have some plan or some framework within which to study the existing system.

Flow block diagrams

A flow block diagram may be developed at an early stage in the investigation to represent the system. Flow block diagrams show the important subsystems in an organization and the flows between them. They provide a good overview of a system, within which more detailed investigation can occur. It is common for flow block diagrams to be based around the traditional functions of a business – sales, purchasing, manufacturing, stores, accounting, planning, control, and so on. These diagrams were treated in detail in Chapter 1.

Kismet case study 11.3

A flow block diagram of Kismet is given in Figure 11.2.

Figure 11.2 **A flow block diagram of Kismet**

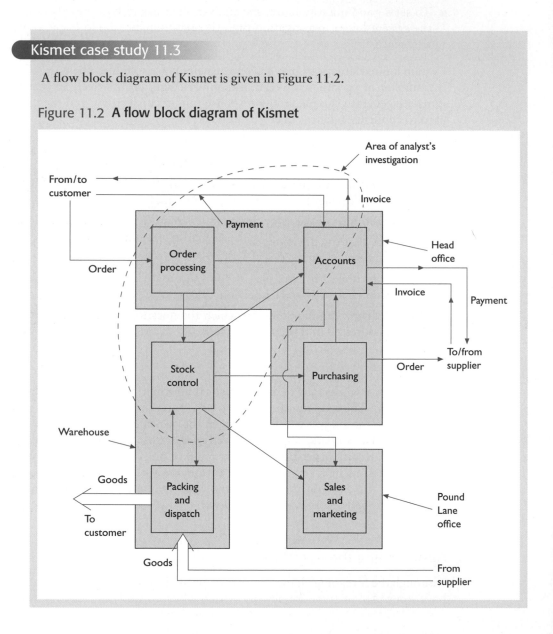

Organization charts

Organization charts show the various roles and their relationships within an organization. They are usually hierarchical in nature, reflecting relationships of control, decision flow and levels of managerial activity between the various elements of the hierarchy. The chart enables the analyst to establish key personnel for interview.

Kismet case study 11.4

An organization chart for Kismet is given in Figure 11.3.

Figure 11.3 **An organization chart for Kismet**

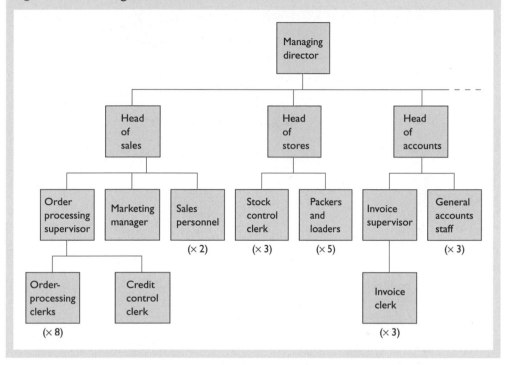

Task identification

The analyst will identify key tasks within each subsystem. A useful model to adopt is the system model (see Figure 11.4), where the task is regarded as a process for converting an input into an output. There may be intermediate storage requirements, and there will be some control over the operation of the task. This gives the analyst a template by which a task can be investigated. Key questions that should be satisfied are:

- What different types of input are there into the task?
- And for each input:
  - What is the structure of the input?
  - Where does it come from?
  - What is the rate of input (how many per hour)?
  - Is it regular, or are there peaks and troughs?
- What different types of output are there to the task?
- And for each output:
  - What is the structure of the output?
  - Where does it go to?
  - What is the rate of output (how many per hour) required?

Figure 11.4 **A systems model of a task (task template)**

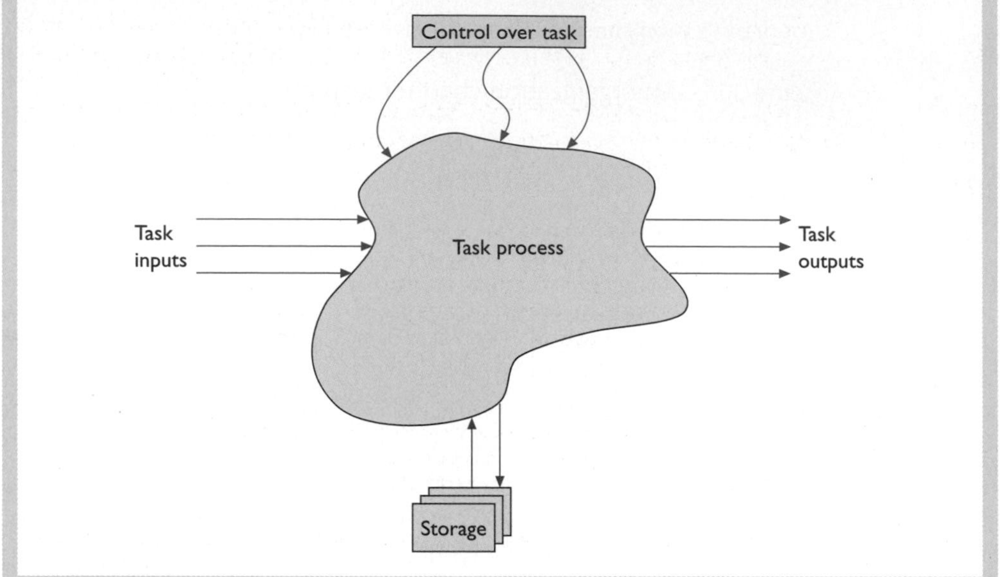

- Is it regular, or are there peaks and troughs?
- What is the purpose of the output?
■ What is the logic of the process?
■ Does it require discretion, or is it rule-governed?
■ What is the purpose of the process?
■ What experience or training is necessary to become competent at it?
■ What level of accuracy is required?
■ What stores, files or records are consulted in performing the task?
■ How often are these consulted?
■ What indexes or keys are used for selecting the correct record?
■ How many records are in the available record store?
■ What types of control are exerted over the task?
■ Who is responsible for each control?

After investigation, the analyst should have a good understanding of:

■ Who does what.
■ Where it is done.
■ Why it is done.
■ When it is done.
■ How it is done.

This framework provides a useful outline on which the analyst can base questions during an interview.

Kismet case study 11.5

Figure 11.5 gives an example of some of the questions to be asked of the sales order processing supervisor at Kismet. These are based on the framework outlined above.

Figure 11.5 Examples of questions to be asked of the Kismet sales order processing supervisor during a systems investigation

Inputs

What is the content of a customer sales order?
Does the company transcribe customer orders to company documentation?
How many sales orders are received per day?
Are there heavy/light times of the week/year?
What do you do if a sales order is incomplete in its specification?

Process

What is done with the sales orders?
How are they divided among the sales order processing personnel?
At what stage is it established that stock exists?
What is done if stock is not currently held?
How are the orders priced?
What happens to an order for an item of stock not held by the company?

Outputs

What is produced by the process?
Where does it go?
Are reports, summaries or totals provided?
How quickly are the priced sales orders produced from the customer orders?

Control

What accuracy controls operate over the transcription of the orders to company documentation?
What controls operate to ensure that all customer orders received are processed?
How is it established that customers have not exceeded credit limits?

Storage

What catalogues, records, files are consulted?
What information is obtained from them?
Whose responsibility is it for ensuring the accuracy of the information?

Staffing

How many staff are involved?
What are their roles?
How do the controls operate over staff?

Costs

What is the budgeted cost for processing an order?
What is the actual cost of processing an order?
How are costs split between variable and fixed costs?

Growth

Is it envisaged that there will be growth in demand for sales order processing?

11.4 The feasibility study and report

One of the purposes of carrying out a systems investigation, perhaps *the* main purpose, is to establish the feasibility of introducing a computer system. Among other things, this will provide some estimate of the likely costs and benefits of a proposed system. The reason for the study is to establish at as early a stage as possible whether the project is realistic. This must be determined with the minimum of expenditure. If the project turns out not to be feasible then all the time and money spent on the systems investigation will be 'down the drain'.

There is a conflict here. On the one hand, the earlier the feasibility study is done the less money will have been sunk, but the less likely it will be that the feasibility study gives an accurate estimate of costs and benefits. On the other hand, a more accurate assessment can only be made if more money is spent on the feasibility survey.

There is no completely satisfactory way of resolving this dilemma. In practice, the analyst is more likely to recommend an extensive feasibility study in more unusual and innovative projects. This is because the degree of uncertainty in success, costs and benefits is greater. However, many analysts become familiar with certain types of project, such as the computerization of a standard accounting system. In these cases, it will be possible to make reasonably accurate feasibility assessments quickly.

There is inevitably an element of guesswork at the feasibility stage (despite what some analysts might claim). The long history of notable failures of computerization is testimony to this fact, as they can, in part, be put down to unrealistic feasibility studies. The more effort put into the study, the less the guesswork. Sometimes, parts of the stages of systems analysis and systems (high-level) design may be undertaken using the structured tools such as data flow diagrams and entity relationship models explained in Chapters 12 and 13, prior to producing a feasibility report.

Kismet case study 11.6

It is assumed here, in the case of Kismet, that the analyst has established enough information after investigation and initial interviews to have a thorough understanding of the present physical system and is able to recommend the feasibility of a computer system. The suggestion will be based on an understanding of the tasks to be performed, the volume of transactions processed and the types of information to be produced.

In looking at feasibility, the analyst considers three main areas – economic, technical and organizational feasibility.

11.4.1 Economic feasibility

As with any project that an organization undertakes, there will be economic costs and economic benefits. These have to be compared and a view taken as to whether the benefits justify the costs. If not, then the project is unlikely to be undertaken.

Economic costs

There are a number of different types of cost associated with a computer project. These are:

1. **Systems analysis and design:** The cost of the analyst must be taken into the calculation of the total cost of the project. Of course, the analyst's costs in carrying out the stages up to and including the feasibility study will not be included in this calculation. These are already a sunk cost of the project.

2. **Purchase of hardware:** Alternatives to purchase, such as leasing or renting, may be considered here.

3. **Software costs:** These are often the hardest to estimate. Software may be written from scratch, developed using fourth-generation tools or purchased, in the form of an applications package.

4. **Training costs:** Staff need to be trained to use the new system.

5. **Installation costs:** This may be a significant cost if new rooms have to be built, cables laid and work environments altered.

6. **Conversion and changeover costs:** These concern the loading of data from the existing system into the new system in a secure manner. There are also costs associated with the resulting changeover from the old to the new system.

7. **Redundancy costs:** If the purpose of computerization is to replace people with machines then redundancy money may have to be paid.

8. **Operating costs:**
   (a) maintenance costs for hardware and software;
   (b) costs of power, paper, and so on;
   (c) costs associated with personnel to operate the new system – for example, computer centre staff, data input clerks, and so on.

Economic benefits

These are often very varied. Some may be estimable with a high degree of accuracy, others may be uncertain. Many benefits will be completely non-measurable. Examples of benefits are:

1. **Savings in labour costs:** These may be predictable, allowing for uncertainties in future wage rates, and so on.

2. **Benefits due to faster processing:** Examples of these might be a reduced debtor period as a result of speedier debtor processing, or reduced buffer stock due to better stock control. These may be estimable.

3. **Better decision making:** Computerized information systems provide more targeted and accurate information more quickly and cheaply than manual systems. This leads to better managerial decisions. It is generally not possible to put a figure on the value of better managerial decisions. Even if it were, it would be impossible to assign what percentage of this improvement was the result of better information and what was the result of other factors.

4. **Better customer service:** Once again, it will generally not be possible to estimate the economic benefits of either better customer service or more competitive services. This will be only one factor affecting customer choice.

5. **Error reduction:** The benefits of this may be estimable if current losses associated with erroneous processing are known.

Comparison of costs and benefits

Both costs and benefits occur in the future, although not usually in the same future periods (see Figure 11.6). The costs occur largely during the initial stages of the systems' development, whereas the benefits occur later in the useful life of the system. These must be compared.

One method is to discount the future streams of costs and benefits back to the present by means of an assumed rate. This will be near to the prevailing rate of interest in the

Figure 11.6 The time profile of costs and benefits for a typical systems life cycle

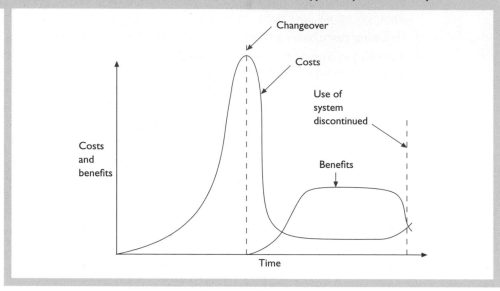

financial markets, although its exact determination will depend on the project, the company undertaking the project and the sector within which the company functions. This discount rate is arbitrary within certain limits.

All of the following factors:

- the non-measurable nature of some of the costs and benefits;
- the fact that many of the benefits occur far into the uncertain future; and
- the degree of arbitrariness associated with the choice of the cost–benefit comparison calculation

mean that the estimation of economic feasibility must be made with much reservation. It is tempting to regard the figure in the net present value calculation of the economic feasibility of the project as the 'hard' piece of data on which a decision to continue the project can be made. This would be a mistake. It ignores not only the non-measurable nature of certain costs and benefits but also other aspects of feasibility covered in the following sections.

11.4.2 Technical feasibility

This is concerned with the technical possibility and desirability of a computer solution in the problem area. Some of the issues will overlap with points brought out in the discussion on costs and benefits in the previous section. Many suggestions are not technically impossible per se. Rather, it is a question of how much money an organization is prepared to invest in order to achieve a technical solution. The following categories are important in determining the technical feasibility of a project.

1. **Rule-governed tasks:** If the tasks undertaken in the area of investigation are not governed by rules but require discretion and judgement then it is unlikely that computerization

will be feasible. For example, the processing of a sales order, the production of a summary of aged debtors report or the calculation of creditworthiness on a points basis are all rule-governed. The selection of candidates for jobs is not. This could not be incorporated into a computer system (although new developments in expert systems raise the possibility that this might not always be so).

2. **Repetitive tasks:** If a task is performed only rarely then it may not be feasible to invest the time, effort and money in developing a program to carry it out. The tasks that are most suitable for computerization are those that are repetitive.

3. **Complex tasks:** If a complex task can be broken down into simple constituent tasks then it is generally easy and desirable to computerize.

4. **High degree of accuracy:** Humans are quite good at making quick estimates based on 'rule of thumb' assumptions in flexible circumstances. Computers are not. However, if a high degree of numerical accuracy is required then computers outstrip humans by both speed and low error rates.

5. **Speed of response:** Computer systems give fast responses if required and are designed to do so.

6. **Data used for many tasks:** Once data is inside a computer it is generally easy and cheap to use it repeatedly for different tasks.

11.4.3 Organizational feasibility

Organizational feasibility, or as it is sometimes called, 'operational feasibility', concerns the viability of the proposed system within the operational and organizational environment. The issues to consider vary from organization to organization, but the analyst is wise to address at least the following questions:

1. Does the organization for which the information system is to be supplied have a history of acceptance of information technology, or has past introduction led to conflict? Some sectors are notorious for their opposition to computerization. For instance, in the UK the print industry unions fought an extended battle opposing the introduction of computer technology. Other sectors, such as banking, have a history of acceptance of and adaptation to information technology. A previous history of opposition to the introduction of computer systems may have taken the form of a formalized union opposition, or it may have been revealed in the attitude of users. High levels of absenteeism and high turnover rates subsequent to a previous introduction of new technology are good indicators of future poor acceptance.

2. Will the personnel in the organization be able to cope with operating the new technology? It is unrealistic, for instance, to expect staff with long-established working practices to adapt readily to new technology no matter how much training is given.

3. Is the organizational structure compatible with the proposed information system? For example, a highly centralized autocratic management structure is generally not compatible with a distributed computer system. Decentralized systems inevitably lead to local autonomy and local management of computer resources. Similarly, if departments or divisions in an organization have a history of competing with one another rather than cooperating, it is unlikely that it will be easy to develop a successful integrated system.

These are all issues in the area of organizational behaviour and 'people problems'. Analysts often have a training in programming or other technical areas, and it is easy for them to ignore this vital component of feasibility.

11.4.4 Feasibility report

A feasibility report will be written by the analyst and considered by management prior to allowing the project to continue further. It will go to the steering committee in the case of a large organization. In a smaller organization without a steering committee structure, the report will be assessed by senior managers as part of their normal activities.

As well as providing information on the feasibility of the project, the systems investigation will have provided much information that will also be incorporated into the feasibility report. In particular:

- The principal work areas for the project will have been identified.
- Any needs for specialist staff to be involved in the later stages of the project will have been noted.
- Possible improvement or potential for savings may have become apparent during the investigation.

Outline headings for a typical feasibility report are given in Figure 11.7. Once the feasibility report has been accepted, the project can proceed to the next stage. This is to

Figure 11.7 The contents of a typical feasibility report

Title page: Name of project, report name, version number, author, date.

Terms of reference: These will be taken from the statement of scope and objectives.

Summary: This gives a clear, concise statement of the feasibility study and its recommendations.

Background: Statement of the reasons for initiation of the project, the background of the current system, how it features in the organization, how it figures in the organization's development plans, what problems it encounters.

Method of study: Detailed description of the systems investigation including personnel interviewed and documents searched, together with any other channels of information. Assumptions made and limitations imposed.

Present system: Statement of the main features of the current system, including its major tasks, its staffing, its storage, its equipment, its control procedures, and the way it relates to other systems in the organization.

Proposed system(s): Each proposed system, if there is more than one, is outlined. This will include a statement of the facilities provided. (Data flow diagrams, explained in Chapter 12, and other charting techniques may be used as a pictorial representation of the proposal.) For each proposal, its economic, technical and organizational feasibility will be assessed. Major control features will be included.

Recommendation: The recommended system will be clearly indicated with reasons why it is preferred.

Development plan: A development plan for the recommended system is given in some detail; this will include projected costs for future stages in the life cycle with estimates of the time schedule for each.

Appendix: This will provide supporting material to the main report. It will include references to documents, summaries of interviews, charts and graphs showing details of transaction processing, estimates of hardware costs and so on. In fact, anything that is likely to be of use to those reading the report that will enable them to make a more informed decision will be included.

provide an analysis from which a new system can be designed and implemented. Chapters 12 and 13 cover the two main aspects of analysis – analysis of processes and analysis of data. Various tools and techniques will be explained; although these are normally used in analysis, there is nothing to stop the analyst using them in the stages of systems investigation. The various charts and diagrams can then be included in the feasibility report. This is tantamount to carrying out broad aspects of *systems* analysis and *systems* design (as opposed to *detailed* design) prior to the provision of the feasibility report. This makes possible a more comprehensive development of a proposal or range of proposals. It also allows better communication of these proposals within the feasibility report as the techniques used are designed to facilitate communication.

Summary

After senior management or the steering committee has recognized the need for the development of an information system, it is necessary to carry out a formal feasibility study. This will involve an analyst. The analyst will need to have an understanding of the scope and objectives of the proposed systems project. It is customary for a written statement in this area to be agreed between the analyst and those who are commissioning the project. Although this will only give the broadest indication of the scope of the intended system, it will provide the analyst with a direction in which to proceed in systems investigation. Also, importantly, it will give the analyst a budget and schedule within which to provide a feasibility report.

During systems investigation, the analyst will obtain information by interviewing key personnel, searching current documentation and reports, observing the existing system, measuring various key variables such as the number of transactions processed and the time taken for each transaction, and possibly using questionnaires for response from large groups. All of these channels of information suffer from distorting influences that devalue the accuracy and use of the information gathered through them.

In order to organize the way that the information is obtained, it is helpful for the analyst to have a framework of reference. This is provided by the systems model. At the highest level, flow block diagrams will aid the analyst in representing the major components within the organization and the flows between them. At the more detailed level, when key tasks are considered, it is appropriate to view them as processes for converting inputs into outputs using storage while being subject to control. Organization charts give the relationships between the various roles in the organization.

A feasibility report is provided by the analyst for the systems project. As well as giving a description of the present and proposed systems it contains an assessment of the feasibility of the proposal(s). This will not only take account of the economic feasibility – the economic costs and benefits – but will also look at the technical and organizational feasibility. The feasibility study and report is essential for proper project control. It enables senior management, which is responsible for major resource decisions, to take a decision on the continuation of the project with a minimum of sunk cost. The more unusual the requirements of the proposed system or the greater the sums involved in its development, the more extensive will be the systems investigation prior to the feasibility report. Various charting and diagrammatically based techniques such as data flow diagrams and entity–relationship models, explained in Chapters 12 and 13, may also be used. After acceptance of the feasibility study the analyst, together with a project group in the case of larger systems, will proceed to full-scale analysis and design.

Review questions

1. What is the purpose of a statement of scope and objectives?

2. During systems investigation, what channels are open to the analyst in gathering information about a system? What are the strengths and weaknesses of each?

3. What is the purpose of a feasibility study?

4. Explain the terms *economic feasibility*, *technical feasibility* and *organizational feasibility*.

Exercises

1. Why is it difficult to undertake an economic assessment of a project at an early stage in its development?

2. What features of a task (or group of tasks) are likely to make it technically non-feasible?

3. 'In the feasibility report, it is common for the analyst to outline more than one proposal and recommend just one of these.' Surely the analyst should either give only the recommended option or, alternatively, outline several proposals with their implications and let management decide the most suitable?

4. What benefits are likely to result from:
   (a) computerizing the records system in a library?
   (b) computerizing a sales order and invoicing system (as in Kismet)?
   (c) providing a computerized point of sales system in a supermarket?

CASE STUDY 11

Shared services feasibility

The feasibility study is finished. Suppliers and customers have agreed as to what shared services can achieve. A deal has been signed. So what comes between that happy moment and actually making it happen? If clarity was the watchword for the start-up phase, engagement could be the one for getting the project going.

In short, it requires a governance strategy that coordinates and manages all the streams of the work being undertaken. Suppliers and customers must engage via what might be called a project management ecosystem. From assessing progress weekly and managing issues, to steering the project at the highest level and assessing the realization of benefits, this is a mutually reinforcing system of reporting committees and managers that bear responsibility for the programme in every aspect.

'Most shared services implementation involves a mix of partners', says Alan Richell, head of transformation leadership at Capgemini. 'It is, therefore, essential to establish a collaborative working environment for success. Making shared services happen is not a one-off event. Continual innovation and collaboration needs to be built into the delivery model.'

Capgemini advises breaking the management down into four streams: business transformation; IT; applications; and service provision. 'You need the business transformation partner to support organisational and process changes, whether dealing with internal shared services or BPO', continues Tony Kelly, BPO director, Capgemini. 'The IT transformation partner is needed to manage technology changes, working with the applications partner. Finally, if the decision is to outsource, then you need a BPO or service provision partner to deliver the services. The key point to remember is: do not assume one delivery partner. All of these are very important streams and must be managed appropriately. If any one of these is not given the right attention, the project can easily fail.'

It is the transformational element that lies at the heart of this. It is so important because it seems somewhat counterintuitive. The assumption of management might be that to opt for shared services is to take a load off their mind. This is not so. It is rather to change the responsibility they must bear.

Outsourcing adds another layer of complexity to the management of shared services. The point about these relationships is that they are both deep and long term. Even if it is 'only' administration and back-office management that is outsourced, they are still functions that are crucial to the success of the business. They will also change over time. So, it is vital that the provider is open with the customer as to what they require for commercial success: they must avoid foisting any unpleasant surprises upon the customer farther down the line, and ending up squeezing the client in order to make their own ends meet.

Even when an in-house department is set up, it should be treated as an external supplier to ensure that the best processes are set in place and strict service-level agreements are adhered to. In short, contracts should be put in place whether the supplier is internal or external to ensure that the service meets the required criteria and that if it doesn't, action can be taken to rectify the failure.

Adapted from: **Partners**
Mark Vernon, FT.com, 7 September 2006

Question

1. Taking a step back from the starting point of this case study, construct a skeleton feasibility report evaluating the introduction of a shared service for IT provision.

Recommended reading

Avison D. and Fitzgerald G. (2007). *Information Systems Development: Methodologies, Techniques and Tools*, 4th revised edn. McGraw Hill

A leading textbook that provdes extensive coverage of the area. Practical examples are provided and contextualized through consideration of social and business factors.

Harris D. (2003). *Systems Analysis and Design for the Small Enterprise*, 3rd edn. Dryden Press

This is a business-focused book that uses mini case studies and running case studies throughout. It is very readable and well illustrated.

Wiley W. (2000). *Essential Business Requirements*. Addison-Wesley

This well-illustrated and easy-to-read book covers business events and system developments, looking at system data processes and behaviour. The book considers the estimation of project costs and has a business focus.

Chapter 12

Process analysis and modelling

Learning outcomes

On completion of this chapter, you should be able to:

- Explain the need for systems analysis and describe the techniques typically employed
- Create a logical model of a system comprising levelled data flow diagrams
- Explain the need for a data dictionary
- Create process specifications comprising decision tables, logic flow charts and structured English.

Introduction

In Chapter 11 the first stages of the life cycle for a systems project were described, namely the feasibility study and the collection of information. The analyst now has a large amount of documentation on the existing system. However, to be of use this information must be organized and analysed before a new design, probably involving computerization, can be developed.

The purpose of this chapter is to illustrate the method to be adopted by the analyst in analysing and modelling the processes that handle the data and information within the organization. The approach taken is to move from a description and analysis of the existing physical system and to derive a logical model of the processes involved. Physical analysis is illustrated using manual systems flowcharts, which picture the formal document flows within departments and processes in an organization. The logical model is derived in the first instance using data flow diagrams, which show the relationships between logical data flows and processes. The content of each data flow together with other useful information on it is contained in a data dictionary. The logical content of the processes can be described using structured English, decision tables and logic flowcharts. These are all covered in this chapter. In order to be of use in systems design, the process model of the system must be supplemented with a data model. The production of this is considered in Chapter 13 on data analysis and modelling.

12.1 Systems analysis

The purpose of systems analysis is to ascertain what must be done in order to carry out the functions of the system. This will involve a decomposition of the functions of the

Figure 12.1 Tools used during the stage of systems analysis

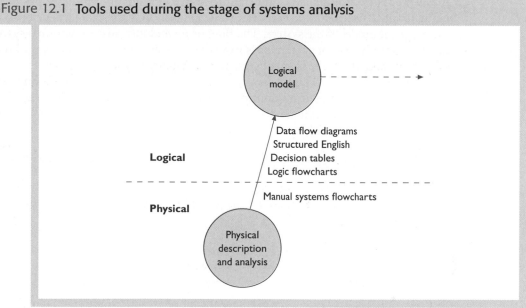

system into their logical constituents and the production of a logical model of the processes and of the data flows necessary to perform these. The logical model will be illustrated by data flow diagrams at the various levels of process decomposition. The algorithms will be revealed by structured process specification techniques such as structured English, decision tables and logic flowcharts. The importance of concentration on the logical features of a system (what logically needs to be done in order to carry out the functions) as distinct from the physical features (who does what, where, with which file, and so on) is to avoid making premature commitments to physical design. The rationale for adopting this approach was covered in Chapter 10, which outlined the need for an information systems development methodology.

Prior to production of the logical analysis, it is often helpful to carry out a physical analysis of the document flows between processes and departments within the existing system. As well as enabling the analyst to identify key tasks, these charts can be used to evaluate control and efficiency aspects of the current system.

The output of the stage of systems analysis will be a logical model of the functioning of the system. This will consist of diagrams, charts and dictionaries, which are the product of the techniques used in the analysis. An important feature of a structured approach to systems analysis and design is the generation of clear and helpful documentation that can assist communication not only between the programmer and analyst but also between management and users and the analyst. The fact that a logical model is produced in systems analysis removes complicating and distracting physical elements that would hamper communication. The movement from the physical to the logical model and the techniques used are illustrated in Figure 12.1.

12.2 Manual systems flowcharts

After investigation, the analyst may have collected an unwieldy batch of interview notes, details of observations, questionnaire responses and sundry documents. In the initial stages of analysis, it is important to arrive at a methodical description of the existing manual system and to carry out some analysis at a physical level prior to developing a logical model of the system. The flow of *formal* information within a system often occurs through documents that pass from one department to another. A traditional tool of systems analysis is the manual systems (document) flowchart.

The basic idea is that certain tasks performed on documents are common to many applications – filing, preparing multiple copies, collating, sorting. These are given specially agreed symbols (Figure 12.2). The life history of a document from origination

Figure 12.2 Basic symbols used in the preparation of manual systems flowcharts

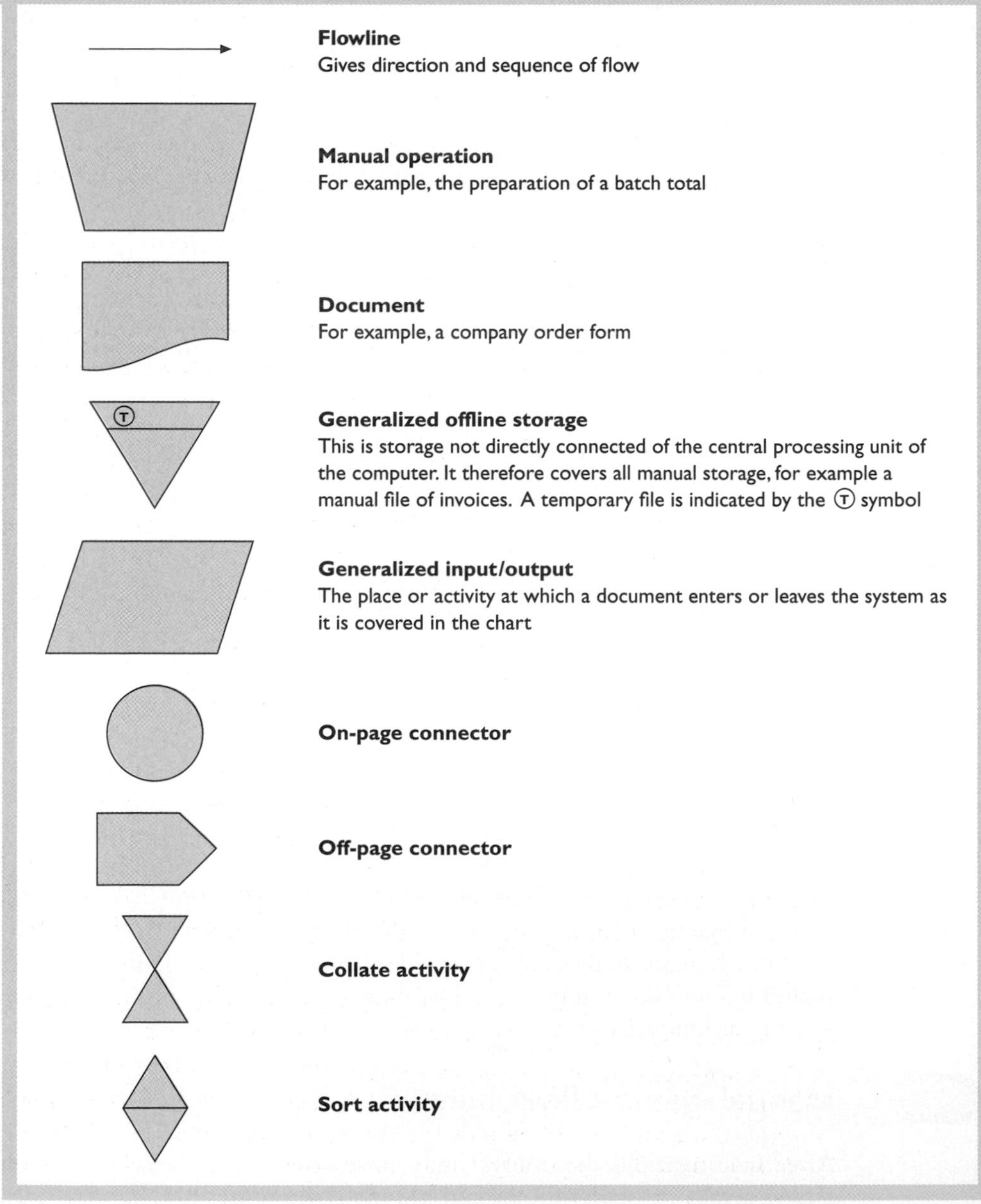

Flowline
Gives direction and sequence of flow

Manual operation
For example, the preparation of a batch total

Document
For example, a company order form

Generalized offline storage
This is storage not directly connected of the central processing unit of the computer. It therefore covers all manual storage, for example a manual file of invoices. A temporary file is indicated by the Ⓣ symbol

Generalized input/output
The place or activity at which a document enters or leaves the system as it is covered in the chart

On-page connector

Off-page connector

Collate activity

Sort activity

(entry from outside the system or preparation within) to destination (exit from the system or filing) is recorded on the flowchart. The passage of the document from department to department is also shown.

Kismet case study 12.1

The best way to understand a manual systems flowchart, sometimes called a document flowchart, is to study one. Here the Kismet case study is developed giving a detailed description of the processes occurring during order processing. A manual systems flowchart covering these is shown in Figure 12.3.

Order processing

Customers mail their orders to Kismet HQ. On receipt of an order in the sales order department, a five-part company order form is filled in giving (among other information) the *order#, order date, customer#, customer name, item 1 code#, item 1 quantity, item 2 code#, item 2 quantity*, and so on. The top copy of this form is filed temporarily in *customer#* sequence for customer enquiry purposes (rather than *order#* sequence, as when customers enquire about a recently placed order they will not be in possession of the *order#*). Each item is provisionally priced on the remaining copies of the form from a sales catalogue held in the order department. The priced copies are sent to the credit control section.

The credit control section provisionally calculates the order value. Brief details of the customer account are then consulted to establish that the customer exists and is correctly named and that the total value of the order, when added to the current balance, does not exceed the credit limit of the customer. If all these conditions are met then the order copies are stamped 'approved', signed and returned to the sales order department, one copy of the order being retained in the credit control department filed by *customer#*. If the above conditions are not met, the order copies are filed temporarily to be dealt with later by the credit control manager.

On receipt of the approved order copies in the sales order department, the top copy is extracted from the temporary file and sent to the customer as an acknowledgment. One of the 'approved' copies is filed in the order department in the 'approved order' file under *order#* to enable staff to retrieve details of the order in the event of further customer queries. The remaining two copies are sent to the stores department and the invoicing department. The invoicing department files the copy under *order#*.

The stores department selects the goods as ordered and enters the quantities supplied on the order form. A two-part dispatch note is made out giving the goods supplied together with their quantities. One copy of this is sent to the invoicing department, and the other is sent with the goods to packing and dispatch. If the entire order is supplied then the order form is filed in the stores department under *order#*, otherwise the goods supplied are noted on the form and it is filed in *date* sequence. Periodically, the stores department goes through the unsatisfied back orders and attempts to supply the goods ordered. The stores department also updates the inventory records.

On receipt of the dispatch note, the invoicing department prepares a three-part invoice using the sales price of the goods from the catalogue. The discount applicable to a customer is calculated. This is based on the customer's geographical location, total purchases during the last 12 months and the total value of the order. Sales tax is added and totals formed. One copy of the invoice is sent to the customer, and one is sent to accounts

▶

to update the customer accounts and other ledgers. The remaining copy is filed in the invoicing department with the order copy and dispatch note under *order#*.

The flowchart for order processing and dispatch in Kismet is given in Figure 12.3. Note that the flow lines indicate flows of *documents*.

Figure 12.3 **The manual system flowchart for order processing/dispatch in Kismet**

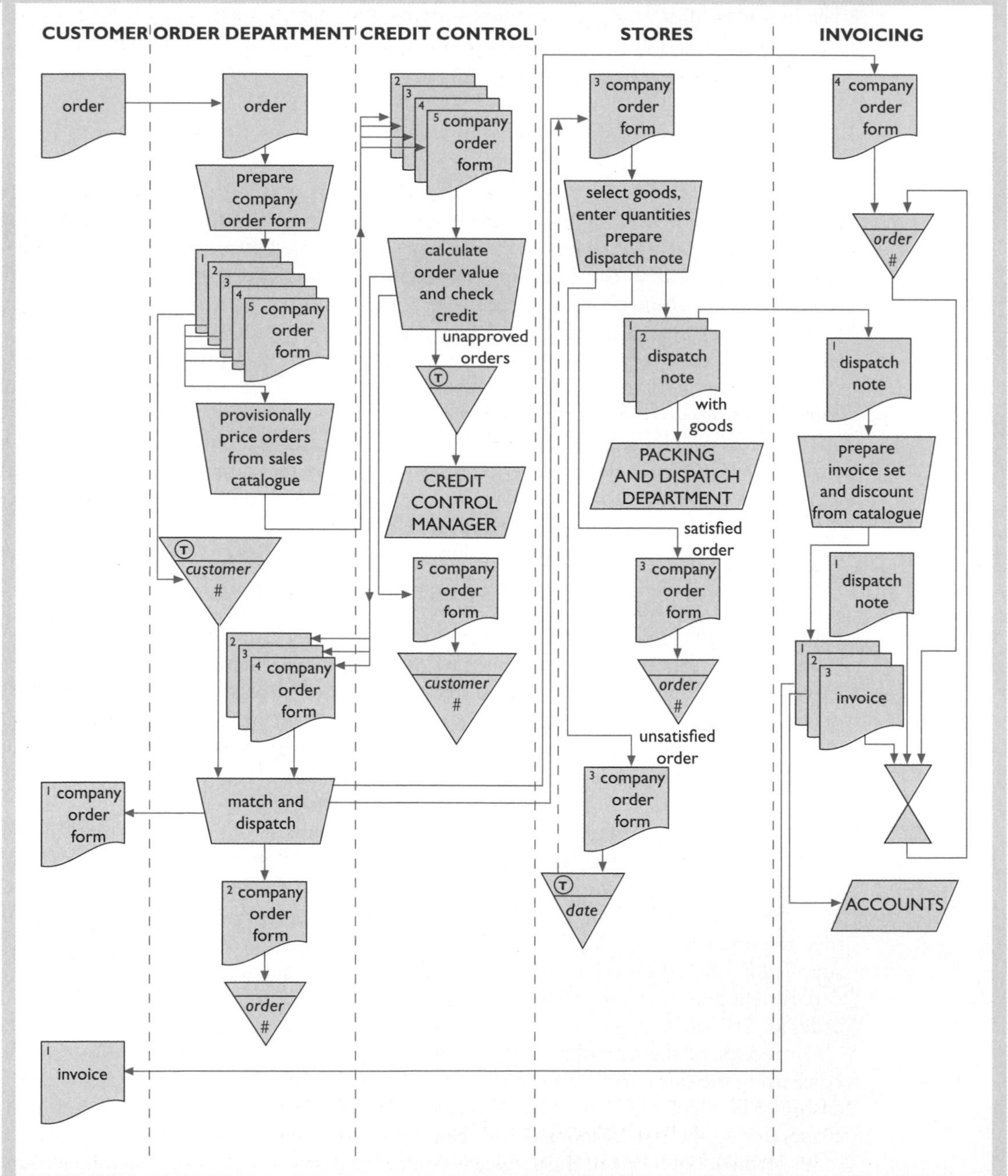

The following practical points will assist in the drawing of flowcharts:

- The chart is divided into vertical sections representing different locations for operations.
- Although not shown, a far-left section may be used for additional (brief) narrative.
- The chart proceeds as far as possible from left to right and top to bottom.
- Documents are shown at origination, on entry into a section and then again only as required to avoid confusion with other documents.
- Ensure that all documents are accounted for by being permanently filed, being destroyed, leaving the system as charted (for example to the credit control manager in Kismet) or transferring to another flowchart.

There are a number of advantages and disadvantages in the use of manual systems flowcharts.

Advantages

- Flowcharts are easier to understand and assimilate than narrative. This becomes more pronounced with increasing complexity of the system.
- The preparation of a chart necessitates the full understanding by the analyst of the procedures and sequences of operations on documents.
- Incompleteness in tracing the destination of a document is easily discovered, indicating the need for further investigation on the part of the analyst (in Kismet, where does the customer's original order go?).
- Little technical knowledge is required to appreciate the document, so it can be used as a communication tool between the user of the system and the analyst in order to check and correct the latter's understanding.
- Weaknesses in the system, such as preparation of unnecessary documents, lack of control, unnecessary duplication of work and bottlenecks, are easily located.

Disadvantages

- With heavily integrated systems, flowcharts may become difficult to manage (large sheets of paper!). The use of off-page connectors and continuation is sometimes necessary but tends to reduce the visual impact and clarity of the chart.
- They are difficult to amend.
- It must be realized that when analysing an existing system informal information is an important part. The flowchart does not incorporate any recognition of this.

The systems flowchart is not only of use to the analyst when carrying out the stages of analysis and design of a computerized information system. Management may also use the flowchart to impose uniformity on groups of systems as the structure of the processes surrounding document handling are revealed. This may be necessary to ensure that, say, one branch of an organization handles order processing in the same way as another. The flowchart may be used as an aid in the preparation of internal audit and procedures manuals. In the former case, it is possible to ensure that essential information is provided to management at the correct stage. Auditors may use the flowchart in a review of internal control as a guide to determining auditing procedures in the annual audit.

The task of evaluation of the system is often considered as part of analysis. As has been pointed out, flowcharts assist in this task.

Kismet case study 12.2

A typical approach to evaluation of the order and dispatch system of Kismet would use the chart to answer a number of questions. Note how easy it is to answer the following typical list of questions by using the flowchart:

1. Can goods be dispatched but not invoiced?
2. Can orders be received and not (completely) dealt with?
3. Can customers be invoiced for goods that are not dispatched because of low stocks?
4. Can goods be dispatched to customers who are not creditworthy?
5. Can invoicing errors occur?
6. Can sales be invoiced but not recorded?

12.3 Data flow diagrams

Although systems flowcharts provide a useful tool for analysing a physical description, they may impede the design process. This is because they draw attention to physical detail. It is important to realize that the systems analyst will be designing a system to *do* something. This 'something' can be specified by describing its logic and the actions on data. To concentrate on existing physical detail will obscure the functions of the system, restrict the designer's creativity and cause premature commitments to physical design in the early stages of the project.

Kismet case study 12.3

An example of the concentration on physical detail described above is given here. It is of little importance to a computer design that one copy of a Kismet company order form is filed temporarily in the order department while four copies go to credit control, where, after approval, one is filed, the remaining copies being returned to the order department, after which the first copy is sent to the customer.

If the whole procedure is to be computerized, including the order approval, the process will occur within the computer as an exchange of data between files or a database and programs. But again, to assume total computerization is to make a possibly premature physical design decision. It may be more effective to retain parts of the old manual system or design new manual procedures.

The point to realize is that the processes, the exchanges of data and the stores of data, are important, not their particular physical representation, whether it be, for instance, a sequential file on tape, an indexed file on disk or a composition of two manual files in two separate locations.

Figure 12.4 Symbols used in data flow diagrams

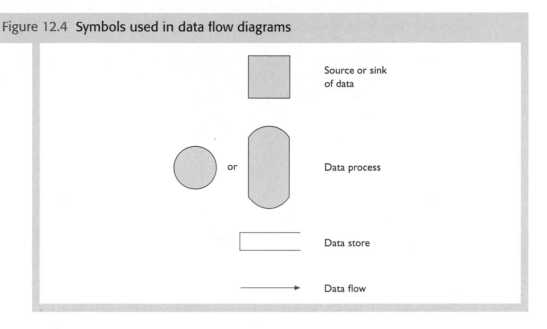

Data flow diagrams assist in building a logical model of the system independent of physical commitments. They show the various flows of data between the processes that transform it. Data stores and the points at which data enters and leaves a system are also shown. The basic symbols used in drawing data flow diagrams are shown in Figure 12.4.

- **Data source** or **data sink:** The square indicates a source or sink for data and is a reflection of the ignorance as to what happens to the data prior to its emergence from the source or after its disappearance into the sink.

- **Data process:** The circle or rounded rectangle indicates a data process. In this, a brief but meaningful identifier of the process is written. It is important to realize that only *data* processes occur in a data flow diagram. Physical processes are not mentioned. For instance, the fact that goods are selected from their stock locations to satisfy an order is not a data process but a material task. A data process is one that transforms only data. It may be that this process will be carried out by a computer program, a part of a computer program, a set of computer programs or manually. The data flow diagram is neutral on this point.

  The identifier used in the data process symbol should, ideally, be both meaningful and succinct. It is good practice to restrict identifiers to a concatenation of imperative verb and object. For example *process stock transaction* or *check credit status* are both acceptable. It is bad practice to try to describe the process. For example, it is a great temptation for the novice to 'name' a data process as *check the application for the account against the credit point list to establish the creditworthiness and the credit limit of the customer*. This is not acceptable.

- **Data store:** A data store is represented by an open-ended rectangle with a suitable identifier. This is distinguished from a data sink by the fact that the data is stored and it (or some part of it) will be retrieved. A sink indicates ignorance, as far as the

Figure 12.5 Part of an erroneous data flow diagram

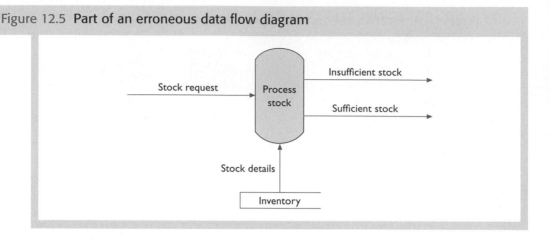

diagram is concerned, of the fate of the data. No particular storage medium is implied by the data store symbol. It could be a magnetic tape or disk, a document or even some person's memory. Once again, it is a great temptation for the newcomer to represent material stores. This is a mistake.

- **Data flow:** The line represents a data flow. The nature of the data is indicated by a name (or names). Wherever that piece of data flows within the diagram it should be tagged with the same name. Once again, it is important to realize that these are flows of *data* and not material flows. If a data flow diagram is drawn representing part of a system in which goods accompanied by a dispatch note are moved, it is the dispatch note, or to be more exact the dispatch note details, that appear on the data flow diagram. There is no mention of the goods.

It is also a common error to confuse data flows with flows of control. This is illustrated in Figure 12.5. Obviously, what the designer of the diagram intended is that the exit data flow travels one way if there is sufficient stock and the other way if there is insufficient. It is not usual to indicate the conditions under which data flows on a data flow diagram. This would tempt the analyst into thinking of the system from the point of view of control rather than data flows.

The difference between a data store and a data flow often confuses the beginner. It is helpful to think of an analogy with water. Water flowing down a pipe is analogous to a data flow, whereas water in a reservoir is the analogy for a data store.

12.3.1 Data flow diagrams in detail

In systems investigation, the analyst will have collected a great deal of information on tasks performed on document flows within the system. These tasks will be involved in the processing of business transactions and the generation of management information. The document processing will probably have been charted in a manual systems flowchart. In drawing data flow diagrams a logical approach is taken. It is important to ignore the location of processes in the manual system, the documents involved and who is responsible for the tasks. The designer should concentrate on the functions that are carried out.

If Kismet is considered, as described in Section 12.2, it can be seen that one very general course of action is taken. Orders from customers are processed to generate dispatch notes (which eventually accompany goods sent to the customer) and to make up invoices (sent to the customer and to the accounts department). In doing this, a price catalogue and customer account details are consulted and inventory records are updated.

This is indicated in Figure 12.6. In itself it is not very informative, although, even at this level, in a more comprehensive analysis of all Kismet's functions there would be other interfacing subsystems, such as purchasing, payroll and accounting. If the analyst had seriously misunderstood the structure of the system, this would be obvious at a glance.

Further progress can be made by decomposing this order-processing function into its component parts. Three different types of task occur when Kismet processes a customer order. First, the company order is generated and approved. Second, stock is selected, inventory updated and a dispatch note prepared. Finally, invoices are made up and sent to the customer and to accounts. Involved in this are various data flows, stores, processes, sources and sinks.

Figure 12.6 **A high-level view of order processing for Kismet**

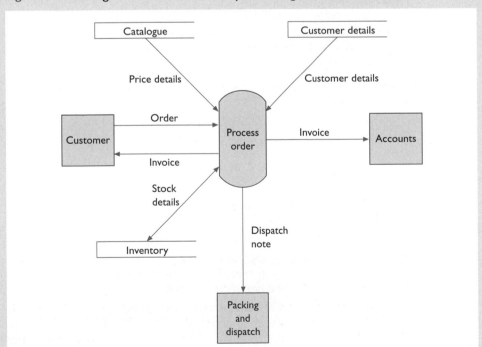

Read the case study and note where the sources, sinks, processes, stores and flows occur. These are:

1. Sources/sinks:
   (a) customer
   (b) credit control manager
   (c) packing and dispatch department
   (d) accounting.

2. Processes:
   (a) generate approved company order
   (b) process stock transaction
   (c) make up invoice.

3. Data stores:
   (a) inventory
   (b) catalogue
   (c) customer details
   (d) company order store
   (e) company order/invoice/dispatch note.

4. Data flows:
   (a) customer order
   (b) company order
   (c) price details
   (d) stock details
   (e) customer credit details
   (f) invoice
   (g) customer invoice details
   (h) dispatch note.

The data flow diagram at the first level can now be drawn (Figure 12.7). The following points should be noted:

1. The diagram can be thought of as starting at the top left and moving downwards and to the right. This gives some idea of the sequence of tasks performed, although it is not a rigid rule.

2. Each data flow, source/sink, process and store is labelled. It is a convention that where source/sinks or stores are repeated they are given a diagonal line at the corner of the symbol (see the CUSTOMER source/sink). A data flow that is repeated is given the same name.

3. Certain tasks are left out of a data flow diagram. Any error-handling routine is usually omitted. For instance, although not stated, there would be a procedure for handling an incorrectly prepared company order form when the *customer name* and *customer#* were found not to correspond.

4. Departments and physical locations are ignored in the data flow diagram, except where they appear as sources or sinks. For instance, although the processing of the stock transaction occurs in the stores and the generation of the approved company order occurs in the order department, this information does not appear in the diagram.

5. Although the goods would accompany the dispatch note to PACKING AND DISPATCH, this is not shown on the data flow diagram as it is not a data flow.

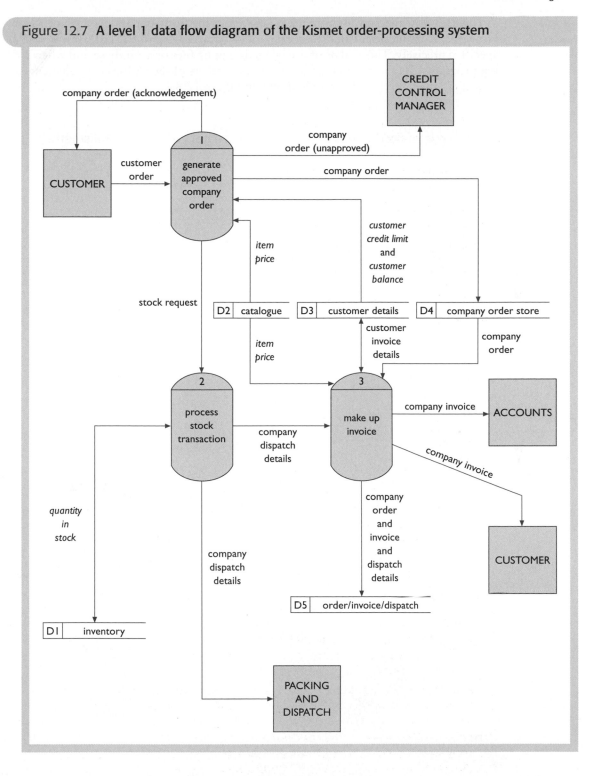

Figure 12.7 A level 1 data flow diagram of the Kismet order-processing system

The data flow diagram shows a great deal about the flows of data between processes. However, it is important that the contents of data flows and the data stores also be specified precisely. This will be of use when designing files or a database and when writing programs. A tabular representation of the contents of the various data elements appearing in the data flow diagram is shown in Figure 12.8.

Figure 12.8 Table of descriptions of the data flow diagram elements for Kismet

Source/sink	Process
Customer	(1) Generate approved company order
Credit control manager	(2) Process stock transaction
Packing and dispatch	(3) Make up invoice
Accounting	

Data flow

Customer order	Company order	Company dispatch details
customer#	*order#*	*dispatch#*
customer name	*order date*	*order#*
[item#	*customer#*	*customer#*
item quantity]*	*customer name*	*customer name*
delivery address	*customer address*	*delivery address*
	delivery address	*dispatch date*
	[item#	*[item#*
	item quantity	*item quantity]**
	item price]*	
	total	

Company invoice	Stock request	
invoice#	*order#*	
invoice date	*customer#*	
customer#	*customer name*	
customer name	*delivery address*	
customer address	*[item#*	
order#	*item quantity]**	
[item#		
item price		Customer invoice details
item quantity]*		*customer#*
subtotal		*customer name*
sales tax		*customer address*
discount%		*turnover year to date*
total payable		

Data store

D1 Inventory	D2 Catalogue	D3 Customer details
item#	*item#*	*customer#*
quantity in stock	*item price*	*customer name*
.	.	*customer address*
.	.	*[delivery address]*
.	.	*customer balance*
.	.	*customer credit limit*
.	.	*turnover year to date*
.	.	*registration date*
		.
D4 Company order store	D5 Order/invoice/dispatch	.
see Company order	see Company order	.
	and invoice	.
	and dispatch details	

The following points arising from this diagram should be noted:

- The description in the case study does not go into much detail on the contents of each document or file (except in the case of the company order form). These contents are either implied by the nature of the task (*customer address* must be present to dispatch the invoice) or should be found on the 'document description form' prepared by the analyst during investigation.

- Extra detail will be stored for other tasks that are not part of the case as documented. For instance, under inventory there would be reorder levels. This omission does not matter as it would be remedied when the procedures for purchase and reorder of goods were incorporated into a data flow diagram.

- The exact content of the data stores and flows will be recorded in a **data dictionary**. This is often described as a store of data about data. The dictionary is of considerable importance in analysis and design and is covered in Section 12.4.

- The meaning of [. . . .]∗ is that the contents of the brackets may be repeated an indeterminate number of times.

Data flow diagrams for simple systems are relatively straightforward to design. However, for larger systems it is useful to follow a set of guidelines. These are:

1. Identify the major processes.
2. Identify the major data sources, sinks and stores.
3. Identify the major data flows.
4. Name the data flows, processes, sources, sinks and stores.
5. Draw the diagram.
6. Review the diagram, particularly checking that similar data flows, stores, sources and sinks have the same name and that different data flows and so on have different names.

12.3.2 Data flow diagrams at various levels

Two interconnected questions arise concerning data flow diagrams. These are:

1. What level of discrimination of processes should be shown on the data flow diagram? For instance, in Figure 12.7 the data process *generate approved company order* could be regarded as consisting of a number of subprocesses, such as *accept order*, *check credit limit* and *price order*. Should these be shown as processes?

2. What is the maximum number of processes that should be shown on a data flow diagram?

A major objective of a data flow diagram is its use in communication of the logical process model of the organization. It is difficult to understand a data flow diagram when it has more than seven to nine processes. This is the practical upper limit. If there is a tendency to overstep this then the data flow diagram should be redrawn, with processes that are logically grouped together being replaced by a single process that encompasses them all. The processes are not 'lost' from the model. They should appear on another data flow diagram that shows how this combined process can be exploded into its constituents. These constituents themselves may be complex and can be broken down into linked data processes shown on a data flow diagram at a lower level. This

Figure 12.9 Data flow diagrams at various levels

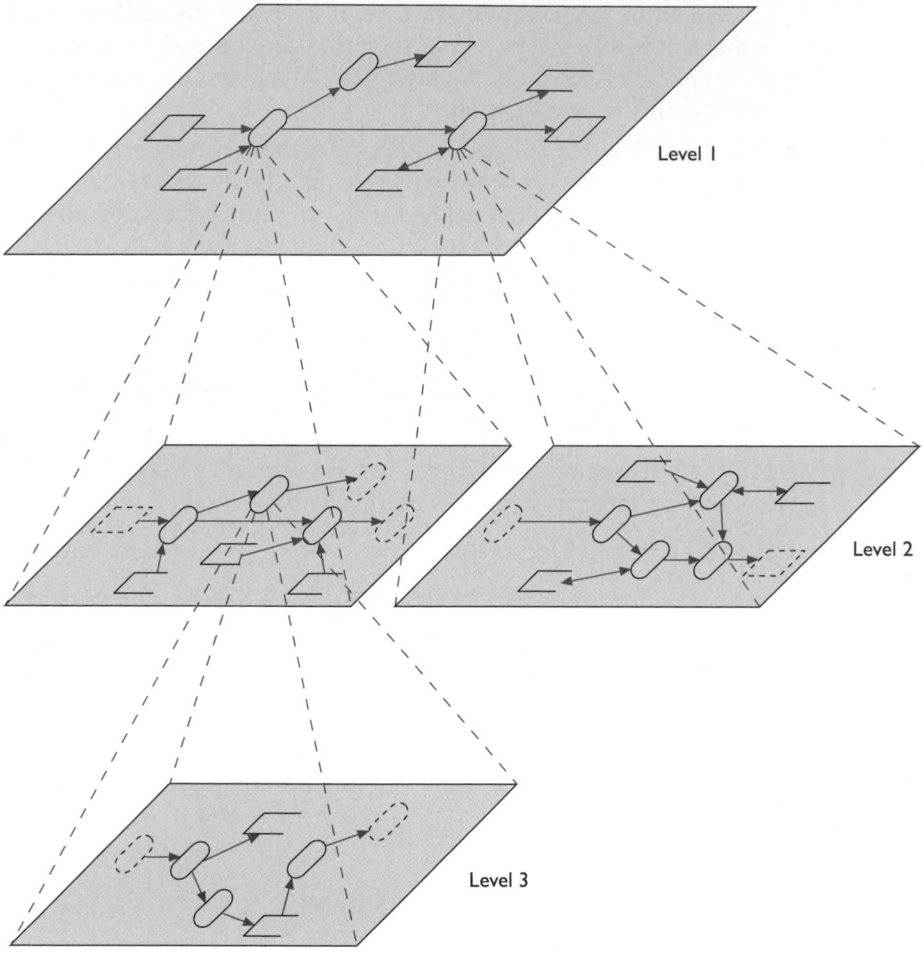

should be repeated until the processes are logically simple: that is, until they cannot be broken down any further. This is illustrated in Figure 12.9.

The generation of levels in data flow diagrams has two other advantages. First, it naturally falls into line with the analyst's approach to top-down decomposition. That is, the analyst considers the major functions and processes first. These are then decomposed into their constituents. The analyst can therefore concentrate on the higher-level data flow diagrams before designing the others. Second, the various levels correspond to the various degrees of detail by which the system is represented. This is useful for the analyst when discussing the results of the analysis with members of the organization. Senior managers are more likely to be interested in a global view as given in a high-level data flow diagram. Other personnel will be concerned with more localized areas but in greater detail.

The person responsible for supervising the generation of approved company orders in Kismet will be interested in a lower-level, more detailed explosion of the *generate approved company order* process.

The processes in the data flow diagram for Kismet (Figure 12.7) can be further decomposed. The generation of an approved company order is really a number of tasks:

1. Accept the order.
2. Prepare the company order form.
3. Price the goods.
4. Provisionally calculate the value of the order.
5. Check the creditworthiness of the customer.

This is shown on a level 2 data flow diagram (Figure 12.10). The number 1 task in level 1 is exploded into seven tasks, 1.1–1.7. The inputs and outputs of this exploded chart must match those of the *parent* for which it is the functional decomposition.

Figure 12.10 **A level 2 data flow diagram of the Kismet *generate approved company order* process**

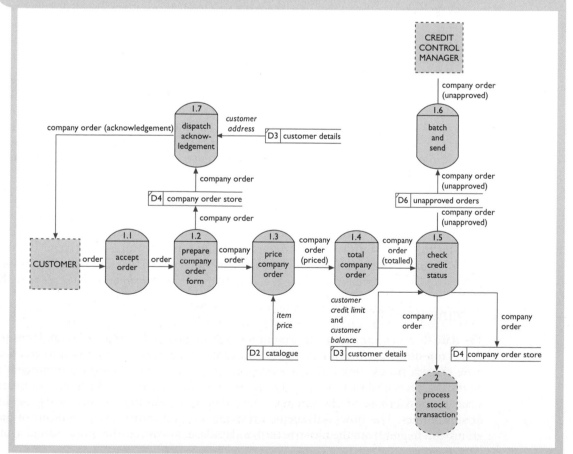

There are two exceptions to this. First, certain local files need not be shown on the parent. In Figure 12.10, the *unapproved orders* store is such a file. It is only used as a temporary repository for the unapproved orders and does not feature in the rest of the system. Second, for the sake of clarity it may be necessary to amalgamate a number of data flows at the parent level. If functional analysis were to be carried out on function number 2, *process stock transaction*, the input/output data flow would be composed of an input flow with *item#* and *quantity in stock* as the data elements and an output with *item#*, *transaction type* and *item quantity* as elements.

If necessary, further analysis of the level 2 diagram could be undertaken by exploding chosen processes to a level 3 diagram.

12.3.3 Design commitments of the data flow diagram approach

It is important to separate the process of analysis from that of design. This may be difficult. The process of analysis goes beyond description, as every case of model building is partly a process of design. Another aspect of design is that the choice of data flows, stores, processes, sources and sinks is just one way of characterizing what is important in an organization's information system. To use these to build a model already commits the analyst to a certain design strategy: that of top-down, reductionist design.

However, within the design implications inherited through the use of structured techniques such as data flow diagrams, there is some separation of analysis from design.

Kismet case study 12.6

In the case of Kismet, the generation of an approved company order follows a certain (unnecessarily repetitive) procedure, which is illustrated in the data flow diagram (Figure 12.10). In an ideal design, it is unlikely that the company order emanating from task 1.2 would be stored in the company order file awaiting the trigger from the successful order vetting (task 1.5) before dispatch of the acknowledgement. Rather, a copy of the approved company order form would be sent to the customer as part of the output of task 1.5.

In analysis, the analyst considers what, logically, *is* done in order to carry out the functions of the organization. In design, the analyst states what, logically, *should* be done for the organization to carry out its functions efficiently and effectively. The data flow diagram, by stripping away the physical aspects of a system and revealing its logic at the appropriate level of detail, makes it easy to see improvements that can be made.

12.3.4 Summary so far

The data flow diagram is an important tool of structured analysis and design. It ensures that a top-down approach is taken. This promotes a logical, as opposed to physical, view of data stores, flows and processes. In this way, no premature commitment to physical aspects of design is made. Eventually, the data stores *may* form part of the file structure or database of the system, and the data processes *may* become the programs or subroutines. The flows will then correspond to the data passed in and out of programs and to and from the file structure or database. However, this can be decided at a later stage.

The levels of data flow diagram correspond to the levels of top-down decomposition and the various levels of detail that management and users will need in order to discuss sensibly the analyst's understanding of processes.

The diagram may also be part of the agreed document provided at the end of analysis. Its non-technical nature means that it can be easily understood by users and agreed upon as a correct analysis of the system. This makes it a powerful communication tool, bridging the gap between analysts and users.

Finally, it makes it easy to sketch out different design alternatives for a future computerized system. How this is done will be covered in Chapter 14 on systems design.

12.4 Data dictionaries

A data dictionary is a store of data about data. It provides information on the structure and use of data in an organization. It is therefore closely connected to the data flow diagram and, as covered in Chapter 13, to the data model. The contents of a typical entry in a data dictionary are given in Figure 12.11.

Figure 12.11 Typical contents of a data dictionary entry

Name:
Included here are all the names by which this data element is known. If there is more than one then these are termed 'aliases'.

Type of data
For example: data flow, data store, data item.

Structure
In the case of a data flow or data store this gives the list of data items, including repeats. If the type of data is a data item its 'picture' may be given – for example. 'AA9999' – together with the range of permissible values.

Usage characteristics:
This details the list of processes that the data flows/data stores interact with. In the case of a data item this list will give the data aggregates which use the item. Information on the data such as the frequency, volume and security issues surrounding the data is often given, as this will aid the designer in deciding on the physical characteristics of the proposed system.

> **Name:**   **Type:**
>   Invoice   Data flow
>
>   **aliases:**
>   customer invoice
>   client invoice
>
> **Structure:**
>   Aggregate: (*invoice#, invoice date, customer#, customer name, order#,* [*item#, item price,*
>   *item quantity*]*, *subtotal, sales tax, discount%, total payable*)
>
> **Usage characteristics:**
>   Output process 3 – *make up invoice*
>   input to sink – *accounts*
>   input to sink – *customer*

The data dictionary provides a precise and unambiguous specification of the data elements within the system. It is normally stored on a computer to facilitate cross-referencing between data elements. The data element *order#* referred to in the entry under invoice can easily be cross-referenced to discover that its structure is, for instance, followed by five digits.

It is important that data descriptions held in a data dictionary not be duplicated in several places. This is done so that if a change is made to some aspect of a data element the alteration is made in only one place in the dictionary, thus ensuring the maintenance of consistency.

The data dictionary is used right through the process of analysis to detailed design and into programming as the reference point to which any questions on the structure of data can be directed. Nowadays, computerized data dictionaries, sometimes called **data encyclopedias,** enable a considerable amount of extra information to be held on data, thus increasing the reliance of analysis and design on an adequate data dictionary.

If a table is made out when a data flow diagram is first drawn (as in Figure 12.8), this will provide much of the information for the data dictionary. Along with the data flow diagrams and process specifications (covered in Sections 12.5–12.7) the data dictionary constitutes the logical model of the system.

12.5 Decision tables

The data flow diagram demonstrates the decomposition of the functions performed in an organization into simpler data processes and flows. Some of these processes may be complex in themselves but are not suitable for further decomposition in the data flow diagram.

Kismet case study 12.7

An example of the use of decision tables might be Kismet's procedure for calculating discounts. Although not given previously in the case study, the firm's policy was summarized by the invoice manager to the systems analyst as follows:

Three factors determine the percentage of discount. The first is the total value of the order (we like to encourage our customers to place large single orders rather than smaller multiple orders as it makes delivery and van scheduling easier). The discount is 3% for orders over £4000. If the delivery is within 50 miles of the warehouse, delivery costs are lower and a 2% discount is given, except if the 3% discount for large orders has been granted. In this latter case, only a 1% discount is given if the delivery is within 50 miles. Customers who have made purchases of more than £100,000 over the past 12 months are granted a further 2% discount. These measures are designed to encourage large purchases from local high-turnover retailers. We would like to offer a more targeted discount policy, although this would be more difficult to administer. We hope that one aspect of computerization is that automated discount calculation will help us to give more personalized encouragement to our customers.

The decision table for this policy is shown in Figure 12.12. The conditions that are important for determining the discount are shown in the top left-hand quadrant. In the top right-hand quadrant are the range of entries for these conditions. In this case, a condition applies (Y = yes) or does not (N = no). Note the pattern of the entries. It makes it

Figure 12.12 A decision table for Kismet's discount policy

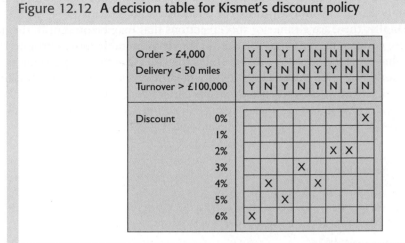

Figure 12.13 The format of a decision table

Conditions being tested	Condition stub	Condition entries
Range of possible actions to be taken	Action stub	Action entries

easy to see that all eight entries have been included. Each column can be thought of as representing a type of order. For instance, column 3 represents a large order (>£4000), not delivered within 50 miles, from a customer with a turnover of more than £100,000. The action to be taken can be found by following the column down to discover that a discount of 5% (X = action) is to be allowed. This is an example of the general format for decision tables. This format is given in Figure 12.13.

Figure 12.12 is a simple decision table. There are only two possible entries for each condition, Y or N. This is called a **limited-entry decision table**. With three conditions there are $2^3 = 8$ columns; with four conditions there are $2^4 = 16$ columns. If there are n conditions there will be 2^n columns. With a large number of conditions, the decision table becomes very wide: for example, seven conditions leads to $2^7 = 128$ columns. Fortunately, it is often possible to collapse the columns. Wherever two columns differ only to the extent of one entry and the action(s) associated with each column are identical, the effect of the Y or N entry is nil. The two columns can be replaced by one column, which has the Y and the N replaced by a single '–' but is otherwise identical to the columns it replaces. The decision table can be collapsed until no two columns satisfy the pairwise condition stated.

As well as limited-entry tables there are **mixed** or **extended-entry tables**. These are used when there is not a simple value yes or no (true or false) associated with a condition. For instance, there might have been three possible ways of differentiating the size of the order as far as discounting was concerned: <£2000, ≥£2000 but >£5000 and ≥£5000. These three entries would appear in the condition entry, and the condition 'order size' would appear in the condition stub.

Finally, there are a range of special actions that may be present in the decision table. These concern the way that the user of the decision table moves around the table or to another table. Perhaps the most useful is the **GOTO** action, which causes the execution of another decision table. This is used when the types of action and conditions applicable to a case divide neatly into exclusive classes depending on the value of some condition. Care should be taken when using this action, as a number of tables interconnected by **GOTO**s can give the appearance of logical spaghetti.

Kismet case study 12.8

The variations on the basic table are illustrated in Figure 12.14. This is the revealed discount policy of Kismet's competitor, Hardy Ltd.

Figure 12.14 Decision tables illustrating Hardy's discount policy

Table A

Retail store chain	Y	Y	Y	Y	Y	Y	Y	Y	N
Order size	<£2,000	<£2,000	£2,000 to less than £5,000	£2,000 to less than £5,000	£5,000 to less than £10,000	£5,000 to less than £10,000	>£10,000	>£10,000	–
One delivery	Y	N	Y	N	Y	N	Y	N	–
Discount 4%		X							
6%				X					
9%	X								
10%						X		X	
11%			X						
15%					X		X		
Note to manager							X	X	
GO TO table B									X

Table B

Order > £3,000	Y	Y	Y	Y	N	N	N
Order > £5,000	Y	Y	N	N	N	N	N
Delivery < 50 miles	Y	N	Y	N	Y	N	N
Turnover > £100,000	–	–	–	–	–	Y	N
Discount 0%							X
3%						X	
4%					X		
5%		X		X			
9%	X		X				
Send note to manager	X	X					

In the case of an order from a retail electrical store chain a discount of 4% is allowed if the order is less than £2000, 6% if the order is between £2000 and £5000 and 10% if the order is £5000 or more. There is a further discount of 5% if there is only one delivery address. A note of the invoice is sent to the manager if the total amount invoiced is greater than £10,000. With all other types of customer, a 4% discount is given if the order is more than £3000. A 5% discount is also allowed if the delivery is within 50 miles, 3% is allowed if no other discounts have been made and the customer has an annual turnover with Hardy of more than £100,000. A note of any invoice in excess of £5000 is sent to the manager.

Decision tables are a valuable tool in analysis. Within the general format of the table conditions are specified unambiguously and separated from actions, which are clearly stated. The declarative style of the table accords well with the way that certain processes are considered as the implementation of a set of conditions.

The straightforward, non-technical character of the tables makes them a valuable communication tool between analysts and users in checking the analyst's understanding of a process. In design, the tables can be used to specify the requirements of a program. They facilitate analyst–programmer communication.

Although it takes intelligence to construct a decision table, it requires a very limited repertoire of mental abilities to use one. They are therefore in a form suitable for incorporation into a computer program. There are programs that accept a decision table as input and produce program code to implement the table as output. The program runs interactively with users by requiring answers to basic questions. These questions correspond to the conditions.

Finally, decision tables cover in a methodical way the totality of possible combinations of conditions that might apply in a particular case and so can be used to check on the completeness and consistency of a policy that involves the taking of different actions when different conditions are satisfied.

Kismet case study 12.9

In order to appreciate the completeness and consistency of a policy, consider the following example:

Kismet's management has decided that computerization offers it the opportunity to offer a more complex and targeted discount policy. It has decided to offer its customers a differential discount depending on whether the order is large (over £5000), whether the year-to-date turnover of the customer is large (over £100,000), whether the order is to be delivered to one address only and whether the delivery, or deliveries, is within 50 miles. After many hours of discussion, the management has arrived at the following policy:

1. A high-priority order is defined to be one from a high-turnover customer who requires a large order or who is using only one delivery address.

2. A low-priority order is defined to be one that is neither large nor from a customer with a high turnover.

3. If the order is large and to be delivered to only one address a discount of 10% is allowed, with an additional discount of 5% if that address is within 50 miles.

Figure 12.15 The use of a decision table to illustrate inconsistency

	H	H	H	H					H	H			L	L	L	L
Large order	Y	Y	Y	Y	Y	Y	Y	Y	N	N	N	N	N	N	N	N
Large turnover	Y	Y	Y	Y	N	N	N	N	Y	Y	Y	Y	N	N	N	N
One address	Y	Y	N	N	Y	Y	N	N	Y	Y	N	N	Y	Y	N	N
Within 50 miles	Y	N	Y	N	Y	N	Y	N	Y	N	Y	N	Y	N	Y	N
Actions																
Give — Rule 3	15	10			15	10										
Rule 4			≤5	≤5			≤5	≤5			≤5	≤5			≤5	≤5
Rule 5									10	10	5	5				
percent — Rule 6	≥5	≥5	≥5	≥5					≥5	≥5						
Rule 7													3	3		
discount — Rule 8							5	5								
Rule 9	≥10		≥10		≥10		≥10									
TOTAL	15	10	(a)	5	15	10	(b)	5	10	10	5	5	3	3	(c)	(c)

Notes

H = High-priority order (Rule 1)

L = Low-priority order (Rule 2)

(a) Rules 4, 6 and 9 are inconsistent

(b) Rules 4, 8 and 9 are inconsistent

(c) There is insufficient information to assign a discount.

4. No order that is to be delivered to multiple addresses may receive more than 5% discount.

5. However, an order that is not large from a customer with a turnover of more than £100,000 should receive a 10% discount except in as far as this conflicts with rule 4, in which case they will obtain the maximum discount applicable under that rule.

6. High-priority orders are to be given at least 5% discount.

7. Low-priority orders are to be given a 3% discount if there is only one delivery address.

8. Orders from customers with a turnover of less than £100,000 to be delivered to multiple addresses shall receive a discount of 5% if the order is large, irrespective of whether the delivery is within 50 miles or not.

9. All large orders that are to be delivered within a 50-mile radius are to receive at least 10% discount.

10. All applicable discounts are to be totalled.

This policy has been analysed in Figure 12.15. Although this does not exactly follow the format of Figure 12.13, it is, in principle, a decision table separating conditions and actions. The effects of each of the rules on each of the types of order (each type of order corresponds to one column in the condition entry quadrant) are shown in the action entry quadrant. The total effect of all rules on a type of order is shown, where possible, in the TOTAL row. For example, column 2 corresponds to a large order from a customer with a turnover in excess of £100,000. The order has one delivery address, which is not within the 50-mile zone surrounding the Kismet warehouse. It is judged to be a high-priority order (rule 1) and so is to be accorded at least 5% discount (rule 6). The order satisfies rule 2 and so is given a 10% discount.

It is clear that the policy is inconsistent. Notes (a) and (b) of Figure 12.15 indicate where the inconsistency arises. This could be eliminated by removing rule 9. It would be the analyst's responsibility to point out to management the inconsistency and advise on possible ways of eliminating it. An inconsistent policy cannot be incorporated into a program. It is ultimately the responsibility of Kismet to decide on the policy. It is a business decision. Normally, all the analyst would do is to comment on the formal properties of the policy.

In summary, there are a number of advantages and disadvantages in the use of decision tables to represent the links between conditions and actions.

Advantages

- They provide a clear tabular representation linking conditions with actions and so act as a communication tool.
- The declarative style corresponds to the way that many processes are understood as conditions that determine actions.
- They ensure an exhaustive coverage of all possible cases.
- They can be used to investigate inconsistency and redundancy in a set of rules.
- They are easy to follow in operation.
- They can be incorporated into program specifications.

Disadvantages

- They can become very large and unwieldy with large numbers of conditions.
- They are only suitable for representing processes where there is little interleaving between the evaluation of conditions and the execution of actions.

12.6 Logic flowcharts

Decision tables are one way of clearly representing the logic of a process and are most suitable when only few actions need to be undertaken as a result of the evaluation of a (possibly complex) set of conditions. If, though, the process is one that involves intermingling the evaluation of conditions with the execution of various actions, then the proliferation of **GOTO** statements to subsidiary decision tables makes it difficult to follow the logic of the process. Logic flowcharts overcome this difficulty. The symbols used in logic flowcharts are shown in Figure 12.16.

Figure 12.16 Basic symbols used in the preparation of logic flowcharts

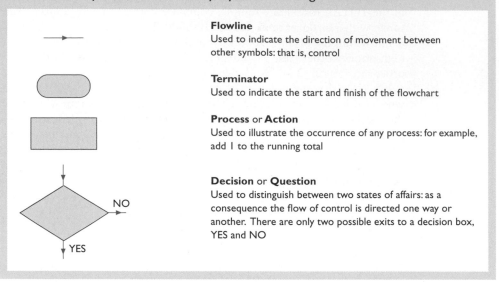

Flowline
Used to indicate the direction of movement between other symbols: that is, control

Terminator
Used to indicate the start and finish of the flowchart

Process or **Action**
Used to illustrate the occurrence of any process: for example, add 1 to the running total

Decision or **Question**
Used to distinguish between two states of affairs: as a consequence the flow of control is directed one way or another. There are only two possible exits to a decision box, YES and NO

Kismet case study 12.10

The use of logic flowcharts can be illustrated by the representation of the following example. It concerns the approval of orders in the credit control section of Kismet. The procedure, stated here, can be regarded as a fuller version of the summary that appeared previously in Case study 12.1. The additions mainly concern the procedure to be followed in the case of error discovery and the maintenance of a running total of the value of approved orders. The order set has been priced and valued. Now is the time for credit approval.

The credit control clerk processes a stack of order sets for which provisional values have been calculated and inserted. The presence of the *customer#* and *customer name* are first checked. If either is absent then the customer file is consulted and the missing entry inserted. If there is no reference to the customer in the file the order set is sent to the credit control manager. If the number and name are found not to match then the order 4 set is sent back to the order-processing section together with an internal company P22 form for investigation. In all other cases, the *order value* is added to the *current balance* and compared with the *credit limit*. If this has been exceeded, the order set is sent to the credit control manager along with the customer records. If the order has passed these tests, the order set is stamped 'OK approved' and put in the out tray. At the end of the stack, the contents of the out tray are returned to the order-processing section, and the total value of all approved orders is entered on the daily totals sheet.

The flowchart is shown in Figure 12.17. The flow lines indicate flows of control, *not* flows of data or documents. When it is said that there is a flow of control between points A and B, all this means is that after the operation at A has been carried out the operation at B is carried out. Nothing passes between points A and B.

Figure 12.17 **The logic flowchart for credit approval in Kismet**

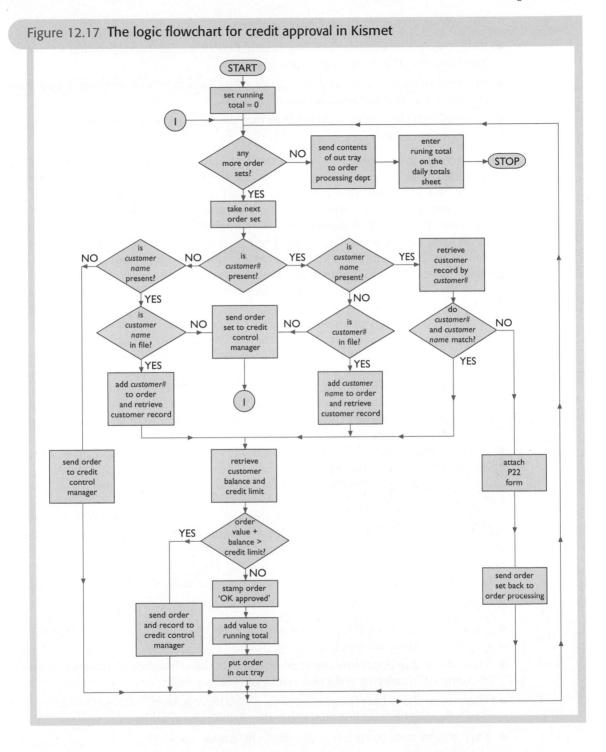

The following conditions apply to flowcharts:

- Each question or decision box has exactly two exits: one corresponding to 'yes' or 'true' and the other to 'no' or 'false'.

- All flows of control must end in a decision box, action box or terminator and must always ensure that the process eventually stops.

- Generally, the flowchart is designed so that the flow of control goes from the top of the page downwards.

The flowchart in Figure 12.17 follows these principles. The repetitious nature of the processing of one order after another is accomplished by directing the flow of control from the end of the approval process, as applied to one order, back to the top of the chart. There, a test is performed to establish whether there are any more orders in the stack before proceeding. A running total is maintained.

Flowcharts have several advantages. Their pictorial representation makes them easy to follow and understand – the different paths through the process are obvious at a glance. They can therefore be used as a basis for agreement between the analyst and the user on the correctness of the analyst's understanding. They may also form part of the firm's procedures manual.

Flowcharts can be given for high or low levels of analysis. For instance, to answer the simple question 'is the customer name in the file?' requires the execution of a number of actions and the consideration of further questions. If the records in the file are ordered by *customer#*, it implies the following type of procedure for the clerk. Go to the filing cabinet, start at the first record, compare the *customer name* with the target *name*, if identical, stop – the *customer name* is in the file, otherwise carry out the procedure on the next record, and so on. The level of the chart is generally high at the analysis stage, and such low-level specifications are ignored.

Logic flowcharts can also be used in the design stage as a way of specifying a procedure precisely. If it is intended that a program be written from this specification, it is called a **program logic flowchart**. The flowchart will be presented generally at a much more detailed level. Variable names will be included, procedures for establishing counts will be outlined, and so on. The presence of the decision box encourages the use of the **GOTO** programming structure, so program flowcharts may lead to programming techniques that result in non-structured programs. This may be a reason to discourage their use at the design stage.

In summary, the main advantages and disadvantages in the use of logic flowcharts are:

Advantages

- They provide a pictorial representation of a series of actions and are therefore easy to understand and natural to follow.

- They are used in procedures manuals to indicate the sequences of actions that are to be followed in carrying out a task – for example, an audit.

- They are very good at representing cases where there is an interleaving of actions and the evaluation of conditions (compare this with decision tables).

- They may be used to specify programs to programmers.

Disadvantages

- They encourage the use of **GOTO** statements if used in program specifications in design. This may lead to programs that have a logic that is difficult to unravel.

- They force the developer to work at a very low level of detail at an early stage of the project, therefore losing the benefit of the top-down approach previously advocated.

- They are difficult and time-consuming to alter once drawn.

12.7 Structured English

As well as using decision tables or logic flowcharts, procedures can be represented through the use of structured English. This also has the effect of imposing a structure on the specification, which encourages the use of structured programming. Structured English is a precise, highly restricted subset of the natural English language. There is no accepted standard for structured English, but all usages have a number of features in common. The vocabulary of the language is restricted to:

- Precise verbs phrased in the imperative mood. All adjectives, adverbs and words with vague or ambiguous meanings are avoided. Complex sentence structures involving subordinate clauses are broken down into their atomic constituents. Irrelevant phrases are dropped. For instance, the sentence 'The large document containing the particular details on the customer should now be edited carefully by the clerk making sure that all entries are made clearly with an indelible pen' would probably be reduced to 'edit document containing customer details'.

- References to items of data should use the same terms as applied in the data flow diagram and the data dictionary.

- Certain reserved words are used for revealing the logical structure of processes.

The logic of any process can be described by using three structures (Figure 12.18):

1. **A sequential block of statements:** The statements should be concise and contain a verb and object. For example:

   (a) Compute total
   (b) Set sales tax equal to total multiplied by sales tax rate
   (c) Set total equal to total plus sales tax
   (d) Compute discount
   (e) Set net total equal to total minus discount
   (f) Write net total on invoice.

2. **Decision structures:** These are used when it is required that one sequence of operations be carried out if a condition is satisfied and another set if it is not satisfied. The structure takes two forms:

   (a) The two-way decision:

   > **IF** ⟨condition⟩
   > **THEN** ⟨block-1⟩
   > **ELSE** ⟨block-2⟩

   where the **ELSE** is not compulsory. For example:

   > **IF** total > credit limit **THEN** refer to credit control manager
   > **ELSE** stamp 'OK approved'

Figure 12.18 **The logical form of structured English**

Structured English

(1) Sequential   [⟨statement⟩]*
    = block

(2) Decision   **IF** ⟨condition⟩
        THEN do block-1
        ELSE do block-2

        CASE ⟨variable⟩
            CASE 1 ⟨value-1⟩
                    do block-1
            CASE 2 ⟨value-2⟩
                    do block-2
            CASE 3 ⟨value-3⟩
                    do block-3

(3) Repetition   **DO WHILE** ⟨condition⟩
            do block

            REPEAT
                do block
            UNTIL ⟨condition⟩

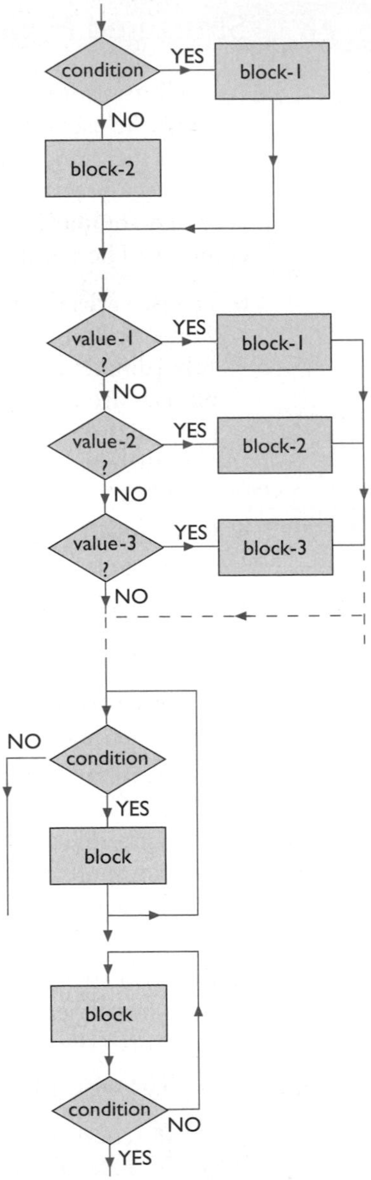

Logical form
statement 1
statement 2
statement 3

(b) The multi-way decision:

> **CASE** ⟨variable⟩
> **CASE 1** ⟨value-1⟩
> > do block-1
>
> **CASE 2** ⟨value-2⟩
> > do block-2
>
> **CASE 3** ⟨value-3⟩
> > do block-3

For example:

> **CASE** invoice value
> > **CASE 1** invoice value <£2000
> > > add 1% to discount percent
> >
> > **CASE 2** £2000 ≤ invoice value <£5000
> > > add 3% to discount percent
> >
> > **CASE 3** invoice value ≥£5000
> > > add 6% to discount percent

3. **Repetition structures:** These are used where a process is repeated until some condition is met. There are two forms of repetition statement:

> **DO WHILE** ⟨condition⟩
> > do block

and

> **REPEAT**
> > do block

> **UNTIL** ⟨condition⟩

In the former, the test as to whether the condition is satisfied occurs before the loop is entered (so the loop will not be traversed at all if the condition fails first time). In the latter, the test occurs after the loop has been traversed, implying that the loop is traversed at least once. For example:

> **DO WHILE** stack of invoices is not empty
> > get next invoice
> > add invoice total to running total

Structured English representations of processes may be a little difficult to follow for the uninitiated, particularly if there is a high degree of internal nesting. However, as mentioned at the beginning of this section they do have the attraction of encouraging structured coding of programs.

Whether decision tables, a logic flowchart or structured English is chosen as the representation of a process depends on its nature. Complex sets of conditions determining few actions with little iteration suggest a decision table representation. Otherwise a logic flowchart or structured English representation will be suitable, the choice being the result of the trade-off between diagrammatic clarity and the wish to encourage structured code in the design stage.

Kismet case study 12.11

The example now discussed illustrates the use of structured English to specify a process. It concerns the task of pricing the Kismet company order sets and is taken from a statement supplied by the clerk responsible for pricing the orders. It covers error cases not given in the case study.

> I get the stack of orders to price from the supervisor. I first of all tidy the pile and then go through the orders one by one until I have finished. After this I put the stack of priced orders in the credit control section's in tray. I carefully price each item in turn by consulting the sales catalogue. Sometimes I cannot find the item because it is a new product and I then have to look at the supplement. If I have no luck there I just put a big query mark by it on the form. After I have finished I put the order in the out tray.

The structured English version is given in Figure 12.19(a). Note how the rambling description of the process, as given by the order pricing clerk, is transformed into a set of precise statements.

The indenting is important as it gives a clear indication of the structure of the logic governing the process. Statements may also be nested, as shown in the example.

Figure 12.19 The structured English representation of the pricing process for Kismet: (a) structured English without ENDIF and ENDDO; (b) structured English with ENDIF and ENDDO

```
(a)  get stack of orders
         DO WHILE there are more orders in the stack
             get the top order
             DO WHILE there are more unpriced items on the order
                 get next unpriced item#
                 IF item# is in the catalogue
                     THEN write item price on the order
                     ELSE IF item price is in the supplement
                             THEN write item price on the order
                             ELSE write? on the order
             put the order in the out tray
         get the stack of orders from the out tray
         put the stack of orders in the credit control section's in tray

(b)  get stack of orders
         DO WHILE there are more orders in the stack
             get the top order
             DO WHILE there are more unpriced items on the order
                 get next unpriced item#
                 IF item# is in the catalogue
                     THEN write item price on the order
                     ELSE IF item price is in the supplement
                             THEN write item price on the order
                             ELSE write ? on the order
                         ENDIF
                     ENDIF
             ENDDO
                 put the order in the out tray
         ENDDO
         get the stack of orders from the out tray
         put the stack of orders in the credit control section's in tray
```

To illustrate the scope of an **IF** statement or a **DO** statement it is sometimes clearer to use **ENDDO**, **ENDIF** and **ENDCASE** statements. These fill a role analogous to brackets in elementary arithmetic. The expression $6 - 3 \times 7 + 3$ can be made much clearer by the insertion of brackets: $(6 - (3 \times (7 + 3)))$. In fact, in many cases the brackets are necessary to indicate the precise meaning of the formula. Similarly, **ENDDO**, **ENDIF** and **ENDCASE** fulfil the role analogous to the right-hand bracket.

The structured English version of the Kismet pricing clerk's routine using **ENDDO** and **ENDIF** statements is shown in Figure 12.19(b).

Summary

The purpose of systems analysis is to arrive at an understanding of a system that is sufficient to design a computerized replacement. This replacement may involve substantial redesign and the integration of physically disparate manual systems. In order to achieve this, a structured approach is taken to systems analysis. This chapter was concerned with structured process analysis and modelling. Its main features are:

- a commitment to a 'top-down' decomposition in which data and processes are analysed into their constituent parts;

- an emphasis on the development of a model of the system as a prerequisite for successful design; and

- an assumption that developing an information system is largely a technical exercise.

The main tool used is the data flow diagram, which models the data flows between data processes, stores and sinks. This diagram reveals the logical model at various levels of detail, depending on the degree of decomposition and the intended recipient of the diagram. The nature of the processes is specified via decision tables, logic flowcharts or structured English, all of which have their relative strengths and limitations. The data dictionary maintains information on the nature of the data itself. The entire repertoire of techniques is aimed at deriving a logical model, independent of physical commitments, and at producing documentation that is precise, thus facilitating communication between users, management, programmers and the analyst.

Much attention has been given to the analysis of the organization into its functional components, the further breakdown of these into individual processes, the charting of the data flows between them and their representation by various tools. What has been missing from the analysis is the treatment of the data stores and the nature of the data itself. Some would regard this as perhaps the most important feature of analysis, and it is to this that the next chapter is devoted.

Review questions

1. What are the scope and objectives of systems analysis?

2. When considering a complex integrated system, why is it important to use a methodical approach to systems analysis and design?

3. What benefits are to be obtained in analysis by initially focusing on processes and functions at a general rather than a detailed level?

4. What are the advantages and limitations of:

    (a) decision tables
    (b) logic flowcharts
    (c) structured English

    as representation tools for processes?

5. What are the advantages and limitations of manual systems flowcharts?

6. Explain the purpose of a data dictionary.

Exercises

1. Can a situation represented by a logic flowchart, decision table or structured English always be represented without loss of information by all three? What determines the choice of method of process specification?

2. 'There is little difference between data flow diagrams and document flowcharts – they both represent the flow of data between processes.' Do you agree?

3. 'At the stage of analysis an understanding of the existing system is more important than technical computer expertise, and as the tools of analysis are relatively easy to understand, it is more effective if existing users carry out the analysis and computer experts are brought in only at the design stage.' Do you agree?

4. 'By concentrating on formal data and processes, the analyst ignores the fact that much useful information in an organization is of an informal nature – opinions, hunches and qualitative approximations. The analyst is therefore bound to produce an inadequate analysis and design of a computerized information system.' What is to be said for and against this view?

5. A large lending library handles book issues, returns and enquiries and sends out notices regarding overdue books to borrowers. All procedures are currently manual. The library deals with a large number of postal and telephone transactions. The majority of its books are stored in underground stacks. The library thus needs a fast response information system and to this end has purchased a database management system.

    Initial analysis indicates that the following information has been stored on books, borrowers and loans in the current manual system:

    – For each book: book number, author, title.
    – For each borrower: ID number, name, address.
    – For each loan of a book to a borrower: date due for return.
    – A record of books reserved for potential borrowers is also maintained.

    The database is to be designed to support the following functions currently carried out manually:

    – *Book issue processing*: On receipt of a request for a loan the librarian makes an enquiry to establish whether the book is held by the library and is available (that is, not on loan). If the book is not held, then that information is given to the potential borrower by a note.

    If the book is held but is on loan the potential borrower is also informed, a note that the book is to be reserved on return is made, and it is established by enquiry whether the book is overdue or not. If it is overdue, a note is sent to the current borrower pointing out the overdue status of the loan and that a request for the book has been made. If the book is directly available then it is issued to the potential borrower and details of this loan, including the date due for return, are stored.

– *Book return processing*: On receipt of a returned book, the librarian cancels the loan and makes an enquiry to establish whether the book is reserved. If it is reserved, then it is issued to the reserver and the reserve note is cancelled. Otherwise, the book is returned to the stack.

– *Enquiry processing*: There are two types of enquiry:

  (a) Given the name of the borrower, establish what books he/she has on loan and when they are due for return.
  (b) Given the name of the book, establish which borrower, if any, has the book and the date due for return.

– *Overdue processing*: When books become two weeks overdue, a notice is sent out requesting their return. A similar note is sent every two weeks until return.

  (a) Draw a high-level combined data flow diagram for the processes.
  (b) Draw an exploded data flow diagram for each of the processes.

6. The daily invoicing routine for an invoice clerk is as follows. At the beginning of the day the stack of sales orders with their associated dispatch notes is taken from the in tray and processed. The details of each order are checked against the details of the relevant customer account and a discount is calculated. A customer in the trade is allowed 15% off the list price. There is also a special 5% discount for any customer who has been ordering regularly for two years, provided that the customer has not received the trade discount. Any order over £1000 is allowed a bulk discount of 10% off the list price in addition to any other discounts. If the total to be invoiced exceeds the customer's credit limit, a note is sent to the manager prior to dispatch of the invoice. When all invoices have been dispatched, a note of the total invoiced is sent to the manager.

   (a) Draw a logic flowchart illustrating the day's procedure.
   (b) Represent the above by using structured English.

7. Design a manual systems flowchart to illustrate a procedure that Kismet might use to handle return of goods. This flowchart should be compatible with Figure 12.3.

8. The following is an account of the manual operations that occur at the head office of a chain of supermarkets:

Each supermarket submits a daily cash report plus supporting documentation to the head office by post. This is passed from the mail room to the area manager. The area manager's staff carry out checks on the arithmetic of the cash reports and on submitted bank deposit slips and petty cash vouchers. All of these documents are then passed to the cashier's department after any queries have been reconciled.

Each day's cash report is summarized and entered into a cash analysis book in the cashier's department. This cash analysis book forms part of the main cash book into which weekly totals are entered. At the end of each week, the cashier's department reconciles the cash book with the bank pass sheets. The cash reports are then sent to the accounts department.

Every week, each supermarket also submits, by post, records of deliveries made by suppliers together with other stock movement details. These are sent to the area manager's office, where the unit costs and sales prices are entered on the document and delivery records. The complete set of documents is then passed to the accounts department. The area manager's office also receives delivery sheets sent from the company's own warehouses. These are for goods supplied to the supermarkets. These sheets are priced at cost and at selling prices before being submitted to the accounts department.

The accounts department receives the stock movement forms, the direct and internal delivery sheets and the cash reports. The department then prepares a monthly report for each supermarket at cost and selling prices.

Draw a document systems flowchart with any necessary narrative showing the various document flows. (Note that many temporary and permanent files are implied in the description without being explicitly stated.)

9. When a library first receives a book from a publisher it is sent, together with the accompanying delivery note, to the library desk. Here the delivery note is checked against a file of books ordered. If no order can be found to match the note, a letter of enquiry is sent to the publishers. If a matching order is found, a catalogue note is prepared from the details on the validated delivery note. The catalogue note, together with the book, is sent to the registration department. The validated delivery note is sent to the accounts department, where it is stored. On receipt of an invoice from the publisher, the accounts department checks its store of delivery notes. If the corresponding delivery note is found then an instruction to pay the publisher is made, and subsequently a cheque is sent. If no corresponding delivery note is found, the invoice is stored in a pending file.

Draw a data flow diagram for this information.

10. As a systems analyst, you have been commissioned by the ABC Company to computerize its sales order processing. It is believed by the board of ABC that the attractiveness of its product to customers can be increased by ensuring that all customers receive a discount off the list price of ABC's products. It is further intended that a maximum discount of 25% on any transaction should not be exceeded. To this end, it has isolated the following customer/transaction features:

   - regular customers
   - cash transactions
   - bulk order
   - trade customers.

   The board suggests the following policy, where (all discounts are off the list price and are to be added together):

   (a) Those customers who are trade receive 15% discount, provided that the transaction is a bulk order; otherwise, the discount is 12%.
   (b) Non-trade customers are allowed 5% discount, provided that the order is bulk.
   (c) Cash transactions receive 13% discount if trade; if not a 10% discount.
   (d) All regular customers are allowed 10% discount unless the total discount allowable under rules (a), (b) and (c) is greater than 10%, in which case the greater discount will apply.

   By means of a decision table, advise the board as to the suitability of its discount policy in the light of its stated aims.

11. A stack of student records, ordered by *student*#, contains up to five records on each student covering the student's exam results in one or more of the following – accounting, economics, law, maths, systems analysis. A clerk is required to process these records and must produce an average for each student, which is then entered on a summary

sheet. Not all students take all five subjects. The clerk also computes an average mark for each exam for each of the five subjects and enters it on the summary sheet.

  (a) Produce a structured English specification of a suitable process to achieve these aims.
  (b) Represent this process by a logic flowchart.

12. A firm pursues the following discount policy on its products (all discounts being offered as a percentage of advertised price).

  (a) Those customers ordering more than ten items receive at least a 1% discount.
  (b) Those customers who are not regular customers receive at most a 2% discount.
  (c) All those regular customers who order more than ten items receive a 2% discount plus an additional 1% discount if they pay cash.
  (d) Any person paying cash and who is either a regular customer or orders more than ten items (but not both) is to receive a 2% discount.
  (e) All customers who satisfy just one of the following conditions – ordering more than ten items, paying cash or being a regular customer – receive a 1% discount in as far as this does not conflict with rules (a)–(d).
  (f) Any customer not covered by the preceding rules receives no discount.

Using decision tables, evaluate the above rules as to their consistency, comprehensiveness and redundancy. Can the rules be replaced by a simpler set?

CASE STUDY 12

Kemsing Theatre

The Kemsing Theatre is a small regionally based theatre in south-east England. For most of the year the theatre stages plays, but it also screens cinema films, hosts visiting speakers and stages musical events. The theatre accepts postal and telephone bookings for its forthcoming performances up to six months in advance. About half of the bookings are directly from the public, the remainder being from agencies. The theatre employs 25 people, whose functions range from set design and special effects through to marketing, box office and accounting functions.

When a member of the public makes a booking by telephone either a credit card number is taken and the booking is firmly made, or a reservation for the seat is taken. In the latter case, the member of the public must collect and pay for the ticket at least half an hour before the performance.

In the case of agencies, on receipt of a block booking request by phone or mail, the theatre runs a credit check on the agency account and makes out a confirmation note for those requested seats that are still available.

This is sent to the agency as both a confirmation of booking and an invoice. At the end of each month, the theatre sends a statement of account to each agency.

Half an hour before the performance starts, all those seats that have been reserved by the public but have not been collected are released for general sale. The theatre also receives enquiries on seat availability from both agencies and the public.

Questions

1. Draw a data flow diagram illustrating the data flows, processes and stores necessary to carry out the invoicing, enquiry and booking facilities of the theatre.

2. For each data flow and data store, illustrate the structure of the data concerned.

Recommended reading

Avison D., Wood-Harper A.T., Vidgen R. and Wood R. (2000). *Multiview*, reissued 2nd edn. McGraw-Hill

This book applies the structured techniques covered in this chapter to a case study. The approach is integrated with other approaches, particularly data analysis as covered in Chapter 13.

Bowman K. (2003). *Systems Analysis: A Beginner's Guide*. Palgrave Macmillan

This provides a helpful introduction to the topic of systems analysis. Concepts are illustrated by case studies that run through the book.

Cutts J. (1997). *Structured Systems Analysis and Design Methodology*, 3rd edn. Blackwell Scientific Publications

This is a standard text on structured systems analysis and design. It is comprehensive, clear and suitable for a detailed understanding of structured methods.

Deeks D. (2002). *An Introduction to System Analysis Techniques*, 2nd edn. Addison-Wesley

A good all-round introduction to the analysis of data and processes in both structured and object-oriented paradigms.

Kendall K. and Kendall J. (2007). *Systems Analysis and Design*, 7th rev edn. Prentice Hall

An accessible and well-illustrated book that covers the topics of data flow diagrams and data dictionaries particularly well.

Langer A.M. (2007) *Analysis and Design of Information Systems*, 3rd edn. Springer-Verlag London Ltd

This is design for professionals and information systems students who need an in-depth view of the process and tools of systems development (particularly documentation) in the analysis stage.

Yeates D. (ed.) (2006). *Business Analysis*. British Computer Society

An interesting and informative coverage of systems analysis from a business perspective. The section on business process modelling is particularly relevant to the topics covered in this chapter.

Chapter 13

Data analysis and modelling

Learning outcomes

On completion of this chapter, you should be able to:

- Compare different approaches to data modelling
- Carry out entity–relationship modelling
- Explain the process of normalization of data
- Identify the linkages between process modelling and data modelling.

Introduction

The data flow diagram shows the data processes and the flows of data between them but does little to represent the contents of the data store. The trend towards the use of integrated databases in business information systems means that the analysis and design of the database is an important stage in the systems life cycle. In this chapter, entity–relationship modelling is introduced to derive a data model of the organization. The resulting data model is 'fine-tuned' through normalization. Finally, the adequacy of this model is tested against the functions that it will be required to service. The aim is to provide a data model that leads to an effective database design, which is sufficient to satisfy the organization's data processing and information needs. The latter part of the chapter deals with the interrelationship between data modelling and process modelling.

13.1 Top-down versus bottom-up approaches to data modelling

A bottom-up approach to designing the data store involves extracting data fields as indicated on the document description forms. These are the forms that the analyst uses to specify the data content of existing documents in the system. Any extra data elements that might be required as inputs to processes that are new to the system are then added. These data elements are then grouped into records. It is quite likely that each of the original documents in the manual system gives rise to a record. For instance, a company order form might give rise to a record, the fields of which are *order#, order date, customer#, customer name, [item1 #*, [item1 quantity]** . . . . (Note: we continue the previous practice of abbreviating *order number* to *order#*, etc.) These records form the basis of files. There is a record for each order, and the collection of these is the order file. Decisions are then made on the medium for each file, on the way the file is to be organized and on the indexes needed to retrieve the information for an application. This approach to analysis and design is called **bottom-up** because the system is developed from the basic building blocks – the data fields – upwards through the records and files.

This approach is adequate if small systems that require little or no internal integration are to be designed. However, if there are a large number of fields, which are shared between many applications, it becomes increasingly difficult to design the system without repeating the same data fields unnecessarily.

Kismet case study 13.1

This issue of repeating data fields can be made by using an example from Kismet. A bottom-up approach leads to the design of a stock file that contains stock records having as fields *item#*, *item description*, *quantity held*, etc. This is the responsibility of the stores department. There is also a catalogue file of records containing fields such as *item#*, *item description*, *price*, etc. This is the responsibility of the sales department. Each time a new item is entered on the stock file it needs to be entered on the catalogue file, and each time a description is altered on one it needs to be altered on the other.

One solution to the problem of repeating data fields is to design a program that will take the contents of one file and reconcile them with the other. However, this is a piecemeal solution to a problem that has been created by designing the data store in a piecemeal fashion to satisfy each of the applications separately.

A deeper problem with this approach occurs if substantial redesign of the system is required. Here, the existing documentation is not a good guide to the final data store contents. It is difficult to decide on the fields required at the outset and the extent to which they are to be shared between applications.

What is needed is a way of developing the data store for the organization so that it does not suffer from the limitations of the bottom-up approach. Data analysis using **top-down** data modelling achieves this. This approach leaves physical design considerations until the last available opportunity in the analysis and design cycle. If the logical rather than physical structure of the data is considered, the analyst is not likely to be sidetracked by details on sequencing of records or indexes on files. In the spirit of decomposition associated with structured techniques, a top-down approach to data analysis first considers the types of object on which the organization would wish to keep data and the relationships between them. This is followed by a consideration of the kinds of data to be kept on these objects and only at a later stage how this is to be physically stored in the computer system.

There are other reasons for taking this approach to data analysis. The functions for which data is used in an organization are likely to change over time, although the structure of the data itself may remain constant. For instance, different types of report may need to be drawn from the data from one year to the next. The data structure can be seen to be the fixed element and the functions as dependent on it. If this is assumed then it becomes clear that to design a data store that satisfies the temporary functional contingencies of the time will be unsatisfactory when these change. It seems more sensible to design the data store in such a way that it mirrors or models the structure of the objects and relationships within the organization and also the data held on these.

Integrated databases and the programs that interact with them (database management systems) have been explained fully in Chapter 8 on databases. It is important to realize that many commercial database systems allow the database to be defined by providing a high-level logical model of the data structure. The storage structure details are (largely) controlled by the database management system. The outcome of top-down entity–relationship data modelling provides such a suitable model.

13.2 Entity–relationship modelling

The fundamental assumption behind entity–relationship modelling is that an organization's data structure can be modelled with the use of just three distinct sorts of object. These are as follows.

13.2.1 Entity type

An entity type is a type of thing that is capable of an independent existence and on which the organization may wish to hold data. This is the key characteristic of an entity type. For instance, the entity type **EMPLOYEE** is the type of thing on which a payroll department may wish to keep data such as *employee#* and *date of birth*. The entity type is an abstract concept of which there are particular entity occurrences. It is on these occurrences, strictly, that data is held. An example of the entity type **EMPLOYEE** is the man called 'Tom Yorke' by his work colleagues and 'father' by his daughter. Entity types may also have as their occurrences documents, such as the entity type **ORDER**, or more abstract occurrences, such as the entity type **ACADEMIC COURSE** (it is not possible to see, touch or feel a BA in business studies). To reiterate, if an organization wishes to keep data on a type of thing that has an independent existence, then it should be regarded as an entity type.

13.2.2 Relationship

The entity types applicable to an organization may bear some relationship to one another. For example, the entity type **EMPLOYEE** will bear some relationship to the entity type **DEPARTMENT** because the structure of the organization requires each employee to be a member of a department. Not all entity types will bear relationships to other entity types – the entity type **ORDER** will not have any special relationship with **EMPLOYEE**, for instance. The relationship between an employee and the department of which he/she is a member will be called the 'membership' relationship – any other meaningful name could have been used. Such relationships exist (in reality), and therefore questions are often asked concerning them, such as 'Which department does Tom Yorke belong to?' or 'Who belongs to the stores department?' This suggests that relationships between entity types form an important feature of an organization, one that is worth modelling.

13.2.3 Attribute

The entity types that are deemed applicable to an organization also have attributes. These can be thought of as properties. The entity type **EMPLOYEE** has the attributes *name, employee#, date of birth, sex,* and so on. For a particular occurrence of the type

EMPLOYEE, say the man Tom Yorke, these attributes have the values *Thomas Edward Yorke, 3123, 7 October 1968, male*. The man, Tom Yorke, will have other properties, such as inside leg measurement, colour of eyes and passport number, but only some of these will be relevant to the entity type EMPLOYEE and so be attributes of that entity type. Each entity occurrence of an entity type must be separately identifiable by some attribute. This attribute is called the **key attribute**. The key attribute of EMPLOYEE would be *employee#*. This is because each *employee#* will identify one and only one employee. Two employees could not have the same *employee#*. If they could, then *employee#* would not be a key attribute.

The use of the categories entity, relationship and attribute is one way of viewing the world, or in this case the organization. Although these terms carry no physical implications about the way that data will be physically represented in the computer, it is often the case that a direct correspondence will eventually be set up. The entity type will be represented by a record type. The attributes will be represented by fields of the record type. An individual occurrence of an entity will then correspond to a particular record with certain values for the fields. So the entity type, EMPLOYEE, and the entity occurrence, Tom Yorke, can be represented by the record type and record:

record structure:
name employee# date of birth sex

record occurrence:
Thomas Edward Yorke 3123 07/10/1968 male

The relationships between the entity types can be represented in different ways. One way is by the use of a pointer from one record standing for one entity to another record corresponding to the second entity involved.

13.2.4 Types of relationship

There are a number of useful distinctions between various types of relationship. These distinctions are determined by the number of occurrences of the respective entity types that play a part in the relationship.

1:*n* relationships

Figure 13.1(a) shows a 1:*n* relationship. This can be understood as stating that each department has *n* employees as members and each employee is a member of one department. A representation of occurrences exhibiting this is shown in Figure 13.1(b). Note that the relationship is still 1:*n* even though Stores has only one member, Salvador Mendez. The restriction on the relationship is that each employee can be a member of *at most* one department. If departments can exist without having any employees as members (a possible though unlikely occurrence) then this may be as shown in Figure 13.1(c). The dotted line indicates that an occurrence of a department need not be attached to any employee. Similarly, Figure 13.1(d) indicates that it is possible for an employee to exist who is not a member of any department.

m:n relationships

Suppose that each item that exists in the stores department may be supplied by many suppliers, and each supplier may supply many items. This is said to be an *m:n* relationship. Figure 13.1(e) and (f) indicate *m:n* relationships.

Figure 13.1 Examples of relationship types

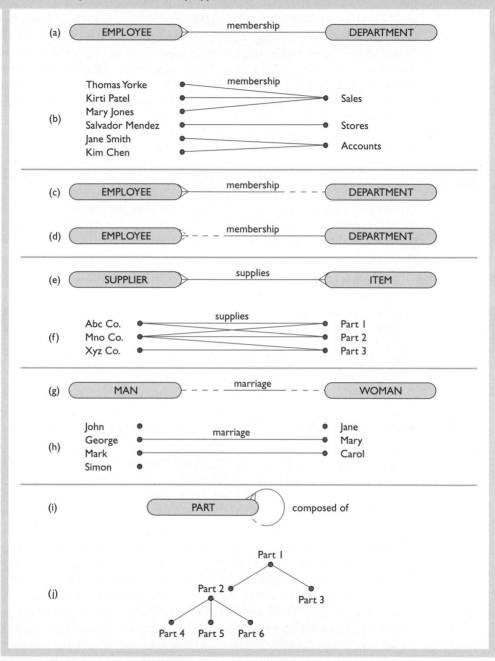

1:1 relationships

There are also 1:1 relationships. In most societies, each man is allowed to be married to at most one woman, and each woman may be married to at most one man. This is shown in Figure 13.1(g) and (h).

Involuted relationships

Relationships may occasionally be involuted. This means that an example of an entity type is related to another example of the same entity type. For instance, it is common for a part used in a later stage in a production process to be composed of parts that are manufactured at an earlier stage. Thus components are made up of components, which are themselves made up of components, and so on. This is shown in Figure 13.1(i), which implies that the parts and composition follow the tree-like structure in Figure 13.1(j). The dotted line is necessary because there must be some parts that will be basic: that is, not composed themselves of parts.

13.3   Data analysis and modelling – an overview of the method

In top-down data analysis using entity–relationship modelling the analyst follows the steps outlined in Figure 13.2. As an example, this method is later applied in Section 13.3 to the Kismet case study. First, an overview of the method is given:

1. **The analyst defines the major data areas to be covered by the model.** These major data areas will usually be determined by the major functions of the organization. Sales order processing, marketing, accounts, purchasing, manufacturing, inventory and administration are all examples of major functional areas. The analyst will then concentrate on each of these areas in turn and develop a data model for each. Later, the models will be amalgamated. This division into functional areas is only carried out if the organization is complex. With a simpler organization, the development of a data model will be attempted without division.

2. **The analyst selects all the important entity types for the chosen data area in the organization.** There is no mechanical rule that can be applied to determining the selection of entity types. However, a good rule of thumb to determine whether something is an entity type is to ask the question 'Is this the sort of thing that the organization is going to wish to keep information on for any reason?' The analyst will obviously be guided by the results of the systems investigation phase. It is clear that an organization like Kismet holds information on orders, items, invoices, and so on. The analyst lists these entity types. At this stage, the analyst should specify the key attribute for each entity.

3. **The analyst determines what relationships exist between the entity types.** At this stage, the analyst determines what relationships within the organization hold between the entity types previously identified. In deciding what relationships exist, the analyst must look not merely at what actually is the case but also at what could be the case. Suppose that PART and SUPPLIER have been isolated as entity types and that they stand to one another in the relationship 'supplies' – suppliers supply parts. Suppose further that *as a matter of fact* each supplier supplies many parts, and each part is supplied by only one supplier. The relationship would not be regarded as $1:n$ if it *might be* the case that a part could be supplied to the organization by more than one supplier. It would properly be regarded as $m:n$. The analyst has to determine not just the factual position concerning entity occurrences but also the semantics of the relationships themselves, for example the business policy or business rules concerned.

4. **The analyst builds the entity model and draws an entity diagram.** The entity model is the aggregation of all entities and the relationships that exist between them. The

Figure 13.2 The method of data analysis

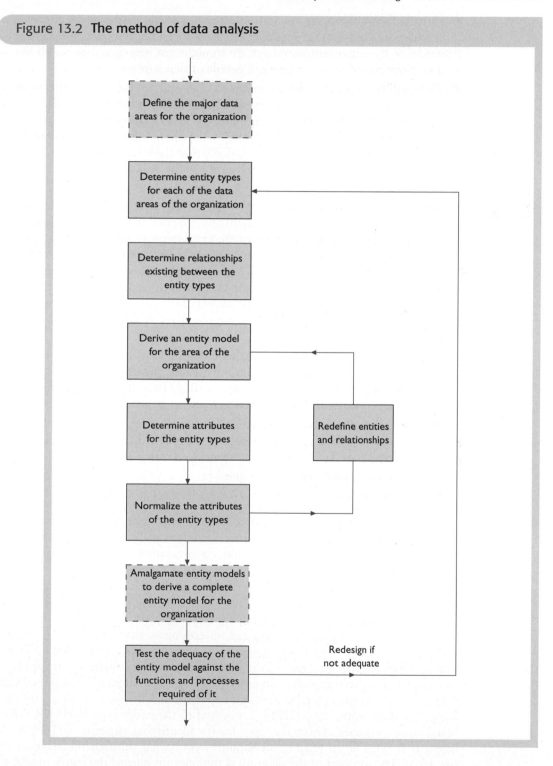

entity diagram is the representation on paper of the model, using the symbols and conventions displayed in Figure 13.1. It has been developed as a high-level logical model of the organization. As yet, no thought has been given either to the detailed data to be stored or to the physical details of that storage.

5. **The analyst determines the attributes of each entity.** Having decided on the overall structure of the model, the analyst will begin to fill in the detail by listing attributes of each of the entities. These will correspond to data that will be stored on each entity. Although it is a good idea to make these attributes as comprehensive as possible – it assists later stages – it is likely that there will be additions and deletions to the attribute list attaching to each entity as the design continues.

6. **The attributes on the entity model are normalized.** Normalization ensures that the entity model consists of entity types in their simplest form. This is important for the design of a data model that will lead to an efficient database as an end product of design. The effect of normalization will be to decompose entity types into their simpler constituent parts. These parts are themselves entity types. The process of normalization continues until certain formal constraints have been met. Normalization is explained in its application to Kismet in case study 13.2. Normalization is also used at the later stage of detailed design to ensure that the final database exemplifies a structure that minimizes duplication of data and so avoids inconsistencies and other anomalies in the database.

7. **The separate entity models are amalgamated into an entity model for the organization as a whole.** This step is relevant only if separate data areas were previously defined for the functions within the organization. In a simple organization, the entity model initially developed is for the organization as a whole.

8. **The adequacy of the entity model is tested against the functions and processes required of it.** How can the analyst be sure that the entity model that has been developed is adequate? There are two questions to be answered:

   (a) Will the required data be present?

   (b) Can the data be accessed?

A clear idea of the data that is required for the functions and processes of the organization has been established during process analysis and modelling (Chapter 12). The data flow diagrams and the specification via structured English, logic flowcharts and decision tables give a clear picture of what data is required. The analyst should check that all the data required is present in the data model. This will mean establishing that data required for processes is contained as attributes. It will also mean that paths through the model to extract the data are present.

To see this, consider the following example. Suppose that a process for automatic re-ordering of an item in stock is triggered every time that the quantity held falls below its reorder level. In order to carry out the application, a list of suppliers that supply the item must be available to the process. In other words, given an item it needs to be ascertained that the set of suppliers for the item can be retrieved. The most obvious way for this to happen is if the entity type **ITEM** is connected to the entity type **SUPPLIER** through the relationship 'supplies'. Given the value for the identifying attribute of **ITEM**, in this case *item#*, it is possible to retrieve all suppliers connected through the relation (see Figure 13.3). The top part of the diagram is the relevant part of the entity model showing that the **ITEM** entity is accessed (illustrated by the double-ruled arrow) and retrieved. Then the **SUPPLIER** entity is accessed through the relationship 'supplies' (illustrated by

Figure 13.3 An example of a functional entity model

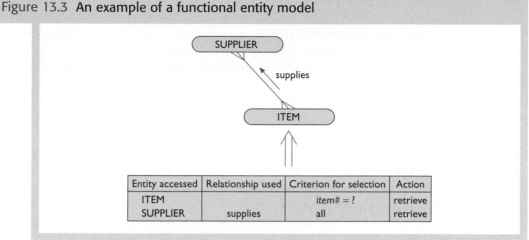

Entity accessed	Relationship used	Criterion for selection	Action
ITEM		*item# = ?*	retrieve
SUPPLIER	supplies	all	retrieve

Figure 13.4 Marriage as (a) a relationship, (b) an attribute and (c) an entity type

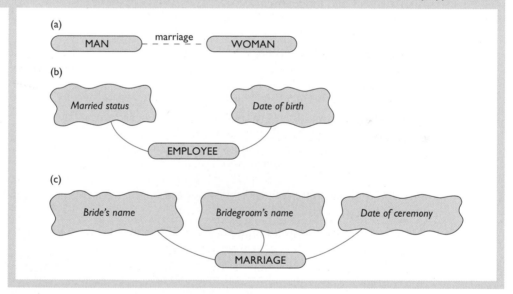

the single-ruled arrow). All occurrences of the entity type attached to the selected **ITEM** entity are then also retrieved.

Once all these steps have been carried out, the analyst will have produced a data model of the organization sufficient for the provision of data for the various functions and processes that the information system will need to fulfil.

The foregoing is portrayed as a clear-cut, straightforward process, but in practice development of the entity and functional entity models may be messy. One problem is that it is not always clear whether something should be treated as an attribute, an entity or a relationship. To see this for a simple example, consider the treatment of marriage:

1. **Relationship:** 'Marriage' can be regarded as a relationship between two entity types – **MAN** and **WOMAN**. This is a one-to-one relationship, as shown in Figure 13.4(a).

2. **Attribute:** Marriage, or rather *married status*, can be regarded as an attribute of a man, woman or employee. Married status is shown in Figure 13.4(b) as an attribute.

3. **Entity type: MARRIAGE** can also be regarded as an entity type. After all, marriage is an event and data on it can be stored – its date, the church or registry office where officiated, the name of the bride, and so on. The entity type **MARRIAGE** is illustrated in Figure 13.4(c).

There is no single answer as to the correct way to treat marriage. It all depends on the circumstances. If the marital status of an employee is to be recorded for tax calculation purposes then marriage, or more accurately *married status*, will be an attribute. If, when given details of a person, details of the spouse need to be established then marriage will be represented as a relationship between entity types. However, the public records office will wish to keep information on marriages, and for it marriage is appropriately modelled as an entity type.

Part of the skill in conceptual data modelling is deciding on these categories. It is not uncommon for an analyst to revise a decision and redesign an entity model treating a former attribute as a relationship.

The remainder of this section uses the Kismet case study to illustrate the techniques of data analysis and modelling.

Kismet case study 13.2

1 The analyst defines the major data areas to be covered by the model

In Kismet, the case study is restricted to the sales order processing subsystem. In a complete system to Kismet, other areas would also be involved. The major data areas correspond to the major functional areas of the system. Examples of these would be purchase order processing, stock control and dispatch scheduling.

2 The analyst selects all the important entity types for the chosen data area in the organization

If the Kismet case study given in Section 12.2 is consulted, it is seen that the following are good candidates for entity types for the order-processing function area. It is important to remember that the crucial question to ask is 'Is this the type of thing that the organization would want to keep information on?'

CUSTOMER	MAIL ORDER	COMPANY ORDER	ITEM
SALES CATALOGUE	GOODS	DISPATCH NOTE	INVOICE

On further consideration, it is clear that some deletions can probably be made from this list.

The mail order from the customer is probably a document that is filed for future reference. All of the information on the order is transferred to the company order form. The company order is therefore the obvious entity type, and the mail order can be removed. The company order entity type will be referred to now as the **ORDER**. This could only be realistically checked by the analyst by asking such questions as 'Is all the information on the mail order transferred to the company order form?'

The terms 'item' and 'goods' refer to the same type of thing. So this would be one entity type – **ITEM**.

The sales catalogue might be an entity type in itself, with such attributes as *date of preparation* and *person responsible for preparation*. Conversely, it may be no more than a selection from the set of data that is already held on the items, such as *item#, item description, selling price*. If the latter is true, then it should be removed from the list of entity types and viewed as the output of a process that selects certain attributes of ITEM.

No reference has been made to an entity type DEPARTMENT. This would obviously be an entity type in a complete data analysis of Kismet but has been left out here for simplicity.

The list of entity types is CUSTOMER, ORDER, ITEM, DISPATCH NOTE, INVOICE.

The analyst determines that the key attributes, that is the attributes by which the entities are to be identified, are:

customer#, order#, item#, dispatch#, invoice#

3 The analyst determines what relationships exist between the entity types

The various relationships in which the entity types are involved can be obtained by consulting the case study in Chapter 12. The analyst may be tempted here to use his/her general knowledge of the semantics of business entity types, but it can be dangerous to assume that what is true in most business organizations is true in all. The analyst should be relying heavily on interviews. For the purposes of Kismet, it is assumed that the details of relationships have been established or checked by the analyst. Most will be obvious. Here, two examples are considered:

- Each customer may place many orders, but each order can be placed by only one customer. The relationship is therefore $1:n$.

- Each order requests many items, and each item can appear in many orders. The relationship is therefore $m:n$.

In the latter case, it is important to be clear that an occurrence of the entity type ITEM is itself an abstract object. An example of an occurrence is the Glauckman 20-watt hi-fi speaker (of which there may be many physical examples in stock). An attribute of the Glauckman 20-watt hi-fi speaker is *quantity held*, the value of which might be six. Individual examples of the Glauckman 20-watt hi-fi speaker have not been referred to. (This is very different from the example EMPLOYEE used in Section 13.2, which has as an occurrence the physical object Tom Yorke.)

The relationships between the entities are listed in Table 13.1.

Table 13.1 Relationships between entity types for sales order processing in Kismet

Entity	Entity	Relationship name	Degree
CUSTOMER	ORDER	places	$1:n$
ORDER	ITEM	requests	$m:n$
DISPATCH NOTE	ITEM	comprises	$m:n$
DISPATCH NOTE	ORDER	relates	$n:1$
INVOICE	ITEM	bills	$m:n$
DISPATCH NOTE	INVOICE	relates to	$1:1$
DISPATCH NOTE	CUSTOMER	sent to	$n:1$

Wherever possible each relationship is given a name that is meaningful. Customers place orders. An obvious name for the relationship between **CUSTOMER** and **ORDER** is 'places'. Other names are more artificial. Difficulties arise when the relationships do not have natural names or where the same name would normally be used for different relationships. Apart from clarity, the reason for naming is that there may be more than one relationship between two entity types, and it is necessary to distinguish them.

4 The analyst builds the entity model and draws an entity diagram

The entity diagram is shown in Figure 13.5. This is a representation of the listing of entity types, relationships and their degrees as established in Table 13.1. The purpose of the diagram is to reveal clearly the structure of the relationships between entities. It is much easier to see the nature of the data model from the diagram than from the table.

The dotted connections exist on the relationships 'requests', 'comprises' and 'contains' as it is possible that there are items that have not been ordered and therefore not been invoiced and dispatched. The dotted connection on 'relates' is a recognition that time delays can occur between the placing of an order and its dispatch, so the former may exist without the latter.

It is sometimes possible to collapse the entity types involved in a 1:1 relationship and form an amalgamated entity type. This has not been done here with **DISPATCH NOTE/INVOICE** as they are independent and take part in separate and different relationships.

5 The analyst determines the attributes of each entity

It is necessary to establish what data is to be kept on each entity: that is, the attributes of the entity that are of interest to the organization. The existing documentation and interviews provide the analyst with key information. For Kismet, the attributes of the various entity types are shown in Table 13.2. Notice that some of these are repeated sets of attributes – those indicated with a *. At this stage, it may be discovered that new entities need to be defined. The attributes of each entity should be defined within the data dictionary. Remember that a data dictionary is a store of data about data. This enables a consistent development of the data model and also ensures that data flows to and from data stores, as indicated in the data flow diagram, can be serviced.

Figure 13.5 Entity diagram for order processing at Kismet

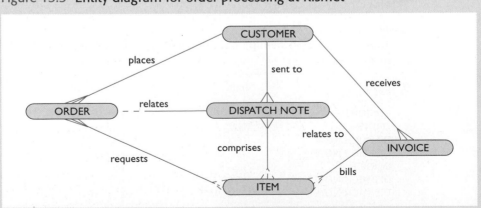

Table 13.2 Attributes associated with the entity types in Kismet's processing

Entity	Attributes
ORDER	order#, order date, customer#, customer name, [item#, item quantity, item price]*
CUSTOMER	customer#, customer name, customer address, [delivery address]*, contact name, contact telephone number, customer analysis code, credit limit, credit terms, standard discount, turnover year to date, current balance
DISPATCH NOTE	dispatch#, dispatch date, order#, customer#, customer name, customer address, [item#, quantity]*
INVOICE	invoice#, invoice date, order#, customer#, customer name, customer address, [item#, item description, item price, item quantity]*, subtotal, discount, sales tax, total payable
ITEM	item#, item description, quantity in stock, average item cost, item price, reorder level, stock analysis code

6 The attributes on the entity model are normalized

Normalization results in a fine-tuning of the entity model. It may lead to more entities and relationships being defined if the entity model does not contain entities in their simplest form. The analyst is moving away from considering a high-level logical model of the organization to the detailed analysis of data and its impact on that model. Looking ahead to the design stage of the data store, a normalized entity model will lead to a normalized data model. This ensures that data is organized in such a way that (1) updating a piece of data generally requires its update in only one place, and (2) deletion of a specified piece of data does not lead to the unintended loss of other data.

Normalization is a formal technique. It is not described here with formal rigour but, rather, it is sketched in order to provide an overview of the process. Normalization applied to entities is aimed at ending up with a set of entity types, attributes and relationships that are normalized. An entity type with a key attribute, or key set of attributes, is normalized if

each non-key attribute is a 'fact' about the key attribute, the whole key attribute and nothing but the key attribute.

This normalization is called **third normal form** (3NF). To obtain normalization of the entity types to third normal form, the entity types and attributes are analysed into their constituents. Initially, first normal form (1NF) is achieved, then second normal form (2NF) and finally third normal form (3NF). Normalization for the entity type ORDER is carried out as an example. This is illustrated in Figures 13.6–13.9.

Figure 13.6 shows the entity type ORDER, the attributes of ORDER with the key attribute underlined, and a set of example data on three orders.

First normal form

An entity is in first normal form if there are no repeating groups of attributes.

It is clear that for each ORDER, item#, item quantity, item price are repeated for each item ordered. These repeating groups can be removed by recognizing that each order contains a number of order details. Thus ORDER DETAIL is an entity type. Each order is made up of many order details. So the relationship is 1:n. This is shown in Figure 13.7. Note that the entity type ORDER DETAIL contains the order# of the ORDER to which it relates. This ensures that the order details are always linked to the relevant order where

Figure 13.6 Entity type ORDER showing repeating groups of attributes

ORDER

ORDER (order#, order date, customer#, customer name, [item#, item quantity, item price]*)

ORDER

order#	order date	customer#	customer name	item#	item quantity	item price
123	11/09/2004	101	Smith's	12	19	23.78
				14	2	145.99
				15	5	200.00
				23	1	96.00
126	11/09/2004	102	HI-FI Ltd	11	2	67.89
				14	3	145.99
127	12/09/2004	101	Smith's	13	1	99.99
				14	2	145.99

Figure 13.7 Entities in first normal form

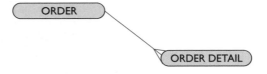

ORDER (order#, order date, customer#, customer name)
ORDER DETAIL (order#, item#, item quantity, item price)

ORDER

order#	order date	customer#	customer name
123	11/09/2004	101	Smith's
126	11/09/2004	102	HI-FI Ltd
127	12/09/2004	101	Smith's

ORDER DETAIL

order#	item#	item quantity	item price
123	12	19	23.78
123	14	2	145.99
123	15	5	200.00
123	23	1	96.00
126	11	2	67.89
126	14	3	145.99
127	13	1	99.99
127	14	2	145.99

the non-repeating attributes, such as *order date* and *customer#*, appear. The key for **ORDER DETAIL** is the set of attributes consisting of *order#*, *item#*. Each on its own will not identify a unique occurrence of **ORDER DETAIL**, but together they guarantee this.

Second normal form

An entity is in second normal form if it is in 1NF and every attribute that is not part of the key depends on the whole key.

In Figure 13.7, the entity type **ORDER** has only one attribute as its key, so all the other attributes depend on this attribute. Considering **ORDER DETAIL**, *item quantity* depends on the whole key. This is because the quantity of an item in an order does not depend only on the item (the item is ordered in other orders) or only on the order (there are other items ordered in the order). However, the combination of *order#* and *item#* fixes *item quantity*. The same is not true of *item price*. This depends only on *item#*. When it is realized that order details are about items ordered, it becomes clear that **ITEM** is an entity type.

This is shown in Figure 13.8. Each order detail is about only one item, but each item may be referred to by many examples of order detail from different orders. The relationship is 1:*n* as shown. The advantage of second normal form is that data on an item

Figure 13.8 **Entities in second normal form**

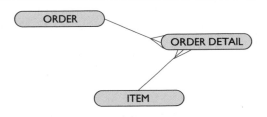

ORDER (*order#*, *order date*, *customer#*, *customer name*)
ORDER DETAIL (*order#*, *item#*, *item quantity*)
ITEM (*item#*, *item price*)

ORDER

order#	order date	customer#	customer name
123	11/09/2004	101	Smith's
126	11/09/2004	102	HI-FI Ltd
127	12/09/2004	101	Smith's

ORDER DETAIL

order#	item#	item quantity
123	12	19
123	14	2
123	15	5
123	23	1
126	11	2
126	14	3
127	13	1
127	14	2

ITEM

item#	item price
11	67.89
12	23.78
13	99.99
14	145.99
15	200.00
23	96.00

such as its price occurs only once. This contrasts with the repeated prices for items with *item#* 1 and 2 in Figure 13.7. The data model will be used to design an effective database. A good database design minimizes the duplication of data.

Third normal form

An entity is in third normal form if it is in 2NF and each attribute (or set of attributes) that is not part of the key depends on nothing but the key.

In Figure 13.8, both **ORDER DETAIL** and **ITEM** contain only one non-key attribute each. So each of these attributes can depend, by definition, only on the key. However, the entity type **ORDER** has an attribute *customer name* that depends on the *customer#*. Customer name is a fact about the customer. Customers place orders.

This is shown in Figure 13.9. A new entity type **CUSTOMER** is introduced. This has a key, *customer#*, and one non-key attribute, *customer name*. Each customer may place

Figure 13.9 Entities in third normal form

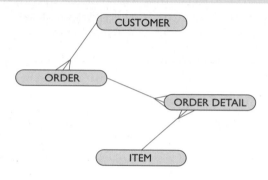

ORDER (*order#*, order date, customer#)
ORDER DETAIL (*order#*, *item#*, item quantity)
ITEM (*item#*, item price)
CUSTOMER (*customer#*, customer name)

ORDER

order#	order date	customer#
123	11/09/2004	101
126	11/09/2004	102
127	12/09/2004	101

CUSTOMER

customer#	customer name
101	Smith's
102	HI-FI Ltd

ORDER DETAIL

order#	item#	item quantity
123	12	19
123	14	2
123	15	5
123	23	1
126	11	2
126	14	3
127	13	1
127	14	2

ITEM

item#	item price
11	67.89
12	23.78
13	99.99
14	145.99
15	200.00
23	96.00

many orders, but each order is placed by only one customer. The relationship is 1:*n*. Note once again that the new model avoids repeating data. The customer name, Smith, appears only once.

Another important feature of normalization is that a fully normalized set of entities and attributes ensures that data on entities is not dependent on the existence of other entities. Returning to Figure 13.6, it is clear that if there had been no order with *order#* = 126 then data on customer 102, such as the customer's name, HI-FI Ltd, and data on item 11, such as the item price, £67.89, would not appear. The normalized form of the entity–relationship model allows maintenance of this data because it is in its 'proper' place connected with the entity to which it relates.

In summary, normalization of entity types leads to a data model that will form the basis of a good database design because it:

■ decomposes entity types into their simple atomic constituents;

■ ensures that data is not unnecessarily repeated; and

■ allows data on entities to be independent of the existence of other entities.

It is also important to realize that the data that was associated with the original un-normalized entity is still recoverable. All the data in Figure 13.6 on individual orders can be reconstructed from the entities and attributes in Figure 13.9. The entities are connected at the table level by their key attributes.

Having normalized each of the entity types in the model, it is possible to amalgamate them to provide a new comprehensive entity model for the data area under analysis. This is shown in Figure 13.10. The decomposition of the entity type **ORDER** has given rise to only one new entity type, **ORDER DETAIL**. Both **CUSTOMER** and **ITEM** already appeared in the model, and their attributes were already in the attribute list.

Figure 13.10 Entity diagram after normalization for order processing at Kismet (relationship names have been omitted)

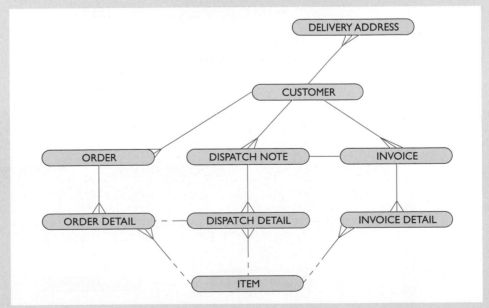

7 The separate entity models are amalgamated into an entity model for the organization as a whole

If the system for which the data model was being derived was relatively simple, then the result of stage 6 will be the entity model for the organization, or rather that part of the organization that is the subject of investigation. If, though, division into separate data areas was carried out, these must now be amalgamated to provide a comprehensive data model. In doing so, it will be discovered that entity types appearing in one area also appear in others. Obviously, the resulting attributes of the entity type will be the combined set of attributes appearing in every data area in which the entity type occurs.

A combined entity diagram for Kismet dealing with stock control and purchase order processing, as well as sales order processing, is given in Figure 13.11.

Figure 13.11 A combined entity diagram for Kismet (relationship names have been omitted)

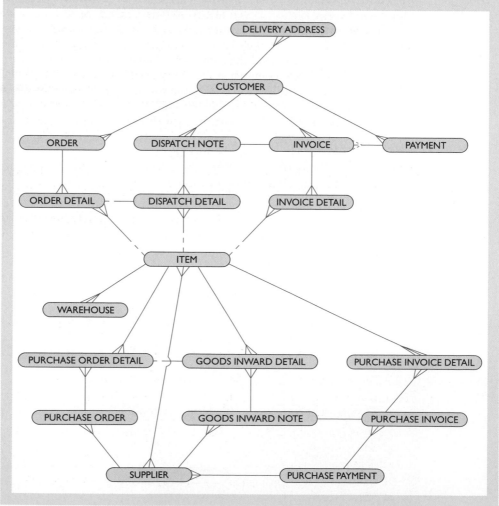

8 The adequacy of the entity model is tested against the functions and processes required of it

Top-down data analysis produces an entity model that is a representation of the entities on which the organization may wish to hold information and of the important relationships between them. The model will form the basis for design of a computerized data store and is derived independently of any analysis of the functions or processes that will require access to the data. Although the functions and processes that use the store may change over time, it is important to establish that the current needs can be met. Functional analysis is concerned with the way that functions and processes map on to the data model. It acts as a test of adequacy of the model.

The processes that are going to need data from the data store have been established in the course of process analysis and modelling, which was covered in Chapter 12. For each of these processes, functional analysis applied to the data model provides:

- a list of entity types that need to be accessed to provide the data for the process;
- the order in which the entities are accessed;
- the criteria used to select the entities – for example, an order might be selected by a given *order#*, or all orders connected via a relationship to a customer might be selected;
- the nature of the access to the entity (retrieve, update, delete and create).

A functional diagram is then drawn. This is a diagram of the relevant subset of the entity model. It shows the direction and movement around the model to access the entities needed to satisfy the function or process. A table of the criteria and resulting actions is also given. This is illustrated with two examples from Kismet.

After the investigation stage of Kismet has been performed, the analyst has established the following functions (among others):

- **Function 1:** For a given customer, a list of those items ordered is needed together with their order dates and order # (*order#, order date, item#, item description, item price, item quantity*) where the items have been ordered more than four days previously and have as yet not been dispatched. This is needed for management information purposes to ensure that good customer service and relations can be maintained.

- **Function 2:** Create an order for a customer after determining the credit status of the customer.

When checking the model to ensure that the data can be supplied for the function, it is important to realize that the purpose of the test is not to carry out the function or process, as that will be achieved by a program working with the data, but merely to establish the accessibility of the needed data.

In order to carry out Function 1, the following has to be performed:

1. Retrieve the given CUSTOMER entity, selected by *customer#*.

2. Retrieve all orders placed by that customer through the CUSTOMER/ORDER relationship where the *order date* is less than today's date minus four days.

3. Retrieve the details of all those orders through the ORDER/ORDER DETAILS relationship.

4. Establish which of those order details have not as yet been satisfied by retrieving the related dispatch details via the relationship ORDER DETAILS/DISPATCH DETAILS.

▶

Figure 13.12 Functional entity diagram for Kismet – Function 1

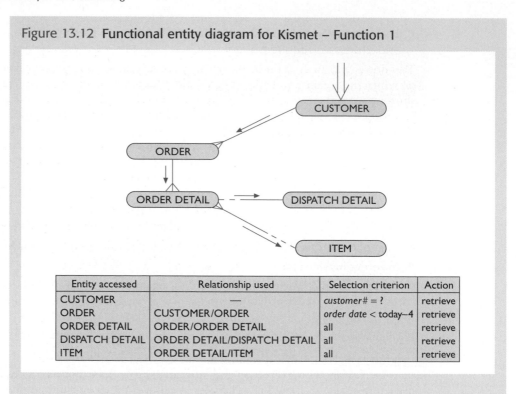

Entity accessed	Relationship used	Selection criterion	Action
CUSTOMER	—	*customer# = ?*	retrieve
ORDER	CUSTOMER/ORDER	*order date < today–4*	retrieve
ORDER DETAIL	ORDER/ORDER DETAIL	all	retrieve
DISPATCH DETAIL	ORDER DETAIL/DISPATCH DETAIL	all	retrieve
ITEM	ORDER DETAIL/ITEM	all	retrieve

Figure 13.13 Functional entity diagram for Kismet – Function 2

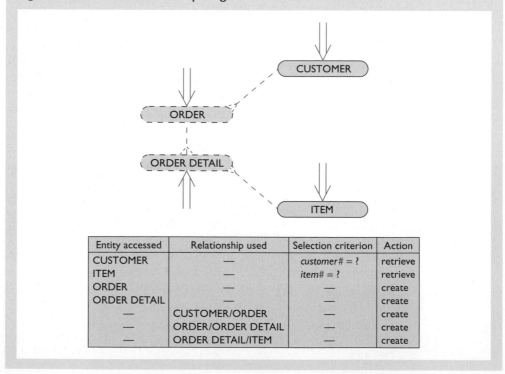

Entity accessed	Relationship used	Selection criterion	Action
CUSTOMER	—	*customer# = ?*	retrieve
ITEM	—	*item# = ?*	retrieve
ORDER	—	—	create
ORDER DETAIL	—	—	create
—	CUSTOMER/ORDER	—	create
—	ORDER/ORDER DETAIL	—	create
—	ORDER DETAIL/ITEM	—	create

5. Retrieve the required details of those items that have not been dispatched through the ORDER DETAILS/ITEM relationship.

This is shown in Figure 13.12. The diagram and the accompanying table show only the entities accessed and paths taken but do not show what is done with the retrieved data. The single arrow indicates a path through the data model, whereas a double arrow implies access from the outside. The analysis and specification of the processes are covered in process analysis and modelling in Chapter 12.

For Function 2, the CUSTOMER and ITEM entities are accessed. ORDER and ORDER DETAILS are created. The order can now be priced, as all the necessary information has been obtained. The value is compared with *credit limit* and *current balance* obtained on the CUSTOMER entity. The relationships between CUSTOMER, ORDER, ORDER DETAILS and ITEMS can now be created. This is shown in Figure 13.13. Once again, note that the path only guarantees that the data can be accessed; it does not show what use is made of this data. The dotted lines are used to show that an entity or relationship is being created rather than being used.

13.4 Process modelling and data modelling – the links

It would be wrong to think that process analysis and modelling as described in Chapter 12 and data analysis and modelling as described in this chapter are rival approaches to systems analysis. Rather, each has evolved in response to particular problems and conditions.

Structured process analysis was developed in an attempt to overcome the difficulties of designing large integrated systems. Such systems cannot be designed by individuals by themselves. The task is too complex and time-consuming. Instead, teams of programmers and analysts are assigned to a project. A large project will require several teams, each dealing with a particular aspect or subsystem of the total system considered. In the development of an integrated system, the interests of each individual and each team overlap and it is necessary to establish effective communication. The problem is that agreements between parties on some aspect of analysis or design are likely to impact on the work of others. Multi-way communication is necessary. It is all too easy to develop a tower of Babel, where communication and project control, rather than the system under investigation, become the problem. It was common for projects to drift over budget and fail to meet time deadlines. An initial response to a project that was slipping behind its schedule was often to add more manpower in the form of extra analysts or programmers. This often aggravated, rather than alleviated, the problem by increasing communication difficulties.

One of the aims of structured process analysis and design is to respond to these software engineering problems by providing an approach that makes effective project control easier. This is achieved by concentrating initially on the logic and not the physical detail of the processes in an organization. These processes are systematically decomposed into manageable chunks or modules. At the program development stage, the individual modular specifications can be coded separately in a form that is easy to test. Various standards for documentation go with this approach, which in the early stages emphasizes features important to the eventual users.

In contrast, top-down data analysis was developed in order to take account of the fact that processes often share the same data and that the data stores need to be designed in an integrated manner that allows this. To do this, an effective data model of the organization is developed. With the realization that the data structure of the organization is unlikely to change much over time, although the processes that use the data might alter, came the emphasis on the importance of data analysis and even on the priority of data analysis over process analysis.

It is impossible for an analyst to concentrate on either process or data analysis to the exclusion of the other. The degree of attention paid to each will depend on the nature of the system under investigation. A system in which there is a high degree of integration and shared data, and for which it is intended to design a database that can service not only the present but the future needs of an organization, will require a heavy initial input of data analysis in conjunction with process analysis. By contrast, complex processes using simple data structures will require only cursory attention to data analysis.

The way that data and process analysis and design interact is shown in Figure 13.14. Here, the approach taken has been that structured process analysis and modelling is complementary to data modelling.

Figure 13.14 The interaction of data analysis and process analysis

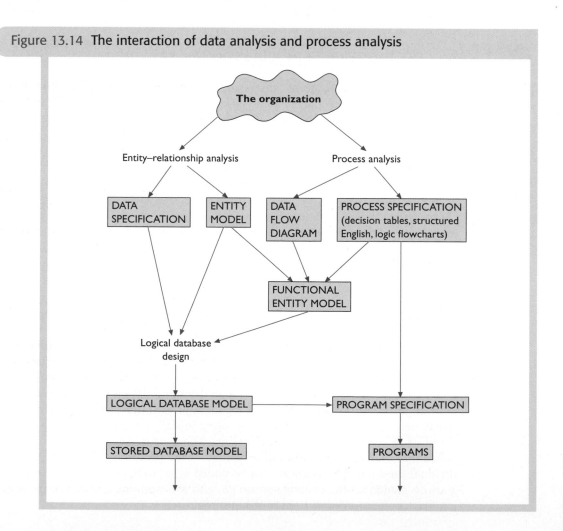

One point of contact is in the development of the functional entity model, where the entity model, as derived from a 'snapshot' picture of the entity–relationship structure of the organization, is tested against the requirements of the existing processes, as analysed and revealed through data flow diagrams, structured English descriptions, decision tables and logic flowcharts. If it is found to be lacking, then the entity model may be changed at this stage.

Another point of contact is via the data dictionary (not shown). Lists of attributes on each entity type, arrived at during data specification, are reconciled with the data needs of processes as revealed in the data flows in the data flow diagram.

The logical model of the database is designed from the entity model and data specifications. This will incorporate any constraints imposed by the limitations of the chosen model type: for example, hierarchical database model. Eventually, this gives rise to the stored database model and the database itself. Process specifications lead to the program specifications. From these, the programs are written that carry out the required data and information processing for the organization. These will require stored data and so will make calls on the database.

The approach to analysis taken in this chapter and in Chapter 12 can be considered 'scientific' in that it is based on some of the fundamental assumptions of natural science and engineering. The approach has the following characteristics:

- **Reductionist:** Progress is achieved by the decomposition and analysis of problems and processes into their constituents.

- **Importance of technical considerations:** Data and processes are the subjects of analysis and design; people are seen as important only as far as they interface with the system.

- **Technology oriented:** It is expected that the end result of analysis and design is to provide a computerized system that overcomes the shortcomings of the existing system.

- **Realist:** The system being analysed, its objectives, its structure and processes, are taken as having an existence and form independent of any subjectivity of the analyst.

This approach has a great deal to recommend it but, as will be seen in Chapters 16 and 17, there are limitations and alternatives.

Summary

The aim of analysis is to summarize and model key elements of a system in a way that facilitates understanding, enables evaluation and aids design. Data analysis is concerned with the development of an abstract data model of an organization appropriate for the design of an effective database.

The importance of data analysis has been increased by:

- the increase in the use of integrated databases;

- the treatment of data as a resource of an organization rather than an input/output product;

- the recognition that although processes change over time the structure of the data held by an organization is relatively stable.

Data modelling is specifically aimed at creating a structure for the store of data that meets organizational requirements. This is achieved by identifying the basic entities and relationships in an organization. Attributes are determined and a normalized set of entity types derived. The entity model is then designed. Its adequacy is established by testing it against the data requirements of the processes that it will serve. This leads to the construction of functional entity models, which indicate the order and selection criteria for data access during a process. The entity–relationship model and its associated data specification of entity attributes are the basis from which the logical database model is designed.

Data analysis and process analysis are complementary activities in the analysis of a system. Although the first concentrates on deriving a data model of the organization, while the second concentrates on modelling processes, the adequacy of the data model is dependent on its ability to serve the processes with the required data. The links are established through the functional entity model and the data dictionary.

The approach to analysis in this chapter and in Chapter 12 is often regarded as 'scientific'. It has all the hallmarks of an engineering philosophy. The approach is reductionist; it concentrates on data and processes by restricting the scope of analysis to technical rather than social aspects of a system; it views the problem solution in terms of computerization; and, finally, it assumes a realist philosophy with respect to the systems, their functioning and their objectives.

Review questions

1. Explain the difference between *bottom-up* and *top-down* data modelling. Why is top-down data modelling generally preferable? Under what circumstances is bottom-up modelling appropriate?

2. Explain the difference between an *entity type*, a *relationship* and an *attribute*. Give examples of each.

3. Give examples of $1:n$, $m:n$ and 1:1 relationships.

4. What is a *key attribute*?

5. What is the purpose of normalization?

6. Explain the differences between 1NF, 2NF and 3NF.

7. What is the purpose of deriving a functional entity model?

8. What reasons might an analyst give for carrying out data analysis prior to attempting process analysis?

Exercises

1. Given that Thomas Yorke is both an employee in an organization and a project leader, he is an occurrence of both the entity types EMPLOYEE and PROJECT LEADER. If the same data (values of attributes) is kept on Thomas Yorke at two occurrences, is this a weakness of entity–relationship modelling?

2. Entities have attributes and stand in relationships to one another. However, relationships also may have attributes. For example, an employee (entity) works (relationship) on a

project (entity). Not only do both the employee and the project have attributes but so does the relationship – works. Mary Jones works on Project A from February to April. This period of work is not an attribute of Mary Jones or of Project A but of the relationship of Mary Jones to Project A. Can entity–relationship modelling handle this difficulty?

3. An object may fall under two distinct entity types. This is particularly true of people who play different roles in an organization. For instance, John Black is both a lecturer to students and a course director. Can the entity–relationship model deal with this adequately, or does it need a new category – that of role?

4. Using the data given in Exercise 5, Chapter 12:

   (a) Identify entities, attributes and relationships for the library.
   (b) Design a suitable entity model and functional entity models for the system.

5. Each department in an organization consists of a manager and several departmental staff. Each manager is in charge of only one department, and departmental staff are assigned to a single department. Attached to each department are several projects. All departmental staff are assigned to projects, with some staff being assigned to several projects, not necessarily in the same department. Each project is run by a management group consisting of the manager of the department together with a selection of staff working on the project. No departmental staff member is ever required to sit on more than one management group.

   (a) Draw an entity diagram for this information.
   (b) Draw a functional diagram for the function: determine which departmental staff working on a given project are not attached to the department responsible for that project.

6. A local hospital consists of many wards, each of which is assigned many patients. Each patient is assigned to one doctor, who has overall responsibility for the patients in his or her care. Other doctors are assigned on an advisory basis. Each patient is prescribed drugs by the doctor responsible for that patient. Each nurse is assigned to a ward and nurses all patients on the ward, although they are given special responsibility for some patients. Each patient is assigned one nurse in this position of responsibility. One of the doctors is attached to each ward as an overall medical advisor.

   (a) Draw an entity diagram representing these relationships.
   (b) Draw a functional diagram representing:

      ■ Function 1: Determine which nurses are responsible for those patients that are the responsibility of a given doctor.
      ■ Function 2: Determine the drug usage prescribed by a doctor.
      ■ Function 3: Determine the range of wards covered by a doctor in any of his/her roles.

CASE STUDY 13

Lift Express

Lift Express is a nationwide organization concerned with the servicing and repair of lifts supplied and installed by its parent company. Lift Express divides the UK into five regions; all service and repair operations within a region are handled by the regional headquarters. At present, all operations are based on a manual system.

▶

On discovery of a lift fault or of the need for it to be serviced, a customer telephones or writes to the regional headquarters. Details of the request for service/repairs are made on standard company documentation by clerical staff at the HQ. Service engineers are all home-based, and details of the customer's requirements are phoned (fault) or posted (service request) to a selected engineer who is based in the same region as the customer. (In the case of faults, documentation detailing the fault is posted later to the engineer.) After visiting the customer, the engineer produces a charge sheet for the job, a copy of which is sent back to the regional HQ, where it is stapled to the original request details. An invoice for the customer is generated and then posted.

Currently, Lift Express is losing work to a rival company. The reason has been located as an inadequate customer request- and information-processing system. Specifically, there are significant delays in paperwork, leading to an unacceptable period occurring between a customer request and an instruction to the engineer, and between a job being completed and an invoice generated. There are difficulties in scheduling engineers' workloads – some are overworked, while others are not fully employed. Management is finding it difficult to extract decision-making information from the system, for instance given a customer – the number of calls booked not as yet completed, or an individual engineer – the amount of income generated per month by the engineer.

In order to remedy these faults, it has been decided to implement a computerized information system.

Questions

1. Explain the principles of data analysis and suggest how these can be applied in designing the information system for Lift Express.

2. Define entity types and relationships important to the functioning of the system and then design an entity model.

3. Design a functional model and data access table for the following: determine the number of calls handled by a given engineer for a given customer.

Recommended reading

Allen S. (2005). *Beginning Data Modeling and Relational Databases for Everyone*, 2nd edn. Springer-Verlag Berlin and Heidelberg GmbH & Co. KG

This book provides a straightforward approach to developing an effective logical model from which a relational database may be designed and implemented. All the key concepts are covered in the 17 chapters. Earlier chapters introduce ideas of modelling and relational databases which are utilized later.

Avison D., Wood-Harper A.T., Vidgen R. and Wood R. (2000). *Multiview*, reissued 2nd edn. McGraw-Hill

This book applies data analysis to a case study. The approach is integrated with other approaches, including structured process modelling as covered in Chapter 10.

Benyon D. (1996). *Information and Data Modelling*, 2nd edn. McGraw-Hill

This covers in detail methods of information analysis and modelling. Aimed at students of management and business studies, this is a clear text extending the contents of the current chapter.

Benyon-Davies P. (2004). *Database Systems*, 3rd edn. Palgrave Macmillan

This updated text gives coverage of databases, database management systems and database development. Later chapters cover trends in database technologies, especially concerning distributed and parallel processing, and chapters on data warehouses and data mining. Although this book goes beyond the needs of many business studies programmes, its clarity would render it useful.

Bowman K. (2003). *Systems Analysis: A Beginner's Guide*. Palgrave Macmillan

This provides a helpful introduction to the topic of systems analysis. Concepts are illustrated by case studies that run through the book.

Connolly T. and Begg C. (2004). *Database Systems: A Practical Approach to Design, Implementation and Management*, 4th edn. Addison-Wesley

A comprehensive text covering databases, SQL, transaction management, data warehouses and data mining, and advanced concepts.

Deeks D. (2002). *An Introduction to System Analysis Techniques*, 2nd edn. Addison-Wesley

A good all-round introduction to the analysis of data and processes in both structured and object-oriented paradigms.

Halpin T. (2001). *Information Modeling and Relational Database: From Conceptual Analysis to Logical Design*. Morgan Kaufmann

This adopts an interesting approach to arriving at the well-understood data models which can then be employed to generate a relational database.

Krogstie J. (ed.) (2004). *Information Modeling Methods and Methodologies*. IGI Publishing

This book presents a research-informed view of modelling methods and methodologies. It provides an overview of current approaches.

Chapter 14

Systems design

Learning outcomes

On completion of this chapter, you should be able to:

- Explain how new system requirements and inefficiencies in the logical model are addressed in the systems design
- Suggest alternative designs for an information system
- Delimit a system in terms of automation boundaries
- Define the walkthrough and the formal review and explain their function as part of systems design.

Introduction

In Chapters 11, 12 and 13 it was seen how the analyst proceeds from the collection of descriptive material on the functioning of the existing physical system through to the analysis and development of a logical model of that system. Data flows between processes were represented and analysed using data flow diagrams at various levels, data processes were specified using decision tables, structured English and logic flowcharts, and a conceptual data model for the system was derived.

This chapter deals with the transition from analysis to design. This initially involves the recasting of the high-level models to eliminate any remaining physical aspects and to take account of any additional requirements that a new system must satisfy. These models can be used to design, in outline, various proposals for the new system. At this stage, the extent of computerization will be decided, together with which processes are to be carried out in batch as distinct from online mode. Decisions will also be taken on whether to centralize or distribute the system and on whether to opt for a file-based or database system. Design considerations for these alternatives are outlined in this chapter. Two or three alternative designs are submitted and assessed through a formal review. As soon as one of these outline proposals has been accepted, then detailed design work can commence. Detailed design is covered in Chapter 15.

14.1 The transition from analysis to design

The aim of analysis is to derive a logical model of the way that the existing system works. This is on the assumption that the existing system provides a good guide to *what* is required of a new system (as distinct from *how* the new system is to achieve these requirements). Certain limitations should be obvious:

1. There may be requirements of the new system that are not being satisfied by the current system – these need to be taken into account.

2. Inefficiencies in the existing system may become translated into the logical model; ideally, the model should reveal the logic of an efficient system and so should be amended.

3. It is often the case that physical aspects creep into the logical analysis – these should be removed.

These three points are now dealt with.

14.1.1 Treatment of new requirements

It is desirable to review the requirements to be made of an information system when it undergoes a major change, such as computerization of a manual system or replacement of an existing computer system by another. This review may throw up new requirements. These will be established by interviews with management and users. By definition, the logical model of the existing system cannot contain these. It is important, then, that the logical model be amended to reflect these new requirements.

These additions are likely to lead to new processes, which will be added to the higher-level data flow diagrams. They will interact via data flows with existing data stores and/or processes. Added processes are decomposed into their exploded functional constituents on lower-level data flow diagrams. If their operation is governed by sophisticated logic, then this must be specified using one of the tools of specification, such as structured English.

Often, new requirements concern the extraction of new types of management information from data stores rather than the alteration of the existing pattern of transaction processing. This can be accomplished simply at the data flow diagram level by inserting a process that accepts as input the data flows from the relevant data stores and produces as output the required data. It will also be necessary to establish that the entity model, as revealed by the entity diagram, is sufficient to provide the data for the function. In other words, the access path through the model must be checked by drawing a functional entity diagram.

Kismet case study 14.1

With the Kismet case study, one of the problems that management listed with the existing document-handling system was the difficulty of deriving useful management information. For example, management needed a regular report on the total value of goods sold, analysed by each item type within customer types. This is vital information to establish which sectors of the market are growing and which are declining with respect to sales. Examples of customer types might be specialist retail chains (chain stores dealing with electrical goods only), non-specialist retail chains, specialist single shops (the local hi-fi shop) and non-specialist single shops. Examples of item types are compact disc, turntable, mini rack system and graphic equalizer. An example of a partial report is given in Figure 14.1.

▶

Figure 14.1 Sales analysis report by customer type within item type

Start date 12/09/2004	Stop date 12/10/2004	
Stock analysis code	Customer analysis code	Value
A1	1	45,123
	2	100,876
	3	1,122
	4	0
A2	1	107,879
	2	232,112
:	:	:
:	:	:

Figure 14.2 A data flow diagram for the production of the sales analysis

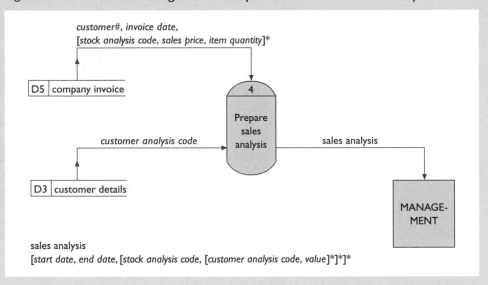

It is a notable weakness of the existing system that such reports are difficult to extract. The documents are stored in a manner that makes it time-consuming and costly to obtain this information. One of the benefits of computerized information systems is that information for use in decision making can be extracted quickly and cheaply from the results of transaction processing.

The process for generating this report can be incorporated in a straightforward way into a data flow diagram (see Figure 14.2). In order to produce this report for any selected invoice it is necessary to extract the invoice details (and hence the stock analysis codes of the items sold), and the customer for whom the invoice is generated. The analysis code of the customer can then be obtained.

This may be established by reference to the entity diagram developed in Chapter 13 and shown in Figure 13.10. The new functional entity diagram governing this process is

Figure 14.3 Functional entity model showing the entities accessed for the sales analysis report

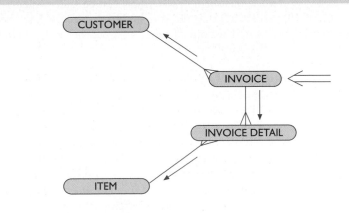

CUSTOMER   (*customer#, customer analysis code, ...*)
INVOICE   (*invoice#, invoice date, customer#, ...*)
INVOICE DETAIL   (*invoice#, item#, item quantity, sales price*)
ITEM   (*item#, stock analysis code, ...*)

Entity accessed	Relationship used	Selection criteria	Action
INVOICE	—	by invoice date	retrieve
CUSTOMER	INVOICE/CUSTOMER	all	retrieve
INVOICE DETAIL	INVOICE/INVOICE DETAIL	all	retrieve
ITEM	INVOICE DETAIL/ITEM	all	retrieve

shown in Figure 14.3. For any selected invoice it is possible to retrieve the customer receiving the invoice through the **CUSTOMER/INVOICE** relationship and hence determine the *customer analysis code*. For the invoice, it is also possible to retrieve the invoice details through the **CUSTOMER/INVOICE DETAILS** relationship. This gives the *item #*, *sale price* and *item quantity* for each item sold under the invoice. The value of that item can then be calculated. The item can then be retrieved via the **INVOICE DETAIL/ITEM** relationship and hence the *stock analysis code* obtained. There is now sufficient data to derive the analysis of all invoices between specified dates by customer analysis code within the stock analysis code and so provide the report.

14.1.2 Treatment of inefficiencies

The development of data flow diagrams has been accomplished using top-down decomposition of the major processes, such as those occurring in the Kismet order-processing system. Inevitably, the decomposition as revealed by lower-level data flow diagrams is not purely a result of a logical analysis of the nature of the major processes. Rather, the lower-level structure tends to be determined partly by what is done in the existing system to fulfil a function as well as by what needs to be done as determined by the logic of the function. If what is done is unnecessary or inefficient, this may have unfortunate repercussions on the logical model. It is at this transition stage that the model should be adjusted.

Kismet case study 14.2

An example of this adjustment of the model can be seen in the Kismet case study. From Figure 12.10, process 1.2 and the surrounding processes have been extracted and are shown in Figure 14.4. The copy of the company order is stored temporarily in the company order store D4. Another copy is priced and then a credit check is performed on the customer. If successful, the credit check triggers the dispatch of the stored company order to the customer as an acknowledgement of receipt of the order. This is clearly unnecessary. Why not send the acknowledgement company order as an output of process 1.5, the credit check? Historically, the reason for the temporary store is to maintain a record of the order in the sales department while the company order is sent to the credit control section and back. This would take time, and the sales department might need to answer a query on the customer order while it is in transit (the enquiry process is not shown). If the entire system is to be computerized (perhaps a premature judgement) then this time lag may not occur. In fact, in an online system the aim is to eliminate this time lag completely. The logical model of the system has inherited the inefficiency of the physical system on which it is based.

Figure 14.4 A partial data flow diagram illustrating the process of generating an approved order

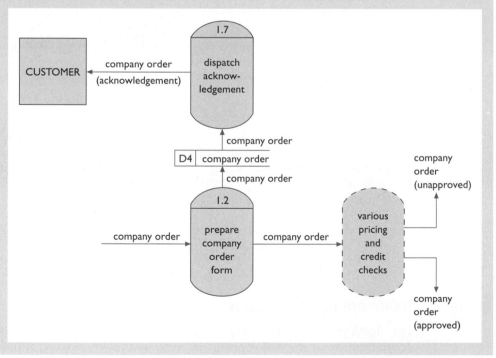

The important point to be made here is not to reach a definite answer on the peculiarities of the Kismet case but rather to reinforce the observation that there is nothing sacrosanct about a logical model derived from the study of an existing system – it can be changed as seen fit. Nor is there any clear-cut set of rules as to how to modify the model before design can start. Indeed, any modification could be considered to be part of design, although here these changes are referred to as a transition from analysis to design.

14.1.3 Treatment of physical aspects

Certain physical considerations may have crept into the logical model.

Kismet case study 14.3

Data store D5 in Figure 12.7 contains the order/invoice/dispatch note trio. These are disallowed as bedfellows in the logical model and should be indicated on the data flow diagram as separate stores. They have been thrown together purely for convenience in ▶

Figure 14.5 An amended data flow diagram of the Kismet order-processing system

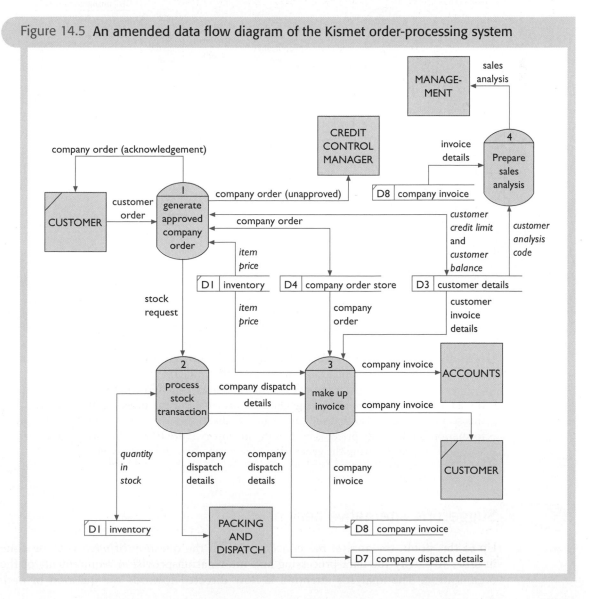

Figure 14.6 An amended level 2 data flow diagram of the generation of an approved company order

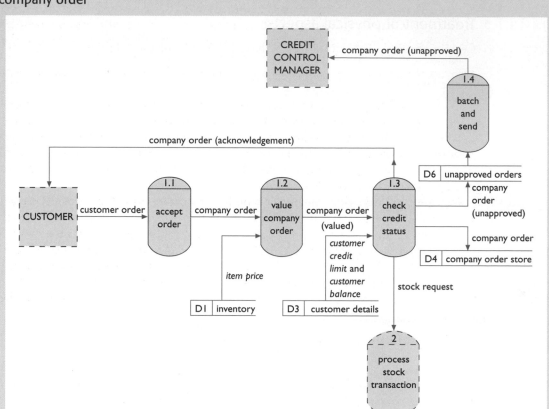

the physical manual files. There is no fear that by separating these the connection between them will be lost. The links remain at an attribute level, as each of the trio contains the attribute *order#*. Also, each order is linked to its relevant invoice(s) and dispatch note(s) through relationships in the entity model.

Amended data flow diagrams are shown in Figures 14.5 and 14.6. These incorporate the addition of the sales analysis generation process and the other comments given in this section. Notice also that the catalogue has disappeared as a separate store. The information on item sale prices is held in the inventory store (the **ITEM** entity), and this is accessed for prices during the generation of a company order and invoice.

14.2 Suggesting alternative designs

Up to this point, the analyst has concentrated on the question of *what* is to be done in order to satisfy the data-processing and information-provision requirements of the organization. The analyst's attention is now directed towards the question of *how* to do it. This is a two-step process. First, the analyst suggests, in outline, two or three alternatives. This is termed **systems design**. One of these is selected by management. Second, the detailed design of the chosen system is carried out. Detailed design is covered in Chapter 15. Is it worth emphasizing that the authors are deliberately separating the stages of systems analysis and design in this book. It is thought that by exaggerating the issues particular to each stage a clearer understanding can be formed. In reality, the stages are often much more blurred and the transition between them less obvious.

Why should the analyst be presenting general alternative systems when there has already been a costed proposal in the feasibility study? The analyst now has a much greater understanding of the system than earlier on in the investigation. There may be new opportunities for a different extent or type of computerization from what was previously envisaged. Having developed a logical model, it is also easy to sketch and present these alternatives to management.

In preparing a design, the analyst will need to make various choices. There will be decisions on the extent of computerization – which processes in the process model will be computerized and which will be manual – and decisions on the type of system for those processes that are computerized. Although this is the stage where the decisions are made explicit, it is likely that some consideration of the type of system will already have been made throughout the process so far. This is inevitable given that the decisions represent important strategic choices for the organization. The principal choices concern:

- centralized or distributed systems;
- file-based or database systems;
- batch or online systems;
- input methods;
- applications packages or specially designed programs;
- hardware.

General design considerations on each of these are summarized here and then applied to Kismet.

14.2.1 Centralized and distributed systems

A distributed computer system is one where:

- there are two or more geographically separated computers;
- these are linked by telecommunications; and
- the network of computers serves a single organization.

A centralized computer system is one with a single computer servicing the needs of the organization. There may be remote terminals connected by telecommunications.

A large organization on many different sites may decide to have a distributed system because most of the data processing and information provision is localized to each site. Local data storage and processing are then feasible. The need for distributed computing (as distinct from several standalone computers) comes from the requirement that data and the results of processing at one site are available to computers at other sites.

A single-site organization may also decide to have a collection of micro/minicomputers and connect these via a local area network. This is possible if no large centralized processing power is needed. It has the advantage that each node on the network can be devoted to local needs such as decision support using spreadsheet modelling or word processing, and nodes can be added to the network when needed.

Advantages of distributed computing

- Telecommunications costs between several sites are reduced, provided that most of the processing is locally based.
- There is greater flexibility, as additional computers can be added to the networks as needed.
- The organization is not reliant on a single computer, which might break down.

Disadvantages of distributed computing

- Commonly used data is often replicated at many sites – changes in this data, unless happening to all occurrences, can lead to an inconsistent organizational data store.
- With several computers at dispersed sites, lack of standardization of equipment, software and data storage is possible.
- Control is more difficult.

14.2.2 File-based and database systems

The data store serving the programs with data can be designed either as a series of independent files or as an integrated database. The choice will depend on a number of factors. The differences between file-based and database systems have been extensively covered in Chapter 8. Here, only summaries of the main points are made. The following features suggest that a database system is more appropriate:

- The same data is commonly shared by several applications.
- Data in one part of the organization is related to, and integrated with, data in other parts.
- The data structure for the organization is stable.
- The applications for which the data is to be used are likely to change over time.
- There is a need for flexible enquiry and reporting facilities.

The following features suggest that a file-based system may be suitable:

- There is little or no common data usage between different applications.
- There is a need for fast transaction processing.
- Sophisticated, flexible enquiry facilities are not required – reports are standard and unchanging.

Database systems, if appropriate, offer substantial advantages over file-based systems in the same circumstances:

- Data redundancy is minimized, and database consistency is maintained.
- Application programmer productivity is enhanced.

- Control over data is centralized, leading to better data management.
- Data can be shared easily between different applications.
- The physical details of data storage are hidden from users, who are presented with tailor-made logical views of relevant data.

Difficulties and disadvantages of database systems include:

- The need for integrated initial design (difficult) rather than piecemeal design of files to meet problems as they arise (easy).
- Processing is usually slower than with file-based systems.
- The need to purchase costly database management software and extensive disk storage.

14.2.3 Batch and online systems

Another choice to be made by the analyst is between batch and online systems. Some parts of the system can be designed in batch mode, whereas others may use online processing.

In **batch mode**, transactions are entered into the computer system and held temporarily before processing until a batch has been input. The entire set of transactions is then processed. The advantages of batch processing are:

- **Control:** Because data is not processed immediately on entry there is a further chance to detect and correct errors before processing. The following controls are possible:
  - **Control totals:** A total for, say, the value of all invoices in a batch is generated manually and then compared with a computer-generated total before processing.
  - **Hash totals:** This is the same as a control total, except that the figure is meaningless – for example, the sum of all account codes in a batch.
  - **Visual checks:** A list of all input transactions can be printed after batch input and compared with the source documents before processing.
  - **Transaction counts:** A computer-generated count of the number of input transactions is compared with a manual total.
- **Efficient processing:** Data can be held and then processed at a time when there is little demand on computer resources.

Batch-processing systems are used for processing large volumes of repetitive transactions where control considerations and the efficient utilization of computing capacity are important. Typical applications are payroll, sales and purchase ledger processing, and stock movements. The drawback of this form of processing is that it may take some time after input for a transaction to change relevant files or a database. This is only a disadvantage where up-to-date reports or enquiry results are needed.

Online processing occurs when a transaction is processed immediately on input. Batch controls over erroneous input are not possible, because each transaction is handled one by one. The requirement that immediate processing occurs implies that the computer must be available at all times to accept and process. This leads to under-utilization of resources during slack periods. Any application that requires an immediate response, as many enquiries do, must be carried out in online mode. Similarly, some applications require the effects of an updating transaction to be immediate. Airline booking systems and current stock systems are examples.

14.2.4 Input methods

At this stage, the analyst will also specify the main types of input media and methods that are to be used. The main considerations are:

- volumes of transactions to be input;
- speed of input required;
- initial and operating costs of the chosen method;
- degree of accuracy required over input;
- special characteristics of the application.

The input method will be intimately connected with the decisions on batch and on-line processing. Those methods associated with fast, high-volume, repetitive input are more likely candidates for batch processing. A detailed range of input devices and media was provided in Chapter 3; the main alternatives are:

- **Keyboard:** Keyboard input is cheap on initial cost but high on operating costs because it is a heavily labour-intensive form of input. Without sophisticated computer-operated checks (check digits, master-file checks, and so on) there are likely to be high error rates unless batch entry with its associated controls is chosen. The main advantage of keyboard entry is that it is very flexible on the kinds of data that can be input.

- **Preprinted character recognition:** The main examples are optical character recognition (OCR) and magnetic ink character recognition (MICR). The input equipment 'reads' the input document and converts the characters to a machine-understandable form. There is a high initial cost for the purchase of the equipment but very low operating costs, as little labour is used for input. This means that this method is suitable for high-volume input. Low error rates are also a feature. The method is limited to those applications where known identifying data can be preprinted on documents – for example the cheque and account number together with the bank sort code on a cheque, or the account code and amount on an electricity bill. The method is inflexible on the kinds of data to be input.

- **Optical mark recognition:** This is used where a preprinted document is produced that contains selection boxes. These are marked indicating choices and can be 'read' by special equipment, which is preprogrammed as to the location of the boxes. The presence or absence of a mark is converted to a machine-understandable form. Once again there are high initial costs, low operating costs and low error rates. This method is suitable for high-volume applications where selection between alternatives is required. Typical applications are market research surveys, automated marking of multiple-choice examination questions and stock selection.

- **Bar-code reading:** Bar-codes that identify items are preprinted and attached to the items. The bar-codes are read in by special readers, often using laser light. Bar-codes need to be attached to items, so the method is associated with data input over the movement of material goods. Examples are the sale of goods in supermarkets, library loans and stock movements. Input of data is simple to achieve, needs no skill and is error-free. The applications to which it is put are mainly in the handling of items of stock.

- **Voice input:** Speech input is now widely available. A number of simple applications where a limited vocabulary is employed, such as navigating the menus of a call centre, can already be controlled completely by voice. Developments in speech recognition are leading to the use of speech input for more general activities such as word processing.

- **Remote input:** If the system can be accessed remotely, for example by Internet access to a web server, input data may be transmitted directly to the system by the customers or employees themselves. The data input process may be automated, as in the case of EDI, or may entail a manual submission, as in the case of a business-to-customer e-commerce site.

14.2.5 Applications packages and specially designed programs

It may be possible to purchase an applications package rather than writing special programs for the system. Packages are written by a third party and sold to many customers, so the cost of this alternative is considerably lower than designing, coding and testing programs from scratch. Packages also have the advantage that they are quick to implement, can be demonstrated in action prior to purchase and generally have good documentation. They will also have been tried and tested by many previous purchasers. These can be consulted on the quality of the package and the support given by the software house or dealer selling it.

However, packages may not integrate easily with existing software that has been written especially for the organization. The package may also not suit precisely the data-processing and information needs. The software house selling the package will attempt to introduce as much flexibility as possible into it, thus accommodating as wide a market as possible. However, this may introduce unwanted inefficiency into the program.

More recently, the trend has been away from 'purpose-built' software and towards the use of packages that can be customized to fulfil the differing requirements of particular organizations. Some of these products are aimed at quite specific markets, such as the student record-keeping systems produced by software vendors for use in colleges and universities. The core of the system is retained for each implementation, but additional modules or different functionality can be purchased; the system can be customized to take into account the particular regulations and procedures of each institution. Other examples are more generic in function. Examples are the enterprise resource planning software produced by companies such as SAP and Oracle. These packages attempt to bring together the information systems supporting the different functional areas in an organization. These were described in detail in Chapter 2. Also, the accounting software produced by vendors such as Sage is sector-independent but can be tailored to meet specific local conditions. The business reasons for this approach provide advantages for both the purchaser and the vendor. For the purchaser, the costs of production are shared between many, thereby reducing the purchase price. Also, the ability to tailor the package to local needs is an attractive option. For the vendor, the opportunity arises to resell the core of a product that has already been developed. In addition, the flexibility to adapt the product often leads to ongoing contracts with the purchaser for maintenance and enhancement.

The analyst is more likely to recommend a package if:

- Cost is a major consideration.
- The system needs to be implemented quickly.
- The data-processing and information requirements are standard ones for the type of business function to be computerized.
- The organization does not have a mature computer centre that can write and maintain software.
- Well-established packages from reputable companies exist.

Some business functions are more amenable to packages than others. For instance, all businesses have standard accounting activities – sales, general and purchase-ledger processing, and payroll. It is common to buy packages for these. Even quite large companies will purchase mainframe software in these areas.

14.2.6 Hardware

Different designs will have different hardware requirements. Some of these factors have been taken into account in the choice of input method and equipment. The analyst will need to take decisions on suitable processing, output, communications and storage hardware. This will depend largely on the amount of processing required by the system, the complexity of the software and the number of users attached to the system. Choices on whether to develop a centralized or distributed system will obviously have hardware implications. The amount of data to be stored and decisions over adopting a file-based approach as opposed to a database with a database management system will affect storage hardware needs.

The analyst suggests two or three alternative systems to management. All the factors discussed in this section will be taken into account in each design. Management will need not only an explanation of the alternative designs but also estimates of the costs and time schedules associated with each alternative. The data flow diagrams will provide a valuable tool for the analyst in developing alternative high-level designs, as they can be used to indicate which features of a system are to be computerized and how this is to be achieved. The way that data flow diagrams do this is treated in the next section.

14.3 Automation boundaries

As well as revealing the logic of data flows between processes in process modelling, the data flow diagram can be the basis of design in selecting and communicating which processes are to be computerized and how this is to be achieved. Automation boundaries are used. The data flow diagram as a design aid can best be understood by a consideration of the following examples.

Kismet case study 14.4

In Figure 14.7(a), the automation boundaries suggest that the entire order-processing system for Kismet is to be computerized. Customer orders flow into the system, and company invoices, dispatch notes, and approved and unapproved company orders flow out.

In contrast, Figure 14.7(b) shows the automation boundaries as encompassing the production of the company order (approved as a customer acknowledgement or unapproved and sent to the credit control manager) together with the company invoice. ▶

Figure 14.7(a) Automation boundaries for the Kismet system suggesting a fully computerized order/stock/invoice processing system

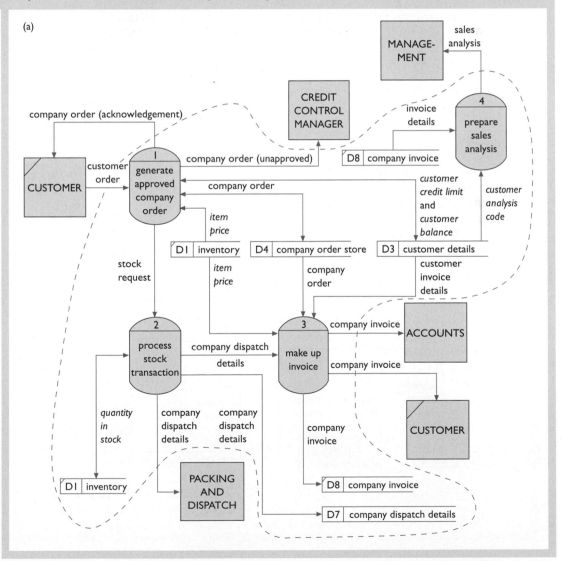

Stock processing and generation of the dispatch details are carried out manually. The computer system produces a stock request, which is (presumably) sent to the warehouse, where the goods are picked and a dispatch note generated manually and sent with the goods to packing and dispatch. The dispatch note details are then input into the computer system, which retrieves a copy of the order from the company order store and generates a company invoice. These two alternative approaches can be presented clearly and discussed with the aid of the data flow diagram.

Figure 14.7(b) Automation boundaries for the Kismet system suggesting a computerized order/stock/invoice system with a manual stock control system

Figure 14.8 provides two alternatives for process 1 – that of generating an approved company order. The diagrams show the difference between the representation of a batch-processing system and an online real-time system.

Figure 14.8(a) illustrates an online system for the processing of approved orders. The customer order details when input are immediately subject to pricing and credit checking and if successful a stock request is output to process 2 – process stock transaction. The unapproved orders are stored temporarily in D6, where they are output in a batch for the credit control manager.

In Figure 14.8(b) the orders are input and stored temporarily prior to pricing and credit checking. The automation boundaries suggest that the input of the orders is distinct from the processes that follow. In the data flow diagram it is also easy to see that the unapproved orders are stored and then output in a batch for consideration by the credit control manager. Likewise, the stock requests from the approved orders are stored and later used as input to the stock process.

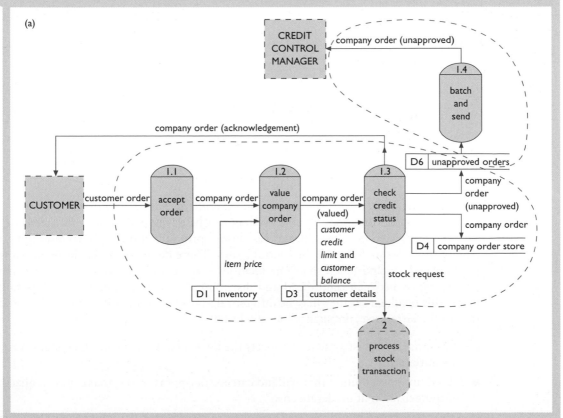

Figure 14.8(a) Automation boundaries for the process of generating an approved company order (process 1) showing online order processing of customer orders

Figure 14.8(b) Automation boundaries for the process of generating an approved company order (process 1) showing batch processing of customer orders

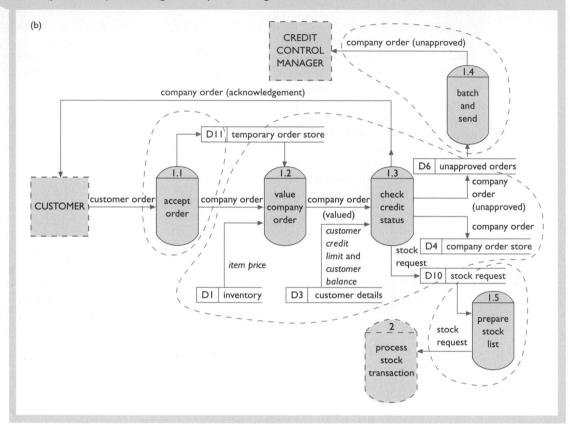

At this stage, the analyst should present several alternative designs as suggestions for the way in which the new computer system can be developed to meet the needs of the organization. Two or three alternatives should promote sufficiently wide-ranging debate without losing focus on the central issues. These designs may be different ways of physically providing much the same facilities – the choice between online and batch processing or between centralized and distributed systems can be regarded as falling under this heading. Or they may be different designs providing different levels of facilities. In the latter case, the suggestions might be:

- A minimal, low-cost system that meets the basic needs for which the systems project was initiated.

- A medium-cost solution that will indicate extra opportunities that can be realized by computerization at moderate cost.

- A grander system that illustrates how the organization can exploit the full benefits of computerization in the area of the system under consideration.

A basic design for Kismet would cover just the order processing and invoicing, as in Figure 14.7(b). A medium-cost solution (Figure 14.7(a)) will handle stock control as well. This can include an automatic reordering system that produces purchase orders for suppliers when stocks of an item fall below a certain level. In other words, the analyst may provide a basic design and also one that provides extra facilities (at extra cost). A more extensive computerization would involve the integration of the accounting system with the order-processing system and stock control systems, would have facilities for accepting credit card purchases direct from the public by phone or through a website, and would have programs that optimally schedule van deliveries.

In presenting the various alternative designs, the analyst will have made decisions on all the features listed in Section 14.2 – online and batch, centralized versus distributed systems, file-based versus database systems, packages and specially written programs, hardware, and input methods. For each design, the analyst will be required to submit cost estimates and a schedule for the time to be taken to complete the project. It is crucial in systems design that the analyst always maintain a clear idea of the management constraints and organizational objectives under which the project is being developed.

The suggested systems designs will be presented to management at a structured formal review. At this stage, management will select one system and will give the 'go ahead' to the analyst to start the work of deriving a detailed design for this system. Walkthroughs and formal reviews occur at several stages during a project's life cycle. Section 14.4 covers these.

14.4 Walkthroughs and formal reviews

At various stages, the analyst may wish to present aspects of his or her work to others. This is achieved through walkthroughs and reviews. The difference between them is that a walkthrough is an interactive presentation of some part of the system by the analyst. The aim is for the analyst to present ideas or problems and receive useful feedback from the participants. In contrast, the formal review is a public presentation of some aspects of analysis and design and is used as a milestone in the computer project. Formal reviews are often used as exit criteria from one stage in the analysis and design process so that progress may be made into the following stages.

14.4.1 Walkthroughs

A walkthrough consists of perhaps three or four people, including the analyst, who will present some aspect of the system in the stages of analysis or design. Data flow diagrams, entity–relationship models and flowcharts may be used to illustrate points. Each walkthrough should last no more than 20 to 30 minutes – much longer and the participants' attention will wander. The participants, other than the analyst making the presentation, may be other analysts or programmers, users or management.

The purpose of the walkthrough is to communicate some particular aspect of systems analysis or design to the group so that useful feedback may be provided for the analyst.

The walkthrough is often used when analysts run into particular problems or wish to check out their understanding of a part of a system with users. They are informal, semi-structured meetings that occur on an ad hoc basis throughout analysis and design. Communication is of the essence in a walkthrough, so structured tools, with their emphasis on logic rather than physical details, are indispensable aids.

14.4.2 Formal reviews

Formal reviews may occur at many points during the systems analysis and design of a project and are used as a formal recognition that some major point has been reached in the process. A successful formal review implies that the next stage may be started, an unsuccessful one that some failure in analysis or design has been noted and needs to be reworked.

At formal reviews (sometimes called **inspections**), the analyst or team of analysts make a formal presentation. This will be backed up by documentation, which will have been previously circulated to participants. It is the purpose of the review to find errors or shortcomings in the stage of analysis or design presented.

The participants in a formal review are generally as follows:

1. **The moderator or review leader:** This individual is responsible for organizing the review after being notified by the analysts that the required stage has been achieved. The review leader circulates the documentation, schedules the meeting and ensures that all relevant and interested parties are invited as inspectors.

   During the inspection, the review leader ensures that all the relevant points are covered in a proper manner. Given that the nature of the inspection process is fault finding, it is important that all participants in the project realize that finding faults at this stage is beneficial to the project as a whole. To discover these later will need redesign, which will undoubtedly be both expensive and troublesome. Equally, it is important for the inspectors to realize that an over-critical stance may be counter-productive. Either analysts will be induced to cover up or minimize the importance of errors, or they may not wish to make a presentation until everything is '110% perfect'. Political considerations may also influence the review session. Participants may have a vested interest in delaying, blocking or changing the course of development of a project. It is the responsibility of the review leader to ensure that the review is conducted in the most unbiased, constructive way possible.

2. **Inspectors:** The inspection group consists of:
   (a) technical people who may be brought into the review for their experience in the area;
   (b) representatives of those who will use and be affected by the new system;
   (c) specialists who will have an interest in the system once it is working.

   Auditors are the most important examples of this last group.

   The role of the inspectors is to assess the proposed stage with a view to locating errors or shortcomings. They will base their examination mainly on documentation provided beforehand by analysts.

3. **Systems analysts:** The systems analyst provides beforehand the documentation on which the presentation will be based. During the presentation, the analyst may provide a brief overview of the contents of the documentation. The main part of the presentation, though, will revolve around questions on the documentation raised by the inspectors and answered by the analyst.

After the formal review (at which a secretary may take notes on the major points raised), it is the responsibility of the analyst to rework areas that have been found to be lacking and to satisfy the review leader that this has been done. In the event of serious shortcomings, another review will be required.

Formal reviews may occur at a number of points during the development of a project. Major reviews will probably occur at the following:

1. **Systems design:** To consider alternative designs.

2. **Detailed design:** To consider the systems specification consisting of:

   (a) hardware specifications;
   (b) database or file specifications;
   (c) program specifications;
   (d) input/output specifications;
   (e) identification of procedures surrounding the system;
   (f) implementation schedules.

3. **Implementation:** To consider the results of a formal systems test.

Reviews are one of the important controls that may be exercised over the development of the project.

Summary

The purpose of systems design is to present alternative solutions to the problem situation. High-level logical models have been developed for the system, involving no prior physical design considerations, so it is easy to illustrate and communicate different approaches in outline for new systems.

The logical model of the system needs to be amended to incorporate any new requirements. At this stage, inefficiencies in the model and any physical aspects are removed. Both of these are legacies of having used an existing physical system as the basis for analysis and design. Alternative designs are illustrated using automation boundaries on the data flow diagrams. In deriving these designs the analyst must pay attention to physical design features. The most important of these concern decisions over centralized and distributed processing, file-based and database systems, online and batch processing, packages and programs, input methods and hardware. The analyst will restrict the number of suggested designs to two or three. For each, a cost estimate and implementation schedule will be given. The presentation of these suggestions will be made during a formal review. Management will decide on which, if any, of the presented systems is to be undertaken. The analyst will carry out a detailed design of the chosen system. This work is covered in Chapter 15.

Review questions

1. What are the objectives of systems design?

2. How is *systems analysis* distinguished from *systems design*?

3. In providing alternative systems designs, what considerations should a systems analyst employ?

4. How do automation boundaries help in the design process?

5. How is the difference between online and batch processing shown with the use of data flow diagrams and automation boundaries?

6. What is the difference in purpose between a *walkthrough* and a *formal review*?

7. What roles do the participants in a formal review play?

Exercises

1. What are the specific advantages and disadvantages for Kismet in adopting a batch system as distinct from an online system for order approval as shown in Figure 14.8?

2. What are the specific advantages and disadvantages for Kismet in adopting a more highly automated system as indicated in Figure 14.7(a) as compared to that shown in Figure 14.7(b)?

3. 'A proposed system was given in the feasibility study along with its associated costs and benefits. It is a waste of time and money to present alternatives at this stage when a system has already been agreed.' How would you answer this criticism?

CASE STUDY 14

Kemsing Theatre

Go over your answers to the data flow diagram produced for Case Study 12 (the introduction to the Kemsing Theatre booking system):

Questions

1. Eliminate reference to any physical aspects that have entered the model.

2. Suggest additional processes/functions that would be useful to a theatre booking system and incorporate them into the data flow diagrams.

3. Derive two alternative designs and illustrate them by automation boundaries in the data flow diagrams.

Recommended reading

Avison D. and Fitzgerald G. (2007). *Information Systems Development: Methodologies, Techniques and Tools*, 4th revised edn. McGraw Hill

This well-established book covers a range of techniques and methodologies for systems analysis and design. The book provides a comprehensive coverage of data, process, rapid, blended, and people-oriented methodologies. This edition contains new material on ERP and the development of e-commerce applications. The book is suitable for those covering an information systems course at undergraduate level.

Bittner K. and Spence I. (2002). *Use Case Modeling.* Addison-Wesley

This book provides an interesting context to the topic of automation boundaries which are covered in this chapter.

Evans E. (2003). *Domain-driven Design: Tackling Complexity in the Heart of Software.* Addison-Wesley

This tackles the issues of systems design in the context of a particular approach called domain-driven design. The book provides examples of best practice in design and includes a number of case studies.

Flowers S. (1999). *Software Failure, Management Failure: Amazing Stories and Cautionary Tales.* John Wiley & Sons.

This book is a collection of case studies of systems failures such as the Performing Rights Society, the London Ambulance Service and the Taurus London Stock Exchange system. The book encourages the reader to learn lessons about good and bad systems design by analysing systems developments that have failed.

Flynn D. J. (1997). *Information Systems Requirements: Determination and Analysis*, 2nd edn. McGraw-Hill

This is a comprehensive coverage of information systems analysis and design suitable for the student of computing studies who wishes to become acquainted with management and non-technical issues in analysis and design.

Weaver P., Lambrou N. and Walkley M. (2002). *Practical Business Systems Development using SSADM.* FT Prentice Hall

A clear, straightforward text suitable for reference on SSADM.

Yourdon Inc. (1993). *Yourdon Systems Method: Model Driven Systems Development.* Prentice Hall

This is useful as a statement of a systems development methodology by one of the founding father companies of structured systems analysis and design. It is suitable as an example reference of a commercial methodology.

Chapter 15

Detailed design, implementation and review

Learning outcomes

On completion of this chapter, you should be able to:

- Describe how the high-level logical model derived from analysis of a system is converted into a physical design and systems specification
- Use a range of techniques to specify the physical design of a system
- Appreciate the importance of input and output design
- Explain the advantages of adopting a modular approach in systems design
- Define the function of schema in database design
- Evaluate different approaches to and plan effectively for systems changeover
- Describe the role and importance of evaluation and maintenance in systems development.

Introduction

In Chapter 14, it was seen how the system developer (or analyst) uses the logical model of the system to suggest design alternatives for the new physical system. Broad decisions were taken over the extent of computerization and the types of system that could be developed for this. Having obtained agreement from the relevant management authority on the choice of system, the analyst must now carry out detailed design of the new system. This chapter covers this and subsequent stages in the systems life cycle.

The detailed design of the system includes specification of the hardware, software, database, user interface and schedule for implementation. The detailed specification is analogous to an architect's or engineer's blueprint – it is the document from which the system will be built. Once agreement has been obtained on the detailed design, steps will be taken to acquire and install the hardware, write or purchase and test the software, train staff, develop the database and convert and load the contents of existing files. The system is then ready to take over from the current one. Various methods of changeover are discussed. After changeover, a post-implementation review considers the effectiveness of the system and its relation to its specification and original objectives. Finally, ongoing maintenance and development will be needed during the useful life of the system.

15.1　Detailed design

Data flow diagrams were used to develop a high-level logical model of the processes and the data flows between them in the system. They were particularly helpful in sketching design alternatives using automation boundaries. The logic of the processes themselves has been captured in structured tools such as decision tables, structured English or logic flowcharts. The data model of the organization has been produced using entity–relationship modelling.

The use of this logical approach has ensured that no premature physical design decisions have been taken. The concentration has always been on the question 'What logically is required of the system and what logically must be achieved in order to do this?' not 'How are we physically going to accomplish this?' However, the time has come to move away from these logical models towards the detailed physical design of the computerized system (see Figure 15.1). The data flow diagrams and logic representations developed so far will be invaluable in producing program specifications. The entity model will be essential in designing a database model.

Figure 15.1　Tools used during the stages of systems analysis and design

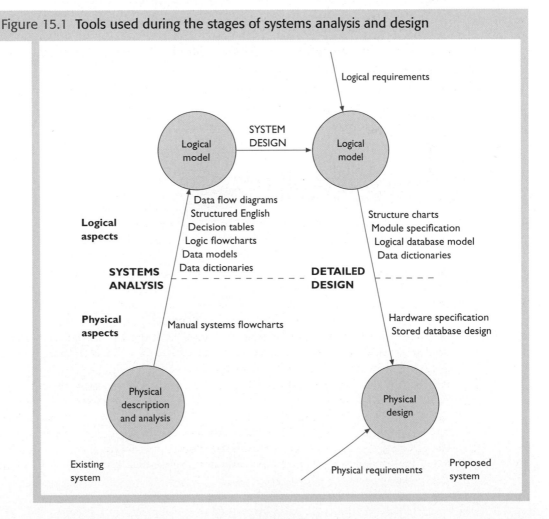

Any system can be considered as being composed of input, output, storage and processing elements. This approach is used in looking at the various tasks to be covered in detailed systems design. Control in systems has been covered extensively in Chapter 9. Control features figure prominently in the design of all the other elements.

15.1.1 Process design

Process design covers the need to design and specify the processing hardware, and to design and specify the software to run in the central processing unit.

The specification of processor hardware is a technical skill beyond the scope of this text. The analyst will need to consider the demands to be made on the processor. In particular, the volume of transactions to be processed per day and the processing requirement for each, the speed of response needed for interactive enquiries, the number of simultaneous users, the types of peripheral devices required, the amount of RAM, the complexity of programs, and the extent to which the system should be able to cope with future increases in demand are all determinants of the processing power required. Decisions taken on whether to centralize or distribute computing and the mix between batch and online processing will all affect the decision.

Figure 15.2 Part of a structure chart dealing with payslip preparation for a payroll application

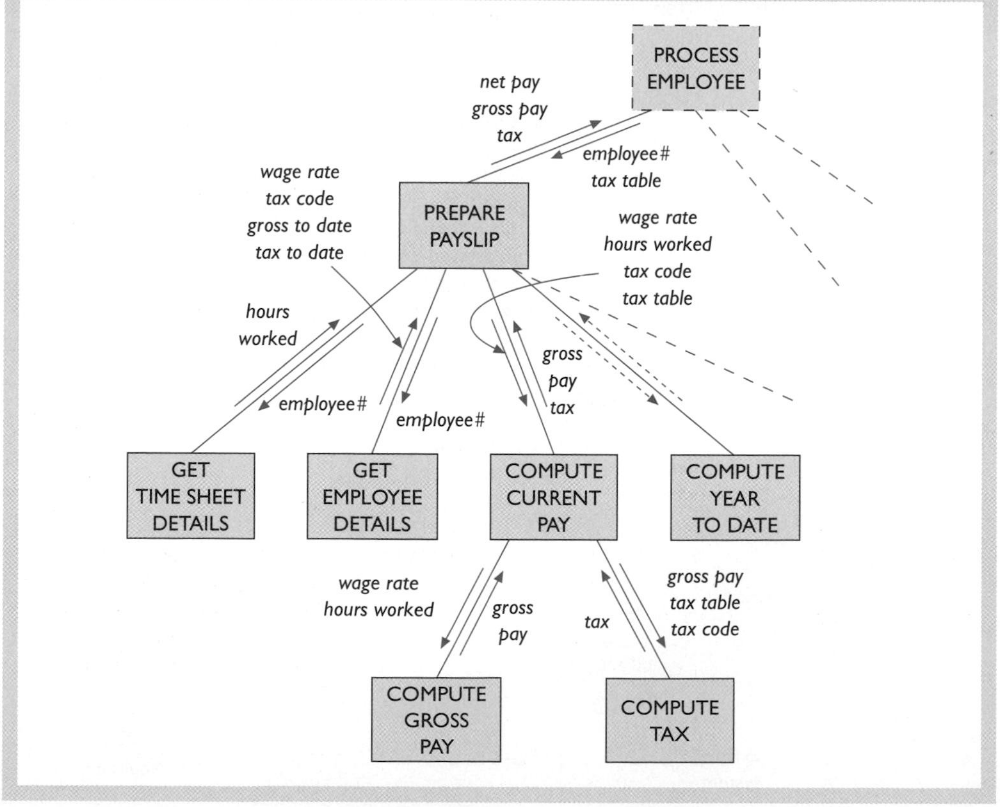

The development of program specifications is facilitated by the structured tools used so far. Programs are regarded as being composed of various modules. These program modules should be constructed so that each performs a single independent function, is independently testable and leads to code that is easy to understand and amend at a later date if necessary. The modular design should also facilitate the addition of extra modules if needed later and so aid the flexibility of the system. Connections between **modules** can be illustrated with a **structure chart**. These terms will now be explained. An example of part of a structure chart and a module specification can be seen in Figures 15.2 and 15.3.

Modules

A module contains a set of executable instructions for performing some process. At the design stage, these instructions may be specified using structured English or decision tables. At a later stage, this specification will be converted into program instructions in the chosen programming language.

Figure 15.3 **A module specification for the input/process/output for the PREPARE PAYSLIP process**

SYSTEM	PAYROLL PROCESS
MODULE NAME	PREPARE PAYSLIP
AUTHOR	J. SMITH
DATE	03/07/2004
MODULE CALLS	GET TIME SHEET DETAILS
	GET EMPLOYEE DETAILS
	COMPUTE CURRENT PAY
	COMPUTE YEAR TO DATE
	: : : :
	: : : :
MODULE IS CALLED BY	PROCESS EMPLOYEE
MODULE INPUTS	*employee#*
	tax table
MODULE OUTPUTS	*gross pay*
	tax
	net pay
PROCESS	**DO** GET TIME SHEET DETAILS
	DO GET EMPLOYEE DETAILS
	DO COMPUTE CURRENT
	SET *net pay = gross pay − tax*
	DO COMPUTE YEAR TO DATE
	: : : :
	: : : :

Data may be passed from one module to another. This is akin to being passed from one data process to another in a data flow diagram. In Figure 15.2, part of a set of interconnected modules handling a payroll process is shown. Each module is named, and the data flows between modules are illustrated.

The chart shows that the module PREPARE PAYSLIP requires that four other modules be executed. These are GET TIME SHEET DETAILS, GET EMPLOYEE DETAILS, COMPUTE CURRENT PAY and COMPUTE YEAR TO DATE. The module COMPUTE CURRENT PAY is said to be called by the module PREPARE PAYSLIP. COMPUTE CURRENT PAY itself calls COMPUTE GROSS PAY and COMPUTE TAX. The inputs and outputs from any module are shown entering or leaving the module box. Needless to say, all the data inputs and outputs will be in the data dictionary.

A module is independently specified in a module specification as illustrated in Figure 15.3. This is sometimes called an **input/process/output (IPO) chart**. The module specification, together with the data dictionary entries, is sufficient on its own for the programmer to write code. It is not necessary when coding a module to have any understanding of the other modules in the system or to have them fitting together.

This is very different from traditional programming methods, where monolithic code would be produced. The integration between functions then allowed programmers to produce a code that was very efficient in its use of central processor time. However, programs were difficult to understand, and bugs were frequently time-consuming to find and correct. Alteration of the code at a later stage, for example to introduce an additional function, might lead to unpredicted effects elsewhere in the program. It soon came to be the case that over 50% of the cost of a project over its life cycle was concerned with debugging, amending and generally maintaining software.

Central processing power is now cheap. It is not necessary to produce monolithic code designed to be efficient in its use of computing power. Rather, the aims have been to maximize flexibility so that programs are easy to alter, to enable programmers to produce code that is readily understandable once written and to ensure that addition of new functions is straightforward. The programming task as a consequence becomes more predictable. This is one of the advantages of the structured approach – the programming task is more easily controlled (and, incidentally, more easily costed). As will be seen in Section 15.1.2, data flow diagrams can be translated directly to produce interconnected modules.

Structure charts

The structure chart, part of an example of which is shown in Figure 15.2, is a diagrammatic representation of the way that modules are connected. For each module, it shows what data is input and output and what other modules call it or are called by it. There is no more information (in fact considerably less) in a structure chart than in the set of module specifications. However, the structure chart does give a picture of the system that is easy to understand. Frequently, the data flows between modules are omitted for the sake of clarity. The structure chart is hierarchical. The use of hierarchical charts together with input/process/output specifications is called the **HIPO (hierarchical input/process/output) technique.**

Looking at Figure 15.3, it can be seen that the module PREPARE PAYSLIP calls up the four modules GET TIME SHEET DETAILS, GET EMPLOYEE DETAILS, COMPUTE CURRENT PAY and COMPUTE YEAR TO DATE in that order. These will each be specified independently. Figure 15.2 shows these as occurring in order from left to right. This is the implied sequence of execution of modules.

Corresponding to the three basic structures of structured English:

sequential (DO A, DO B . . .)

decision (IF ⟨condition⟩

       THEN DO A

       ELSE DO B)

repetition (REPEAT A

       UNTIL ⟨condition⟩)

there are notational variants in the structure chart. These are illustrated in Figure 15.4.

    Each module is normally considered to call its submodules and execute or perform them from left to right, as shown in Figure 15.4(a). Each submodule may itself call submodules and is not considered to have been executed until all its submodules have been executed. This order is shown in Figure 15.5.

    Wherever a decision has to be made to execute one module rather than another, this is indicated by a diamond placed at the connection point, as in Figure 15.4(b).

Figure 15.4 **The relation between structure charts and structured English:
(a) sequence; (b) decision; (c) repetition**

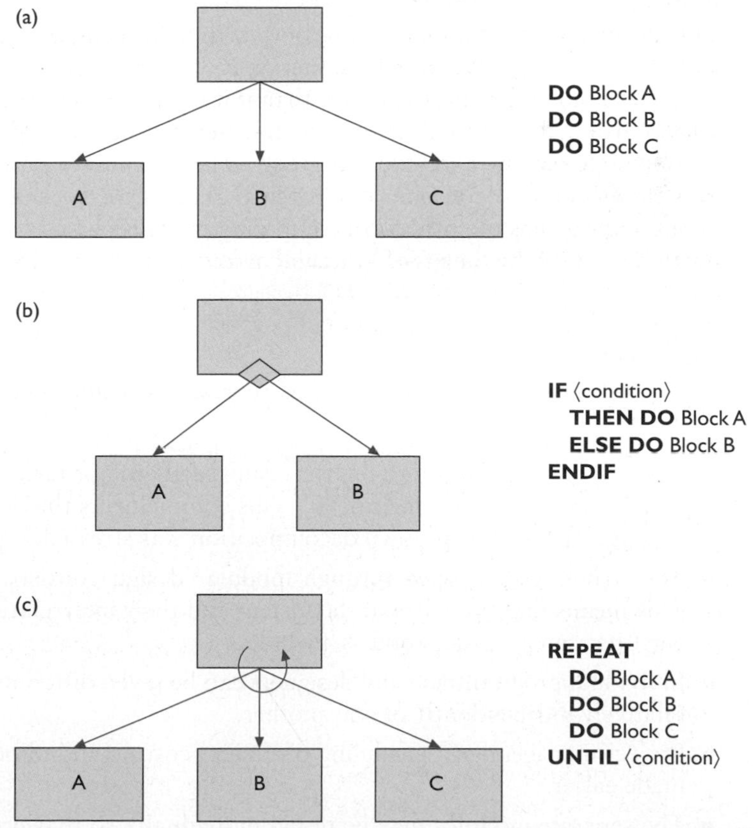

Figure 15.5 Order of module calling in a structure chart

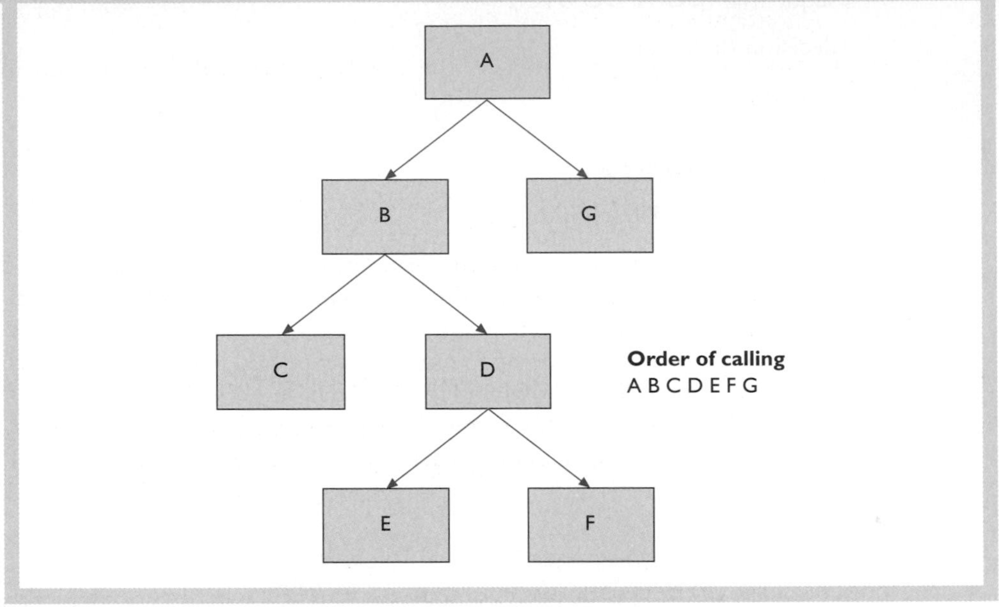

Order of calling
A B C D E F G

For instance, a part of a module dealing with processing a stock transaction will carry out different procedures if the transaction is an increment to stock (receipt of a delivery corresponding to a purchase order) than if it is a decrement (dispatch corresponding to a sales order). The parent module will test the transaction to determine its type.

A module may be executed repeatedly. This will be the case with batch transaction processing, where each one of a batch is treated in the same way. For instance, in preparing payslips the process of computing pay is repeated for each employee. This iteration is shown by means of a circular arrow, as in Figure 15.4(c).

15.1.2 Modular design

The advantages of modular design as represented using hierarchical structure charts and module specifications are:

- Easier design of programs: analysts can specify major tasks at a high level and later break these down into their detail. This complements the development of the analysis stage, in which top-down decomposition was stressed.

- The structure developed through modular design consists of manageable chunks. This means that the parts of the system and their interrelations are represented in a way that can be understood as a whole.

- Individual programmers and designers can be given different modules and can work relatively independently of one another.

- Project management, scheduling of design, costing and allocation of manpower are made easier.

- The separate modules may be tested individually so that errors can be located precisely and easily corrected.

- The final system will be modular. Individual modules can be 'lifted out', altered or inserted easily with the confidence that their effect on other modules is specified by input and output data and the processes that occur.

In order that design may achieve these ends, it is crucial that modules are loosely coupled and cohesive.

Coupling

The idea of coupling was introduced in Chapter 1, where the degree of subsystem coupling was defined in terms of the extent to which a change in the state of one subsystem led to a change in the state of another. Modular decoupling is similar in concept. As data is what passes between modules, it is data connections that are important.

Two modules are less coupled:

- the fewer the number of types of data item passed from one to the other;
- the less they share the same data from a data store.

A module that is only loosely coupled to other modules has a simple interface and is therefore easy to design, code, change and test independently.

Cohesion

Modules, as well as being loosely coupled, should be cohesive. This is harder to define. A module is more cohesive if:

- It consists of one single function, such as **COMPUTE GROSS PAY**.
- It consists of more than one function, but each is executed in sequence: for example, **PREPARE PAYSLIP** consists of four sequentially executed modules.
- It performs a set of independent actions that are linked by being performed at the same time. Examples of this are initialization and termination routines concerned with data structures used by a set of processes.

The advantages of modular design as stated can only be fully realized with modules that are loosely coupled to one another yet highly cohesive internally.

Kismet case study 15.1

This part of the Kismet case study introduces the development of the structure chart and module specification. The level 1 data flow diagram for the Kismet order-processing system is given again in Figure 15.6(a) and the level 2 breakdown in Figure 15.7(a). These will be used to generate a (partial) structure chart for the Kismet system.

The main part of the level 1 data flow diagram suggests that there are three separate functions. The first deals with the generation of approved orders. The second processes stock transactions to update stock records and produce dispatch notes. Finally, invoices are made up and dispatched. This can be seen in the simple structure chart of Figure 15.6(b).

The structure chart dealing with the generation of approved orders is shown in Figure 15.7(b). As is common in the production of hierarchical structure charts, the data flows between the various modules are omitted. This is usually done to simplify the chart. However, there is another reason. The structure is prepared before the individual module specification, and it is at this point that the analyst's attention is devoted to the

515

Figure 15.6 (a) A data flow diagram of Kismet's order-processing system; (b) part of a structure chart for the Kismet order-processing system

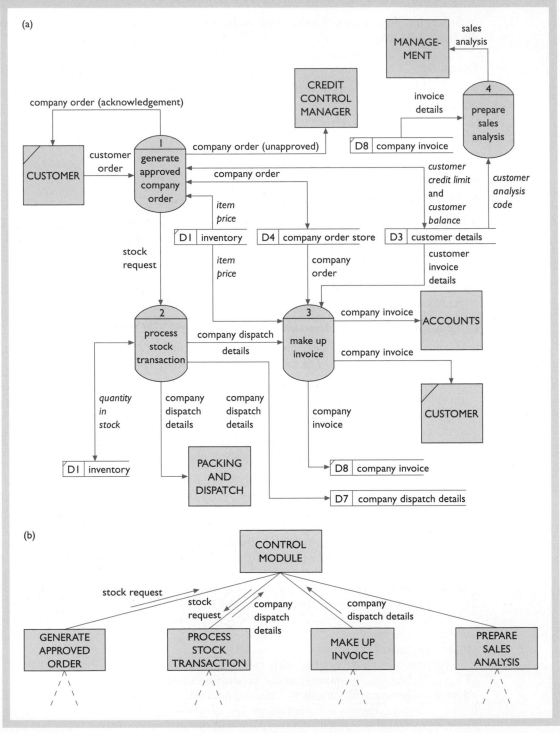

Figure 15.7 (a) The data flow diagram for the generation of an approved order;
(b) a structure chart for the generation of an approved order

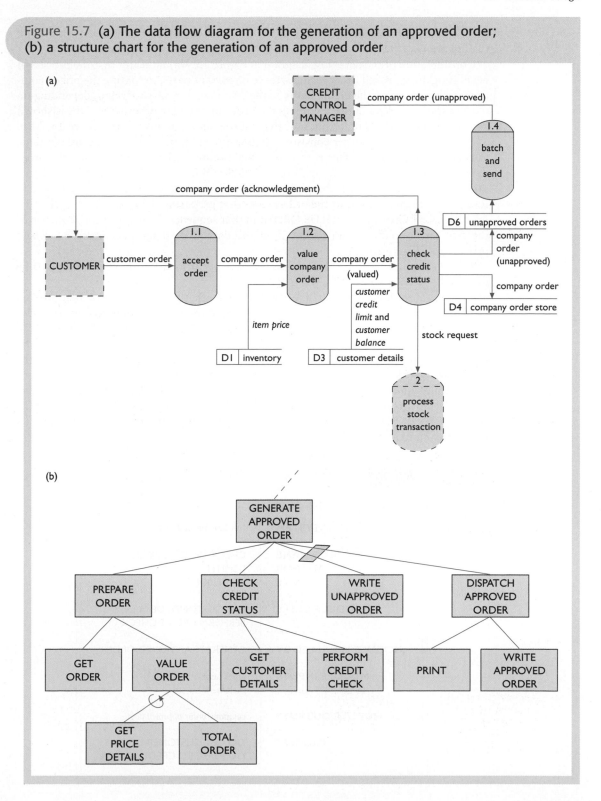

precise description of the data flows. Structure charts are then first derived without all the data flows.

Consideration of the data flow diagram in Figure 15.7(a) indicates that the process of generating an approved order includes three important parts: preparing the priced company order, checking the credit status of the customer for the order and, depending on the result of the credit check, handling the order in one way or another. This is shown by the second-level decomposition of the tasks in the structure chart (Figure 15.7(b)).

Preparing the priced order consists of two tasks. First, the order details are obtained through keyboard entry. This is shown by the module **GET ORDER**. Second, the order details are then used to value the order (**VALUE ORDER**). This itself consists of two tasks. The first is to obtain the price details for each item ordered, and the second is to calculate the total value of the order. Note that preparing the order involves the two processes **GET ORDER** and **VALUE ORDER** in that sequence. This is just the sequence of the two corresponding data processes in the data flow diagram – process 1.1 and process 1.2 (Figure 15.7(a)).

The next process in the chain, process 1.3, is performed by the next module to be executed – **CHECK CREDIT STATUS**.

Finally, depending on the outcome of the credit check, the order is stored (unapproved) in store D6 or printed for dispatch to the customer and stored (approved) in store D4. This corresponds to the alternatives shown on the structure chart (Figure 15.7(b)).

The approved order is also needed by the module concerned with processing the stock transaction. It is passed, minus its price details, as the output 'stock request' of the **GENERATE APPROVED ORDER** module via the control module.

A sample of a module specification is given in Figure 15.8. The data inputs and outputs will be defined in the data dictionary. Note that the position of the module **CHECK CREDIT STATUS** in the hierarchy chart is determined by identifying the module that calls it, and the modules that it calls.

Figure 15.8 **A module specification for CHECK CREDIT DETAIL**

SYSTEM	ORDER PROCESSING
MODULE NAME	CHECK CREDIT STATUS
AUTHOR	J. SMITH
DATE	03/07/2004
MODULE CALLS	GET CUSTOMER DETAILS PERFORM CREDIT CHECK
MODULE IS CALLED BY	GENERATE APPROVED ORDER
MODULE INPUTS	*order total* *customer#*
MODULE OUTPUTS	*company order approval flag*
PROCESS	**DO** GET CUSTOMER DETAILS **DO** PERFORM CREDIT CHECK

15.1.3 Summary so far

The way a data flow diagram is used for the preparation of a structure chart can be summarized as follows:

1. View the diagram to establish whether the data processes fall into groups, each associated with a type of process. View the resulting grouped collections of data processes to establish the key functions in each group. If each group has only a single data process in it, this is straightforward.

2. Decompose these functions to obtain modules that are highly cohesive and loosely coupled. Note that the sequence of data processes will indicate the left-to-right ordering of modules. Data flows that are conditional on a test performed in a data process will correspond to alternative module selections. This can be indicated using the diamond symbol. Lower-level data flow diagrams are to be used in this decomposition.

3. Now specify each module separately ensuring that named data items and data collections are entered in the data dictionary and that the data produced by major modules corresponds to the data being passed between processes in the data flow diagrams.

This gives a general idea of the development of a hierarchical structure chart and module specification. Do not form the impression that once the data flow diagrams have been developed the production of the modular structure chart is a mechanical task. It is not. The analysis of high-level diagrams can often be difficult. Most important is the realization that to discover key functions and to decompose these into their constituents, each of which performs a single logical function that is translatable into a cohesive module, requires more than an uncritical reading of a data flow diagram. It is necessary for the analyst to obtain a deep appreciation of the system and the functions it performs. Although structured methods attempt to replace the art of design by the science of engineering, there is still a place for creative understanding.

15.1.4 Data store design

During systems analysis and design, a conceptual data model of the organization was developed. This was based on modelling entities and their relationships. Later, attributes of the entities were established. A normalized entity model was then developed to third normal form. The resulting normalized entities have been checked by deriving functional entity models to ensure that the various processes can be served with the data that they need. During systems design, a decision will have been made as to whether to service the future data needs of the organization via a database approach using a database management system or via an application-led, file-based approach. The considerations involved in this choice were covered in Chapter 14. Either way, detailed design of the data store will be required, and this will be aided by the normalized data model.

File-based systems

In general, a file-based approach will have been chosen if there is little or no common data usage between applications and there is a need for fast transaction processing. The analyst will need to design record layouts. This involves specifying the names of the fields in each record, their type (for example, text or numeric) and their length. Records may be of fixed or variable length. In the latter case, this is either because fields are allowed to vary in length or because some fields are repeated. Record structures can become quite complicated if groups of fields are repeated within already repeating groups of fields.

As well as record design, the storage organization and access for each file must be decided. This will determine the speed of access to individual records and the ease with which records can be added and deleted within the file. The most common types of storage organization are sequential, indexed, indexed-sequential, random storage with hashing, lists and inverted files. Different file organizations have different characteristics with respect to ease and speed of data storage and retrieval. Depending on the type of application, the most appropriate organization is chosen. The topic of files, file organization and file design was covered extensively in Chapter 8 and the reader is referred there for further information.

The analyst will need to specify suitable backing-store hardware. This is likely to be optical or magnetic disk-based unless the system is concerned with archiving data, in which case magnetic tape might prove a cheaper option. In order to select appropriate hardware, the analyst must take into account the number of files and within each file the number of records and the storage required for each, the file organization chosen, the response time required and likely future developments, especially in terms of increases in size. These characteristics will allow the analyst to calculate the total storage requirements and to specify appropriate hardware.

Database systems

It is likely that a database approach will have been selected if the same data is shared between many applications, if there is a large degree of integration of data and if flexible reporting and enquiry facilities are needed.

The analyst will use the conceptual data model as a guide to selecting the appropriate database model. Relational database systems allow great flexibility in the storage and retrieval of data. Although their relatively slow access times and high storage overheads can be a disadvantage, current developments in both hardware and relational database management systems are diminishing these drawbacks.

Relational databases have now established themselves as the most popular choice for database solutions. Relational database management software is usually accompanied by sophisticated query/fourth-generation languages, interfaces with spreadsheet models and networking facilities with other relational databases. Pre-written template software produced by fourth-generation languages for standard business functions, especially accounting, can also be purchased and tailored to the needs of the organization. An example is ORACLE, a relational database system, with SQL.

Databases, database management systems and data models were covered extensively in Chapter 8 on database systems. The reader is referred to this chapter for a fuller account of the terms and concepts used in this section.

Provided that the database management system intended for purchase is known, the analyst can begin to design the **conceptual schema**. This is an overall logical view of the data model cast in terms of the data definition language of the database management system. It will contain integrity and authorization rules. In the case of a relational model, this will be a relatively straightforward translation of the normalized entity model. Each entity and each relationship will become a table. Each attribute of an entity will become a column in the table corresponding to the entity. The derivation of a conceptual model for hierarchical and network systems is less straightforward. This is partly because the notion of a genuine conceptual schema does not strictly apply.

For each user of the database an external schema is defined. This is part of the database that a user is entitled to access in order to carry out a function. The analyst will have determined the data needs of the users for their various tasks during systems analysis. This can now be accommodated in the database design. The access will correspond to certain entities, attributes of those entities and paths through the database via relationships.

The analyst must also design the internal schema. This describes how the database is physically stored. It will make reference to record ordering, pointers, indexes, block sizes and access paths. Good internal schema design will ensure an efficient database. Unlike conceptual and external schemas, an internal schema makes reference to physical aspects of the database. The way that external schemas relate to the conceptual schema, and the way this in turn relates to the storage schema, is specified in terms of external/conceptual and conceptual/internal mappings.

The design of the database must proceed in tandem with the module design as the programs specified need access to the database. There are therefore intimate relationships between the data flow diagrams, data models, structure charts, module specifications, database schemas and data dictionaries. For a large organization, there will be many data flow diagrams. The entity model may have several *hundred* entity types. It is a complicated task coordinating the interrelations between the various elements in analysis and design. **Computer-aided systems engineering (CASE)** software packages help in this. They also semi-automate the design process. See Chapter 17 for a longer discussion.

As in the case of file-based systems, the analyst will need to estimate sizes and types of hardware required.

Kismet case study 15.2

We can now consider the data store design for Kismet. The analyst has decided to develop a relational database system for Kismet. Although the organization carries out transaction processing, one of the major requirements of the new system is that it will be able to provide flexible enquiry and reporting facilities. This, together with the stable and integrated nature of the model, suggests that a relational database is appropriate.

The analyst will convert the fully normalized conceptual data model to produce the relational conceptual schema. Part of this schema is shown in Figure 15.9(a). It is defined within a typical relational data definition language (DDL). This definition should be compared with the corresponding normalized entity model for Kismet developed in Chapter 13, which covered data analysis and modelling. As can be seen, the derivation is straightforward. The fields *order#* and *item#* are character fields, each composed of six characters. The fields are not allowed to be empty for any row of the table. The *item quantity* is an integer.

One of the functions required by Kismet is online enquiry of the status of any customer order. Given a customer *order#*, it is required that the contents of the order and the items and quantities dispatched against this order be accessible. This is defined as a view or external schema in Figure 15.9(b). The fields selected and tables accessible are specified. The relational join ensures that an *order#* is followed through the three tables. Once again, the reader should compare this with the conceptual schema and the entity model developed in Chapter 13.

▶

Figure 15.9 Conceptual and external schema definitions for Kismet: (a) part of a relational conceptual schema for Kismet; (b) an external schema definition for a user making enquiries on the status of customer orders at Kismet

```
(a)
CREATE TABLE    ORDER DETAIL    (order# (CHAR (6), NONULL
                                 item# (CHAR (6), NONULL
                                 item quantity (INTEGER))

CREATE TABLE    ORDER           (order# (CHAR (6), NONULL
                                 (order date (DATE)
                                 customer# (CHAR (8))

(b)
DEFINE VIEW    ORDER ENQUIRY

     AS SELECT        ORDER.customer#, ORDER.order#, ORDER.order date,
                      ORDER DETAIL.item#, ORDER DETAIL.item quantity,
                      DISPATCH DETAIL.dispatch#, DISPATCH DETAIL.item#,
                      DISPATCH DETAIL.dispatch quantity

     FROM             ORDER, ORDER DETAIL, DISPATCH DETAIL

     WHERE                ORDER.order# = ORDER DETAIL.order#
                      AND ORDER DETAIL.order# = DISPATCH DETAIL.order#

     ORDER BY         customer#
```

15.1.5 Input/output design

There are two main aspects of input/output design. One is the specification of the hardware. The other is the design of the user–machine interface.

In the specification of hardware, many decisions will have already been determined by the data input methods broadly outlined in systems design, by the choices between batch and online systems and between centralized and distributed systems. The analyst will need to determine the number and range of input and output devices required in line with these decisions.

User interface design

The design of the user interface is a crucial aspect of program design. Most programs require data entry screens and screen or printed output. This will be controlled by software. However, design of this interface will not normally fall out of data flow diagrams but should be determined by an understanding of the types of user, their requirements and their levels of ability – in short, a model of the user.

The following factors have to be considered, along with a model of the user, in interface input design.

Screen design

The format and presentation of material on the monitor screen will affect the way that a user interacts with the system. Bad layout will result in errors of input, user fatigue and a tendency towards user rejection of the system.

Screen presentations should ensure that the material presented on screen is relevant, is provided in a logical manner and is simple and coherent. If data is to be input from documents, then the screen should mirror the layout of the document as far as possible.

Screens can be presented to the user in the form of:

- **Menus:** to allow simple selection.
- **Form filling:** where a cursor jumps from field to field on the screen waiting for data input at each field.
- **Interactive commands:** where a user keys in individual commands and data.

Controls

Users make mistakes. This occurs in transcription. Also, the source data from which they work can contain errors. Controls need to be built into the user interface to cover input. Controls were dealt with extensively in Chapter 9. The major controls over input are:

- **Batch controls:** such as sequencing, control totals, hash totals, listings for visual comparison.
- **Software controls:** such as check digits, master-file checks and echoes, range checks and layout checks.
- **Screen design:** sensible screen design prevents the errors already stated.
- **Codes:** the coding of items, accounts, and other entities can be accomplished to cut down data entry costs and at the same time ensure greater accuracy.

User guidance

Novice users will be unable to sit in front of a computer screen and achieve much without considerable guidance and help from the system. In particular, users should always be capable of ascertaining where they are in a system – this is particularly important deep into a menu structure – and what the purpose is of the present facility. Even expert users may 'become lost' in a complex system and need guidance.

Help facilities should be available at all times to the user. There should be general help on the system and how to use it. Contextual help is also important. This is where pressing the 'help' button yields help based on the command that was used prior to the call for help. As well as aiding legitimate users, well-designed help systems unfortunately aid the unauthorized user in trespass.

Where a common entry is needed the system may suggest a default or at least a type of entry. For example:

DATE - - - - - - - -

is much less helpful than

DATE *DD/MM/YYYY*

or

DATE *04/07/2004*

where the current date is presented as default.

Error messages

Error messages should always be helpful in identifying the error. Messages such as 'UNIDENTIFIED COMMAND' or 'PARAMETER NOT RECOGNIZED' are unhelpful, although not as bad as 'ERROR 243 @45'. A helpful error message should not only analyse the error but also provide help to the user in recovery; for example, 'NUMERIC ACCOUNT CODE NOT EXPECTED. ALL ACCOUNT CODES BEGIN WITH A CHARACTER. PLEASE TRY AGAIN (FOR LIST OF ACCEPTABLE ACCOUNT CODES PRESS FUNCTION KEY 1)'.

Response time

Generally, response times to commands should be short. Lengthy response times, particularly for regular users, lead to irritation, errors and non-acceptance of the system. For complicated tasks and requests, though, especially with inexperienced users, rapid response times may increase errors and prevent learning.

Given all these considerations, the analyst will design the user interface with a model of the user in mind. Users can be categorized in several ways that affect the design. Three important categories are:

1. **Casual *v*. regular users:** Regular users become more knowledgeable about the system through use. They are also more likely to be provided with training if interaction with the computer system occupies much of their job. For such users, fast response times, interactive commands and defaults are important.

2. **Passive *v*. interactive users:** Interactive users are those who either develop systems or build decision support models. They are liable to have or want to have the facility to navigate around the system. Those responsible for using the system to answer online enquiries also often fall within the category of interactive user. These users rely heavily on a systematic knowledge of command structures. Passive users are best served with menus and form filling, which restrict their area of choice. Data input personnel fall into this category.

3. **Novice *v*. expert users:** This category is not the same as casual *v*. regular users. For instance, it is possible for both a novice and an expert to be a casual user of the system. Expert casual users are likely to require targeted but unobtrusive help facilities, whereas novices will need a complete step-by-step set of screen instructions.

The design of the user interface is one aspect of the design of the total system involving the user. **Human–computer interaction,** covered in a previous chapter, locates issues in user interface design within the much broader framework of the function of the system and the place of technology and people within this.

Reports and input documents

The analyst will also be responsible for designing documents that are used for input and for reports produced as output by the system. Many of the same considerations apply as for user interface design. Input documents should match screens as far as possible. Printed reports should always be designed with the aim of logical presentation and clarity in mind.

Kismet case study 15.3

Kismet users fall into a number of categories. There are data input personnel such as those concerned with order entry, payments received, purchase orders, and so on. These will be regular users passively responding to forms as presented on the screen. There will also be staff dealing with and tracing particular orders, dealing with customer enquiries and the like. These may be the same people as the order entry staff, although they need different and more flexible skills.

Middle management will use the system for monitoring and predicting the performance of the company. For example, the sales manager will wish to draw off reports of sales by customer type, by geographical area, by type of item, by date and by other parameters. This user is not likely to be a regular user of the computer system. Other members of the sales and accounts departments involved with sales and profit forecasting will interactively use and develop spreadsheet models fed by actual data. These will become expert interactive users.

An example of a specification of a form to appear on a screen is given in Figure 15.10. The customer order entry is carried out by a regular user of the system. A number of points should be noted and would be included along with the specification. The system generates the date, time and order number. This not only saves time but is done for reasons of security and control. The data entry clerk is presented with a customer number data entry field. The customer name is then displayed as an error control. The delivery address is extracted from the customer account details and displayed on screen, but the

Figure 15.10 A screen layout design for customer order entry

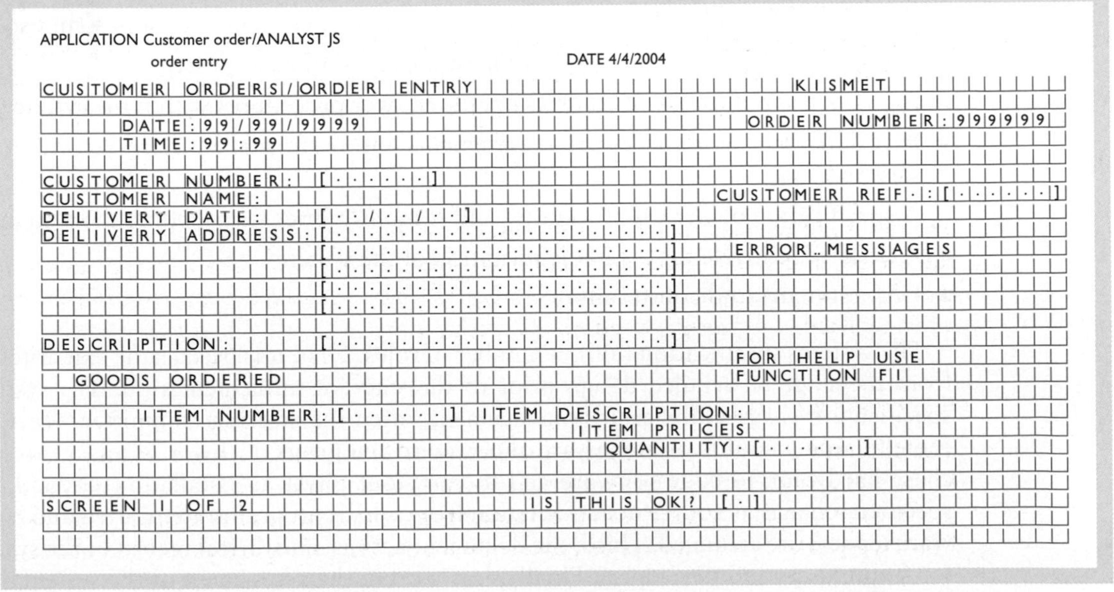

```
APPLICATION Customer order/ANALYST JS
          order entry                              DATE 4/4/2004
CUSTOMER ORDERS//ORDER ENTRY                              KISMET
      DATE:99/99/9999                  ORDER NUMBER:999999
      TIME:99:99
CUSTOMER NUMBER:[[·····]]
CUSTOMER NAME:                         CUSTOMER REF.:[[······]]
DELIVERY DATE:   [[··/··/··]]
DELIVERY ADDRESS:[[···················]]
                 [[···················]]   ERROR MESSAGES
                 [[···················]]
                 [[···················]]
                 [[···················]]
DESCRIPTION:     [[···················]]
                                           FOR HELP USE
   GOODS ORDERED                           FUNCTION F1
   ITEM NUMBER:[[······]] ITEM DESCRIPTION:
                          ITEM PRICES
                          QUANTITY·[[······]]

SCREEN 1 OF 2            IS THIS OK? [[·]]
```

operator has the ability to overwrite this. The items ordered are entered by item number with a flashback description check. This screen is one of two. The second screen would allow more items to be ordered. The data entry clerk has the option to accept or reject the entered data as displayed on the screen. Various other checks would be performed. For example, the data would be validated as being possible: for example, not 31 June. The user is a regular user, so no on-screen help is given. If help is required, particularly as a result of error messages, this can be called up as described using keyboard function F1.

There will be a large number of such layout designs specifying the complete user interface. The analyst will have designed these with the different types of user in mind.

15.2 Systems specification

Detailed design results in a **systems specification**. This is a comprehensive document describing the system as it is to be produced. There is no agreed format for this specification, but it is likely to include the following:

- An executive summary: this provides a quick summary of the major points in the specification.
- A description of the proposed system and especially its objectives. Flow block diagrams and data flow diagrams can be used. The work to be carried out by the system and the various user functions should be covered.
- A complete specification of:
  - Programs: these will include module specifications and structure charts, together with test data.
  - Input: this will include specimen source documents, screen layouts, menu structures and control procedures.
  - Output: this will include specimen output reports, contents of listings, and so on.
  - Data storage: this is the specification of file and database structure.
- A detailed specification of controls operating over procedures within the system.
- A specification of all hardware requirements and performance characteristics to be satisfied.
- A specification of clerical procedures and responsibilities surrounding the system.
- A detailed schedule for the implementation of the system.
- Cost estimates and constraints.

The systems specification fulfils a number of roles. First, it is used as the exit criterion from the stage of detailed design prior to the stage of implementation. The systems specification is agreed by senior management, often the steering committee. Once accepted, large amounts of money are allocated to the project. This is necessary to purchase hardware, to code software and to carry out physical installation. Second, the specification acts as source documentation from which programs are written and hardware tenders are arranged. Third, the document acts as a historical record of the system for future users and developers. Finally, it is used in the assessment of the system once the system is being used. Does the system meet its response times? Is it built according to design? These are examples of questions that can only be answered in consultation with the systems specification.

15.3 Implementation

Once the systems specification has been agreed, its implementation can begin. This is the stage when things are done rather than analysed or designed. There are various separate but related tasks to be accomplished. Programs are written and tested, hardware is acquired and installed, staff are trained, the system is tested, and historic data from the old manual system or computer system is loaded into the files or database. Many of these tasks are carried out simultaneously. It is important that they are all completed before changeover to the new system is effected.

15.3.1 Program development and testing

One of the outputs of the detailed physical design stage was a set of program specifications. These are used by programmers as the blueprint from which to write the software. Program development and testing is one of the most costly phases in the systems life cycle. Historically, it was also the phase most likely to be over budget and completed late. Early programming techniques compounded these difficulties. The software produced was often unreliable and costly to debug and maintain.

Structured techniques, though, have produced a set of specifications for cohesive decoupled modules. These reduce programming complexity and ensure reliability and easy maintenance of software. Each module can be coded and tested separately. Structured analysis and design facilitates structured programming.

Structured programming allows only a small number of logical coding structures. In particular, the **GOTO** command, so popular with novice programmers, is disallowed. The use of **GOTO** commands, which direct a change in the order of program statement execution, leads to logical spaghetti in program execution. It becomes extremely difficult to understand and debug programs once written. The coding structures allowed correspond to those in structured English. It is common for programming languages to use instructions such as **REPEAT . . . UNTIL** and **IF . . . THEN . . . ELSE . . .** statements. Blocks of code are nested within these logical structures in the program. Internally, the blocks themselves will exhibit the same allowable logical structure (see Figure 15.11). The other main feature of structured program code is that although variables (containing data) are passed in and out of a module, all variables used only within that module have no meaning outside it. In structured programming, the variables are declared in the code. This corresponds to structured module specifications and structure charts, where data flows are stated explicitly.

Program testing is of critical importance in the development of software. It is one of the tasks of the analyst to specify test plans for the software. Individual modules are tested as they are written. This ensures that separately they perform to specification. Modules are then tested grouped together. This enables an assessment of their successful integration to be made. Finally, the entire set of programs is tested.

It is difficult to state what constitutes an adequately tested program. For instance, a program may perform perfectly well with standard data input, but how does it perform with erroneous data – a negative-value sale for instance? How will the program react to an unusual set of input data? Much program code is devised to deal with these situations.

Figure 15.11 Allowable coding structures and their relation to structured English

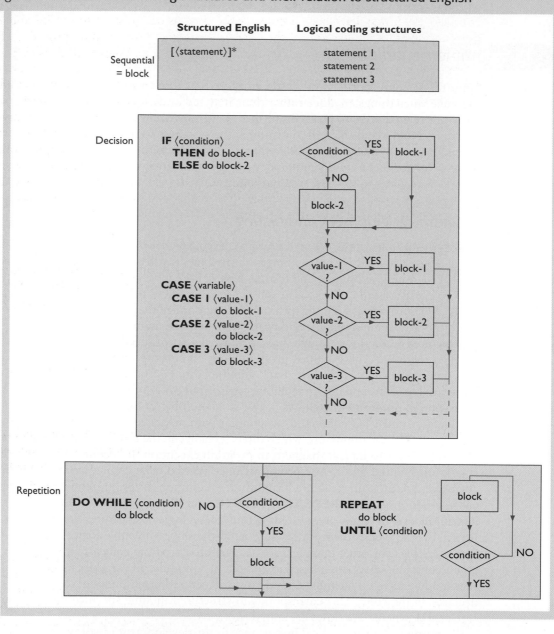

It has been estimated that from 50 to 80% of program code is devoted to error handling of one sort or another. There are a number of types of testing:

- **Random test data** can be generated, processed and the accuracy of processing checked.
- **Logical test data** may be developed using the logical limits for acceptable and unacceptable data.
- **Typical test data** assesses the performance of the software using actual past data.

It has been assumed that programs are to be developed especially for the system using conventional high-level languages and structured techniques. There are other approaches. For example, it may have been decided at the systems design stage to opt for applications packages for some or all of the data-processing and information provision. The benefits and limitations of this approach were covered in Chapter 3. A decision to adopt a package will have been taken on the basis of an analysis of the organization's requirements and the existence of the appropriate software package. It is unlikely that this software can be just loaded into the system and run. It is usual for the package to require tailoring to meet the needs of the organization. This is not to say that programs must be written. Rather, the package will have routines already available for customization. Examples are the design of reports, the determination of an account-coding structure and the setting of password controls. Alternatively, it may have been decided at an earlier stage to adopt a prototyping approach to software and systems development using a fourth-generation language. Prototyping and the use of fourth-generation languages were covered in Chapters 3 and 7.

Extreme programming

Extreme programming, sometimes called **XP** (not to be confused with Windows XP), is a methodology for software design and development initiated in the late 1990s. It stresses customer involvement and emphasizes success through customer satisfaction. Extreme programming is most applicable for projects where

- systems requirements are expected to change regularly;
- systems requirements are often difficult to specify completely in advance;
- systems need to be developed quickly;
- systems are relatively small.

Extreme programming projects involve small groups of developers (at least 2 and typically no more than 12) together with selected managers (customers). The smallness of the development group is the key to its success as it facilitates communication and feedback. Use of the methodology, though iterative, can be classified in four stages:

Planning

During this phase short **user stories** (often each a few lines of text) are developed for each of the requirements of the system. These are produced by the customers and are accompanied by a specification of an acceptance test – a test which will determine whether the code when produced performs what is required of it. These user stories are different from the large formal systems specifications developed in some methodologies, e.g. structured systems analysis and design. A group of user stories (e.g. containing 70 stories) forms a release plan which is used to schedule the rest of the project. This release plan may go through several iterations.

Design

During systems design great emphasis is placed on simplicity. Functionality is not added until and unless it is scheduled. Care is taken to name classes of objects and methods consistently. Generally, object approaches are used in design. These may be facilitated by techniques such as the use of Class, Responsibility and Collaboration

(CRC) cards, each of which captures for each class of objects the responsibility it fulfils and the classes with which it interacts. Design sessions involve verbal simulations of message passing between objects and investigating processes. There is not generally a formal document design coming out of this phase but rather a deeper understanding, amongst the small team of developers, of the ways to implement the user stories in code.

Coding

During the coding process the customer is always available to clarify any questions on functionality required. The test code is developed first, before producing the main code, thus emphasizing the focus of the development. All code is produced to agreed formal standards. A key feature of the programming is the use of **pair programming**. All code is produced by programmers working in pairs, each programmer side by side on the same computer. One of the pair concentrates only on the detailed implementation of the code and has control of the keyboard and mouse. The other programmer, the observer, concentrates only on tactical issues (e.g. syntax checking, defects) and, importantly, on strategic issues about how the code fits together in the larger picture of the system being developed. The programmers frequently switch roles. Pair programming yields results almost as quickly as two programmers working separately. The main advantages are in terms of the reliability and customer satisfaction of the software produced, together with the sense of common ownership and a lack of programmer alienation. Code when produced is held in a central repository and can and should be accessed and amended by the pair to ensure integration with code produced by other pairs.

Testing

Unlike traditional methods where testing is a function that is performed *after* code has been produced, within extreme programming the development of unit test code occurs *before* the program code is developed. This is viewed as essential to the development process. The process of extreme programming also allows for changes to be implemented as the system is developed. This requires reconsideration of unit tests and frequent reintegration using the central repository of code reflecting the sum total state of development. A system is regarded as acceptable when it passes all acceptance tests to the customer's satisfaction.

Extreme programming, as a methodology, is gaining importance where fast development of (relatively) small systems in a dynamic environment is required. It is often linked with the systems development approach called Rapid Applications Development (RAD) which is discussed in more detail in Chapter 16.

15.3.2 Hardware acquisition and installation

The characteristics of the hardware required were included in the systems specification. The analyst may have had certain manufacturers of hardware in mind. This is likely to be true if the organization already has a commitment to an existing manufacturer in its current and ongoing systems. In other cases, the hardware specification can be put out to tender and it is up to different suppliers to make contract offers.

Hardware is usually purchased new, although an alternative to purchasing is leasing. This is recommended in circumstances where there are tax concessions to be gained.

Computer rental is sometimes used when extra hardware is needed for peak periods or where the system has a short designated lifespan.

Installation of hardware is costly. It may require building new rooms that are air-conditioned and dust-free. It will almost certainly involve laying data communication and power cables. Physical security such as fire alarms, video monitoring and secure rooms for data file libraries will also be installed.

15.3.3 Training and staff development

Users are the key element in any successful computer system. Their knowledge and understanding will have been tapped during systems investigation and analysis. Models of users will have influenced the user–machine interface design, but unless staff are adequately prepared for the new system it will have little chance of being used effectively. This requires staff training and education.

Education is to be distinguished from training in that the former involves providing staff with a general understanding of the system, the way it functions, its scope and its limitations. They will be informed of how the system can be used to provide information for their needs or carry out processing tasks for them. Training, in contrast, involves the familiarization of staff with the skills necessary to operate the computer system to perform tasks. In either case, there are several approaches:

- Lectures and seminars can be used for instructive overviews. Their advantage is that a large number of staff are reached using one instructor.

- Simulation of the work environment is used for training. This is a costly, though effective, training technique.

- On-the-job training involves supervision of personnel as skills that are progressively more complex are gradually mastered. This is a popular way of training new staff on an existing system.

- Software packages are used for training personnel in applications software. For example, there are tutorial programs for most of the major word-processing packages.

- The information centre should devise training courses for staff involving some, if not all, of these techniques.

Staff training and education need to take account of the abilities of the trainees as well as the tasks for which training is provided. Staff will have different requirements and expectations of training. Insufficient attention to staff development is one certain way of ensuring that an information system will fail.

15.3.4 Data store conversion

The file or database structure will have already been designed. In the case of a database, the conceptual, internal and external schemas were defined using the data definition language of the database management system. An organization will have historic data that must be entered into the files or database of the new computer system before it can be used for the organization's needs.

In the case of computer-held data, this generally involves writing programs that accept data from the old files or database and convert it to the format required for the new system. This data is then written to the new system.

With manual files, the task is more time-consuming. Decisions are made as to what data to transfer. This data is unlikely to be in the format required for input into the new system. It is common for data to be transcribed on to intermediate documentation prior to data entry. Although costly, this minimizes errors in transcription. Careful attention must be paid to control during this conversion. Batch and hash totals can be used in the transfer of accounting data. Balances should be agreed with clients of the system, whether such clients are internal or external to the organization. Listings of input are produced and maintained for later queries and visual inspection.

During data store conversion, the organization is continuing to function as nearly normal as possible. The old data store itself will be changing rather than remaining static. This adds further problems.

15.4   Systems changeover

At some stage, the new computerized system will be brought into operation. How and when this is done will depend on the confidence that management has in its reliability. All systems will have undergone a **systems test** involving the use of the installed software and hardware. However, this is very different from the situation that the system is likely to encounter in practice – peak loading, many users and many users committing errors in interacting with the system.

Four changeover strategies are considered here (see Figure 15.12). They are not mutually exclusive. Each has its benefits and limitations. They have varying degrees of safeguards against the effects of system malfunctions on the organization.

15.4.1 Direct changeover

With direct changeover, the new system is brought into operation in its entirety on a designated date. This has the advantage of being quick but depends heavily on the reliability of the systems design, implementation and testing, and on how the staff were trained. It is not generally recommended, although it may be unavoidable in cases where the system does not replace an existing one.

15.4.2 Parallel approach

The parallel approach, or some version of it, is very common in practice. It can be used when there is a great deal of similarity between the old and the new systems. This similarity needs to exist between inputs and outputs. Both systems are run in parallel until there is enough confidence in the new system to dispense with the old.

Parallel running can take weeks or months. An advantage is that if the new system malfunctions then there is a backup system on which to rely. The output of the old and the new systems can also be compared. If there is any discrepancy, then this can be investigated.

It is easy to stress the advantages of the parallel approach while ignoring its limitations. Staff will be put under enormous pressure if they not only have to use the old system but must also repeat the same operations with an unfamiliar new system. If staff were working near to capacity prior to the introduction of the new system, it is doubtful whether they will be able to handle the extra load. Overtime working and temporary staff are possible solutions, although each carries dangers. In the former

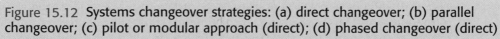

Figure 15.12 **Systems changeover strategies: (a) direct changeover; (b) parallel changeover; (c) pilot or modular approach (direct); (d) phased changeover (direct)**

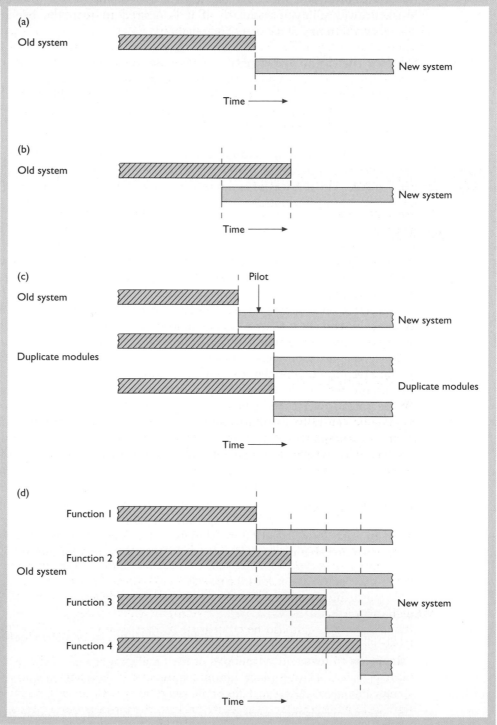

case, staff will not be performing at peak efficiency – not a desirable situation in which to run a new system. In the latter, the temporary staff will need to be trained. Should they be trained to use the old or the new system, or both? These difficulties cannot be brushed away glibly, particularly if it is desired to reap the benefits of parallel changeover in terms of its safety and reliability.

15.4.3 Pilot or modular approach

Some systems can be broken down into several identical and duplicate modules. For instance, an automated point-of-sale and stock-updating system for a supermarket chain will be repeated in many branches. A stock control system for handling 10,000 types of item performs identical functions on each type of item, independent of its type. Changeover to these systems can be effected by first changing over to one module either in parallel or directly. If this proves satisfactory, then changeover to the entire system can be made. This is a way of minimizing the risks. The pilot system can also be used for on-the-job training of staff.

15.4.4 Phased changeover

Where a system is composed of different self-contained modules performing different functions it may be possible to phase in the new system while gradually phasing out the old. For example, a system involving nominal, sales and purchase ledger accounts, stock control, financial planning, sales forecasting and payroll can be phased in gradually, one function at a time. Although in the final integrated system there will be data flows between these various modules, each is sufficiently self-contained and directed towards a recognized business function that it is possible to phase in modules gradually.

This creeping commitment to computerization need not be restricted to changeover but can involve the whole development process. Its advantage is that cash flow outlay can be spread over time, analysts and programmers are employed consistently, resources are generally distributed more evenly over time, and the gradual commitment to the computerized system ensures that any difficulties in changeover are more easily handled. The drawback is that interfacing modules will need to have continuously changing modes of interface. For example, between a financial planning and sales ledger system there will initially be a manual–manual interface. If the ledger system is computerized, then a computer–manual interface will need to be developed. Finally, a computer–computer interface is required. The continuous changeover process experienced by users, while distributing resources over time, can also give the feeling that computerization is a never-ending process. This can be bad for morale.

Kismet case study 15.4

The central purposes in developing a computerized information system for Kismet were to:

- process customer orders quickly;
- be able to satisfy customer enquiries in such areas as the status of orders, prices of goods and delivery availability;
- provide management with a greater variety of relevant, up-to-date information on company performance.

Kismet is a firm that is beginning to embark on computerized systems. It does not currently have the experience or confidence gained by organizations that have a continuing systems development policy, possibly over 20 years or more. Kismet therefore wishes to embark on as risk-free a changeover strategy as possible. Much of the new system, such as the part dealing with transaction processing, is very similar to the old system. A parallel changeover will allow the necessary processing checks to be carried out and at the same time will allow a manual system to be provided as backup. There will be difficulties performing these checks, as the computerized system works almost instantaneously, whereas the manual system took many days to process orders – that was one of its faults. With respect to order enquiry, it has been decided to rely entirely on the new system, although sample checks are to be recorded and verified later. Similarly, the management reports as generated by the new system will be used. Sample checks against reports from the old system are to be made, but given the limited number of types of report that were generated, this part of the system will rely heavily on the adequacy of systems testing prior to changeover.

The parallel run is to be initially for a period of one month. There will then be a formal review of the system prior to its final acceptance and the discarding of the old manual system.

15.5 Evaluation and maintenance

No computerized system once implemented remains unaltered through the rest of its working life. Changes are made, and maintenance is undertaken. Hardware maintenance is usually carried out under a maintenance contract with the equipment suppliers. Hardware maintenance involves technical tasks often requiring circuitry and other specialized parts.

Software maintenance is also carried out. In time, bugs may be discovered in the programs. It is necessary to correct these. Modular program design, structured code and the documentation techniques of structured systems analysis and design ensure that this task can be effected efficiently.

Software maintenance continues to be a complex and costly contributor to the entire systems project. Many project managers are now recognizing the **total cost of ownership** of information systems. This incorporates the entire cost of software, from initial feasibility studies through analysis and design to post-implementation maintenance. Eventually, the new development will become outdated, and for completeness the cost of creating and dealing with that legacy system must also be included. The importance of good documentation and design, and the reusability and maintainability of the code generated, are all important factors in calculating the total cost of ownership.

User needs also evolve over time to respond to the changing business environment. Software is amended to serve these. New applications programs must be written. It is the responsibility of the computer centre or information centre to ensure that the system is kept up to date.

Some time after the system has settled down, it is customary to carry out a **post-implementation audit**. The purpose of this audit is to compare the new system as it actually is with what was intended in its specification. To ensure independence, this audit will be carried out by an analyst or team not involved in the original systems project.

The audit will consider a number of areas:

- The adequacy of the systems documentation that governs manual procedures and computer programs will be checked.
- The training of personnel involved in the use of the new system will be assessed.
- Attempts will be made to establish the reliability of systems output.
- Comparison of the actual costs and benefits incurred during implementation is made against the estimated costs and benefits, and significant variances are investigated.
- Response times will be determined and compared with those specified.

The original purposes of the systems project will once again be considered. Does the system as delivered meet these objectives? The post-implementation audit will yield a report that will assess the system. Suggestions for improvements will be made. These may be minor and can be accommodated within the ongoing development of the project. If they are major, they will be shelved until a major overhaul or replacement of the system is due.

During the course of the useful life of the system, several audits will be made. Some of these will be required by external bodies. Examples are financial audits required by the accountancy profession for accounting transaction-processing systems. Other audits are internal. They will deal with such matters as efficiency, effectiveness, security and reliability. The topic of auditing of computer systems was covered in Chapter 9 on control.

Great achievements can be made using structured systems analysis and design. Information systems have been produced that:

- involve integrated redesign rather than piecemeal copying of old manual systems;
- are based on the logical information requirements of the organization rather than the physical dictates of old processing patterns;
- are more likely to be delivered on time and on budget because of the added control that modular development confers on the project;
- contain software that is reliable, well documented and easily amendable.

However, there are some who point to limitations in structured analysis and design. They comment on its lack of suitability in all cases. These reservations are founded on three implicit assumptions:

1. A technical solution to an organization's information problems is always desirable and possible.
2. The experts in systems analysis and design are the analysts and programmers. Users come in only to provide information about the existing system during investigation and as a consideration in interface design. They themselves do not design and develop the system.
3. The correct approach to development is to progress in a linear fashion through a number of clearly definable stages with exit criteria.

Chapters 7 and 17 consider how these assumptions have been challenged by soft systems analysis and design, user participation in socio-technical analysis and design, and prototyping as an approach to systems development.

Summary

Having selected the overall systems design, detailed design of the system then commences. Programs are defined by the use of structure charts and individual module specifications. These ensure that the programming task can be carried out in a controlled and reliable way. The data store is designed. In the case of file-based systems, this involves the specification of file and record layouts. For databases, schema design is required. An important aspect of input/output design is that of the user interface. This is determined not only by the types of task for which input or output is used but also by a model of the user. There are various categories of user. In all these areas, hardware requirements must be established, given the data-processing and information-provision requirements of the organization as identified during analysis.

The systems specification is an important landmark between detailed design and implementation. This is a report covering all aspects of the systems design in detail. As well as giving cost estimates, it will also provide a schedule for the implementation stage of the project. Once the specification has been agreed with management then implementation can commence.

During implementation, large sums of money are allocated and spent. Hardware as specified is acquired and installed. Programs are coded and tested. The structured hierarchical input/process/output design facilitates the use of structured programming. Targeted training and education are provided for staff. Historical data is loaded into the system. The systems test is a major step in the implementation stage prior to changeover to the new system.

Systems changeover can be effected in a number of ways, each of which has certain benefits, drawbacks and areas of application. After the system has been running for some time, a post-implementation audit compares the system as delivered with that as specified. Suggestions for further improvements are made. As the information needs of the organization evolve so the system is amended, programs adapted and new applications software written to take account of this.

Review questions

1. Outline the areas to be covered in the detailed design of a system.

2. What benefits accrue when software has been developed as a result of modular design?

3. Explain the terms *module decoupling* and *module cohesion*. Why are they desirable characteristics in modular software design?

4. What is the role of a systems specification?

5. Distinguish between the various types of test carried out during implementation.

6. What security features must be present in the conversion of historic accounting data for entry into a new system?

7. What are the purposes of a post-implementation audit?

Exercises

1. Using the data flow diagrams developed for the library example (Chapter 12, Exercise 5) derive a hierarchical structure chart for the system.

2. What is the difference between a *conceptual data model* and a *conceptual schema*?

3. What features of interface design affect the acceptance of computer systems by users?

4. How do structured techniques in systems analysis and design aid systems development in the later stages?

5. How could each of the following be analysed according to the categories of systems users covered in the text:

    (a) customer order data input personnel?
    (b) customer cashpoint users?
    (c) flight booking and reservation enquiry personnel?
    (d) spreadsheet model developers?
    (e) programmers?
    (f) middle-management users of summary accounting decision support information?

6. Which of the following should be incorporated into a systems test: hardware, software, data storage, manual procedures, backup facilities, computer operations staff, users, data communications, security and control?

7. Explain *four* different changeover strategies. Are they mutually exclusive? In each of the following cases, suggest a changeover strategy. Explain its merits and drawbacks. Justify your choice by giving reasons why other strategies are not appropriate.

    (a) A computerized inventory control system is to replace antiquated manual methods. It is to be installed in eight warehouses and deals with 10,000 types of item.
    (b) A major high street bank has commissioned an automated cheque and cash deposit system for its branches. It is to be operated by the bank's counter personnel and will allow instant account updating for deposits.
    (c) A new company has developed a computerized lottery system to be installed in lottery ticket offices throughout the country.

8. Why is software maintenance, as distinct from software creation, traditionally regarded as an arduous, unpopular task?

9. Why is software maintenance necessary?

CASE STUDY 15

Evaluation and maintenance

1. Consider the first month of operation of the new Kismet system. A formal review will take place at the end of that period and an evaluation will be made as to whether the parallel running of old and new systems will come to an end. You have been commissioned to write this report for managers at Kismet. Draft an outline of the report, making your recommendations.

2. Consider now the first year of operation. What might be the maintenance issues in hardware and software during that time? What about the issues over a five-year period?

Recommended reading

Astels D. (2003). *Test-driven Development: A Practical Guide*. Prentice Hall PTR

This book introduces an approach to software design which encourages the developer to plan test routines for code before the code is written, thereby predicting and anticipating where errors could occur and avoiding them.

Budgen D. (2003). *Software Design*, 2nd edn. Addison-Wesley

This is a clear, comprehensive text suitable for final-year undergraduates in systems analysis and design. Part 1 explores the nature of the design process and the various roles played in software development. Part 2 gives a detailed examination of well-established structured approaches – JSP, SSADM and JSD.

Buxton B. (2003). *Sketching User Experiences: Getting the Design Right and the Right Design*, 2nd edn. Morgan Kaufmann

This book adopts a challenging approach to the way new products are designed and implemented. The author proposes a range of methods for HCI and other design decisions.

Galitz W. (2007). *The Essential Guide to User Interface Design: An Introduction to GUI Design Principles and Techniques*, 3rd edn. John Wiley & Sons.

This describes the fundamentals of good interface design. The book covers a range of GUI applications, including design for the Web.

Isaacs E. (2002). *Designing from Both Sides of the Screen: A Dialogue Between a Designer and an Engineer*. Sams

This is equally relevant to software engineers and designers. It covers the principles of good interface design and provides many examples of good and bad practice. An extended case study provides the context for much of the theory.

Riordan R. (2005). *Designing Effective Database Systems*. Pearson Education Limited

This text is intended for those who are not experienced database developers but may have to develop their own database systems. Although there are coding examples it is intended that the book be accessible to non-programmers. Most of the examples are either Access or SQL. An introduction to relational theory is provided as well as development steps.

Snyder C. (2003). *Paper Prototyping: Fast and Simple Techniques for Designing and Refining the User Interface*. Morgan Kaufmann

This provides an innovative approach to user interface design employing tools which encourage low cost and rapid development.

Somerville I. (2006). *Software Engineering*, 8th rev. edn. Pearson Education

This classic text covers many topics, including systems design, user interface design, validation, evolution and management of software, legacy systems and configuration management.

Chapter 16

Object oriented approaches

Learning outcomes

On completion of this chapter, you should be able to:

■ Characterize object oriented approaches

■ Define UML and outline its essential aspects

■ Produce and refine UML diagrams

■ Make qualitative judgements about the quality of a UML model

■ Differentiate between dynamic and static modelling

■ Compare object oriented approaches to other systems development methodologies.

Introduction

This chapter introduces the object oriented paradigm. Object orientation offers an alternative to the structured, procedural methods that have been presented in Chapters 11–15. Proponents of object oriented approaches claim that they provide a more intuitive way of modelling and developing systems. It is claimed that the concepts and language employed form a closer match to the real-world elements and processes that are being modelled thereby making the task of systems development more readily accessible and fit for purpose.

The standard approach to system specification now universally adopted for object oriented development is the Unified Modelling Languge (UML). This chapter introduces UML and some of the key aspects of its vocabulary. At the early stages of information systems project management the allocation and scheduling of activities to teams is usually undertaken. The first stage of UML modelling is often the modelling of use cases. This use case modelling not only provides the starting point for the system design process but also offers a project management opportunity whereby work allocation and team responsibilities can be established.

The next stage of object oriented development is to consider the static modelling of the classes that comprise the system. Classes must first be discovered and then the class members, the contents of the classes, need to be defined. Different techniques can be applied to this process and two alternative styles are considered in this chapter.

As well as locating classes, the system developer will discover associations that exist between the classes. The combination of classes and their associations will result in the production of class models.

Throughout this stage it is essential to remember that it is only the static aspects of the system that are being modelled. Consideration of timing, sequencing activities, ordering events etc. comprise the dynamic aspects and must be suspended until the next stage.

The dynamic models represent and explain the interaction between the classes as they collaborate to carry out the functionality of the system. These models capture the message passing that takes place between objects to perform the various tasks required. They show when objects are created, updated and destroyed if no longer required.

This chapter introduces some of the UML techniques for modelling the dynamic aspects of the system. From the toolkit of interaction diagrams that are provided in UML, two are highlighted: the collaboration diagram and the sequence diagram.

The iterative nature of object oriented development will become more apparent as in producing the dynamic models, the system developer will continually revisit the use case models, class diagrams and CRC cards that have already been produced.

16.1 The emergence of object oriented approaches

Systems development in the earliest days was usually centred around the programmer. Those who had learned, often by teaching themselves, how to write programs were invested with great power. Their knowledge of the newly emerging programming languages gave them a huge earning potential and much freedom in deciding how systems development projects would be carried out.

As projects became more complex, the success rate for some was less than for others. Increasingly the new systems required maintenance and the hitherto rather secretive world of program development needed to be opened up to greater scrutiny. The result was the increasing arrival and uptake of systems development methodologies: these were standardized and widely accepted ways of tackling the complex task of solving problems in information systems.

The first methodologies were described as 'structured' approaches. These normally adopted a variation of the classic waterfall approach. Typically they provided tools and techniques that allowed systems designers to model systems and to turn those models into artefacts that would assist in software development. Some approaches focused on the modelling of data. These data-driven approaches would require the developer to focus on input and output documents, to locate stores of data and to investigate the way that data was transformed and modified within a system. Consideration of the processing of the data was added at a later stage. Alterative methodologies focused on the processes that a system was required to carry out. These process-driven approaches concentrated first on the functionality of systems; the activities and processes in a system were identified and modelled first. Considerations of the data requirements were added later.

Whichever viewpoint was adopted, eventually the development team would at some stage be required to bring together both the data and the functions that needed to be modelled and that the system needed to embody. The defining feature of structured approaches is that the consideration of data and functions was carried out independently with a rendez-vous at some later point in the project.

This separation of data and function was not only a feature on the development approach but was mirrored in the syntax of the programming languages available. For example the language COBOL contained a DATA DIVISION where data items were declared and a separate PROCEDURE DIVISION where actions were performed and data was operated upon. A similar demarcation was evident in other high-level languages.

This style of programming is, to an extent, analogous to a recipe in a cookery book or the instructions in a car maintenance manual. A recipe usually starts with a list of ingredients and utensils (the 'data' for the recipe). Then in a following section a set of actions describe operations to be carried out such as: put the milk and flour in the bowl, whisk for 10 minutes etc. (the procedures or methods). In describing how to change a spark plug, a car maintenance manual might first outline a list of tools and spare parts required, such as a 10 millimetre spanner, a spark plug (the data) followed by a set of annotated photographs illustrating and describing how to effect the repair (the procedures or methods).

The separation of data from functions had a number of benefits for developers and programmers but at the same time led to a number of problems. Particular difficulties were evident in the maintenance of legacy program code and in re-using existing code in the construction of new systems.

16.1.1 Advantages of object oriented approaches

In the late 1980s and through the 1990s serious attention was turned to the object oriented (OO) programming languages such as Smalltalk, C++ and Java. These languages adopted a fundamentally different approach in that the data and functions for individual objects (as opposed to the entire programme) were combined at the earliest stage. This focusing on objects, rather than data or actions in isolation, appeared to reap dividends in providing a more natural way of expressing a solution to a real-world problem. After all, the real world is comprised of objects. These objects can be thought of as carrying out a small set of actions and storing items of data. In addition, it quickly became apparent that objects could be treated as fundamental building blocks; they can be maintained and updated more easily than entire programs or sections of programs. Also, once designed, objects could easily be reused in different situations.

Once the potential benefits were communicated amongst the wider community a number of object oriented analysis and design approaches began to appear. These approaches were readily adopted as a further advantage became apparent: the conceptual modelling and vobaculary required at each stage in object oriented analysis, design and programming was the same. Unlike the structured approach which required a switch of toolsets and documentation styles between stages of the development process, object oriented approaches retained the basic core concepts and terminology throughout, namely representation of classes and objects and the communication (message passing) between them. This persistence of concept meant that a seamless development approach through analysis, design and programming was possible. This further enhanced the status of the increasingly popular object oriented approach.

One possible limiting factor to the growing popularity of OO was the number of competing diagrammatic notations and development approaches being used. This problem was eliminated, however, when the three major proponents of competing approaches, Grady Booch, Ivar Jacobson and James Rumbaugh (the so-called *three amigos*), collaborated and pooled the best features of their respective approaches to develop the Unified Modelling Language (UML). This rapidly became the de facto standard for OO development. The overall development has, since then, been overseen by the Object Management Group (OMG), a standards body which has taken over responsibility for development of UML.

16.1.2 Hybrid approaches

Many different approaches can be taken in information systems development. To a certain extent the approach selected will determine the underlying system architecture implemented. Traditional structured approaches will invariably lead to implementation using a procedural programming language. Data modelling, carried out using entity/relationship diagrams and normalization, will invariably lead to a database solution implemented using a relational database system. Object oriented approaches will normally see an implementation in an object oriented language such as C++ or Java. That is not to say that hybrid approaches are not possible. Many systems developed using object oriented approaches result in the attributes (the data) of the objects being stored in relational databases, thereby breaking the data and action link that was discussed above. Hybrid approaches that require transformations of data between fundamentally different paradigms are not uncommon. They attempt to gain maximum advantage by exploiting the best features of both.

16.2   The Unified Modelling Language

The Unified Modelling Language (UML) is often defined as a system specification language. Although UML is defined as a language, it is very visual in nature. It provides a range of diagrams and other techniques that allow developers to specify a system. Like all languages it has a set of rules (a grammar) that must be followed so all users can comprehend what is being expressed. It can therefore be summarized as a visual specification language. Although UML is generally part of a development process that ultimately results the production of program code, it is not a software generating device, and is certainly not a programming language. Some software packages do exist, however, that allow designers to model problems and then automatically generate skeleton program code based on that model. These software packages take the model beyond the platform independence that UML can offer and produce an outline solution or framework with which the programmer can work and enhance. This is discussed further in the next chapter.

UML preserves the terminology that proponents and enthusiasts of object technology have always used such as **object, class, operation, attribute** etc. The key stages in systems development using UML are captured in a number of models, each progressively adding detail:

- User modelling – use case models;
- Analysis model;
- Design model;
- Deployment model;
- Implementation model;
- Test model.

The modelling can also be delineated into:

- Static modelling – use case diagrams, class diagrams and models;
- Dynamic modelling – iteration diagrams, collaboration diagrams, state diagrams.

Figure 16.1 The UML views

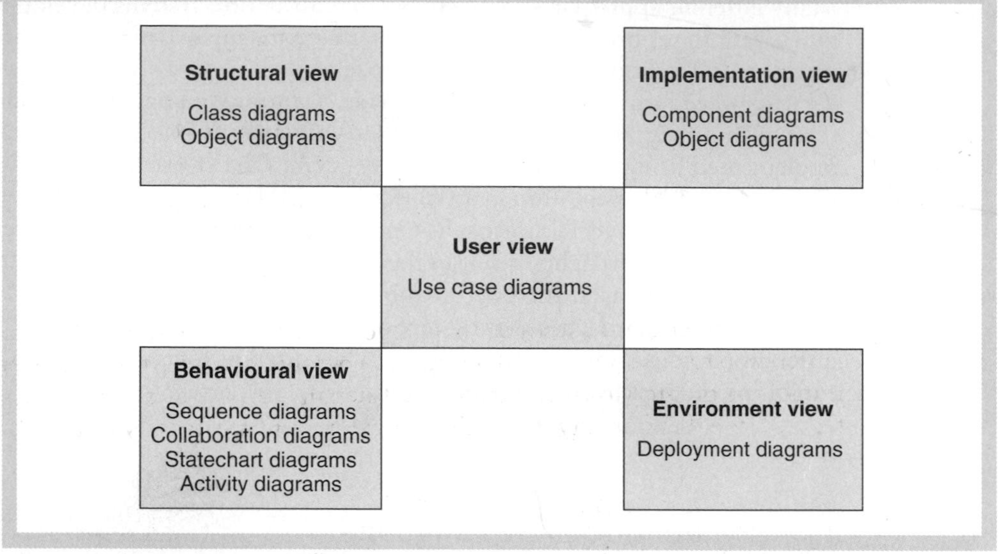

Structural view		Implementation view
Class diagrams		Component diagrams
Object diagrams		Object diagrams
	User view	
	Use case diagrams	
Behavioural view		Environment view
Sequence diagrams		
Collaboration diagrams		Deployment diagrams
Statechart diagrams		
Activity diagrams		

(Adapted from Sinan Si Alhir, 2003. Permission from O'Reilly Media Inc.)

In total, UML defines nine different types of diagrams: use case, class, object, sequence, collaboration, state, activity, component and deployment. Each diagram coveys a different viewpoint on the system being modelled through the use of labelled symbols (rectangles, circles, ellipse etc.) often connected by labelled connectors (solid or dashed lines or arrows).

Sinan Si Alhir (2003) provides a model which divides UML into a number of 'views'; each view is drawn with its associated diagrams. The model is shown in Figure 16.1. A key feature of this model is the placement of the User view at the centre, emphasizing the importance of the user at the heart of the development process.

16.3 Use case modelling

At an early stage it is essential to establish the use cases that are required in the development of a system. Many authors, in describing the management of a project, emphasize the importance of use case modelling at this point. For example, in their description of project management Fowler and Scott (2003) make plentiful use of use case modelling at the 'elaboration phase' and state that they are an essential tool in requirements capture.

A number of guidelines exist to assist the system developer. Bennett *et al.* (2006) suggest that it is conceptually easier to focus on people and other existing systems rather than attempting to identify more abstract roles. They suggest asking the following questions:

- Who are the people who will use this system to enter information?
- Who are the people who will use this system as recipients of information?
- What are the other systems that this system will interact with?

Figure 16.2 A generic use case diagram

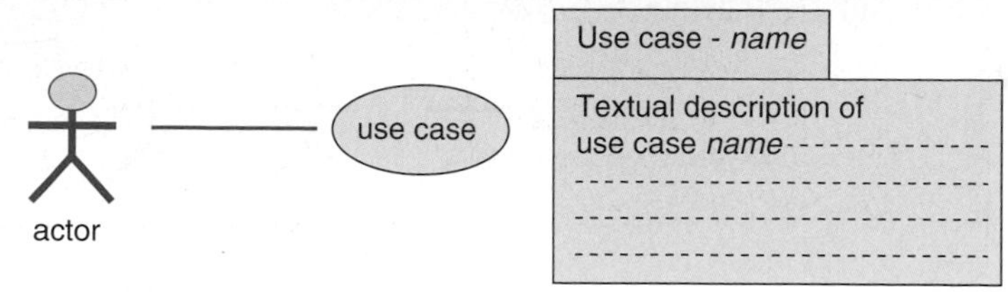

To help answer these questions the developer might return to the documents produced at the outset of the investigation stage: the organization chart, the flow block diagram, transcripts of interviews, results of questionnaires etc. At this point the emphasis needs to be on the functionality: the actions that the system will carry out.

16.3.1 Use case diagrams

A usual starting point for an object oriented systems development project is the generation of use case diagrams. Use cases allow the developer to get a very quick but very clear impression of the behaviour of an existing system and the requirements of the proposed one. An important point to note is that although they are concerned with capturing behaviour, use cases are not intended to describe how that behaviour is actually carried out.

The basic components of a use case diagram are:

- Actors;
- Use cases;
- Relationships.

In addition, each use case will contain an accompanying textual description.

Figure 16.2 shows a simple generic use case diagram. In the diagram, a single actor is shown, drawn as a stick person. A single use case is represented, drawn as an elipse. The connecting line between actor and use case represents a relationship; this illustrates the participation of this actor in this use case. The accompanying text provides additional detail about the use case being modelled.

Actors

Actors are represented on a use case diagram by a stick person. The role carried out by the actor is given a name; a label containing this role name is placed underneath the actor. Although an actor is represented as a stick person, the role does not have to be carried out by a human participant. An actor can either represent one or more people carrying out a role, or can be another system that interacts with or provides a service for the use case. Figure 16.3 shows examples of three different actors.

When first presented with the concept of an actor it is easy to confuse the role which is being presented with an actual person who might be carrying out that role. This can be clarified by considering Figure 16.3. In a system representing a General Practice there may be several roles identified. There may be a number of doctors practising within the system and a number of patients being treated. However, the role of doctor only needs to be represented once; that actor represents all doctors in the practice.

Figure 16.3 The role of doctor, patient and the electronic prescription system, each represented as actors

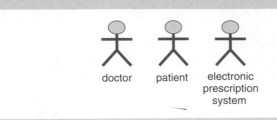

Similarly for patients, a single patient role is all that needs to be shown. The separation of person from role is reinforced in the situation where a doctor may fall ill and require treatment. In that case, the person who normally operates in the role of doctor temporarily steps out of that role and steps into the role of patient. In the role of patient they are then treated by another person acting in the doctor role. This illustrates the separation of a general role that can be fulfilled by many different people, and the different roles that individuals can adopt at different times.

The emphasis of this section has been on people and roles, but it should be remembered that an actor can also represent the role played by an external system, not just by human participants. In the example above, data may be transferred to and from an electronic prescription system. Although this is an external system, it is still represented as a stick person.

Use cases

A use case is represented by an ellipse with the use case name written inside. As a use case represents an aspect of functionality, the name ascribed normally has an active feel: usually a descriptive verb forms part of the name. In addition to the diagrammatic representation, a use case will also have an associated block of descriptive text. Although this text is normally entered 'free form' it is written in a terse and precise way to avoid ambiguities and aid the specification process. An example of a use case can be seen in Figure 16.4. The use case is named and represented in Figure 16.4(a) and the accompanying text can be seen in Figure 16.4(b).

Figure 16.4 (a) Use case and (b) accompanying text

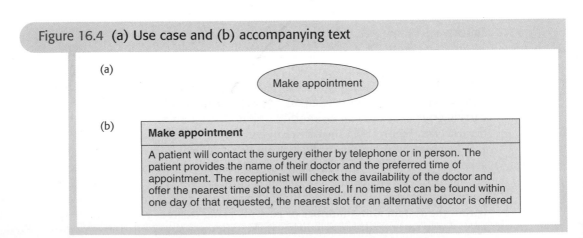

When using an OO software development tool the designer would typically draw the diagrammatic part of the use case and then double-click on the use case to open a window into which the text can be entered. The tool would preserve the link between the diagram and the accompanying text.

Relationships

A single undecorated line represents the relationship between an actor and the use case in which they participate. An actor can participate in one or more use cases and a use case can have a relationship with more than one actor. In Figure 16.5 the patient actor participates in both the appointment and the prescription use case. The doctor actor, however, only participates in one use case: writing prescriptions. The Organize surgery use case only has one actor: the receptionist. The other two use cases both have two actors participating in them.

An interesting issue to consider at this stage is whether a relationship between an actor and a use case is actually required. Looking at Figure 16.5 it is reasonable to question whether or not a relationship between the *doctor* actor and the *Make appointment* use case should be shown. After all, both patient and doctor will be expected to attend the appointment. The decision hinges upon the participation of the actor in the use case and whether they are a beneficiary. If the use case provides some value for a particular actor then a relationship will be required. The *Make appointment* use case clearly will involve a requirement for a doctor but at this level and at this point in the specification of the system the clear beneficiaries are the receptionist, who will discharge the duty of making an appointment, and the patient, who will come away satisfied that their appointment has been arranged.

16.3.2 Use cases and use case diagrams

As shown above, each use case represents a functional aspect of the system and is represented by the labelled ellipse and accompanying text. The combination of a set of related

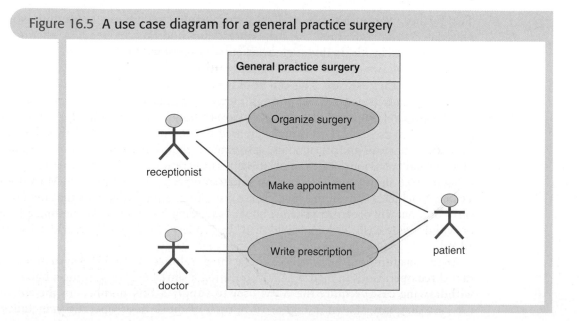

Figure 16.5 A use case diagram for a general practice surgery

use cases (with associated relationships and actors) enclosed within a rectangle forms the **use case diagram**. Figure 16.5 shows a simplified use case diagram for a general practice surgery. At the highest level, use cases describe very broad functionality. In order to capture greater detail, an individual use case may be further elaborated. This can be done either by adding additional detail, in terms of further use cases and relationships, on the same diagram. Alternatively an individual use case may become the subject of a new use case diagram. Within that diagram the detail of the use case can be expressed in much greater detail without excessively crowding the higher-level diagram.

16.3.3 Advantages of use cases

A number of advantages of use cases are cited, namely that they:

- are straightforward to generate;
- are a simple way to capture high-level functionality;
- are comprehensible to non-experts;
- focus on users, thereby encouraging fulfilment of requirements;
- focus on users, which can assist development of the HCI;
- can be a useful project management aid in estimating and scheduling activities.

Amongst the disadvantages are that they:

- place an early emphasis on functionality which distorts the intention of object orientation;
- do not capture the non-functional requirements;
- may be an unfamiliar device for the developers and/or the client.

16.3.4 Enhancing the use case

Two further relationships are available which enable the use case to capture more sophisticated behaviour: these are the <<includes>> and the <<extends>> relationships. Each is labelled inside double angle brackets (<<. . .>>) for emphasis. The <<includes>> relationship allows one use case to incorporate (or include) functionality that is encapsulated in another use case. This can be of benefit, for example, where one system function has already been specified and can therefore be reused across several others. The <<extends>> relationship allows one use case to build upon (or extend) the functionality of another use case. This is typically used where one use case describes the normal expected behaviour and a second use case extends that to incorporate some variant case of less usual behaviour, for example unsuccessful completion of the use case.

Figure 16.6 shows high-level use case diagram representing a typical ATM (Automatic Telling Machine), or cash machine. There are four top-level functions that the user can carry out, namely ordering a cheque book, requesting a statement, requesting a balance or withdrawing cash. Having established the top-level functions, further details can be added.

After consulting further with the client the developer of the ATM system discovers that three operations in Figure 16.6 (requesting a statement, requesting a balance and withdrawing cash) require the ATM user to supply a PIN number. In the enhanced use case diagram, shown in Figure 16.7, each of those three operations includes the

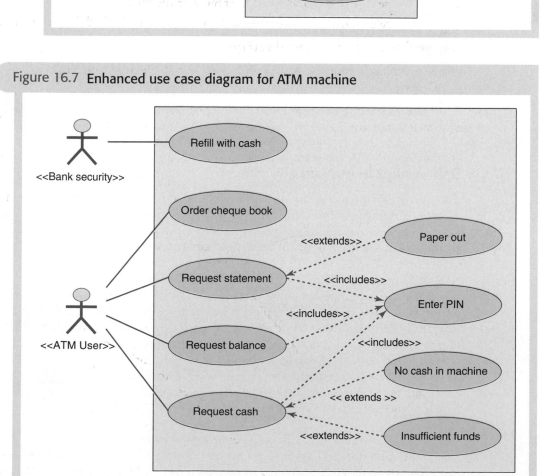

Figure 16.6 Initial attempt at use case diagram for ATM machine

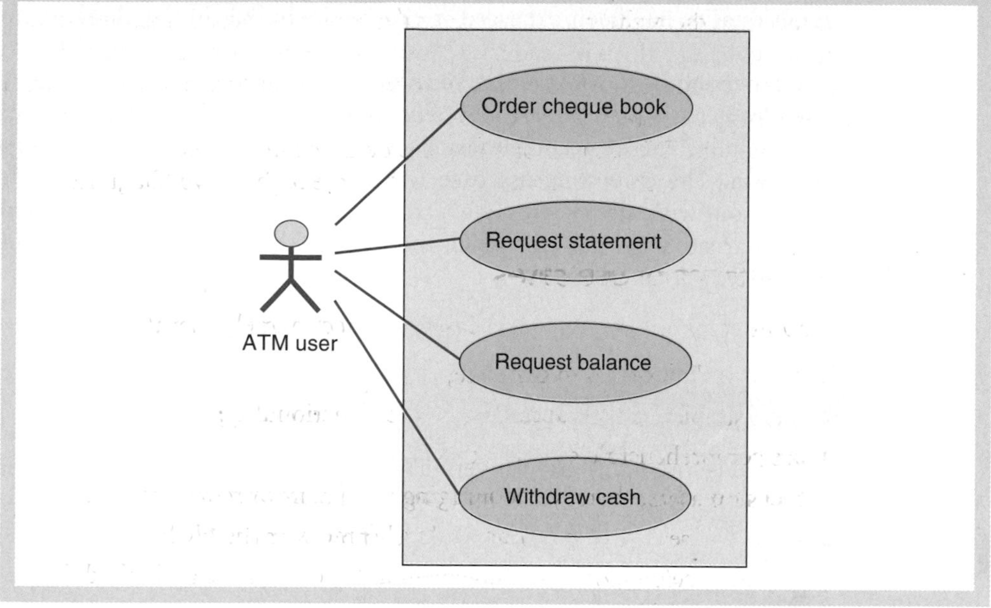

Figure 16.7 Enhanced use case diagram for ATM machine

enter PIN use case. This reusing of modelling features makes the diagram more readable and simplifies the design process by reducing duplication. Once the *enter PIN* functionality has been captured it can be 'included' in the three operations that require it.

On occasions a cash machine may be out of money or out of paper. In that case the *withdraw cash* and the *request statement* use cases will not be able to complete successfully. These variant situations are recorded as use cases that extend the normal situation. The extending use case will override the actions that would normally be carried out with alternatives, e.g. error messages explaining the problem encountered. A similar situation pertains when the user has insufficient funds for the operation to complete.

Kismet case study 16.1

Using Figure 11.2 as a key driver, the following use cases might be identified:

- Place customer order;
- Request stock;
- Construct invoice;
- Invoice customer;
- Receive payment.

Note that this list is limited to the area designated as that under the area of investigation by the analyst (encircled in a dotted line). A first-draft diagram can be constructed from this information.

In Figure 16.8 the roles have been discovered from the organization chart and also from the flow block diagram. The use case names have been derived from the flow block diagram and the interviews with staff.

Figure 16.8 **First cut at use case diagram for Kismet order processing system**

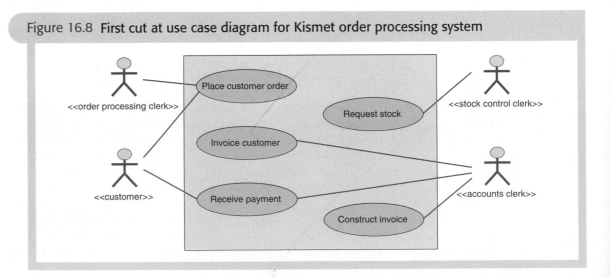

16.3.5 Reading a use case diagram

A common error of novice designers in constructing or interpreting use case diagrams is to attempt to capture or deduce flow of control. For example in Figure 16.7 the use cases *Request Statement* and *Enter PIN* are connected by an <<includes>> relationship. That does **not** imply an ordering (in either direction). Intuitively we might deduce that a user might first enter their PIN and then request a statement. Indeed the client might have informed us that this sequence is to be rigidly enforced. However, the purpose of a use case diagram is not to represent sequencing of activity. All we can deduce from that part of the diagram is that there are two aspects of functionality: *Request Statement* and *Enter PIN*. The diagram tells us that the latter activity is contained within the former (and that the latter is available for inclusion in other use cases too). It says nothing about the ordering of activities. Flow of control will be represented in the dynamic aspects of the system model which are covered later.

16.3.6 Developing use case diagrams

The analyst will adopt a strategy for deriving use case diagrams. As with all aspects of object oriented development this will be an iterative process. The key stages are:

1. Model the actors.
2. Model the use cases graphically and create textual description.
3. Model the relationships between actors and use cases.
4. Model the enhancements through <<extends>> and <<includes>> relationships.
5. Combine the elements onto a single use case diagram.
6. Elaborate the more complex use cases by creating a new use case diagram for each use case.

These stages will be repeated until all individual use cases are of a sufficiently simple level that they can be fully documented in a few sentences of text. It is important to remember, however, that use cases are rarely an end in themselves. They usually form the framework for the next stages of the development. As such there is not a need to capture every last detail of the system in the use cases themselves. The detail will emerge in the class modelling that will follow. The use cases should capture the functionality at a level that facilitates that modelling.

Actors as constituent parts of the system

The placement of actors outside the perimeter rectangle of a use case diagram is a clear statement that they are outside the system. There are occasions where this may seem contentious. Some actors interact with the system in a very peripheral way; others seem to be intrinsic, almost indispensable to the running of the system. The system developer might have difficulties with this. The conundrum will be returned to when modelling the classes of the system. At that point the placement issues can be more easily considered and attempts made at a resolution.

Once a first-draft use case diagram has been produced, further work can commence on fleshing out the detail of these top-level use cases. By inspecting the results of the manual systems flowchart in the operations manual the use case diagram can be enhanced.

Iterative application of use case modelling techniques and further consultation with the users of the system reveals further detail. This allows for an enhanced use case model to be developed.

In Figure 16.9 further detail has been added, in particular to explain the process of placing an order. This provides more richness in the modelling of the system. A difficulty for the developer is that if increasing detail is continually added to the diagram it may become overwhelming and difficult to read. This problem is addressed in the next section.

Figure 16.9 **Enhanced use case diagram for Kismet order processing system**

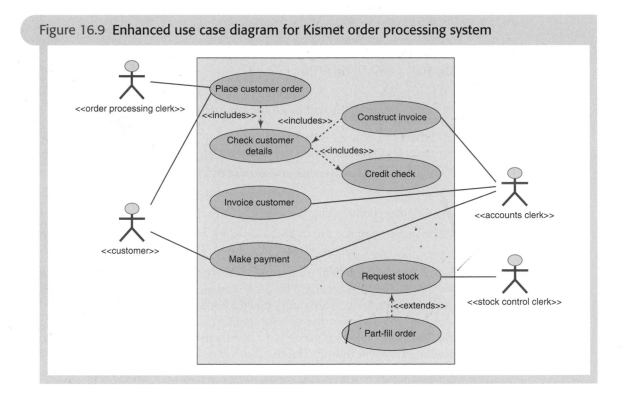

Two interconnected questions arise concerning use case diagrams. These are:

1. What level of discrimination of functions should be shown on the use case diagram? For instance, the use case *generate approved company order* could be regarded as consisting of a number of contributory use cases, such as *accept order*, *check credit limit* and *price order*. Should these be shown as use cases?

2. What is the maximum number of use cases that should be shown on a use case diagram?

In all but the very smallest systems it will not be possible to incorporate all the enhanced detail on a single use case diagram. The additions shown in Figure 16.9 do refine the representation of the system but further analysis is still required.

A major objective of a use case diagram is its use in communication of the logical functional model of the organization. It is difficult to understand a use case diagram when it has more than about seven use cases. This is the practical upper limit. If there is a tendency to overstep this then the use case diagram should be redrawn, with use cases that are logically grouped together being replaced by a single use case that encompasses them all.

A helpful device to accomplish this further refinement is the UML package. A package in UML is a general-purpose mechanism for grouping related elements. At the use case modelling stage, packages can be used to create use case diagrams that are of manageable size. In creating a package, the detail previously captured in a single use case appears on another use case diagram that shows how this use case can be exploded into its constituents. These constituents themselves may be complex and can be further broken down into packages at a lower level.

The creation of packages to elaborate upon complex use cases has two other advantages. First, it naturally falls into line with the analyst's approach to top-down decomposition. That is, the analyst considers the major functions and processes first. These are then decomposed into their constituents. The analyst can therefore concentrate on the higher-level use cases before designing the others. Second, the various packages correspond to the various degrees of detail by which the system is represented. This is useful for the analyst when discussing the results of the analysis with members of the organization. Senior managers are more likely to be interested in a global view as given in a high-level use case diagram. Other personnel will be concerned with more localized areas but in greater detail.

Kismet case study 16.3

The activities involved in a customer placing an order can effectively be grouped into a UML package. Figure 16.10 shows the package created. This is an example of consolidating related activities: the parent use case diagram will become clearer to read as a result.

The activities involved in processing a payment can be further expanded into a UML package. Figure 16.11 shows the package created. This is an example of refining a more complex use case diagram: the resulting package will provide the detail that the parent   ▶

Figure 16.10 UML package for the place order use case

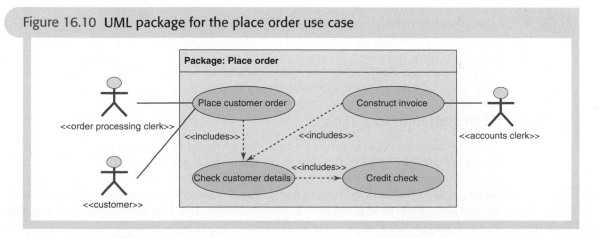

Figure 16.11 UML package for the process payment use case

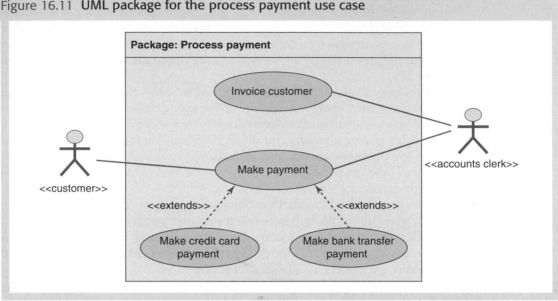

use case represents. The use cases representing the placing of a customer order have been refined and separated out into their own package. The process payment functionality has also been placed in a separate package; this allows for further refinement to be introduced to both new packages without overcomplicating the use case diagrams for each.

16.4 Static modelling

The fundamental building block of any object oriented system is the class. The collection of classes in a system and the collaboration between those classes provide the essence of an object oriented solution.

Class diagrams, which contain representations of the individual classes, allow the system developer to model the static aspects of a system. In that sense they follow on naturally from the use case modelling already undertaken. At the early stages the intention is not to establish flow of control or ordering of activities: that will come later on. In the modelling of classes, the system developer is simply focusing on the attributes and behaviour of each individual class, and which classes are required to collaborate with each other in order to carry out the tasks of the system.

16.4.1 Representation of a class

The diagrammatic representation of a class in UML is a rectangular icon. In its simplest form a rectangle containing the class name is sufficient to represent a class. Figure 16.12 shows the classes for a customer and a customer order. The naming convention for classes is to capitalize the first letter (e.g. Item). Where more than one word is used to name a class, the first letter of each word is capitalized and all words are joined together without spaces (e.g. CustomerOrder).

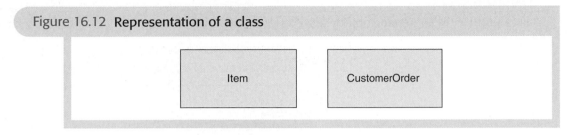

Figure 16.12 **Representation of a class**

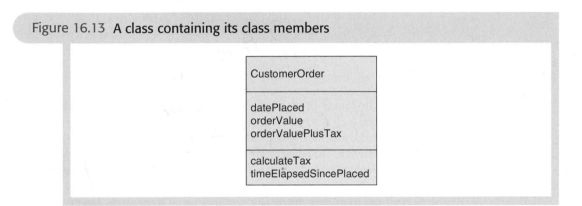

Figure 16.13 **A class containing its class members**

Class members

A more detailed version of a class would also include its attributes, its operations or both. These attributes and operations are collectively described as the class members. The attributes represent the data item that a class will maintain. Dates, names, money values or, indeed, other classes are all examples of items that a class might hold as its attributes. In Figure 16.13 three attributes of a customer order have been identified, namely the date the order was placed (*datePlaced*), the total value of the order (*orderValue*) and the gross value of the order including purchase tax (*orderValuePlusTax*). The collection of all the attributes of a class viewed as a snapshot is called the **state** of a class.

Operations are the activities or processes that a class can carry out. These are often referred to as the responsibilities of the class or the methods of the class. Some operations change the state of a class, others do not.

The naming convention for attributes and operations is the same as for class names with the exception that the first letter is written in lower case.

Clearly the decision whether or not to include any particular class member in a class, or whether a class member would be better omitted or included in a different class, is crucial in the production of a successful design. It is important that only the relevant, essential class members are included. This ensures that classes are tightly specified and clearly focused. Conceptually, this is referred to as **cohesion**; the topic is returned to later in this chapter.

16.4.2 Objects

At the specification stage a class can be thought of as providing a template data type. When a system has been built and is running, actual instances of the class will be generated. These instances are called objects (and hence the name Object Orientation!). As

Figure 16.14 **A generic object based on the class CustomerOrder**

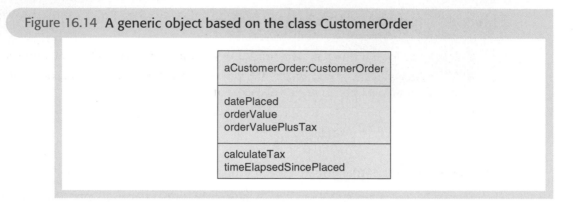

objects are simply instances of classes it is unsurprising that a similar UML diagram is use to represent both.

An object is named by including both its name and, separated by a colon, the class from which it was instantiated. The object name follows the naming convention for data members. It is rare to refer to particular instances of objects at design-time; it is run-time where objects are created. However, there are times when the developer will refer to objects collectively, as opposed to classes. In those cases it is usual to provide a generic name of the form aObject:Classname. In Figure 16.14 the name aCustomerOrder:CustomerOrder is used to refer to any object of the Class CustomerOrder. In Figure 16.15 two individual named objects of the Class CustomerOrder (one representing customer Fred, one representing customer Jo) are shown.

Figure 16.15 **Specific named object diagrams based on the class CustomerOrder**

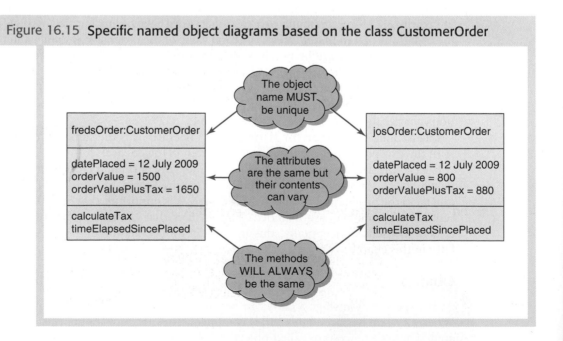

Figure 16.15 illustrates the degree of commonality between the various elements that comprise different objects of the same class.

- All objects must be uniquely identifiable. The names of all objects must therefore differ.
- All objects of a class share exactly the same set of attributes. The actual data contents stored, however, can vary from object to object.
- All objects of a class share exactly the same set of operations. These must therefore be identical for all objects of a class.

16.4.3 Message passing

In order to function, an OO system relies on the communication carried out between the classes. The communication is carried out by message passing. The operations of a class effect this message passing and the attributes often comprise the data element of the message.

To understand message passing it can be helpful to think of a class as a black box. A black box is an abstract device: the internal contents of the black box are hidden but an interface exists through which we can communicate with it (see Figure 16.16). Messages can be sent to the black box. These messages cause some activity to be triggered. The result of the activity might be a responding message from the black box back to the message sender.

Figure 16.17 shows a simple message-passing communication with a black box; the black box calculates the Value Added Tax (VAT) that is due on a given item. The

Figure 16.16 The black box concept

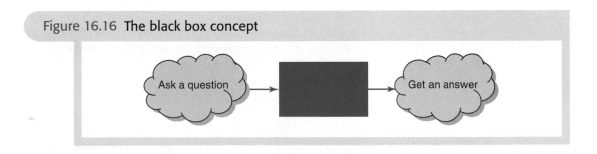

Figure 16.17 The black box responding to a message

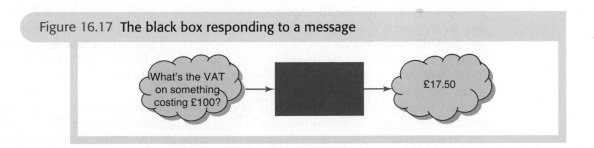

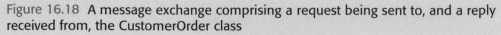

Figure 16.18 **A message exchange comprising a request being sent to, and a reply received from, the CustomerOrder class**

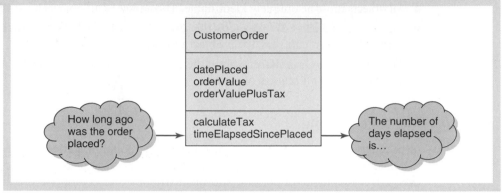

message sent to the black box includes some data (the price of the item). The black box performs a calculation (we are not privy to the internal workings of this) and responds with a message response which includes some data (the amount of VAT due).

An object oriented system is comprised of many classes, all acting as black boxes. Each class has its own responsibilities which are hidden internally. Classes are dependent on their communication with other classes and with the outside world. Each class is unaware of the internal specification of the others. However, through the system of message passing the overall system objectives are achieved.

Figure 16.18 shows a message being sent to the CustomerOrder class. The message enquires about the time that has elapsed since the order was placed. The class acts as a black box and a message is returned containing some data. The reply tells us the number of days that have elapsed. As far as the sender and receiver of the message are concerned, the class is a black box: the mechanics of calculating the number of days that have elapsed is of no concern to them, only the resulting figure.

When a system is actually executing the message will be sent to a particular object of the CustomerOrder class. In that case the calculation comparing today's date to the real date the order was placed will result in the actual number of days being calculated and returned.

The sender and recipient of these messages could be an external actor communicating through an interface, or could be another class within the system. For example in Figure 16.18 the questioner asking how long ago the order was placed might be a user of the system selecting a menu item from a data interrogation screen to satisfy a particular query. In that case the message reply might be sent to a notification dialogue box on the screen. Alternatively the sender might be a class which has the responsibility for collecting information about overdue items. This class might be trawling through all orders and collecting together a copy of those that exceed a specified maximum number of days. In that case the message reply might be returned to the sender with a copy of the order where appropriate.

The syntax of the message is not important at this stage but it is worth noting that often a message sent to a class will have a corresponding method within the class that carries out the desired operation. The message and the corresponding method are therefore usually given the same name.

Figure 16.19 **An association between the Customer and CustomerOrder classes**

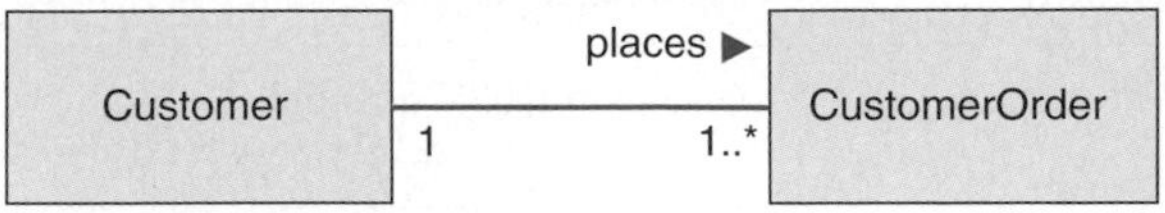

16.4.4 Associations

Classes do not work in isolation. We have already seen examples of message passing between classes in previous sections. This implies an element of connectedness between classes.

In a UML model, instances of classes may be related to each other; where classes are related an **association** exists. Associations are conceptual links between classes and reflect the responsibilities of a class. They are modelled in UML as a connecting line between two classes.

Associations are provided with a **role name** which describes in active language the nature of the association. A solid arrowhead attached to the role name provides the direction in which the association can be read. Figure 16.19 shows an association between customers and orders. Reading from left to right the association captures the link that a customer places an order. It is not essential to label the association in both directions; this will be determined by the context in which the association manifests itself within the system. If a role name is not shown then the name of the target class is taken to be that role name.

Each end of the association is connected to a class. At the point of connection an indication of the cardinality of the relationship is provided. This is termed the **multiplicity** of the association. The multiplicity indicates the number of occurrences of the class that can participate in the association.

In Figure 16.19, reading towards the right, the multiplicity of the association shows that a customer can place 1 or more orders, indicated by 1..* (the minimum and maximum values of 1 and * respectively). Reading towards the left, the multiplicity of the association shows that each customer order has been placed by a single customer, indicated by the lone digit 1.

Table 16.1 illustrates the range of multiplicities that can be employed.

16.4.5 Inheritance

One of the defining features of object oriented approaches is the facility to capture and take advantage of **inheritance**. In the natural world we take this for granted. For example all animals eat, sleep, reproduce, move around etc. If you consider more specific categories (or classes) of animal, such as mammal, fish, bird etc., each of those classes of animal will be able to eat, sleep, reproduce, move around etc., albeit in slightly different ways. Indeed, if you look at specific examples of animals (objects), regardless of whether you are considering an earthworm, an elephant or an eagle, the fact that it is an animal means that you know it will be able to eat, sleep, reproduce, move around.

Table 16.1 **The range of multiplicities that can be employed**

Multiplicity	Explanation	Possible example
1	Only permissible quantity	Number of customers involved in placing a particular order
52	Only permissible quantity	Number of cards in a standard deck
6,12	Two permissible quantities (6 or 12)	Number of strings on a rhythm guitar
4,5	Two permissible quantities (4 or 5)	Number of strings on a bass guitar
1..8	Range of permissible quantities (any value from 1 to 8 inclusive)	Number of carriages comprising a train
0..6	Range of permissible quantities (any value from 0 to 6 inclusive)	Number of library books you have checked out at any particular moment
1..*	Range of permissible quantities (1 or more)	Number of books in the library
*	Range of permissible quantities (zero or more)	Number of calls taken by a call centre in a day

In the same way, when engaged in OO modelling, the attributes and operations of a 'child' class can be inherited from a 'parent' class. In addition to that, a child class can also add further attributes and operations, or refine the way that the parent operation is implemented. This increasing specialization from parent to child ensures the diversity of classes required but reduces duplication by maintaining the common aspects at the more general level. It also ensures that common features will be inherited and become available to all subclasses (children) of the superclass (the parent).

In UML, inheritance is shown as an association with an open arrowhead pointing from child to parent class. Figure 16.20 shows an inheritance hierarchy. In this example different categories of customer are shown: corporate customers and private individuals. This diagram can be read as 'a corporate customer is a kind of customer' and 'a private customer is a kind of customer'. This 'is a kind of' relationship typifies inheritance.

Figure 16.20 shows that customers are handled differently depending on their category. An example of this can be seen in the payment methods available. Private individuals are limited to settling payment by debit card only. Corporate customers are invoiced and can settle invoices in a variety of ways. However, both corporate and private customers can inherit the attributes of name and address and the operation of placing an order. This is because these class members appear in the superclass called Customer.

Where the complete set of child classes is known, they are joined to the parent by a shared connector. For example, if it transpires that there are only two categories of

Figure 16.20 An inheritance hierarchy

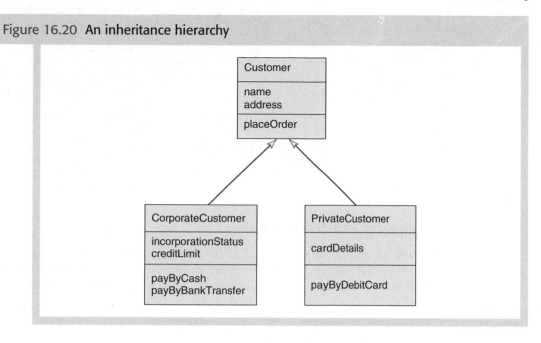

Figure 16.21 An inheritance hierarchy (alternative notation)

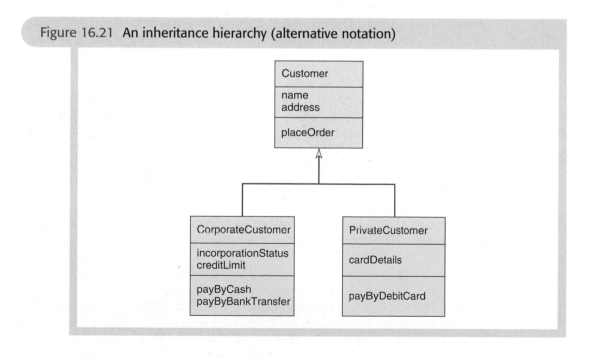

customer, corporate and private, the inheritance would be more properly recorded as shown in Figure 16.21. This can be read as 'a customer is either a corporate customer or a private customer', or 'a corporate customer or a private customer are the only two kinds of customer'.

Figure 16.22 Two examples of the aggregation relationship

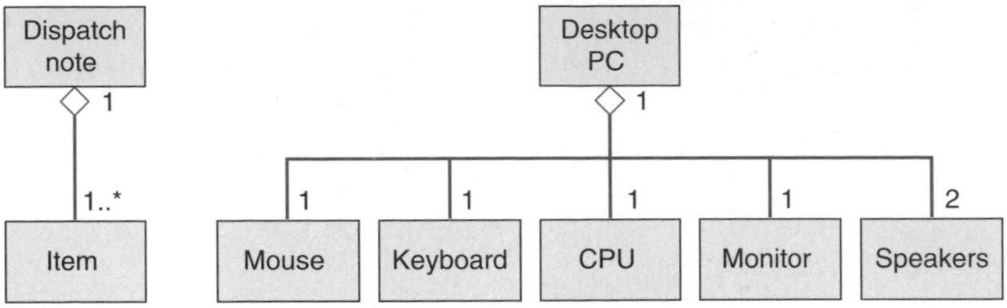

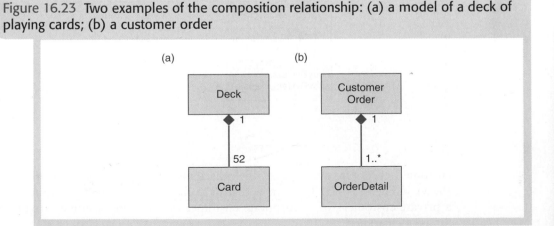

16.4.6 Aggregation and composition

Although all associations represent a relationship between classes, some associations can be specified further and allow the reader to infer that one class is a component of the other. UML provides two variants on this theme: **aggregation** and **composition**.

Aggregation

In an aggregation relationship, a class is comprised of one or more other classes. Aggregation is sometimes referred to as a whole-part relationship; the classes that represent the parts can be combined together to make the whole. Figure 16.22 shows two examples of aggregation. The first shows a Dispatch note class comprised of a number of items. The second shows a typical desktop computer as an aggregation of its component parts. Here the desktop computer comprises a mouse, a keyboard, two speakers etc.

Composition

A composition relationship is stronger than an aggregation. The composite parts can only belong to one particular whole. If the whole were to be removed from the system, the composite parts would have no separate existence and would be removed too.

Figure 16.23(a) shows a model of a deck of playing cards. The *deck* class (the whole) is composed of the individual *card* classes (the parts). An individual playing card would serve no purpose if removed from the deck. If a deck were deleted from a system, all the

Figure 16.23 Two examples of the composition relationship: (a) a model of a deck of playing cards; (b) a customer order

individual cards would be deleted simultaneously. Figure 16.23(b) shows the various 'lines' of detail that collectively make up a customer order. The Customer Order class (the whole) is composed of the individual Order Detail classes (the parts). An individual Order Detail serves no purpose if disaggregated from the Customer Order. If a Customer Order were deleted from a system, all the individual lines of Detail would be deleted simultaneously.

Both examples illustrate the differentiation between the composition and the aggregation relationship; in the latter the whole and the parts can exist independently.

16.4.7 Class diagram

The UML **class diagram** presents various classes and the different static relationships that exist between them. It brings together on a single diagram the elements described above, namely the classes and the associations between classes.

If a class diagram were drawn for the entire system it would be extremely complex and difficult to interpret readily. For that reason class diagrams are usually packaged in a similar way to that previously shown for use cases.

A common device for the system developer in packaging classes into class diagrams is to be guided by the use case diagrams. Each use case diagram provides a logically cohesive set of functions; an individual class diagram can therefore be drawn for each of the use case diagrams. There may be some overlap where classes and associations appear in more than one class diagram. This is not problematic. Indeed, when using an OO software development tool the designer would typically select a use case diagram and then from a menu of options be able to display the relevant class diagram, i.e. the classes and associations that appear in that diagram and that are involved in carrying out the use case.

Kismet case study 16.4

Figure 16.24 shows a class diagram that reflects the use case *Place Order*. The classes that are required to carry out the use case and the associations between those classes are shown on this diagram.

Figure 16.24 **A class diagram**

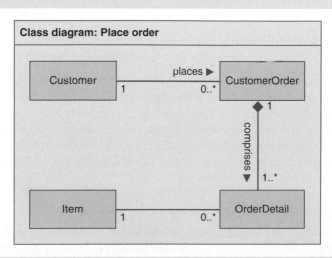

A particular class diagram forms just one view on the system. Clearly other aspects of the system will be captured in other class diagrams, in turn reflecting other use cases. This connection between class diagram and their relevant use cases allows the developer and the client to view the system in a systematic but manageable way.

16.4.8 Modelling strategies

The process of identifying classes and associations, attributes and operations, aggregations and generalizations in order to produce a class diagram is an iterative process. The various elements will often have been derived from the systems investigation, described in Chapter 11, Section 11.3. This information allows the system developer to capture those classes that are clearly identifiable and also to capture intuitive beliefs about how the system operates. The model developed will cycle between use case, class and class diagram, refining and improving again and again. More importantly, the accessibility of the diagrammatic and other features of UML enable the client to be intrinsically involved in the process and to participate fully at this stage of the development.

Discovering classes

Clearly the importance of the class in the OO modelling approach means that identifying classes is a fundamentally essential activity. A primary resource for discovering classes is the use case diagram. If modelled in sufficient detail the use case, through its name and its accompanying textual description will contain the source information for identifying classes. However, this source alone cannot suffice as omissions in the use case diagrams would perpetuate into later modelling. Again the application of iterative techniques and constant involvement of the client with their detailed knowledge of the problem domain will assist in ensuring correctness throughout.

Various approaches to discovering classes have been proposed. Bennett *et al.* (2006) suggest an approach where the outputs of the systems investigation stage are scrutinized by categorization. They suggest exploring under the following categories:

- Specific instances of a general type: e.g. People ('Louis Earle'), organizations ('Sheffield Insurance Services'), organizational units ('The sales team').
- Structures: e.g. 'preferred suppliers', 'delivery packing instructions'.
- Abstractions: e.g. 'account holder', 'requirement'.
- Enduring relationships between classes: e.g. 'agreement'.

Stevens and Pooley (1999) suggest two approaches, data-driven design and responsibility-driven design. They describe these two approaches as the ends of a continuum and suggest that an iterative approach which combines both is likely to be the most successful. They also point out that although many authors refer to 'class identification', really the process here is concerned with 'key domain abstractions'. We are discovering features and facts about the system that could identify classes but could equally identify associations, actors, attributes etc.

Data-driven design

As the name implies, **data-driven design** focuses more at the outset on the data requirements of the system. The system developer looks less at the activities that the system is carrying out and more at the information requirements. Proponents of this approach claim that it is particularly suitable at initial stages given that the major UML artefacts being generated here represent static views of the system.

One technique for data-driven design is that of noun identification. The textual output from system investigation and the resulting use case diagrams encapsulate the requirements of the system. This textual data is inspected and all nouns and noun phrases are underlined and extracted. This process provides a list of candidate classes. Further refinement of that list then produces the initial class list for the system.

The refinements usually take a format such as this:

- convert plurals to singular
  - orders > order
- remove synonyms
  - choose one of 'customer invoice' and 'invoice'
- remove anything vague/ambiguous, or clarify
- usually remove events or actions, notably if they have no state or identity
- remove anything outside the scope of the system: e.g. actors
- remove attributes: items that are relevant but have no behaviour
- gives list of possible classes.

Kismet case study 16.5

Using the text of Kismet case study 12.1 (the order processing system) the following initial list of nouns and noun phrases can be extracted

Table 16.2 **Results of noun phrase analysis**

customers	total value of the order	unsatisfied back orders
orders	current balance	goods ordered
Kismet HQ	credit limit	stores department
order	order copies	inventory records
sales order department	credit control department	dispatch note
company order form	credit control manager	invoicing department
order#	approved order copies	three-part invoice
order date	top copy	sales price
customer#	temporary file	goods
customer name	'approved order' file	catalogue
item 1 code#	staff	discount
item 1 quantity	customer queries	geographical location
item 2 code#	two copies	total purchases
item 2 quantity	stores department	total value of the order
top copy	invoicing department	sales tax
form	the copy	totals
recently placed order	quantities supplied	Accounts
item	order form	customer accounts
remaining copies	dispatch note	ledgers
sales catalogue	goods supplied	remaining copy
order department	quantities	invoicing department
priced copies	One copy	order copy
credit control section	the goods	dispatch note
order value	packing and dispatch	
customer account	entire order	

565

This list can be refined to provide a list of possible classes

Table 16.3 **Candidate classes**

customer, order, item, customer account, dispatch note, invoice

Other noun phrases might suggest external systems that might be represented by actors (sales catalogue, credit control section) or attributes of classes already identified (customer#, customer name).

Responsibility-driven design

An alternative to data-driven design is **responsibility-driven design**. Proponents of this approach point out that although information requirements are an essential aspect, each class is responsible for maintaining that data and that system operation can only be effected by message passing between classes. The data within the system is formed, maintained, amended, and made accessible only through the communication between collaborating classes; the responsibility for this, the proponents claim, must be captured at an early stage.

A textual analysis of the verbs in the documentation produced so far can provide a starting point to identifying activities and operations. However, this quickly leads to questions of whether these operations are active solely within an individual class or whether a collaboration with other classes is required.

16.4.9 CRC cards

The most popular technique for carrying out responsibility-driven design is through the use of CRC cards, pioneered by Beck and Cunningham (1989). CRC stands for Class, Responsibilities, Collaborations. CRC cards do not form part of UML but they are a very popular tool with OO system developers nonetheless. They provide the system developer with a simple but potentially powerful tool in identifying classes and associations.

Kismet case study 16.6

Based on the classes discovered in the text analysis of nouns and noun phrases a set of CRC cards is constructed (three are shown in Figure 16.25). In drawing up the cards the systems developers realize that an additional class *OrderDetail* is required to store the lines of detail that comprise each invoice.

Figure 16.25 **Three examples of CRC cards**

CustomerOrder	
Responsibilities	Collaborators
• Accept order	• Customer
• Cancel order	• Customer
• Calculate total order value	• OrderDetail
• Check credit status	• CustomerCredit

Figure 16.25 (cont'd)

Customer	
Responsibilities • Maintains customer details	**Collaborators** • Order • CustomerAccount

Order detail	
Responsibilities • Records items ordered	**Collaborators** • Item

A single CRC card is a small (typically 15cm × 8cm) piece of card with a pre-printed layout. The card is ruled off into three sections. The top section, across the width of the card, contains the name of the class. Below that, the remaining space is divided into two vertical sections. On the left, the various responsibilities of the class are listed. On the right are listed all the other classes with which this class must collaborate in order to satisfy those responsibilities. Cards are usually single sided.

Usually, developers line up the various responsibilities on the left with the relevant collaborators on the right. An alternative is just to make two lists, one on each side of the card. Given that the 'work' has been done in thinking through the collaborations required for each responsibility, it seems wasteful to then lose the connection by making two unrelated lists. The most effective approach is therefore to preserve a link between each responsibility and the collaborators required to ensure it is carried out.

The process by which CRC cards are produced and developed is very much a participatory activity that works best for a team rather than an individual system developer. Typically classes would be shared between developers; ideally each would take just one or two classes. Each developer then engages in a role play activity where they represent their class in a negotiation with others.

The whole process is usually conducted as a brainstorming session; all ideas are welcomed and then tested out. An iterative approach is adopted as cards are written and rewritten to respond to the various ideas put forward. Developers often adopt an anthropomorphic approach to the CRC cards and take on the role of the card themselves. These sessions can often be very animated as developers request services and information from others to satisfy the requirements of the card (or class) that they are representing.

In this enactment, new fuctionality might emerge requiring a class to decide where the new responsibility might reside. Negotiation can take place which may result in responsibility being placed in a different class and a further collaboration being required.

To manage the process, the team may decide to enact separately each of the use case diagrams previously identified. By focusing on a use case diagram the process is given an appropriate level of contextualization. The iterative nature of the development approach might for example result in redefining the use cases packaged in the diagram or in discovering new classes. A typical discovery at this stage might be the realization that two classes share a number of responsibilities and collaborators. This identification of generalization might then lead to an inheritance association and the creation of a new superclass.

16.4.10 Further aspects to object orientation

Association classes

Sometimes the association between two classes contains so much contextual information that there is a need to delegate responsibility to a separate class. The term for a class performing this function is an **association class**.

Figure 16.26(a) shows an association between suppliers and the items that are ordered. Often additional discounts can be gained if orders are placed in a systematic way. To take advantage of those discounts the association needs to contain additional detail such as the preferred supplier. Because an association class represents the association, it is usually given the same name as the association role name. An alternative way of representing the relationship between items and suppliers is to create a new class. This is shown in Figure 16.26(b).

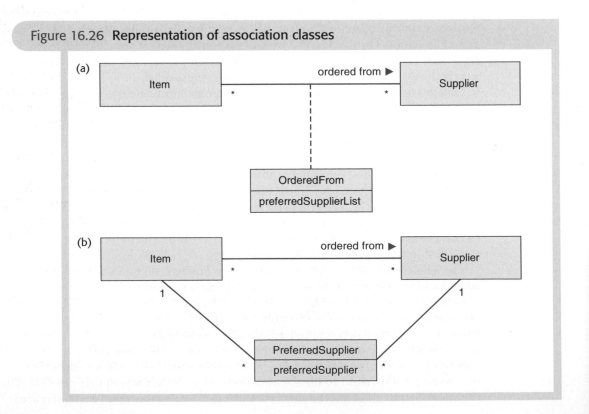

Figure 16.26 Representation of association classes

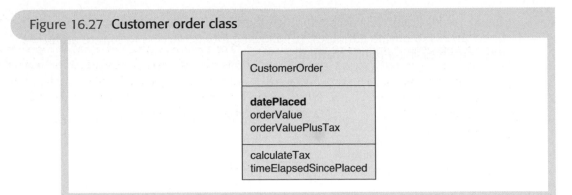

Figure 16.27 Customer order class

Visibility

An important aspect of object orientation is that of **information hiding**. This means that attributes and methods are only available at the point where they are required. Moreover access to those class members is constrained and limited so that they are only visible in the appropriate context.

Figure 16.27 shows a Customer Order class. The class contains an attribute called datePlaced: this has been highlighted. It would be possible, although inadvisable, to allow this attribute to be directly accessible from outside of the class. The reason this could be dangerous is that the designer of another class might inadvertently alter the contents of this attribute, believing that it referred to a different *datePlaced*, say the date that an order with a supplier was placed. This problem is called a **side effect**. Errors that arise as a result of these side effects are notoriously difficult to locate but they can be limited and controlled through information hiding.

Even simply accessing the contents of an attribute from outside the class can be problematic as it ties different classes together in an unnecessarily close way. The degree of interdependency of this kind is known as **coupling**; as a general rule components of software should limit the degree of coupling, thereby encouraging modularity, facilitating maintenance and promoting reuse.

To help address this, attributes of classes can be given **private** visibility. If given a private **access specifier**, an attribute is only accessible from within its own class, i.e. only an object instantiated from that class can access it. That poses the question, what if we want message passing between two classes to involve one of these private attributes? The resolution is to create a method that can access the attribute and give the method **public** visibility. Other classes can then pass a message that invokes that method; the method is made responsible for managing and controlling access to the attribute. In UML a plus character (+) preceding the class member name indicates a public access specifier and a minus character (−) indicates a private access specifier.

In Figure 16.28(a) an external request to interrogate the contents of the orderValue attribute is not valid as the attribute has a private access specifier. Figure 16.28(b) shows the class with the addition of a further method *getOrderValue*. This method is given a public access specifier and therefore an external message *getOrderValue* can be sent which invokes the method and provides for controlled access to the attribute.

Visibility is also an issue for the operations of a class. Some operations may only be responsible for internal activity within a class, others will be triggered by messages sent

Figure 16.28 **Controlling access through the use of access specifiers: (a) preventing direct access to private attributes; (b) allowing indirect access to private attributes through accessing a public method**

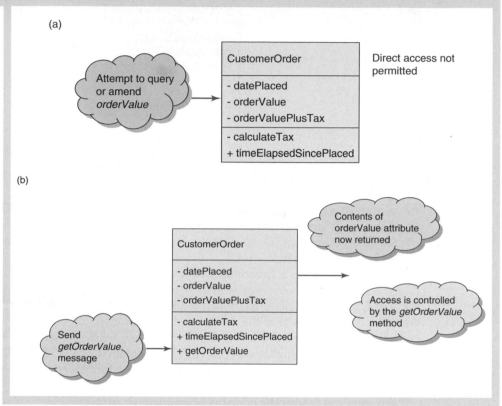

from other classes or from user commands. In Figure 16.28(b) the method *calculateTax* is used to generate the value for attribute *orderValuePlusTax* in a calculation based on the contents of the attribute *orderValue*. This method has no relevance outside the class itself. In this case the method can be given private visibility. It is therefore not possible to send a message originating from outside the class to calculate the tax. Because of the private access specifier, only an object from the CustomerOrder class can send the message, thereby carrying out the operation completely internally.

The operation *timeElapsedSincePlaced*, however, might need to be available to another class which, say, is responsible for compiling a list of all outstanding orders. In order to receive this message and respond to it *timeElapsedSincePlaced* needs to be publicly visible.

A final level of visibility that UML provides is the **protected** access specifier. This is indicated by prefixing a hash (#) symbol to a class member. Attributes or methods with protected visibility are accessible from the class or from any subclass that appear in specializations of that class. This halfway house between public and private visibility reflects that fact that sometimes we want to prevent open access to a class member from other classes, but that inherited classes, although different to the original class, are

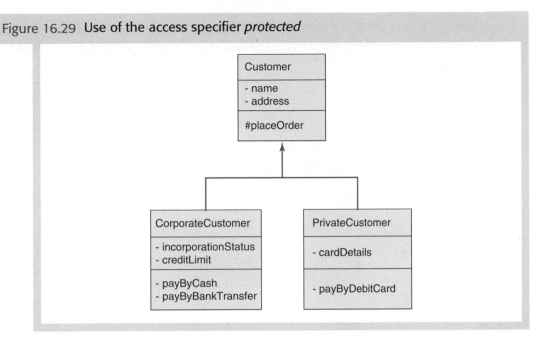

Figure 16.29 **Use of the access specifier** *protected*

related and might be an exception. Private access would exclude the inherited class from accessing the item but protected access does not.

In Figure 16.29 the method *placeOrder* has a protected access specifier and is therefore visible in the corporate and private customer classes. A message to *placeOrder* can therefore be sent to a corporate customer or a private customer and will be successfully and appropriately dealt with.

Visibility is an important issue to get right at the design stage, particularly if amendments or modifications to classes are likely to be made later on. A typical modification might be to create new classes which are further specializations of classes already designed. If class members are given protected access specifiers then they will be available for any new subclasses that subsequently inherit from the original class.

For example, if some years later it is decided to specialize the CorporateCustomer class in Figure 16.30 into *NationalCorporateCustomer* and *InternationalCorporateCustomer* the methods *payByCash* and *payByBankTransfer* would not be visible as they were designed with private access. If the source code for the CorporateCustomer is available, the maintenance can be carried out but it is an avoidable additional cost, and could open up the class, which has by now been tried and tested for new errors or side effects during the maintenance process. In some circumstances the source code is not even available. In those cases the need for careful foresight and planning in design are even more obvious.

Abstraction

The visible class members provide an interface to the class. If considered as a black box, the interface can be seen to be the entry point for communication to the hidden class contents. The concept of a client of a class (the sender of a message to the class) not needing to know any more than that provided by the interface, is termed **abstraction**. Developers of object oriented systems make use of abstraction in their design of classes and their associations. Where a design makes best use of abstraction there is invariably

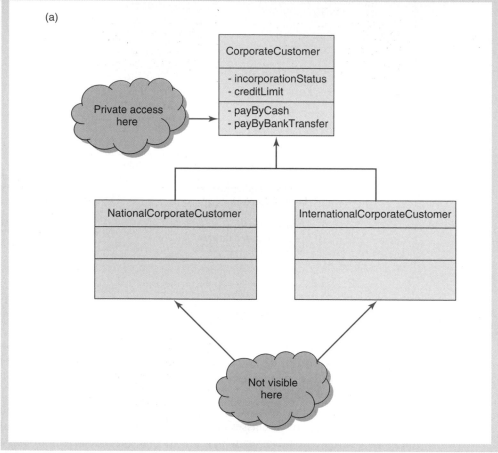

Figure 16.30 **Making use of the protected access specifier: (a) designing without use of the protected access specifier; (b) designing with the protected access specifier**

evidence of highly cohesive classes and low coupling between classes (cohesion and coupling were both defined earlier). This facilitates a system architecture comprised of components that can be easily maintained or replaced and that can be readily reused.

Encapsulation

In a good design, modifications to one module should have a minimal effect on others. Earlier in this chapter the degree of dependency between classes was defined as coupling; as a general principle it was stated that coupling should be kept to a minimum. In object oriented systems communication between classes is fundamental; however, dependency is a different issue. By restricting the visible elements of a class through the techniques of information hiding, and by enforcing visibility through access specifiers, a designer is applying the principle of **encapsulation**. Encapsulation ensures that the interface to the outside world is restricted only to that which is absolutely essential. The possibility for dependency between classes is therefore minimized. For example, a Customer class might provide a method which searches through the objects of that class to locate a particular

Figure 16.30 *(cont'd)*

(b)

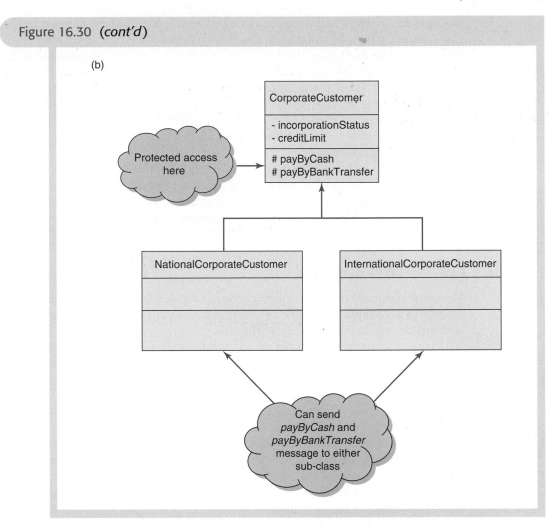

instance of a customer. The interface to the Customer class, and therefore the means by which to perform this search, is through the method signature: the name of the method and the expected parameters supplied, e.g. the item required as the search criterion. The actual search algorithm is encapsulated within the Customer class; any class requesting the search is completely unaware of the algorithm used to carry out the search. Indeed the search algorithm could at a later date be completely rewritten, say to improve performance. Other classes using the Customer class continue to send messages using the unchanged message signature unaware that the underlying code has been amended.

16.5   Dynamic modelling

The class diagrams seen previously show the associations between the classes within the system; these identify the relationships within that static structure. Within individual classes some functionality can be deduced, e.g. it can be deduced that a method *calculateTax* will perform operations upon the contents of an attribute *orderValue* to produce the contents of a different attribute *orderValuePlusTax*. However, where use cases require classes to collaborate together to perform tasks it is far more difficult to deduce the operation from the static models seen so far. The diagrams introduced in this chapter focus on the dynamic aspects of the system. Where communication between objects takes place, this will be captured and portrayed. Where operations must take place in an ordered fashion, e.g. in sequence, this can also be clearly represented. The combination of static and dynamic models will provide a system specification that can readily be programmed using an object oriented programming language and produce a working system.

A number of UML models are provided to represent the dynamic aspects of a system. Collectively they are termed **interaction diagrams**. In particular there are two diagrams which are particularly used: the **sequence diagram** and the **communication (or collaboration) diagram**. Although different in appearance, both of these diagrams capture similar information.

16.5.1 Collaboration diagrams

The combination of the objects performing a given action and the links between them is defined as a **collaboration**. The collaboration diagram captures these elements along with any actors that are involved in the task.

There is a synergy between the class diagrams that are produced to model the static aspects of the use cases, and the collaboration diagram. The collaboration diagram can be thought of as an animated version of the class diagram. The result of the message passing that was represented on the class diagram by the target methods in the classes is shown actually taking place on the collaboration diagram. There is one significant difference between the two diagrams, however; to model communication in the actual system, the collaboration diagram must be a representation of activity at *run time*. The elements that appeared as classes and associations on the class model must therefore be replaced by the actual objects that are communicating at run time. The collaboration diagram therefore comprises objects, associations and, if required, the actors that initiate or participate in the communication.

The representation of objects was introduced in the previous chapter. Figure 16.31 shows two classes, *Customer* and *CustomerOrder* joined by an association called *list*.

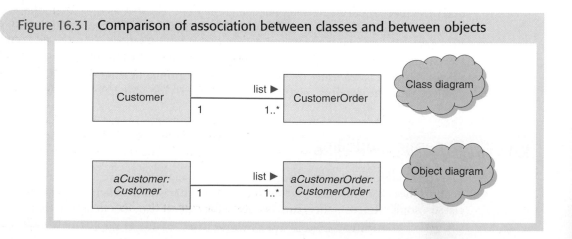

Figure 16.31 **Comparison of association between classes and between objects**

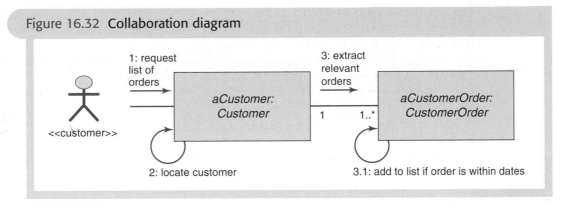

Figure 16.32 Collaboration diagram

Below the classes, two objects are shown. These objects have been given the generic names *aCustomer* and *aCustomerOrder*. The link between the objects represents the association shown on the class diagram.

Often a collaboration diagram omits the association role name as the passing of messages will replace this detail. The multiplicity in the object version of the diagram clearly must be the same as in the class diagram. If an inconsistency is detected then further iterations of the static modelling stage will be revisited to correct the difference. It is not compulsory to show the multiplicity in a collaboration diagram. In less complex diagrams it is less of an issue, but in more complex ones it can appear to clutter and detract from the purpose of the diagram. A collaboration diagram should realize a use case. It should show the sequence of messages that are exchanged between the linked objects.

Figure 16.32 shows a collaboration diagram which is a realization of a use case *ListAllOrdersPlaced*. This use case allows a customer to log on to a web-based interrogation system to obtain a list of all the orders that have been placed between two given dates. The service is only available to certain categories of customer.

The collaboration diagram shows the interface with the customer actor, where the request is submitted. The system will first need to locate the relevant customer records to verify that the customer is entitled to use the system. This is achieved by searching through the customer objects to find the correct one. Once the correct customer object has been found, the association between that customer and all the orders placed by that customer is used to navigate to each order in turn. The date criteria is applied to establish whether the current order is within the desired range. If so the order object is added to a list of those meeting the required criteria and a navigation to the next customer order is performed. This process is repeated until all the customer orders for that customer have been inspected. In this example the process has been simplified by ignoring (a) the user interface and (b) how the list of orders fulfilling the criteria is handled and made available to the customer.

Often a collaboration diagram will be accompanied by text written in a structured form of natural language such as that shown in Figure 16.33. This provides further detail explaining the activity that must be performed. The developer should be aware of the following points:

- Each use case will usually have a principal beneficiary. The collaboration diagram will usually feature the actor that plays the role of this beneficiary.
- Often the actor is the instigator of the activity shown in the collaboration diagram.

Figure 16.33 Structured text to accompany collaboration diagram

1. Customer provides customer reference number and requests orders placed between dd1/mm1/yy1 and dd2/mm2/yy2.
2. Locate customer object using customer reference number.
3. For all orders associated with this customer object
   3.1 if order date attribute in customer order object is between dd1/mm1/yy1 and dd2/mm2/yy2 then add order object to list

- The messages sent between actor and object, or from one object to another, replace the association role names. In each collaboration diagram the navigation between objects must map to a corresponding association. Again, if an inconsistency is detected then further iterations of design at the static modelling stage must be conducted to address the problem.
- The direction of navigation of the messages reflects the direction of the association role name in the class diagram.
- The numbering of the messages allows the sequencing of activities to be established. This allows for the capture of the dynamic aspects of the system.
- Detailed procedural design can be recorded in accompanying text written in **structured English.** This facilitates the creation of a more rigorous design and also provides a more seamless progression to the programming phase.

Developing the collaborations

The introduction of the dynamic aspects of a system requires detailed understanding of the behaviour of that system. In creating an interaction diagram such as the collaboration diagram, the system developer will return to the CRC cards previously developed. These will indicate where the responsibility for certain aspects of functionality resides and will show which classes join to collaborate and carry out a task. Once again the development process is expected to be iterative in nature; the classes expected to collaborate and function may not in practice be those ideally placed so to do. It may require revising the CRC cards and/or the class diagram again to be clear how that part of the model actually functions.

A typical problem that might be identified at this stage might be a message sent to an object that has no method available that can understand that message. In Figure 16.32 the message *extractRelevantOrders* is being sent to an object of the *CustomerOrder* class. If no method has been provided to carry out this message request then the CRC card for the *CustomerOrder* class will need to be revisited. This further responsibility of the *CustomerOrder* class will need to be added and a collaboration with the *Customer* class will be identified to discharge this responsibility. The class diagram for the use case *ListAllOrdersPlaced* may need to be checked to ensure the association is identified and that its multiplicity is correct.

Message types

In its simplest terms, only one object in a collaboration diagram is actively working at any one time. This is termed **synchronous** message passing. When an object receives a

Figure 16.34 UML representations of messages

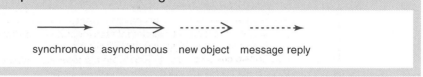

synchronous asynchronous   new object   message reply

message its activation state becomes live and it starts actively working. While the methods that respond to the message are invoked and carry out the required operations, the object remains in this live activation state. Once the object has completed it will send a response to the sender of the originating message and the live activation state ends. However, during its operation an object may send a message to another object. In that case the message sender remains in live activation state but ceases actively working. The receiver enters live activation state and starts actively working until it completes and returns a response. Alternatively, it too may send a message to a further object. In this way a stack of objects may all be live but each one temporarily suspended awaiting a response from the recipient of its message which will allow it to continue and complete its tasks.

In more complex system operation, an object may send a message but carry on actively working, i.e. it does not wait for a response. This is known as **asynchronous** message passing. This form of operation allows for procedures to continue in parallel threads of activity.

Figure 16.34 shows four UML representations of messages. The solid arrow with a solid head indicates a synchronous message. The solid arrow with an angled arrowhead indicates an asynchronous message. Two other styles are shown. The dashed arrow with an angled arrowhead shows a message from one object which results in the creation of a new object. Finally the dashed arrow with a solid head indicates a message reply.

As all messages have a logical response, the responses do not have to be shown on the collaboration diagram and often they are omitted. The structured numbering of the messages allows a reader of the diagram to deduce which objects are live and actively working at any point. UML provides methods for representing active objects and asynchronous communication.

In Figure 16.35, object *a* of class A is drawn with a thickened border to show that it is active. As described above, an active object can send messages to passive objects or can communicate with other active objects. This is very much a snapshot style of representation and is normally used to explain a particular, often complex, aspect of a collaboration. It is a particularly pertinent device where software support tools are used in the development process. Typically the software tool will animate the collaboration diagram and the various objects can be shown to become active or passive as the use case under scrutiny is played out.

Also Figure 16.35 shows that messages 1 and 2 are sent from object *a* synchronously, i.e. object *a* issues message 1 but does not wait for a response before issuing message 2. Objects *b* and *c* then both become active simultaneously. As part of its functioning object *c* is required to issue message 3. However, in order for it to perform correctly it is essential that object *b* has completed and made its reply to object *a*. This rendezvous point is established by preceding the message with a list of the messages that must have completed. This list is terminated with a slash character. In the example above message 1 is shown in that way (1/).

Figure 16.35 Synchronization in message passing

a:A

1: do this

2: do that

b:B

c:C

3: 1/ do the other

d:D

Further detail

Depending on the complexity of the use case being modelled, further detail can be added to the collaboration diagram.

In Figure 16.36 the mechanics of extracting the required orders is clarified. The iteration of checking through each order is shown: the test condition *while more orders to check* shown in square brackets and the prefix of an asterisk indicates a repetition. At a sublevel of numbering, the test condition *date in range* is shown in square brackets. If the test condition is true then the operation *add to list* is performed. The placement of *add to list* at level 3.1.1 is below (i.e. within) the level of *while more orders to check*, namely 3.1. This confirms that the operation at level 3.1.1 is iteratively performed for each and every occurrence of an object discovered at level 3.1.

Creating new objects

During program execution, new objects will be created. These new objects will be created in response to a message request. In order to correctly instantiate a new object a class may contain a special method known as a **constructor** function. By convention the constructor is given the same name as the class itself. The constructor takes responsibility for any initialization routines and in particular setting the initial values of attributes.

Figure 16.36 Enhancing the collaboration diagram

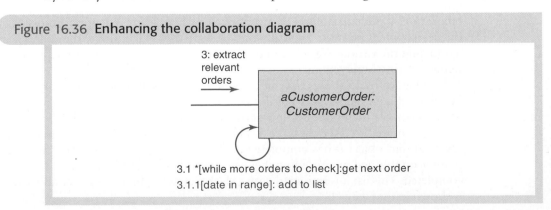

3: extract
relevant
orders

*aCustomerOrder:
CustomerOrder*

3.1 *[while more orders to check]:get next order
3.1.1[date in range]: add to list

Kismet case study 16.7

Figure 16.37 shows the classes for *Customer* and *CustomerOrder*. A use case has been identified by the system developer called *PlaceOrder* whereby a customer can via a web interface place an order for goods. A fragment of the class diagram representing that use case is shown. The *receiveOrder* method will be responsible for accepting the order requirements and sending a message that creates the new *CustomerOrder* object. The constructor function which responds to this message can be seen in the *CustomerOrder* class. These dynamic aspects are more easily represented in the collaboration diagram.

Figure 16.37 Use of the constructor function

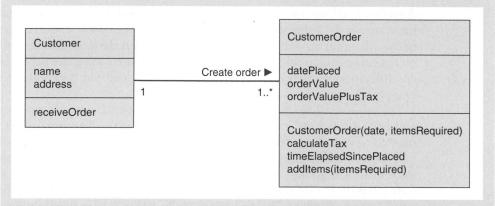

Figure 16.38 shows a collaboration diagram for the *PlaceOrder* use case. When a customer places an order the customer details are first checked. Then a message is sent to create a new *CustomerOrder* object. The message includes detail about the items

Figure 16.38 Collaboration diagram for the *PlaceOrder* use case

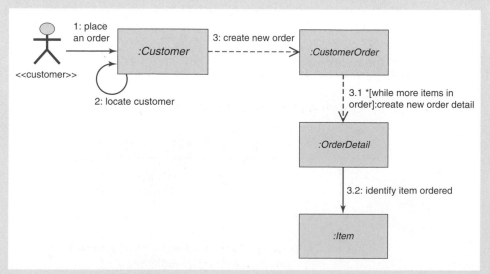

required and the date the order was placed. A new *CustomerOrder* object is created and the constructor function initializes the attribute *datePlaced* to the value of *date*, which was provided with the message that was initiated from the *Customer* class. The constructor function of the *CustomerOrder* class then sends a message to its own *addItems* method which begins the process of building the order. A message to create a new *orderDetail* object is repeated and sent once for each of the items ordered. The *orderDetail* class may also have its own constructor function to handle the operation (this detail is not shown here). Each order detail is associated with a particular item.

16.5.2 Sequence diagram

A further UML interaction diagram that can be used to capture the dynamic aspects of the system is the **sequence diagram**. In many ways the collaboration diagram and the sequence diagram are semantically similar; it is often the case that the information presented using one could just as effectively be presented using the other. However, there are differences in the presentation and these may lead the system developer to choose one over the other.

The sequence diagram captures the objects and the communication between them to realize a use case. As it represents dynamic aspects, the diagram utilizes objects rather than classes to animate the runtime situation. As with the collaboration diagram, actors may also be included: typically an actor will instigate the activity being represented in the sequence diagram.

The layout of a sequence diagram is more prescribed than is the case for a collaboration diagram. As seen above, the latter can be laid out 'free-from' on the page or screen where development takes place. The sequence diagram has a timescale running vertically from top to bottom. Activities are placed on timelines to indicate their order (or sequence). The objects involved are placed horizontally across the top of the diagram. The ordering of the objects is not important. Each object is provided with its own timeline, running vertically down the page parallel to the other timelines.

Figure 16.39 shows three objects and the respective timelines for each. The timeline represents the duration of the use case. There is no scale to this line; intervals on the line

Figure 16.39 Framework for a sequence diagram

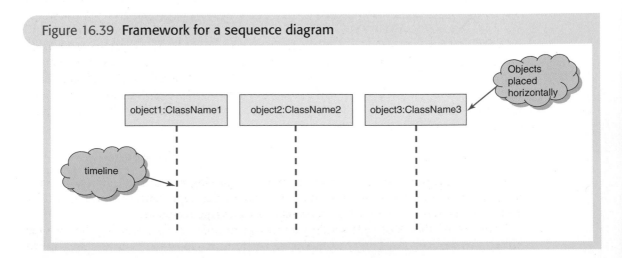

Figure 16.40 Sequence diagram showing active objects

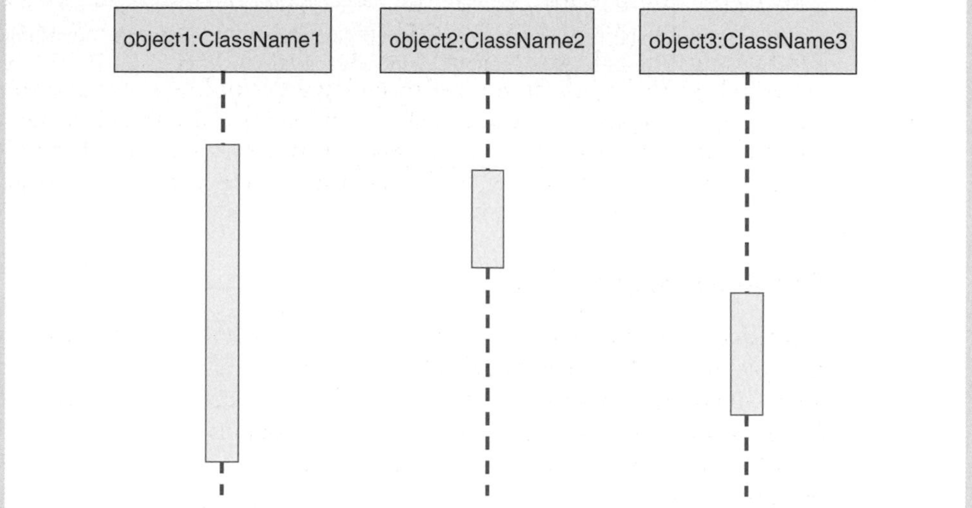

do not reflect proportionate durations of time. However, the ordering along the line persists such that for any two given points, the one that is lower on the diagram occurs after the one above it.

Object activity

Each timeline represents the lifetime of the object within the use case being elaborated. Objects are shown as being active or inactive during this timeline by being represented as a rectangle superimposed on the timeline. At the topmost side of the rectangle an object becomes active. This might be as a result of receiving a message. Then, as the reader of the diagram travels downwards through the rectangle, the object remains in an active state. At the bottommost side of the rectangle the object ceases to be active. This might be because the method that was invoked by the object as a result of receiving a message has fully completed and terminated.

In Figure 16.40 *object1* becomes active first with *object2* becoming active next. Both objects remain active until eventually *object2* terminates its operation and becomes inactive. *Object1*, however, continues to be active. After a delay, *object3* becomes active and starts processing. *Object1* still continues to be active. After a time *object3* also terminates and becomes inactive. *Object1* still continues to be active but after a time it terminates and becomes inactive.

Message passing

The communication between objects by message passing is indicated by a horizontal solid arrow. The arrow originates from the rectangle that represents the message sender and connects to the rectangle that represents the message recipient.

Figure 16.41 shows *object1* sending a message to *object2*. On receiving the message *object2* becomes active. Later, after *object2* has terminated *object1* sends a message to

Figure 16.41 Sequence diagram showing message passing

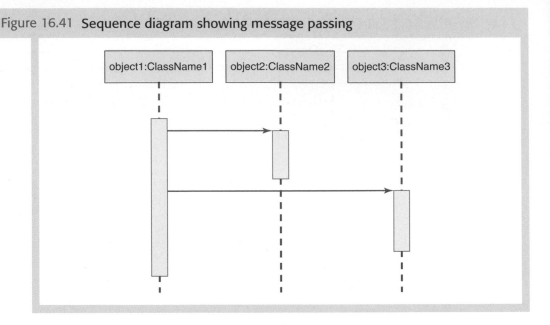

object3 causing it to become active. The vertical placing of the messages and the rectangles representing activity clearly indicates the sequence of events.

Including actors and responses

Often a use case includes an invocation by an actor. This interaction can be included by adding the actor at the leftmost side of the diagram. Figure 16.42 shows an actor sending a message and initiating the activity in the use case. This diagram also introduces a further feature: the dotted arrow; these represent responses or return values as a result of the method carried out. The inclusion of return messages is a design decision for the system developer. Often a client object will be requesting data from another object acting in the server role. Once the data has been produced by the server its subsequent delivery might benefit from being included. However, an alternative view is that the return of results is implicitly shown in the rectangle representing activity. At the end of the period of activity, the consequence must be that the results are provided. In other cases there is no data to be returned, for example when the client requests the server to carry out a task on its behalf. In that case the only return expected might be an acknowledgement that the server has completed. Again the rectangle representing activity provides that information. There is a stronger case for including the return message in the former example compared to the latter. The system developer needs to make a decision whether the inclusion of return messages adds to the knowledge provided in the diagram or clutters it by providing excessive detail.

Creating and deleting objects

Although some objects persist through the lifetime of a use case, others are more transient and either come into existence or are deleted during its execution. The creation of an object is shown by placing the object rectangle at the vertical position on the timeline when it comes into existence, rather than at the top of the diagram. An object can be

Figure 16.42 Sequence diagram showing interaction with actor

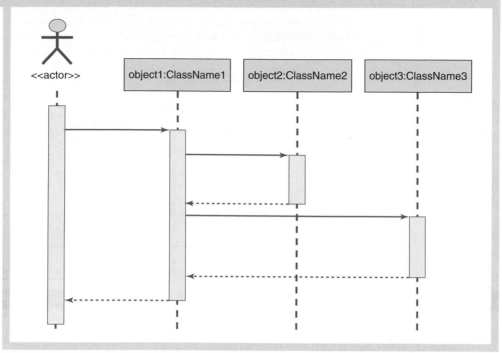

shown to be deleted by placing a large cross through the dashed timeline for the object and ending the timeline at that point.

Figure 16.43 shows *object3*, a temporary object which is only created after *object2* has become inactive. The new object is created in response to a *create* message sent from *object1*. A message is then sent to *object3* causing it to carry out some tasks. After these tasks have completed the object sends the results back to *object1*. Finally *object1* sends a *delete* message causing *object3* to be destroyed and removed from the system. The placement of a large cross on the timeline of an object indicates that it has been deleted.

The technique of labelling the message arrows with the name of the message sent is quite usual in the production of sequence diagrams.

Message types

The notion of an object sending itself a message is not uncommon in sequence diagrams. Often methods are devised which carry out some internal processing. An example of this was seen earlier in the *calculateTax* method of the *customerOrder* class in Figure 16.28.

A *customerOrder* object can send itself a message *calculateTax* to invoke the method and generate the value for attribute *orderValuePlusTax* in a calculation based on the contents of the attribute *orderValue*. This can be seen in Figure 16.44. Where an object sends a message to itself the active section of the object is illustrated by an offset rectangle which receives the message. The bottom edge of the offset rectangle shows where control is passed back.

The same set of message types as indicated previously for collaboration diagrams in Figure 16.34 can be applied to sequence diagrams.

Figure 16.43 Sequence diagram showing creation and deletion of objects

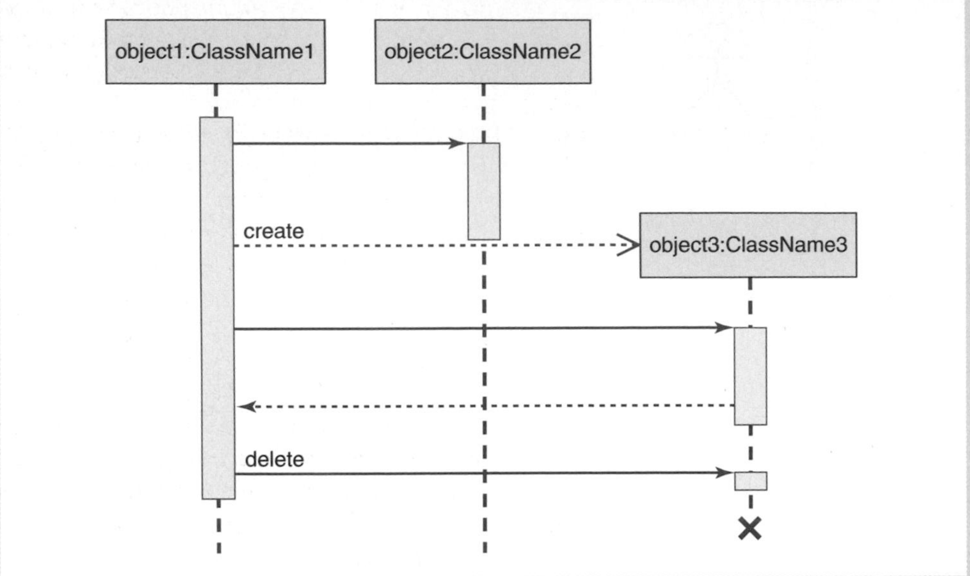

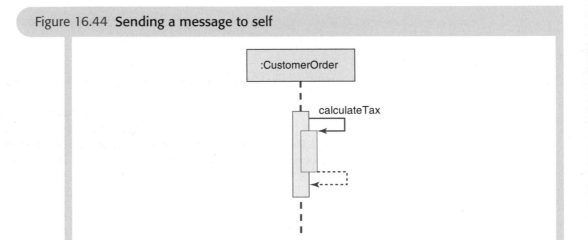

Figure 16.44 Sending a message to self

Control structures

At points in a sequence diagram there may be a need to show alternative execution paths (selection) or repetitions of activity (iteration). Selection and iteration are examples of basic **control structures** and both can be shown on sequence diagrams. There are many different ways of representing these control structures; the one chosen here introduces the notion of a **fragment;** this is a popular device as it mirrors the packaging technique already introduced.

In a sequence diagram a fragment is captured by enclosing it within a thick solid framed rectangle. A control structure can then be imposed on the fragment by indicating in a panel in the top left corner the structure and any controlling condition. Figure 16.45(a)

Figure 16.45 (a) Single attempt password entry; (b) multiple attempt password entry

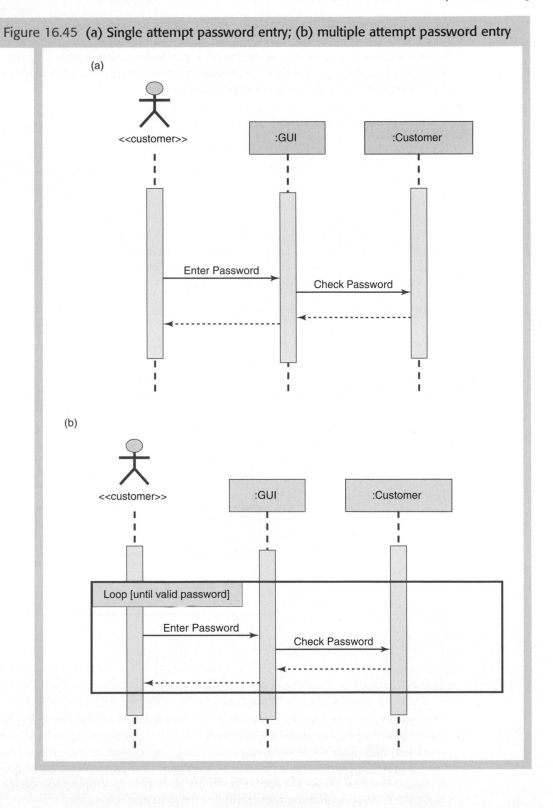

shows the sequence diagram for the entry of a password with a confirmation reply indicating whether the password was entered successfully. Figure 16.45(b) shows the enhanced sequence diagram for the entry of a password where a user is given limitless attempts to re-enter the password each time an unsuccessful attempt is made. The fragment is repeated until the successful condition is met.

Kismet case study 16.8

As part of the order processing system a report is required to evaluate whether a particular customer is entitled to a discount on the basis of having placed a large number of high-value orders. The specification of the reports requires that for the customer in question the total value of all the individual invoices that each have a value greater than £1000 is calculated.

Figure 16.46 shows a sequence diagram which represents this sales analysis. The nested fragments show the iteration through all invoices (the outer fragment) and the extraction of those invoices that meet the criterion. The grand total is made available to the customer through the user interface.

Figure 16.46 **Sequence diagram representing a sales analysis**

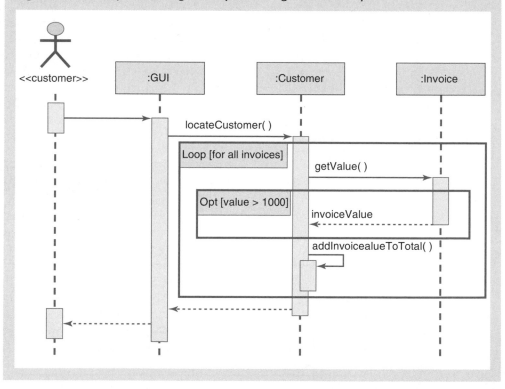

By judicious use of nested control structures any level of complexity in expressing an algorithm can be captured. As the use cases being described should be at a level of simplicity that makes for meaningful understanding, the level of nesting should not be too deep. Where it appears to be becoming too complex a further refactoring of use cases or an increased use of the <<includes>> relationship may help simplify the design and increase the robustness and maintainability of the system implemented.

Summary

This chapter has introduced the object oriented paradigm. In particular it has focused on the use of UML as the de facto standard approach for the development of systems using the object oriented paradigm.

The first stage of modelling using the Unified Modelling Language is invariably the modelling of use cases. Use case modelling provides a project manager with an early opportunity to allocate duties and responsibilities to the various participants in the project team.

Use case modelling is also the starting point for the object oriented system design process. At this stage, high-level functionality is established. Actors are identified and their relationship to the use cases is established. Textual descriptions are added to provide greater richness to the use case.

Use case diagrams are produced and then refined as detail is increasingly added. The UML packaging technique allows diagrams to kept logically coherent and preserve readability.

Static modelling is the process of discovering and establishing classes, class members, and associations between classes. A packaging approach that was already started at the use case modelling stage is continued whereby each use case model is further explained in terms of the classes and associations involved in carrying out that particular subset of system functionality. Different approaches to static modelling can be utilized; generally, these focus either on the data or on the responsibilities of a class and a number of techniques, such as noun identification or CRC cards, can be employed. A good design will evidence high levels of cohesion within classes and low levels of coupling between classes. This will enable the system to be more easily maintainable and facilitate reuse. Throughout the static modelling stage consideration of the dynamic aspects such as sequencing activities and ordering events must be suspended. These dynamic aspects are the subject of the next stage.

A recurring aspect of object oriented approaches is that the entire development must be viewed as an iterative process. Although static modelling has been presented as a 'stage', it is quite likely that during the static modelling some rethinking about the use case modelling will occur. New use cases may emerge or existing use cases may be refactored. This in turn may result in further static modelling. The reference to a static modelling stage must not assume a single start point (being the end of use case modelling) and a single end point (being the start of dynamic modelling). The developer may return many times to any or all of these stages.

The dynamic models introduced in this chapter represent and explain the interaction between the classes as they collaborate to carry out the functionality of the system. These models capture the message passing that takes place between objects to perform the various tasks required. They show when objects are created, updated and destroyed if no longer required.

Review questions

1. What differentiates object oriented approaches from the structured methods introduced in earlier chapters?

2. What are the advantages of object oriented approaches?

3. What are the key components of a use case?

4. Define the <<includes>> and the <<extends>> relationships that can be used in use case diagrams.

5. How can packages be used to facilitate use case design and improve the readability of use case diagrams?

6. Define the terms class, object, message passing, association, inheritance, aggregation, composition.

7. What techniques can be employed to discover the classes in a system?

8. Describe the contents of a CRC card. How are CRC cards used to flesh out the requirements of a system?

9. Define the three access specifiers: public, private and protected. Suggest examples of their use.

10. What is meant by information hiding? How do systems developers use encapsulation to aid the design process?

11. What are the key aspects of the static and dynamic modelling phases in an object oriented development?

12. How can control structures be shown on a sequence diagram? Compare this to the representation of control structures on a collaboration diagram. What are the merits of each approach?

Exercises

1. Section 16.3.4 introduced the Automatic Teller Machine (ATM) example and provided a top-level use case diagram. Work up this example into a full object oriented design for two of the use cases. You should produce classes, class models, a sequence diagram and a collaboration diagram for the two use cases you have chosen.

2. Using Kismet Case Study 16.8 as a guide, produce a sequence diagram to represent a sales order analysis for Kismet. The report should list the names of any customer who has placed an order in the last month. Compare the use of the sequence diagram with the collaboration diagram for this report.

3. Employees that work for a company are either full-time (salaried and paid monthly) or part-time (paid weekly by the number of hours worked). Create an inheritance hierarchy showing an employee superclass and subclasses for part-time and full-time employees. Create attributes for each of the three classes and provide access specifiers for the attributes. Create get and set methods where appropriate to allow the attributes to be accessed and amended.

CASE STUDY 16

Further develop the Kismet order processing system using object oriented approaches and UML.

References and recommended reading

Beck K. and Cunningham W. (1989). A Laboratory for Object-Oriented Thinking. In: *Proceedings of OOPSLA 89*, New Orleans, Louisiana
This paper was an early and important contribution to the development and uptake of CRC cards in object oriented approaches.

Bennett S., McRobb S. and Farmer R. (2006). *Object-oriented Systems Analysis and Design Using UML*, 3rd edn. McGraw Hill
A well-written book that takes the reader through the background to information systems design and object oriented approaches and then applies UML to a number of case studies to illustrate its use.

Booch G. *et al.* (2007). *Object Oriented Analysis and Design with Applications*, 3rd edn. Addison Wesley
An extensive coverage of the topic co-authored by one of the founding fathers of the Unified Modelling Language. The book provides sufficient range of content to be accessible to novice or experienced developer alike. A number of case studies provide context from a variety of problem domains.

Fowler M. and Scott K. (2003). *UML Distilled: A Brief Guide to the Standard Object Modelling Language*, 3rd edn. Addison Wesley
Although this book suggests an overview only, the coverage of topics is sufficiently expansive to provide a good coverage for the novice developer.

Larman C. (2004). *Applying UML and Patterns: An Introduction to Object-Oriented Analysis and Design and Iterative Development*, 3rd edn. Prentice Hall
Although the book provides a thorough introduction to UML it goes further and presents the software development process in a holistic way. Designers are encouraged to look beyond the current project or system in hand and consider the design of systems in the wider context of object oriented development.

Pilone D. and Pitman N. (2005). *UML 2.0 in a Nutshell*. O'Reilly.
This well-written book not only acts as an excellent primer to get the novice developer up to speed in creating UML designs but also is a useful reference manual for the more experienced user.

Rosenberg D. and Stephens M. (2007). *Use Case Driven Object Modelling with UML: Theory and Practice*. APress, US.
The book covers object oriented approaches by emphasizing the importance of use cases. As well as providing a good coverage of UML, the focus on use cases provides a context of project management, and staffing issues.

Si Alhir S. (2003). *Learning UML*. O'Reilly
This book provides a very thorough guide to the Unified Modeling Language.

Stevens P. and Pooley R. (1999). *Using UML: Software Engineering With Objects and Components*, Revised edn. Addison Wesley.
This book provides a straightforward guide to the Unified Modelling Language. It is particularly aimed at the novice student.

Chapter 17

Systems development: further tools, techniques and alternative approaches

Learning outcomes

On completion of this chapter, you should be able to:

- Evaluate approaches to project management for information systems
- Define CASE, explain what CASE tools are and describe the role played by CASE in systems development
- Outline the concept of rapid applications development as a framework for the development of information systems
- Compare and contrast hard and soft approaches to systems analysis.

Introduction

This chapter introduces and examines some additional tools and techniques and approaches that have attracted significant interest and gained importance with the developers of information systems. In some cases they are complementary to the approach described in Chapters 10–16, in others they are alternatives. First the concept of project management is introduced. A number of approaches, including the popular PRINCE2™ approach, are described and their applicability to information systems development is discussed.

Next, the increasingly important use of computers themselves as tools in the process of analysis and design is described. The power of modern hardware and software has brought about an increasing reliance upon computer-aided software engineering (CASE) to address the complexity of managing large systems development projects.

Next, rapid applications development (RAD) is considered as a framework for employing the chosen systems development methodology. Like CASE, the interest in RAD also reflects concerns over the management of large projects and the failure in some cases of traditional methodologies. RAD is not necessarily an alternative to these methodologies, as it does not claim to be a complete methodology itself. However, it does provide a framework of techniques that proponents claim allows the chosen methodology to be implemented more effectively.

Different approaches to the analysis and design of computerized information systems have differing strengths and weaknesses, differing areas of applicability and differing objectives. It is the purpose of this chapter to outline some alternatives and highlight their points of difference. Those already introduced are in the category of 'hard' approaches to systems development. By way of contrast, two 'soft' approaches will then be introduced: the first is due to Peter Checkland and generally known by his name; the second is a socio-technical approach stressing the participation of users in analysis and design. Here, both of these will be termed 'soft' approaches, compared with the 'hard' approaches, of which the structured and object-oriented methodologies considered so far are exemplars.

This chapter will also provide a general comparison between hard and soft methodologies. The underlying philosophies of each will be explained and contrasted. It is not intended to treat these additional approaches in detail but rather to give the reader a flavour of the debate that occurs between the proponents of hard and soft methodologies. This is a fruitful topic for discussion. It not only reveals deep and important divergences in attitudes to the analysis and design of information systems, particularly those in which people as social beings are heavily involved, but also sets the framework for a debate that is likely to persist for several years and may mark an important turning point in the development of attitudes to systems analysis and design.

17.1 Project management

The success rate of IT projects over time makes for mixed reading. Estimates have been made that as much as 30% of the money spent on software development is used rescuing failed projects and reworking software that does not satisfy the initial requirements. Many explanations have been provided for project failure, for example:

- the project scope was not fully appreciated;
- the user needs were not completely understood;
- lack of management continuity;
- over-optimistic estimates of the benefits that can be attained;
- high user expectations;
- poor alignment between IT departments and business users.

The classic benchmarks are that a project is considered successful if:

- it meets the specification;
- it is delivered on time;
- it comes in within budget.

The history of IT project management is littered with projects that have failed in one or more, even all, of the above criteria. The adoption of standard, recognized methods in developing information systems, such as structured methodologies or object oriented approaches, has been cited as a factor in improving in project success rate. Other factors that can improve project success include the adoption of a standard project management approach, and paying due attention to the human factors in team management.

17.1.1 Project management approaches

A number of authors have commented on project management techniques. Fowler (2004) states that it is not possible to have a single process for software development. He believes that the multitude of factors associated with software development lead to different

Figure 17.1 **High-level model of systems development**

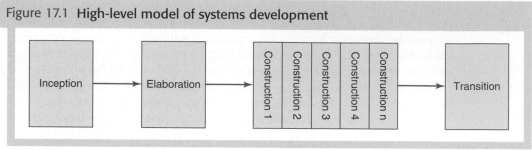

(Adapted from Fowler, 2004)

processes. This might include the type of software being produced (such as real-time systems, information systems etc.) the size of the project (single developer, small team, large team – 100 plus) and so on. Figure 17.1 shows his high-level view of the process.

Under this model the process of systems development is intended to be iterative and incremental. During the inception phase the business case for the project and its scope are established. The elaboration phase sees detailed requirements gathering and high-level analysis. The construction phases consist of iterations of software construction, testing and integration. The transition phase involves final handover, performance tuning and user training.

Larman (2004) defines a model comprising three macro-level steps: Plan and elaborate – Build – Deploy. He then subdivides these three steps to further describe the development process.

He describes a model of stages but one that is very iterative in deployment. The Plan and elaborate step, shown in Figure 17.2, is analogous to the Analysis phase in more

Figure 17.2 **The *Plan and Elaborate* step**

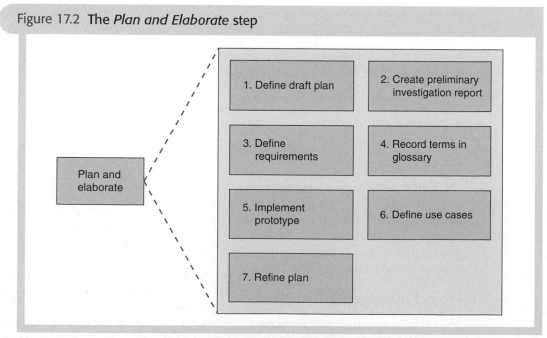

(Adapted from Larman, 2004. Larman, Craig, *Applying UML and Patterns: An Introduction to Object-Oriented Analysis and Design and Iterative Development*, 3rd, © 2005. Reproduced by permission of Pearson Education, Inc., Upper Saddle River, New Jersey.)

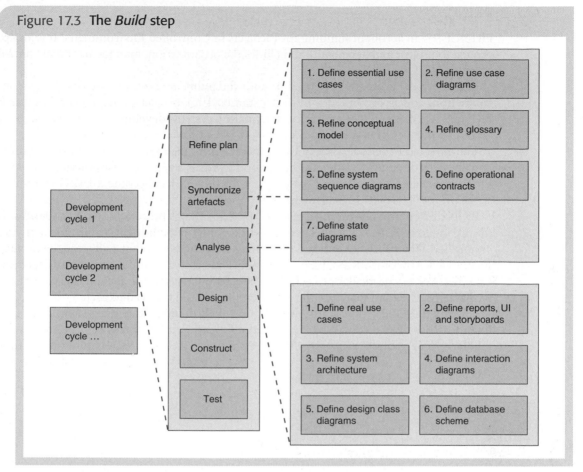

Figure 17.3 **The *Build* step**

(Adapted from Larman, 2004. Larman, Craig, *Applying UML and Patterns: An Introduction to Object-Oriented Analysis and Design and Iterative Development*, 3rd, © 2005. Reproduced by permission of Pearson Education, Inc., Upper Saddle River, New Jersey.)

traditional approaches. It includes the initial project conception, investigation of alternatives, planning, requirements specification etc. It focuses on producing the higher-level use cases (these are defined in more detail in Chapter 16) that capture the business processes.

The Build step, shown in Figure 17.3, is analogous to the design stage in more traditional approaches. An iterative rolling out of development cycles takes place, each progressively extending the system. Within each development cycle a series of stages is identified: Refine plan, Synchronize artefacts, Analyse, Design, Construct, Test. The development cycle made up of this series of stages is usually subject to **time-boxing**, i.e. a rigid time frame is applied within which all work must be completed. A range of two weeks to two months is typical for time-boxing a development cycle.

Some steps are identified as being optional, for example prototype implementation (step 5) in the *Plan and evaluate step* and the state diagram production (step 7) in the *Build step*.

17.1.2 PRINCE2™

PRINCE® is an acronym standing for **PRojects in Controlled Environments**. It is an approach to project management that includes the organization, management and control of projects.

PRINCE has become widely used in both the public and private sectors since its introduction, and is becoming a de facto standard for project management. Although PRINCE was originally intended for information systems development, it has also been used on a number of non-IT projects.

The most recent release, PRINCE2™, incorporates the requirements of existing users and has been designed to enhance the method towards a generic, best practice approach for the management of all types of projects. PRINCE2 has become a UK Government standard for IT project management.

PRINCE2 offers a project management approach that is process-based. Each process is framed in terms of the key inputs and outputs together with the deliverables and activities anticipated. The processes indicate the management activities that will steer the project. Figure 17.4 shows the PRINCE2 process model and the various constituent management activities. For any particular project it will be essential to establish the importance of each of these processes and therefore the attention that should be given to each.

Under PRINCE2 a project is divided into well-defined stages; at each stage it is intended that resources will be controlled efficiently and progress will be monitored regularly. The project management team members' roles and responsibilities are fully

Figure 17.4 The PRINCE2 Process Model

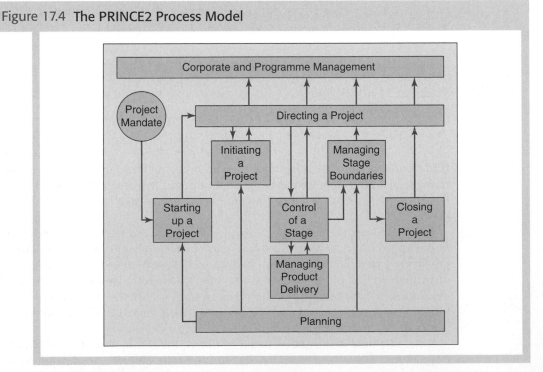

(© Crown Copyright 2007 – Reproduced under licence from OGC. http://www.ogc.gov.uk/prince2/about_p2/about_intro.htm)

described. Project planning using PRINCE2 is product-based, which means the project plans are focused on delivering results and are not simply about planning when the various activities on the project will be done.

The UK Office of Government Commerce cites the benefits of PRINCE2 to be:

- a controlled and organized start, middle and end;
- regular reviews of progress against plan and against the business case;
- flexible decision points;
- automatic management control of any deviations from the plan;
- the involvement of management and stakeholders at the right time and place during the project;
- good communication channels between the project, project management, and the rest of the organization.

PRINCE2 focuses on the business benefits that can be obtained from a project. These often take the form of financial benefits but can also be strategic (e.g. the fulfilment of an overarching organizational strategic aim) or legislative (e.g. fulfilling a requirement of a government body or of the organization's head office).

To account for the changing environment in which projects are carried out, PRINCE2 includes a system of version control which is termed **configuration management**. This allows for tracking of the products being delivered, knowing their current status and which version is the latest.

Although PRINCE2 is very popular for projects concerned with the development of information systems it is in fact applicable to any project type, regardless of its environment. However, although the set of concepts and processes are laid down, the way they are applied to each particular project will vary and a successful implementation will inevitably entail some tailoring of the method.

17.2 Computer-aided software engineering

Computer-aided software engineering (CASE) provides new tools for the rapid development of reliable computer systems. The traditional cost curve for the design and development of a business information system locates most of the cost as falling within the area of implementation, particularly coding. Fourth-generation languages (4GLs) and other applications-generation tools are an attempt to cut the cost in this area by enabling speedy development of systems through the automation of the production of code.

The success of this can be measured by the fact that it is now possible to build a system and, if it fails to meet user needs, to redevelop it quickly and cheaply. This, in essence, is the philosophy behind prototyping. A problem with the approach is that it diminishes the role of formal requirements specification and systems design. This may be acceptable or even desirable for small systems, particularly for decision support, but the approach cannot cope with larger projects unless considerable design effort has been undertaken.

Structured methodologies, developed in the late 1970s and early 1980s and covered elsewhere in this book, were a significant improvement in approaches to systems analysis and design compared with previous methods. By clearly identifying stages, tools and

Figure 17.5 The place of CASE tools in software development

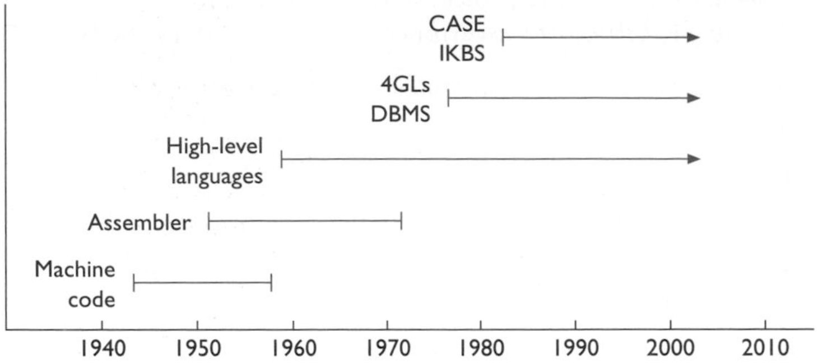

techniques, and documentation standards, consistency and quality control were maintained for systems design projects. Design errors were significantly reduced.

However, requirements analysis, especially if linked to strategic requirements, is not readily accessible to structured techniques. This dysfunctionality is developed later in this chapter. Errors still occur as a result of inaccurate requirements analysis and specifications, and changes in requirements mean lengthy redesign. But just as the computer itself has been utilized to assist the coding process (4GLs and application generators), the next step is to use the computer in the requirements specification, analysis and design process itself. This is the place of computer-aided software engineering (CASE) (Figure 17.5).

CASE automates various stages of the analysis and design process with the assistance of software tools. The CASE philosophy involves the use of these software tools working together with a methodology of systems analysis and design to:

- develop models that describe the business;
- aid in corporate planning;
- provide support for systems specification, documentation and design; and
- aid in the implementation process.

CASE tools are used by computer professionals to carry out some part of the systems analysis/design process. They are not end-user oriented, although they may be used in conjunction with end users. The tools are normally run on high-performance development workstations.

CASE support

CASE tools provide assistance in the following ways (see Figure 17.6):

1. **Corporate planning of information systems:** Software is used to describe the organization, its goals, resources, responsibilities and structure. These descriptions may be used to create strategic plans. The software will be used to indicate and track relationships between the various components of the plan. The planning specifications will identify activities for incorporation into information systems developments. Many CASE tools also include facilities for cost estimation calculations. Outline

Figure 17.6 CASE assistance in the systems development process

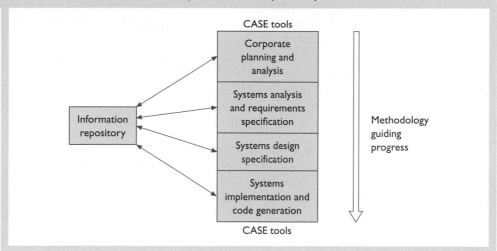

design parameters are fed in, and an indication of the expected cost and duration of the project is generated.

2. **Creating specifications of requirements:** This corresponds to the non-strategic stages of systems analysis. At this stage, an information system is analysed into its component activities and data requirements. Many diagrammatic tools familiar to the reader from the stages of structured process and data analysis are used – for example, data flow diagrams and entity models.

3. **Creating design specifications:** CASE tools can be used to specify a design for a new system. These tools include software for producing HIPO (Heirarchy, Input, Process, Output) charts, structured module specifications and decision tables.

4. **Code-generation tools:** CASE support in this area will accept the outputs of the design specification and produce computer-generated code for direct execution.

5. **An information repository:** Central to any CASE assistance in systems analysis, design and implementation is the information repository. This stores information on entities, processes, data structures, business rules, source code and project management data. It is important, as at any one stage of development consistency and completeness must be maintained in descriptions of data, processes, rules, and so on. Throughout the various stages of analysis and design it is vital that as each component develops, for example from an item in a high-level plan through to a record type in a database, it can be tracked. In short, the information repository does for the CASE process what the data dictionary, in a more limited way, does for structured process analysis and design.

6. **A development methodology:** Underlying any CASE approach is a development methodology. The CASE tool provides the developer with support for the various development stages identified by that methodology. Automated facilities allow for the production of the particular style of diagrams expected of the methodology. The cost estimation routines will similarly reflect the philosophy of the methodology.

CASE terminology

There are no agreed international or de facto standards on CASE. This is a problem not least because the terminology can be used in widely varying ways. However, the following are in common use.

Front-end CASE/upper CASE/analyst workbench

This refers to a set of tools that aid productivity in the analysis, design and documentation of systems. These tools are used to define the systems requirements and the systems properties. Typically, the outputs of front-end CASE are:

- process and data structure specifications: data flow diagrams, state transition diagrams, flowcharts, entity–relationship diagrams, data dictionaries, pseudo-code, structured English, decision tables, decision trees, structure charts, module specifications, Warnier–Orr diagrams;
- screen definitions;
- report definitions.

In order to achieve this, there will be a wide variety of highly interactive screen-based prototyping facilities, including:

- diagram editors;
- screen painters;
- dialogue prototyping aids.

Back-end CASE/lower CASE/code generator/4GL generator

This refers to tools that automate the latter stages of the implementation process. As input, back-end CASE tools may take the output specifications of front-end CASE tools. The outputs of back-end CASE might be:

- source and object program code;
- database and file definitions;
- job control language.

Life cycle CASE/I-CASE

This encapsulates tools covering the entire process of corporate analysis and planning, systems analysis and design, and implementation. For example, the unified modelling language (UML), proposed as a standard for object oriented development, is incorporated into several I-CASE tools.

Reverse engineering/re-engineering

Reverse engineering is the opposite of the standard implementation process for the production of code. Reverse engineering takes existing unstructured code as input (often COBOL programs that can be found in legacy systems) and produces restructured code as output. In particular, the reverse engineering process produces output where:

- Common subroutines and modules are identified.
- Conditional branches and loops are simplified in structure.
- Blocks of code are collapsed into single-line statements for ease of reference and use.

- Subroutines are called in hierarchies.
- New source code is generated fitting the above conditions.

The need for reverse engineering is generated by the recognition that most software used in an organization needs enhancement from time to time. Unless this was produced using a rigorous methodology (and many systems still in use based on COBOL code were not), the task facing the programmer is immense. Complex spaghetti logic structures are impossible or, at best, time-consuming to disentangle and alter. If the software has undergone amendment, the side effects of code alteration are not easily identifiable. The software tends to be bug-ridden and difficult to validate. Reverse engineering creates code that is structured and easily amendable. It thus enables existing software to be enhanced rather than abandoned when update is necessary.

CASE benefits

CASE has grown rapidly in use over the last decade and is predicted to continue to increase in importance over the next decade. Some of the benefits of CASE are as follows:

1. **Enhancement of existing applications:** This can occur in two ways. First, systems produced using CASE tools can be rejuvenated when required by altering the systems specifications, already incorporated into the previous use of CASE, to take account of new needs. These can then be fed into back-end CASE tools to produce new code. The process is considerably quicker than attempting alterations via manually held systems specifications. Second, using reverse engineering tools, existing applications can be recast in a way that makes them suitable for amendment.

2. **Complete, accurate and consistent design specifications:** Most errors in the development of a new system occur in the systems specification stage. Most of these are not picked up until acceptance testing by users has taken place. CASE, by the use of computer specification tools and a central information repository, forces certain aspects of consistency and completeness on the design process.

3. **Reducing human effort:** CASE tools reduce human effort in analysis and design by offloading development work on to computers.

   Diagramming and charting tools cut the development time, especially when it is considered that each diagram may have to undergo several versions before completion.

   By keeping track of the development process, CASE tools can relieve the human of considerable project management burdens. These tools keep note of authors, versions of models and a calendar. CASE tools also provide for consistency and completeness checking across various stages of the development process. They do this by tracking entities, processes, data definitions, diagrams and other things that would otherwise take up much human effort.

   Back-end CASE tools significantly reduce the human programming requirement by generating source and object code, and database definitions.

4. **Integration of development:** CASE tools, particularly I-CASE tools, encourage integration of the development process from the early stages of corporate analysis through information systems specification to code implementation. This is a trend that has been emerging in paper-based methodologies and is now mirrored in CASE tools and methodologies. It is based on a recognition that the design of an information system is not merely a technical issue deriving from a clear understanding of where we are now and where we want to go, but rather an activity that has to link and translate corporate information systems requirements into deliverable systems.

5. **Speed:** CASE tools speed up the development process for a project. The tools also allow considerable interactive input from systems developers during the process. This is compatible with a prototyping approach to systems development.

6. **Links to object oriented analysis:** Object oriented analysis and design are rapidly gaining support. Object oriented methods are particularly suited to incorporation into CASE tools as the terminology and diagrammatical requirements are similar throughout the stages of development. The emphasis in object oriented methodologies on team development, reuse of code and message passing between objects are all facilitated by the central repository, libraries and group support found in CASE tools.

17.3 Rapid applications development

Rapid applications development (RAD) grew out of the recognition that businesses need to respond quickly to a changing and often uncertain environment in the development of their information systems. RAD is directly opposed to the traditional life-cycle approach, which is characterized by a completely linear development of a system and a concentration on technical perspectives. In traditional approaches, the *requirements* of a project are fixed at an early stage, but the *resources* and *time* tend to vary to fulfil those requirements. In RAD, the opposite view is taken. *Time* is fixed and *resources* are fixed as much as possible, but *requirements* are allowed to change as the project develops to meet the real business objectives.

RAD borrows from other approaches and uses prototyping, participation and CASE tools as well as other formal techniques. It recognizes the importance of gaining user participation, particularly senior management involvement, in its evolutionary approach to information systems development. RAD was first separately identified and introduced by James Martin (1991). His exposition was set clearly within his information engineering approach to the development of business information systems. Now, however, the term 'rapid applications development' is used much more loosely to encompass any approach which emphasizes fast development of systems. Rather than being a methodology itself, RAD is a framework for systems development that can be applied to a range of methodologies. In the UK, a consortium of systems developers have defined a set of standards for RAD called the dynamic systems development method (DSDM).

17.3.1 RAD concepts

Central to the concept of RAD is the role of clearly defined workshops. These should:

- involve business and information systems personnel;
- be of a defined length of time (typically between one and five days);
- be in 'clean rooms' – i.e. rooms set aside for the purpose, removed from everyday operations, provided with technical support, and without interruption;
- involve a facilitator who will be independent, control the meeting, set agendas and be responsible for steering the meeting to deliverables;
- involve a scribe to record.

RAD has four phases:

1. **Requirements planning:** The role of joint requirements planning (JRP) is to establish high-level management and strategic objectives for the organization. The workshop will contain senior managers, often cooperating in a cross-functional way. They will have the authority to take decisions over the strategic direction of the business. The assumption behind RAD is that JRP will drive the process from a high-level business perspective rather than a technical one.

2. **Applications development:** Joint applications development (JAD) follows JRP and involves users in participation in the workshops. JAD follows a top-down approach and may use prototyping tools. Any techniques that can aid user design, especially data flow diagrams and entity modelling, will be employed. I-CASE (see Section 17.2) will be used at this stage. The important feature of applications development is that the JAD workshops short-circuit the traditional life-cycle approach, which involves lengthy interviews with users and the collection of documentation, often over considerable time periods. In JAD, the momentum is not lost and several focused workshops may be called quite quickly.

3. **Systems construction:** The designs specifications output by JAD are used to develop detailed designs and generate code. In this phase, graphical user interface building tools, database management system development tools, 4GLs and back-end CASE tools are used (see Section 17.2). A series of prototypes are created, which are then assessed by end users, which may result in further iterations and modifications. The various parts of the system are developed by small teams, known as SWAT teams (*s*killed *w*ith *a*dvanced *t*ools). The central system can be built quickly using this approach. The focus of RAD is on the development of core functionality, rather than the 'bells and whistles' of the system – it is often claimed that 80% (the core) of the system can be built in 20% of the time.

4. **Cutover:** During cutover, users are trained and the system is tested comprehensively. The objective is to have the core functioning effectively. The remainder of the system can be built later. By concentration on the core and the need to develop systems rapidly within a 'time box', the development process can concentrate on the most important aspects of the information system from a business perspective. If the process looks as though it is slipping behind schedule, out of its time box, it is likely that the requirements will be reduced rather than the deadline extended.

Rapid applications developments make the assumptions that:

- Businesses face continuous change and uncertainty.
- Information requirements and therefore information systems must change to meet this challenge.
- Information systems development should be driven by business requirements.
- It is important that information systems be developed quickly.
- Prototyping and development tools are necessary to ensure quick responses.
- Users should participate in development.
- The 'final system' does not exist.

17.3.2 RAD and e-commerce

The growth in web-based technologies has led in many businesses to a review of their approaches to information systems development. With its focus on fast development, prototyping and user involvement, RAD appears to be an attractive candidate as a framework for developing e-commerce activities. Proponents of RAD, who believe that it is ideally suited to electronic business activities, give the following reasons for its adoption:

- **Time to market:** The fast-changing technology of e-commerce requires a rapid development cycle to preserve competitive advantage. Business needs must often be met within weeks rather than months.

- **Whole system solutions:** A move into electronic business requires significant changes in work practices. As a consequence the system needs to be developed and introduced collaboratively in order to be successful.

- **Fast-changing requirements:** The constant change in the electronic economy means that it is almost impossible to establish the business requirements at the outset of the project. RAD, unlike the traditional methodologies previously discussed, does not insist on a complete understanding of the requirements at the outset of the initiative.

- **Decision taking:** Many hard decisions have to be taken as the requirements of the project change. RAD provides effective frameworks for taking and implementing these difficult decisions.

17.4 An evaluation of 'hard' approaches to systems analysis and design

Several approaches to the analysis and design of information systems have been termed 'hard' approaches. What do they have in common? In answering this, it is useful to take a look at three central examples of hard systems approaches as applied to the analysis and design of computerized information systems. The common features of these will then be more apparent. The three examples chosen here are structured functional/process analysis and design, data analysis and the object oriented approach to the development of computer systems. The first two of these have been covered extensively in Chapters 11–13. There, though, the emphasis is on an explanation of the tools and techniques and how these are applied through the systems life cycle. The focus of the remainder of this chapter is different in concentrating on the underlying assumptions, philosophies and typical areas of application of each approach. The aim is to compare and assess them rather than explain how to undertake practical projects.

17.4.1 Structured functional/process analysis and design

This has spawned many commercial methodologies. These are highly detailed, giving precise instructions as to the tools to be used at each stage and the documentation to be completed. Although each of these methodologies will differ, they all share most of the following characteristics:

- **Function/process oriented:** The attention of the analyst is concentrated on analysing and designing what are seen as the most important elements in systems analysis and design. These are the functions and processes that are carried out in the existing system and are designed to be present in the new system. Once these are clearly specified, the remainder of analysis and design is seen to follow naturally.

- **Top-down:** In analysis and design, the approach taken is to concentrate on the most general processes and functions in the initial stages. Only then are these decomposed again and again until a fine-grained representation of the systems processes is obtained.

- **Logical has priority over physical:** Compatible with a top-down approach is the emphasis on a logical analysis of the functions/processes of the existing system and on the design of a logical model of the desired system. Physical aspects of design – file, program and hardware specifications – are postponed for as long as possible. This lack of early commitment to the physical aspects of design is seen as preventing premature physical decisions that would constrain design alternatives. In the early stages, physical analysis is seen as a necessary stepping stone to deriving a logical model of what the existing system does. It then plays little role in the remainder of the project.

- **Stages and exit criteria:** In common with other hard approaches to systems analysis and design, the process is seen as a linear development from the initial systems investigation and feasibility study, through analysis and design, to implementation and review. Each of these has its own exit criteria. For instance, the feasibility study is completed by the production and agreement of a feasibility report. This staged approach with objective deliverables is a characteristic of approaches that place a high emphasis on project control.

- **Tools and techniques:** Structured tools and techniques emphasize the general philosophy of the approach. Processes, top-down analysis and design, and the development of logical models are encouraged by use of the techniques. Data flow diagrams illustrate the logical flow of information and data between processes, structured English represents the logic of a process, and data dictionaries specify the logical content of data flows and data stores. The emphasis is always on the logical rather than on the physical aspects of information systems, so these paper representations are clear communication devices between users, analysts and programmers. Repeated use of these structured tools ensures a program specification suitable for structured programming techniques and the use of structured programming languages. Hierarchical input/process/output charts ensure that complete modular specifications are developed. Different programmers can work independently on different parts of the system.

The movement to develop structured methods arose from severe problems in software engineering. It was not uncommon for computer projects to run considerably over budget on both time and costs. This often arose out of the difficulty of coordinating large teams of programmers. By concentrating on a top-down approach leading to modular specifications, structured approaches make possible a more accurate estimation of costs and schedules.

Another area in which structured approaches attempt to overcome difficulties is in the design of complex, highly integrated systems. Traditional methods are unsuitable for these. By concentrating on the overall logic of an information system it is possible for the analyst to transcend the barriers imposed by physical departmental divisions.

Structured techniques in analysis and design, backed up by structured programming, ensure that the final software is modular in nature. This means that not only individual programs but also parts of programs are testable separately and can be amended easily. The modular nature of the program specifications also allows more adequate project control. The scope of the programmer for ingenuity and creativity is significantly reduced. Quality control techniques are more easily applicable to the programmer's end product. This changes the nature of the programmer's task. The 'art' of programming has been deskilled to meet the needs of 'scientific' management.

17.4.2 Data analysis

All approaches to systems analysis and design require attention to be paid at some stage to the data store aspects of the information system. What distinguishes approaches that are said to be based on data analysis is the importance and priority attached to the analysis and design of a logical *data* model of the organization in the design of an information system.

Up to now, an entity–relationship approach to data modelling has been taken. This is the most common, although there are now alternatives that attempt to overcome some of the limitations imposed by the oversimplicity of the entity–relationship structure. The various methodologies based on data analysis share the following features:

- **Data model oriented:** The emphasis is on deriving a data model of the entities and relationships within the organization rather than attempting to analyse or model the functions and processes. The thinking behind this is that the overall structure of an organization changes little over time. Once an accurate data model of this has been established and incorporated into a computer-based data store, it will be the foundation on which applications programs can be written. These programs will carry out the various data processes required by the organization. Applications change over time. It is therefore sensible to analyse and design around a common database rather than on the shifting sands of changing functions.

- **Logical has priority over physical:** The emphasis is on building a logical data model of the organization prior to taking any physical decisions on how this is to be incorporated into a physical database, how many records there are, what file sizes will be, and so on. The logical model is later translated into a form suitable for implementation, using one of the commercial database systems.

- **Top-down:** Data analysis approaches stress the need to concentrate on an overall analysis prior to detail. For example, in entity–relationship modelling the important entities and their relationships are identified first. The structure of the model is then specified. Only at a later stage will attention be directed to attributes. This is to be contrasted with a bottom-up strategy, in which the concentration would be on the attributes at an earlier stage.

- **Documentation:** All approaches based on data analysis emphasize the importance of structure. The clearest way of revealing structure is pictorially. Diagrammatic representations play an important role in data analysis at the early stages.

The impetus to develop methodologies based on data analysis came from a number of areas. Modern commercial databases allow the sharing of common data by different applications and users within an organization. They also allow for considerable complexity in storage structures and retrieval. It is crucial to ensure that the best use is made of these facilities. Entity–relationship modelling and other data analysis modelling approaches assist the design of the complex models suitable for modern database management systems.

Another reason for the emphasis on data analysis is the recognition that data structures, if they are to be enduring, should mirror the real world of the organization. Organizations have complex structures. It requires more than a piecemeal approach to deal adequately with the modelling task.

17.4.3 Object oriented approaches

The distinctive way of modelling and implementing a system using object oriented approaches has already been described in Chapter 16. The characteristics of object oriented approaches are:

- **Logical has priority over physical:** The emphasis is placed on building a logical object model of the organization and establishing the necessary associations and communications between the logical objects prior to taking any physical decisions on how the objects are to be implemented.

- **Top-down/bottom-up:** The modelling of the system usually starts with a top-down partitioning into related groups of classes. The terminology for these groups differs; Bertrand Meyer (1995) calls them **clusters**, whereas Coad and Yourdon (1991) describe them as **subjects**. This initial partitioning is then followed by a combination of top-down and bottom-up development activities. The top-down development can be illustrated by the inheritance mechanism, whereby abstract classes are created and then refined into more specialized classes that implement specific activities in the system. The bottom-up development is evidenced by the use of primitive (building block) classes, which are aggregated together into larger so-called container classes to implement increasingly complex levels of the solution.

- **Transition between stages:** A major attraction of object oriented approaches is the uniformity of terminology and concepts throughout the development process. The analyst searches for candidate classes and considers the data (attributes) and functions (methods) that each class must implement. The designer puts detail into the implementation of the methods and considers the associations and the message passing between classes. The programmer implements the classes, their attributes and methods. Because of the uniformity, it is said that transition from one stage to the next is **seamless**.

- **Documentation:** At each stage of analysis and design detailed documentation is produced. This is often generated by a CASE tool. The seamless nature of the transition between stages described above means that the same diagrams produced at the analysis stage can be enhanced at the design stage. Many CASE tools can then generate skeleton code from those diagrams, extending the seamless feel throughout the development process. The documentation, automatically generated by a CASE tool, is particularly beneficial in recording the libraries of classes, both newly created and reused.

17.4.4 Characteristics of 'hard' approaches

The examples of 'hard' systems approaches covered in the previous sections of this chapter may seem to have little in common. Why, then, are they characterized together as 'hard' approaches?

1. They all assume that there is a clearly identifiable existing system in some state or other. To make this discovery is essential to the process of systems analysis and design. No major problem is presented by this task; it is a matter of investigation and documentation.

2. There can be a clear and agreed statement of the objective of systems analysis and design. Generally, this is established in conjunction with the 'owners' of the system. It is the role of the systems analyst/designer and programmer to provide this system on time and within cost.

3. It is assumed that the end result of the process of analysis will be a design that will incorporate a technological system. In other words, the problem – that is, the disparity between the existing system and the desired system – is seen to be soluble by technical means. In most cases, this means a computer.

4. Just as it is clearly possible to describe the existing system objectively, it is possible to determine whether the designed system, once implemented, meets the objectives set of it. Thus there is a measure of performance.

5. The process of analysis and design needs to be carried out by experts. This follows from the general assumption that the solution to the problem will be technical. The client/expert dichotomy is essential to 'hard' systems approaches.

As a summary, it can be said that 'where we are now' and 'where we want to go' can be clearly established. The problem facing the analyst is 'how to get there'. The solution is in terms of a prescribed progression from the current state to the desired state through several stages. Four distinct phases can be identified:

1. Investigating the existing system – information gathering, problem identification, feasibility study.

2. Analysis of the existing system and the provision of a solution to the problem by designing a new system on paper or using a CASE tool.

3. Implementing the solution.

4. Evaluating its effectiveness.

Although 'hard' approaches have been presented as applying to the analysis and design of information systems, their scope is much larger. They are similar to a general engineering approach to problem solving. The assumptions and overall strategy are similar whether one is designing a transport network, building a bridge, running a project to put someone on the Moon or designing a computer system.

Hard systems approaches have their antecedents in engineering and military applications. They emphasize a scientific approach towards problem solving rather than intuition or experience. A high premium is placed on logic and rationality. Philosophically, they assume a realist view – the world is 'out there' independent of us; all that has to be done is to discover it and alter it to meet our desires. In so far as people enter analysis and design considerations, they are either sources of information about the current system or operators of the new system. In the latter case, their importance is taken into account in the design of the human–computer interface.

17.4.5 Criticisms of 'hard' systems approaches

Hard systems approaches have vastly predominated in the development of computer systems. Project control failures, difficulties in designing highly integrated systems and the increasing importance of data model design for databases have led to the evolution of hard methodologies, which have superseded the more traditional approaches. Hard systems analysis and design has been hugely successful. However, there have been some notable failures. Systems that have been designed, implemented and are technically perfect but nobody uses them, systems that seem to be built to solve a problem that does not exist – these are two such examples. These failures may be located not in the poor application of systems analysis and design techniques but rather in the (mis)application of these techniques in the first place. Hard approaches make certain assumptions that limit their applicability. They do not provide fix-all methodologies that are universally applicable to all situations.

1. Hard systems approaches assume that an engineering perspective is applicable in all cases. This is unlikely to be true in situations that are unstructured. This may occur when there is no common agreement about the cause of the current problem. There may not even be a clearly identifiable problem. Once again, there may be no agreement about a desired solution. In these circumstances, hard approaches find it difficult to get off the ground. They assume that there is no difficulty in defining the existing and desired states of the system. When this assumption fails, they provide no help in further analysis.

2. Hard systems approaches are mathematically/logically based. This limits the range of problems that can be tackled. Moreover, they assume that factors and models to be used in remedying problems also have this orientation. Decision tables, entity–relationship models and logic flowcharts are all cases in point from the area of systems analysis and design. However, it goes further than this. As one might expect from their antecedents in engineering, operational research techniques play an important part in suggested aids to decision making. Linear programming, queuing theory, Monte Carlo simulation and statistical sampling theory are used. These all presuppose that a mathematical model is useful in the decision process. However, problems in an organization may not be amenable to this type of approach. For example, a failure to coordinate production schedules may not be the result of poor information flows and scheduling, which can be solved by the use of a computerized system with computer-based operational research-scheduling techniques. It may be caused by disagreement about the role of production and sales in the organization, personality conflicts, individual interests not coinciding with company objectives, or any number of things. To use a hard approach is already to straitjacket the problem as one soluble by mathematical/logical techniques when it may not be.

3. The emphasis on mathematics and logic presupposes the importance of quantitative information as compared with qualitative or vague information, intuition and psychological models of decision making. This may be acceptable when there is clear agreement on problems and solutions and the task is seen as one of moving from the

given undesirable state to a new desired state. In other cases, however, the range of useful types of information is broader. Closely connected to this is the assumption that quantitative information equals objectivity, whereas qualitative information equals subjectivity. From the scientific outlook, the latter is to be avoided. Whether subjectivity is to be avoided is a moot point. However, the proponents of a hard approach often ignore the fact that the requirement to provide quantitative information where none is accurately known often leads to unjustified assumptions being made. Claims to objectivity can then be seen to be spurious.

4. Closely allied to the previous points is the lack of recognition given to the organizational context in which a problem lies. Hard approaches tend to concentrate on data, processes, functions, tasks, decisions, data stores, flows, entities and relationships. They do not pay any attention to the social or organizational aspects of the system.

5. The emphasis is always on linear problem solving: there is a problem, it is solved, the next problem arises, it is solved, and so on. This leads to a reactive approach to management. An alternative is an ongoing developmental approach that stresses proactive attitudes.

6. The dichotomy between the client and the expert can act as a barrier to successful systems analysis and development. This may happen in a number of ways. There may be communication problems. The client is an expert in the area for which systems analysis is being carried out. The expert is probably from a technical background, so they do not share the same language. Tools used in structured approaches help to overcome this limitation. By stressing the logical aspects of the system and using diagrammatic tools that illustrate this, technicalities that may confuse the clients are removed. However, there is a more subtle effect of this dichotomy. The expert is seen to be outside the problem area. He or she observes it objectively. Not so! Once involved, the analyst interacts with the system – particularly the people operating within it. The analyst brings his or her own set of experiences, knowledge, prejudices and background to bear on the problem area.

These comments on hard approaches to systems analysis and design are not meant to be damning. Rather, they illustrate the need for caution before adopting a hard methodology. In particular, the applicability of the chosen methodology should first be established. Areas that are unstructured, with a lack of agreement on problems and what would count as a solution, are just those areas that are not suited to a technical approach to systems analysis and design.

17.5 'Soft' approaches to systems analysis and design

Hard approaches to systems analysis and design have been very successful in developing computer systems that, viewed from a technical perspective, are efficient and effective information providers. However, there have been cases when new information systems have not had user acceptance or have seemed to be misplaced as a solution to a spurious problem. These difficulties have led to developments that challenge the assumptions made by approaches deriving from a 'hard' view of systems.

Two approaches are outlined in this chapter. Each perceives different weaknesses in the approaches considered so far, so each has a different remedy. They both identify the presence of people in a system as leading to complications not acknowledged by proponents of hard approaches.

Checkland's (1999) approach recognizes that different people have different perceptions of problems and of the systems in which they lie. It is therefore a mistake to assume automatically that there is agreement on 'where we are now' or even on 'where we want to go'. Rather, problems are much less structured, much fuzzier than supporters of hard approaches would have us believe.

The socio-technical approach stresses the recognition that computerized information systems are part of interacting social and technical systems. If one part is changed, for example the technical system, by means of computerization, then the other will be affected. It is important to realize that the social and technical systems (the socio-technical system) cannot be designed independently of each other. One way to ensure that sufficient weight is given to the social aspects of the system is to involve users in the process of analysis and design. This undercuts the assumption of 'hard' approaches that the end product of design is a purely technical system. It also challenges the assumption of the necessity or desirability of the expert/user division.

17.5.1 Checkland's approach

In order to understand the rationale for Checkland's approach, it is helpful to look at some of the underlying philosophical assumptions made.

First, the assumption is that problems are not regarded as being 'out there' in a realist sense. There are no objectively given problems. Different people may see different problems in the 'same' situation.

It is, perhaps, misleading to talk of the 'situation' as though it were objectively given. A situation is a combination of the external world together with the way that it seems to the observer. This will be influenced by the background and beliefs of that observer. For example, an experienced doctor will unconsciously interpret an X-ray photograph and see shapes of importance in it. However, to the untrained observer there is very little of substance. Or again, different cultural backgrounds interpret voice inflections in different ways. So the same sentence uttered by two different people may be variously interpreted as being hostile or friendly.

Not only will different people disagree over the 'neutral' description of a situation but they will also disagree as to its problematic nature. For example, the student may regard end-of-course failure rates in professional exams as a problem – another hurdle to cross on the way to a career. However, a qualified professional may regard them as a non-problematic essential for the maintenance of small numbers of qualified professionals. This guarantees high incomes for those who are qualified. The professional institute setting the exams has a third view – the failure rates are taken as evidence that standards are being maintained.

It should be clear not only that different people may see the same situation as problematic in different ways but also that some may not see any problem at all. One man's meat is another man's poison. What determines an individual's view of a situation is the nexus of beliefs, desires and interests that the individual has. It is the combination of beliefs about 'what is' and 'what ought to be' that is so important in determining a situation as 'problematic' for an individual.

Second, just as problems are intellectual constructs, so are solutions. Two people may agree on a problem and yet disagree as to what constitutes a solution. Take an examination for example. Very high failure rates on a course may be regarded as problematic by both students and the course director. Students see the solution in terms of easier examinations and more effective teaching. The course director sees the need to raise entry qualifications.

The third assumption states that problems very rarely come singly, neatly packaged and ready for a solution. It is more likely that there are several interlocking problems. Moreover, if one problem is solved, this may generate a problem elsewhere. Problems are often messy and not amenable to simple solutions such as the installation of a computerized information system. This is another reason why the term 'problem situation' rather than 'problem' is used to describe what confronts the analyst.

Fourth, it is obvious from these points that it is important that the problem area be investigated and analysed prior to any decisions on the desirability of computer systems. The role of the systems analyst is seen, at least initially, as much more akin to a therapist than to a technical computer expert. The analyst encourages participants in the existing system to examine their own perceptions of the system and its interconnections with others, its objectives, their role in it and the role of others. This learning process is an essential prerequisite for development. It is recognized at the outset that a computer system may not be suitable for the organization, or at least not a total solution.

The final assumption implies that the analyst cannot be divorced from the system and the participants involved in it owing to the early therapeutic role of the analyst.

The methodology

Checkland's methodology (Figure 17.7) evolved out of the area of management consultancy. The analyst is not an expert in any particular area so is therefore not employed to give technical advice. Rather, the analyst should be thought of as a change agent or therapist who is able to stimulate others to new perceptions of the problem situation. The approach is particularly effective compared with other methodologies in cases

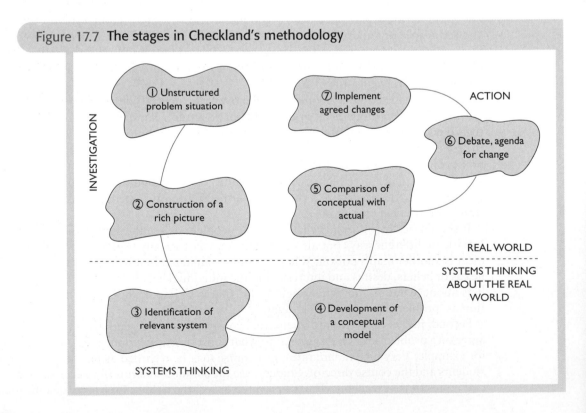

Figure 17.7 **The stages in Checkland's methodology**

INVESTIGATION

① Unstructured problem situation

⑦ Implement agreed changes

ACTION

⑥ Debate, agenda for change

② Construction of a rich picture

⑤ Comparison of conceptual with actual

REAL WORLD

SYSTEMS THINKING ABOUT THE REAL WORLD

③ Identification of relevant system

④ Development of a conceptual model

SYSTEMS THINKING

where there are messy problems. The stages are now outlined. Although progression is from one stage to the next, there is not the same rigidity and control over stage exits as in the structured life-cycle approach. Stages may be re-entered once left. The process is iterative rather than linear.

Stage 1 The development of rich pictures

The first task of the analyst is to become acquainted with the problem situation, and an attempt is made to build up a **rich picture** of the problem situation. This is a cartoon of the important influences and constituents of the problem situation. The analyst collects information to incorporate into this picture. Not only is hard information collected, such as facts and other quantitative data, but soft information is also obtained. Here are included the participants in the problem situation, any worries, fears and aspirations they have that are thought by the analyst to be relevant, conflicts and alliances between departments or individuals, and hunches and guesses. In particular, the analyst is looking for structure, key processes, and the interaction between process and structure.

It is important that the analyst does not impose a systems structure on the problem situation at this stage. The analyst will be interested in determining meaningful roles that individuals fulfil, such as boss or counsellor. In drawing the rich picture, the analyst will identify primary tasks and issues and will attempt to see varying perspectives. At this stage, the analyst should take particular care not to pigeonhole the problem, say as a marketing problem or a communications problem. This will limit the types of change that may ultimately be suggested.

Three important roles in the problem situation are identified. The **client** is the individual who is paying the analyst. The **problem owner** will be the individual who is responsible, or the area within which the problem situation arises. It may not be clear initially who the owner is. Different perceptions of the situation will assume different problem owners (we are all familiar with the conversation 'that's your problem', 'no it's yours'). The analyst may need to experiment with several individuals in order to establish a realistic problem owner. The **problem solver** is normally the analyst. These three roles may be held by three different people, or they may coincide in two individuals. It is common for the client and problem owner to be the same person.

Kismet case study 17.1

An example of a rich picture is shown in Figure 17.8. It corresponds to the Kismet case study covered in Chapter 11. A few details have been added in order to make the problem area more unstructured, and the picture therefore richer, since the original case as presented was fairly 'cut and dried'. Unlike the models produced so far, the rich picture attempts to capture the roles played by various participants. Examples are the customers who might take their business to Hardy, or the soon-to-retire head of the accounts department, who may be the sole source of information about key aspects of control in the current system. The diagram also acts as a prompt for further investigation, such as the logjam of back orders or the out-of-date price lists. It also poses certain questions as to the interaction between roles and events; for example, 'is the back-order logjam causing customers to turn to a competitor?'

▶

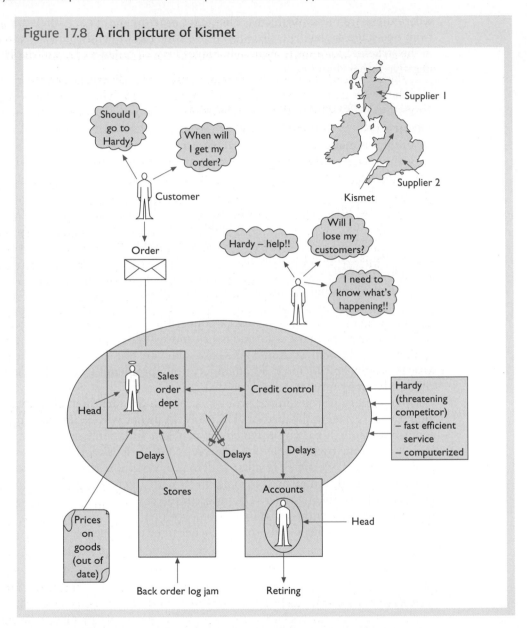

Figure 17.8 A rich picture of Kismet

The purpose of a rich picture is:

- To help to visualize a complex mess of interacting people, roles, threats, facts, observations, and so on. Its purpose is to facilitate understanding of the problem situation.

- To avoid imposing a rigid structure on the appreciation of the problem situation. A systems perspective is to be avoided at this early stage. It would tend to force perception of the problem through systems concepts such as inputs/outputs, systems objectives, feedback and the like. This may not be appropriate for the situation.

- To aid an investigative approach by the analyst towards the problem situation.

■ To act as a communication tool between participants. This will aid a consensus perception of the problem situation. It is all too easy for the fact that different participants have importantly divergent views of the situation to go unnoticed.

It should already be clear that there is considerable divergence between this approach and the structured approach taken in Chapters 10–15. There, the initial stages were restricted to the identification of key functions and processes, key entities in the organization and their formal relationships.

Stage 2 Identification of the relevant system and the root definition

The rich picture is a pictorial representation of the problem situation. In order to progress, it is necessary to view the problem from a systemic point of view. This is where the idea of a **relevant system** comes in. This is the most appropriate way of viewing the problem situation as a system. It is not always clear what the relevant system is. The relevant system is extracted from the rich picture. There is no one correct answer to the question 'what is the relevant system?' Several suggestions may be made. The one that is accepted is agreed by negotiation, often between the problem owner and the problem solver. This relevant system should be the one that provides most insight into the problem situation and is most appropriate for stimulating understanding and change in the organization – the ultimate goal of the methodology.

Kismet case study 17.2

Discussions take place with the managers of Kismet to establish the relevant system. In the case of Kismet the task is reasonably straightforward. It is a system for processing orders effectively and efficiently.

Other cases where things are less structured may require consideration of several 'relevant' systems before one that fits becomes apparent. For instance, a local technical college might be regarded alternatively as 'a system for educating pupils in order to meet the labour need of the local area' or 'a system for removing local unemployed adolescents at their potentially most disruptive and destructive age from the streets'. Or again, the owner/manager of a small business may regard it as 'a system for maintaining a stable financial income', 'a system for maintaining a stable and interesting employment for himself and his employees' or 'a system for providing a valued community service'.

Generally, relevant systems are issue-based or primary-task-based. When agreed on, they may come as quite a revelation to some of those participating in the problem situation. Identification of the relevant system may help to cast light on the otherwise seemingly non-understandable behaviour of their colleagues.

Just to name the relevant system gives a highly generalized specification of the area associated with the problem situation. It is important to be more precise. This is done by developing a **root definition** of the relevant system. The root definition gives a precise description of the *essence* of the relevant system.

Producing a root definition is not a mechanical task. It can only be achieved through trial and error. However, there is a checklist, called by its mnemonic CATWOE, which every adequate root definition should satisfy. All the CATWOE components should be present (or at least their absence needs to be justified and acknowledged).

1. **Customers:** These are the group of people or body who are served by or who benefit from the system. In the Kismet case, it is not only the customers of Kismet but also the stores and accounts functions.

2. **Actors:** These are the people, or rather types of people, who carry out the essential activities in the relevant system.

3. **Transformation process:** This is what the system does – that is, the process that converts inputs into outputs.

4. *Weltanschauung*: The *Weltanschauung* or 'world view' that is relevant to the system is specified somewhere in the root definition. In the case of Kismet, this is indicated by the assumption of performance according to cost and time constraints.

5. **Owners:** The owners of the system are those to whom the system is answerable. They have power to change the system or make it cease to exist. In the case of Kismet, this will probably be the management of the company.

6. **Environment:** This is the environment in which the relevant system is located.

Kismet case study 17.3

The CATWOE components for Kismet are now discussed. The following summary is produced:

- Customers: For Kismet, it is not only the customers but also the stores and accounts functions that must be considered.

- Actors: The task of identifying actors can be assisted by the work done on the creation of rich pictures. For example, a number of actors are present in Figure 17.8.

- Transformation process: The processing of inputs and outputs can be summarized as transforming the orders placed by customers into requests for stock and notifications to accounts.

- The 'world view': In the case of Kismet, this is indicated by the assumption of performance according to cost and time constraints.

- The owners of the system: For Kismet, this will probably be the management of the company.

- The environment in which the relevant system is located must be established.

This leads to a root definition of the Kismet sales order processing as follows:

A business function within Kismet operated by sales and credit control staff to accept and process orders provided by customers, transforming them into validated requests to stock and notifications into accounts, within speed and cost constraints set by Kismet management.

The purpose of identifying the relevant system and deriving a root definition is to concentrate on the *essence* of the system covering the problem situation. It is then easier to proceed to develop a logical model of a system that meets this description.

Stage 3 Building a conceptual model

Given that the relevant system has been identified and a root definition has been provided, the next stage of the methodology is to develop a conceptual model. This is a logical

Figure 17.9 A conceptual model

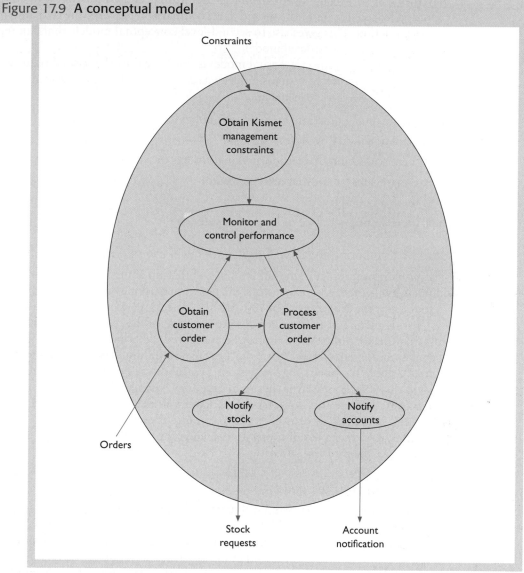

model of the key activities or processes that must be carried out in order to satisfy the root definition of the system. It is not a model of the real world. It may bear no resemblance to what occurs in the problem situation and is not derived by observing it. Rather, it consists of what is logically required by the root definition. The distinction between what *must* be done in order to satisfy the root definition and what *is* actually done in the system is of fundamental importance. Its recognition is at the heart of the usefulness of the methodology in stimulating organizational learning and change.

The key activities are shown in the conceptual model in Figure 17.9. Each of these key activities themselves represents a subsystem that would carry the activity out – for example, the subsystem to monitor and control performance. These high-level activities give rise to second-level activities that must be performed in order that the high-level activities can be executed. For instance, monitoring and control require collection of the standard, collection of the sensed data, comparison between the two and taking the necessary action. This gives rise to second-level conceptual models that can replace the relevant part of the first-level model.

When completed, the conceptual model is tested against the formal requirement of a general systems model (a systems model was covered in Chapter 1). Examples of typical questions that need to be asked are:

- Does the model illustrate an activity that has a continuous purpose?
- Is there a measure of performance?
- Is there some kind of decision-making process or role?
- Are there subsystems that are connected?
- Is there a boundary?
- Is there some guarantee of long-term stability?

Stage 4 Comparing the conceptual model with the real world

The previous two stages have attempted to build up some ideal model of what should happen in a system that carries out the essential activities required by the agreed root definition of the relevant system. Now is the time to see what actually happens.

The rich picture provides a good representation of the real situation, and it is against this that the conceptual model must be compared. Alternatively, the conceptual model may be compared directly with the problem situation. Differences should be highlighted as possible points for discussion. Typical of the questions considered by the analyst at this stage are 'Why is there a discrepancy between the conceptual model and the real world at this point?' and 'Does this activity in the conceptual model really occur?' The point of this investigation is not to criticize the way that things are actually done but rather to derive a list of topics – an **agenda for change** – that can be discussed with the actors in the problem situation.

Stage 5 Debating the agenda

This stage involves a structured discussion of the points raised on the agenda with the participants in the problem situation. It is important to realize that this is a consciousness-raising exercise as much as anything. The analyst should restrict discussion to changes that are systemically desirable and culturally feasible. That is, the changes should not run counter to the thinking that has gone into the selection of the relevant system and the root definition. Nor should they ignore the particular organizational culture within which the participants have lived and worked. The aim is to obtain agreement on a list of changes to be implemented.

Stage 6 Implementing agreed changes

Checkland is not very specific on how this stage is to be carried out. This is understandable in that a large range of changes might be agreed as feasible and desirable. It may be the case that a need for a computerized information system that will serve specific functions has been identified. In this case, it is probable that formal information modelling and structured analysis and design techniques will take over. However, the need for other types of change may be agreed. For instance, it may be thought necessary to change aspects of the organizational structure such as departmental responsibilities, the degree of centralization, or even the physical layout. Changes in overall policies, strategies or procedures may be agreed. The process of analysis may have revealed divergent attitudes concerning the problem situation. The outcome of the debate on the agenda may be an agreement to foster changed attitudes within the problem situation.

The stages in Checkland's methodology are not necessarily carried out in a linear fashion. It is often necessary to re-enter an earlier stage for revision. For instance, when comparing the conceptual model with the real world it may become apparent that the relevant system has not been identified correctly. This will require backtracking. There is another important way in which Checkland's methodology is not linear. It would be a mistake to assume that once the stages have been executed the problem in the problem situation has been resolved. It is not a problem-solving methodology but rather aims at *improvement* of situations through organizational understanding, learning and change.

17.5.2 Participation in socio-technical analysis and design

The socio-technical approach grew out of work started in the Tavistock Institute for Behavioural Research in the 1950s. This derived from the introduction of new technology in the coal mines. The approach recognized that successful introduction of new technology required the identification of social needs and goals as well as technical/economic objectives. The underlying assumption was that a system will only function effectively if human needs such as job satisfaction are acknowledged.

In the 1970s, the socio-technical approach began to be adopted in various guises for the development of computer systems in organizational environments. The common element in these approaches is the recognition of the interdependence of four factors – technology, tasks, people and the organization (Figure 17.10). If one of these is altered, for example the introduction of new computerized technology, it will have an impact

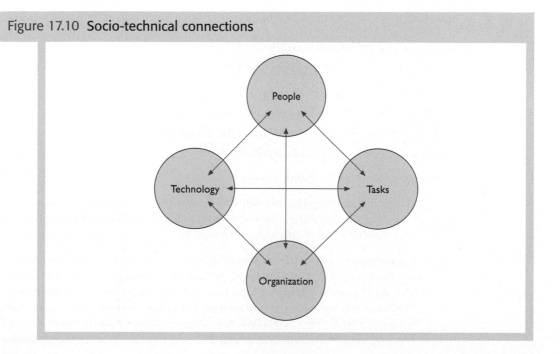

Figure 17.10 **Socio-technical connections**

on all the others. It therefore makes sense to take account of all aspects of the socio-technical system in computerization so that harmony can be maintained.

One socio-technical approach, due to Mumford (2003, and colleagues) (Land and Hirscheim, 1983), sees the best way of obtaining this harmony as involving users participatively in the process of analysis and design. This idea meshes neatly with the general trend towards industrial democracy experienced over the last 20 years, together with the increasing acceptance of humanistic values as applied to the workplace.

Benefits of participation

From the management point of view, participation in analysis and design enables the valuable knowledge and skills of the workforce to be incorporated into the final system. The analyst may be a technical expert in the area of computers but is unlikely to be familiar with the organization, tasks and people within which the final system must fit. Participation is seen as a more effective way of obtaining this experience than the 'classical' approaches such as the formal interview or questionnaire.

Also, from the management perspective, it is more likely that users will show commitment to and confidence in the final installed system if they have had a hand in its development. This stems from two sources. First, it is difficult for an individual to participate in the design of a system and not establish a psychological investment in and therefore commitment to it. Second, the continued presence of the participants in the process of analysis and design educates them in an appreciation of the final system and also allays their fears of its likely effects. Users may fear job deskilling, removal of job satisfaction or their ability to cope with the new system. Even if groundless, these fears lead to resistance to the implementation of the new system and ultimately to its ineffective use or failure. Participation allays these fears by providing information as the system is developed.

From a 'worker' point of view, participation can be seen as a way of maintaining control over the introduction of new technology. By being involved at all stages of the process participants can ensure that jobs and job satisfaction are maintained. It also serves as a public recognition of the importance of participants' knowledge and skills in the workplace.

Issues involved in participation

Several issues are involved in participation:

1. What role do participants play in the design process?
2. At which stage in the life cycle are participants involved?
3. Which groups should participate in the design process?
4. How are participants to be selected?

These questions are dealt with below:

1. **What role do participants play in the design process?** Three different levels of involvement can be identified for participants. These correspond to deepening degrees of commitment to the participative approach.

   (a) **Consultative:** The participants are consulted for their views and understanding by an expert. The expert analysts note these responses and take account of them at their discretion. This is little different from the 'traditional' approach towards interview as a source of information about the system. Where this differs in a socio-technical approach is that the analyst will be interested not only in the technical aspects of analysis and design but also in a complete socio-technical design.

(b) **Representative:** Selected users from relevant interest groups join the design teams. Their views are taken into account, although it is still recognized that the analysts are the 'experts' and ultimately they are responsible for design.

(c) **Consensus:** With consensus participation, the interest groups take over responsibility for the analysis and design. Analysts are now regarded as just another interest group whose responsibility it is to provide technical knowledge and to ensure that the design is technically sound.

2. **At which stage in the life cycle are participants involved?** This may happen at any or all stages of the project. Major stages are as follows:

    (a) Project initiation – it is unlikely that management will allow participation at this stage. It is traditionally regarded as the province of strategic decision making.

    (b) Definition of systems objectives.

    (c) Description and analysis of the existing system.

    (d) Identification of problem areas within the existing system.

    (e) Suggestion, design and evaluation of alternative solutions to the problems identified in (d).

    (f) Detailed design of the human work (social) and computer (technical) systems.

    (g) Preparation of systems specification.

    (h) Implementation of the human work and computer systems.

    (i) Evaluation and monitoring of the working system.

3. **Which groups should participate in the design process?** The answer to this is 'any group that will be significantly affected by the computer system'. This may include outside groups in the early stages (such as watchdog committees for the nationalized industries) as well as groups from within the organization. Examples of the latter are trade unions, clerical and shopfloor workers, middle management, and programmers and analysts.

4. **How are participants to be selected?** Interest groups may elect their own members, or participants may be chosen by management. Both approaches may be politically sensitive. With the former method, it may be the case that only those with the most strongly militant anti-technology views are put forward, whereas with the latter, management's buddies may be chosen.

The presupposition so far has been that participation is to be thought of as being limited to analysis and design. There is no reason why participants should not be involved in the decision-making process. However, this is unlikely to be agreed by management at the major decision points – when global terms of reference are being established for the project or when stop/go decisions are needed. At other points – fixing of local terms of reference or choice between alternative solutions – the decision-making process is almost invariably interwoven with analysis and design. Then participation in decision making goes hand in hand with analysis and design.

Methodology

In order to gain the benefits promised by participation it is necessary to have an effective methodology. Without this those involved in participation will be directionless. The methodology outlined here is due to Enid Mumford. It involves various procedures such as variance analysis, job satisfaction analysis and future analysis to aid the participative approach: these procedures are briefly described. However, it does not preclude the use of other tools or techniques, such as data flow diagrams or entity–relationship modelling, particularly in the latter stages of systems design. Mumford has given her approach to IS development the acronym ETHICS (*effective*, *technical* and *human* *implementation* of *computer* *systems*). The important components in the approach advocated by Mumford are now discussed.

The diagnosis of needs and problems

Three diagnostic tools are used here, variance analysis, job satisfaction analysis and future analysis:

1. **Variance analysis:** This involves identifying weak parts of the existing system that produce operational problems. The design group will identify key operations within a department and note those areas where there is a systematic deviation of the results of those operations from the standards set. This may often occur on the boundaries of a system, where there are coordination problems. Variances may affect one another; therefore it is important to reveal connections and dependencies. A variance matrix may be of assistance here. In systems design, the aim is to control these variances where they originate rather than by control at a later stage.

2. **Job satisfaction analysis:** The amount of job satisfaction obtained in a work situation may be explained in terms of the fit between what participants expect from their jobs and what they are obtaining. Three important needs should be considered. These are connected with the personality of the individual, the personal values held by that individual and the need for competence and efficiency. If systems are designed with these in mind, job satisfaction will be improved. This is a necessary condition to ensure that the socio-technical system will function effectively.

3. **Future analysis:** Large systems take a long time to design. If a large project is undertaken, it may be three or four years or even longer from initiation to the start of the successful operation of the new system. The life of the new system will need to be more than three or four years in order to recover the costs of the project. This implies that in analysis and design the time horizon with which the project is concerned is many years. In order to achieve a system that will meet the needs of the future, then the future has to be predicted. This becomes more difficult and uncertain the greater the forecasting period. Future changes may not be just in volumes of transactions processed or types of information required of the information system. Changes in the economic climate, new technology and changes in organizational structure such as decentralization or merging of companies will all have a significant impact on the satisfaction of future needs by the system currently being designed.

Many traditional approaches do not take the need to design for the future seriously and have consequently produced systems suffering from the 'dinosaur syndrome'. The requirement of a system to meet future demands can be achieved by:

(a) **Predicting the future by modelling and simulation:** The predictions are then catered for in current design.

(b) **Designing a system that is robust:** This means that the system has built-in redundancy and flexibility to deal with uncertain future requirements. The system is also designed to be modular for easy adaptation.

(c) **A structured approach to future analysis:** This involves the design team(s) drawing up a list of factors of relevance to the system that may be the subject of change. The likelihood of each of the factors changing over the lifetime of the system is then evaluated. The impact of these changes on the system is then assessed. The components of the system that are subject to these effects should be identified so that the stage of design can take account of them.

The consideration of the groups affected by the system

The groups that will be affected by the system are identified. The goals of these are then established by consultation with company policy and the diagnosis of user needs and job satisfaction analysis. An attempt is made to establish the weightings to be associated with each goal. Ideally, this would be by consensus between the various groups as a result of negotiation.

Socio-technical approach to the analysis and design of the system

The purpose of socio-technical analysis and design is to produce an end system consisting of social and technical structures that satisfies both technical and social goals. This proceeds by using a general stage, which is followed by a detailed one.

Initially, alternative systems strategies are suggested. The effects of each of these are forecast for the period of the planning horizon. The impact of each strategy is then compared against both the goals of the system and the predicted performance of the existing socio-technical system up to the planning horizon. Optimistic and pessimistic estimations are made for each strategy by changing the values of uncertain parameters. The strategy with the best fit to the social and technical goals is selected.

Detailed design progresses through social and technical analysis. In technical analysis, logically integrated sets of tasks, called **unit operations**, are identified. These unit operations consist of tasks that are logically cohesive in transforming an input into an output in preparation for the next unit operation or stage. For example, a unit operation would be the batching, error checking and input of sales data into a daybook preparatory to updating the sales ledger. Each design group receives one or more operation within its scope. In the analysis of the social aspects of the work system the relationships between individuals and the roles they play are investigated. The results of job satisfaction analysis would be used at this point. Each work group has the responsibility for eliminating variances that have been discovered in variance analysis. Within the work group, the existing and future users of the system are of particular importance in the development of the social system and the earlier stages of technical analysis. The impact of the computer analysts is felt most during the latter stages of technical design.

Implementation

Once designed, the system can be implemented. This may occur as a linear process or may take the form of prototyping. In prototyping, an experimental smaller version of the system is built. This will not have the full functionality of the final system and will probably not be technically efficient in a computing sense. However, it does enable an evaluation to be made of the extent to which it meets some of the social and technical goals of the design. This will provide a direction for improvement of the final system before any major expenditure has gone into its weaknesses. Indeed, several prototypes may be built before a satisfactory version on which the final design can be based is reached.

Post-implementation evaluation

After the system has been installed and is running, some assessment of its performance in the light of its social and technical goals is made. This allows correction as part of normal ongoing maintenance or provides valuable knowledge that is relevant in the design of a future system.

In summary, the participative approach differs from 'hard' approaches in a number of ways:

1. There is a recognition that technical systems cannot be treated independently of the social systems with which they interact.

2. Following from point 1, in the design of computer-based information systems the social system within which the work occurs must be the subject of analysis and design as much as the technical system itself. Without this harmonious design, any resultant technical system is subject to a high risk of failure on the grounds of its inadequacy from a social point of view.

3. The current and future users of the system possess a knowledge of existing work practices and deficiencies that makes their experience valuable in the process of analysis and design. In order to utilize this experience, it is necessary to use a set of diagnostic procedures (job satisfaction analysis, variance analysis, and so on). The traditional role of the expert systems analyst is restricted to technical aspects of analysis and design.

4. Participation in analysis and design is a prerequisite for a successful implementation of technical systems as it reduces users' fears over the introduction of new technology.

5. There is an ethical commitment to the belief that users of technology and those affected by it have a right to have some say on the design and operation of these systems.

17.5.3 Checkland's methodology and the participative approach: reservations

Both Checkland's methodology and the participative socio-technical approach offer alternatives to the 'hard' approaches covered in previous chapters. How realistic are they? Although they both have their supporters, there are serious questions that need to be addressed.

Checkland

The main criticism levelled at Checkland's methodology is its lack of comprehensiveness, particularly in the later stages of analysis and design. This has led critics to argue that it is not a methodology that takes the analyst through the life cycle. The idea of a 'life cycle' is not one that fits well with Checkland's approach, although it is undeniable that the methodology is strongest in the early stages of problem identification and analysis. At the very least, proponents would argue that it explores possibilities for organizational learning and progress in problem situations that are neglected by 'hard' approaches. The methodology from this viewpoint is regarded more as a front-end approach to carrying out the necessary problem analysis prior to the technical analysis that would imply a computerized system.

Another comment made on the methodology is that the analyst is not only in the position of attempting to understand an existing system but is also required by the methodology, via root definitions and conceptual models, to be an originator of systems. Although this remark has some foundation, it is not clear that it does not also apply to structured methods if properly carried out. In these, during the transition from analysis to systems design, there is always an element of assessing what needs to be done logically in order to perform a function, as well as analysing what actually is done.

Although Checkland's methodology has been used commercially, it does not have the same extensive track record as is associated with the structured methods covered in Chapters 10–15. This is not to say that there have been significant failures using the methodology but rather that the number of times it has been employed provide an insufficiently large sample from which to draw conclusions. It remains to be seen whether the methodology will have a lasting impact on approaches to analysis and design.

Participative socio-technical approaches

The participative element of this has been criticized from the point of view of its heavy cost. To involve users participatively in analysis and design places a great burden on the personnel in an organization. Proponents of the approach would not argue with this but would point out that the extra cost is more than justified by the production of systems that are accepted by and meet user needs – it produces effective and not merely technically efficient systems.

The emphasis on participation and the omission of specific tools is seen as a shortcoming by critics. However, the approach should be seen as setting a framework within which successful analysis and design can be carried out. It does not preclude the use of data flow diagrams, entity modelling or any other technique that aids analysis and design. Participation is seen as a recognition of the importance of implementing a system that meets socio-technical as well as purely technical goals.

There may be resistance to the use of participation in its fullest forms. From one quarter, management can see it as a way of losing managerial control; from another, analysts can view it as diminishing the importance of their status and roles. This is not an objection to the approach, but resistance to its use will weaken its effectiveness, so it is important that a commitment to participation be obtained from all parties involved.

Finally, in common with Checkland's methodology, there are too few cases in which the approach has been applied to judge its success from an empirical standpoint.

Both Checkland and those who have developed the participative approach have undoubtedly identified weaknesses in the universal applicability of 'hard' approaches. It remains to be seen whether their solutions will fulfil the promises they intend to keep.

Summary

This chapter has expanded on the material covered in Chapters 11–16 by introducing and examining additional systems development tools, techniques and approaches.

Project management is an essential element to the successful implementation of a project. Indeed in many system developments, particularly state-funded projects, the use of a specific project management approach is a contractual requirement without which sponsorship is not made available. The PRINCE2 method, a well-established approach, was described.

CASE tools are an essential aid for the analyst/designer. Initially they offered a tool for the generation of the diagrams that model the logical system. As they have matured CASE tools now provide an entire environment for the capture of the required aspects of the physical system, for the modelling of the logical system and often the generation of code that will comprise the physical solution.

Approaches to systems analysis and design have been divided into two categories – 'hard' and 'soft'. Although this is a useful division, it must always be remembered that there are many differences in the underlying assumptions and practices between different methodologies within each category.

'Hard' approaches seek to develop a technical solution to problems through the implementation of a computer system (Table 17.1 – structured, data analysis, object oriented). They assume the possibility of a clear and agreed statement both of the current situation and its problems and of the desired state of affairs to be achieved. The problem for systems analysis and design is then seen as designing a solution that will take us from where we are now to where we want to go. The assumptions underlying this approach are akin to those in engineering. Users of the existing system are seen as providers of useful information about it. Users of the proposed system are seen in terms of their information requirements and as devices for input of data. The role of the analyst is as *the* expert brought in on a client–consultant basis to design the system.

Traditional methodologies concentrate on the automation of existing business processes. They do this by recommending procedures and documentation to describe the current system and turn this into a set of program and file specifications. Structured process analysis and design grew out of the failure of traditional methods when designing complex integrated systems or when providing systems that involve substantial redesign of functions or procedures. The emphasis is on transcending the physical limitations of the current system by developing a logical model of data flows, functions and processes prior to design. The perspective of approaches based on data analysis acknowledges that databases are a corporate resource and consequently need careful design. This is achieved by deriving a logical data model of the organization from which a database structure can be defined.

'Soft' approaches recognize the impact of human beings in the area of systems analysis and design (Table 17.1 – Checkland, socio-technical participation). First, these methodologies deny the premise that it is easy to specify current and desired systems – problem situations are messy, and the solutions are intellectual constructs as perceived by actors within the system (Checkland). Second, the role of the analyst is not one of an expert to give definitive knowledge on systems analysis and design but rather that of a therapist (Checkland) or as just one of a design team involving users (participative approach). Third, the role of participants in the existing system is integral to successful system development. Checkland's approach concentrates on enriching the systems participants' perceptions of the current system. This is aimed at stimulation of change and improvement of the problem situation in the fuzzy system within which it occurs. The participative approach emphasizes the need to obtain a harmonious design of interacting social and technical systems by involving users in the process of analysis and design. Both deny that a computer system is the *only* solution: the former by recognizing that not all problems require computer-based solutions; the latter by asserting that designing a technical computer system independently of people's needs will lead to failure.

Approaches to development are not static. The influence of CASE tools on the process of analysis and design is becoming increasingly significant. These are likely to be centred on object oriented approaches, which concentrate on a perspective of the world as being composed of objects, relationships between objects and operations using those objects. CASE may cover the entire spectrum of systems analysis and design from the

Table 17.1 Comparison of approaches

Approach	Reasons for development	Aim	Area	Method	Key words/concepts examples
Structured	Failures at developing large integrated systems and inability to coordinate programmer teams	To develop a technically efficient, modular, integrated system	Functions, total systems	Development of a logical model of a system emphasizing functions, data processes and data flows	Data flow diagrams, data dictionaries, structured HIPO charts
Data analysis	Development and increasing importance of database technology	To develop a database structure suitable for supporting the organization's changing applications	Organizational data structures	Development of a logical data model of an organization emphasizing entities, relationships and structures	Entity–relationships models
Object oriented	Failures of structured methodologies to produce systems on time, within budget and future-proofed	To develop and maintain applications with greater ease and higher quality	Objects, total systems	Development of static and dynamic object models emphasizing associations, inheritance structures and message passing	Class/object model, object interaction diagram, state transition, inheritance, reuse of previous designs and code
Checkland	Failure to take account of fuzzy problems in organizational contexts	To achieve user understanding of organizational problem situations, thereby leading to learning and improvement	Fuzzy systems, problem situations	Development of a conceptual model of an ideal system through which participants can identify weaknesses and stimulate change	Rich pictures, conceptual models, root definitions, CATWOE, agenda for change
Socio-technical participation	Failures of systems as a result of user non-acceptance	To develop a fit between social and technical systems by participation, thereby ensuring systems acceptance	Socio-technical system	Involvement of the user in the process of analysis and design	Participation, consensus, job satisfaction, variance analysis, autonomous work groups
Rapid applications development	The need to develop systems quickly to respond to changing business needs	To develop an effective core system quickly to meet user needs	Functions, end-user needs	Involvement of management and users in an iterative development process, which may involve a variety of tools, including CASE	Joint requirements planning, workshops, joint applications development, prototyping

strategic planning of information systems to the automatic generation of executable code.

The recent development of rapid applications development (RAD) has emphasized the need for fast core systems development to meet rapidly changing business needs. RAD is gaining popularity, particularly in the development of e-commerce solutions.

Review questions

1. Explain the difference in the meanings of the terms *hard* and *soft* as applied to approaches to systems analysis.

2. State *four* main features of:

    (a) structured process analysis and design
    (b) structured data analysis and design
    (c) object oriented systems analysis and design.

3. What are the limitations of 'hard' approaches to systems analysis and design?

4. Outline the stages in Checkland's methodology.

5. What is the purpose of drawing rich pictures?

6. What is a CASE tool? What benefits can be gained from using a CASE tool? What are the drawbacks?

7. Describe the PRINCE2 approach to Project Management.

Exercises

1. What is meant by 'a participative approach to socio-technical design'?

2. Explain and distinguish the different possible levels of involvement of participants in the analysis and design stages of a project.

3. What benefits are claimed for user participation in analysis and design?

4. What roles do variance analysis, job satisfaction analysis and future analysis play in socio-technical analysis and design?

5. The hard approaches to analysis and design are often criticized for assuming that by using a technical solution it is possible to solve, or at least alleviate, problems in an organization. But if a technical solution is what the organization wants, why should this be a criticism?

6. 'User participation is an advantage in analysis and design, but the real benefits for the work-force and ultimately management would occur if users also participated in the decision process involving new technology and information systems.' Do you agree?

7. What are the key features of a RAD approach? Why has RAD been described as being 'well suited' to e-commerce systems developments?

8. This chapter, in common with many texts, uses the term *methodology* frequently. Provide and justify a definition of a methodology.

9. Why is PRINCE2 project management well suited to information systems projects?

CASE STUDY 17

Rapid applications development

Post Office IT (POiT) supplies technology solutions to the Post Office and its businesses and as such is one of the largest IT suppliers in the UK. POiT had investigated ways of improving productivity and understood that rapid application development (RAD) could deliver benefits such as:

- reducing time to market for new applications by cutting development times;
- getting more for less by improving productivity;
- building greater user buy-in by including end users from the word go.

But the challenge facing POiT staff was how to put RAD into practice and realize these benefits.

POiT had an ideal opportunity to use RAD as it needed to demonstrate reduced lead times and costs for one of its main clients, SSL. SSL (Subscription Services Ltd) is a customer management and telemarketing specialist and is particularly well known as the organization that collects the TV licence fee on behalf of the BBC under the brand TV Licensing. POiT had been retained to develop a system to automate a small specialist licensing section, which it had not previously been cost-effective to automate; SSL and POiT jointly chose this as the pilot RAD project. When they had investigated RAD in the past, POiT had chosen the dynamic systems development method (DSDM) – the industry-standard, public domain methodology for RAD. POiT was already an active member of the DSDM Consortium, the body that promotes the method, and decided that DSDM would underpin the approach that it adopted for the pilot project.

When it started out on the pilot, POiT was given a rigorous set of targets. This included doubling productivity against traditional methods and developing the new system to a very tight development budget. In fact, the entire project took seven and a half months – for an application that would have taken 13 months to develop by normal methods, thus halving the labour costs of the project. As everyone becomes more and more price-conscious, the need to deliver to fixed cost is becoming an ever more important driver, and users are beginning to expect this for IT as well as other services and products they purchase. The POiT pilot was no exception. Once the functional model had been defined, the project was supplied to a fixed price, yet it delivered almost 50% more function than was planned.

To outsource or mentor?

To implement a new way of working and deliver significant quantifiable benefits in one project is a very tall order. If POiT was to be successful, it had to get up to speed fast. It felt that, while it could have hired expertise to deliver the project in double-quick time, when the 'hired guns' left, it would have found itself back at square one. POiT wanted to retain RAD knowledge at the end of the project.

Mentoring is an excellent way of investing in in-house staff so that they retain knowledge and experience gained from the real world in real projects. To this end, POiT looked around for a partner who could not only transfer expertise and knowledge but also support it as it worked through the pilot. Like POiT, IBM is an active member of the DSDM Consortium, and as a founder member has worked with the method since its inception. This, combined with its willingness to work in true partnership with customers, made IBM the natural choice.

Shortening the learning curve

In order to get everyone 'singing from the same hymn sheet', the IBM consultants implemented an intensive programme of training and education. Equally important as education is building team spirit and motivation, which is vital to a successful RAD project. These intensive education sessions, which included users and IT staff, provided the ideal catalyst.

POiT was well aware that the best way to learn is not necessarily in the classroom. Indeed, its experience was that learning 'on the job' was often more useful, so it was delighted with IBM's approach.

IBM followed up the initial education sessions with regular health checks. These sessions reviewed the entire project, including the people, the development environment and the technology. These reviews formed the basis of a positive feedback loop, which meant that lessons learned throughout the life of the pilot were acted on as it progressed. This positive feedback loop enabled vital fine-tuning of the development process, helping to ensure that all members of the team were able get the most from the learning experience that the pilot project provided.

Building assets for the future

It is one thing to retain the knowledge and experience once the consultants have left, but what about the process? POiT was keen to build a repeatable process so that when the next project came along it would not have to 'reinvent the wheel'. With this in mind, IBM set up a DSDM workbench, comprising techniques and guidelines based on its wealth of experience in traditional and RAD projects. This meant that through the pilot, although the first using RAD and DSDM, POiT was already building work practices and an environment that could be expected to be found in companies with far more experience.

The way forward

The project was successful as a pilot and pioneered many new tools and techniques that POiT can use in the future. One of the benefits of combining IBM's mentoring with DSDM is that POiT is now in a position to pick and choose from the DSDM elements available without being tied to the entire structure. It can do this safe in the knowledge that it knows what it is doing.

Both POiT and SSL are keen to use RAD again and to continue developing and refining their processes and standards. In fact, a senior SSL manager was heard to ask 'When are we doing the next project?'

Questions

1. In what ways did the RAD approach followed in the PoiT project differ from the traditional structured analysis and design approaches introduced in earlier chapters?
2. Identify the features of the PoiT project that made it particularly successful.
3. Were there any aspects of the PoiT project that made it particularly suited to an RAD approach? Can RAD deliver better-quality solutions in all situations?

References and recommended reading

Avgerou C. and Cornford T. (1998). *Developing Information Systems: Concepts, Issues and Practice*, 2nd edn. Palgrave (formerly Macmillan)

This provides an interesting introduction to approaches and issues in information systems development. The book adopts a conceptual and critical perspective. It is suitable as a supplementary to a detailed explanatory text.

Avison D. and Fitzgerald G. (2003). *Information Systems Development: Methodologies, Techniques and Tools*, 3rd edn. McGraw-Hill

This well-established text covers a range of techniques and methodologies for systems analysis and design. The book provides a comprehensive coverage of data, process, rapid, blended, and people-oriented methodologies. This edition contains new material on ERP and the development of e-commerce applications. The book is suitable for those covering an information systems course at undergraduate level.

Bennet S., McRobb S. and Farmer R. (2002). *Object Oriented Systems Analysis and Design using UML*. McGraw-Hill

This text for undergraduate courses presents various life cycle models and develops object oriented approaches using UML. The book contains two extensive case studies with end of chapter summaries, questions and case reviews.

Bittner K. and Spence I. (2006). *Managing Iterative Software Development Projects*. Addison-Wesley

This book acknowledges the environment of change within which projects are usually developed and provides strategies of dynamic planning and iterative development including extreme programming.

Checkland P.B. (1999). *Systems Thinking, Systems Practice*. John Wiley & Sons.

This book develops the thinking behind the Checkland methodology.

Coad P. and Yourdon E. (1991). *Object-oriented Analysis*, 2nd edn. Prentice Hall

A straightforward introductory text covering the major tasks associated with object-oriented analysis.

Cobham D., Harston J., Kretsis M. and Kyte J. (1999). *The Uptake and Usage of Object Technology*, Proceedings of BIT Conference

Fettke P. and Loos P *et al.* (2007). *Reference Modelling for Business Systems Analysis*. IGI Global

The starting point of referencing modelling is to identify various conceptual modules for different types of industry and use these as a guide to commonality in systems development. This text provides insights into languages and models for reference modelling. There are a large number of contributors. It is suitable for advanced readers.

Fowler M. (2004). *UML Distilled: A Brief Guide to the Standard Modelling Language*. Addison-Wesley, Pearson

This is a short practical book enabling readers to become up to speed with UML 2.0 and learn the essentials of the UML language. The book gives a clear coverage of UML diagramming tools and a useful introduction to OO techniques in software development.

Land F. and Hirscheim R. (1983). Participative systems design: rationale, tools and techniques. *Journal of Applied Systems Analysis*, **10**

Larman C. (2004). *Applying UML and Patterns: An Introduction to Object-Oriented Analysis and Design and Iterative Development*, 3rd edn. Prentice Hall

An excellent step-by-step guide to UML and object oriented development.

Martin J. (1989). *Information Engineering*. Prentice Hall

A clear and comprehensive statement of the main ideas behind the influential methodology of information engineering.

Martin J. (1991). *Rapid Applications Development*. Prentice Hall

This is an important text as the first identifiable approach with the underlying theme of rapid applications development. Other texts on RAD have diverged from Martin's original approach, and the term 'RAD' is now more loosely defined.

Meyer B. (1995). *Object Success*. Prentice Hall

A very clear exposition of Meyer's view of object oriented approaches, illustrated with many real case studies and some amusing anecdotes. The book contains a useful section on managing projects in an object oriented environment.

Mumford E. (2003). *Redesigning Human Systems*. IGI Publishing

A fascinating view on systems design and the management of change. The author emphasizes the need for an ethical approach in implementing changes to systems.

Newman W.M. and Lamming M.J. (2004). *Interactive Systems Design*. Addison-Wesley

This text provides a coherent framework for user oriented design covering all stages of analysis, design, implementation and evaluation. It illustrates points with examples from air traffic control, police detective work and medical practice. Prototyping and evaluation play a major role in this approach, and this is fully explained.

Office of Government Commerce (2005). *Managing Successful Projects with PRINCE2*. Her Majesty's Stationery Office

This well-illustrated official guide lays out the PRINCE2 method in its entirety. It is a manual for successful adoption and usage of PRINCE2.

Chapter 18

Expert systems and knowledge bases

Learning outcomes

On completion of this chapter, you should be able to:

- Define artificial intelligence and expert systems
- Describe the typical architecture of an expert system
- Contrast alternative ways of representing knowledge
- Explain how inferences are drawn in an expert system
- Give examples of the application of artificial intelligence in the World Wide Web.

Introduction

In Chapters 7 and 8, various ways to store and retrieve information were considered. Important though data and information handling are to an organization's information system, they are only one component. Modern developments allow the storage and use of expert knowledge as well. These are known as expert systems. It is the purpose of this chapter to explain the nature of expert systems and knowledge bases together with features of these systems that distinguish them from traditional information processing using file-based and database structures. It is important to treat (in some depth) the internal working of expert systems and the way that knowledge is stored in them. Unlike traditional information systems, where the business person or accountant will need a broad understanding of aspects of analysis and design but is little concerned with the technical implementation of the system, it is increasingly common for the expert to take a major role in the detailed aspects of the development of an expert system.

The chapter begins with an introduction to the role of an expert and the nature of expertise. This allows a definition of the basic ideas lying behind expert systems. More detailed coverage involves explanation of the important distinction between procedural and declarative knowledge. This is used as an introduction to the idea of the representation of knowledge in the form of rules and leads to an explanation of the basic components or architecture of an expert system. Various forms of knowledge representation are described, and their particular applications and limitations are highlighted. Reasoning with certain knowledge is dealt with by providing classical rules and methods of inference. The representation of uncertainty and its use in reasoning are also covered. The chapter as a whole acts as an introduction to the ideas behind expert systems.

18.1 Expert systems architecture

For many years there has been a prediction of rapid growth in artificial intelligence (AI) in business as projects currently under development come to fruition. One of the greatest limitations of current information-processing systems is that their scope has been restricted to the fast and accurate processing of numeric and text data. Broadly speaking, this processing has involved numeric and algebraic functions on numbers, or various forms of insertion, deletion and retrieval of text. The processing is controlled by a program working on the numeric and text data. This mimics many tasks that were performed manually in the past. The accountant added debits and credits to arrive at balances, the scientist performed statistical tests on survey data, or the office clerk inserted or deleted data in files in cabinets. Other sorts of task, though, cannot be regarded as falling into these categories.

The doctor having a knowledge of diseases comes to a diagnosis of an illness by reasoning from information given by the patient's symptoms and then prescribes medication on the basis of known characteristics of available drugs together with the patient's history. The solicitor advises the client on the likely outcome of litigation based on the facts of the particular case, an expert understanding of the law and a knowledge of the way the courts work and interpret this law in practice. The accountant looks at various characteristics of a company's performance and makes a judgement as to the likely state of health of that company. All of these tasks involve some of the features for which computers traditionally have been noted – performing text and numeric processing quickly and efficiently – but they also involve one more ability: reasoning. Reasoning is the movement from details of a particular case and knowledge of the general subject area surrounding that case to the derivation of conclusions. Expert systems incorporate this reasoning by applying general rules in a knowledge base to aspects of a particular case under consideration.

What is an expert system? The short answer is that it is a computerized system that performs the role of an expert or carries out a task that requires expertise. In order to understand what an expert system is, then, it is worth paying some attention to the role of an expert and the nature of expertise. It is then important to ascertain what types of expert and expertise there are in business and what benefits will accrue to an organization when it develops an expert system.

An expert typically has a body of knowledge and handles that knowledge in its application to problems in a way not possessed by the layman. An expert:

- has a body of knowledge in a particular subject area;
- can apply this knowledge to problem situations, often in conditions of uncertain or incomplete information;
- can deliver effective and efficient solutions, such as the diagnosis of a problem, an assessment of a situation, advice, planning, or recommended courses of action and decisions;
- is able to provide explanations and justifications for these solutions;
- can provide information on the subject area of expertise;
- is able to identify his or her limitations in this subject area and know where to obtain further advice;
- can interact with a person requiring the expert's assistance;
- can improve their knowledge and expertise by learning.

For example, corporate tax specialists:

- will have a body of tax knowledge on tax legislation and principles, together with the way that government taxation boards apply them;
- will be able to apply this expertise in particular situations given corporate facts to, for instance, recommend ways of classifying corporate assets to minimize tax liability;
- will be able to justify and explain their recommendations to government tax authorities and internal management in the organization for which the expert is acting as tax specialist;
- will be able to answer specific tax enquiries;
- will be aware of the limitations of their own tax expertise;
- will be able to interact with those requiring tax advice at a level that takes account of the enquirer's level of knowledge and interests;
- will be able to update their expertise in the light of new tax legislation or precedent.

Organizations have experts in many areas. A business organization will probably have general expertise in such areas as tax, accounts, marketing, production and personnel as well as specific expertise in the narrow area of its activity – for example, the design, production and retailing of motor cars. As well as 'high-level' expertise, there will be 'low-level' expertise. An example of this might be the knowledge possessed by a clerk of the way that an organization stores its records with cross-referencing and the handling of exceptions.

In order to justify the cost of an expert system, an organization will want to realize benefits. Among many possible benefits of an expert system are:

- A cost-effective consultant system to aid or replace existing expertise within the organization. Being computer-based, expert systems perform consistently unlike human experts, who may have 'off days'.
- An archive of specific skills that the organization possesses and on which it is dependent for its successful functioning – experts may leave or retire.
- A training aid for 'future experts'.
- A standard for expertise against which human experts can be compared.

The characteristics of an area of expertise that make it suitable for the design of an expert system are:

- The area of expertise should involve the analysis of a complex set of conditions and the application of these to a specifiable area of knowledge that is amenable to computerized representation (see Sections 18.1.1 and 18.1.2).
- The area of expertise is narrow and clear-cut and can be made explicit. It does not, for instance, involve the expert in using general knowledge or 'common sense'.
- The expert's task typically takes between a few minutes and, say, three hours. Less than this and the use of computer input will slow the task; more than this and the task is likely to be too complex.

What is an expert system? We can return to this original question. Although a detailed answer is provided by the rest of the chapter, a brief answer follows from the previous considerations of the role of an expert and the nature of expertise. An expert system typically:

- incorporates expert knowledge in a particular subject area, usually by storing and representing this as rules or other representation forms (**knowledge base**);
- separates the general knowledge from the details of a particular case under consideration to which the knowledge base is applied (**particular context**);
- clearly distinguishes the knowledge from the mechanism of reasoning (**inference engine**);
- possesses an interactive user interface for providing explanations, justifications and questions to the user; and
- provides, as its output, advice or decisions in the area of expertise.

In addition, an expert system may be able to handle uncertain or incomplete information. It may also be able to learn – that is, modify its knowledge base or inference engine.

Expert systems have been developed and are currently being developed for a wide variety of areas of expertise in business. A few examples are:

- a system that provides advice to employers on the dismissal of employees;
- a system that provides advice on registration under the Data Protection Act in the UK;
- a system that develops investment plans for personal clients tailored to their needs;
- a system that aids auditors in providing an effective and complete audit of a company's accounts;
- a system that provides an assessment of a company's health from various perspectives such as the auditor, the trade creditor and the financier of loans.

Before embarking on the remainder of the chapter, a word of warning is appropriate. Vendors of software and systems sometimes describe their products as 'expert systems' for marketing reasons. The reader should be wary. As one software vendor of a major mainframe package explained:

> Our software has gone through various upgradings over the last ten years, but it is still essentially the same product. Ten years ago we called it a 'management information system', five years ago a 'decision support system' and now we sell it as an 'expert system'.

Expert systems are sometimes known as 'knowledge-based systems' or 'intelligent knowledge-based systems'. The architecture of a typical expert system is shown in Figure 18.1. Each of the parts is considered separately in the following sections in order to give an overview of the way an expert system works. Knowledge representation in the domain-specific knowledge base and the ways that inferences are drawn are also considered in more detail in Sections 18.2 and 18.3.

18.1.1 Domain-specific knowledge base

This is one of the two logically distinct components of the knowledge base. Domain-specific knowledge is the representation of the static expertise of the experts. As most experts are knowledgeable in limited areas, this is reflected in the term 'domain-specific'. An example of expertise might be how to interpret a complex tax law in such a way that it is most advantageous to a client. This is to be distinguished from general

Figure 18.1 Architecture of a typical expert system

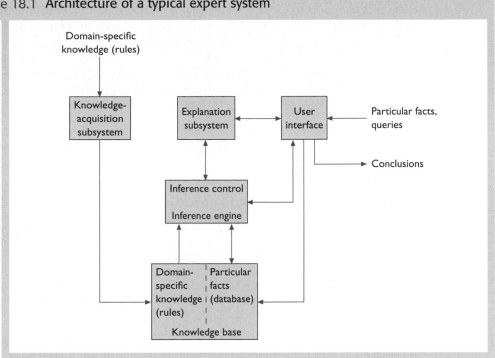

or common-sense knowledge, which we all have. The latter is often mundane. The fact that all objects fall to the ground when released, except if they are lighter than air or are fairly light and there is a strong wind blowing, is an instance of common-sense knowledge. Another example is that one might bring a bottle of wine, flowers or a box of chocolates to a friend's dinner party but not a plate of cold, uncooked liver. This latter sort of common-sense knowledge, although widespread among people, is most difficult to represent and use in reasoning in expert systems, because common-sense knowledge often involves a mixture of pictorial and verbal, general and specific, and uncertain and vague knowledge from many areas. It is linked to an understanding of the meanings of natural-language terms that surpasses that of any computer of today. Common-sense knowledge may be inextricably interwoven with moral beliefs, complex social attitudes and individual interests. All of this makes it difficult to represent such knowledge in a way that is accessible to automated reasoning. Common sense is widespread but not simple.

Declarative and procedural knowledge

Fundamental to any expert system is the assumption that much knowledge is declarative rather than procedural. To see the difference, it is illustrative to consider an example. The following is from a recipe for making moussaka:

> First slice the aubergines, pack into a colander and then sprinkle with salt. Place a plate on top and a large weight on the plate and leave for half an hour. Meanwhile, fry the garlic and onions in olive oil for about 5 minutes before adding the minced meat. In a basin, mix together the tomato puree, parsley and wine, season it with salt and pepper and when the meat has browned pour the mixture over it.

The knowledge contained in the above is largely procedural. With procedural knowledge, it is common to see statements such as '**DO** ⟨this⟩ . . . **THEN DO** ⟨that⟩ . . .' or 'meanwhile **DO** ⟨this⟩ . . . **UNTIL** ⟨that⟩ occurs'. The knowledge consists of actions or activities linked by temporal connections. Procedural knowledge can be easily incorporated into conventional programs, which execute code (activities) in the order in which they appear in the program. Cooking knowledge may still be beyond the computer of today, but numeric computation is procedural. In order to find the average of a set of numbers, the following recipe can be followed:

Set a running total and count to zero. Take the first number and add it to the total and add one to the count. **DO** this with each successive number **UNTIL** there are no more numbers. **THEN** divide the running total by the count. The result is the average.

A computer program could provide a coded version of this requested set of actions. In contrast, declarative knowledge, illustrated in the following example, is rather different:

IF the student has successfully completed level 1 of the examination **OR** has been exempted from level 1 by virtue of satisfying *any* of the conditions laid out in paragraphs 3(a) to 3(f) below, **THEN** the student is entitled to register for level 2 of the examination. A student registered for level 2 is exempt from examination papers 2.3 **AND** 2.4 **IF** he/she has obtained exemption from level 1 by virtue of satisfying the conditions 3(a) **OR** 3(b) below, **OR** satisfying 3(d) **AND** being in possession of an honours degree awarded by a British university **OR** accredited by the Council for National Academic Awards.

Here, the knowledge consists of propositions linked together by logical relationships. It is common to find expressions of the form '**IF** ⟨such-and-such⟩ **THEN** ⟨so-and-so⟩ is the case' or '⟨so-and-so⟩ **UNLESS** ⟨this⟩ **OR** ⟨that⟩'. There is no sense in which one activity is performed before another. Rather, there is a set of conditions or area of knowledge that is declared.

Rules

It is often possible to represent this declarative knowledge in the form of rules. Figure 18.2 is an example of a set of rules representing declarative knowledge in the area of the assessment of a company's financial health. It is this set of rules that forms the domain-specific knowledge in the knowledge base.

Figure 18.2 Rules from a knowledge base dealing with a company's financial health

Rule 1 **IF** the quick ratio is higher than the industry average quick ratio
AND the inventory turnover ratio is higher than the industry average turnover ratio
THEN short-term liquidity is good

Rule 2 **IF** the debt to equity ratio is low
AND the dividend cover is high
THEN the medium-term insolvency risk is low

Rule 3 **IF** the short-term liquidity is good
AND the medium-term insolvency risk is low
AND EITHER the market is likely to expand
OR the market is stable
AND the company has a majority market share
THEN the company is financially stable

The rules given in Figure 18.2 are often known as **if–then rules**. They have the form:

IF ⟨antecedent condition⟩ **THEN** ⟨consequent⟩

where the antecedent condition is any sentence or set of sentences connected by 'and', 'or' or 'not'. These are known as **Boolean operators** and give the structure of the rule. The simplest expert systems will treat expressions such as 'short-term liquidity is good' as simple and unanalysable atomic units. Their sole function is to be assigned a truth value (true or false). More complex systems might be capable of treating this expression as saying of the attribute 'short-term liquidity' that it has the value 'good' – it might have had the value 'poor' or 'average'. The presence of attribute–value pairs allows more complex reasoning to be undertaken by the system. This will be seen later in Section 18.2.1.

However, not all knowledge can be represented in the form of if–then rules. It has already been seen that some knowledge is procedural; also, much declarative knowledge cannot easily be cast into the if–then mould either. Any knowledge that relies on pictorial representation, such as the relative positioning of streets on a street map, cannot appropriately be represented as propositional knowledge and therefore not as if–then rules. Some declarative knowledge is best understood as knowing that certain entities have attributes; they inherit these attributes by virtue of being instances of other entities. It is unnatural to attempt to encode this in the form of rules. For example, salmon have fins by virtue of being fish, as do trout. Rather than represent this as if–then rules about salmon and trout separately, this knowledge can be represented as being facts about fish, which salmon and trout then inherit. Other suitable forms of representation such as semantic networks and frames are treated in Sections 18.2.3 and 18.2.4. However, for the explanation of the architecture of the expert system, a rule-based representation will be assumed.

The knowledge base may consist of several hundreds or even thousands of rules for complex areas of expertise. As a rough guide, it is convenient to class expert systems as small if they have between 50 and 200 rules and as large if over 1000 rules. With many fewer than 50 rules, the area covered is becoming so small that it will hardly qualify as expertise.

18.1.2 Knowledge-acquisition subsystem

The domain-specific knowledge in the form of rules, or some other chosen representational form, needs to be entered into the system. This is achieved by the knowledge-acquisition subsystem. In the simplest case, rules are entered at the keyboard. The rules are required to follow a specified syntax called the **knowledge-representation language** (KRL). As well as rules, other information can be added. For instance, in Figure 18.2, rule 1 requires that the quick ratio, a measure used in accounting, is higher than the industry average as a necessary condition that liquidity is good. When this rule is considered by the expert system in a later consultation the system will attempt to determine the truth of that antecedent condition. It may be the case that whether the quick ratio is higher than the industry average or not is determined by further rules. Alternatively, the expert system may need a basic piece of evidence in order to establish the company's financial health, and the only way of finding this is to ask the user of the expert system a question. The exact text of the question can be specified when the rule is first input into the knowledge base. This may lead to the following representation in the KRL:

The quick ratio is higher than the industry average: **ASK TEXT** 'Is the quick ratio for the company higher than the average quick ratio for the industry as a whole?'

The user might require further explanation in order to be able to answer the question. The KRL can provide the facility for this. It is also clear that the condition is Boolean – TRUE or FALSE (or possibly UNKNOWN) should be assigned to the value of the proposition. All this can be incorporated, leading to the following full specification in the KRL:

> The quick ratio is higher than the industry average: **ASK TEXT** 'Is the quick ratio for the company higher than the average quick ratio for the industry as a whole', **YES/NO**, **EXPLANATION** 'The quick ratio may be determined from the company's financial accounts and is given by the following formula:
>
> quick ratio = ⟨current assets less inventory⟩/current assets'.

These rules and other details can be entered via a standard word-processing package. The text file is created and then compiled, the syntax is checked and the rules and other information are converted into a form suitable for storage in the knowledge base. Alternatively, the rules may be entered interactively during a rule-building consultation with the expert system. Each rule is checked for correct syntax as it is entered, and checks are made immediately to ensure that the rule is consistent with the existing rules. The process is analogous to interpreting a program in a high-level language rather than compiling, although this analogy should not be taken too far.

The methods of entry mentioned in the previous paragraph are typical of knowledge-acquisition subsystems associated with expert systems built from application packages called **expert system shells**. These are expert systems that initially contain no knowledge in their knowledge base. The knowledge is entered by the builders of the expert system.

The kind of knowledge acquisition just described is similar to rote learning. Just as scientific progress does not occur through rote learning of new rules (where do they come from?), so expert systems imbued with greater power may obtain knowledge in additional ways. Perhaps the most common is by deriving rules from a large number of cases. Given, for example, many cases of plant disease symptoms and other environmental conditions, together with the diagnosed disease in each case, a pattern connecting certain symptoms and environmental conditions with a particular disease can be established. The knowledge-acquisition subsystem scans details of these cases, often held on a conventional database, and derives this pattern in the form of rules, which are automatically generated and entered into the knowledge base. The process is called **rule induction**. Although automated machine learning is gradually being developed, there are still technical and theoretical difficulties that restrict its use to very specialized applications.

By far the most common method of acquisition is direct rule entry via the keyboard. To do this requires overcoming one of the major problems involved in building an expert system. That problem is to obtain the knowledge and represent it in the required form (for example, as a set of rules) when the knowledge originally resides in the mind of an expert and, as any psychologist will confirm, the way knowledge is represented to the human in the mind is still a mystery. The process of extracting the knowledge in the required form is called **knowledge elicitation**.

Knowledge elicitation

Although some expert systems are derived from source documentation, such as legislation, the vast majority of expert systems rely, partly at least, on expertise that is resident in the mind of an expert(s). It shows itself in behavioural terms only when required to perform a task. In the process of knowledge elicitation, this is extracted and displayed in a form suitable for incorporating into a computerized system.

The systems analyst relies heavily on interviewing personnel in an existing system in order to identify key tasks, information flows, data stores, and so on. This interview model has formed the basis of initial attempts at knowledge elicitation. However, even if the expert is willing to spend the considerable time and effort with the knowledge engineer in order to pass on the expertise, there are major obstacles to a smooth, orderly and exhaustive elicitation stage.

1. Many areas of expertise are highly technical, and unless the knowledge engineer is familiar with the area he or she will have great difficulty in understanding and representing it correctly.

2. A knowledge engineer may attempt to become familiar with the domain by textbook research. Unfortunately, it is often the non-textbook heuristic approaches taken by experts, based on experience, that make their expertise so valuable. A little learning on the part of the knowledge engineer may be a dangerous thing. It can force the expert into the position of providing 'textbook' answers to questions asked from a textbook background.

3. An expert's time is precious, and knowledge elicitation is a lengthy task.

4. The expert may be a competent practitioner but may not be used to verbal discussion of the domain area in the manner required for knowledge engineering.

5. The chosen tool may affect the way that the engineer attempts to elicit the expertise. The expert, though, may not represent the knowledge internally in the form in which the engineer is attempting to extract it. This creates a difficulty, and the expert may need to rethink the domain. However, this can be an instructive educational process for the expert. It forces valuable systematization and the adoption of new perspectives on the domain.

6. There is a temptation on the part of the expert to wish to discuss the more unusual and difficult areas that he or she deals with, whereas the primary purpose of the knowledge engineer is to concentrate on the central and often more mundane cases.

These problems have prompted the development of a number of knowledge elicitation techniques that go beyond the traditional interview.

Forward scenario simulation

This is rather like a structured interview in which the expert is given a series of hypothetical case study problems and asked how to solve them. The expert is required to explain what facts are being considered and how they are being treated as the problem is solved. The major advantage of this approach is that by a judicious selection of problems by, for example, another expert or even the expert subject of the elicitation process, the engineer can ensure a comprehensive coverage of the central types of problem in the domain area.

It is usual to conduct the interview on each problem in two stages:

1. Ask the interviewee to outline the task to be accomplished in solving the problem, including a description of the possible outcomes, variables and rules used.

2. Establish how general and how specific each of the discovered rules are.

Typical questions from the knowledge engineer might be:

- When do you do (such-and-such)?
- Why do you do (such-and-such)?
- Under what circumstances would this rule apply?
- Under what circumstances would this rule not apply?
- How did you establish (such-and-such)?

Protocol analysis

In protocol analysis, the knowledge engineer observes and probably audio/video tapes the expert in the course of performing tasks. These records are searched for key variables, rules and the order of approach taken during problem solving. This has one advantage over the structured interview in that the expert is not required to give explanations and justifications for every decision. The pressure that is present during the interview may generate spurious responses – experts do not like to say 'I just don't know why I did that' or 'It was no more than a guess'. However, unless all major types of case come up, protocol analysis techniques will not lead to a complete knowledge elicitation.

Goal decomposition

This is a set of techniques most suitable where the knowledge domain is structured in a hierarchy. The techniques derive from use in psychology. 'Laddered Grid' and '20 Questions' are two examples of goal decomposition. In the latter, the expert is confronted with an interviewer who has a set of hypothetical problems. The expert is provided with no initial information, and by a series of questions attempts to establish as much as possible about the problem. The types of question asked and the order in which they are put gives the knowledge engineer valuable insights into the way that the expert perceives the structure of the knowledge domain. This technique can only be used by an engineer with some familiarity with the domain.

Multidimensional techniques

These techniques provide some kind of map as to how the elements in a knowledge domain are put together where there are complex interactions. Many of these techniques also derive from the discipline of psychology, where they are used to build a model of the way that a person perceives the world. The techniques often involve determining ways in which two things are alike and different from a third. If this is repeated many times with different objects, a set of differentiating concepts that are important to the expert is established. Techniques such as repertory grid, factor analysis and multidimensional scaling fall into this category. Details of these may be obtained from the references at the end of this chapter.

Automated elicitation and acquisition

In the future, expert systems may be able to abstract general principles and rules applicable to knowledge domains directly from sets of given examples. However, the current state of the art is many years behind such developments, although primitive **induction** techniques are already used to infer straightforward rules governing a domain. Some expert system shells may have this induction facility, the aim being to bypass much of the work of the knowledge engineer and produce working expert systems rapidly.

Figure 18.3 An automatic induction to provide a set of rules governing job selection

CASE	ATTRIBUTES			DECISION
	DEGREE CLASS	*QUALIFICATION*	*EXPERIENCE*	
1	1	YES	1 YEAR	OFFER
2	3	YES	2 YEAR	REJECT
3	2	YES	2 YEAR	OFFER
4	1	YES	*	OFFER
5	2	YES	2 YEAR	OFFER
6	*	NO	*	REJECT
7	2	YES	3 YEAR	OFFER
8	3	NO	3 YEAR	REJECT
9	3	*	*	REJECT

(Note * = Unknown)

Rules

IF *DEGREE CLASS* = 1 **AND** *QUALIFIED*
  THEN *OFFER*

IF *DEGREE CLASS* = 2 **AND** *QUALIFIED*
    AND (*EXPERIENCE* = '3 YEAR' **OR** *EXPERIENCE* = '2 YEAR')
  THEN *OFFER*

IF *DEGREE CLASS* = 3 **THEN** *REJECT*

IF NOT *QUALIFIED* **THEN** *REJECT*

These shells typically work by requiring the expert (or some person) to select key attributes that are applicable to a task and then input a large number of instances of the task while giving the associated values of attributes and outcomes. The automated induction module of the shell is called up, and a set of rules is inferred. There are standard algorithms for this, and an example is given in Figure 18.3. Here, it is intended to determine the rules governing the selection of candidates for a post. Nine previous cases and their decisions lead to the four rules shown in the figure being inferred.

These systems will only be useful when theoretical issues surrounding induction have found algorithmic solutions. In particular:

- How can an automated system decide upon the relevant attributes that are to be used in the induction, having been given a number of cases?
- How can the system derive probabilistic rules governing attributes that take real-number values?
- How can the system identify and ignore freak cases without upsetting the existing system of rules?

18.1.3 Case-specific knowledge base (database)

The other component of the knowledge base contains details relevant to a particular consultation of the expert system. An expert system used to diagnose a company's financial health will have permanent rules governing the factors that affect company financial health in general (domain-specific knowledge) but during use will have factual details on the company under consideration (XYZ Company). Details on XYZ will be stored in the case-specific knowledge base. The facts are either input directly by the user, for instance in response to a question, or taken directly from an external conventional database holding company data, or derived from the content of the factual knowledge base by reasoning with the rules.

The term 'database' is sometimes used to refer to the case-specific knowledge base. It must be realized that this is not the same use of 'database' as in Chapter 8 but refers merely to the store of case-specific data.

18.1.4 Inference engine

Given details of a particular case and general domain-specific rules, what conclusions can be drawn? The process of drawing conclusions is not a static one. It involves the application of sound methods of reasoning to evidence as it currently stands in the knowledge base.

The inference engine (or interpreter) applies the domain-specific knowledge base to the particular facts of the case under consideration to derive these new conclusions. Principles govern the work of the inference engine. Some of these concern the allowable types of inference that can be performed. The strictest inference principles are logically sound. That is, if we are given initial data as true, then the inferences drawn with the use of the principle must also be true. Some principles of inference, particularly those concerned with probabilistic or uncertain reasoning, do not meet this requirement.

In a rule-based system, the most common example of a sound inference principle is logical derivation by *modus ponendo ponens* (usually shortened to *modus ponens*). This is an obvious inference principle known to the ancients. A simple example of *modus ponens* is:

Given rule	*If* it is raining *then* the ground is wet
Given fact	It is raining
Derived new fact	The ground is wet

A similar though perhaps slightly less obvious inference is *modus tollendo tollens* (usually shortened to *modus tollens*). Using a weather example again:

Given rule	*If* it is raining *then* the ground is wet
Given fact	The ground is not wet
Derived new fact	It is not raining

In most formal systems, these can be shown to be logically equivalent forms of reasoning (specifically those systems in which we are entitled to assume the negation of an assumption if that assumption leads to a contradiction – another intuitively sound move known as *reductio ad absurdum*). However, some expert systems make use of *modus ponens* without *modus tollens*. This implies that they are unable to derive certain obvious and particularly useful conclusions from a given set of rules and particular facts.

Common inference principles for Boolean algebra given in Figure 18.4(a) and (b) have already been considered, while (c) and (d) are trivial but important for those systems that allow antecedents of rules to contain conjunctions and disjunctions (as in rule 1 concerning short-term liquidity in Figure 18.2). They generate complex propositions from simple ones; (e) is known as the resolution principle and can be used to reduce a set of complex propositions to simpler ones, and (f) can be used to eliminate a

Figure 18.4 Some inference principles for Boolean algebra: (a) *modus ponendo ponens*; (b) *modus tollendo tollens*; (c) conjunction introduction; (d) disjunction introduction; (e) resolution; (f) disjunction elimination

		Principle	Example
(a)	Rule	**If** A **then** B	**If** the creature has feathers **then** it is a bird
	Fact	A	the creature has feathers
	New fact	B	it is a bird
(b)	Rule	**If** A **then** B	**If** the creature has feathers **then** it is a bird
	Fact	not B	it is **not** a bird
	New fact	not A	the creature does **not** have feathers
(c)	Fact	A	it is a fish
	Fact	B	it weighs 10 kilograms
	New fact	A **and** B	it is a fish **and** weighs 10 kilograms
(d)	Fact	A	it is raining
	New fact	A **or** B	it is raining **or** snowing
(e)	Fact	(**not** A) **or** B	either it does **not** have gills **or** it is a fish
	Fact	(**not** B) **or** C	either it it is **not** a fish **or** it lives in water
	New fact	**not** A **or** C	either it does **not** have gills **or** it lives in water
(f)	Fact	(**not** A) **or** B	either it does not have gills **or** it is a fish
	Fact	A	it does have gills
	New fact	B	it is a fish

disjunction. All expert systems will use some or all of these or their equivalents in the inference process.

These abstract inference principles need to be applied selectively in order to achieve a useful derivation of new facts during the consultation. At any given time there may be many ways of proceeding from the set of rules and particular facts in the knowledge base. There must not only be principles for deriving new facts but also a way of choosing which principle is to be used at any moment. And given that, for example, *modus ponens* is chosen then which rules and existing facts should be used if there is more than one possible use? In short, there must not only be sound inference principles but also an inference control strategy for selecting which principles are to be applied to which rules in the knowledge base at a given time. ('Inference principles' has been used in the text to mean any method of inference. It is common elsewhere also to refer to these as 'inference rules'. This has been avoided as it may lead to confusion with rules held in the knowledge base that are domain-specific and provide empirical knowledge or definitions, such as in Figure 18.2. The matter is further complicated by the inclusion of inference rules in the rule base of some expert systems.)

An example of inference control is shown in Figure 18.5. This is a model of a very simple expert system illustrating the way that the inference engine dynamically interacts with the rule base and the fact base (database) to derive new facts. The inference engine is a set of activities that is incorporated into a computer program. The inference engine is procedural – the rules and facts are declarative.

The expert system attempts the identification of creatures based on certain characteristics such as whether they live in the sea, have stripes, eat meat, and so on. (No claim is

Figure 18.5 Model of a simple expert system for classifying creatures

RULE BASE

(1) **IF** eats meat **THEN** carnivore
(2) **IF** suckles young **AND** warm-blooded **THEN** mammal
(3) **IF NOT** warm-blooded **AND** lives in sea **THEN** fish
(4) **IF NOT** carnivore **AND** striped **AND** mammal **THEN** zebra
(5) **IF** carnivore **AND** striped **AND** mammal **THEN** tiger
(6) **IF** mammal **AND** lives in sea **AND NOT** pinniped **THEN** whale
(7) **IF** fish **AND** striped **THEN** tiger fish
(8) **IF** pinniped **AND** mammal **THEN** seal
(9) **IF** hind flippers **THEN** pinniped

INFERENCE ENGINE

(1) Find all rules whose antecedents are satisfied by the database
(2) Ignore rules found in (1) whose consequents are in the database
(3) Execute lowest numbered rule remaining, **if** no rule **then** quit
(4) **Go to** (1)

DATABASE

Initial: suckles young, warm-blooded, lives in sea, hind flippers

	Pass 1	Pass 2	Pass 3	Pass 4
Rules relevant	2, 9	2, 9	2, 8, 9	2, 8, 9
Rule fired	2	9	8	
Database at end of pass	suckles young warm-blooded lives in sea hind flippers mammal	suckles young warm-blooded lives in sea hind flippers mammal pinniped	suckles young warm-blooded lives in sea hind flippers mammal pinniped seal	suckles young warm-blooded lives in sea hind flippers mammal pinniped seal QUIT

made for the sophistication of the system!) The inference engine works by executing instructions (1) to (4). As (4) is a **GOTO** instruction, the engine just loops until the exit condition is met in line (3).

Initial data is supplied on the beast to be identified. This is held in the database. In the example, the facts given are that the subject:

- is warm-blooded;
- suckles young;
- lives in the sea;
- has flippers.

During **pass 1**, line (1) is executed and matches the data in the database with each rule in turn to establish whether the antecedent is satisfied. This results in rule 2 and rule 9 being selected. A check is made to ignore the rules that add nothing to the database, line (2). This leaves both rules still operative, so some method of resolving which rule to operate (or **fire**, as it is sometimes called) must be used. In the example, the simple expedient of executing the lowest-numbered rule is chosen – line (3). This is rule 2, which allows the inference engine to derive the conclusion of the rule, 'mammal', and add it to the database. Line (4) is executed, returning control to line (1).

In **pass 2**, both rule 2 and rule 9 have their antecedents satisfied, but as 'mammal' is already in the database rule 9 is fired (line (3)) and 'pinniped' is added to the database.

In **pass 3**, rules 2, 8 and 9 have their antecedents satisfied (line (1)). Only rule 8 adds new facts to the database (line (2)). So rule 8 is fired (line (3)), and control is returned to line (1) (line (4)).

In **pass 4**, rules 2, 8 and 9 have their antecedents satisfied, but as their consequents are in the database no operative rules remain, and line (3) ensures that the process ends.

The rule base can be given an alternative representation, as in Figure 18.6. This representation highlights the logical connectives **AND**, **NOT** and **OR**. It also serves to establish a hierarchy of rules based on dependence. For instance, rule 8 can be seen to be dependent on rules 2 and 9. This kind of representation may be used when developing the knowledge base. Some people prefer it as they find it easier to work with a picture than the linguistic statement of rules.

A number of features are worth noting about the model in Figure 18.5:

1. The order of rules in the rule base is irrelevant to the final outcome. Reordering the rules might lead to facts being derived in a different sequence during the inferring, but on completion the same set remains in the database. This is characteristic of some, although not all, expert systems and corresponds to the fact that rules do not appear to be ordered in the human brain (except possibly by dependence).

2. The inference engine contains no domain-specific knowledge but only procedural rules for generating inferences. The rule base contains only domain-specific knowledge.

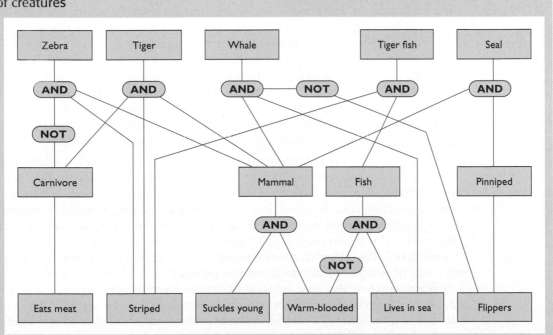

Figure 18.6 An intermediate representation of the knowledge base for the classification of creatures

Put another way, the inference engine could be used on a set of rules diagnosing a company's financial health – the strategy is the same. This feature explains why it is possible to have expert system shells.

3. Rules can be added to the rule base as more knowledge is incorporated. For instance, the following can be added:

Rule 10 **IF** warm-blooded **AND** feathers **THEN** bird

This does not require any other change in the rule base or the inference engine. In the latter case, the inference strategy works for 9 or 900 rules. The knowledge base can grow. This would not be so easy if rules in the knowledge base were not purely declarative.

4. The expert system in Figure 18.5 is very primitive. This is not just because the rules are naive and cover only a fraction of the taxonomy of the animal kingdom. Rather, the inference control strategy (using *modus ponens*) is simple: given the antecedents of conditionals then derive the consequents. This strategy when applied repetitively is called **forward chaining**. Looked at from the point of view of Figure 18.6, it can be seen that given baseline facts, such as 'eats meat' and 'suckles young', the strategy amounts to moving forwards (upwards) through the chart until no more progress can be made. This may be unwieldy if there are a large number of rules and facts to be handled, and it is often better to adopt a different inference control strategy.

An alternative is to take a conclusion as a working hypothesis. In the case of Figure 18.6, this might be to take as the initial assumption that the creature is a tiger. The inference strategy is to look for rules that 'prove' that it is a tiger. If one of the rules is found (rule 5), the next step is to attempt to prove the antecedent – in this case that the creature is a carnivore, is striped and is a mammal. The inference control strategy will attempt to prove each of these in turn. To prove that it is a carnivore, it is sufficient to show that it eats meat; this does not depend on a further rule as a basic element. If the fact is not in the database then the creature is not a carnivore and not a tiger. The inference strategy then selects another goal – for example, it is a whale – and repeats the entire backtracking process.

However, if 'eats meat' is in the database, then it can be proved that the creature is a carnivore. This is the first step to proving that it is a tiger. The inference control strategy then attempts to show that the creature is striped and then that it is a mammal. If either of these fails, the strategy is to move on to another goal as before. This involves backtracking from conclusions to attempt to establish the facts that would prove them, so the inference strategy is known as **backward chaining**.

5. There is no facility for adding data from the user once the system has started its processing. The typical expert will, in the course of a consultation, ask for further information to back up a line of reasoning that he or she is pursuing. Here, the system just proves all it can from the initial data using forward chaining. It might be argued that there is nothing wrong with this provided that all the relevant facts are given at the beginning. This is inappropriate, because the relevant facts may only be established as relevant in the course of a consultation. For example, in a medical expert system it is not of much relevance to know if a patient is a rock musician, accountant or shop assistant in diagnosing the cause of spots, a high temperature and a sore throat. However, matters change if the symptoms are deafness. To say that all the facts should be given initially if they are relevant to the proof of some conclusion (relevant to the diagnosis of some disease) is just not practical – there are often too many, and

only the expert knows which facts are relevant. In any case, the aim of an expert system is to simulate the behaviour and knowledge of experts, and they proceed by selective questioning having been given an initial set of facts. The vast majority of expert systems follow this approach. It is generally associated with inference strategies other than forward chaining.

18.1.5 Explanation subsystem

The explanation subsystem typically provides the following features.

HOW questions

An important feature of experts is that they are able to justify their conclusions. Indeed, it is this ability that leads us to have confidence in their advice. If a doctor concludes that a patient, X, has, say, appendicitis, this conclusion may be justified by saying that:

> X's appendix has not been removed. The patient has a high temperature and vomiting, and the abdomen is sensitive to touch on the lower right-hand side. Under these conditions, a patient probably has appendicitis. This probability is further increased by the fact that none of the following range of foods has been eaten in the last 24 hours: shellfish, mushrooms, . . .

The doctor is providing an explanation of *how* these conclusions were reached. It is important that doctors can do this. If they could not, we would regard them as merely successful clairvoyants – that is, assuming they were right most of the time in their diagnoses.

Expert systems incorporate the possibility of *how* explanations in their explanation subsystem. The user of the system may at any stage interrupt the workings of the expert system to establish how a conclusion or intermediate derived fact has been derived. In the model system in Figure 18.5, after the consultation, the user might query the expert system with the keyboard input '**HOW** seal'. The expert system would respond:

> The conclusion 'seal' was reached because rule 8 applied '**IF** pinniped **AND** mammal **THEN** seal'. Rule 8 applied because 'pinniped' was derived using rule 9 '**IF** flippers **THEN** pinniped'. Rule 9 applied because 'flippers' was given initially. Rule 8 also applied because 'mammal' was derived using rule 2 '**IF** suckles its young **AND** warm-blooded **THEN** mammal'. Rule 2 applied because 'suckles young' and 'warm-blooded' were given initially.

The output given is typical of a response to a **HOW** question provided by an expert system. The proposition for which an explanation is being sought is treated by citing the rules in a backward line of reasoning, together with intermediate conclusions provided by these rules, until 'basic' facts are established – that is, those facts given initially or given in response to questions. The explanatory subsystem inserts expressions such as:

> The conclusion '. . .' was reached because rule . . . applied

in order to make the explanation more readable.

In a large expert system, the line of reasoning to a conclusion may be long and complex. It is usually possible to restrict the explanation facility to a shortened version.

WHY questions

Another form of question that is asked of the expert is a **WHY** question. The doctor may ask patient X whether they had eaten shellfish recently. The patient may wish to know why the doctor is interested. The doctor responds (perhaps rather insensitively):

> I am trying to establish whether you have appendicitis. I have already established that you have a high temperature, vomiting and sensitivity to pressure in the lower right abdomen. This makes appendicitis possible. This possibility is increased if I can rule out the possibility of food poisoning. I can do this if you have not had one of a range of foods recently. Shellfish is one of this range.

Here the doctor is citing a possible diagnosis (conclusion) and explaining how the answer to the question will impact on the proof of this diagnosis. It is important that expert systems provide this possibility. It is achieved by means of a **WHY** question. The system in Figure 18.5 does not ask questions of the user during a consultation. However, imagine that it had this facility – no initial facts were given and it derived its conclusions by attempting to prove that the creature in question was each of the possibilities in turn. (This means that the inference engine cannot be identical to that in Figure 18.5.) Suppose further that the system is trying to prove that the creature under investigation is a whale. The expert system needs to establish, if it has not already done so, whether the creature is warm-blooded. The system will generate a suitable question to ask the user. In response, the user may type '**WHY** warm-blooded' at the keyboard. The **WHY** explanation facility provides the following on the screen:

> I am trying to establish 'whale'.
> 'Mammal' is a necessary condition for a creature to be a 'whale', rule 6, and 'warm-blooded' is a necessary condition for a creature to be a 'mammal', rule 2.

Once again, text is inserted by the expert system to make the explanation more readable.

It is important to see that the explanation follows a template, and the rule numbers and the facts or potential facts are added in a standard way to the template. This means that the explanation facility would be of the same form even if the knowledge base were more complex or had a different subject matter.

Requests for further explanation

A third form of explanatory facility has been covered in Section 18.1.2. This is when the system is attempting to establish a fact by questioning the user. The question itself may need further explanation (what does the term 'quick ratio' mean in the question 'Is the quick ratio higher for the company than the quick ratio for the industry as a whole?'). This is provided by explanatory text added to the original text of the question. The explanation is optional, as it would be irritating and confusing to the experienced user to see large amounts of unnecessary additional text.

Consultation traces

A final explanation facility that may be provided generates a record of the inference paths taken by the system during a consultation. This is generally not so important to the user but may be of considerable help to the person building or testing the expert system. This trace is often graphic, showing the rules executed and the facts established in the chronological order of the consultation. For example, part of the graph of Figure 18.6 traversed during a consultation may be traced on the screen.

In summary, four forms of explanatory facility are generally provided:

1. **How:** how has a conclusion been established? What facts and rules were used in deriving it?

2. **Why:** why is a particular question being asked? What is the impact of the answer to the question on a proof to a conclusion?

3. **Further explanation:** provide more text accompanying the question as a further explanation.

4. **Trace:** provide a 'picture' of the consultation. Display the rules fired and the conclusions established in the order in which these events occurred.

18.2 Representation of knowledge

The ways that people represent their knowledge are rich and varied. There are pictorial representations, as in maps and diagrams; there are graphic representations showing relationships; and, most common and most powerful of all, there are representations in natural language. This book is written in a natural language, English, and can be regarded as representing knowledge on various aspects of business information systems – their analysis, design and use. The only limits imposed in the representation are those governed by the rules of English and the amount of existing knowledge that is assumed to be possessed by the reader. English is a comprehensive natural language in terms of its vocabulary and its structure (the structure of a language is the set of its semantic categories, together with rules for assembling complex wholes such as sentences out of simpler parts – nouns, verbs, and so on). English is so rich that its rules have never been completely formalized. Attempts are being made, and success in this area is a prerequisite for the development of computers with genuine natural language interfaces. Large subsets of English have been formalized, although computers still have difficulty in treating idiomatic expressions. Few English representations adequately distinguish the fact that 'the whisky is good but the meat is bad' is not an example of 'the spirit is willing but the flesh is weak' (or so the joke goes).

The representation of knowledge used in Figures 18.2 and 18.5 has been very simple. If–then rules have been employed, together with the limitations that the constituents of these rules be simple sentences (bearers of truth and falsity and sentences made out of these by the logical connectives **AND**, **OR** and **NOT**).

Although knowledge representation in expert systems has not approached the power of expression of the English language, it has advanced beyond these simple structures. The next sections consider some of the limitations of these simple structures and the ways that they may be overcome using alternative knowledge representation techniques.

18.2.1 Attribute–value pairs

Imagine that the three rules in Figure 18.7 occur in an expert system that has been set up to deal with applications for credit cards. Part of the system determines whether the applicant's credit status is acceptable, while another part analyses the income to

---

Figure 18.7 **Some rules governing entitlement to credit cards**

> **Rule 1: If** income > £30,000 **then** credit type = gold card
> **Rule 2: If** income ≤ £30,000 **and** credit status = OK **then** credit type = normal
> **Rule 3: If** income > £10,000 **then** credit status = OK

determine the type of credit card to which the applicant is entitled. The rules are simplified for the sake of the example.

If the representation is taken as being composed of complete propositions with no internal structure then the fact that an applicant's income is £15,000 would not be applicable to these rules. 'Income = £15,000' does not occur as the antecedent to any of them. To ensure that rule 3 fires, the information 'income > £10,000' must be entered as a unit in the database. But still neither rule 1 nor rule 2 has its antecedents satisfied. It is also necessary to add the fact 'income < £30,000' to ensure that rule 2 fires after 'credit status = OK' has been proved by rule 3.

The simple representation has the following disadvantages:

- It is necessary to translate the details of the applicant, namely that income = £15,000, into the two facts 'income > £10,000' and 'income < £30,000' in order to ensure that the knowledge base works with the particular facts of the applicant who is the subject of the consultation. The level of income may be used in many other rules as well, but it is then necessary to make sure that income is rendered in the correct form to satisfy each.

- The value of the attribute 'income' for the applicant is £15,000. Intuitively speaking, this is what should be entered. It should then be possible for the expert system to derive implied income statements such as 'income < £30,000' from this.

- If the thresholds in the rules change, for example the critical income level in rule 3 is increased to £12,000, then the income fact as entered for an individual would need to be altered to take account of this.

These considerations lead to the attribute–value (A–V) pair as a common method of expressing knowledge in expert systems.

Applied to the rules in Figure 18.7, the A–V construction can be expressed as follows. There are three attributes – 'income', 'credit status' and 'credit type'. The value of 'credit status' can be 'OK' or 'not OK', the value of 'credit type' can be 'normal', 'gold card' or 'platinum card' (not shown), and the value of 'income' can be any number greater than zero. The user of the expert system inputs the value for the attribute 'income', which is £15,000 in this particular case. The expert system tests this value of income against the rules and assigns the value 'OK' to the attribute 'credit status' (rule 3) and 'normal' to the attribute 'credit type' (rule 2). The rationale behind the A–V representation is that much expert knowledge and reasoning concerns treatment of an example of an object type and its associated attributes where these attributes can have values. The credit card system is concerned with one type of object, a card applicant, and, for each consultation, one example of the applicant, say John Smith. There are a range of attributes of John Smith. Some have values that are entered into the system, whereas the values of others are derived using the rules.

Many common expert system shells work by using A–V pairs in an if–then rule format. It is uncommon, except in the simplest systems, to restrict the representation form to if–then rules containing conditions that are not capable of being further decomposed into constituents such as A–V pairs.

18.2.2 Object–attribute–value triples

Frequently, it is important to depict more than one object in an expert system. The attribute–value representation is then inadequate as all attributes are assumed to be of one object. This limitation may be overcome by using the object–attribute–value

> **Figure 18.8** (a) A rule from MYCIN; (b) the representation of the rule as an object–attribute–value triplet
>
> (a) RULE 85
>
> **If** The site of the culture is blood, and
> The morphology of the organism is rod, and
> The Gram stain of the organism is Gram-neg, and
> The patient is a compromised host
>
> **Then** there is suggestive evidence (0.6) that the identity of the organism is
> *Pseudomonas aeruginosas*
>
> (b)
>
> | | Object | Attribute | Value |
> |---|---|---|---|
> | **If** | Culture | Site | Blood |
> | | Organism | Morphology | Rod |
> | | Organism | Gram stain | Gram-neg |
> | | Patient | Compromised host | True |
> | **Then** | Organism | Identity | *Pseudomonas aeruginosas* |

(O–A–V) model of representing knowledge. For example, the expert system that assesses a company's financial health may need to encode and work with information on each of the company's outstanding loans. Each loan will be treated as an object and will have attributes such as 'rate of interest', 'call-in date', 'amount', 'creditors' and 'redeemable', with values such as: '10%', '1 Jan 2004', '£1m', 'Federated Bank' and 'true'.

One of the earliest expert systems was MYCIN. This system was developed to aid doctors in the diagnosis and treatment of meningitis and bacterial infections of the blood. MYCIN is an example of a system that represents its knowledge as O–A–V triples within rules. Rule 85 is given in Figure 18.8(a), and its analysis using the O–A–V framework is given in Figure 18.8(b).

Object–attribute–values may be represented in diagrams. Figure 18.9 is the O–A–V triplet representation for two loans to a company. As a company may have many loans, both may be present during a current consultation in Figure 18.10. The blanks indicate where the values of attributes will be added in order to depict an instance of the loan type. Figure 18.10 is the static representation of a generic loan. Figure 18.9 is the dynamic representation of instances of loans during a consultation. The working expert system can be thought of as filling these value slots during the consultation. Some will be filled by the user entering values; others will be entered as a result of the inference process.

Object–attribute–value triples are a fundamental component of the resource development framework which is fuelling the growth of the semantic web and was discussed previously.

18.2.3 Semantic networks

O–A–V triplets go some way towards representing the complexity of knowledge with which experts deal, but they are a long way from the flexibility needed to build models for all knowledge domains. O–A–V triplets are a special and well-defined limitation of the more general semantic network. If the subjects of objects, attributes and values are

Figure 18.9 O–A–V triplets representing two loans

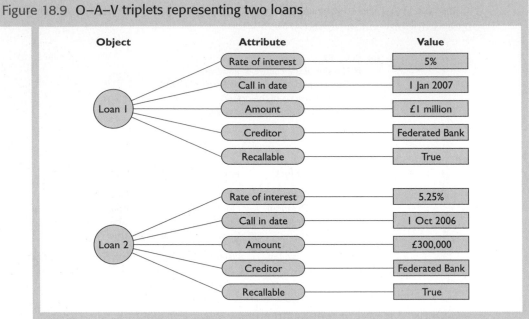

Figure 18.10 Structure of a typical loan

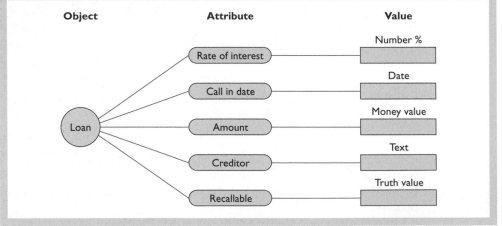

left and attention is focused on the network representation of Figure 18.9, then Figure 18.11 is arrived at. Here no distinction is made between the nodes (unlike Figure 18.9, where the different types of node have different semantic roles). There are, however, directed links between nodes. 'Has-a', 'is-a' and 'is-a-value-of' are the names of these directed links.

Figure 18.11 A semantic network representation of an O–A–V triplet

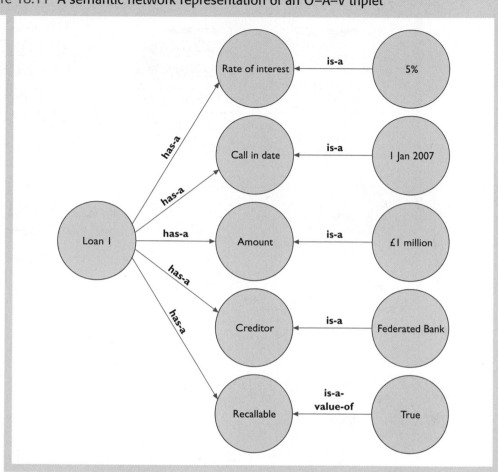

Figure 18.12 is an example of a general semantic network. Its formal composition is a network of nodes connected by directed links or arcs. There are well-known methods of representing this kind of structure at the physical level. Virtually no limitation is placed on what can be the content of a node or link, but it is usual to restrict the representation to the following:

Nodes

Nodes can be classified into the following categories:

1. Objects are generally represented as nodes. In the example in Figure 18.12, Anita Patel, John Smith and Jack Jones are all physical objects. Abstract objects are also placed in nodes. The number 40 is an abstract object. Some objects seem to fall between the two. 'Accounts department' names an object that is more abstract than Jack Jones but less abstract than the number 40. It is also represented as a node.

2. General terms such as 'employee' or 'accountant' are placed at nodes. These terms correspond to classes of individual objects. (In the terminology of data analysis and the development of the entity model covered in Chapter 13, these classes can be

Figure 18.12 **A semantic network**

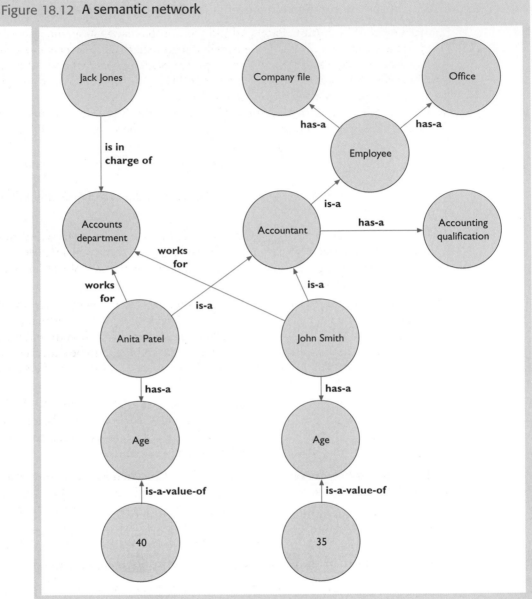

regarded as entity types, while the objects themselves will be entities, perhaps as some occurrence of an entity type shown in Figure 18.12.)

3. Attributes can be considered to be of two types. There are attributes that require values, and there are those that do not. 'Age' is an example of the former in that it needs a numeric value. 'Accounting qualification' and 'office' are attributes of 'accountant' and 'employee' respectively that do not require values in the illustrated semantic network. The distinction between attributes and objects is not always clear.

Generally speaking, those attributes that do not require values will rise to the highest possible level of abstraction associated with general terms. In Figure 18.12, it is a property of each employee that he or she has a company file. Therefore it is also a property of each accountant that he or she has a company file (because they are employees) and of both Anita Patel and John Smith that each has a company file (because they are accountants). It would be possible to associate the property individually with each object employee of the company – that is, with Anita Patel and John Smith – but this would waste space and miss the generality of the association of the property of having a company file with being an employee.

On the other hand, 'age' cannot rise through the hierarchy, because it requires a value. Although each employee has an age, it is not the same age. Age is really a function from the class of employees to the class of numbers.

Links

Links are one-way, directed connections between nodes. They generally fall into one of a number of categories:

1. 'Has-a' links relate attribute nodes to general-term nodes or to object nodes. They state that a general term has an attribute, such as an employee having an office or an accountant having an accounting qualification, or that an object has an attribute. Anita Patel has an age (40).

2. 'Is-a' links represent relations between object nodes and general-term nodes or between general-term nodes and other general-term nodes. In the former case, the relationship is similar to class (set) membership. In the latter, it is the subclass (subset) relationship. John Smith is an accountant and can be said to be a member of the class of accountants. The accountants are all employees, and the set of accountants is a subset of the set of employees.

3. Other links may be present. In the semantic network of Figure 18.12, the link between Anita Patel and the accounts department represents a relationship between two objects. The relationship is 'works for'. Similarly, Jack Jones is in charge of the accounts department – another relationship between two objects.

Two types of link are of especial importance. Causal links are relationships between individual events or states and occur in many knowledge bases. Part links are also a common feature of the world and so appear regularly in semantic networks. (The dynamo is part of the engine, which is part of the car.)

Examples of common link/node structures and inheritance are shown in Figure 18.13.

Advantages: The advantages of semantic network representations are:

■ They are extremely flexible. New nodes and links can be added as required. The lack of restriction on what the nodes and links mean makes it easy to add knowledge in a natural way.

■ ⟨node: is-a link : node⟩ and ⟨node : has-a link : node⟩ correspond to common structures in English. Examples are Tweety is a robin (⟨object⟩ *is a* ⟨general term⟩), a robin *is a* bird (⟨general term⟩ *is a* ⟨general term⟩) and a bird *has a* beak (⟨general term⟩ *has a* ⟨attribute⟩).

■ As mentioned earlier, it is possible to store information at the most abstract level possible. Nodes at lower levels inherit properties from nodes at a higher level through is-a links. In Figure 18.12, it can be inferred that accountants have company files and offices. Both Anita Patel and John Smith have accounting qualifications, company files and offices by virtue of is-a links. As well as minimizing redundant

Figure 18.13 Some semantic network features: (a) common link/node semantic structures; (b) is-a and has-a inheritance

(a)

Structure	Example
Object ——relates——▸ Object	Smith works in London
Object ——is-a——▸ Class of objects	Smith is a lawyer
Class of objects ——is-a——▸ Class of objects	A lawyer is a human
Class of objects ——has-a——▸ Attribute	A lawyer is well paid
Object ——has-a——▸ Attribute ◂——is-a—— Object	Smith has an age of 34

(b)

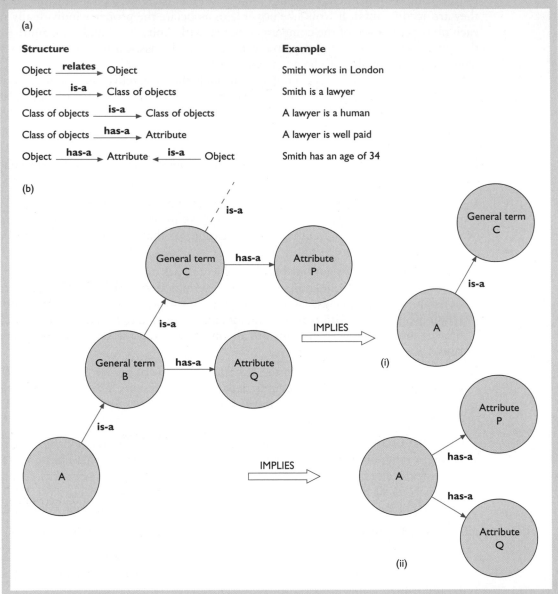

duplication of attributes, the inheritance corresponds to a natural way of reasoning in English.

■ Semantic networks and inheritance hierarchies are closely linked to current artificial intelligence research into how humans store knowledge. Figure 18.14 is an example of the type of semantic net that Collins and Quillian (1969) used in an experiment to study memory. In general, if the subject of the experiment was asked 'Can canaries sing?' it took less time to answer than to answer the question 'Can

Figure 18.14 Semantic network hierarchy that explains human question response times

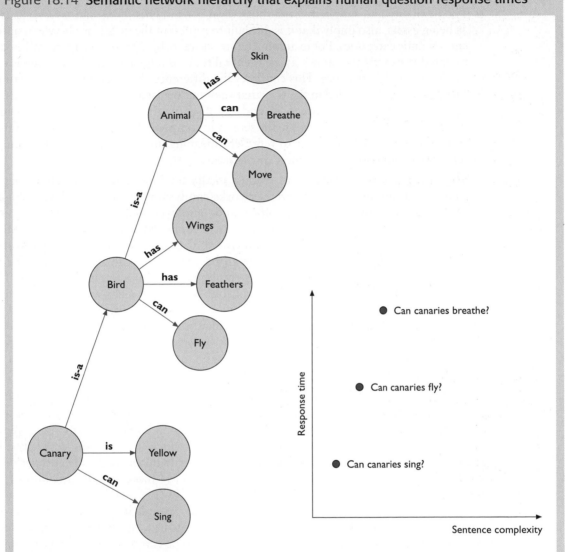

canaries fly?' This in its turn took less time to answer than 'Can canaries breathe?' Collins and Quillian argued that information stored in the memory was stored at the most abstract level possible. This can be seen in the semantic network of Figure 18.14. The difference in response can be explained by the need to determine an inheritance in order to answer the question 'Can canaries fly?' but not to answer 'Can canaries sing?'

Semantic networks as a method of storage have some properties that simulate human knowledge storage and retrieval characteristics and to that extent are a useful representation technique.

Disadvantages: The disadvantages of semantic networks are:

■ The flexibility and simplicity of the structural constituents (links and nodes), as well as being assets, also imply that it is difficult to represent the difference between different semantic categories. For example, the structure ⟨⟨object⟩ *is a* ⟨general term⟩⟩ is represented in exactly the same way as ⟨⟨general term⟩ *is a* ⟨general term⟩⟩ by means of a ⟨node:link:node⟩ structure. This conflates the differences between the two structures. The difference is revealed in the way that they can be used to carry out inferences, or simply in the difference between '∈' and '⊆' of set theory. One of the aims of linguistic philosophy has been to analyse the semantic components of propositions into their constituent categories in order to represent meaning and facilitate inference. Simple semantic networks obliterate these distinctions.

■ They are particularly efficient as storage media for inheritance hierarchies, but as soon as exceptions occur semantic networks can become overly complex. In Figure 18.12, the has-a link connecting 'office' and 'employee' is a particularly convenient and efficient way of storing information that Anita Patel, John Smith . . . , all of whom are employees (as illustrated by the is-a link hierarchy), have offices. However, if there are exceptions, then these have to be encoded separately. Suppose, for instance, that John Smith is one of the few employees who does not have an office. This needs to be stored as a special property of John Smith with a has-a link so that the inheritance by John Smith of the 'office' property through the hierarchy is blocked. As long as there are a few exceptions, then a semantic network may be an advantageous storage representation, but once exceptions become common it becomes unwieldy.

18.2.4 Frames

Frames are an alternative way of representing knowledge. They use the basic idea of the object–attribute–value representation but build in refinements that overcome some of the limitations of the O–A–V form. The rationale behind frames is that experts represent their knowledge as various concepts (frames), which are interconnected. For instance, 'employee' is a concept that has various attributes, and 'storekeeper' is a connected concept, a type of employee, which will have more specific attributes than those of employee.

The use of frames can be understood by using the example in Figure 18.15. This is a frame for a long-term loan. The frame consists of slots in which entries are made for a particular occurrence of the frame type. The frame type can be thought of as an object type, the slots as attributes and the entries as attribute values. The frame is more developed than the O–A–V triplet in the following ways:

■ The frame may have pointers to other frames. These pointers may indicate hierarchies of the is-a link sort typical of semantic networks or they may indicate other frames that have some bearing on the frame under consideration. In Figure 18.15 the 'long-term loan' is a kind of 'loan'. This corresponds to an is-a link.

■ It is common for an expert to have incomplete knowledge of the facts of a particular case. What does the expert do? In many cases, the expert will assume that the missing information is typical for the kind of object under consideration – a 'best guess' philosophy. Frames allow this to be built into the description. In Figure 18.15, the 'rate of interest' of the loan needs to be specified. If it is not then a default is inserted – the current rate of interest. This may be a defined variable or may itself be another frame. Frames may point to other frames elsewhere. At any later stage, the default

Figure 18.15 A frame for a long-term loan

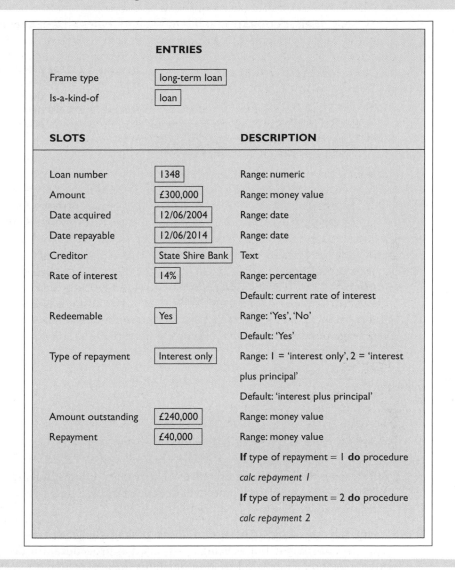

value may be overridden by known complete information being added. The 'type of repayment' also has a default value. In the case of particular long-term loans it is unlikely that the default values will be used, but in many other business examples they will be an integral part of the representation.

■ The difference between declarative and procedural knowledge was explained in Section 18.1.1. Although it is true that expert systems emphasize declarative aspects of knowledge, experts themselves will sometimes use procedures. When reasoning about a company's long-term loan structure, an expert may be required to calculate a future repayment against a loan. This is essentially a procedural task unless the repayment is found by simply looking up tables containing dates, rates of interest and loan amounts. Frames allow slot entries to be filled by the output of procedures, as in

Figure 18.16 Procedural and declarative knowledge

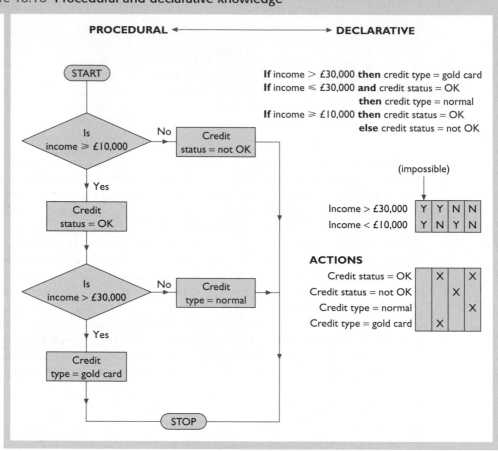

the 'repayment' slot in Figure 18.15. The frame contains in its specification the procedures to be called and under what circumstances. These procedures are defined in the knowledge base.

Generally speaking, it is best to speak of knowledge not as either procedural or declarative absolutely but as being represented as procedural (or declarative) for a particular purpose. Frames allow this flexibility in a way that O–A–V triplets do not. Figure 18.16 gives one procedural and two declarative representations of the same piece of knowledge. It uses a slightly extended version of the rules in Figure 18.7 covering the granting of credit cards.

18.2.5 Logic

Knowledge may also be represented in the form of logic. Philosophers since Aristotle have been interested in correct and incorrect forms of reasoning and have found that valid reasoning conforms to various patterns of argument. In order to reveal these patterns, systems of formal logic have been developed as powerful symbolic representation tools. As expert systems are concerned with reasoning correctly in using knowledge, it is not surprising that formal logic has been an influence on the representation of knowledge.

Figure 18.17 Representation of grandparent relations

Grandparent (x,y):-child (x,z) & child (z,y)

Child (George, Sarah)
Child (Sandra, Mary)
Child (George, Sandra)
Child (Sandra, James)
Child (Sarah, Ian)

The influence of formal propositional logic has already been looked at. If–then rule representation using the Boolean logical connectives **AND**, **OR** and **NOT** is an example of this. The decomposition of the structure of the individual sentences involved in the rule may also be achieved using predicate logic.

An example of this is shown in Figure 18.17. The property of being a grandparent is defined in terms of being a child of a child. Individual facts are added to the database as illustrated. This form of representation facilitates drawing inferences according to the canons of classical logic. Each entry is either a rule defining a term or a fact.

The artificial intelligence language PROLOG is based on the predicate calculus. The expressions in Figure 18.17 are in a PROLOG-like form. The language contains within it its own inferential procedures. If 'grandparent (George,x)' were to be entered, a list of names satisfying the individual fact together with the rule definition of grandparent would be produced by the PROLOG system. PROLOG is forming the basis of the artificial intelligence kernel language of Japanese fifth-generation computers.

18.2.6 Knowledge representation – conclusion

The main forms of knowledge representation have been covered. Many expert systems allow a mixture of techniques, recognizing that each has its own area of suitability and limitations. The most general technique is the semantic network, of which frames, O–A–V triplets and A–V pairs are specializations. Most expert systems to date have employed O–A–V triplets together with production rules for the general knowledge base, although it is becoming increasingly common to use frames as well (especially as more low-cost expert system shells using frames are released on to the market). The influence of logic techniques has not yet been fully realized, although developments in this area are likely with the advent of Japanese fifth-generation computers.

18.3 Drawing inferences

The knowledge base contains domain-specific knowledge and particular facts. As can be seen from Section 18.2, these may be represented as production rules, object–attribute–value triplets, semantic networks, frames or statements in logic. The aim of an expert system is to apply the domain-specific knowledge to the particular facts to draw conclusions or give advice. It is the purpose of this section to sketch the ways in which this may be carried out. Principles of inference are considered, together with inference control strategies that apply these principles systematically, so ensuring that, wherever they exist, the expert system will arrive at proper conclusions.

18.3.1 Principles and methods of inference

Several principles and methods of reasoning are used in expert systems. Two of the most common are *modus ponens* and the resolution principle. These are now explained.

Modus ponens

The principle of *modus ponens* and the closely connected principle of *modus tollens* were considered in Section 18.1.4. They are basic to the understanding of most expert systems, as some reasoning in virtually any area of expertise is best captured using these principles with if–then rules. *Modus ponens* also reflects an obvious form of human reasoning (unlike *modus tollens*). It is so basic that even to question its validity has often been taken as evidence of a failure to understand the if–then construction and the words contained in it.

The strictest requirement on principles of reasoning is that these principles must lead to true conclusions when applied to true premises. Some principles dealing with reasoning and propositions were given in Figure 18.4. How do we know that these will meet this strict requirement? In other words, does proof from truth always lead to truth in these cases? To answer this, it is necessary to give meanings to the logical connectives.

Truth (T) and falsity (F) are employed for this task in Figure 18.18(a). It can be read by looking at a combination of T and F for A and B together and then determining the given value for A and B joined by the logical connective. For instance, **IF** 'A' is true **AND** 'B' is false then 'A **OR** B' is true. The figure defines the meanings of '**IF–THEN**', '**AND**', '**OR**' and '**NOT**'. Put another way, if a Martian had the concept of truth and falsity, then it would be able to understand the meaning of our words '**IF–THEN**', '**AND**', '**OR**' and '**NOT**' purely from Figure 18.18.

Figure 18.18 Truth tables: (a) a truth table for the logical connectives; (b) a truth table for *modus ponendo ponens*; (c) a truth table for the resolution principle

(a)

A	B	if A then B	A and B	A or B	not A	not A or B
T	T	T	T	T	F	T
T	F	F	F	T	F	F
F	T	T	F	T	T	T
F	F	T	F	F	T	T

(b)

	A	B	If A then B,	A	∴ B
*	T	T	T	T	T
	T	F	F	T	F
	F	T	T	F	T
	F	F	T	F	F

(c)

	A	B	C	Not A or B,	Not B or C	∴ not A or C
*	T	T	T	T	T	T
	T	T	F	T	F	F
	T	F	T	F	T	T
	T	F	F	F	T	F
*	F	T	T	T	T	T
	F	T	F	T	F	T
*	F	F	T	T	T	T
*	F	F	F	T	T	T

Figure 18.18(b) illustrates why *modus ponens* is a valid principle of reasoning. Here truth tables are used to assign T or F to each premise and to the conclusion in an inference. All possible combinations of truth and falsity are assigned to A and B. The truth value is then calculated for each premise and each conclusion. The requirement on a sound reasoning principle is that true premises lead to true conclusions. The starred line (*) is the only case where all the premises are true. Hence the conclusion is true.

Resolution

The resolution principle is given in Figure 18.4(e) and is shown to be a sound principle of reasoning in Figure 18.18(c). Once again, the starred lines (*) represent cases where the premises are true. In each of these lines, the conclusion is true.

The resolution method is a systematic way of establishing whether a proposition can be proved from a set of if–then rules and other facts. Central to the resolution method is the resolution principle. Here is a simple example of the method in practice. The following is assumed:

(1) *If* it is raining *then* the road is slippery	**IF** A **THEN** B
(2) *If* the road is slippery *then* motor accidents increase	**IF** B **THEN** C
(3) It is raining	A

and we wish to establish whether the following can be proved:

(4) Motor accidents increase	C

The resolution method involves four steps.

1. Rewrite all if–then statements as or statements. The equivalence '**IF** A **THEN** B' and '(**NOT** A) **OR** B' is shown in Figure 18.18(a). (1) and (2) become (5) and (6):

(5) Either it is *not* raining *or* the road is slippery	**NOT** A **OR** B
(6) Either the road is *not* slippery *or* motor accidents increase	**NOT** B **OR** C

2. Assert the negation of the proposition under test – that is, assume the negation of (4) is true:

(7) Motor accidents do *not* increase	**NOT** C

3. Use the resolution principle (see Figure 18.4(c)) on (5) and (6) to derive (8):

(5) Either it is *not* raining *or* the road is slippery	**NOT** A **OR** B
(6) Either the road is *not* slippery *or* motor accidents increase	**NOT** B **OR** C
(8) Either it is *not* raining *or* motor accidents increase	**NOT** A **OR** C

Now use the disjunction elimination principle (see Figure 18.4(f)) on (3) and (8) to prove that motor accidents increase (9):

(8) Either it is *not* raining *or* motor accidents increase	**NOT** A **OR** C
(3) It is raining	A
(9) Motor accidents increase	C

4. Show that a contradiction has been reached between (9) and (7):

Motor accidents increase *and* motor accidents do *not* increase	C **AND NOT** C

so the supposition in (7) must be false, that is

Motor accidents increase	C

has been proved.

The resolution method always follows this four-step strategy. The resolutions in step 3 can be many and complex. The method is very important in expert systems because (1) it can be automated easily and (2) those expert systems that attempt to prove goals from sets of rules and facts (referred to in Section 18.1.4 as 'backward-chaining systems') can do so easily by asserting the negation of the goal to be proved and using the method to derive a contradiction.

The resolution method can handle expressions in the predicate calculus equally well, although it becomes more complex. This is important, as predicate logic is one of the standard representation techniques for the knowledge base.

18.3.2 Uncertain reasoning

So far, the principles and methods of inference that have been considered all deal with cases that involve certain truth or certain falsity, and the principles always lead from truth to truth. However, much human expertise is concerned with reasoning where propositions are not known with certainty, and conclusions cannot be derived with certainty, or with rules that are themselves perhaps not certain. Indeed, the presence of uncertainty in a real-life situation is for many people the chief reason for using an expert. As was mentioned at the beginning of this chapter, there are some who regard the handling of uncertain reasoning as an essential feature of an expert system.

1. An example of the first case of uncertainty mentioned might occur when a doctor attempts to diagnose the cause of fever-like symptoms. Neither the doctor nor the patient knows with certainty whether the patient has been in contact with a Lassa fever carrier from Nigeria. Probably not, but it is still a possibility and one of the factors that needs to be considered if the patient is suffering from some of the symptoms of Lassa fever.

2. An example of the second type of uncertainty concerns credit card applications. If the credit card applicant has an income of more than £30,000 per annum and a mortgage then the credit status is probably 'OK'. If it is known that the applicant has not defaulted on any other loans or credit card payments in the past then credit status increases to almost certainly 'OK'.

3. An example of the third case can happen on the frontiers of a discipline, where heuristic reasoning is carried out by experts using several rules, each of which may be doubted. This may happen where events are supposed, but not known, to be linked as cause and effect.

The implied format for each of these cases is:

(1) Probably A
(2) **IF** A **THEN** probably B
(3) Probably (**IF** A **THEN** B)

Some mixture of these may be present in the same case.

Reasoning with uncertainty is a treacherous area. Many plausible reasoning principles turn out to be ill-founded. A student thought that the following was an acceptable reasoning method (note its similarity with the example used to explain resolution):

If it is raining *then* probably the road is slippery	**IF** A **THEN** probably B
If the road is slippery *then* probably accidents increase	**IF** B **THEN** probably C
It is raining	A

therefore

    Probably accidents increase   probably C

The student thought again when the following instance of the reasoning method was provided:

If there is shortly to be an avalanche *then* probably it has been snowing recently	**IF** A **THEN** probably B
If it has been snowing recently *then* probably I will go skiing	**IF** B **THEN** probably C
There is shortly to be an avalanche	A

therefore

    Probably I will go skiing   probably C

There are two major areas to be looked at with respect to uncertainty in expert systems. First, how is uncertain knowledge represented? Second, how is uncertainty handled in reasoning? The way that uncertainty is represented will impact on the way it is handled in reasoning.

Certainty factors

This is the method used in MYCIN and several other expert systems. Each proposition (or value associated with an attribute of an object) is assigned a certainty factor in the real number range -1 to $+1$: -1 indicates certainty that the proposition does not hold, $+1$ indicates certainty that it does, and 0 indicates ignorance.

There are different ways that reasoning using certainty factors may be carried out. One method is to regard the certainty factor of a pair of propositions to be the minimum of the two factors if they are connected by **AND** and to be the maximum if connected by **OR**, and to regard the certainty of the conclusion of an if–then rule to be the certainty of the antecedent multiplied by the certainty of the consequent. The rule normally has some threshold certainty associated with the antecedent. Below this, the rule will not fire. 0.20 is a typical threshold that is used in MYCIN. Consider the following example. Given:

A (certainty = 0.6)
B (certainty = 0.4)
IF A **AND** B **THEN** C (certainty = 0.9)

therefore

A **AND** B (certainty = min (0.6, 0.4) =0.4)
C (certainty = $0.9 \infty 0.4 = 0.36$)

Necessity and sufficiency factors

The certainty factors in MYCIN's rules indicate how sufficient the evidence (antecedent) is for a conclusion (consequent). In many areas of expertise, the absence of evidence for a conclusion is often taken as indicating that the conclusion does not hold. The evidence is therefore necessary for the conclusion. So, as well as sufficiency factors there are necessity factors. PROSPECTOR is an expert system that contains rules with both of these factors. From PROSPECTOR:

If there is hornblende pervasively altered to biotite *then* there is strong evidence (320, 0.001) for potassic zone alteration.

Without going into the exact meaning of these dual factors, the value of 320 indicates that the altered hornblende is highly sufficient for potassic zone alteration, but 0.001 indicates that the absence of this evidence does little to rule out the possibility. Necessity and sufficiency factors are particularly important where a condition may be associated with one of a range of circumstances.

Fuzzy sets

The use of fuzzy sets is a formal approach to inexact reasoning that diverges from the basic assumptions of classical logic. In traditional set theory, predicates such as 'is red' or 'is a bad debtor' are assumed to denote sets – the set of red things and the set of bad debtors. Each object in the world is either in the set or it is not. Thus Jones is in the set of bad debtors, whereas Smith and the Eiffel Tower are not. Fuzzy set theory, in contrast, interprets predicates as denoting fuzzy sets. A fuzzy set is a set of objects. Some objects are definitely in the set. Some are definitely not. And some are only probably or possibly in the set.

Uncertain reasoning – conclusion

Three forms of representing uncertainty and reasoning with uncertainty have been covered. This coverage is only superficial. The treatment that each gives to handling uncertainty is too complex for the scope of this book. References are given at the end of the chapter for the interested reader. There are a number of features that must be highlighted:

1. There is no one agreed method of handling uncertainty. This is not because of technical disagreement but rather reflects deep and theoretical differences of opinion. Moreover, there seems to be little basis for adjudicating between the competing views, as criteria for comparison are not agreed.

2. The strict requirement that sound principles of reasoning must lead from truth to truth cannot apply in cases of uncertain reasoning.

3. There may be no one (or even several) correct model of uncertain reasoning to be applied *in vacuo*. It may be the case that the way uncertainty is handled is domain-dependent. That is, although accountants, doctors and car mechanics use terms like 'probable', 'unlikely' and 'possible', these are used in different ways in different areas of expertise (domains).

4. Empirical research in each domain of expertise may indicate the models of inexact reasoning that are used there. These models can then be built into an expert system. Nowadays, even expert system shells may not impose predefined methods of handling uncertainty upon the expert systems builder. They allow the architect to design control over the way in which uncertainty is handled in the final expert system.

5. Some expert systems provide 'friendly' user interfaces that use terms like 'probable' and 'likely'. These will be working with some numerical model of inexact reasoning behind the friendly and uncomplicated façade presented to the user. In understanding how an expert system arrives at its conclusions, it is important to penetrate this mask.

6. Reasoning under uncertainty is, and will remain, one of the most important and controversial theoretical and practical areas in expert systems.

18.3.3 Inference control strategies

Using a principle to draw an inference will yield a new fact or probabilistic conclusion. In order to carry out a consultation, however, an expert system needs to draw many inferences. These cannot be made randomly or else the inference system will 'wander' logically around the knowledge area. Preferably there needs to be some pattern or strategy to decide which inferences to draw at which time. The purpose of an inference control strategy is to determine this. The strategy used will obviously determine the performance characteristics of the expert system.

Forward chaining

This strategy takes the established current facts and attempts to use the rules (or whatever representation form the domain-specific knowledge base takes) to derive new facts. The new facts are added to the set of established facts, and the strategy then attempts to derive further new facts to add to this set. The system is said to be data-driven. This is most obvious in the application of *modus ponens*, where the antecedent conditions are among the set of established facts and the conclusions when drawn are added to this set. At any one time it may be possible to use more than one rule to derive more than one conclusion. In order to resolve the conflict, the inference control strategy must decide between the competing rules. A simple way of doing this is to number the rules and fire the lowest-numbered rule that has its antecedent satisfied. More complex conflict-resolving techniques are used in larger systems. An example of a forward-chaining system has been given in Figure 18.5, the model expert system dealing with creature classification.

Forward chaining is a useful strategy if there are a large number of possible outcomes given a small number of values for the initial data. This characteristic of an application is typical of expert systems dealing with planning where relatively few basic constraints are given.

Backward chaining

By far the most common inference control strategy is backward chaining. This is used in MYCIN and all the major systems. In backward chaining, a goal is selected and the system establishes the facts that are needed to prove the goal. Each of the needed facts becomes a subgoal, and the system establishes the facts that are needed to prove these, which, in their turn, become sub-subgoals, and so on. Eventually, a basic proposition is reached. A basic proposition is a sub-sub . . . goal that does not depend on other facts.

There are now three possibilities. The proposition required is in the database, in which case the system will go on to establish, if it can, the other facts needed to prove the initial goal; the negation of the proposition is in the database, in which case the system will need to prove the initial goal, if it can, by a different route; neither the proposition nor its negation has been established. In this last situation, it is normal for the expert system to interrogate the user. The answer provided can then be used in the reasoning.

In a consultation with an expert, say a doctor, it is usual for the patient to volunteer information at the start of the session ('I have been feeling tired for a week with loss of appetite and a sore throat. I also have a bad headache, which comes in the evening . . .') The doctor will use this initial information to select a most likely goal (diagnosis) and then seek to establish this by backward reasoning – performing laboratory tests, asking the patient particular questions, checking reflexes, and so on. This form of approach is quite common. Suppose that a client consults an investment adviser when seeking a planned portfolio. The client will start by proffering information such as the amount of money involved, why they wish to invest, what special requirements are needed (for example, lump sum capitalization in 15 years to pay for a university education), constraints (such as no wish to invest in companies involved in military hardware), and so on. The investment adviser will use this to select likely strategies, which will require further elicitation of facts from the client.

Both of these examples can be characterized by initial forward chaining followed by backward chaining. It is common for modern expert systems to allow this mix of inference control strategies.

Much research work is yet to be done on inference control strategies. These strategies become particularly important when dealing with large expert systems. The hundreds or even thousands of rules involved may use large chunks of computer processing during searching unless efficient control strategies are adopted. This is crucial with the current trend towards large multi-user expert systems in the areas of finance and insurance.

18.4 Intelligence and the Internet

The expert systems that have been described so far in this chapter represent one particular implementation of artificial intelligence. In general, they are tools designed within a particular problem domain and based upon a knowledge base limited by the expert knowledge acquired and stored. An example of their use is the assessment of insurance risk leading to selection of an appropriate policy.

Intelligent agents are another application of artificial intelligence. Unlike the bounded knowledge base servicing an expert system, the source data for an intelligent agent can be located on any traversable route on the Internet. Another distinguishing feature of intelligent agents is their need and ability to relocate from node to node across networks of computers and to communicate with other pieces of software such as other intelligent agents.

Intelligent agents

The quantity of information available through application of the Internet is already huge and continues to grow exponentially. The sheer amount of information available is itself becoming a prohibitive factor in effective and efficient searching.

The use of intelligent agents was introduced in Chapter 6. An intelligent agent is a piece of software that performs a task on behalf of the user; the task is invariably mundane or highly repetitive in nature and often concludes with a result or a suggestion.

Intelligent agents can be either closed or open in their activity. A closed agent operates in a particular system environment reacting to goal setting in this limited domain. A simple example is the desktop computer's own system agent, which checks internal performance, such as the degree of disk fragmentation, and makes recommendations for more effective operation of the system. An open agent, however, can interface with other intelligent agents and work cooperatively in a multidisciplinary environment. This environment is called an **agent society**. Many of the search agents that trawl websites for information operate in this collaborative way. Some work has already been undertaken to establish standards for communication between intelligent agents. An example is the development of a Java standard for intelligent agent applets, called **aglets**.

Functionality of intelligent agents

Intelligent agents appear in many forms. The range of functions that they carry out can be evaluated under three main headings:

1. **Autonomy:** While human interaction is essential at key stages of the activity of an intelligent agent, a desirable feature is that the agent can reach its goals without intervention. Similarly, when interaction with other intelligent agents occurs, autonomy in deciding whether and how the exchange of information is to take place is another distinguishing feature.

2. **Intelligence:** This is usually manifested by an appreciation of the agent's own environment. An ability to recognize features of the environment, to respond to changes in the environment and to modify the goal if appropriate are all desirable attributes. These characteristics confer intelligence on the agent's activity.

3. **Relocation:** An intelligent agent must be able to move effectively between nodes on a network and across the Internet using the autonomous characteristics and intelligence outlined above. Ease of travel is an essential feature.

Intelligent agents and the value chain

Examples have already been given in previous chapters showing the application of intelligent agents to business, particularly in the e-commerce arena. Applications are already available to enable consumers to compare prices and products, for businesses to interact with suppliers and retail outlets and to facilitate more effective electronic negotiations and transactions. In particular, the most effective applications have applied the intelligence to other problem domains to add value to the solutions provided. An example can be found in push and pull marketing.

The concept of push and pull technology was introduced in Chapter 6. Push marketing is characterized by the unsolicited approaches made by business systems to existing or potential customers. The combination of intelligent agent technology with data warehouses and sophisticated mining techniques has enabled customer relationship management to become far more focused and thereby more successful. The intelligent agent can locate potential customers; these customers can then be matched with existing profiles held in data warehouses. The net result is to cut down on the poor targeting often associated with unwanted, mass-distribution e-mail, often referred to as **spam**.

Intelligent agents that can assist in pull marketing are the best developed of these technologies. Web crawlers and gophers have a long history in the evolution of the web. Modern search agents are often called **bots**. The word is an abbreviation of **robot**, derived from the Czech word *robota* meaning *work*. Common uses are in locating the best price for a particular product, often achieved by employing the combining efforts of several existing search engines. Another example of the use of intelligent agents in pull technology is in the subscription to an information provider. Users request a particular service, such as news features about a particular topic or books of a particular style or by a named author. The intelligent agent supporting the marketing pull will search for relevant sites and download the required information in an ongoing fashion. As changes occur, the latest updates are constantly retrieved as long as the intelligent agent is active.

Mini case 18.1

Shopping Bots

Anyone looking for the best price for a laptop computer, camera or book can use a slew of specialist comparison shopping tools, or 'shopping bots'. These specialized search services have an estimated 60m users a month and include Pricegrabber, Shopzilla and Shopping.com. Most provide comparison guides for different geographic markets including the US, UK and other European countries.

Generally, shopping bots help users search quickly for goods across a wide variety of sites and can be useful for researching products and finding the best deal. However, most services also include 'pay for placement' retailers at the top of the results lists, so you usually need to reorder results by price. Most also include user ratings and shop ratings that help users to avoid dodgy stores. Shopzilla was one of the first to include user ratings and feedback. It also has services tailored to the US, UK, French, German and Australian markets and draws results from a large number of stores. Shopping.com also offers international sites and includes extensive product details, making it a good research tool as well as a buying guide. But typically the first results are from 'featured merchants' so, again, you should re-sort by price.

My own favourite is Pricegrabber (www.pricegrabber.co.uk). Pricegrabber's innovations include bottom-line price calculations that take account of tax and shipping, making direct comparisons between stores much easier. Pricegrabber also supplies lots of product information and user feedback on merchants.

Adapted from: **Short cut to the cheapest deals**
Paul Taylor, *Financial Times*, 30 March 2007

Questions

1. What advantages do shopping bots offer?
2. To what degree do these systems display intelligence or expertise?

Summary

Expert systems are a rapidly expanding area in the application of artificial intelligence in business. It is estimated that investment in expert systems will continue to increase in the twenty-first century. Expert systems incorporate the expertise or competent skills of one or many experts. They do this in a way that separates the general knowledge of the expert from the particular details of a case under consideration. The expert system then applies this knowledge to the case and uses reasoning to come to conclusions, gives advice, makes planning decisions, or suggests analyses and diagnoses.

The main components of an expert system are the knowledge base, the inference engine, the explanation subsystem and the knowledge-acquisition subsystem. The knowledge base stores the domain-specific knowledge of the expert, together with particular data obtained during a consultation. The inference engine is responsible for dynamically applying the domain-specific knowledge to the particular case during use of the system. The explanation subsystem allows users to interrogate the expert system with requests as to *how* a specific conclusion has been derived or *why* a question is being asked. The knowledge-acquisition subsystem enables the entry of knowledge by the expert or generates general rules from a database of past cases by automated induction. The major problems in knowledge acquisition occur in the earlier stages of knowledge elicitation from the expert and the representation of this in a suitable form for the system.

The choice for the form of representation is an important one. Different forms have different areas of suitability. Rule-based representations are common in many expert systems, particularly small systems. This structure may be combined with the representation of attributes and values of objects (A–V pairs) in the rules themselves. If many objects are used in a system, it may be convenient to use an object–attribute–value representation strategy. Semantic networks provide a general way of representing the connections between various objects and concepts. Frame-based representations, in which concepts are modelled as frames with slots for attributes, are now becoming widely used. The ability for default values to fill the slots, references to procedures and the way that frames can be linked together, and in so doing model the interconnections between concepts, enable knowledge to be represented in a powerful way.

Different principles of inference can be used in different systems. Where the reasoning is concerned only with certainty there is some agreement about the constraints that inferences should meet. However, matters become more complex when, as is common with many areas of expertise, the luxury of a certain world disappears. The way that uncertain knowledge is represented interacts with the techniques of reasoning with uncertainty. Various approaches are common. Certainty factors, necessity and sufficiency measures and fuzzy sets have all been used. There is still a large area of disagreement about the representation and patterns of reasoning to be used with uncertain knowledge. It may be the case that what counts for adequate uncertain reasoning cannot be based on analytical or mathematical investigation but will rely on empirical research, which may deliver different results for different areas of expertise.

Inference control strategies ensure that the inference engine carries out reasoning in an exhaustive and efficient manner. Systems that attempt to prove selected goals by establishing propositions needed to prove these goals, which in themselves become secondary goals, are backward-chaining or goal-driven systems. This is in contrast to forward-chaining systems, which attempt to derive conclusions from established facts.

It is important for the business person involved in the development (and use) of expert systems to have an understanding of their components, the way that knowledge is represented in them and the forms of reasoning used. This is because it is likely that in the development of such systems they (the experts) will be more intimately involved than they would in the development of traditional information systems.

Intelligent agents can be used to enhance activities along the supply chain and help to add value. Agents can be either open or closed in operation. Examples are found in push and pull marketing, with the use of bots being the most common application.

Review questions

1. Briefly explain the following terms:

knowledge base	HOW question	has-a link
inference engine	backward chaining	inheritance hierarchy
inference principle	declarative knowledge	forward chaining

inference strategy	procedural knowledge	uncertain reasoning
if–then rule	object–attribute–value triple	certainty factor
knowledge-acquisition subsystem	frame	expert system shell
	semantic network	artificial intelligence
explanatory subsystem	is-a link	WHY question

2. What is meant by *reasoning with uncertainty* in the context of knowledge systems?

3. Using an example, explain the difference between *declarative* and *procedural* knowledge.

4. Explain the difference between a system that uses attribute–value pairs and a system that uses object–attribute–value triplets to represent knowledge. Give an example where it is necessary to use O–A–V representation rather than A–V representation.

Exercises

1. 'There is little difference between an expert system interrogating a knowledge base and a database management system accessing a database.' Do you agree?

2. Select a familiar task that requires the use of knowledge to be carried out successfully. Specify the central knowledge areas involved in performing the task and represent these as if–then rules. A partial example is now given:

Task: Decision on the purchase of a second-hand car.

Areas: (1) Is a car needed?
(2) Is the car that is being considered sound?
(3) Is the car that is being considered priced reasonably?
(4) Can I finance purchase of the car?

if–then rules (Area 2)

(2.1) *If* the bodywork is sound
and the engine is sound
and the suspension is sound
and the steering is sound
and the general condition is satisfactory
then the car is considered sound.

(2.1.2) *If* there is not knocking from the engine when idling
and there is not blue smoke from the exhaust
and . . .
and . . .
then the engine is sound.

3. Explain, using a simple example, what is meant by a *frame-based representation*. In what ways does a frame-based representation differ from a semantic network? Explain the advantages and disadvantages of a frame-based representation over:

(a) O–A–V triplets
(b) a rule-based representation.

4. (a) Explain what it is for a pattern of reasoning to be sound.
   (b) Consider the following argument forms:

   (1) No As are Bs
       Some Bs are Cs
       ∴ No As are Cs

   (2) All As are Bs
       Some Bs are not Cs
       ∴ Some As are not Cs

   (3) Some As are Bs
       No As are Cs
       ∴ Some Bs are not Cs

   (4) Not all As are Bs
       Some Bs are not Cs
       ∴ Some As are Cs

   (5) Some As are Bs and some are not
       Some Bs are Cs and some are not
       ∴ Some As are Cs

   (6) All As are Bs
       No Bs are Cs
       ∴ No As are Cs

   In each of these cases, decide whether the pattern of reasoning is sound. (Hint: Represent each predicate by a set drawn on a Venn diagram constructed to reveal the argument form. Attempt to produce a Venn diagram where all the premises are true yet the conclusion is false. If this can be done, the argument form is unsound. Why? See Figure 18.19.)

   For unsound patterns of reasoning, suggest an English example where the premises are true and the conclusion false.
   (Example for (1)
   No women are men TRUE
   Some men are doctors TRUE
   No women are doctors FALSE)

5. Explain the resolution method of proof. Why is it particularly applicable to backward-chaining strategies?

Figure 18.19

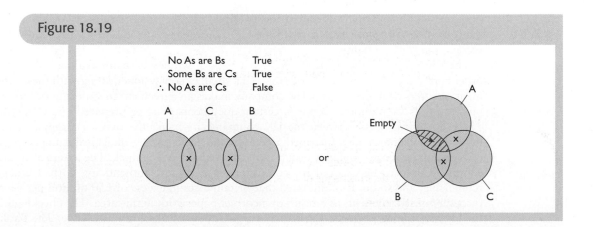

6. The resolution principle may be stated as:

   A **OR** B
   NOT B **OR** C
   ∴ A **OR** C

   Show that this is a sound principle by using a truth table.

7. Represent the following paragraph (taken from the main text of the chapter) as:

   (a) Boolean if–then rules
   (b) O–A–V triplets within rules.

   If the student has successfully completed level 1 of the examination, *or* has been exempted from level 1 by virtue of satisfying *any* of the conditions laid out in paragraphs 3(a) to 3(f) below, *then* the student is entitled to register for level 2 of the examination. A student registered for level 2 is exempt from examination papers 2.3 *and* 2.4 *if* he/she has obtained exemption from level 1 by virtue of satisfying the conditions 3(a) *or* 3(b) below, *or* satisfying 3(d) *and* being in possession of an honours degree awarded by a British university or accredited by the Council for National Academic Awards.

8. Are intelligent knowledge-based systems (expert systems) really intelligent in the sense that we use the word 'intelligent' to apply to human beings? If so, by virtue of what characteristics are they to be regarded as intelligent? If not, could a computer-based system be regarded as intelligent, and what would constitute the justification for applying the term?

9. 'Backward chaining is an efficient reasoning strategy when the number of goals is small relative to the number of rules to be considered. As technology advances, however, the increase in the speed of making inferences using facts and knowledge in the knowledge base will blur the importance of the distinction between forward and backward chaining as far as the user of the expert system is concerned.' Is this true?

CASE STUDY 18

Expert systems

Banking and finance are prime areas for investment in expert systems projects, although many of these have not yet come to fruition and the area is one naturally associated with secrecy and confidentiality.

The UK branch of the Bank of America acts as a 'wholesale' bank dealing only with other banks and companies. It has developed a small expert system dealing with the treatment of letters of credit. When a UK company makes an agreement to export goods to or import goods from another country, certain documents must be prepared and checked. These documents pass between the UK company, its bank, the overseas company, its bank, and sometimes other intermediary banks and agencies as well. This documentation is often quite extensive and may occupy a file more than an inch thick. The letters of credit contained need to be checked for completeness, accuracy, authenticity, correct cross-referencing, and so on. It is estimated that Britain loses in excess of £50 million per year through refused payments as a result of incorrect paperwork in this area. The checking of the letters, although mechanical, requires a great deal of obscure knowledge. The Bank of America requires that its employees have at least ten years' experience before allowing them to authorize payments of substantial sums of money involved in overseas trade. It takes up to two years to train junior clerks. This seemed suitable as an expert system domain as the task was clear-cut, the expertise was at least worth archiving if not developing as a system for expert assistance, and there was a commitment from those involved, including the bank's head of marketing and development, for cash management and electronic banking services in the UK. Originally, it had been intended that the domain would cover the entire set of documents relevant to granting letters of credit, and it had been hoped that a system could be designed that would detect all the shortcomings in the supporting documentation. It soon became clear that this area was too large, at least for the bank's first attempt to build an expert system, so the domain was pruned by restricting the system to the seven most important documents. These included the invoice, certificate of origin, insurance certificate, drafts and the transportation documents. It was decided to use an expert systems shell (Expert Edge) together with an experienced knowledge engineer and one expert – the head of documentary services at the bank. Expert Edge is a backward-chaining PC shell written in C. It took about six weeks of knowledge elicitation and six weeks of testing to arrive at a working system. There were 270 rules, perhaps a large number to count as a small system.

The knowledge elicitation began by developing a structure similar to a semantic network, although in the form of a tree (called a name tree). This had a root called 'discrepancy', with branches for each of the document types. Each of these also had branches. For instance, 'transportation document' had branches called 'signature', 'endorsement' and 'quantities'. The name tree is part of the knowledge base and is referred to during a consultation. The rules are either added via standard word-processed text in the knowledge representation language of the shell or are added through a facility of Expert Edge that prompts users for the various parts of a rule. This is simpler for 'uneducated' users as it avoids the need to master the syntax of the knowledge-representation language.

A number of problems were encountered in development. First, there was a shortage of available expert time. This was particularly noticeable in the testing stage of the system, and it was difficult to choose a comprehensive set of test examples. Second, there was a trade-off concerned with the use of technical terms. These terms are preferable as they have a precise meaning and they often aid conciseness in the final system. Unfortunately, however, their use makes the system less comprehensible to inexperienced users.

This is also connected with a third problem area. It was initially intended that the system be used as a training medium for the bank's personnel and that it be sold to outside import/export companies. Both of these aims required the use of different questions and recommendations, depending on the nature of the end user. For instance, a particular discrepancy should lead to a recommendation that the bank refuse payment if it is using the system but lead to the recommendation that the export/import company correct the inaccurate documentation if it is using the system. Much of the knowledge would be most naturally represented in tabular form, but the particular expert system shell had no facility for this, although interfacing with a desktop database package was possible.

A consultation with the system typically takes about 20 minutes and involves the system interrogating the user to obtain answers to yes/no, numeric or menu selection questions. There are no questions that require a text response. Complex calculations may be performed by the system during a consultation. Whenever a rule governing the correct use of documentation is found to be infringed an error message is displayed on the screen, normally detailing the type of error found and a recommended course of action. The system allows WHY questions, and it answers them by proceeding up the rule trees of ▶

dependent rules as far as the user wishes. Most trees are broad and shallow, reflecting the nature of the task – carrying out checks over a wide range of areas where each check does not exhibit much depth. As was explained earlier, the system covers only the seven most important documents. What happens if other documentation is involved? This is handled by the system asking the question as to whether the letters of credit require other documents. If the answer is 'yes', then the user is directed to a senior officer.

The system is now used for training purposes, and it is estimated that the previous training period of one and a half to two years can be reduced to about two weeks with the system – a substantial saving. The system always performs reliably and makes the user think about the task in a systematic way. It is simple to use; even the typist is using it. However, it is not being used as a live system. There are two reasons. First, the system is slower than the human being. The need to input data at the keyboard means that the time taken in a consultation is (slightly) longer than the average time taken for a manual check of the documentation. Second, and more importantly, the system has not, as yet, passed the test of confidence. Whether it does so subsequently depends on its performance in continued future use. The bank has been favourably impressed by its first expert system development and intends to continue with other developments if suitable domains are found. The main lessons learned by the participants in the process seem to be that it is necessary to establish that the chosen area is representable as a set of rules prior to the start of the project, that time should be made clearly available by the expert, and that the project should proceed with an interactive prototyping approach combined with clear checkpoints along the development trail.

Questions

1. What features of the handling of letters of credit lend this system to an expert system solution?

2. The system was developed using an expert systems shell. What is an expert systems shell?

3. What advantages are there to developing a solution using a shell rather than a programming language such as PROLOG?

4. The expert systems shell used backward chaining. What is meant by this?

5. Explain how knowledge acquisition took place in this system.

6. The system allowed 'why' questions to provide an explanation of how a decision has been reached. Describe in general terms how this is accomplished by the explanation subsystem. Define a semantic net. How might semantic nets have been used in developing this system? What problems were encountered in implementing the system? Would you consider the project to have been a success?

References and recommended reading

Beerel A. (1993). *Expert Systems in Business: Real World Applications.* Ellis Horwood
This is a readable text that combines an introduction to theoretical aspects of expert systems with the practical knowledge and experience of an expert systems builder. The book also has case studies. Included is material on the relationship between corporate culture and expert systems, project management of expert systems and investment decisions on expert systems development.

Brighton H. (2007). *Introducing Artificial Intelligence.* Icon Books
This provides a straightforward and very readable background to AI.

Chorofas D.N. (1998) *Agent Technology Handbook*. McGraw-Hill

This is a thorough coverage of the use of intelligent agents in networks and mobile computing. The book contains sections on reliability and diagnostics issues. The book is mainly business-focused, with relatively little complex technical content.

Cohen P.R. and Feigenbaum E.A. (eds) (1990). *The Handbook of Artificial Intelligence*, Vol. 3. William Kaufmann

These are invaluable reference books on all aspects of artificial intelligence.

Collins A. and Quillian M.R. (1969). Retrieval time from semantic memory. *Journal of Verbal Learning and Verbal Behaviour*, 8, 240–7

Negnevitsky M. (2004). *Artificial Intelligence: A Guide to Intelligent Systems*, 2nd edn. Addison-Wesley

An accessible book which introduces the topic of AI and concentrates on the concepts without dwelling excessively on the mathematical foundations. The book describes the building of a system and the evaluation and selection of appropriate tools.

Newell A. and Simon H. (1972). *Human Problem Solving*. Prentice Hall

Turban E. (2004). *Decision Support and Expert Systems*, 7th rev. edn. Prentice Hall

This is a comprehensive textbook covering all aspects of DSS and expert systems from the perspective of a manager wishing to know about management support technologies. It has several case studies and chapter-end questions.

Wooldridge M. (2002). *An Introduction to Multi-agent Systems*. John Wiley & Sons.

Suitable for undergraduate and some postgraduate courses, this book provides a non-technical exploration of intelligent agents and multi-agent systems.

Index